Praise for *Foundations™ of World Wide Web Programming with HTML and CGI*

"This is an excellent text for readers seeking in-depth understanding of HTML, along with a glimpse into its future. Clear exposition leads the reader step by step through the elements of HTML and CGI. The authors provide a wealth of advice on how to engineer and manage CGI applications, with plentiful and realistic examples. The writing style is delightful, sometimes even reminiscent of K&P's classic *Software Tools*.
— *Alan Richmond, President, CyberWeb SoftWare*
http://www.stars.com/CWSW/

"This crack team has written a must-read for anyone who runs a serious Web site, demonstrating how to use advanced HTML and CGIs to make Web programs truly powerful."
— *Jeff Evans, President, Versacom*

Here's what people say about Ed Tittel's *HTML For Dummies®*

"Everything we needed and then some! We started with no knowledge of writing HTML... We bought *HTML For Dummies*, and by the next day our Web page looked and operated as we had hoped."
— *Neal L. Martin, Grand Forks, ND*

"A lot of sound advice on do's and don'ts for designing HTML and Web pages, and for building complex Web sites."
— *Cye H. Waldman, Technical Editor, WWWiz Magazine*
http://wwwiz.com

"An excellent balance between breadth and depth, covering the art — as well the science — of creating Web pages."
— *Steven L. Mullen, Spectroscopist, University of Illinois*

"I've read other books on HTML programming that were confusing, but *HTML For Dummies* was right on the mark!"
— *Christopher J. Hollenbeck, Salestech, PC Upgrades International*

"Plenty of HTML pages to access and see what's going on."
— *Lee Hopkins, Psychology Dept., University of Surrey, UK*

"Very complete — great for 'proper' page structure!"
— *Dave Culp, Real Estate Broker, Walnut Creek, CA*

FOUNDATIONS™ *of*

World Wide Web Programming

WITH HTML & CGI

FOUNDATIONS™ *of*

World Wide Web Programming

WITH HTML & CGI

PROGRAMMERS PRESS

Foundations of World Wide Web Programming with HTML and CGI

Published by
IDG Books Worldwide, Inc.
An International Data Group Company
919 East Hillsdale Boulevard, Suite 400
Foster City, CA 94404

Copyright

Library of Congress Catalog Card No.: 95-077530

ISBN 1-56884-703-3

Printed in the United States of America

Second Printing, November, 1995
10 9 8 7 6 5 4 3 2

Distributed in the United States by IDG Books Worldwide, Inc.

  Published in the United States of America

FROM THE PUBLISHER

The *Foundations* series is designed, written, and edited by working programmers for working programmers. We asked you what you needed from a book to become productive using a programming tool, technique, or language. You told us to publish a book that:

- Is written from the perspective of a professional programmer
- Provides great coding examples that can be readily applied to your programs
- Serves as a tutorial that facilitates mastery of complex techniques, features, and concepts
- Serves as a comprehensive reference, achieving "dog-eared" status on your short-shelf of must-have books
- Provides a comprehensive index (programmers always go to the index first!)
- Includes either a fully indexed and linked electronic reference for quick and portable reference or valuable software that helps you get your job done better.

Our goal is to deliver all of this and more. We offer no gimmicks; no promise of instant proficiency through repetition or oversimplification. Sure, it's okay to learn the basics of driving a car doing 20 MPH with your dad in an empty parking lot. But if you're competing the next day in the Indy 500, you need entirely different preparation. You need to know the capabilities of your machine, the idiosyncrasies of the course, and how to translate that knowledge into a competitive advantage.

Like all Programmers Press books, this book is written by professionals. It is meticulously edited for technical accuracy, completeness, and readability. It is a book you will come to trust and rely on.

Thank you for choosing our product.

Christopher J. Williams
Group Publisher and Vice President

Welcome to the world of IDG Books Worldwide.

IDG Books Worldwide, Inc. is a subsidiary of International Data Group, the world's largest publisher of computer-related information and the leading global provider of information services on information technology. IDG was founded more than 25 years ago and now employs more than 7,500 people worldwide. IDG publishes more than 235 computer publications in 67 countries (see listing below). More than fifty million people read one or more IDG publications each month.

Launched in 1990, IDG Books Worldwide is today the #1 publisher of best-selling computer books in the United States. We are proud to have received 3 awards from the Computer Press Association in recognition of editorial excellence, and our best-selling *...For Dummies*™ series has more than 18 million copies in print with translations in 24 languages. IDG Books, through a recent joint venture with IDG's Hi-Tech Beijing, became the first U.S. publisher to publish a computer book in the People's Republic of China. In record time, IDG Books has become the first choice for millions of readers around the world who want to learn how to better manage their businesses.

Our mission is simple: Every IDG book is designed to bring extra value and skill-building instructions to the reader. Our books are written by experts who understand and care about our readers. The knowledge base of our editorial staff comes from years of experience in publishing, education, and journalism — experience which we use to produce books for the '90s. In short, we care about books, so we attract the best people. We devote special attention to details such as audience, interior design, use of icons, and illustrations. And because we use an efficient process of authoring, editing, and desktop publishing our books electronically, we can spend more time ensuring superior content and spend less time on the technicalities of making books.

You can count on our commitment to deliver high-quality books at competitive prices on topics consumers want to read about. At IDG, we value quality, and we have been delivering quality for more than 25 years. You'll find no better book on a subject than an IDG book.

John J. Kilcullen

John Kilcullen
President and CEO
IDG Books Worldwide, Inc.

About the Authors

Ed Tittel is the author of numerous books about computing, and a columnist for *MAXIMIZE!* magazine. He's the coauthor (with Bob LeVitus) of three best-selling books: *Stupid DOS Tricks*, *Stupid Windows Tricks*, and *Stupid Beyond Belief DOS Tricks*. He's also a coauthor (with Deni Connor and Earl Follis) of the best-selling *NetWare For Dummies*, now in its second edition, and (with Steve James) of the brand-new *HTML For Dummies*. These days, he's turning his focus to Internet-related topics and activities, both as a writer and as a member of the NetWorld + Interop program committee.

Ed's last "real job" was as the Director of Technical Marketing for Novell, Inc. In this position, he tried his best to control technical content for Novell's corporate trade shows, marketing communications, and presentations. He has been a frequent speaker on LAN-related topics at industry events, and was even a course developer for Excelan in San Jose, where he designed and maintained several introductory LAN training classes.

Ed has been a regular contributor to the computer trade press since 1987 and has written more than 100 articles for a variety of publications, with a decided emphasis on networking technology. These publications include *Computerworld, InfoWorld, LAN Times, LAN Magazine, BYTE, Macworld, MacUser, MAXIMIZE!, NetGuide*, and *IWAY*.

You can contact him at

```
etittel@zilker.net
```

Mark Gaither is currently a Software Engineer at HaL Software Systems in Austin, Texas. He is part of a five-person team in charge of maintaining and extending an SGML filtering gateway for the wonderful tech writers at HaL. Mark's experience with SGML all started by chance when he was volunteered to aid Steven DeRose, who was delivering an introduction to SGML and Hypertext at Hypertext '91 in San Antonio, Texas. As a result, Mark's SGML experience has blossomed in the Web world. He righteously evangelizes valid HTML, sometimes to his own detriment. He maintains the HaL HTML Validation Service and the HaL HTML Check Toolkit, available at

```
http://www.halsoft.com/html/
```

Mark can also be found religiously answering Dr. Web technical queries from HTML and WWW neophytes worldwide (http://www.-stars.com/Dr.Web/). Finally, Mark is a cofounder and the current director of the Austin WWW Users Group, whose membership is nearing 200; and he is a member of the Board of Directors of the Austin Area Multimedia Alliance.

Mark was graduated by Texas A&M University in Computer Science in 1990 (Bachelors) and is nearing the completion of his Masters in CS. Mark can be found on the weekends laying waste to rust and grime on his nearly complete frame-off restoration of a 1970 Chevelle SS 454 LS-5 (grunt, grunt!), while reciting quotes from favorite movies like *Fletch*, *Raising Arizona*, *Tombstone*, *Stripes*, and the *Blues Brothers*.

You can contact Mark at

`markg@gaither.com`

Sebastian Hassinger is an independent consultant and programmer who concentrates on all things Internet, with a special affinity for CGI programming and World Wide Web wackiness. Currently, clones of Sebastian can be seen working part-time at Apple Computer, Inc., and at OuterNet Connection Strategies. He is occasionally sighted around his supposed home, in beautiful south Austin, Texas.

Sebastian is a graduate of Concordia Unversity, Montreal, Canada, with a B.A. in English received in 1989. Before his tenure at Apple Computer, he worked for Simon Fraser University in Vancouver, BC, Canada, in the Macintosh Multimedia Laboratories (EXCITE) as a jack-of-all-programming-trades and disciplines. He also contributed the CGI programs for *HTML For Dummies*, and has written manuals and technical white papers for a number of high tech organizations in Canada.

You can contact Sebastian at

`singe@outer.net`

Mike Erwin is an independent consultant and programmer who is frankly obsessed with the Internet, with a focus on CGI programming and Internet connectivity at any speed (the faster, the better). Mike also works part-time at Apple Computer, Inc., and is the president and CEO of OuterNet Connection Strategies, an Austin-based Internet service provider.

Mike is a graduate of UT Austin, with a BBA in Finance received in 1989, and a B.S. in Computer Science in 1991, also from UT Austin. Before his tenure at Apple Computer, he worked as a contract programmer for companies like IBM, Microsoft, the state of Texas, and other industry heavyweights. He also contributed to the CGI programs in *HTML For Dummies*, and has written science fiction and fantasy for publications like *TSR* in the mid-1980s.

You can contact Mike at

`mikee@outer.net`

For More Information

For general information on IDG Books in the U.S., including information on discounts and premiums, contact IDG Books at 800-434-3422. For information on where to purchase IDG's books outside the U.S., contact Christina Turner at 415-655-3022.

For information on translations, contact Marc Jeffrey Mikulich, Foreign Rights Manager, at IDG Books Worldwide; fax number: 415-655-3295.

For sales inquiries and special prices for bulk quantities, contact Tony Real at 800-434-3422 or 415-655-3048.

For information on using IDG's books in the classroom and ordering examination copies, contact Jim Kelly at 800-434-2086.

Foundations of World Wide Web Programming with HTML and CGI is distributed in Canada by Macmillan of Canada, a Division of Canada Publishing Corporation; by Computer and Technical Books in Miami, Florida, for South America and the Caribbean; by Longman Singapore in Singapore, Malaysia, Thailand, and Korea; by Toppan Co. Ltd. in Japan; by Asia Computerworld in Hong Kong; by Woodslane Pty. Ltd. in Australia and New Zealand; and by Transword Publishers Ltd. in the U.K. and Europe.

Credits

Group Publisher and Vice President
Christopher J. Williams

Publishing Director
John Osborn

Senior Acquisitions Manager
Amorette Pedersen

Editorial Director
Anne Marie Walker

Production Director
Beth A. Roberts

Technical Editor
Anu Garg

Composition and Layout
Ronnie K. Bucci

Proofreader
Jeannie Smith

Indexer
Liz Cunningham

Cover Design
Draper and Liew, Inc.

Cover Photo
Donovan Reese/Tony Stone Images

Acknowledgments

We have way too many people to thank for this book to get it all right in a short space, so we'd like to start out by thanking everybody who helped us. Actually, we couldn't have done it without you, even if we didn't mention you here! Thanks, anyway.

Ed Tittel

There are too many people to thank and compliment to give everyone the recognition they deserve, but here goes, anyway. To my family: Suzy, Austin, Chelsea, and Dusty — thanks for putting up with me when things got weird! Special thanks to Michael Stewart, who did most of the really hard running around and fact-checking. It's a pleasure working with you, as always. To my coauthors, Mark, Mike, and Sebastian: they said it couldn't be done, but we went ahead and did it anyway. It's been a privilege to work with each of you; I hope our next one is even more fun!

Mark Gaither

Ed Tittel patiently helped me turn my experiences into something that I hope is useful to the rest of the WWW community. He continues to be an inspiration. Thanks Ed, for believing in me (also to his wife Suzy for putting up with our meetings in their kitchen). And thanks to Mike Erwin and Sebastian Hassinger for their CGI and networking expertise and enthusiasm.

I'm thankful to Dan Connolly at W3C for teaching me to truly understand the power of the Web. Thanks to those WWW pioneers who responded to my e-mail queries: Tim Berners-Lee, Dave Raggett, and Peter Flynn. Thanks to Tony Sanders at BSDI for the invaluable feedback on my HTML Validation Service. Thanks to Nelson Beebe at the University of Utah for his expert input about valid SGML. Thanks to Anne Marie Walker at IDG Books for taking a chance on someone with such a silly and skewed sense of humor.

Thanks go to my family: my brother Paul, who instilled in me that hockey defenseman mentality when it comes to business; my brother Adam, who taught me about software engineering and fishing; my mother Lynda, who continues to support her number–one son no matter what; and my father Norman, an author himself, who prepared me for this endeavor.

Thanks to Dr. Bart Childs and John Leggett at Texas A&M University; Dr. Childs for the "do the right" attitude and Dr. Leggett for turning me on the history of hypertext. They both also made me work very, very hard!

Sebastian Hassinger

I'd especially like to give thanks and much love to Nina, Eyre, and Haefen for their patience, support, and love. Without them, I'm nothing.

Thanks are also due to Ed Tittel, for pulling the writing team together, both at the onset of the project and at various points during the process when it looked like we might all come apart. Thanks also to Mike Erwin and Mark Gaither for their fine writing and hard work.

Mike Erwin

I want to personally thank a few individuals, without whose assistance and guidance this book would not have been possible. First, hats off to Alex Sirota, whose expert skill at database management systems helped keep me straight in writing my discussion of database CGI scripting. Second, a very rich thank you to Ed Tittel, who held the reins close when managing the overall direction of this book. He was able to aggregate the writing of four unique and different contributors into a single flow. Finally, my heartfelt thanks to the folks at OuterNet (especially Paul Wolfe and Charlie Scott), who were happy to help with providing test systems and top-notch service to go along with them.

From all of us

There's a whole crowd of other folks whose information has helped us over the years, especially the originators of the Web — most notably, Tim Berners-Lee and the rest of the CERN team, as well as Earl Hood, Brigitte Jellinek, and Tom Boutell. We'd also like to thank the geniuses, sung and unsung, at NCSA, MIT, Netscape Communications, Stanford, HaL, and anyplace else whose Web collections we visited, for helping to pull the many strands of this book together. Thanks to our intrepid technical editor, Anu Garg, who survived the simultaneous rigors of job-hunting and editing this book to provide us with pointed and witty feedback. You helped make this book better than it already was! Our extra-special thanks to Amy Pedersen and Anne Marie Walker, our partners in grime from IDG, who not only made this project possible, but stuck with us until it was finished!

The final word of thanks goes to all of the many software authors whose work we mentioned in the book (and included on the CD whenever possible). Without your work, this book would have been nothing! We only hope that the exposure you gain from this work is positive, and that we can continue to draw on your efforts in the future. Thanks again!!

The publisher would like to give special thanks to Patrick McGovern, without whom this book would not have been possible.

Contents Overview

If you're tackling World Wide Web (WWW) programming for the first time, it's hard to know where to start. Part I introduces the fundamentals of HTML and the Web's Common Gateway Interface (CGI), the keys to building enhanced Web services and capabilities.

A quick overview of the philosophical and technical underpinnings for the WWW, including a look at the history and evolution of the Web as we know it today. This chapter introduces all the basic ingredients involved in delivering information via the WWW.

The Standard Generalized Markup Language provides the foundation for the HTML; understanding what SGML is and how it works is essential to a deep understanding of HTML. This chapter provides an overview of the basics of SGML grammar and syntax, and sheds ample light on markup languages in general.

The Document Type Definitions (DTDs) that govern HTML are SGML documents that describe each variant of the language. This chapter reviews the history and differences among the variants, examines the HTML 1.0 and 2.0 DTDs in detail, and touches briefly on HTML 3.0 and the Netscape Mozilla DTDs.

Chapter 11 Testing and Installing CGI Applications 225

Once a CGI program is built, it must be thoroughly tested before it can be unloosed on the Web; this chapter builds a test plan for the sample application designed and constructed in the two preceding chapters. It also discusses the issues that must be addressed in installing a CGI for production use.

Chapter 12 Our Foundations Development Environment 241

An overview and analysis of the programming platform, languages, and tools that the authors used to build and test the many examples in this book, including a discussion of what motivated these particular choices.

Chapter 13 Locating CGI Resources... 247

A guided tour of the tools and techniques that you can use to identify and capture some of the many terrific CGI resources available on the Web and elsewhere.

Chapter 14 CGI Return Page Templates.................................... 263

Most of the information created by CGI programs must be delivered to end users in the form of HTML documents ("return pages"). This chapter explores techniques to speed the coding of the framework for such documents.

Chapter 15 The Major CGI Libraries... 277

There are numerous valuable collections of prefabricated CGI code available on the Web; this chapter covers what the authors found most valuable and interesting.

Chapter 16 <FORM> Alternatives... 291

While the most common stimulant for CGI programming is to handle HTML <FORM> input, some users can't take advantage of these services. Here, you learn about valuable alternatives to capture input from users who couldn't otherwise respond to requests for input on Web pages.

Chapter 17 Gotchas, Warnings, and No-Nos 307

There are numerous common problems, pitfalls, and gotchas that can trap the unwary Web programmer. This chapter covers the most common ones based on the authors' own CGI development experiences.

PART III BASIC CGI PROGRAMMING ELEMENTS AND TECHNIQUES 315

Part III moves into an exploration of some of the basic elements and topics that Web programmers must wrestle with as part of their development efforts.

In order to deliver documents created in other formats to the WWW, organizations must recreate them as HTML documents (or, more typically, as document collections). This chapter explores the approaches used in this process and describes some tools to help automate this time- and resources-intensive activity.

This chapter explains how to use graphics as navigational tools within HTML documents, and explores and describes several tools to help automate the process of creating the image map files that let CGI programs convert mouse clicks into hypertext links.

Building customized HTML documents as the output of CGI programs is entirely routine; this chapter explains how to pull this everyday programming feat off with panache and style.

The platform that hosts a Web site determines many of the programming details necessary for its successful operation. This chapter explores some of the choices available and explains the trade offs involved.

Part IV covers advanced WWW programming tools and topics, including some emerging areas of intense activity sure to interest programmers in search of a real challenge.

The WWW can be an effective front end for all kinds of routine Internet information-gathering activities; this chapter explains how to spice up file access and retrieval with a CGI-based Web interface.

There's more to information access on the Web than WAIS; this chapter explores some nascent CGI-based interfaces to those engines of organizational information manipulation — database management systems.

Table of Contents

PART IV   ADVANCED CGI PROGRAMMING TOOLS AND TECHNIQUES 479

Introduction

Welcome to *The Foundations of WWW Programming with HTML and CGI* (*TWF*, The Web Foundation)! This book is shamelessly devoted to informing and educating programmers who seek to extend the capabilities of their Web server and its services. Our primary goal is to provide you with sufficient information to enable you to tackle any Web-related basic programming task.

TWF will arm you with pointers to online resources (code, tools, and techniques) and other sources of information, so that you can tackle just about any kind of Common Gateway Interface (CGI) programming project. *TWF* includes a CD-ROM that contains all the code included in the book, as well as a broad collection of public domain and shareware tools, libraries, and ready-to-run CGI programs. For more information on the CD-ROM, please consult Chapter 34, "The Foundations of World World Wide Web Programming with HTML and CGI."

Parts Is Parts

This *Foundations* book is divided into four parts. Part I covers the terminology and programming tools, interfaces, and techniques employed throughout the rest of the book. Part II builds a bridge from these fundamentals to prepare you for real-world CGI, including implementation and testing of a sample set of forms-handling CGI programs. Part III covers basic CGI programming elements and techniques, with an emphasis on the basic services and operations that CGI programmers need to learn and use. In Part IV we'll introduce you to some advanced CGI programs and techniques, including Web-based audio, video, multimedia, DBMS access, real-time interaction, and more.

PART I: THE FOUNDATIONS OF HTML AND CGI

Part I introduces the basic concepts, standards, and technologies to handle Web programming tasks. It includes a discussion of the Standard Generalized Markup Language (SGML), the descriptive ISO-standard metalanguage used to define HTML (HyperText Markup Language) for creating online Web documents. It also includes an in-depth discussion of the historical, current, and planned versions of HTML, to help you understand what you can do with Web pages today (and what you might be able to do with them tomorrow).

Part I also covers the Common Gateway Interface (CGI), the primary interface that supports delivery of input from Web clients to their servers. Since this defines the mechanisms whereby Web servers handle user input, and defines extended or enhanced services, it is the key component for the entire book. In Chapters 6 through 9, we cover the CGI specification in detail and discuss the options available for selecting a CGI programming language (with specific recommendations to help you make a good choice). We also discuss CGI's parameter-passing conventions and its input/output characteristics and behavior. We conclude our CGI introduction with a walkthrough of the CGI design process, including an in-depth requirements analysis that drives the design for a set of forms-handling CGI programs.

PART II: THE BRIDGE TO CGI IMPLEMENTATION

Part II provides the concepts and information you'll need to begin mastering the elements of CGI implementation. Here, we begin by taking the design for the forms-handling CGIs discussed in Chapter 9, proceed to implement the necessary code in Chapter 10, and take you through the testing and debugging process in Chapter 11.

In the remaining five chapters, we discuss our own CGI development environment while explaining the reasons for our choices, along with possible alternatives. This is followed by a short tutorial on mining for information about CGI on the Web, including pointers to the major electronic watering holes, gathering spots, and other sources of information. Next we examine tools and techniques to let you locate and use prefabricated CGI code and libraries in your programs, to advance your own development efforts. We conclude Part II with a review of the common traps and pitfalls that CGI programmers may encounter, based almost entirely on our own experiences.

PART III: BASIC CGI PROGRAMMING ELEMENTS AND TECHNIQUES

In Part III, we discuss common programming elements for CGI programs and examine some basic canned functionality that most CGI programmers will want to understand and use. This includes discussion of the Multipurpose Internet Mail Extensions (MIME) formats used to create Web files and documents, as well as information on how to index, access, and search large collections of data using the Web. This part also includes a discussion of activity monitoring and reporting, image map handling, and the principles of effective hypertext document design.

PART IV: ADVANCED CGI PROGRAMMING TOOLS AND TECHNIQUES

In Part IV, we investigate some more advanced tools and techniques for CGI programming, including creating interfaces to online file archives and database management systems (DBMS). We also look at the issues and practices involved in delivering audio and video via the Web, as well as the problems involved in using the Web for "near real-time" interactivity in applications. We continue with discussions of on-the-fly HTML creation and usage, and managing security (and secure communications) on the Web. The final chapter covers the book's accompanying CD-ROM — how it is organized and how it should be used.

How to Use This Book

If you're a relative newcomer to Web programming and CGI, we'd strongly recommend that you read Parts I and II in their entirety. You can then pick and choose among those topics in Parts III and IV that catch your interest, and dip in again from time to time as other topics catch your eye.

If you're a seasoned Web hand, you'll probably just want to skim the first two parts. Even though they might be somewhat familiar, we're pretty sure that even an experienced WebMaster will be able to glean some useful information in Part I about things like HTML 3.0, SGML browsers, HTML validation tools, and new programming languages. In the same vein, Part II includes useful coverage of some online resources and search techniques that you might find interesting. We also strongly recommend a look at Chapter 17, which discusses the pitfalls and gotchas that lurk in wait for all CGI programmers, no matter how long they've been at their work.

But it's in Parts III and IV that you'll probably get the most value from this book, especially in the discussions of tools for WAIS, indexing, activity monitoring and status reporting, and document Webification. We'd recommend reading a chapter or two any time the mood strikes you, or using the book's index and table of contents to search for information on specific topics.

Conventions Used in This Book

We've tried to be clear and consistent about what's what in this book. This can get tricky, so we used the following typographical conventions to distinguish among a variety of elements that you're likely to encounter while programming.

 The CD-ROM symbol placed next to a URL or program name indicates that the item is included on the CD-ROM that accompanies this book.

- When we include fragments of code or whole programs, we'll often set them off from the rest of the text, like this:

```
# Because these lines start with a '#' they're valid comments in a
# variety of programming languages (like Perl and the UNIX shells)
```

- Sometimes when we set code off from the rest of the text, it will include special comments named callouts. We use these comments to draw your attention to special language capabilities or cool tips and tricks. Here's an example:

```
foreach $elem (elements) { #start callout here, OK to drop down 1-2
    $elem *=2;                #lines
}
```

foreach statement applies the same operation to each array element

- When we quote an element of code in running text, you'll see a different typeface used to set it off, as in "the **chop** command in Perl provides a tool for extracting and manipulating substrings, based on definition of specific delimiter character."

- When we name UNIX or other programs, system commands, or special terms, they'll be printed in italics, as in "the *grep* command provides a way to manipulate data based on pattern-matching and regular expressions."

- When we name an environment or program variable, we'll surround it with single quotes, as in "The variable 'DocumentRoot' is important to define for an NCSA *httpd* server, because it controls access to the Web server's document tree." (Note: because *httpd* is the name of a UNIX program, we set it in italics.)

- Filenames, including full filenames as well as stem names and extensions, and directory paths, both partial and full, will be bracketed in double quotes, as in "The file named "home.html" has a stem name of "home" and an extension of ".html"." Notice that the final period in this sentence falls between the two double quotation marks, because there's no period in the extension of the filename (whatever's inside is a literal representation of the name). Also, because we use double quotes for their normal purposes (as we did above to quote a sentence), we always try to indicate with words when a file or directory term is being used (as we also did above).

If you can follow — and master — these simple rules, you'll be well equipped to keep up with the content of this book. It's not too much harder than mastering the details of any programming language we know of, so we're pretty sure you can handle the job!

But Wait, There's More!

In addition to the materials you'll find in this book, we've established a Web server that includes the materials on the CD-ROM, with an interactive search engine, an online registration form, and the opportunity for you to give us some feedback (and suggestions, we hope) about the book or related topics and activities.

On the "live" Web pages, you'll find pointers to the most current versions of the tools, libraries, and code. (We're still waiting for somebody to figure out how to update a CD-ROM after it's shipped!). You'll also be able to share your code, ideas, or suggestions for additional online materials or resources with us, using an electronic suggestion box. Please drop by our pages and share your comments and experiences with us — we can't promise you fame or fortune, but you might very well get a plug in the next edition of this book, or in one of the others we'll be working on soon!

To visit the *TWF* Web server, point your browser at this URL:

```
http://www.idgprogrammer.com/
```

While you're there, don't forget to register your purchase and tell us what you liked and didn't like about the book. If you've located any cool resources, mailing lists, libraries, or other information that we didn't include, please let us know about those, too. We'll be adding some of your suggestions to our "official" Web pages (after we check them out, first), and your suggestions will be visible to the whole world as soon as you offer them.

Bon Voyage!

We hope you find the materials, code, pointers, and information in this book useful. Please share your thoughts and ideas with us, pro or con (our e-mail addresses are listed in the "About the Authors" section). At this point, we're finished with the introduction, so we'd like to close by saying — thanks for buying our book — enjoy your reading!

I

Foundations of HTML and CGI

*T*he nine chapters in Part I introduce and explain the subject matter for this book. In Chapter 1, we begin with a look at the philosophical and technical underpinnings for the World Wide Web (WWW) and the Internet. In Chapter 2, we examine the Standard Generalized Markup Language (SGML) used to define the World Wide Web's HyperText Markup Language (HTML). Then, in Chapters 3,4, and 5, we take a close look at the SGML-derived Document Type Definitions (DTDs) for the historical, prevailing, and emerging versions of HTML. We also discuss the need for formal HTML validation and describe several tools and techniques to use in this process.

Chapters 6 through 9 focus on the Common Gateway Interface (CGI) — the set of parameter-passing and communications conventions defined for the WWW, that lets users send input to servers for further processing by special-purpose programs. Chapter 6 covers the basic interface definition, and Chapter 7 explores the variety of programming languages suitable for CGI implementation. In Chapter 8, we explain the details of CGI input, output, and parameter-passing conventions. In Chapter 9, we discuss the process of designing a CGI application and tackle a typical set of forms-handling tools as an example.

CHAPTER

1

Basics of the World Wide Web

Vannevar Bush penned an inspiring, forward-looking, seminal treatise entitled "As We May Think," published by *The Atlantic Monthly* in July 1945. Yeah, that's right — 1945 — at the end of World War II! His basic thesis was to urge his fellow scientists to begin the paramount task of making the world's staggering wealth of knowledge and experience more accessible.

In this article, Bush pressed his cohorts to cast aside the machines of war and present the common man with access to, and control over, the "inherited knowledge of the ages." Somewhere in this treatise, the notions of hypertext and hypermedia were born. Today, the World Wide Web (also known as WWW or W3) is the major knowledge dissemination system that implements these notions.

Many pundits have since tickled the keyboards of their computers, creating new and exhilarating hypermedia systems: Doug Englebart's Augment in the 1960s (he invented the mouse), Ted Nelson's Xanadu in the 1970s, and now in the 1990s Tim Berners-Lee (affectionately known as TBL) brings us the World Wide Web. Each of these men ran with Bush's dream of harnessing all of mankind's knowledge and experience, but some were tackled near midfield, while others shot wide of the goal. It looks like WWW might actually sneak past the goalkeeper...

Each of these scientists had a problem that called for a new and unique solution. Tim Berners-Lee needed a collaborative environment to let physicists exchange vital research information without suffering the delays inherent in communications such as electronic mail (e-mail), file transfer protocol (ftp), snail mail (the United States Postal Service and its equivalents), or the fax. Like Bush, TBL envisioned a new way of harnessing man's thinking power to the whiz-bang speeds of new computers. Thus, the WWW was created in the basement between three steam pipes and a rusty valve at the European Laboratory for Particle Physics (CERN) in Geneva, Switzerland in 1990.

The Internet: An Amorphous Blob

The Internet as we know it today is similar in its appearance and through-put to the roadways in any middling-sized metropolis. Every major thor-ough fare appears to be under construction and the overall transportation system is ever-expanding to handle more and more automobiles, trucks, and buses.

But as each new construction is completed, it's time to start expanding again or resurfacing those streets that were just completed five years earlier. If there's one sensation that's familiar to commuters in these circumstances, it's best summed up as "hurry up and wait!"

The WWW is an interactive hypermedia system built upon the Inter-net, which itself has grown from a tiny band of DARPA (Defense Advanced Research Project Agency) machines to its full-blown glory today. We're not gonna tell you how big the Internet is, because nobody really knows! All we know is that there is a large, fuzzy blob out there at the end of our phone lines where packets of data are passed amongst servers on the Internet backbone at breathtaking speeds. Somehow they manage to arrive at the correct destinations in the correct order and that's all anybody really cares about.

When we speak of hypermedia, we're talking about four basic docu-ment components — text, images, audio, and video. The WWW sup-ports all of these one way or another. Software is readily available to let some images be viewed alongside text as part and parcel of the Web's online documents. Other images, along with audio and video, must be viewed (or rendered) using add-in external helper applications (these are platform- and client-specific but usable nonetheless) to supplement the basic software's capabilities.

To perform all this chicanery and to support the desired collaborative aspects of TBL's solution to the problem of delivering the sum of human knowledge and experience, he borrowed from many sources:

- a little from the TCP/IP knowledge base
- a smidgen from the MIME shelf
- a little from the SGML pool
- a bunch from open systems and client/server architectures

In short, Berners-Lee leveraged some of the more common UNIX protocols and extended others, to come up with simple but efficient pieces to create the WWW. As a result, two de facto standards have emerged, the HyperText Transfer Protocol (HTTP) and the HyperText Markup Language (HTML). Together, these two lay the foundation for the magnificent successes that the Web has wrought.

The HyperText Transfer Protocol (HTTP)

The HyperText Transfer Protocol (HTTP) is a network protocol built for the WWW. HTTP is nothing less than a distributed collaborative hypermedia information system. In TBL's words, HTTP is a "generic stateless object-oriented protocol." This kind of network protocol is both simple to use and easy to implement, sentiments that capture two of the driving forces behind HTTP.

Certain operations, called *methods*, are associated with the object-oriented HTTP protocol. These methods define extensions to the HTTP commands and can be associated with particular types of network objects such as documents, files, or network services.

The purpose of HTTP was to make available many sources of related, networked information via the Internet. It is possible to browse these information stores, to rapidly follow references from any source of information to other pertinent sources which may themselves be located at multiple remote locations.

As with any hypermedia system, response times should be fast: Berners-Lee indicates that no more than 100 milliseconds should be required for a hypermedia link or jump. This requires a very fast, stateless, information retrieval network protocol. While this goal has not been fully realized (especially for dial-up Web surfers), the Web is still easy to navigate, with little effort required to move across links from one document to another.

HTTP's functionality includes search and retrieval, front-end updates, and document annotation. HTTP allows an extensible set of methods to be designed and deployed. It builds on the discipline of reference provided by the Universal Resource Identifier (URI), a well-thought-out scheme that originated with the Internet Engineering Task Force (IETF). There are two types of URIs, the Universal Resource Name (URN) and the Universal Resource Locator (URL).

HTTP also features dynamic data representation through client/server negotiation. This allows WWW information systems to be built independent of the development and deployment of new information representations. The way information is represented can be worked out as part of the process of shipping data from servers to clients, and vice versa.

How HTTP Works

On the Internet, network communications occur via TCP/IP connections. Occasionally, certain situations may arise where this protocol suite is implemented atop another network protocol. In this case, HTTP objects may be mapped onto foreign transport mechanisms or networks. This is a simple, straightforward process, one that usually goes unnoticed by WWW users.

It's a testament to the Web's ease of access and use that service providers like CompuServe and America Online have been able to graft Internet (and Web) access onto their basic services, which use completely different networking protocols, without disturbing the basic interface that users have come to expect from the Web.

The HTTP protocol is *stateless* — that is, neither the client nor server stores information about the state of the other side of an ongoing connection. The server does not need to store information about the last client it serviced, nor does a client need to track a server's state of affairs. Each minds its own business and manages state information for itself. This supports the simplest kinds of client and server applications, and helps to account for the broad reach and platform support found in the Web community.

Most networking protocols depend on the notion of a transaction, which consists of the following elements:

- the establishment of a *connection* between a client and a server, to permit communications to occur,
- a *request* from a client to a server, for specific services, resources, or other known "topics of communication,"
- a *response* from the server to the client's request, supplying the requested resource or an explanation as to why it can't be delivered, and
- the termination of the connection, at the *close* of request/response communication.

This rhythm (connection, request, response, close) describes the basic form of interchange between clients and servers the world over, both on and off the Web.

Connection

This is the establishment of a networked TCP/IP connection from the client to an Internet WWW server. Historically, UNIX has been the dominant operating system on the Internet. When using TCP/IP on a UNIX server, port 80 is the "well-known" port address for WWW communications. Other nonreserved ports may be specified in the server's URL, but they must be specifically requested in order to be used.

Request

The request initiates from a WWW client in the form of a request message aimed at a particular server. This request includes the method to be applied to the requested network object, that object's identifier, and the HTTP protocol version utilized, followed by further information encoded in a particular header style.

Response

The response emanates from the server, back to the requesting client. It consists of three parts: a response status line, a response header, and the response data.

The status line contains the following fields:

- an identifier for the HTTP version used by the server
- a status code that describes the results of the server's attempt to decipher and understand the client's request
- a hard-coded explanation from the server about the response

The response header may contain specific information about the requested object, plus whatever Multipurpose Internet Mail Extensions (MIME) declarations (like Content-Type) may be required to deliver the response. A response header normally contains nothing different from the request header information supplied by the client (and is viewed, therefore, as a form of confirmation).

The response data supplies any additional information that follows the response header. This data is normally encoded in the form of a MIME message body. The relevance of this data depends entirely upon the status code returned by the server. Also, the MIME 'Content-Type' declaration used for the data may be any Content-Type that the requesting client has specified that it can accept. The two main Content-Types are 'text/plain' (normal ASCII) and 'text/html' (normal HTML documents). According to the HTTP specification, it's safe to assume that any WWW client can handle these two Content-Types.

Close

This is the termination of a TCP/IP connection, which may be initiated either by the client or the server.

The specific formats of the request and response elements defined in the HTTP specification can be found at:

```
http://www.w3.org/hypertext/WWW/Protocols/HTTP/HTTP2.html
```

All HTTP header information is normally represented using the ISO-Latin-1 character set, where each line is terminated by a carriage return/line feed pair (usually written CrLf). In the HTTP specification, object transmission in a variety of binary forms is also possible.

HTTP CHARACTER SETS

In all cases in HTTP where RFC 822 characters are allowed, these may be extended to use the full ISO-Latin-1 character set. 8-bit transmission is always used.

For more information about the HTTP/1.0 specification, consult this URL:

```
http://www.w3.org/hypertext/WWW/Protocols/HTTP1.0/draft-ietf-http-spec.html
```

The Common Gateway Interface

The WWW contains a plethora of static hyperdocuments like those that probably describe your organization and its products or services. But this is not enough. Today, dynamically created hyperdocuments are the rage. To support dynamic interaction on the Web, you need an interface for running external programs under the direction of an HTTP server. The Common Gateway Interface (CGI) supplies this functionality; it is a gateway between the WWW and other sources of data, like your company's SQL database of products. With a CGI application, you can provide a delivery mechanism for SQL queries from the Web, back to the Web clients that made those queries.

CGI defines an interface for running external applications and programs on behalf of a Web server. You can think of CGI as a mechanism for extending the capabilities and functionality of any WWW server. With CGI applications at your site, you can add external functionality to your server that can make your site unique.

Currently, CGI supports only access to HTTP servers. This does not preclude the future extension of CGI to include other networking protocols, but that's where things stand today.

Gateways are really applications that handle information requests on a server's behalf. The server hands client requests off to referenced CGI applications, including the appropriate data from the requesting client. The CGI application executes using this input data, and returns its results back to the server. The server, in turn, passes this back to the requesting client. This relationship is depicted in Figure 1-1.

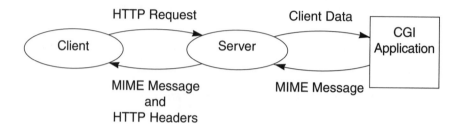

Figure 1-1
For CGI, the client/server relationship introduces a back-end CGI program that provides services to the client on behalf of the Web server.

Such gateways can be used for a wide variety of applications on the Web, but the most common CGI applications by far handle HTML <FORM> and <ISINDEX> requests.

In Chapter 6 we will dissect CGI and look at all of its internals.

The HyperText Markup Language (HTML)

HTML is an application of the Standard Generalized Markup Language (SGML). SGML (ISO-8879) was approved as an international standard in 1986. SGML provides a way to represent document and hyperdocument structure. It is also a way to encode hyperdocuments so they can be interchanged. This is similar to the exchange of documents during a collaborative authoring effort between multiple authors at different remote sites.

SGML is also a *metalanguage* for formally describing document markup systems. In fact, HTML uses SGML to define a language that describes a WWW hyperdocument's structure and interconnectivity.

Following the rigors of SGML, TBL bore HTML to the world in 1990. Since then, many of us have found it to be easy to use but sometimes quite limiting. These limiting factors are being addressed by the World Wide Web Consortium (aka W3C) at MIT. But HTML had to start somewhere, and its success argues that it didn't start out too badly!

HOW TO READ AN HTML DOCUMENT

There are several important things you'll need to know when interpreting HTML documents:

- Line breaks and indentation exist solely for human readability.
- Tag names are sacred:
  - <HEAD> cannot be changed to <HEADER>
  - <NAME> cannot be changed to <NAMES>
- Document elements are indicated by a start tag at the beginning <NAME> and an end tag at the end </NAME>:
  - <HTML> — start tag of HTML document
  - </HTML> — end tag of HTML document
  - <A> — start tag of anchor
  - </A> — end tag of anchor
- Element attributes are written as:

  name = "*value*" — in the start tag only

- Tag names and attributes are case insensitive:
  - <Head> = <hEAD> = <HeAd> = <Head> = <HEAd> = <HEAD>
  - <A NAME=" "> = <A Name=" "> = <A name=" ">
- Markup minimization is allowed but should be avoided. For example, the <HTML> ... </HTML> tag set can be excluded in the earlier example and it would still be considered valid HTML. (More about valid HTML in Chapter 3.)
- HTML presumes a Document Type Definition (DTD), which specifies valid tag names, attributes, and uses of minimization.

Here is an example of an HTML document:

```
<!DOCTYPE HTML PUBLIC "-//IETF//DTD HTML 2.0//EN">
<!- That is an SGML prologue. More about this later ->
<HTML>
<HEAD><TITLE>A Sample HTML Document</TITLE></HEAD>
<BODY>
<H1>Table of Contents</H1>
<!- an ordered list ->
<OL>
```

```
<!- a list item which is a link to another anchor
    in the same document named 'intro' ->
<LI><A HREF="#intro">Introduction</A>
<LI><A HREF="#concepts">Concepts</A>
<LI><A HREF="#conclusion">Conclusion</A>
</OL>
<!- a horizontal rule; a divider ->
<HR>
<A NAME="intro"><H2>Introduction</H2></A>
<P> All good documents include introduction material.
<A NAME="concepts"><H2>Concepts</H2></A>
<P> Concepts are a good idea to present to the reader.
<A NAME="conclusion"><H2>Conclusion</H2></A>
<P> Any good writer tells them what they just read.
</BODY>
</HTML>
```

In the preceding example, you should be able to decipher something of the document's structure. It has an <HTML> container around the whole document. It has major sub-elements, that is, a <HEAD> followed by a <BODY>. Within the <BODY> envelope, you should notice paragraph markup (<P>), list markup (<OL> ... </OL>), and header-level markup (<H1> and <H2>). This provides valuable clues about how to read an HTML document.

In fact, HTML has four primary characteristics:

- It uses descriptive markup.
- It defines hierarchical document structures, plus both intra- and inter-document hyperlinks.
- HTML is governed by a formal specification.
- HTML's specification, plus the language itself, is both human- and computer-readable.

In the sections that follow, we'll explain what each of these characteristics means and why they are important.

DESCRIPTIVE MARKUP

HTML is a simple descriptive markup language. This means that parts of documents are marked or tagged with *descriptive* names, like

<CHAPTER> or <TITLE>, that are applicable to any proper instances of a document's data.

Tags can give visual clues to the reader that certain words or phrases are special, as in this example which describes the title of a law firm:

```
<TITLE>Dewey, Cheatum, and Howe — Attorneys at Law</TITLE>
```

By contrast, a procedural markup language defines separate markup for a multitude of specialized applications like "bold, centered, 20 point times roman." In Chapter 2, you will learn more about descriptive markup, what descriptive markup languages can do, and how they differ from procedural markup langauges.

HIERARCHICAL DOCUMENT STRUCTURE PLUS INTERCONNECTIONS

Links between documents or document elements invariably accompany an HTML document's structure. An interconnection or link is a unary relationship between two document elements. These two elements are called *link anchors*.

The source link anchor "links to" a target link anchor. In HTML, link anchors can be named or not, through the attribution of link tags. For example, the anchor tag in HTML has an attribute to declare an anchor's name. In the following example, the anchor takes the name "tranny":

```
<A NAME="tranny">12 Bolt Posi-traction</A>
```

The NAME attribute is controlled and maintained by an HTML document's author.

Document elements may be coarse-grained, like a phrase or sentence, or fine-grained, like a word or pixel of a display unit. Document elements may refer to other document elements, or to external objects through a hypertext link mechanism, according to the reference discipline for documents in use. For HTML, this means that links can point to other document elements in the same document (intra-document linking) or to elements in a different document (inter-document linking).

THE FORMAL SPECIFICATION

HTML has a Document Type Definition (DTD) that states its formal specification. The DTD defines HTML's syntax, describes each individual HTML document element, states the attributes permitted for any element, and describes each element's legal data content model (a data content model defines which, if any, other elements may occur within a given element). In addition to element information, the DTD also supplies definitions for any external entities that may be referenced within HTML (for example, the ISO-Latin-1 character set used to represent characters on-screen).

Historically, the HTML DTD has gone through three levels, numbered zero (0) through two (2). Currently, level 2 is the HTML specification supported by the Internet Engineering Task Force (IETF), one of the chief standards bodies that governs the Internet (and by extension, the World Wide Web).

Level 3 HTML is expected to emerge from its nest at W3C soon, while the Mozilla DTD from Netscape seeks to lure everyone to jump aboard and follow Netscape to Web Nirvana. Dave Ragget, Dan Connolly, and TBL, with a cast of supporting characters, are pushing the level 3.0 DTD closer and closer to the edge of the nest.

The unfortunate side effect of three competing HTML specifications is that organizations and developers have to pick a particular version to use. The consequences of making a wrong choice are fraught with peril and can lead to wasted efforts of mammoth proportions. In Chapter 3, you'll learn all about the competing HTML DTDs and what makes each worthy of consideration.

HUMAN- AND COMPUTER-READABLE REPRESENTATION

HTML represents document structure that is readable by humans, as well as computers. Because *markup* — the descriptive tags that help to define HTML and its behavior — is separated from text by a collection of special delimiter strings, all of which are printable, text and markup can coexist peacefully and meaningfully.

In fact, readers who are completely ignorant about HTML could probably still decipher this HTML code fragment:

```
<TITLE>The Tale of the One-Blanks</TITLE>
```

That's because tag names use ordinary terminology that's intelligible to most people (or abbreviations for such terminology, which make sense once they're expanded and explained). Tags could be written in Latin, but that wouldn't help readability one little bit!

Summary

The WWW is built upon numerous protocols and existing Internet technologies. Its cornerstones are HTTP, CGI, and HTML, which is itself an application of the metalanguage, SGML. In the next chapter, we'll look at SGML up close and in person. Freshen up your coffee, push random play on your CD player, and pull up your chair. Here we go into SGML land.

2

An Introduction to SGML

Networked information repositories are today's equivalent of the late 19th Century Placer Gold Mines in the Sierra Nevadas (in other words, "there's gold in them thar hills!"). These data stores are growing in breadth and depth at breakneck speed.

In keeping with the California Gold Rush, everybody and his brother is staking a claim somewhere on the WWW. While some are striking it rich, others are going bust because of their ignorance about online information delivery and management. If you want your claim to pay off, you should know that managing and organizing your stake of networked information is paramount for success.

In this chapter we'll give you an overview of Standard Generalized Markup Language (SGML), including its applications, the underlying standard that governs and describes SGML, and its relationship to HTML.

What Is SGML?

SGML is an international standard used for the formal definition of device-, system-, and application-independent electronic text. In other words, SGML is a metalanguage (a language used to describe languages in general), that formally defines a descriptive markup language. The power of SGML is its cross-platform, structure-driven approach to describing the contents of a document. In other words, SGML identifies every part of a document by its purpose in the document. SGML does not describe the appearance of the document. Instead, it leaves presentation up to browsers and print-formatting applications.

Since SGML is a language, it has special terms and phrases like *international standard*, *formal definition*, *metalanguage*, and *markup language*. We'll start by taking a closer look at some of these terms.

Historically, the word "markup" has been used to describe annotations within a text file. These annotations instruct a typesetter how a particular document element should be laid out for printing. Printing has become more and more automated, so the idea of markup has been extended to cover other annotations and instructions in documents, which are used to control format and output.

Today, *markup* — or *encoding* as it's sometimes called — is a mechanism for making a particular interpretation of a body of text clear and explicit. In everyday writing, we are already familiar with implicit types of text markup: that is, with things like punctuation, font changes, initial caps, and white space on the page.

The function of implicit markup is to provide visual clues to readers. This kind of markup indicates the beginnings and endings of words, or the division of structural document elements like paragraphs, sections, and chapters.

Encoding text for electronic processing takes this implicit information and turns it into an explicit process: that is, the markup is included right in the flow of the text. Explicit markup instructs computers how to interpret the content of the text, and how to render it on a page, a screen, or a file.

Thus, a markup language defines a formal mechanism for preparing text for electronic interpretation and presentation. In its most basic form, therefore, a markup language consists of a set of conventions used to encode text. Such a language must specify the following information:

- the elements of the markup
- in what contexts markup elements may occur
- any markup that is required (rather than optional) to create a properly defined document
- the delimiters of the markup text, to distinguish markup from body text
- the semantics that describe what markup elements signify

SGML provides mechanisms for the all of these except for markup semantics. Typically, additional documentation, like a set of user guidelines, is required to enable readers (and software developers) to make sense of the markup.

The SGML Philosophy

SGML is a formal metalanguage for defining descriptive markup languages. Using the constructs of SGML, you can create an infinite number of descriptive markup languages. One example of an SGML-derived language is the HyperText Markup Language (HTML) used in the WWW.

SGML provides a means to encode hypertext documents intended for easy, straightforward interchange among systems and software. Since SGML documents are application-, system-, and device-independent, you can read someone else's SGML document with your SGML application, or vice versa. This eliminates the need for specific, one-to-one (or one-to-many) conversion utilities to transform a WordPerfect document into a WordStar document, for example.

As a stamp of global approval, SGML was adopted by the International Standards Organization (ISO) and approved as an official ISO Standard in 1986. SGML's standard designation is ISO-8879-1. Because of ISO's rigorous standardization process, many commercial institutions, as well as entire sectors of U.S. government and industry, have adopted SGML as a required component in their document production systems.

SGML's Primary Characteristics

SGML has five primary characteristics:

1. It allows you to create descriptive markup languages.
2. It is hierarchical with interconnected elements and components.
3. There is no implied set of markup conventions, so it supports flexible tag sets.
4. It has a complete formal specification.
5. It is human- as well as machine-readable.

These characteristics combine to create a document definition and description tool that is powerful, flexible, and general enough to accommodate any kind of electronic publishing.

DESCRIPTIVE MARKUP

A descriptive markup system uses embedded codes to describe or annotate document elements, like paragraphs or quotations. These codes or tags are the names for a document's structural elements.

SGML uses markup codes like <PARA> ... </PARA> to identify a particular document element. The <PARA> ... </PARA> tags dictate that the text inside them must be treated as a paragraph. SGML doesn't care how this paragraph is rendered, only that the text inside these tags be kept together and treated as a unit. By contrast, a procedural markup language defines specific processing instructions on a document element. These instructions are to be executed at particular points in a document: "execute the function named PARA with parameters 'left justify' and '10 point times roman font' here." Descriptive markup leaves the rendering up to the document production system.

In fact, SGML discourages *procedural* markup, which might take the form of a specific instruction within a particular application to make a chunk of text "bold, centered, 20 point times roman." As an example, here's the procedural markup for a block quote in *troff*, a UNIX document-formatting language:

```
.sp 1; .ss; sin +12 -12
```

By contrast, in SGML a block quote looks like this:

```
<BLOCKQUOTE>I'm pink, therefore I'm Spam.</BLOCKQUOTE>
```

Now you can appreciate why an SGML hacker was heard to say, "When I convert a *troff* document to SGML, I feel like I'm liberating data. Like I've rescued it from a foreign prison and it's going to hear English spoken again." (Hey, what can we say, he was working long hours.)

The procedural markup for a hyperlink could be specified as:

```
on mouseUp go to card 419.7
```

And the SGML version:

```
<LINK TARGET="419.7">
```

Procedural languages such as *troff* and T$_{\mathrm{E}}$X impose additional formatting overhead on writers, distracting them from doing what they're better at — namely, writing, not formatting.

Descriptive markup, on the other hand, allows writers to concentrate on the problems at hand — namely, creating good, readable, well-organized content. It is concerned with the *what* of building documents, not the *how*.

Descriptive markup also allows display software to render individual document components differently, without violating the integrity of the content. Where one browser might render <EM>Howdy!</EM> as "italics, 12 times roman" another might render it as "magenta, 14 helvetica, underlined." Yet both would succeed in emphasizing the word "Howdy."

When it comes to distinguishing markup from body copy, markup comprises everything in a text document that isn't content. Historically, markup referred to the handwritten annotations and symbols that a page designer added to a typewritten manuscript. These annotations supplied instructions to a typesetter that dictated how to lay out the copy, including typeface selections, point sizes, etc. This is procedural markup and requires each document to be specified in detail by hand.

Unfortunately, nearly all word processing software and desktop publishing software in use today creates procedural markup. Furthermore, document markup will commonly be unique within specific electronic publishing applications like FrameMaker and Microsoft Word. Because applications like these employ their own unique set of proprietary markup codes, their markup applies only to their own specific way of presenting text (usually limited to on-screen and printed forms). This markup method provides no capabilities for porting and presenting the same text in other forms or media such as online displays, CD-ROM, or the WWW.

On the other hand, descriptive markup makes documents both application- and platform-independent. It separates a document's structural representation from any specific application's formatting instructions or search-and-retrieval capabilities. This separation is particularly important, since it increases SGML's portability and reduces the costs of document conversion that can chip away at your bottom line.

Descriptive markup allows disparate applications to manipulate and operate on elements without having to expend significant effort to interpret proprietary procedural markup. This is particularly useful when building a document that includes conditional sections. For example, you could write one user's manual with conditional sections for the 32- and 64-bit versions.

Then, when a user launches the build application to construct a 32-bit version of the user's manual, only those sections typed "32-bit" would be included in the output, along with all non-conditional sections of the text. This would require manual creation of multiple versions in most procedural markup systems, but can be completely automated using descriptive markup.

In SGML, text processing instructions are distinguished from the descriptive markup occurring in a document. Typically, these instructions are collected outside the SGML document in separate procedures or programs. SGML Style Sheets, accompanied by Architectural Forms, provide the methods and information necessary to implement these processing instructions. These are beyond the scope of this book, but worth investigating should you wish to construct a completely descriptive document management environment (please consult the bibliography at the end of this chapter for more references on SGML).

With descriptive markup, a document can be processed by many different kinds of software applications. Each application can apply different processing instructions to document elements that it considers relevant. For example, a document management system might only process those tags that indicate the author's name, the document's creation date, or the date and time of its last modification. An application concerned with formatting and printing the document might disregard this markup entirely, as well as any hyperlink markup.

On the other hand, different processing applications might work with the same document elements. For example, one application that builds master documents from a configuration definition might look only at the markup describing the current revision level of the document while another application might use the same markup to manage multiple versions of the same document.

Descriptive markup is an effective approach because it lets writers concentrate on a document's structure and content. It minimizes the distractions inherent in document formatting and lowers the formatting knowledge required from the writer. Descriptive markup saves effort that might otherwise be wasted prior to starting the publication cycle. It also insulates documents from unnecessary editing solely to oblige different systems' capabilities such as formatting, navigation, or printing.

Descriptive markup also ensures consistent processing of document element types across many different documents. It permits distinguishing document element types, even when they appear similar in behavior or presentation. Finally, descriptive markup expresses structural information that is useful for various kinds of document processing, like document revision control or document browsing/navigation.

The power of descriptive markup is that it accurately represents document structure and can be used to build a tree (or an outline) from the document's DTD, that shows how the document is structured.

This representation is called a "parse tree" — a term borrowed from compiler writers. For instance, a <BOOK> might be defined to contain <FRONTMATTER>, one or more <CHAPTER>s, and then zero or more <APPENDIX>es.

In turn, each <CHAPTER> contains a <TITLE>, followed by one or more <SECTION>s. Each <SECTION> contains a <TITLE> and one or more <PARA>s, <LIST>s, or <IMAGE>s. Each <PARA> contains character data plus <LINK>s or <FOOTNOTE>s. Put them all together and you've got a set of elements that make up any book; create multiple specific instances of each one, and you can describe a particular book.

Multiple simultaneous trees are possible. For example, here are two different ways to organize the same material:

- Story, Pericope, Paragraph, Sentence
- Book, Chapter, Verse

Both of these document structures represent a piece of literature and describe the document's structure, but each describes that structure in a very different way.

HIERARCHICAL PLUS INTERCONNECTIONS

Hypertext links complement linear structure or organization — which might very well be viewed as a hierarchy — with interconnections among document elements. Add hyperlink relationships among SGML elements and they can refer to other data objects using explicit links, interpreted according to the reference discipline for a particular document.

In fact, the identification mechanism for links lets them point to other document elements in the same document (intra-document linking) or to points in altogether different documents (inter-document linking).

Hyperlink connections might even point to files on a remote machine elsewhere on the network. These connections could also point to data stored using a named foreign organization like multimedia files. SGML allows type information in link identifiers to be resolved and handled according to their designations.

When it comes to understanding SGML in the context of general document representation schemes, it's important to realize that there are alternative document models in wide use today. These include representational schemes like bitmapped pages, page description languages (PostScript and PCL), embedded format commands (T_EX, *troff*, and most desktop word processors), and non-hierarchical descriptions (word processor plus spreadsheet) but they are beyond the scope of this book. Here again, please consult the bibliography at the end of this chapter if you'd like to investigate these subjects in detail.

Flexible Tags

SGML is a metalanguage. It is a language of languages, or a language for creating other languages. Thus, with SGML you can create document languages: for example, HTML is a language created using SGML concepts and constructs. If you wanted to, you could even use SGML to create "My Markup Language" (MML). Essentially, this is exactly what happened with HTML, except they didn't ask for your input at the time (or did they?).

With SGML, you can create a custom language that reflects the structure of your document. SGML's flexibility means there is no requirement for a particular set of markup tags. This is not the case for HTML, but that's because HTML is a specific markup language with a specific application and interpretation scheme, not a metalanguage.

For SGML, each document type definition (DTD) uses its own set of tags, appropriate for a document defined using that DTD, and describing its hierarchical structure and content. As instances of a definition based on a small set of DTDs, HTML documents follow a particular structure.

For instance, an HTML document may contain one and only one <HEAD> element, and one and only one <BODY> element. This structure is dictated by the HTML's DTD.

SGML can be used to represent any kind of document structure. You can develop a BOOK's structure to consist of one and only one FRONTMATTER, followed by a BODY which consists of one or more CHAPTERs that can include zero or more SECTIONs. We can cook up our own BOOK's structure which would differ from yours by our insistence that it require one or more SECTIONs within a CHAPTER.

With SGML, you can make optional features available — for instance, if you want to include zero or more SECTIONs in a CHAPTER, SECTION could be stated to be optional within a CHAPTER in your particular document definition. Even though you might share the same DTD with another document, using optional features can result in multiple hierarchies emerging from the same document type definition.

Besides being platform- and software-independent, SGML is also language- and character set-independent. European and Pacific Rim implementations of SGML permit tag names specified in French or Japanese, because individual or multiple character sets can be included through an external entity mechanism within SGML (we'll cover this in more detail later in this chapter).

Finally, the syntax of your document's structure can be altered to meet any new requirements. If you decide to require new documents to include a BACKMATTER section at the end of each of your SGML documents, you can alter your DTD. This will have adverse effects on previously created documents that conformed to the old DTD, so you'd either have to make the BACKMATTER element optional, or alter all the old documents to include a BACKMATTER section to make them conformant.

The three DTD faces of HTML

At present, there are three HTML DTDs in use:

- the IETF level 2 HTML DTD
- the World Wide Web Consortium's level 3 HTML DTD
- Netscape's Mozilla DTD

These DTDs will be scrutinized and dissected in Chapter 3. All you need to know right now is that in order for a browser or HTML validation tool to work, it has to either know — or assume — that a document conforms to one and only one of these different DTDs.

FORMAL DOCUMENT SPECIFICATION

The formal definition of a document's structure is accomplished through an SGML concept called the Document Type Definition (DTD). A DTD is required for each language created with SGML. As we mentioned earlier, HTML currently has three DTDs resulting in three distinct but related hypertext languages, all of which are more or less compatible with various WWW clients and servers.

A DTD defines the syntax of a markup language by specifying:

- any abbreviation conventions used for markup tags
- names and helper applications for any foreign notations (or non-HTML file or data types that will be linked into HTML documents)
- every named markup element, with information about its legal context (i.e., where it can be used)
- external system objects referenced in the document

The DTD provides numerous capabilities. First, it provides a formal specification for all markup conventions particular to a type of document.

Second, an application known as an SGML parser can ensure that a document is compliant to its DTD. This process is known as validation. Applications that export or create SGML typically validate documents, whereas document conversion and SGML importing applications may not perform validation. We will look closer at validation in Chapter 4.

HUMAN AND COMPUTER READABLE REPRESENTATIONS

SGML represents a document's structure in human- and computer-readable form. The descriptive markup is separated from the text within the flow of a document by some special, printable delimiter strings. In HTML, these delimiters are strings of length one and are < and > (less-than and greater-than signs).

People who are unfamiliar with SGML can still read and probably understand an SGML document. For instance, a human reader would be able to figure out this SGML chunk:

```
<CHAPTER><TITLE>Introduction to Bracket Racing</TITLE> ...
```

Also, a dumb terminal running a character-mode Web browser could give an interpretable but ugly rendering of an HTML document. You can't do this with any non-SGML What-You-See-Is-What-You-Get (WYSIWYG) word processor.

Even primitive but powerful applications such as *awk, sed, lex, edlin, emacs,* or *vi* can read and process an SGML document. Another plus is that no harm comes to SGML data when it's necessary to translate to and from character sets like those found on a Mac, PC, or UNIX workstation. You can even divide an SGML file into smaller pieces without harming the data (unless you forget how to put it back together). There are no byte-order problems like our favorite porting gotcha, encountered when representing floating-point numbers, known as "big/little-endian" (taken from *Gulliver's Travels,* but pointing to byte ordering of high-order and low-order digits when describing numbers, rather than indicating which end of a soft-boiled egg one cracks open to eat).

Document element names can act as natural-language mnemonics (that means you can understand and remember them!). Nor are they cryptic, application-specific commands. Instead they can be interpreted independent of any application-specific knowledge. Finally, the markup is included directly within a document's text flow. It therefore stays with the current context right along with the document's content, rather than being supplied by an external application. Because everything necessary to render or interpret such a document travels together, the principle of locality is preserved; that is, the ability to act locally on the data in order to process it.

SGML Document Structure

An SGML document consists of some required pieces, but can also include other optional bits and pieces of information. For the record, here's what these bits and pieces are:

- an optional SGML declaration
- a required DTD
- instances of document elements and their attributes
- references to entities
- marked sections

Let's take a closer look at each of these elements, to better understand how they interconnect and interoperate to describe a document.

The SGML Declaration

An SGML declaration includes changes to syntax that might include changes to delimiter characters. These are seldom altered, but they can be. You can also alter the maximum length of tag names. This is often increased to a very large value rather than the default 8-character restriction. Finally, the SGML declaration is optional and is often omitted from an SGML document.

The SGML declaration permits alternate markup conventions like the base character set to be altered or expanded. It also permits an SGML parser to determine if it has sufficient capacity (memory available) for a document, as might be indicated by the storage requirements based on the maximum length of tag names.

The syntax of an SGML declaration looks like this:

```
<!SGML gobs-of-declarations  >
```

Most SGML declarations typically occupy files by themselves. A declaration could be included at the head of each SGML document, but this would be inefficient. Say you have 10,000 SGML documents that include an identical SGML declaration in its entirety. If you ever needed to change it, then you'd have to change all 10,000 documents! That's why most folks omit it from their SGML document source and install it in a well-known place in their file systems.

SGML applications — like a parser — can be instructed to use this file as the SGML declaration when validating an SGML document. For example, with the *sgmls* parser, there is a command-line option to specify the path to the SGML declaration file. This approach lessens the impact of changing the SGML declaration and also helps to maintain system-wide consistency.

For an example of the SGML declaration used for HTML, see Chapter 3. For more information about the SGML declaration itself, the ultimate reference is section 13 of the ISO-8879 standards document, but Goldfarb's *SGML Handbook* (see the bibliography at the end of this chapter) includes an annotated version that is much more readable.

THE DTD

A DTD is a formal description of the structure of a particular class of documents. For instance, the Davenport Group created the DocBook DTD that is applied to technical documents to be displayed electronically. This DTD was fine-tuned for computer software documentation, namely user manuals and programming references. The Davenport Group's Archive is available online at:

```
http://www.ora.com/davenport/README.html
```

A DTD declares a document's elements. This dictates what elements a document can contain and their structural relationships to one another. For each element in the document, the DTD specifies its name, plus its content data model.

SGML's element content data model

In the DTD, most elements are specified so as to contain other elements, but elements can also contain parsable character data (#PCDATA). Speaking generically, elements can contain either other elements, #PCDATA, or both. For each and every element, the specifics of what's legal are declared in the element's content data model.

Content data models strongly resemble what computer scientists call *regular expressions*. Not surprisingly, they are defined using regular expression conventions. The occurrence indicator of an element is a symbol appended to the element name. Here are the three indicators that you will encounter when reading an SGML DTD:

- \+ means one or more occurrences
- * means zero or more occurrences
- ? means zero or one occurrence

Note, if an element that occurs within a content data model does not include an occurrence indicator, that means it must occur only once in that context. In other words, its presence is required or mandatory, and it cannot be repeated.

If you re-examine the example of the content data model for an HTML definition list <DL> tag that we presented earlier in this chapter, it looks like:

```
(DT*, DD?)+
```

If you examine this statement closely, it indicates the following information:

1. <DT> stands for definition term; <DD> stands for definition description.

2. If a <DL> tag occurs in a document, it must be followed by at least one definition term <DT> and one definition description <DD>, as indicated by the plus sign around the parentheses that enclose those two elements.

3. If a tag pair occurs, it must consist of one definition term <DT>, but the definition description is optional, as indicated by the ? after <DD>. However, the ? also indicates that only one <DD> may follow any <DT>.

4. A definition term may occur zero or more times in a definition list, as indicated by the asterisk following <DT>, but this is overridden by the plus sign outside the parentheses, to indicate that an empty definition list (with no definition terms inside it) is illegal.

Multiply the effort in decoding this syntax for an average of half-a-dozen elements per individual element's context in HTML, and you'll begin to understand how this dry notation can still produce a rich and varied syntax.

Here are some examples of occurrence indicators in a sample DTD that are sure to be near and dear to the heart of every serious programmer:

```
<!ELEMENT pizza      - - (crust,sauce,topping+) >
<!ELEMENT crust      - - (flour,milk,salt?) >
<!ELEMENT salt       - - (grain+) >
<!ELEMENT topping    - - (cheese,item+) >
<!ELEMENT item       - - (mushrooms | sausage | pepperoni) >
```

Parentheses are used to group elements. There are three special connectors that may occur between elements:

- | means one of the elements in the list must occur
- & means both elements must occur in any order
- , means both elements must occur in a specific order

There is one special content data model. The "ANY" content data model permits the element to contain other DTD elements directly. ANY is not parenthesized. It is not a type of content data model. It is a specification of sub-elements.

In the DTD, there is also an element "declared" content data model. This is done with reserved words specific to SGML. The reserved words for a declared content data model are:

- CDATA — markup within a tag is ignored except </
- EMPTY — the element can never have content or an end tag
- RCDATA — entity references are recognized but no content is allowed

This is an example of an "anchor" element type with a declared content data model:

```
<!ELEMENT anchor      - -    EMPTY>
```

Elements can have mixed content models. This permits a mixture of sub-elements along with character data. Mixed content data models can lead to language ambiguities and should therefore be avoided. This is especially true when elements are separated by the | connector in the content data model, or when an element is minimized and does not require (or accept) an explicit end tag.

Here's an example of an element with a mixed content data model:

```
<!ELEMENT trash    - O (#PCDATA | quote)*>
```

Reading a DTD

Reading a DTD follows the guidelines we presented for reading an HTML document. Here's an example of a DTD for a document type "book":

```
<!DOCTYPE book
<!ENTITY % chunks "para | list | figure">
<!NOTATION gif          SYSTEM      "xv">
<!ELEMENT book          - -         (frontmatter,body)+(link)>
<!ELEMENT frontmatter   - -         (title,author,copyright?)>
<!ELEMENT (title,author,copyright)
                        - -         (#PCDATA)>
<!ELEMENT body          - -         (chapter*)>
<!ELEMENT chapter       - -         (title,section*)>
<!ELEMENT section       - -         (title, (%chunks;)*)>
<!ELEMENT para          - -         (#PCDATA | emph)*>
<!ATTLIST (chapter,section,para)
                   id   ID          #IMPLIED>
<!ELEMENT list          - -         (item*)>
<!ATTLIST list          type        (unord|ord|plain)
"plain"
                        id   ID                      #IMPLIED>
<!ELEMENT item          - -         (para*)>
<!ELEMENT emph          - -         (#PCDATA)>
<!ATTLIST emph          type        CDATA            #IMPLIED>
<!ELEMENT figure        - 0         (caption)>
<!ATTLIST figure        type        NOTATION (gif)   #REQUIRED>
<!ELEMENT caption       - 0         (#PCDATA)>
<!ELEMENT link          - 0         EMPTY>
<!ATTLIST link          rid         IDREF            #REQUIRED
                        type        CDATA            #REQUIRED>
]>
```

A DTD does not specify semantics for any of its elements. Understanding meanings and interpreting document elements is left up to human readers. Therefore, SGML applications — like structured editors — cannot appreciate the meanings of terms like <CHAPTER> or <TITLE>. But they can (and do) test all documents they parse to make sure they're DTD-compliant.

Typically, DTDs are used to:

- define an organization's rules governing document structure, or to codify what constitutes an acceptable "official" document.
- formalize all document markup conventions to enable other applications to parse conforming documents.
- permit parsing tools to analyze and depict the structure of conforming documents.
- allow parsing tools to validate documents and report any deviations.
- declare names for external data and their notations (in SGML-speak, notation means "the format and structure in which data collections occur" — this would identify graphics files for proper rendering or sound files for playback, from the appropriate helper applications).

In short, the DTD defines all the legal markup elements for a document type and states the rules for required or optional terms, and the order in which these terms may occur.

The SGML document prolog

The name (or location) of a governing DTD is required for an SGML document and must be specified at the beginning of the document. As we mentioned earlier, the DTD could even be physically included, but the smart thing is to include it by reference.

Here's an example of an SGML prolog to an HTML document indicating that the document conforms to the IETF HTML 2.0 DTD:

```
<!DOCTYPE HTML PUBLIC "-//IETF//DTD HTML 2.0//EN">
```

The DTD reference occurs within the SGML DOCTYPE declaration and has the following syntax:

```
<!DOCTYPE root-tag PUBLIC public-id system-id [
   ...—any additional markup declarations occur here—
]>
```

Element markup declarations take the form:

```
<!element-type name characteristics >
```

For more information about markup declarations in a DTD, please consult section 11 of the ISO-8879 standard (also covered in Clause 11 in Goldfarb's *SGML Handbook*).

ELEMENTS

In the HTML prolog, "PUBLIC" is the *root-tag*, and the string "-//IETF//DTD HTML 2.0//EN" is the *public-id*. From the public-id you can determine that the DTD was developed by the IETF, that it is DTD version 2.0 for HTML, and that it is written in English.

An element in a DTD is a distinct part of a document and must be declared in the DTD. Working from our book example, some of its elements include <CHAPTER>, <TITLE>, and <LINK>.

Every element in a DTD is realized as an instance of the element type within the SGML document. In SGML terms, an element is called a *generic identifier* (GI). Elements can also contain other elements, as specified in an element's content data model.

For instance, in HTML, the content data model for <DL> is:

```
<!ELEMENT DL      - -  (DT*, DD?)+>
```

This example shows that one or more occurrences of the <DT> and <DD> tag pair must occur. This is indicated by the + symbol outside the parentheses. Content data models are read from left to right, so that the DL element's content data model reads as follows:

> *The element type named DL may contain the DT element type, which can occur zero or more times. The DT element type can be followed by a DD element type which can occur zero or one time.*

Elements in a DTD form a tree, created from the combination of all the element types and their corresponding content data models, as specified in the DTD. Element types cannot legally cross each other's boundaries. An example of this kind of rule violation is:

```
<PARA>Badges, we don't need no <EM>stinkin' badges!</PARA></EM>
```

This is considered invalid because the closing </PARA> tag occurs in the data stream before the closing </EM> tag. This violation is called "improper nesting of tags."

The correct SGML for this example is:

```
<PARA>Badges, we don't need no <EM>stinkin' badges!</EM></PARA>
```

Figure 2-1 shows an example of our sample "book" DTD in a tree form.

Elements are used to provide names or handles for components of a document's structure like <SECTION>, <LIST>, and <FOOTER>. They provide mnemonic names appropriate to the particular document type. You probably wouldn't find a structural component called <VERSE> in a technical computer manual, but you would in a document about poetry.

Elements provide placeholders for information like location markers or named anchors within a document. An example might be where a named anchor would be placed in a document at the head of each section so it could be referenced from the table of contents or the index.

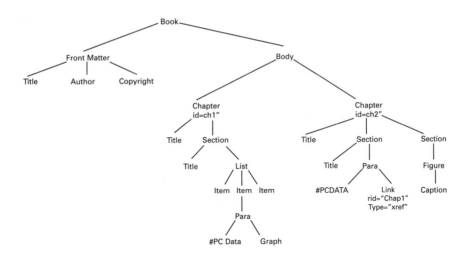

Figure 2-1

The book DTD forms a tree that shows the relationship between chapters, sections, and paragraphs; and the ordering of front matter and chapters.

In HTML, the markup looks like this:

```
<A NAME="rendering">Rendering 3-D Models</A>
```

The <A> element type includes an attribute type, NAME. NAME's value contains location marker information and provides a unique name for an anchor (which is the destination of a link elsewhere, either from within the same document or from another document altogether).

Element types can also specify how an external application should process its content. For example, WWW clients decide how to render element types of the HTML DTD, or whether an external helper application will be necessary, based on an element's type. That's why <EM>Party on!</EM> is rendered by some WWW clients as:

Party on!

while other browers might render the phrase in the color magenta.

The syntax for an element begins with a start tag that contains the name of the element type (its generic identifier, or GI). <CHAPTER> is an example of a start tag. The end of an element instance may be marked by an end tag, so that </CHAPTER> is the end tag for <CHAPTER>.

Start/end tags usually appear in pairs, the exception to this rule occurs when the DTD allows minimization for a particular element type. In this case, the start tag need not be matched by an end tag.

For example, the HTML 2.0 DTD allows minimization of the <P> tag. That is why you seldom see a </P> tag in HTML text. The <P> tag declaration from the IETF level 2 HTML DTD reads as follows:

```
<!ELEMENT P    - O (%text)+ >
```

Minimization creates singleton tags

SGML allows minimization in an element type declaration. Minimization is used to shorten or omit tags for element types, typically for the sake of convenience, but it does have its costs:

- Not all SGML parsers support minimization because it complicates top-down recursive parsing (that is, it will no longer be Look-Ahead-Left-Recursive, or LALR, which is easily implemented with a simple stack algorithm).
- Minimization makes SGML files hard for humans to read because it can introduce ambiguities that a human cannot resolve.
- Markup errors related to minimized elements are more difficult to locate and isolate, both for humans and parsers.
- Non-SGML savvy utilities like *sed*, *awk*, and *emacs* do not have enough information to perform global search-and-replace operations on minimized elements.

Table 2-1 provides a quick reference for the element declarations used in this example:

```
<!ELEMENT chapter   -   (title?,section*)+(footer)>
```

ELEMENT ATTRIBUTES

An attribute gives an element unique characteristics by presenting information specific to an instance of an element type in an SGML document.

This attribute may not necessarily be unique to the element's type (that is, an attribute with the same name may occur for multiple types), but each one describes information that is not common for the element type as a whole.

Table 2-1
SGML Element Type DTD Declaration Quick Reference

Component	Description	Function
<!ELEMENT	start of element declaration	Specifies what element is being declared in the DTD.
chapter	generic identifier	Name of the element type.
-	start tag indicator	"-" means start tag can never be omitted. "O" (uppercase O) allows omission of start tag where unambiguous.
-	end tag indicator	Same as start tag.
(title?,section*...)	content data model	Specifies which other element types in the same DTD can occur with its context.
>	close of markup	Indicates the end of the ELEMENT declaration.

Attribute names

Attributes have names, which are declared in the DTD, and they are usually optional for their related elements. In fact, an element need not have attributes at all. An attribute has a declared value that must also be declared in the DTD. Finally, an attribute has a default value, which may be a specific value, or might simply indicate that the attribute is required for every instance of the element.

Attributes enable parsers to check the uniqueness of instances of element types. Where linking or cross-referencing is concerned, for instance, they allow parsers to resolve link and anchor identifiers uniquely, or to identify (illegal) multiple instances of the same identifier.

In general, attributes indicate the overall characteristics and properties of an element type. Thus, individual instances of an element type may be distinguished on the basis of those characteristics and properties.

Attribute syntax in SGML

The SGML syntax for attributes is as follows:

- Attributes may appear only within start tags.

- All values assigned to attributes must be surrounded by quotes (that is, "black" is a legal attribute value; black is not).

- In an SGML document, every attribute has a name followed by an = (equal sign) followed by its (quoted) value, for example:

```
<CAR COLOR="red" INTERIOR="leather">
```

- Attributes can occur in any order, no matter what their order of declaration.

The declaration format for attributes in the DTD can best be explained using an example:

```
                        Name  Type               Status/Default
<!ATTLIST chapter       id    ID                 #REQUIRED
                        num   NUMBER             #IMPLIED
                        sect  (public|secret)    "public">
```

In other words, this declaration indicates that every chapter must have an id of type ID; that every chapter has a number that is implied by its location in the sequence of chapters; and that chapters have an access rating, called *sect*, that may take the value of "public" or "secret" where "public" is assumed by default.

To ensure a DTD's readability, an element's attributes are usually declared immediately following the element's declaration. This keeps all the relevant information in close proximity, and makes an element's definition easier to follow.

Attributes may have declared values

Like element types, attributes can have "declared" values. These declared values are reserved words in SGML. They are:

- CDATA — All internal markup within the attribute value is ignored.

- ENTITY(IES) — The name of an external entity known to the current document.

- ID — An identifier guaranteed to be unique (that is, it occurs only once) within the document.

- IDREF(S) — An identifier in a document of an element type with an ID as its value.

- NAME(S) — A valid SGML element name must start with a letter, and typically contains only letters, digits, hyphens, or periods, and is typically no longer than NAMELEN (a number indicating the maximum allowable length of a name string).

- NMTOKEN(S) — Same as NAME(S), except that tokens can start with letters, digits, a period, or a hyphen (most NMTOKENs start with a hyphen).

- NOTATION — The name of a foreign data type followed by a parenthesized list of permitted notations.

- NUMBER(S) — Contains only digits.

- NUTOKEN(S) — Starts with a digit, but may contain letters, digits, a period, or a hyphen.

- enumeration — A list of values in the form of quoted strings (e.g., "red","yellow","blue").

Declared values specify the type of values an attribute can take and that is useful for error-checking and improved readability of the DTD.

Attribute occurrence rules

The following designations govern an attribute's occurrence within an element instance:

- #REQUIRED — Required in every instance of an attribute's element type.

- #CURRENT — Defaults to the most recent value supplied for the same attribute in the same element type.

- #CONREF — Indicates that an attribute is empty if specified; if #CONREF is absent from the declaration, the element instance retains its normal content.

- #IMPLIED — Indicates that a value may be omitted; if a value is absent, then applications that require this attribute must infer its value.

- value — An explicit default value may be supplied for an attribute.

#FIXED attributes

A #FIXED attribute identifies that the attribute must have the same value for all instances of its element type. The #FIXED attribute specification in the DTD is placed just before the explicit default value of an attribute, as shown in this example:

```
<!ATTLIST blob   area   NUMBER #FIXED      sq-feet>
```

Table 2-2 provides a quick reference for the SGML attributes defined in the following declaration:

```
<!ELEMENT chapter   - -   (title?,section*)+(footer)>
<!ATTLIST chapter   id    ID                    #REQUIRED
                    num   NUMBER                #IMPLIED
                    sect  (public|secret)       "public">
```

Table 2-2
SGML Attribute DTD Declaration Quick Reference

Component	Description	Function
<!ATTLIST	start of attribute declaration	Specify what part is being declared in DTD.
chapter	generic identifier	Name of the element type in the DTD that has attributes.
id,num,sect	attribute names	These names occur in start tags in document to the left of = sign.
ID,NUMBER, (public|secret)	values of declared attributes; data types of attributes	Identifies the type of data assigned to this attribute.
#REQUIRED, #IMPLIED, "public"	default values	Marks if an attribute is required, optional, or the default value.

ENTITIES

Entities are chunks of data that are self-contained and stored separately from other data. The typical container for an entity (or more normally, a collection of entities) is a file. In SGML there are number, character, general, and parameter entities.

Entities are sometimes used to segment large files into more manageable component files. They can be utilized to incorporate the same data in many places (for example, boiler-plate information like a copyright notice or a disclaimer). Entities also protect non-SGML data from the parser, and allows it to be included in a document by reference. This permits inclusion of non-printable characters like è (a small "e" with a grave accent), as well as frequently used phrases like "National Association of Chevelle Owners."

Entities are declared in a DTD with a name and value. For example, here is a general entity declared in a DTD:

```
<!ENTITY NACO   CDATA     "National Association of Chevelle Owners" >
```

The syntax for referencing an entity within an SGML document is

```
&entity_name;.
```

Here are some examples:

```
&egrave;
&NACO;
```

Character and numeric entities

SGML's character set is taken from the International Standards Organization's body of official international standards. The ISO-Latin-1 character set is called ISO-8859-1. The "Latin" part means that it's derived from the Roman alphabet used so commonly to represent text in many different languages around the world. The number "1" indicates that this is the first version of this character set definition.

Numeric Entities Aren't Portable!

A word of caution: numeric character entities are not portable. Each operating system has its own decimal values for numeric entities. On the Mac, the uppercase Latin A with acute accent (Å) is ç, in ISO-8859-1 the same symbol is Á, and its EBCDIC value is e. If you're writing HTML, though, you'll always want to use the ISO-8859-1 number (at least, until HTML switches over to the Unicode standard, ISO 10646-1, which supports non-Roman alphabets like Japanese, Mandarin, Hanggul, etc.).

ISO-8859-1 specifies character entities using strings of characters to represent other characters such as < for the less-than symbol. It also specifies numeric entities which are strings of numbers that represent characters. These are identified by a pound sign (#) trailing an ampersand. Numeric entities specify a particular character representation by number, so that < is the numeric entity for the less-than sign.

Public entity sets are available that are verbose and unambiguous. These increase portability where entities are concerned. For special handling by the parser, entities can be declared to be non-SGML data.

Two rules of thumb for SGML entities are:

- Declare any external or non-SGML data as an entity.
- Declare entities to represent commonly used acronyms or abbreviations or to encapsulate conventions.

Properly applied, entities increase the representation power of SGML and can provide some labor-saving abbreviations to boot!

Types of entity text

An entity can represent different types of text, but these types must be defined within each entity declared in the DTD. There are four kinds of text types:

- **literal text type:** Literal text types are parsed normally and can include normal markup.
- **data text type:** There are three sub-types of data text:
  - CDATA — no markup or entities recognized
  - SDATA — character data specific to an application
  - PI — content of entity is an application specific instruction
- **bracketed text type:** Bracketed text entities have their content surrounded by SGML delimiter strings. If you need more information about bracketed text entities, consult section 9.6 of ISO-8879.
- **external text type:** External entities are files identified by a PUBLIC or SYSTEM identifier succeeded by an optional sub-type. There are three sub-types:
  - SUBDOC — SGML from another DTD
  - NDATA — entity is a named foreign notation
  - literal — parsed same as SGML

Parameter entities

Parameter entities are declared in the DTD which are intended only for use as macros within the DTD itself. General entities are used in an SGML document and are completely separate from parameter entities.

Parameter entities are referenced with a % (percent sign) rather than the & (ampersand) used for general entities in an SGML document proper. Here's how a parameter entity is declared and used in a DTD:

```
<!ENTITY % emphasis     "italic | bold | red">
<!ELEMENT %emphasis;    - - CDATA>
```

Make sure you pay close attention to the space following the % in the entity declaration; it's required, not a typo!

Table 2-3 supplies a quick reference for SGML entities for the entity declaration:

```
<!ENTITY NACO   CDATA "National Association of Chevelle Owners">
```

Table 2-3

SGML Entity DTD Declaration Quick Reference

Component	Description	Function
<!ENTITY	start of parameter entity	Specifies what is being declared in DTD.
%	parameter entity reference open delimiter; must be followed by a space	Not present in this example; indicates parameter entity used in DTD only; not used in document.
NACO	entity name	Case-sensitive name that references entity.
CDATA	entity type reserved word	Identifies type of value; if omitted, entity parsed when referenced.
"National Association of Chevelle Owners"	entity text	Declares the replacement text for the entity; also can be external identifier for external entities.

MARKED SECTIONS

Marked sections are specially-parsed elements within an SGML document. They are used to conveniently exclude parts of an SGML document, and are similar to the conditional text sections found in desktop publishing applications like FrameMaker. They are also comparable to the #ifdef in C.

Marked sections are used to enclose sections of an SGML document meant for optional inclusion. For instance, if you would like to build a 32-bit version of your UNIX operating system Installation Guide, you could instruct an application to create a temporary SGML file that excludes 64-bit marked sections. Here's an example:

```
For the <![ INCLUDE [ <EM>32-bit</EM> ] ]>
<![ IGNORE [ <EM>64-bit</EM> ] ]> operating system, ...
```

If you had to produce a 64-bit version of this guide, you would have to flip the status keywords, INCLUDE and IGNORE.

A better way to do this would be to declare in the DTD a general entity for each condition:

```
<!ENTITY 32-bit    CDATA     "INCLUDE" >
<!ENTITY 64-bit    CDATA     "IGNORE" >
```

Then the preceding SGML example could be rewritten as:

```
For the <![ &32-bit; [ <EM>32-bit</EM> ] ]>
<![ &64-bit; [ <EM>64-bit</EM> ] ]> operating system, ...
```

To produce a 64-bit version of the document, all you do is switch the status keywords in the DTD, not the document:

```
<!ENTITY 32-bit    CDATA          "IGNORE" >
<!ENTITY 64-bit    CDATA          "INCLUDE" >
```

These marked sections also prevent parsing of the content to protect SGML examples. These meta-information sections do not represent normal document structures. You can also control versions of a single SGML document by using marked sections.

Marked sections take the general form:

```
<![ status-keywords    [ ... anything ... ] ]>
```

Marked section keywords

There are five status keywords used in marked sections:

- IGNORE — exclude this content

- INCLUDE — parse and include text normally

- CDATA — do not recognize tags or entities

- RCDATA — do not recognize entities

- TEMP — flags section as temporary; no effect on parsing

Rules for marked sections

There are a few special rules for marked sections. First, they can be nested and they can cross boundaries. For instance, this example is valid but discouraged, nevertheless:

```
<PARA>Totally a really <![ IGNORE [ <B>terrible concept</B>.</PARA>
<PARA>Public flogging to those who ]]> think this is great!</PARA>
```

The content of a marked section does not have to be valid at all!

General SGML Rules

We thought we'd present some general rules we hope you'll find useful for your Web programming education:

- Entity and element names are typically restricted to the character sets including: a-z A-Z 0-9 and they must start with: a-z A-Z 0-9.

- Typically, element names are case insensitive.

- Typically, entity names are case sensitive (à versus À).

- Delimiters are strings, not characters (< is a string of length one; it could be changed to <** in the SGML declaration).

- Delimiters are not recognized across entity boundaries.

- You can use either single or double quotes for quoted values.

- There is no default escape character for including quotes within quotes; use either a character or numeric entity.

- Tag, entity, and attribute names are eight characters in length by default, excluding delimeter strings.

- Redefining an entity is an ignored non-error; that is, it is not treated as an error, but it has no effect.

- SGML comments take the form:

```
<!-- comment goes here --
   -- and here -->
```

If you can just remember and apply these rules, you'll bypass a lot of potential grief in your HTML and other Web programming!

SGML and HTML

HTML isn't an extension of SGML; it's an application of SGML. HTML was developed utilizing the ISO-8879 standard and defines a markup language for hypertext electronic documents served on the WWW. It could have been called the "World Wide Web Markup Language (WWWML)" if Tim Berners-Lee had deemed it so. It was given a name so that everyone in the WWW community could use a common handle to place on a Web document's structure. In Chapter 3 we will examine the HTML DTD in detail.

Summary

While it is complex and completely formal, SGML is an important standard and represents significant document technology. SGML allows documents to be rigorously described and defined and includes methods for defining and referencing elements, means for governing their order and relationships, and even provides tools to import external data sources and entities as needed.

In fact, SGML is being embraced daily by large commercial institutions and government agencies. They produce rafts of documentation explicitly or as a by-product of building other products such as hardware and software.

Why have they chosen SGML? Because it enables them to produce documents that are portable to other platforms. These documents are application- and system-independent. This independence is crucial because it almost eliminates the "transformation, translation, and conversion" problem plaguing them today. It lets them concentrate on content and assume that form is taken care of, once it's been properly defined.

A Brief SGML Bibliography

Charles F. Goldfarb, **The SGML Handbook** *(edited and with a foreword by Yuri Rubinsky), Clarendon Press, Oxford, UK, 1990. (ISBN 0-19-853737-9; List Price: $90.00.) Written by one of the fathers of SGML, this book contains an excellent introduction to SGML and a nicely annotated version of the ISO-8879 standard. It's incredibly dense and complex, but valuable nonetheless.*

Eric van Herwijnen, **Practical SGML***, 2nd edition, Kluwer Academic Publishers, Norwell, MA, 1994. (ISBN 0-7923-9434-8; List Price: $40.00.) Aimed at helping novices become proficient in SGML syntax, terminology, and applications, this book is a great place to start learning about the subject.*

This Web page:

```
http://www.sil.org/sgml/sgml.html
```

is maintained and sponsored at SoftQuad (a leading vendor of SGML tools and technology) on behalf of the company and the Summer Institute of Linguistics, an academic group focused on providing SGML-related training. It is an outstanding jumping-off point for SGML investigations and points to nearly every useful SGML resource available on the Web.

CHAPTER 3

The HTML DTDs

*T*he goal of all Webheads, WebMasters, and institutions that disseminate online information is to offer a Web space that constantly evolves and provides readers with up-to-date information. But this dedication requires making many decisions prior to unleashing information out of their company's pipe into the Internet sea. One of the most important is, "Which HTML DTD should we adopt and follow?"

While there are many options possible, the most reasonable ones include:

- Follow the current IETF level 2 DTD.
- Follow the ever-changing level 3 draft DTD.
- Follow the Netscape extensions to the level 2 and 3 DTDs.

There are currently three HTML DTDs of particular interest. In this chapter, we will discuss the IETF level 1 and level 2 DTDs; briefly review the IETF level 3 DTD (which we'll investigate in depth in Chapter 5); and cover the Netscape extensions (also known as the Mozilla DTD).

History of HTML

HTML's evolution continues to be a fascinating story. Starting with a simple set of basic markup and text elements, HTML is evolving into a complex hypermedia markup language. Along with this evolution from simple to complex, there have been some digressions from the original basic markup model to today's complex collection of table definitions, mathematical notations, and complex markup requirements.

For instance, HTML+ is one branch of the HTML tree that reached a dead end (but not before exerting a major influence on level 3 development). In fact, many artifacts from HTML+ have been integrated into the level 3 DTD, while numerous others met their demise. Figure 3-1 depicts a timeline for HTML, depicting its development and evolution.

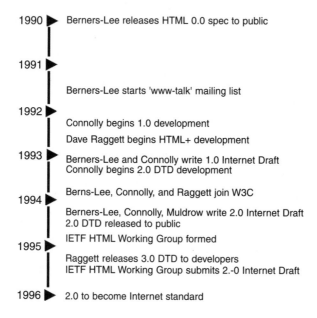

1990 ▶ Berners-Lee releases HTML 0.0 spec to public

1991 ▶

Berners-Lee starts 'www-talk' mailing list

1992 ▶
Connolly begins 1.0 development
Dave Raggett begins HTML+ development

1993 ▶ Berners-Lee and Connolly write 1.0 Internet Draft
Connolly begins 2.0 DTD development

Berns-Lee, Connolly, and Raggett join W3C
1994 ▶
Berners-Lee, Connolly, Muldrow write 2.0 Internet Draft
2.0 DTD released to public
IETF HTML Working Group formed
1995 ▶
Raggett releases 3.0 DTD to developers
IETF HTML Working Group submits 2.-0 Internet Draft

1996 ▶ 2.0 to become Internet standard

Figure 3-1
The evolution of HTML.

Initially, the HTML specification was made available (as an HTML file) in 1990 by Tim Berners-Lee (TBL) while he worked at CERN, the European Particle Physical Laboratory in Switzerland. This specification was basic in scope and supported only elementary text-handling capabilities.

In October of 1991, TBL began the *www-talk* mailing list. Its intent was to allow others to participate in the refinement and evolution of the WWW. In March 1992, Dan Connolly began the development of the level 1 HTML DTD. It went through numerous revisions before July 1992, when Dan released it to the WWW community. He continued work on this specification with input and constructive criticism from many participants of the *www-talk* mailing list. Finally in 1993 TBL took Dan's DTD and wrote an Internet draft RFC for HTML that was released in July 1993. HTML was finally out to the public!

As soon as level 1 was publicly introduced, work began on the level 2 DTD. It rolled support for forms and image maps into the level 1 DTD, and also obsoleted certain elements like <XMP> and <LISTING>, which had become deprecated through experience and use.

HTML 2.0 also provided more advanced text-handling capabilities and permitted the kinds of documents that led to the Web's astonishing growth in the recent past. Dan Connolly and Tim Berners-Lee of the W3 Consortium are members of the IETF HTML working group, and they continue to lead the efforts to complete the HTML 2.0 specification as it nears completion (expected in July 1995).

HTML 3.0 is already under development by the IETF HTML working group. If the current state of its draft proposal is any indication of what the DTD will ultimately contain (and it usually is), HTML 3.0 will incorporate new features like tables, text flow around figures, mathematical equations, and style sheets. Because the specification is still very much in flux, level 3 HTML is primarily of interest to WWW application developers. Dave Raggett of the IETF HTML working group is leading the current development (we cover the current state of HTML 3.0 in Chapter 5).

Workings of the IETF HTML Working Group

Most proposed Internet protocols never become standards. Some do become standards, but not before they are subjected to a series of rigorous development stages conducted by the IETF. For a protocol to qualify, it is typically submitted to the IETF as a detailed specification, sometimes accompanied by a prototype implementation. Table 3-1 depicts the levels of Internet standards.

Table 3-1

Internet Standards Levels

Level of Standard	Description
experimental	implemented for experimental purposes
proposed	submitted by IETF for consideration (expires in 6+ months)
draft	accepted as draft by steering group (expires in 4+ months)
standard	accepted as standard by steering group
required	must be included to meet U.S. government standards
elective	exclude/include at the desire of the developers
recommended	inclusion in implementations recommended but not required
historic	obsolete protocol
information	documentation on standards process

During the *experimental* stage, the IETF and its affiliated institutions try out interesting protocols. At this point the IETF can decide that a protocol does not need to become a standard, which results in the proposed protocol being removed from the standards track. Even so, that same protocol may be resubmitted at a later date for further consideration, should circumstances warrant.

To move from *proposed* to *draft* status, a protocol must have its status advanced by the Internet Engineering Steering Group (IESG), and it must be a *proposed* standard for at least six months. Evolving from *draft* to *standard* status requires a nod from the IESG, but it must also have been in *draft* status for at least four months, and it must have been the subject of at least two successful implementations during the *draft* period.

Upon gaining *standard* status, a protocol can be:

- *required* — that is, the standard must be included in any implementation of TCP/IP.

- *elective* — the standard is optional, left to the developer's discretion.

- *recommended* — the standard is not required, but is highly recommended, probably because of wide use or high demand.

- *historic* or *information* — these rarely occur; the former indicates a standard that has passed from use, while the latter describes some aspect of the standards process itself.

By now, it should be obvious that the IETF does not fool around when developing a standard, which is what HTML will soon become. Currently, HTML 2.0 is in the *draft* stage and its trial period expires November 31, 1995. Only then can HTML 2.0 be considered for adoption as an Internet standard.

HTML 3.0 is currently in the *experimental* stage of standardization. It is well suited to follow in its predecessor's footsteps, because the IETF (in cooperation with W3C) has developed a test bed of applications for developing and deploying HTML 3.0. They have also implemented a proof-of-concept HTML 2.0 browser named *Arena*. For more information about Arena, see this URL:

```
http://www.w3.org/hypertext/WWW/Arena/Status.html
```

The Netscape (Mozilla) DTD is not undergoing this level of development, scrutiny, or testing. Netscape is hoping that the masses will follow them into the sunset and live happily ever after. Maybe this will happen; maybe it won't. Nevertheless, Netscape has implemented unique extensions to the HTML 2.0 DTD that have attracted lots of interest.

IETF Level 1 DTD

HTML allows document producers to conjoin vastly different sources into a single document, while avoiding the interoperability problems inherent to proprietary formats. The first versions of HTML were designed with simplicity as their primary characteristic. Simplicity, availability, and ease of use are the reasons for the Web's explosive growth over the past five years.

The designers of the HTML DTDs considered many possible features and functions. One major consideration was to keep HTML simple, so that multiple applications — like editors and browsers — could easily be developed for many different computing platforms.

The HTML designers also had to work under a few constraints, most notably, the lack of "nestable document structure." So many word processors and desktop publishers handle text in a spectrum of styles, but none of them handle document objects as SGML can. Therefore, HTML has to map into a sequence of styled paragraphs. If the text of a paragraph is then edited, the author should be able to map the sequence of styles back onto a sequence of HTML elements in a prescriptive manner.

Hindsight Is 20-20

We found this interesting mail excerpt in the *www-talk* archives. It is dated 9 Dec 91, and it's from Tim Berners-Lee to Pei Wei:

Pei wrote:

```
> I'm now seriously considering writing an X11 browser
> for HTML files by extending a program I've been
> working on (called VIOLA, a program somewhat like
> HyperCard)...
```

TBL responded with:

```
Ok.. sounds like a good idea.  Dan Connolly (Convex Inc) has put together a
W3 browser for X but could not release the code. A group of students in
Finland were also going to do this for a project — I don't know the status
of that work. Anyone who makes a good X11 W3 browser will be very popular.
```

... and the rest is history!

This constraint also facilitated the design and implementation of conversion filters to take a document format such as Rich Text Format (RTF) and convert it to HTML. This led to trivial and limited element nesting. In the end, this design restriction was removed because it did not provide general element nesting within an HTML document. Paragraph styles are now a function of element nesting rather than selection from a rigid set of elements.

TERMS

Before we tear apart the level 1 DTD, we'll define some terms you will see throughout the HTML DTDs and specifications:

- *deprecated* — some elements in a DTD are marked as deprecated; these are elements that are used and implemented inconsistently. The only reason they are included is to assure backward compatibility with previous specifications. An example of this will appear in the level 1 DTD later in this section.

- *obsoleted* — some elements fade from use because of poor definition and implementation, or because of their lack of expressiveness — in other words, they just plain don't work like they're supposed to!

- *enhanced* — over time, some elements evolve and take on new characteristics or behaviors. This can be attributed to the desires of the WWW community or simply to intentionally augment HTML's expressiveness.

- *recommended* — some elements might be loosely used or implemented (like the <HTML>, <HEAD>, or <BODY> tags) and this could jeopardize a document's structural completeness. The parameter entity of any HTML DTD 'HTML.Recommended' can be used for a more rigorous version of a DTD. This is usually to accommodate SGML tools and applications.

For instance, the recommended style of marking up text in an HTML document must be preceded by a <P> tag. Naked text in a document — text not included in some element container like the <P> tag — is frowned upon. The following bit of HTML demonstrates the preferred and the nonpreferred markup for text:

```
<!-- Recommended style for text in a paragraph -->
<!-- The text is included in a recognizable container -->
<H1>Heading One</H1>
<P>Paragraph starts here ...

<!-- This one is not preferred or recommended -->
<!-- The text is naked in the text flow. Only assumptions -->
<!-- can be made about the text -->
<H1>Heading One</H1>
Paragraph starts here ...
```

THE LEVEL 1 DTD

Let's peek under the hood of the level 1 DTD to get a feel for where we've been and where we must go. The first part of the DTD is the SGML declaration. It defines basic system specifics such as the character set for the tags, the maximum length of a tag name, and the hexadecimal equivalent for a blank character.

```
<!SGML  "ISO 8879:1986"
--

  Document Type Definition for the HyperText Markup Language
  as used by the World Wide Web application (HTML DTD).
NOTE: This is a definition of HTML with respect to
  SGML, and assumes an understanding of SGML terms.
--


CHARSET
        BASESET  "ISO 646:1983//CHARSET
                   International Reference Version (IRV)//ESC 2/5 4/0"
        DESCSET  0    9   UNUSED
                 9    2   9
                 11   2   UNUSED
                 13   1   13
                 14   18  UNUSED
                 32   95  32
                 127  1   UNUSED
      BASESET   "ISO Registration Number 100//CHARSET
                 ECMA-94 Right Part of Latin Alphabet Nr. 1//ESC 2/13 4/1"
      DESCSET   128 32 UNUSED
                160 95 32
                255  1 UNUSED


CAPACITY  SGMLREF
          TOTALCAP     150000
          GRPCAP       150000


SCOPE     DOCUMENT
SYNTAX
        SHUNCHAR CONTROLS 0 1 2 3 4 5 6 7 8 9 10 11 12 13 14 15 16 17 18
19 20 21 22 23 24 25 26 27 28 29 30 31 127 255
        BASESET "ISO 646:1983//CHARSET
                   International Reference Version (IRV)//ESC 2/5 4/0"
        DESCSET  0 128 0
        FUNCTION RE          13
                 RS          10
                 SPACE       32
                 TAB SEPCHAR  9
        NAMING   LCNMSTRT ""
                 UCNMSTRT ""
                 LCNMCHAR ".-"
                 UCNMCHAR ".-"
                 NAMECASE GENERAL YES
                          ENTITY  NO
        DELIM    GENERAL  SGMLREF
                 SHORTREF SGMLREF
        NAMES    SGMLREF
        QUANTITY SGMLREF
                 NAMELEN     34
                 TAGLVL      100
                 LITLEN      1024
                 GRPGTCNT    150
                 GRPCNT      64
```

```
FEATURES
  MINIMIZE
    DATATAG   NO
    OMITTAG   NO
    RANK      NO
    SHORTTAG  NO
  LINK
    SIMPLE    NO
    IMPLICIT  NO
    EXPLICIT  NO
  OTHER
    CONCUR    NO
    SUBDOC    NO
    FORMAL    YES
  APPINFO     NONE
>
```

Next comes the meat of the DTD. We'll first look at the parameter entities that define almost all the macros for the DTD. A couple of other entities are defined later in the DTD. We have added SGML comments where necessary for clarification.

Parameter entities

```
<!DOCTYPE HTML [
<!-- Jul 1 93 -->
<!--      Regarding clause 6.1, SGML Document:

    [1] SGML document = SGML document entity,
        (SGML subdocument entity |
        SGML text entity | non-SGML data entity)*

    The role of SGML document entity is filled by this DTD,
    followed by the conventional HTML data stream.
-->

<!-- DTD parameter entity definitions -->

<!-- These are typical headers leveled from 1 to 6. -->
<!ENTITY % heading "H1|H2|H3|H4|H5|H6" >
<!-- There are four types of lists. -->
<!ENTITY % list "UL|OL|DIR|MENU">
<!-- These are elements to be rendered "as is" -->
<!ENTITY % literal "XMP|LISTING">

<!-- This macro defines an enumerated list of valid head sub-elements -->
<!ENTITY % headelement    "TITLE|NEXTID|ISINDEX" >

<!-- This is an enumerated list of a bunch of elements allowed with the con-
text of a document body -->
```

```
<!ENTITY % bodyelement "P | HR | %heading |
   %list | DL | ADDRESS | PRE | BLOCKQUOTE
   | %literal">

<!ENTITY % oldstyle "%headelement | %bodyelement| #PCDATA">

<!-- This macro defines a URL to have no tags within it, only character data -->
<!ENTITY % URL "CDATA"
   -- The term URL means a CDATA attribute
      whose value is a Uniform Resource Locator,
      as defined. (A URN may also be usable here when defined.)
   -->

<!-- This defines the attributes of a hypertext link from opening double
quote to the closing double quote. These parameter entities are typically
defined for ease of DTD implementation much like creating a function to sort
an array of elements if you have to do it numerous times. They do hide a lot
of the details and make it hard to read a DTD. -->
<!ENTITY % linkattributes
      "NAME NMTOKEN #IMPLIED
      HREF %URL  #IMPLIED
      REL CDATA #IMPLIED -- forward relationship type --
      REV CDATA #IMPLIED -- reversed relationship type to
                               referent data:
                   PARENT CHILD, SIBLING, NEXT, TOP,
                   DEFINITION, UPDATE, ORIGINAL etc. --

      URN CDATA #IMPLIED -- universal resource number --
      TITLE CDATA #IMPLIED -- advisory only --
      METHODS NAMES #IMPLIED -- supported public methods of the
                                object:
                         TEXTSEARCH, GET, HEAD, ... --
   ">
```

Document element types

This section of the DTD defines the document element types and the document structure. Each element type will have its declaration, the requirements of opening and closing tags, and its content data model. A list of attributes for the element type may optionally follow the element type declaration.

```
<!-- DTD Document Element Types-->

<!-- This defines an optional container for the entire HTML document. Notice
that this is an optional tag. You can tell by the "0 0" specification for
its open and close tag requirements. -->
<!ELEMENT HTML 0 0  ((HEAD|BODY|%oldstyle)*, PLAINTEXT?)>
```

```
<!-- This defines the container for the head of an HTML document. First notice
the open and close tag specification. It states that the open and close tag
are both required. No minimization is allowed. Also, notice the content data
model. It is an ampersand delimited list of element types. This means that
within the context of a document head, a title element is required that can be
preceded or followed by any of the optional elements listed. No order of ele-
ments is specified (the reason for the logical "anding" of element types) -->
<!ELEMENT HEAD - -  (TITLE & ISINDEX? & NEXTID? & LINK* & BASE?)>

<!-- This defines the document's title. The RCDATA declared content means
that entity references are recognized while sub-elements are not allowed. -->
<!ELEMENT TITLE - -  RCDATA
    -- The TITLE element is not considered part of the flow of text.
       It should be displayed, for example as the page header or
       window title.
    -->

<!-- This element is a clue to clients that an index is available for this
document. The index resides on a known server and it can be searched. -->
<!ELEMENT  ISINDEX - O EMPTY
    -- WWW clients should offer the option to perform a search on
       documents containing ISINDEX.
    -->

<!-- This is a direction for an application to name or number document elements. -->
<!ELEMENT NEXTID - O EMPTY>
<!ATTLIST NEXTID N NAME #REQUIRED
    -- The number should be a name suitable for use
       for the ID of a new element. When used, the value
       has its numeric part incremented. EG Z67 becomes Z68
    -->

<!-- This element is allowed only in the context of the document head element.
It allows to embed a reference to possibly another HTML document related in
some manner to the current document. This is mostly used for the previous and
next relationships with other hypertext documents. Notice the special declared
content of EMPTY. This means this element can never have content. It only has
a start tag with a list of attributes. -->
<!ELEMENT LINK - O EMPTY>
<!ATTLIST LINK
        %linkattributes>

<!-- This element establishes a base HTML document for the current document.
This is to aid in the resolution of relative URLs in the current document. -->
<!ELEMENT BASE - O EMPTY     -- Reference context for URLS -->
<!ATTLIST BASE
        HREF %URL; #IMPLIED
        >
<!-- This parameter entity defines an enumerated list of elements which can
be used for presentational control of inline characters and phrases. Notice
some are procedural (B,I,U) while others a descriptive. -->
```

```
<!ENTITY % inline "EM | TT | STRONG | B | I | U |
                   CODE | SAMP | KBD | KEY | VAR | DFN | CITE ">

<! This is a blanket element definition for all inline character listed
above in the parameter entity. Each element has content of parsed character
data. This means the content can have any other elements which are parsable.
-->
<!ELEMENT (%inline;) - - (#PCDATA)>

<!-- This parameter entity defines an enumerated list of mixed content for
text objects with the current document. -->
<!ENTITY % text "#PCDATA | IMG | %inline;">

<!-- This parameter entity defines an enumerated list of elements for a
hypertext object. -->
<!ENTITY % htext "A | %text" — Plus links, no structure -->

<!-- This parameter entity defines an enumerated list of elements for structured
hypertext elements. -->
<!ENTITY % stext             -- as htext but also nested structure --
            "P | HR | %list | DL | ADDRESS
            | PRE | BLOCKQUOTE
            | %literal | %htext">

<!-- This element is the document body container. Notice that this element
requires an open and a close tag but an optional content. Ain't that weird? -->
<!ELEMENT BODY - - (%bodyelement|%htext;)*>

<!-- Ah, the anchor element definition. This element allows HTML its hyper-
text expressiveness. Try to follow the content model thread from entity defi-
nition to entity definition. -->
<!ELEMENT A    - - (%text)>
<!ATTLIST A
  %linkattributes;>

<!-- This is the image element type. It also has an empty content. The
source attribute can be either an absolute or relative URL. -->
<!ELEMENT IMG - O EMPTY --  Embedded image -->
<!ATTLIST IMG
        SRC %URL;  #IMPLIED      -- URL of document to embed -->

<!-- The paragraph element type. Notice that it has a required open tag and
an optional close tag. It is really a buoy thrown into the text flow to sepa-
rate paragraphs rather than designate the *start* of a paragraph. -->
<!ELEMENT P - O EMPTY -- separates paragraphs -->

<!-- The horizontal rule element. Most graphical browsers render this as a
continuous line across the document. It usually signifies a break in informa-
tion flow or the end/begin of a new concept. -->
<!ELEMENT  HR - O EMPTY -- horizontal rule -->

<!-- This entity is a list of H1 to H6 level of headers. -->
<!ELEMENT (%heading)    - - (%htext;)+>
```

```
<!-- This is the definition list. It is used for glossary style of lists,
each entry has a definition term and its definition. Notice Dan's comment
about messy mixed content. -->
<!ELEMENT DL  - -  (DT | DD | %stext;)*>
<!--    Content should match ((DT,(%htext;)+)+,(DD,(%stext;)+))
        But mixed content is messy.  -Dan Connolly -->

<!-- The definition list term and definition elements. Each has empty con-
tent and is comparable to a buoy cast into the text flow of a document. -->
<!ELEMENT DT    - O EMPTY>
<!ELEMENT DD    - O EMPTY>

<!-- This element declaration is for two very similar elements, the ordered
(typically numbered) list and the unordered (typically bulleted) list.
Structurally, these two elements are identical. The difference between
these two is how the client renders each. -->
<!ELEMENT (UL|OL) - -  (%htext;|LI|P)+>

<!-- These are also similar elements for a directory and a menu list. Notice
the comment about mixed content again. -->
<!ELEMENT (DIR|MENU) - -  (%htext;|LI)+>
<!--    Content should match ((LI,(%htext;)+)+)
        But mixed content is messy. -->

<!-- This is the attribute declaration for all list objects. The only allow-
able attribute directs a client to render the list object in the most compact
method possible. -->
<!ATTLIST (%list)
  COMPACT NAME #IMPLIED -- COMPACT, etc.-->

<!-- This is the list item element. Again, notice the empty content and the
optional end tag. -->
<!ELEMENT LI    - O EMPTY>

<!-- This is a descriptive element which contains a quote. Normally, clients will
render this a block of text with an exaggerated left and right text margin. -->
<!ELEMENT BLOCKQUOTE  - - (%htext;|P)+
  -- for quoting some other source -->

<!-- This element defines a container for other elements which normally are
elements of an address object such as name, voice, email, WWW URL, and land
mail address. -->
<!ELEMENT ADDRESS - - (%htext;|P)+>

<!-- This is the preformatted text element. This container allowed some primi-
tive table creation but was client specific in its rendering. Notice the mixed
content model. With the width attribute, you could control the presentation of
the text within this container. This was a crude control at best. -->
<!ELEMENT PRE - - (#PCDATA|%inline|A|P)+>
<!ATTLIST PRE
  WIDTH NUMBER #IMPLIED>
<!-- The following mnemonic character entities can be used within an HTML
document as per their specification. With these, you can represent a vast
array of non-ASCII characters. -->
```

```
<!ENTITY AElig  "&#198;" -- capital AE diphthong (ligature) -->
<!ENTITY Aacute "&#193;" -- capital A, acute accent -->
<!ENTITY Acirc  "&#194;" -- capital A, circumflex accent -->
<!ENTITY Agrave "&#192;" -- capital A, grave accent -->
<!ENTITY Aring  "&#197;" -- capital A, ring -->
<!ENTITY Atilde "&#195;" -- capital A, tilde -->
<!ENTITY Auml   "&#196;" -- capital A, dieresis or umlaut mark -->
<!ENTITY Ccedil "&#199;" -- capital C, cedilla -->
<!ENTITY ETH    "&#208;" -- capital Eth, Icelandic -->
<!ENTITY Eacute "&#201;" -- capital E, acute accent -->
<!ENTITY Ecirc  "&#202;" -- capital E, circumflex accent -->
<!ENTITY Egrave "&#200;" -- capital E, grave accent -->
<!ENTITY Euml   "&#203;" -- capital E, dieresis or umlaut mark -->
<!ENTITY Iacute "&#205;" -- capital I, acute accent -->
<!ENTITY Icirc  "&#206;" -- capital I, circumflex accent -->
<!ENTITY Igrave "&#204;" -- capital I, grave accent -->
<!ENTITY Iuml   "&#207;" -- capital I, dieresis or umlaut mark -->
<!ENTITY Ntilde "&#209;" -- capital N, tilde -->
<!ENTITY Oacute "&#211;" -- capital O, acute accent -->
<!ENTITY Ocirc  "&#212;" -- capital O, circumflex accent -->
<!ENTITY Ograve "&#210;" -- capital O, grave accent -->
<!ENTITY Oslash "&#216;" -- capital O, slash -->
<!ENTITY Otilde "&#213;" -- capital O, tilde -->
<!ENTITY Ouml   "&#214;" -- capital O, dieresis or umlaut mark -->
<!ENTITY THORN  "&#222;" -- capital THORN, Icelandic -->
<!ENTITY Uacute "&#218;" -- capital U, acute accent -->
<!ENTITY Ucirc  "&#219;" -- capital U, circumflex accent -->
<!ENTITY Ugrave "&#217;" -- capital U, grave accent -->
<!ENTITY Uuml   "&#220;" -- capital U, dieresis or umlaut mark -->
<!ENTITY Yacute "&#221;" -- capital Y, acute accent -->
<!ENTITY aacute "&#225;" -- small a, acute accent -->
<!ENTITY acirc  "&#226;" -- small a, circumflex accent -->
<!ENTITY aelig  "&#230;" -- small ae diphthong (ligature) -->
<!ENTITY agrave "&#224;" -- small a, grave accent -->
<!ENTITY amp    "&#38;"  -- ampersand -->
<!ENTITY aring  "&#229;" -- small a, ring -->
<!ENTITY atilde "&#227;" -- small a, tilde -->
<!ENTITY auml   "&#228;" -- small a, dieresis or umlaut mark -->
<!ENTITY ccedil "&#231;" -- small c, cedilla -->
<!ENTITY eacute "&#233;" -- small e, acute accent -->
<!ENTITY ecirc  "&#234;" -- small e, circumflex accent -->
<!ENTITY egrave "&#232;" -- small e, grave accent -->
<!ENTITY eth    "&#240;" -- small eth, Icelandic -->
<!ENTITY euml   "&#235;" -- small e, dieresis or umlaut mark -->
<!ENTITY gt     "&#62;"  -- greater than -->
<!ENTITY iacute "&#237;" -- small i, acute accent -->
<!ENTITY icirc  "&#238;" -- small i, circumflex accent -->
<!ENTITY igrave "&#236;" -- small i, grave accent -->
<!ENTITY iuml   "&#239;" -- small i, dieresis or umlaut mark -->
<!ENTITY lt     "&#60;"  -- less than -->
<!ENTITY nbsp   "&#32;"  -- should be NON_BREAKING space -->
<!ENTITY ntilde "&#241;" -- small n, tilde -->
<!ENTITY oacute "&#243;" -- small o, acute accent -->
```

```
<!ENTITY ocirc  "&#244;" -- small o, circumflex accent -->
<!ENTITY ograve "&#242;" -- small o, grave accent -->
<!ENTITY oslash "&#248;" -- small o, slash -->
<!ENTITY otilde "&#245;" -- small o, tilde -->
<!ENTITY ouml   "&#246;" -- small o, dieresis or umlaut mark -->
<!ENTITY szlig  "&#223;" -- small sharp s, German (sz ligature) -->
<!ENTITY thorn  "&#254;" -- small thorn, Icelandic -->
<!ENTITY uacute "&#250;" -- small u, acute accent -->
<!ENTITY ucirc  "&#251;" -- small u, circumflex accent -->
<!ENTITY ugrave "&#249;" -- small u, grave accent -->
<!ENTITY uuml   "&#252;" -- small u, dieresis or umlaut mark -->
<!ENTITY yacute "&#253;" -- small y, acute accent -->
<!ENTITY yuml   "&#255;" -- small y, dieresis or umlaut mark -->

<!-- The following elements have been deemed 'deprecated'. -->
<!ELEMENT (%literal) - -  CDATA>
<!ELEMENT PLAINTEXT - O EMPTY>
]>
```

IETF Level 2 DTD

The IETF level 2 DTD is an Internet draft of the IETF HTML working group. It is the result of further enhancement of the level 1 DTD, which was primitive and limited in expressive capability.

Level 2 is the next step in the evolution of the limited level 1 DTD. The level 2 Internet draft was released in May 1995 and expires in November 1995. It was coauthored by Tim Berners-Lee and Dan Connolly from the WWW Consortium (W3C; note that while both gentlemen now work for the W3C, Tim Berners-Lee started out at CERN, the home of the Web, and Dan Connolly at HaL Software Systems and Convex, Inc.).

Today, the HTML 2.0 DTD has become the de facto standard for the WWW community, even though it's still in draft status. The other two DTDs discussed later in this chapter have added extensions to this HTML document type. Just to clarify common usage, please note that an HTML document that conforms to this DTD is normally called either an HTML level 2 or an HTML 2.0 document.

Now, let's begin to look into the level 2 DTD. You will learn first about the standard DTD, the valid variations on it, and how to control these variations.

DTD FEATURE TEST ENTITIES

The HTML 2.0 DTD defines a standard HTML document type. Additionally, the DTD provides the capability to provide several variations on this standard DTD. The impetus for these variations are considerations made for minimal implementations of HTML 2.0. Each variation is controlled by a marked section entity. These are called "Feature Test Entities" in the level 2 DTD. These entities are used as marked sections within the level 2 DTD proper. Table 3-2 shows the feature test entities for the level 2 DTD.

Table 3-2

Feature Test Entities of the Level 2 HTML DTD

Entity Name	Value	Description
HTML.Recommended	(IGNORE* | INCLUDE)	Impacts structural integrity of document.
HTML.Deprecated	(IGNORE | INCLUDE*)	Impacts poorly used or implemented elements; IGNORE for minimal implementations.
HTML.Highlighting	(IGNORE | INCLUDE*)	Impacts highlighting inline characters; IGNORE for minimal implementations.
HTML.Forms	(IGNORE | INCLUDE*)	Impacts form inclusion; IGNORE for minimal implementations.

* indicates the value of the entity in the standard DTD

For instance, consider this fragment taken from the 2.0 DTD:

```
<!- Declaration of marked section entity. ->
<!ENTITY % HTML.Recommended "INCLUDE"

<!- Since the status keyword of the HTML.Recommended entity is INCLUDE, the
following section of DTD will be included in the document type definition.
This is also called 'Strict' style checking. ->
<![ %HTML.Recommended [
  <!ENTITY % body.content "(%heading|%block|HR|ADDRESS)*"
  - <h1>Heading</h1>
      <p>Text ...
    is preferred to
    <h1>Heading</h1>
      Text ...
  ->
]]>
```

In the standard HTML 2.0 DTD, the status of the 'HTML.Recommended' entity is set to "IGNORE". Changing the status keyword for this entity to "INCLUDE" in the preceding example would result in a new variation of the standard DTD. This variation is known as the "Strict" implementation of the HTML 2.0 DTD, and it results in strictly validated HTML 2.0 documents if the document is parsed.

To turn the HTML 2.0 DTD into a strictly checked HTML 2.0 DTD — also known as HTML 2.0 Strict DTD – you would need to modify the DTD by replacing the status keyword for '%HTML.Recommended'. For example, this is programmatically accomplished using the HaLSoft HTML Validation Service.

There is another way to turn on the strict level 2 DTD. It is more desirable than maintaining two versions of the same DTD. For example, if you put the following SGML code at the top of your HTML document, you can enable a stylistic variation for the 'HTML.Recommended' DTD:

```
<!DOCTYPE HTML PUBLIC "-//IETF//DTD HTML 2.0//EN//"
        [ <!ENTITY % HTML.Recommended "INCLUDE"> ] >
```

The additional field in the SGML prolog overrides the status of the 'HTML.Recommended' entity in the level 2 DTD, and it turns on the properly marked sections in the DTD. When an SGML parser validates this HTML document, it externally sets the status keyword for the entity 'HTML.Recommended' to "INCLUDE".

Four feature test entities are defined in the IETF working group HTML 2.0 specification as follows:

- 'HTML.Recommended' — this entity enables a more stylistic DTD while including common markup necessary for generalized unity. The elements included in this variation may compromise the imposed style or structural integrity of other documents. For example, HoTMetaL requires that all imported documents contain an SGML prolog and comply to the plain level 2 HTML DTD.

- 'HTML.Deprecated' — this entity enables the exclusion of document elements that are not implemented consistently or used in perverse ways. The level 2 specification recommends that HTML documents created by conversion applications do not conform to these antiquated idioms.

- 'HTML.Highlighting' — this entity is used to disable inline character highlighting in an HTML document. This is used for minimal implementations of HTML.

- 'HTML.Forms' — this entity is used to control the inclusion of the FORM element and its sub-elements. This is to enable consistent usage by minimal HTML implementations.

For more information about the level 2 HTML specification, see this URL:

```
ftp://www.ics.uci.edu/pub/ietf/html/index.html
```

In the following sections, you will learn about new elements in HTML 2.0, the old HTML 1.0 elements that are enhanced, and the deprecated and obsoleted elements of HTML 2.0.

NEW ELEMENTS OF **HTML 2.0**

FORM

The FORM element type provides a fill-in text form interface to the WWW. The HTML 2.0 DTD defines the FORM element as (SGML comments added for clarification):

```
<!- This is the FORM element type declaration in the HTML 2.0 DTD. Notice it
must have an open and a close tag. No minimization allowed. The content data
model is defined to include elements defined by the %body.content parameter
entity minus the FORM element (no nesting of FORMs allowed) plus an enumer-
ated list of input widget elements. ->
<!ELEMENT FORM - - %body.content -(FORM) +(INPUT|SELECT|TEXTAREA)>

<!- The FORM attribute list contains a specified action (a CGI application
reference) to be carried out when the submit choice is made, a default HTTP
request method of GET, a default encryption type of application/x-www-form-
urlencoded, and then a couple of attributes to aid in the rendering of
speech for the visually impaired per the ICADD specification. ->
<!ATTLIST FORM
        ACTION %URI #IMPLIED
        METHOD (%HTTP-Method) GET
        ENCTYPE %Content-Type; "application/x-www-form-urlencoded"
        %SDAPREF; "<Para>Form:</Para>"
        %SDASUFF; "<Para>Form End.</Para>"
        >
```

Here are some examples of the FORM element and its attributes:

```
<!- Action by be taken to submit form data; typically a CGI application is
called on a server ->
<FORM ACTION="http://www.foo.com/cgi-bin/launch.cgi">

<!- HTTP request method of POST used for submitting form ->
<FORM METHOD="POST" ACTION=/cgi-bin/test")

<!- binary representation of form data ->
<FORM ENCTYPE="application/octet-stream" METHOD="POST"
ACTION="/cgibin/testit">
```

INPUT

The FORM element type has a sub-element named INPUT. This element
is a text input widget. It is defined in the HTML 2.0 DTD as (SGML
comments added for clarification):

```
<!- This parameter entity defines an enumerated list of input widget types. ->
<!ENTITY % InputType "(TEXT | PASSWORD | CHECKBOX |  RADIO | SUBMIT | RESET |
                       IMAGE | HIDDEN )">
<!- This is the input widget element. Notice it has no content and only
requires the opening tag. ->
<!ELEMENT INPUT - O EMPTY>

<!- The attribute list for the input widget element includes optional attribut-
es: the type of input a widget can accept with TEXT as the default; a name
attribute with no tags allowed in its value; a assigned value which cannot
contain tags; and hypertext reference to a document; a checked toggle for check
boxes and radio buttons; the size of the presented input widget; the maximum
length of accepted text input for an input widget; where to align the accompa-
nying text; and a speech rendering attribute per the ICADD specification. ->
<!ATTLIST INPUT
        TYPE %InputType TEXT
        NAME CDATA #IMPLIED
        VALUE CDATA #IMPLIED
        SRC %URI #IMPLIED
        CHECKED (CHECKED) #IMPLIED
        SIZE CDATA #IMPLIED
        MAXLENGTH NUMBER #IMPLIED
        ALIGN (top|middle|bottom) #IMPLIED
        %SDAPREF; "Input: "
        >
```

Here are some examples of the INPUT element type and its attributes:

```
<!- Type of input interaction ->
<INPUT TYPE="checkbox">
```

```
<!- Name of form datum ->
<INPUT NAME="first name">

<!- Default/initial/selected value ->
<INPUT VALUE="Texas A&amp;M Aggies">

<!- Address of image ->
<INPUT SRC="images/warning.gif">

<!- Initial state is "on" ->
<INPUT CHECKED>

<!- Field size hint ->
<INPUT SIZE="40">

<!- Data length maximum ->
<INPUT MAXLENGTH="45">

<!- Image alignment ->
<INPUT ALIGN="TOP">
```

SELECT

The FORM sub-element SELECT allows a user to choose from a list of choices. Here is how it is defined in the HTML 2.0 DTD (SGML comments added for clarification):

```
<!- This element allows a user to select a choice from a list of choices.
This input widget is similar to a menu of choices. The definition requires
the presence of the start and end tag. The content model can include one or
more options excluding three other elements including another SELECT element.
This means you cannot nest SELECT elements. ->
<!ELEMENT SELECT - - (OPTION+) -(INPUT|SELECT|TEXTAREA)>

<!- The attribute list contains optional attributes which include: a name of
the selection input widget; a size of the presented list of choices (if you
have 100 options, you would only want to present 10 to the used and allow
them to scroll through the other 90 options); a toggle if multiple choices are
allowed; and some speech rendering attributes per the ICADD specification. ->
<!ATTLIST SELECT
        NAME CDATA #REQUIRED
        SIZE NUMBER #IMPLIED
        MULTIPLE (MULTIPLE) #IMPLIED
        %SDAFORM; "List"
        %SDAPREF;
        "<LHead>Select #AttVal(Multiple)</LHead>"
        >
```

Here are a few examples of the SELECT element and its attributes:

```
<!- Name of form data ->
<SELECT NAME="us-states">
```

```
<!- Number of options displayed at a time ->
<SELECT SIZE="10">

<!- Multiple selections allowed ->
<SELECT MULTIPLE>
```

OPTION

This SELECT sub-element is a selection option. Here is how it is defined in the HTML 2.0 DTD (SGML comments added for clarification):

```
<!- The selection option element. It requires the start tag with an optional
end tag. Its content is optional parsed character data. ->
<!ELEMENT OPTION - O (#PCDATA)*>

<!- The attributes of a selection option are optional and include: a toggle
to indicate an option is selected initially; an associated value of the
option (by default, the value of the option is its content); and finally
speech rendering attributes per the ICADD specification. ->
<!ATTLIST OPTION
        SELECTED (SELECTED) #IMPLIED
        VALUE CDATA #IMPLIED
        %SDAFORM; "LItem"
        %SDAPREF;
        "Option: #AttVal(Value) #AttVal(Selected)"
        >
```

Here are a few examples of the OPTION element and its attributes:

```
<!- Initial selected option ->
<OPTION SELECTED> USA

<!- A selection option ->
<OPTION> Florida

<!- Form data value for this option ->
<OPTION VALUE="University of Mississippi"> Ol' Miss
```

TEXTAREA

This FORM sub-element allows multiple-line text entry. This input widget is defined in the HTML 2.0 DTD as (SGML comments added for clarification):

```
<!- This is the multiple line text input widget. It requires both start and
end tags. It content data model contains optional parsed character data
excluding specific document elements including TEXTAREA. This means that you
cannot nest TEXTAREA widgets. ->
```

```
<!ELEMENT TEXTAREA - - (#PCDATA)* -(INPUT|SELECT|TEXTAREA)>

<!– This is the attribute list of a multiple line text input widget which
includes: a required name of the widget; a required number of rows and columns
to render; and some speech rendering attributes per the ICADD specification. –>
<!ATTLIST TEXTAREA
        NAME CDATA #REQUIRED
        ROWS NUMBER #REQUIRED
        COLS NUMBER #REQUIRED
        %SDAFORM; "Para"
        %SDAPREF; "Input Text – #AttVal(Name): "
        >
```

Here is an example of the TEXTAREA element and its attributes:

```
<!– Name of form data –>
<--textarea with required attributes-->
<TEXTAREA NAME="text" ROWS="24" COLS="80">
```

BR

This new element controls the line break within a text flow. It is defined
in the HTML 2.0 DTD as (SGML comments added for clarification):

```
<!– This element controls line break. It has a required start tag and has no
content. It is similar to a buoy thrown into the text flow. Its only
attribute is for speech rendering. –>
<!ELEMENT BR     - O EMPTY>
<!ATTLIST BR
        %SDAPREF; "&#RE;"
        >
```

META

This new element is included in an HTML document's HEAD element. It
allows you to mark up generic metainformation.

Its definition is stated in the HTML 2.0 specification: "It is an extensible container for use in identifying, indexing, and cataloging specialized
document metainformation." It has two functions:

- Provide a mechanism for a client such as a robot to discover that the
  document exists and how it can be accessed or retrieved.

■ Identify the content, quality, and features of a document that can identify its intended use.

Here is how the META element is defined in the HTML 2.0 DTD (SGML comments added for clarification):

```
<!- This is the element for document metainformation. It has a required
start tag and an optional end tag with an empty content. Each META element
specifies a name/value pair. If multiple META elements are provided with the
same name, their combined contents —concatenated as a comma-separated list —
is the value associated with that name. ->
<!ELEMENT META - O EMPTY>

<!- The attribute list contains: an optional HTTP equivalent attribute which
binds the element to an HTTP header field; the name of the name/value pair;
the content of the name/value pair.
<!ATTLIST META
        HTTP-EQUIV   NAME    #IMPLIED
        NAME         NAME    #IMPLIED
        CONTENT      CDATA   #REQUIRED >
```

Here is an example of the META element and its attributes:

```
<META HTTP-EQUIV="Expires"
        CONTENT="Tue, 20 Jun 1995 04:13:09 GMT">
<META HTTP-EQUIV="Keywords"
        CONTENT="Gail,Evelle">
<META HTTP-EQUIV="Reply-to"
        CONTENT="hi_mcdunna@globe.az.us (H.I. McDunna)">
```

The following is the result from the server that includes the HTTP header fields as part of the HTTP response to a GET or HEAD request for that document:

```
Expires:  Tue, 20 Jun 1995 04:13:09 GMT
Keywords: Gail,Evelle
Reply-to: hi_mcdunna@globe.az.us (H.I. McDunna)
```

HTTP servers read the contents of the <HEAD> tag to create corresponding HTTP header fields to any elements defining a value for the attribute HTTP-EQUIV.

Finally, the HTML 2.0 specification recommends that the META element is not to be used where another HTML element, such as the TITLE element, is appropriate.

ENHANCED ELEMENTS OF **HTML 2.0**

Nearly all elements from HTML 1.0 were enhanced or modified for HTML 2.0. Table 3-3 lists the important enhancements and their descriptions.

Table 3-3

Element Enhancements of HTML 2.0

Element Type	Description	Enhancement
A	Anchor	added headings to content model; changed NAME attribute values
BASE	Base HTML document referenced	HREF attribute now required
BODY	Document body container	now optional
BLOCKQUOTE	Block quote container	new and improved content model
DIR,MENU	Directory and menu lists	only <LI> valid in content
DL	Definition list	cleaner content data model
DT,DD	Definition term and definition	new content data model
HEAD	Document head	now optional
IMG	Image	add attributes ISMAP and ALIGN
LINK	Reference to a related document	now requires HREF attribute
LI	List item	no longer has an EMPTY content
OL,UL	Ordered and unordered lists	only <LI> valid in content
NEXTID	Next ID to use for link name	attribute now CDATA type
TITLE	Document title	content model now is #PCDATA

DEPRECATION IN **HTML 2.0**

In the HTML 2.0 DTD, some elements as well as some specific document structures have been deprecated. The following are the deprecated document structures (SGML comments added for commentary):

Text markup

```
<!- Text markup for preformatted text. If HTML.Deprecated has the value of
INCLUDE, these elements are valid markup. ->
<![ %HTML.Deprecated [
        <!ENTITY % preformatted "PRE | XMP | LISTING">
]]>
<!- In the standard DTD, only PRE is valid. ->
<!ENTITY % preformatted "PRE">
```

Text flows

This marked section represents an alternate text flow. It has been
marked as deprecated in the level 2 DTD:

```
<!- This is a deprecated text flow. If this is included, notice the
inclusion of other deprecated elements such as XMP and LISTING. ->
<![ %HTML.Deprecated [

<!ENTITY % literal "CDATA"
            - historical, non-conforming parsing mode where
              the only markup signal is the end tag
              in full
            ->

<!ELEMENT (XMP|LISTING) - -  %literal>
<!ATTLIST XMP
        %SDAFORM; "Lit"
        %SDAPREF; "Example:&#RE;"
        >
<!ATTLIST LISTING
        %SDAFORM; "Lit"
        %SDAPREF; "Listing:&#RE;"
        >

<!- <XMP>           Example section       ->
<!- <LISTING>       Computer listing      ->

<!ELEMENT PLAINTEXT - 0 %literal>
<!- <PLAINTEXT>     Plain text passage    ->

<!ATTLIST PLAINTEXT
        %SDAFORM; "Lit" >
]]>
```

Document head

This marked section entity deprecates a particular document structure. If HTML.Deprecated="INCLUDE", the following document structure would be valid:

```
<![ %HTML.Deprecated [
        <!ENTITY % html.content "HEAD, BODY, PLAINTEXT?">
]]>
<!- Standard document structure if HTML.Deprecated="IGNORE" ->
<!ENTITY % html.content "HEAD, BODY">
```

Finally, there are three deprecated elements: <XMP>, <LISTING>, and <PLAINTEXT>; and one deprecated parameter entity: '%literal'.

For a Webified version of the level 2 HTML DTD, see this URL:

```
http://www.halsoft.com/html/
```

IETF Level 3 DTD

The IETF HTML working group is currently working on the successor to the level 2 HTML DTD and specification, level 3. It is in the *experimental* stage as of this writing. This development is under the auspices of Dave Raggett of the W3C, the designer of HTML+ which has now been recast as HTML 3.0.

The IETF HTML working group is responsible for the evolution of the current HTML 3.0 DTD. In a cooperative effort, the W3C is continuing development of a freeware HTML 3.0 browser code-named *Arena*. This effort is intended to encourage the WWW community and developers to road-test level 3 HTML features, and also to give them a model for standards-compliant implementation.

HTML 3.0 builds upon HTML 2.0, which built upon HTML 1.0. This provides HTML document developers a guarantee of full backward compatibility, so that old documents will still be acceptable to new browsers. By far, the most requested new element type was the "Table", so some straightforward, simple support for tables has been added.

In contrast, the CALS initiative — a Department of Defense documentation standards activity — supports a complex and extensive SGML-based table model. Although some members of the HTML working group have argued for its adoption, the majority opinion of the group appears to be that the CALS model is too complex for widespread WWW deployment. Instead, HTML 3.0 proposes a "lightweight" markup for tables. This is intended for rendering on a wide spectrum of display devices including speech synthesizers and Braille printers.

In addition to table support, HTML 3.0 supports text flow around figures. The FIG element can be used for inline figures — figures within a text flow — that allows clients to handle hot zones (like those in image maps) while still providing salient information to text-based browsers.

The last main feature of HTML 3.0 is support for complex mathematical notation, like that needed for equations and formulae. According to the HTML 3.0 specification, this "adds relatively little complexity to a browser." T_EX, a document formatting language developed by Donald Knuth, continues to be a strong influence for math support.

Just as with tables, a "lightweight" math markup is implemented. According to the specification, it's "simple enough to type in by hand." The level of support is comparable to that of desktop publishing applications and avoids the task of converting math equations to images, as is required today.

An optional but powerful feature of HTML 3.0 is its support for style sheets. These are primarily intended to counter the temptation to add more presentation features to HTML — in other words, it's a way of avoiding the inclusion of procedural markup.

Therefore, HTML 3.0 is designed to be used in conjunction with optional style sheets that provide enhanced control over document rendering. This means that client rendering could be influenced by a user's preferences, by the window size, or by display limitations (for instance, by the lack of certain fonts or colors).

The IETF HTML working group encourages external comments about the evolution of HTML 3.0 from the WWW community. For more information, see the IETF HTML working group's welcome page at:

```
ftp://www.ics.uci.edu/pub/ietf/html/index.html
```

There is also a discussion list that you can join by sending a blank message with subject "subscribe" to:

```
www-talk-request@mail.w3.org
```

You will learn more about the details of HTML 3.0 in Chapter 5.

Netscape Extensions

Netscape Communications Corporation — the software company formerly known as Mosaic Communications Corporation — offers their rendition of a widely used HTML DTD affectionately known as the "Mozilla" DTD. Mozilla is Netscape's hypermedia language for the WWW. It is the basis for the development of their WWW client, *Netscape Navigator.*

Mozilla contains numerous extensions to the 2.0 and the 3.0 DTDs. It extends the 2.0 specification in the following areas:

- <ISINDEX> capabilities
- presentation control over horizontal ruling
- presentation control over lists
- presentation control over "floating" images
- presentation control over line breaks

Mozilla also introduces some new element types for presentation control. These include centering of headers, finer control over line breaks, and font control. Mozilla includes presentational controls like the nesting of <I>, <TT>, and <B> tags for finer font-handling effects. These new elements compensate for the lack of style sheet support in 2.0, but will soon be deprecated with the release of 3.0.

More interesting are the Mozilla extensions to the 3.0 DTD, which currently include presentation controls over the browser's background, support for simple tables, and an upload mechanism for frequently changing documents. These are specific to particular versions of the Navigator browser and cannot be viewed properly by any other WWW browsers.

For more information about Mozilla extensions, see this URL:

```
http://home.netscape.com/assist/net_sites/html_extensions.html
```

Migrating from HTML 2.0 to 3.0

The HTML 3.0 specification recommends that authors designate HTML documents delivered by a server through the use of the MIME Content-type: "text/html; version=3.0". This has special implications for HTML 2.0-specific user agents and applications. Some browsers developed against the HTML 2.0 DTD will not render HTML 3.0 documents properly. To prevent this from happening, the appropriate HTML 2.0-compliant browser action is to launch a file dialog box so that users can save the document to a file, rather than incorrectly rendering the (HTML 3.0) document.

The HTML 3.0 specification calls for a file extension designation in order for servers to discriminate between 2.0 and 3.0 documents. For PCs the extension is ".ht3" and for all others platforms it is ".html3".

Another mechanism to inform a server that a requesting client can handle 3.0 documents comes from exploiting the accepted HTTP request headers from the browser. The server can examine these headers and determine if the requesting browser can properly handle and render a 3.0 document.

For example, a browser that can accept HTML 3.0 documents might include an accept header field like this in its HTTP request:

```
GET /index.html HTTP/1.0
Accept:application/octet-stream
Accept:text/plain; charset=ISO-8859-1
Accept:text/html; version=3.0
\015\102
```

In this example, the client explicitly tells the server that it can indeed handle HTML 3.0 documents, as well as other types of MIME Content-types (\015\012 is the CrLf pair in octal).

Information providers who plan to start serving HTML 3.0 documents can exploit these two mechanisms without adversely impacting HTML 2.0 clients. A server can decide whether a requesting client accepts 3.0 documents by examining its 'HTTP_ACCEPT' environment variable. For instance, this Perl code fragment looks at the 'HTTP_ACCEPT' variable for the acceptance of 3.0 documents:

```
# check environment variable for 3.0 document acceptance
if($ENV{'HTTP_ACCEPT'} =~ /text\/html\;[ ]*version=3\.0/) {
    # signal 3.0 document acceptance by requesting client
    $HTML3 = 'yes';
}
else {
    # signal other type of document
    $HTML3 = 'no';
}
```

In this example, a string-match operation is performed on the 'HTTP_ACCEPT' environment variable that looks for a match on the "text/html; version=3.0" accept field of the HTTP request header.

These mechanisms make the transition from 2.0 to 3.0 practical for new HTML 3.0 compliant browsers without impacting older, less sophisticated browsers. The HTML 3.0 specification fosters the vision that HTML 3.0 documents could be transformed into 2.0 documents if a requesting browser cannot handle 3.0 documents. This could be accomplished by an on-the-fly transformation, or by preprocessing 3.0 documents and storing equivalent 2.0 versions.

Summary

HTML started as a simple hypermedia descriptive markup language, which is a primary reason for the success and proliferation of the WWW. Since its inception, HTML has evolved painfully and slowly. Today, there are three standards to choose from: the level 2, the level 3, and the Mozilla DTDs. We strongly recommend that you adopt the level 2 standard and keep an eye on the level 3 standard so you'll know when to think about making the switch.

4 HTML and Validation

As the World Wide Web evolves, valid HTML documents will become a paramount ingredient of Web life. Why is valid HTML so important? First, it ensures document portability across different computing platforms and applications. Second, it increases the fidelity of information exchange (that is, what they see is what you wanted them to get). A valid HTML document conforms to a specific SGML DTD. Any conforming HTML document can be validated by an SGML parser, or by other tools constructed to check syntax and semantics against the HTML DTD.

What Is HTML, and How Should You Use It?

Basically, HTML is a descriptive markup language that behaves very much like a programming language. Creating hypertext documents in HTML really involves using an SGML-based language. Writing HTML without using a compiler to provide rigorous syntax checking will seldom produce correct results on any but the most trivial documents.

The widespread use of HTML in many forms, standard and nonstandard, increases daily with the introduction of numerous new Web sites all over the Internet. Today some organizations are jumping onto the WWW at light-speed, using it as a venue to republish their thinly disguised marketing blitzes and their endless supply of frivolous info-babble.

Still other organizations are choosing the slow lane. They'd prefer to sit back and let others zoom past, to flush out the bad guys who might be lurking in the bushes just around the next bend. For them, progress itself sometimes happens too fast.

Each of these approaches demands careful scrutiny. It's essential to pay close attention to document creation and maintenance processes, both for conventional printed documents and for their electronic analogs (like Web documents). To publish the highest-quality Web pages, organizations must make HTML validation part of their electronic publishing process.

Even so, the validation effort is not without its own peculiar challenges: As this book is under construction, the current HTML specification is in a state of flux, as the current version (1.0) is about to be superseded by the nearly complete next version (2.0).

The good side of the collision between versions is that some WWW application developers continually "push the envelope" defined by the latest emerging HTML standard (often, in every conceivable direction — and beyond). The bad side of this story is that some developers make unlucky choices and implement elements that later fall by the wayside.

By the time the next level of the HTML standard is officially submitted, tested, and deployed, these unlucky developers' chosen elements may no longer be part of HTML's ever-changing collection of rules and formats. This begs a very interesting question — namely, what can legitimately be considered HTML when it's taken from that part of an emerging standard that has yet to be finalized? Inevitably, developers have to anticipate new developments to speed their products to market, but they take a risk if they get too far ahead of the curve.

What Is Valid HTML?

Valid HTML means that an HTML-tagged document complies with a specific DTD. As we discussed in Chapter 2, a DTD describes the syntax of a descriptive markup language. Because HTML is an application of SGML, SGML provides a formal framework within which HTML is defined and described.

DOING THE "DTD THING"

Because of its SGML lineage, HTML inherits a DTD that declares its syntax and delineates its internal structure. The HTML DTD describes its syntax in a form similar to the Backus-Naur Form (BNF) for context-free grammars often used to describe programming languages and other computing formalisms.

The HTML DTD contains the names for valid and supported HTML elements (the main building blocks of HTML), defines each element's allowable content model (i.e., it lists all the other HTML elements allowed within any particular HTML element's context), and enumerates the list of named attributes for each HTML element. The DTD also defines any allowable external objects that HTML can "recognize" — like the ISO-Latin-1 character or numeric entities.

TESTING FOR COMPLIANCE

You test an HTML document's compliance to a DTD either by proofreading the syntax or by using an SGML parser. Since humans are notoriously inconsistent and unreliable, especially when rigorously enforcing complicated formalisms, we'd strongly recommend sticking with the parser.

To use an SGML parser, you submit the HTML document along with its associated DTD and any external declarations for its perusal and analysis. The parser returns either a valid parse tree depicting the lexical structure of the document, or a list of error statements that enumerate the discrepancies between the document source and the DTD.

If corrections are required, you can then revert back to the HTML document to make required edits. Once the edits are complete and the document is saved, you resubmit the document to the parser. This cycle — which strongly resembles the edit-compile cycle so typical for software development during the code-writing stage — continues until the HTML document is deemed *valid* by the SGML parser.

The Benefits of HTML Style

As with most other types of documents, there's a difference between formal and stylistic correctness. That's why some organizations choose to define a formal institutional style. Even though this requires time and effort, and ultimately, an institutional policy for consistency and readability, we strongly recommend that you define a style and then follow it religiously.

One of the Web's originators, Tim-Berners Lee, created an HTML style guide that is located at the following URL:

```
http://www.w3.org/hypertext/WWW/Provider/Style/Overview.html
```

Daniel LaLiberte has collected a large number of style guides that are referenced at this URL:

```
http://union.ncsa.uiuc.edu/HyperNews/get/www/html/guides.html
```

Once again, we'd suggest that you investigate these alternatives and consider developing a style of your own to follow, especially if your organization faces the possibility that it will have to create and maintain a sizable collection of Web documents. LaLiberte's collection gives plenty of options and guidelines to choose from.

HTML 2.0: THE REIGNING DTD

Level 2.0, the current defacto HTML DTD, was developed, tested, and deployed by the Internet Engineering Task Force (IETF) HTML working group in 1993.

Since then, there have been several splits in the HTML evolution tree. Dave Raggett immediately began developing HTML+ in all its glory. Dave extended the notion of simple HTML to a full-blown online information delivery standard that included table definitions, math equations, and much, much more. To his credit, Dave also planted the seeds for the level 3.0 DTD which is now under development at the World Wide Web (W3) consortium at MIT in Cambridge, Massachusetts. The W3 folks are borrowing heavily from Dave's HTML+ work and incorporating these features into Level 3.0. Dan Connolly and Tim-Berners Lee, both now working for the W3, are guiding this effort, but Dave remains heavily involved.

HTML 3.0: THE COMING DTD

Level 3.0 is a working draft intended for use by WWW application developers only. Many of these developers anxiously and cautiously follow the progress of 3.0's evolution while others, like the Netscape legion, continue to develop their own flavor of HTML called *Mozilla*. The standards groups continue to develop 3.0 undeterred by Netscape's activities.

IT'S NO ACCIDENT THAT MOZILLA IS NAMED AFTER A MONSTER!

The Mozilla DTD contains all of the level 2.0 structures, plus a long list of Netscape proprietary extensions like <BLINK> and <CENTER>. Netscape is also extending the current HTML 2.0 specification in all directions, hoping that the Web community will follow their lead. They have a legitimate shot at steering the Web community toward their definition of Nirvana — that is, if the shotgun doesn't go off accidentally in their hands!

Given all these choices and the strong sway of the marketplace in Netscape's directions, what should a poor Web developer (like you) do?

Choosing an HTML DTD

The goal of all Webheads, WebMasters, and institutions disseminating online information is to offer a Web space that constantly evolves and provides the reader with timely, up-to-date information. This ongoing commitment requires that any Web development team make some decisions prior to unleashing their flow of information into the Internet sea. The hardest decision to be made is, "What HTML specification are we to adopt and follow?"

As we see it, your choices boil down to one of the following:

- Adhere to the current IETF level 2.0 DTD.
- Closely track the new and unstable level 3.0 draft DTD.
- Track the Mozilla specification, which also undergoes regular change.
- Create your own HTML DTD and leave the pack behind.

To aid your decision, direct the following questions to your marketing legion, your stable of technical writers, and your underpaid and under-appreciated local WebMaster:

What is the estimated life of your Web?

If it is to be short-lived, say only six months, we wouldn't worry too much about standards. If it is to last until your grandchildren graduate from graduate school, you'd better embrace one of the real standards and stick to it until the bitter end.

Will your HTML documents be automagically created on a regular schedule?

If so, your tools people will worship you if they have a stable DTD to work with. If your organization is trying to make Web document construction a normal outcome of their document management process, this structure and stability is extremely important.

Does your audience care that the information is standard compliant?

If not, don't worry; code things as you please. If so, or if you're not sure, make a determination from an analysis of your audience.

Ask them which standard best suits their wants and needs. Sometimes subcontractors will be contractually required to follow a specific DTD. If you are contracting your HTML documentation development, please make it known to your hired Webhead that you require the use of a stable HTML DTD.

Stick to your guns: even if it costs you more to get your way, it will be well worth it. This will allow your technical writers and WebMasters to maintain their HTML documents with structured editors that also understand an HTML standard. SoftQuad's *HoTMetaL* is one example of a level 2.0 compliant structured editor; it simply won't permit its users to create improper or uncompliant HTML.

How much information will have to be massaged by hand?

Much of your online information will have to be developed from scratch or retyped and restructured from ordinary hard copy. This is labor-intensive and time consuming. But it has been proven repeatedly to be much cheaper than scanning the hard copy, applying Optical Character Recognition (OCR) software to turn the resulting bitmaps into ASCII characters, and then finally mapping the ASCII bit streams into HTML. (Like many "good ideas" the scanning route is not as easy as it sounds.)

Tallying Up Web Activity

Internet information miners constantly seek Web sites with nuggets of 24 karat information. Some of these miners consider the actual structure of the information to be a clue to a site's richness and value. They will decide to visit a site repeatedly, as long as it continues to produce valuable information.

Unfortunately, this has led to a new era of Web-upsmanship, where it's not uncommon to see claims like "3,000,000 URLs served to 2,000,000 users a month," in an eerie echo of the "billions served" at the Golden Arches. Compiling astronomical visitation counts has become an important technique for measuring a site's popularity, if not its value, so racking up the numbers is the game everyone's trying to win.

Here's how you play: Many sites provide a counter on their welcome page stating that "You are the 167,432nd entity to access this page." We use the term "entity" advisedly because non-human accesses to Web pages happen on a frequent basis.

In addition to the humans who stop by, the entities that visit Web sites are called Web spiders, robots, or crawlers. These robot-like active agents march around the Web, following their shadowy masters' nefarious agendas (actually, they're usually just looking for descriptive data to add to a database somewhere, but we thought this sounded a whole lot more exciting). In the future, many of these Webcrawlers will not only be looking for content, but also for HTML that complies with a specific standard.

Unfortunately, many WebMasters equate the total number of Web accesses with success. The more accesses, the easier it is for them to justify their Web space and its associated overhead costs.

This numbers game, however, resonates unfortunately with concepts like "body counts" and "confirmed kills." The secret is that the counts for the total number of accesses are blown way out of proportion. The biggest contributor to these spurious counts is that each link traversed within the document set counts as another access: Since most visitors (human or otherwise) will typically access at least four or five pages on their way in and out of a document set, the numbers are automatically inflated by counting accesses.

Really valuable statistics would be produced if you could track a user's Web session and record the unique objects that were accessed and the order of access. What does this have to do with valid HTML at your site? It may be the final factor driving a Web publisher's decision to contact you and offer you money for your Web articles. Just two words: "Cha Ching!"

While these are some of the most crucial issues, there are many more questions to consider during the formal document analysis phase of your online publishing production cycle. For more information on this subject, see the discussion of document analysis in Chapter 24.

Adding Value to Your Web Site

The value added by presenting valid HTML documents to your Web audience is twofold:

- If you want your company's Web space to look good using the "new and improved" Web browsers that continue to pop up almost daily, hewing the "valid HTML" line ensures that your materials can accommodate the broadest range of software and viewpoints.

- If you want to be able to use all the new SGML tools on your existing HTML documents, the only way to guarantee their workability is by ensuring that they conform to the DTD that any SGML tool will demand as input to permit it to analyze and interpret them.

As a wag might put it: "Compliance is its own reward." To be ready to handle the kind of audience you'd like your documents to attract, we think it has other benefits as well!

A site that contains valid HTML documents signals that it is well-organized and -maintained. This often results in repeat visits — the key to winning today's ever-popular Web statistics game.

Advantages of Validation

There are five important advantages to publishing a valid HTML document:

- compliance to a known DTD
- increased portability
- can be validated with a parser
- improved information fidelity
- easy assimilation and categorization by a Webcrawler

First, a valid HTML document complies to a known and supported DTD. This is important because standardization legitimizes the structure and content of the document. This was one of the motivations behind the CALS (Computer Aided Logistic Support) initiative where SGML earned its initial world-wide recognition.

The CALS initiative mandated that all documentation delivered to the U.S. government had to adhere to a class of standards. This guaranteed to U.S. government agencies, like the Department of Defense (DoD), that all documentation from all contractors contained the same structure and was readable and reproducible, no matter what platform it was created on or what platform the agency used to generate output.

Most contracts with the DoD now require a contractor to deliver all documentation in SGML that must successfully parse against a mandated DTD outlined in the contract. Imagine if each subcontractor delivered their documents in Microsoft Word, WordPerfect, and FrameMaker file formats to the DoD and then let them convert the resulting amorphous blob. Hence, the birth of CALS and the proliferation of SGML.

Second, a valid HTML document is immediately portable to other WWW sites. This means that any valid HTML document can be moved to another WWW server, whatever that server's computing platform, and still be served to the Web public with almost no need for tweaking (of course the <BASE> URL must be updated).

Another implication includes the possibility that someone might copy your HTML document (your blood, sweat, and tears) and integrate it into a different Web space. Ignoring the ethical implications, because your HTML complies with a standard, this greatly increases the chances that your article entitled "Climbing El Capitán in Yosemite" might be included in an online Rock Climbing Web publication. This creates the chance that you might once again hear those two thrilling words: "Cha Ching!"

Third, a valid HTML document can be parsed successfully by an SGML parser. A parser is a valuable tool for the local WebMaster. It offers a programmatic solution to validating a Web space rather than relying on human inspection.

Fourth, a valid HTML document improves the fidelity of information. We normally communicate with our readers using Standard American English; this greatly improves the chances of successful communication. As long as we can agree on a common language, our chances of communicating effectively are much greater than if each of us can't understand what the other is saying.

SGML Parsers Ain't No Ordinary Parsers

SGML parsers are not the run-of-the-mill "look ahead, left recursive" (LALR) parsers like those used to parse most conventional programming languages. Rather, SGML parsers are "recursive top-down-descent parsers" that are very difficult to code. Although you'd never know how tough they are to build unless you had to do it yourself, they represent substantial amounts of work and mind-numbing complexity.

sgmls is a freely available SGML parser written by James Clark. He also has a beta version of a new SGML parser called *sp*. Later in this chapter we'll look more closely at *sgmls* in the validation tools section (don't worry, you'll get the URL for it, too).

Another aspect of fidelity becomes important when bits of information must regularly change hands. For instance, some Web authors may be engaged in a collaborative effort where they must routinely exchange HTML documents using a predetermined mechanism, usually via the Internet.

In our example scenario, one author may know nothing about HTML, but she relies on an authoring tool to handle the intricacies of HTML (a structured HTML editor such as *HoTMetaL*). This editor currently relies on HTML 2.0, so she produces valid HTML 2.0 every time!

Another Web author might have an extensive background in HTML and uses a plain text editor such as *emacs* with the HTML-mode enabled. He marks up his HTML document, saves it, and then validates it with an SGML parser. Each author has now guaranteed an exchange of valid HTML and, more importantly, a higher fidelity of information exchange.

Finally, a valid HTML document is easier for a Webcrawler to assimilate and categorize. The Webcrawler jumps from Web site to Web site, indexing HTML documents that match its embedded criteria. Normally these Webcrawlers look at the text between <TITLE> and </TITLE> tags.

If the title contains any keywords that match its criteria, the crawler records the URL, the title, and any headings in the document. If the headings are used in proper HTML style (increments and decrements by 1, starting with <H1>), the crawler can organize a simple table of contents of the current document.

The <HTML>, <HEAD>, and <BODY> tags are also very useful structure descriptors to the crawler. Even a properly used <HR> tag can signal to a crawler that a major division of information has occurred. A graphical image divider cannot present this structural clue to the crawler, even if it does so for a human reader.

Disadvantages of Validation

Validation of HTML documents also has two important disadvantages:

- It requires compliance to a rigid standard.
- It requires validation tools and a process.

First, validation requires compliance to a strict structure that is mandated by the DTD. There is very little built-in slack in any DTD. This occurs as a specific design decision, calculated to ensure control over the document's structure and its resulting content.

Some institutions desire this kind of control, like the DoD contractors in the prior example. Some companies rely on technology to abstract away the details of HTML from the writer (requires less intellectual overhead and no HTML training of personnel). Others rely on the expressiveness of the online medium and spit on standards and all the heavy-handed control they represent.

Unfortunately, limiting imagination and artistic expression is the real downfall of valid HTML documents. A <P> tag within an <H2> tag may not pass an SGML parser's strict interpretations of HTML syntax, but it appears in the manner intended by its authors — some of whom knowingly violate the rules — in some browsers.

Second, validating HTML documents requires a well-defined document creation and management process, a suite of validation tools, mucho CPU cycles on some computer, and a human to run the validation tools and decipher the cryptic error messages. The person executing the validation tools can be either a tools guru or the author.

If the tools person validates HTML documents, document errors have to be communicated to the author. Typically, this requires sending e-mail or placing a phone call. For large, complex documents and lots of errors, this creates substantial additional work for all parties.

If it's the author's job to validate a document, then he or she can fix the problem right away. If HTML authors learn how to interpret error messages on their own, they can relieve the WebMaster of the job. Once the WebMaster has these colleagues trained — and this, too, can create substantial additional work for all parties — he or she may be free to move on to more important tasks — like reading the NCSA "What's New Page."

Validation Tools

By sticking to both the letter and the spirit of the HTML specification, your information will get the maximum benefit from new tools. Why? Because most WWW tools developers start with a handful of great ideas, some pizza and beer, a rainy weekend, and the HTML DTD of their choice. They also look at proposed elements in draft DTDs (such as the IETF level 3.0 or Mozilla).

Armed with this formidable collection of ingredients, these stalwart programmers will develop their tools to a base set of document element types specified in the DTD. Most of their energy, time, and money will be spent developing core functionality to support the most primitive HTML elements.

To make their tools distinctive and hopefully more valuable, they may also adopt a small set of extensions to HTML and add support to their tools for these extensions. This is risky because they could choose elements that might not survive to be incorporated in IETF HTML DTD deployment. Maybe that's why so many browsers show such interesting quirks when they're fully explored!

IGNORANCE ISN'T ALWAYS BLISS!

In case you don't already know this, most WWW browsers ignore invalid HTML tags and make educated guesses about improperly used or invalid tag nesting. While this behavior protects them from crashing in the face of bad HTML, it also lets you do anything your heart desires by way of coding your HTML document. This produces some strange behavior and even stranger appearances for many HTML documents. These browsers are *standards aware* which is less restrictive than *standards compliant*. It's an old trick.

That's why even advanced browsers don't make good validation tools. Most of them are designed to render HTML documents to the best of their ability. Rendering valid HTML is easy, when compared to the guessing that has to be built into a browser to handle invalid HTML. Browser technology would improve much faster if developers simply didn't have to worry about invalid tags.

At least one new browser entering the scene has a "Bad HTML" flag that pops up for non-compliant documents. This is the first step toward ubiquitous validation and standardization. Get out your "Book of Validation" and turn to page 107 and read with us ...

GET THE RIGHT TOOL FOR THE JOB

As more and more WWW tools enter the marketplace, they will not all parse noncompliant documents in the same way (e.g., the graphical HTML editor HotMetaL loads only valid 2.0 HTML documents). It will fall upon the document's author or maintainer to fix any errors (possibly by hand).

Some tools incorporate rules-based syntax checkers, while others are rolling their own truly compliant ISO-8879 SGML top-down recursive parsers. The latter costs about 10 times more than a rules-based checker, but is about 100 times more reliable. This is an important feature of validation that could be paramount to the success of your company's Web development efforts.

The wider the array of tools you plan to have at your disposal (and there are a bewildering number of them in the works) the more DTD-compliant your documents will have to be; we simply can't stress this enough. If you don't want to get stuck down the road with 10,000 HTML documents that are unacceptable to some great new SGML tool, then you need to start writing DTD-compliant HTML documents now.

THE NOT-SO-HIDDEN BEAUTIES OF COMPLIANCE

Tony Sanders at Berkeley Software (BSDI) collected input from users about why they thought validation was important. One user wrote:

"We started with some simple pages 6 months ago done at home on a PC. These pages would display more or less OK with the version of Mosaic we had then on the PC, Mac, and the Suns, but not exactly the same. When I moved these pages to the Sun and started to use HotMetaL I had to spend hours hacking the pages to get them to load and a second round of hacking was needed before I could save any changes."

This user finally saw the importance of compliance with an HTML standard. This user is now a religious Validation Advocate, not by choice, but by sheer necessity. Sometimes we get the point right away; sometimes we have to be hit in the head with a skillet! Which would you prefer?

HaLSoft HTML Validation Service

Dan Connolly and Mark Gaither, with great comments from Tony Sanders, developed an HTML Validation Service and an HTML Check Toolkit for HaL Software, Inc.

The HTML Validation Service allows a user to input an HTTP-based URL in a form, choose one of three DTDs (level 2, level 3, or Mozilla), choose either strict or standard checking, and then submit the form to the service. The service is built upon James Clark's *sgmls* version 1.1.19 SGML parser and a simple WWW client to retrieve a URL. The user can also enter just bits and pieces of HTML in another part of the form. Figure 4-1 shows what the interface to the validation service looks like.

Both queries result in either a pass or a fail. Upon failure, the user sees a list of cryptic *sgmls* error messages that can be helpful in correcting any nonstandard uses of HTML in the document. Upon passing, the server presents the user with a congratulatory page and invites them to place an icon on their page. The icon depends on the DTD the user indicated. Figure 4-2 is an example of the "Valid HTML 2.0" icon.

The HaLSoft HTML Validation Service can be found at:

```
http://www.halsoft.com/html-val-svc/
```

This service has been duplicated around the world at such sites as Georgia Tech University and NASA's Jet Propulsion Labs in California.

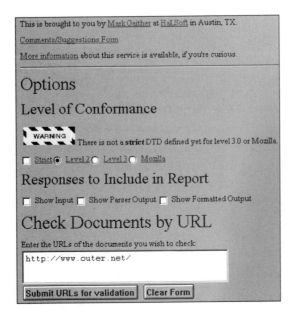

Figure 4-1
The HaLSoft Validation Service in action.

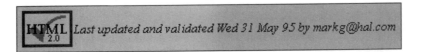

Figure 4-2
HaLSoft's Level 2 Valid Icon.

HaLSoft HTML Check Toolkit

Developed by Connolly and Gaither at HaLSoft, the HTML Check Toolkit allows a user to have HaLSoft's WWW server build a custom validation toolkit and then download it to the user. This results directly from user input into an HTML form that requires the user to determine his or her native UNIX operating system, the directory paths where the binaries and *man* pages should be installed, and the type of compression algorithm needed.

The HTML Check Toolkit allows a user to validate HTML documents locally. This is highly recommended for those Web sites that mandate valid HTML. Highly specialized HTML forms and CGI applications can be developed around this simple toolkit (in fact, the HaLSoft HTML Validation Service is one example of such an application).

The HTML toolkit are free and can be found at:

```
http://www.halsoft.com/html-tk/
```

WEBLINT

Weblint is a Perl script created by Neil Bowers that checks HTML code. UniPress W3 Services created a forms-based interface to *Weblint*. With this interface (shown in Figure 4-3) you can enter your HTML markup and have it checked. You can also supply the URL for an HTML document to be checked.

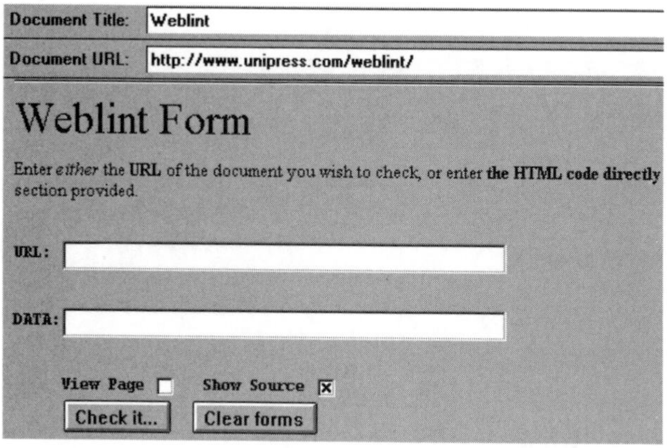

Figure 4-3
Weblint form interface.

Weblint currently performs the following checks:

- document structure
- overlapped elements
- illegally nested elements

- elements that are missing start or end tags
- mismatched tags such as <H1> ... </H2>
- context of included tags
- elements that should only appear once like <HEAD>
- flags obsolete tags like <XMP>
- <TITLE> occurring within a <HEAD>
- ALT attributes for images
- complains at the use of "click here" anchors
- required attributes of element types

Weblint is a rules-based application that does not depend on an SGML parser. *Weblint* has been getting much better at recognizing valid HTML. Its strengths, however, lie in checking document style rather than validation.

Weblint is a free service and tool available at:

http://www.unipress.com/weblint/

HTMLCHEK

This program checks for quite a number of possible defects in the HTML 2.0 documents, but it also checks documents conforming to the Mozilla or the level 3 DTDs. The output from *htmlchek* is divided into two parts, errors and diagnostics.

A very limited form of cross-reference checking is performed for each HTML document. For larger-scale cross-reference checking, *htmlchek* collects all the URLs in an HTML document or collection of documents and stores them in a file. It then builds a link dependency map among the documents in the collection only. It doesn't traverse the Web checking links. It is recommended that you delay your cross-reference checking until you have validated your HTML document collection.

For more information about *htmlchek*, see:

http://uts.cc.utexas.edu/~churchh/htmlchek.html

HoTMetaL

HoTMetaL from SoftQuad is not a standalone validation tool. It is a structured editor that directs the HTML author in creating valid HTML 2.0 documents. HoTMetaL basically controls the structure of an HTML document. The author need not know HTML at all, let alone what is valid level 2.0 HTML. Nevertheless, the resulting HTML document is compliant to the IETF HTML 2.0 document.

HoTMetaL's major drawback is that it can't import invalid HTML documents. So be aware that this is just the first tool to stress validation and that there are more to come. Our advice — choose a DTD today and stick to it.

The free version of HoTMetaL has limited functionality; HoTMetaL Pro is the full-blown version. (We include the shareware version on the CD.)

For more information about HoTMetaL and HoTMetaL Pro, see:

```
http://www.sq.com/products/hotmetal/hmp-org.htm
```

SGMLS AND SP

A free SGML-compliant parser, *sp* (formerly the parser known as *sgmls*), is available from James Clark. *sp* is a completely new, next-generation SGML-compliant parser. Currently, it is in beta testing. Version 0.4, released in April 1995, has the following features:

- It is written in C++.
- It properly supports large character sets.
- It can be compiled to use 16-bit characters.
- The entity manager supports character sets for Unicode and Japanese.
- It includes the *nsgmls* application, which is compatible with *sgmls*.
- It includes a sophisticated SGML normalizer.
- It supports arbitrary concrete syntaxes.
- It can provide other applications with information about an SGML document.

- It supports all varieties of LINK; chains of link processes are limited to a length of one.

- It is fast for large documents compared to *sgmls*.

To build a custom *sp* binary for your site from source code, you need a capable C++ compiler that supports templates. *sp* has been built in at least the following environments:

- SPARC running Solaris 2.3 using gcc 2.6.3

- SPARC running SunOS 4.1.3 using gcc 2.6.3

- SPARC running Solaris 2.3 using Sun C++ 4.0 with gcc

- i486 running Linux 1.2.5 using gcc 2.6.2

- i486 running Windows NT 3.5 using Microsoft Visual C++ 2.0

- i486 running Windows NT 3.5 using Watcom C++ 10.0a targeted for DOS

Both the HaLSoft Validation Service and the HTML Check Toolkit use the antiquated *sgmls* parser by Clark. You can also build a validation application around this parser (we suggest you use the new *sp* parser).

To use the *sp* parser, you need to include an SGML document type prolog on the first line of each HTML document. This can be done by either adding a prolog to each document (which we recommend) or having a script temporarily slap one on top of your HTML document.

The danger of this approach is that over the course of Web site development, you are going to use both level 2 and, hopefully, level 3 HTML documents. Trying to validate a level 2 document against the level 3 DTD will not work.

THE DTD IS PROLOG TO THE FUTURE

You should also get in the practice of adding an SGML prolog to each new HTML document you create. This identifies which DTD the document complies with. As the DTD landscape gets more complicated, WWW servers will have to become much smarter. They will have to recognize an incoming document as either a level 2, level 3, or Mozilla

DTD-based document. If they cannot decipher this information, they will perforce default to some arbitrary DTD, meaning that things could get ugly, fast!

Here's an example of an SGML prolog for the HTML 2.0 DTD:

```
<!DOCTYPE HTML PUBLIC "-//IETF//DTD HTML 2.0//EN" >
```

Look familiar? In fact, you can specify a catalog of DTDs that *sp* can use. Here's the current catalog you get with the HaLSoft HTML Check Toolkit:

```
— catalog: SGML Open style entity catalog for HTML —
— $Id: catalog,v 1.1 1994/10/07 21:35:07 connolly Exp $ —
— ISO latin 1 entity set for HTML — =
PUBLIC  "-//IETF//ENTITIES Added Latin 1 for HTML//EN"  html-latin.sgml
          — fake HTMLicons reference —
PUBLIC   "-//IETF//ENTITIES icons for HTML//EN"  html-icons.sgml
          — fake HTMLmath reference —
PUBLIC  "-//IETF//ENTITIES Math and Greek for HTML//EN"  html-math.sgml
   — Ways to refer to Level 3: most general to most specific —
PUBLIC  "-//IETF//DTD HTML//EN//3.0"              html-3.dtd
PUBLIC  "-//W30//DTD W3 HTML 3.0//EN//"           html-3.dtd
PUBLIC  "-//IETF//DTD HTML 3.0//EN"               html-3.dtd
PUBLIC  "-//IETF//DTD HTML 3.0//EN//"             html-3.dtd
PUBLIC  "-//IETF//DTD HTML Level 3//EN"           html-3.dtd
PUBLIC  "-//IETF//DTD HTML Level 3//EN//3.0"      html-3.dtd
   — Ways to refer to strict Level 3: most general to most specific —
PUBLIC  "-//IETF//DTD HTML Strict//EN//3.0"       html-3s.dtd
PUBLIC  "-//W30//DTD W3 HTML Strict 3.0//EN//"    html-3s.dtd
PUBLIC  "-//IETF//DTD HTML Strict Level 3//EN"    html-3s.dtd
PUBLIC  "-//IETF//DTD HTML Strict Level 3//EN//3.0"  html-3s.dtd
   — Ways to refer to Level 2: most general to most specific —
PUBLIC  "HTML"                                    html.dtd
PUBLIC  "-//IETF//DTD HTML//EN"                   html.dtd
PUBLIC  "-//IETF//DTD HTML//EN//2.0"              html.dtd
PUBLIC  "-//IETF//DTD HTML 2.0//EN"               html.dtd
PUBLIC  "-//IETF//DTD HTML Level 2//EN"           html.dtd
PUBLIC  "-//IETF//DTD HTML Level 2//EN//2.0"      html.dtd
   — Ways to refer to Strict Level 2 —
PUBLIC  "-//IETF//DTD HTML Strict//EN"            html-s.dtd
PUBLIC  "-//IETF//DTD HTML Strict//EN//2.0"       html-s.dtd
PUBLIC  "-//IETF//DTD HTML Strict Level 2//EN"    html-s.dtd
PUBLIC  "-//IETF//DTD HTML Strict Level 2//EN//2.0"  html-s.dtd
   — Ways to refer to Netscape extensions HTML —
PUBLIC "-//Netscape Comm. Corp.//DTD HTML//EN"    html-mcom.dtd
```

With these DTDs available at your site, you can validate a wide variety of HTML documents. The third field in each declaration supplies the filename for the actual DTD. *sp* uses the SGML prolog to verify that the DTD exists in the system. You can add to your local copy of the catalog. You can even include your own DTDs, but before you do, ask yourself why you would want to do this. Take our advice instead: "Don't do it!"

DTD REFERENCE METHODS

Notice that there are several ways to reference a DTD listed in the catalog. For instance, look at the strict section for level 2. Each of these prolog declarations points to the same file containing the strict level 2 HTML DTD. These are synonyms for one another. Choose one and implement it widely; waffling between different prologs is dangerous. We recommend that you use the prologs that contain the actual version number for the HTML DTD:

```
<!DOCTYPE HTML PUBLIC  "-//IETF//DTD HTML 2.0//EN" >
```

Just by visual inspection of the HTML document that includes this prolog, you can determine that it should conform to the level 2 HTML DTD from the IETF (that is, if it passes the validation test).

For more information about *sp* and how to get it, see:

```
http://www.jclark.com/sp.html
```

Validation Alone Is Not Enough

Of course, submitting your HTML document to a validation tool or service is not enough to guarantee that it is well designed (similarly, just because a program compiles doesn't mean that it's bug-free) or follows any suitable style.

But compliance is a very important step on the road to responsible online publishing. Consider the case for using headers (<H1>, <H2>, etc.) just to display a phrase in a larger font than the surrounding text. Can you imagine what your document would look like, using a browser that automatically builds a table of contents (TOC) from the header elements? The TOC would be cluttered up with junk. Not a good idea!

A validation tool is just one important piece of a complete validation process. Without enforcing a validation process on a Web space, documents touted as "Valid HTML 2.0" cannot be assumed valid despite the "Valid HTML 2.0" seal of approval.

Unfortunately, this means that the icon doesn't mean much, if anything at all. This should only underscore your realization that the process through which this document has passed is more important than any labels that attach to it. This leads to the inevitable question:

WHAT'S IN A PROCESS?

The design, deployment, and maintenance of a validation process could be the topic of its own book. Process engineers are highly skilled gurus that cook up detailed functional specifications for processes of all kinds. These processes can quickly become unruly and are usually broken in no time; they can make your life a living hell. Yet you cannot live without them; that's why we suggest that you apply the KISS principle ("Keep it Simple, Stupid!"). Make the validation process a simple procedure that all can understand, follow, and apply.

The simple, manual approach

Here's an example of a simple validation process:

1. Edit the document.
2. Save the document.
3. Validate the document.
4. Update the footer information (includes date, time, and author's name).

This is a non-programmatic process that is not enforceable, but it is easy to explain and understand. Unfortunately, while such a process is easy to deploy, it is also easy to ignore.

The simple, programmatic approach

A programmatic solution is one that includes a document management or version control system like the Concurrent Version System (CVS, which is an extension of the Revision Control System, RCS). Such systems are widespread in most UNIX-based document production operations.

CVS recognizes special variables that an author can embed in an HTML document with comment delimiters (<!-- and -->). For example, in CVS the special variable 'Id' will be expanded once the file is committed to the repository. This variable can be included in the footer information, which will reveal the date, time, and the author who committed the HTML document to the document repository. CVS can also be programmed to execute other applications.

In this case, part of the programmatic solution requires that CVS take the HTML document and run it through a validation tool. If the document validates, it is then installed on the Web site. If it fails, the commit is rolled back — that is, the updated file cannot be referenced by other users, and the previous version remains in place — which triggers an e-mail message to the author, presenting him or her with the error messages from the validation tool.

The beauty of this process is that it guarantees that all documents in the Web are valid (unless someone finds a back door into the Web and inserts non-valid HTML documents through another interface). While we can't completely overlook the sometimes detrimental effects of human ingenuity — especially *Homo hackeris* — this approach clearly improves the odds of maintaining a clean and valid Web site.

This reveals another need — namely, to establish control over a Web space. If the only way to insert HTML documents into the official Web space is through the CVS interface, this can effectively guarantee that the entire Web space will remain valid under the auspices of the current supported DTD. The appearance of the "Valid HTML 2.0 Process" icon on a page at a site that is known to strictly control insertions into its Web is far more believable than at less rigidly controlled sites.

Summary

In case we haven't said it enough, the bottom line for this chapter is: Validate, validate, validate!

The Web is evolving at a mind-boggling pace. Its popularity continues to grow exponentially. With this acceleration come decisions you must make today that will affect your future. Deciding not to validate HTML could result in a 10,000-document Web space that is rapidly approaching obsolescence because the burgeoning number of WWW tools and applications require valid documents.

Those who choose validation and a validation process will quaff brew; those who eschew validation will swallow bitter tears. Take your pick; we'll go for the brew every time. Cheers!

5 The Future of HTML

*H*istory shapes the present. It can also help us predict the future by allowing us to recognize cycles that repeat. The history of explicit markup languages is no different. HTML has evolved from level 0 to level 3 in a matter of just five years, but it has gone through many more cycles in that time.

In Chapter 3 you learned about the history of HTML and the growing pains we all experienced along the road to the present. In this chapter, you'll get a flavor for what's in store for HTML and the WWW, as we look into 1996 and beyond.

A Closer Look at HTML 3.0

The IETF HTML working group is currently developing an Internet draft RFC for HTML 3.0. This specification, once completed and thoroughly tested, will be formally released to the public.

At present, HTML 3.0 is constantly changing, partly due to the input from the handful of developers implementing its features, but primarily because of the rigorous IETF testing process that invariably results in the redesign and re-engineering of features and functions as ideas about what's needed get turned into real implementations. In this chapter, we'll take a closer look at some of the more interesting new elements currently proposed for inclusion in the HTML 3.0 spec.

New HTML 3.0 Elements

As we mentioned in Chapters 3 and 4, what makes HTML 3.0 different from its predecessors is added support for tables, mathematical notation, figures, and a host of miscellaneous capabilities. In the sections that follow, we'll examine these in more detail.

TABLES

The <TABLE> element is the most sought after of the new element types in HTML 3.0. The current 3.0 table model was chosen by the IETF developers because of its flexibility and simplicity. In this model, tables are automatically sized and the default sizing criteria are based on the current window size and the contents of the table's individual cells.

The <TABLE> tag may have an optional table caption followed by one or more rows. A row consists of one or more cells that may be assigned the types 'header' or 'data'. Cells may also be combined across rows and columns and may include attributes for exporting table data or assisting conversion to speech and/or Braille.

Controls over a table's appearance are sparse and are intended to be handled by style sheets or by subclassing the table. This will be discussed a little later in this chapter; for now, it suffices to say that only minimal text layout and style characteristics are supported for tables.

Text flow around tables is also supported in HTML 3.0. If a table is flush with either the left or right margin, any valid 3.0 element can be flowed around the table, depending on the amount of whitespace available. This behavior is controlled by the NOFLOW attribute of the <TABLE> tag, or by the ALIGN attribute, which may be set either to 'center' or 'justify'.

Here are some simple table guidelines, lifted from the HTML 3.0 specification:

- Table cells may include nested tables.
- Missing cells are considered to be empty.
- Missing rows should be ignored; that is, if a cell spans a row and there are no further <TR> elements, then the implied row should be ignored.
- Cells cannot overlap.

What kind of data can a table contain? Here's just a taste:

- lists
- paragraphs
- forms
- figures
- headers
- other tables
- preformatted text

An HTML 3.0 table example

Let's take a look at an example of an HTML 3.0 table instance:

```
<TABLE BORDER>
    <CAPTION>Engine Dynometer Test for 1970 Chevy 454 LS-5</CAPTION>
    <TR><TH ROWSPAN=2>Engine RPM<TH COLSPAN=2>Corrected Data
        <TH ROWSPAN=2>
        <TH ROWSPAN=2>Exhaust Temperature (Fahr.)
    <TR><TH>Torque<TH>Horsepower
    <TR><TH ALIGN="LEFT">3250<TD>465<TD>314<TD><TD>1160
    <TR><TH ALIGN="LEFT">3750<TD>496<TD>371<TD><TD>1208
    <TR><TH ALIGN="LEFT">5000<TD>435<TD>412<TD><TD>1254
</TABLE>
```

Figure 5-1 shows how this is rendered by Arena.

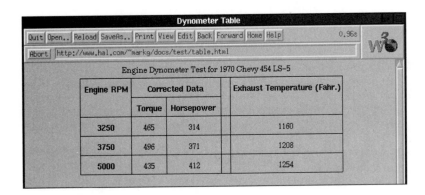

Figure 5-1

Arena's rendering of a sample HTML 3.0 table.

Here's what the HTML code in this sample table will render:

- Cells can be empty.
- Header cells are centered by default.
- Data cells are aligned flush with the left margin (also the default).
- Cells spanning multiple rows appear spanned in the first row.
- Each <TR> tag determines the row count.

You can also build borderless tables which are useful for laying out tabular data. For example, form input widgets could be embedded in a borderless table. Figure 5-2 shows the rendering of the following HTML 3.0 markup for a sample borderless table. This markup represents a table with one row and two columns, one of which is right-aligned, while the other is left-aligned. Here's the sample HTML 3.0 markup:

```
<TABLE>
  <TR VALIGN="BASELINE">
    <TD ALIGN="RIGHT">
        Name:<BR>
        Organization:<BR>
        Voice:<BR>
        WWW:<BR>
    <TD ALIGN="LEFT">
        <INPUT NAME="name" SIZE="20"><BR>
        <INPUT NAME="org" SIZE="40"><BR>
        <INPUT NAME="area-code" SIZE="3"> -
        <INPUT NAME="prefix" SIZE="3"> -
        <INPUT NAME="number" SIZE="4"><BR>
        <INPUT NAME="www" SIZE="40"<BR>
</TABLE>
```

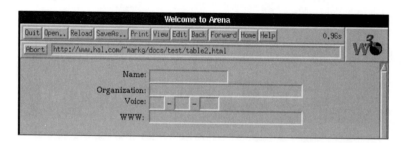

Figure 5-2

Rendering of an embedded form in a borderless table.

In this sample HTML 3.0 table markup, the VALIGN attribute vertically aligns the table from the previous BASELINE. Notice that the 'Voice' input widget consists of three smaller input widgets, one for the area code, one for the exchange or prefix, and one for the number. Also notice the use of <BR> which is typical of inline HTML markup.

<TABLE>

Finally, let's look at each piece of the table section of the HTML 3.0 DTD:

```
<!ELEMENT TABLE - - (CAPTION?, TR*) — mixed headers and data —>
```

This declares an element type called TABLE. Its content data model can have an optional table caption (CAPTION?) followed by zero or more table rows (TR*).

Next is the attribute list for the TABLE element type:

```
<!ATTLIST TABLE
        %attrs; — includes id, lang, and class —
        %needs; — for control of text flow —
        border (border) #IMPLIED — draw borders —
        colspec CDATA   #IMPLIED — column widths and alignment —
        units (en|pixels|relative) en — units for column widths —
        dp      CDATA   #IMPLIED — decimal point e.g. dp="." —
        width NUMBER    #IMPLIED — absolute or percentage width —
        %block.align; — horizontal alignment —
        noflow (noflow) #IMPLIED — noflow around table —
        nowrap (nowrap) #IMPLIED — don't wrap words —
        >
```

In the preceding attribute declaration for TABLE, there are three parameter entity references. Remember, a parameter entity is a DTD macro and is specifically for DTD use only.

'%attrs'

This parameter entity represents common attributes for element types. Here is its declaration from the HTML 3.0 DTD:

```
<!— The CLASS attribute is used to subclass HTML elements for
        rendering purposes, when used with style sheets, e.g. DSSSL
        lite —>
<!ENTITY % attrs  — common attributes for elements —
        'id ID #IMPLIED — as target for hrefs (link ends) —
        lang CDATA "en.us"  — ISO language, country code —
        class NAMES #IMPLIED — for subclassing elements —'>
```

- The ID attribute is an SGML identifier used as a named anchor (the named end of a hypertext link) or to reference elements in an associated style sheet. The ID attribute must be unique within each document.

- The LANG attribute designates an ISO language standard abbreviation, such as "en.uk" for the United Kingdom version of the English language. The language code abbreviations are defined in ISO-639, and the letter country abbreviations in ISO-3166.

- The CLASS attribute is a list of subclass tag names. It is most commonly used to associate a particular presentation style to an element. The list of subclass tags are evaluated from the most general to the most specific and is interpreted from left to right in the list of tags. For example, this bit of HTML defines a paragraph that has the properties and behavior of a couplet in a stanza:

```
<P CLASS="stanza.couplet">
```

'%needs'

This parameter entity represents attributes used to control text flow around document elements. Here is its declaration from the HTML 3.0 DTD:

```
<!ENTITY % needs 'clear CDATA #IMPLIED'>
```

It is used in headers, tables, and other elements to guarantee sufficient room for text flow around the element. The CLEAR attribute tells the browser to move down until there is enough space to render the next element in the document.

'%block.align'

This parameter entity horizontally aligns blocks of elements within the browser window. Here is its declaration from the HTML 3.0 DTD:

```
<!ENTITY % block.align
    "align (bleedleft|left|center|right|bleedright|justify) center">
```

Tables and figures can be horizontally aligned in many ways:

- center (the default) — centered text; text flow around the element is disabled
- right — flush right with the right text margin
- bleedright — flush right with the right window border
- bleedleft — flush left with the left window border
- left — flush left with the left text margin
- justify — the element should stretch to fill within the text margins

Let's now take a look at the rest of the attribute declarations for <TABLE>.

BORDER

This optional attribute controls the inclusion of a surrounding border for a table. To draw a border around your table, use the following HTML statement:

```
<TABLE BORDER>
```

COLSPEC

This optional attribute controls the alignment and widths of table columns. It's a blank-separated list of alignment and column specifications. The columns are listed from left to right starting with an uppercase letter trailed by a number. For example, the following column specification aligns column 1 right with a width of 18 units, aligns column 2 center with a width of 10 units, and aligns column 3 left with a width of 32 units:

```
<TABLE COLSPEC="L18 C10 L32">
```

UNITS

This optional attribute determines the unit of measure for column widths. The default value is 'en' which is a typographical unit equal to half of the current point size of the text. The possible units are enumerated as:

- en (default) — half the point size of an "m"; allows clients to render one row at a time for faster rendering

- relative — client adds the relative width of columns to determine the proportional width of each column
- pixels — atomic unit of your display (because this varies so widely from machine to machine, use of this unit is discouraged)

Here's an example of this attribute set to use relative column widths:

```
<TABLE UNITS="relative">
```

DP

This attribute specifies the character used for the decimal point within the COLSPEC attribute. The two possible values are:

- '.' — period; the default value
- ',' — comma; widely used in Europe and elsewhere around the world

The assignment of the decimal point character is dependent on the current language context, which is set by the LANG attribute for included elements.

WIDTH

This optional attribute specifies the width of a table in units. The UNITS attribute of <TABLE> determines the units of width. If UNITS="relative", the width is calculated as a percentage of the total width between text margins.

NOFLOW

This optional attribute controls the flow of text around a table or figure. When specified, this attribute disables text flow around a table. It is simpler than using the attributes CLEAR or NEEDS on later elements. Here's an example specification:

```
<TABLE NOFLOW>
```

NOWRAP

This optional attribute controls the automatic wrapping of lines within the browser display window. When specified, you can use the <BR> tag to control line breaks within a table. Here's how this attribute might appear in an HTML document:

```
<TABLE NOWRAP>
```

Now let's examine the allowable elements within a <TABLE>. But first let's set this up by looking at three additional parameter entities used in table element declarations. The following DTD fragment is from the HTML 3.0 DTD. We have added SGML comments for commentary and clarification:

```
<!- This parameter entity defines a DTD macro for a cell which can be either
a table header (TH) or table data (TD) ->
<!ENTITY % cell "TH | TD">

<!- This parameter entity defines an enumerated list of types of horizontal
alignment of element types. ->
<!ENTITY % horiz.align "left|center|right|justify">

<!- This parameter entity specifies an enumerated list of types of vertical
alignment of element types. ->
<!ENTITY % vert.align  "top|middle|bottom|baseline">
```

As we'll see later on, the DTD macro and vertical or horizontal alignment of lists can be important aspects of table declarations in HTML 3.0.

<TR>

This sub-element type is the basic unit for <TABLE>. <TR> contains a row of table cells. With the right attributes, you can specify horizontal and vertical alignment of cell contents for the row, or you can disable word wrap.

To format tables, use the CLASS attribute. This sophisticated method allows you to subclass rows in your table to assist with the formatting of the table using style sheet support. As an example, this chunk of HTML specifies a table with three types of rows, each having its own unique formatting and presentation:

```
<TABLE BORDER COLSPEC="L12 C30 R20">
    <TR CLASS="Header"> ...
    <TR CLASS="Body"> ...
    <TR CLASS="Footer"> ...
</TABLE>
```

Each row class can be formatted and presented differently, according to its corresponding style sheet specification. Also, for page-oriented browsers, if a table must be split across pages (a throwback to hard copy), then its footer can be placed appropriately after the entire table has been rendered.

Let's examine the DTD fragment from the HTML 3.0 DTD for <TR>:

```
<!ELEMENT TR - 0 (%cell)* - row container ->
```

This SGML code requires the TR element to have an opening tag, <TR>, and an optional closing tag, </TR>. The content data model specifies the sub-elements defined by the parameter entity '%cell' to be either <TH> or <TD>. Also, TR may contain zero or more cells.

Now we'll investigate the ALIGN and VALIGN attributes for the TR element type (the DP and NOWRAP attributes were discussed earlier). Here's the relevant 3.0 DTD fragment:

```
<!ATTLIST TR
        %attrs; - includes id, lang, and class -
        align (%horiz.align) #IMPLIED - horizontal alignment -
        valign (%vert.align) top  - vertical alignment -
        dp CDATA #IMPLIED  - decimal point e.g. dp="," -
        nowrap (nowrap) #IMPLIED  - don't wrap words -
        >
```

ALIGN

This optional attribute controls the horizontal alignment of paragraphs within the row. Its values can be 'left', 'center', 'right', or 'justify'. For example, to right-align all paragraphs within all cells in a row, you'd write the following HTML 3.0 markup:

```
<TR ALIGN="right"><TH>Header One<TD><P>This paragraph is aligned with the
right text margin for the browser's display window.
```

VALIGN

This attribute specifies explicit vertical alignment for elements within a row. It can take the following values:

- 'top' (the default) — contents of each cell are rendered at the top of each cell

- 'bottom' — contents of each cell are rendered at the bottom of each cell
- 'baseline' — the first line of text in each cell of the row share the same baseline spacing
- 'middle' — contents of each cell are vertically centered in each cell

<CAPTION>

This is an optional element in the content models of elements TABLE and FIG. It is utilized to annotate a table or figure. The caption text can be positioned relative to the table or figure by specifying the ALIGN attribute, which can have the following values: 'top', 'bottom', 'left', and 'right'. In the DTD fragment below, notice that the CAPTION element requires a start and end tag:

```
<!ELEMENT CAPTION - - (%text;)+ — table or figure caption —>
```

The content model is one or more of the elements defined by the parameter entity '%text'. This entity includes many document elements and for brevity is not defined here.

Next is the attribute list for the CAPTION element type:

```
<!ATTLIST CAPTION
        %attrs;
        align (top|bottom|left|right) #IMPLIED
        >
```

This list consists of a list of elements defined by the parameter entity '%attrs' — which we have seen before — and the optional ALIGN attribute. It has no default value.

<TH>, <TD>

'%cell'

The 'cell' is the atomic object of a row. The following DTD fragment specifies that the parameter entity '%cell' (which may take either the TH or TD sub-element type) must have an opening tag:

```
<!ELEMENT (%cell) - 0 %body.content>
```

Both <TH> or <TD> have optional closing tags, </TH> or </TD>, with allowable sub-elements defined by the parameter entity '%body.content'.

'%body.content'

The '%body.content' entity is declared in the HTML 3.0 DTD as:

```
<!ENTITY % body.content "(DIV|%heading|%text|%block|HR|ADDRESS)*">
```

A cursory examination of this entity definition indicates that it includes a plethora of other tags. In fact, this declaration incorporates other parameter entities that are themselves large collections of sub-element types. This entity contains nearly all of the valid tags allowed between <BODY> ... </BODY> tags.

For each row, the contents of its <TH> and <TD> sub-elements comprise the content of its cells. <TH> is used for table headers, while <TD> indicates table data. Clients will usually render headers with a distinctive font. This distinction also helps to render speech or Braille from tables.

The CLASS attribute may be utilized to subclass table cells. For instance, headers could be subclassed into sub-headers, etc. This mechanism could be used in conjunction with associated style sheets for client-side presentation and control over tables, for font selection, color, or style to create visually distinct ways to distinguish header classes from data cell classes.

The vertical and horizontal alignment of cell contents are specified by the cell's optional attributes VALIGN and ALIGN, respectively. If these attributes aren't specified, the alignments are gleaned from the table row parent element type TR.

One recommendation from the HTML 3.0 specification is to use the table attributes COLSPEC and WIDTH for controlling column widths rather than disabling word wrap (NOWRAP) and using the <BR> tag. The COLSPEC attribute has the highest precedence over all other methods when controlling columns widths.

Now, let's investigate all the other attributes for a cell. Here's a fragment of the HTML 3.0 DTD:

```
<!ATTLIST (%cell)
    %attrs; - includes id, lang, and class -
    colspan NUMBER 1 - columns spanned -
```

```
rowspan NUMBER 1 — rows spanned —
align (%horiz.align) #IMPLIED — horizontal alignment —
valign (%vert.align) top — vertical alignment —
dp CDATA #IMPLIED  — decimal point e.g. dp="," —
nowrap (nowrap) #IMPLIED  — don't wrap words —
axis CDATA #IMPLIED — axis name, defaults to element content —
axes CDATA #IMPLIED — comma separated list of axis names —
>
```

COLSPAN

This attribute defines the number of columns a cell may span. Using this attribute, you can also join horizontally adjacent cells on the same row. The default column span is '1'. Our first table example demonstrates how to use this attribute.

ROWSPAN

This attribute identifies the number of rows a cell may span. With this attribute, you can also join vertically adjacent cells across multiple rows. The default value for row span is also '1'.

AXIS

This attribute specifies a header cell's abbreviation, used for rendering speech from HTML for the visually impaired. The default value is the header cell's contents, but this attribute allows a different value to be specified.

AXES

This attribute is a comma-delimited list of axis names. Together, these names identify the column and row headers for any given cell. This attribute is used when rendering a table in speech (for example, for the visually impaired).

For more detailed information about tables, consult this URL:

```
http://www.hpl.hp.co.uk/people/dsr/html3/tables.html
```

FIGURES

The FIG element type is used to mark up figures within an HTML 3.0 document. It contains text for use in nongraphical browsers like Lynx. FIG's ALIGN controls the flow of adjacent elements around a figure. To enable this behavior, set the ALIGN attribute to either 'left' or 'right'. The FIG attributes will be discussed in more detail later in this section.

Here are some examples of the FIGURE element to familiarize you with its structure and usage. The first example places a figure with a caption, a description sentence, and a credit:

```
<FIG SRC="images/build-process.gif">
  <CAPTION><I>localbld</I> process at HaLSoft</CAPTION>
  <P>This is a pictorial definition of the build process including data flow
among processes.
  <CREDIT>Dr. John Daniel (PFJ)</CREDIT>
</FIG>
```

The next example is the welcome page for Wabbit Twacks Wacing, Inc.:

```
<FIG SRC="WTW-logo.gif">
 <H1>Wabbit Twacks Wacing, Inc.</H1>
 <P>Choose one of the following:
 <UL>
    <LI><A HREF="catalog.html">Catalog</A>
    <LI><A HREF="about.html">About WTW</A>
    <LI><A HREF="guide.html">1995 WTW Results and News</A>
 </UL>
</FIG>
```

This example is a weather map accompanied by an overlay:

```
<FIG SRC="weather-doppler-north-america.jpeg">
  <OVERLAY SRC="map.gif">
  <P>Current Doppler weather map of North America.
</FIG>
```

Now that you've seen some examples, let's look at the DTD fragment for the FIG element type.

<FIG>

This is the DTD declaration for the figure element. It requires a start and end tag. Its content data model includes zero or more overlays followed by an optional caption followed by the elements in the parameter entity 'body.content' followed by an optional credit. Notice that nested figures and images are not allowed:

```
<!ELEMENT FIG - - (OVERLAY*, CAPTION?, %body.content;, CREDIT?)
-(FIG|IMG)>
```

Next is the attribute list for the FIG element:

```
<!ATTLIST FIG
    %attrs;
    %needs;                     - for control of text flow -
    src %URI;   #REQUIRED       - URI of document to embed -
    %url.link;                  - standard link attributes -
    %block.align;               - horizontal alignment -
    width  NUMBER #IMPLIED      - desired width in units -
    height NUMBER #IMPLIED      - desired height in units -
    units (em|pixels) pixels - specifies units as em's or pixels -
    imagemap (%URI) #IMPLIED - pass background clicks to server -
    >
```

The preceding attribute declaration for FIG mentions four parameter entity references. We discussed '%attrs', '%block.align', and '%needs' when you learned about tables. Let's look at the other entity used in this attribute list — '%url.link'. Remember, a parameter entity is a DTD macro and is specifically for DTD use only.

'%url.link'

This parameter entity specifies the behavior and syntax of URL-based links. Such links are included when a URL is specified in an HTML 3.0 document and may include the following attributes:

BASE
The BASE attribute is the identification of the base document used to resolve relative URLs.

URN
The URN (uniform resource name) attribute is a location-independent address of a document and is used to check if the referenced object is present in your cache under a different URL (typical for images).

MD
The MD attribute specifies a message digest or cryptographic checksum such as 'md5' for the referenced object and is required to ensure that the

referenced document has not been modified. For example, an attribute/
value pair like:

```
md="md5:jV2OfH+nnXHU8bnkPAad/mSQlTDZ"
```

describes a message digest encoded in base64 by the 'md5' algorithm.
Notice that the prefix in the value preceding the colon denotes the
algorithm.

Here's the DTD fragment for the 'url.link' entity:

```
<!ENTITY % url.link — Attributes associated with URL based links —
   "base IDREF #IMPLIED — which <BASE> to resolve relative links —
   urn CDATA #IMPLIED  — location independent name for object —
   md CDATA #IMPLIED   — message digest for linked object —
   ">
```

Now, let's examine the other FIG attributes starting with SRC.

SRC

This required attribute of the FIGURE element defines the figure's
graphical content. It supplies the specification for the Universal
Resource Identifier (URI) of the referenced object.

UNITS

This optional attribute determines the unit of measure for a figure's
width and height. The default value is 'pixel' which is a single point on
your display. The possible units are enumerated as:

- em — point size for an "m"; allows clients to render one row at a
  time for faster rendering
- pixels (default) — atomic unit of your display (because this varies so
  widely from machine to machine, use of this unit is discouraged)

WIDTH

This optional parameter designates the desired width of a figure. The
units for the width is determined by the value for the UNITS attribute.
Capable WWW clients can scale a figure to this width.

HEIGHT

This optional parameter designates a figure's desired height. The unit for the height is also determined by the value for UNITS. Capable WWW clients can scale a figure to this height.

IMAGEMAP

This optional attribute specifies a URI for processing image events such as drags and clicks. It passes these events to the server.

Here's an example of a FIG element using some of these attributes:

```
<FIG UNITS="em" WIDTH="200" HEIGHT="100" SRC="image.gif">
```

<OVERLAY>

This is a sub-element of the FIGURE element. It can occur zero or more times within the context of a FIGURE. It is used as an extra layer of information layered on a base figure.

An overlay provides a mechanism for caching incremental modifications to a figure in successive documents. This improves the effective rendering speed for figures within a document that changes only slightly from access to access. An overlay that can be significantly smaller than the cached base figure can be retrieved, resulting in better overall client performance. Typically, an overlay originates at the top-left corner of the base image.

Let's take a look at the DTD declaration for OVERLAY and its attributes. The element declaration specifies that a start tag is required while the end tag is optional. OVERLAY has no content. It is similar to a buoy floating within the text flow:

```
<!ELEMENT OVERLAY - O EMPTY — image overlay —>
```

The attribute list comes next. It consists of several attributes that you've already seen, and those you haven't seen yet will be defined later in this chapter. Notice that the SRC attribute is required for OVERLAY, and that the default value for the UNITS attribute is 'pixels'.

```
<!ATTLIST OVERLAY
    src  %URI;  #REQUIRED    — URI of image overlay —
    %url.link;               — standard link attributes —
```

```
units (em|pixels) pixels — specifies units as em's or pixels —
x       NUMBER   0         — offset from left in units —
y       NUMBER   0         — offset from top in units —
width   NUMBER  #IMPLIED   — desired width in units —
height  NUMBER  #IMPLIED   — desired height in units —
imagemap (%URI) #IMPLIED — pass background clicks to server —
>
```

X,Y

These attributes define the origin or offset for the overlay in units that
are defined by the value of the UNITS attribute. By default, the overlay's
origin is (0,0) which is the absolute upper-left-hand corner of the base
figure.

<CREDIT>

This is an optional sub-element of FIGURE and BQ (block quote). It is
used to cite the source for a figure or block quote. Here's the DTD declaration for the CREDIT element type. Notice that it requires a start and
end tag. Its content model contains zero or more text objects defined by
the parameter entity '%text'. Its attributes are defined by the parameter
entity '%attrs' which we have seen before:

```
<!ELEMENT CREDIT - - (%text;)* — source of image —>
<!ATTLIST CREDIT
        %attrs; >
```

Both the <CAPTION> and <CREDIT> contents are rendered on
graphical and text-based browsers. The included text objects within a
FIGURE element, such as <UL> and <P>, communicate a figure's content
to folks cruising the Web using nongraphical browsers. These text
objects are known as "figure description text."

Anchor (<A>) elements in the figure description text play a dual role.
First, you can specify graphical hypertext links similar to the hot zones of
an image map. HTML 3.0 has enhanced the A element to include a new
attribute named SHAPE that designates hot zones in a hypertext link. Second, text-based browsers render hypertext links as highlighted text. This
design of the new and improved <A> tag is to simplify the task of HTML
authors writing for graphical as well as nongraphical clients.

It is the intention of the FIG element to help fight the occasional
alienation experienced by users limited to a VT100 terminal, or the

visually impaired who rely on speech rendering from text. The impetus of the FIG element is to force authors to write figure description text to define graphical hypertext links within an HTML 3.0 document.

Hot zones in a figure for some WWW applications may even be dynamically defined by CGI applications. HTML 3.0 allows drags and clicks to be passed to a CGI application using the IMAGEMAP attribute of the FIGURE element. The Virtual Reality Modeling Language (VRML) allows the definition of hot zones as part of the graphics.

There is a defined protocol for hot zones. For more information about this protocol, see the URL for the HTML 3.0 specification at the end of this section.

For more information about figures, see this URL:

```
http://www.hpl.hp.co.uk/people/dsr/html3/figures.html
```

MATH EQUATIONS AND FORMULAE

The MATH element type in HTML 3.0 is used to render math equations and expressions inline. This element provides expressiveness similar to most desktop publishing systems in use today. MATH can also aid in the rendering of speech for the vision-impaired.

The popular high-level typesetting language T_EX (and its manu-script-handling variant, LaT$_E$X), invented by Donald Knuth of Stanford University, has had a major influence on the design of the HTML 3.0 math functionality. Some of the LaT$_E$X commands, like SQRT and CHOOSE — and their behavior — have carried over to HTML 3.0.

Since HTML is both human- and machine-readable, the design of the MATH element needed to be succinct and human-readable. The use of the BOX element aids this design constraint. Also, multiline equations are not supported but can be implemented by combining MATH elements in a TABLE element.

Math symbols represent yet another design hurdle that the IETF HTML working group must overcome. They continue to labor toward the definition of a set of public SGML math entities, but as of this writing, these entities have not yet taken their final form.

The following SGML code specifies how math entities are included in the HTML 3.0 DTD. This is a series of two statements (SGML comments added for commentary):

```
<!- ISO subset chosen for use with the widely available Adobe math font ->
<!- This is a parameter entity used in the HTML 3.0 DTD for math entities.
Notice the entity's text value - it is a public identifier for an external
object. This object is of type "ENTITIES" that was developed and is owned by
the IETF. Its description is "Math and Greek for HTML" and the tag set is in
English. ->
<!ENTITY % HTMLmath PUBLIC
              "-//IETF//ENTITIES Math and Greek for HTML//EN">
<!- This is the actual instance in the DTD of the math entity. It is similar
to an #include in C. The SGML parser looks for an external public entity
that is identified by its public identifier string.
     Please note: the public identifier is intended to lessen the impact of
changes to the underlying entity definitions. ->
%HTMLmath;
```

<MATH>

Let's look at the DTD declaration for a MATH element in detail. Here's the fragment from the HTML 3.0 DTD that defines the MATH element:

```
<!ELEMENT MATH - - (#PCDATA)* -(%notmath) +(%math)>
```

As of this writing, the attributes for the MATH element are still evolving.

The MATH element requires a start and end tag. Its content model includes zero or more parsable character data while excluding elements defined by the '%notmath' parameter entity and including the elements defined by the '%math' parameter entity. This is a very interesting and convoluted content model. The reasoning behind this approach is to provide the ability to modify content models for these three elements: B (bold), SUP (superscript), and SUB (subscript). These three elements typically appear in math expressions, as well as in general text items.

The following sub-elements of the MATH element are valid markup:

- BOX — a math container element similar to brackets. It can be used for expressions that include placing one expression over another.

- SUP, SUB — superscript and subscript.

- VEC, DOT, DDOT, BAR, TILDE, HAT — used for typical math accents or identifiers.

- ABOVE — draws a line, symbol, or arrow above the current math expression.

- BELOW — same as ABOVE but draws below expression.

- TEXT — used to include textual description with a math expression.

- ARRAY — used for arrays and matrices.

- ROOT, SQRT — root and square root of math expression.

- BT, B, T — used for presentation control of math expression. BT specifies a "bold upright" font, B specifies a "bold" font, and T specifies an "upright" font.

For more information about the MATH element, please consult this URL:

```
http://www.hp.hp.co.uk/people/dsr/html3/maths.html
```

There are many more interesting new features in HTML 3.0, including static banner sections for company logos and navigational images and admonishments. But space and time prevent us from sharing the details with you. For more information about the HTML 3.0 specification, consult this URL:

```
http://www.hp.hp.co.uk/people/dsr/html3/Contents.html
```

HTML STYLE SHEETS

The concept of a style sheet is not new to production of online documentation, but it is a new concept for HTML. In fact, it is such a new concept that the WWW community and the IETF have not yet selected an approach. Several approaches are being considered, too many to list all of them here.

Currently, two possible approaches lead the pack: DSSSL Lite from Dave Raggett, and Cascading Style Sheets from Håkon Lie. Pei Wei has also proposed a style sheet language. For now, these waters are still murky.

Referencing style sheets in HTML 3.0

Rather than analyzing these approaches and dissecting their pros and cons, let's look at how a style sheet is referenced by an HTML 3.0 document via the LINK sub-element of the HEAD element. A style sheet can be associated with an HTML 3.0 document using the LINK element. For example, the following SGML fragment relates the following document to the DSSSL Lite style sheet named 'your-style.dsssl'.

```
<HTML>
<HEAD>
<LINK REL="style" HREF="your-style.dsssl">
</HEAD>
```

With this mechanism, you can control presentation of the HTML 3.0 document. This style can be overridden by using the STYLE element within the document <HEAD>. For example, this SGML fragment can override an externally defined style sheet for this document only:

```
<HEAD>
<STYLE NOTATION="dsssl-lite">
    *** dsss-lite stuff here ***
 </STYLE>
```

Later on in the document, you might see:

```
<H1 CLASS="huge-caps">Heading One in Huge Caps</H1>
<P CLASS="footnote">A uniquely styled paragraph used for footnotes.
```

For more information or to follow the continuing evolution of HTML style sheets, please consult this URL:

```
http://www.w3.org/hypertext/WWW/Style/
```

Summary

All good things must change. But there is a price to pay. Once HTML 2.0 becomes an Internet standard, there will many, many WWW sites that will be forced to spend endless hours migrating their non-valid HTML documents to HTML 2.0. As soon as they can catch their breath from this Herculean catch-up maneuver, along will come HTML 3.0. For the time being, with the addition of new elements to HTML 3.0, the expressiveness of the WWW is blossoming. But only time can tell what some of these flowers will look like, as the specifications for HTML 3.0 begin to be finalized.

6 The Common Gateway Interface

The Hidden Life of HTML

O nline WWW documents lead a completely different life than their conventional, print-bound counterparts. They can change with a single keystroke and the effects are immediately visible to the whole world. Since server programs can generate custom-built Web documents on-the-fly in response to interaction with end users, this makes online WWW publishing much more responsive and open-ended than traditional publishing.

Quick response to change and dynamic behavior are the under-pinnings of the power behind the WWW. But unless you implement the right approach to building and maintaining Web documents, your information can just lie stagnant and be virtually "dead to the world."

Dynamic behavior is a vital aspect of the Web that is sometimes hard to identify or appreciate. This is particularly true when documents are created on-the-fly, usually in response to some event on the WWW. Although what appears to a user in response to a query may look like "just another Web page," it might actually be an evanescent document created for one-time use in direct response to that query.

The same is often true for the results of a Web search, or even when clicking a link or a button on a particular page. The result is a custom-built response, tailored around previous interaction with the user (or from information provided by users, even if they're blissfully unaware of the underlying communications involved).

What makes all this possible is a special mechanism that supports the dynamic creation of HTML documents. This mechanism is based on the invocation of external applications that run under the auspices of a WWW server, called by the browser in the form of an ordinary-looking URL on the Web document currently in use. Each of these external applications can be tailor-made to deliver customized, on-demand HTML documents.

Today, many commercial institutions realize the wealth and value of information that resides in their customer and product databases. Many of them want to provide this ancillary information for public consumption. Some key questions they're grappling with are: "How can we make this information accessible?" and "What's the best way to present it for easy consumption and use?" and "How can we make money on this thing?"

The WWW provides the infrastructure and mechanisms for seamless integration of this kind of information, along with typical sales documents like spec sheets, brochures, testimonials, technical documents, and whatnot (which we'll refer to rather loosely as *collaterals*). A key technology underlying the WWW permits static information to be queried and imported on demand and also supports custom construction of Web documents on-the-fly. This technology is called the Common Gateway Interface (CGI), the subject of this chapter.

What Is the Common Gateway Interface?

The Common Gateway Interface (CGI) supplies the middleware among WWW servers, external databases, and information sources. CGI scripts or programs may be considered to be extensions to the core functionality of a WWW server, like that supplied in the CERN or NCSA *httpd* packages. CGI applications perform specific information-processing, retrieval, and formatting tasks on behalf of their WWW servers. The CGI interface defines a method for the Web server to accommodate additional programs and services that may be used to access external applications from within the context of any active Web document.

The term *gateway* describes the relationship between the WWW server and the external applications that handle data access and manipulation chores on its behalf. This gateway incorporates enough built-in intelligence to guarantee successful communication between the server and the external application. Normally, a gateway handles information requests in some orderly fashion and then returns an appropriate response — for example, an HTML document generated on-the-fly that includes the results of a query applied against an external database.

In other words, CGI allows a WWW server to provide information to WWW clients that would not otherwise be available to those clients in a readable form. This could, for example, allow a WWW client to issue a query to an Informix database and receive an appropriate response in the form of a custom-built Web document. That's why we believe that CGI's main purpose is to support communications with information and services outside the normal purview of WWW, ultimately to produce HTTP objects from non-HTTP objects that a WWW client can render. In short, CGI opens up a door to the whole world of information and services that would otherwise be inaccessible to Web clients and servers alike.

Gateways can be designed and deployed for a variety of purposes, but the most common is the handling of <ISINDEX> and <FORM> HTTP requests. Some common uses of CGI include:

- Gathering user feedback about your product line or your WWW server through an HTML form.
- Dynamic conversion of your system's documentation (for example, *man* pages) into HTML, for easy Web-based access.
- Querying Archie or WAIS databases and rendering results as HTML documents.

Working in tandem with the HTTP server application (*httpd*), CGI applications service requests made by WWW clients by accepting requests for services at the server's behest, handling those requests, and sending appropriate responses back to the client. A client HTTP request consists of the following elements:

- a Universal Resource Identifier (URI)
- a request method
- other important information about the request provided by the transport mechanism of the HTTP

In the sections that follow, you'll have a chance to understand all of these elements in detail as you become familiar with the structure and function of a client HTTP request.

The CGI Specification: Extending HTTP

The CGI specification was created and documented by the main HTTP server authors: Tony Sanders, Ari Luotonen, George Phillips, and John Franks. These folks discovered that they didn't want to keep adding functionality to their HTTP servers every day, in keeping with the needs of one particular Web activity or another. They decided to build a clearly defined core of WWW server functionality and to provide a way to extend services and capabilities from there.

They needed an application programming interface (API) available to any Perl, C, or shell hacker willing to learn the appropriate interface details. Hence, the creation of CGI as a formal, rigorous specification that includes some nasty notation and grammar.

For more information about the CGI specification, please consult the following URL:

```
http://hoohoo.ncsa.uiuc.edu/cgi/interface.html
```

In the subsections that follow, you'll have a chance to cover the elements of the specification, as we prepare you to build CGI programs of your own.

A CAST OF ENVIRONMENT VARIABLES

Environment variables are entities that exist within a particular user's computer environment. Many of these variables attain their values whenever a user logs into a computer, or when the computer is booted for a single-tasking operating system like DOS. Environment variables are pervasive within UNIX, where they are used to pass information to applications from the runtime environment.

Because the environment persists even as execution threads come and go, environment variables sometimes function as placeholders, to pass data from one application to another within the same user session. In the case of CGI, environment variables known to the server and CGI are used to pass data about an HTTP request from a server to the CGI application. These variables are accessible to both the server and any CGI application it may invoke.

The WWW server may also use command-line arguments, as well as environment variables, to pass data about an information request from a WWW client. This allows specific control over program parameters or execution to originate with the server, as well as providing a mechanism for clients to pass short input sequences to the CGI program involved. Likewise, these variables may also be set (or assigned their values) when the server actually executes a CGI application.

ACCESSING CGI VARIABLES

The requirements of a specific WWW server control how CGI applications access variables. If a variable does not have a value, this indicates a zero-length value (NULL in the UNIX realm). If the variable is not defined in the server's system (omitted or missing), it is assumed to have a zero-length value and hence, is also assumed to be NULL. As with variable access, the system requirements for the WWW server dictate the means of value representation for CGI variables.

Likewise, the names for environment variables are system specific. For historic reasons, we will discuss UNIX environment variables in detail. Please notice that these names are case sensitive, so they must be reproduced exactly in order to reference the correct information. Table 6-1 is a quick reference to the standard environment variables that are specific to each request handled by a CGI application.

Table 6-1

Standard Environment Variables Quick Reference

Environment Variable	Description
AUTH_TYPE	access authentication type
CONTENT_LENGTH	size in decimal number of octets of any attached entity
CONTENT_TYPE	the MIME type of an attached entity
GATEWAY_INTERFACE *	server's CGI spec version
HTTP_(string)	client header data
PATH_INFO	path to be interpreted by CGI app
PATH_TRANSLATED	virtual to physical mapping of file in system
QUERY_STRING	URL-encoded search string
REMOTE_ADDR	IP address of agent making request
REMOTE_HOST	fully qualified domain name of requesting agent
REMOTE_IDENT	identity data reported about agent connection to server
REMOTE_USER	user ID sent by client
REQUEST_METHOD	request method by client
SCRIPT_NAME	URI path identifying a CGI app
SERVER_NAME *	server name; host part of URI; DNS alias
SERVER_PORT	server port where request was received
SERVER_PROTOCOL	name and revision of request protocol
SERVER_SOFTWARE *	name and version of server software

* not request-specific (set for all requests).

AUTH_TYPE

This variable is used to provide various levels of server access security. If your server supports user authentication, this environment variable value indicates the protocol-specific authentication method used to validate a user.

HTTP provides a simple challenge–response authorization mechanism. This mechanism can be used by a server to challenge a client's request or by a client to provide authentication information to a server. The variable's value is deciphered from the HTTP *auth-scheme* token in the client's request HTTP header. If no access authorization is required, the value is set to NULL.

For example, a server may require a client to provide a user ID and password to access a specific part of its Web. In order to make this happen, the client must set the AUTH_TYPE environment variable to a value that matches the supported protocol of the server. For HTTP applications, the most common value is:

```
AUTH_TYPE = Basic
```

This provides a basic authentication scheme where the client must authenticate itself with a user ID and password pair. For more information on this (and other) environment variables, please consult section 10.1 of the HTTP 1.0 specification at the following URL:

```
http://www.w3.org/hypertext/WWW/Protocols/HTTP1.0/HTTP1.0/draft-ietf-http-
spec.html#BasicAA
```

CONTENT_LENGTH

This variable's value equals the decimal number of octets for the attached entity, if any. If there is no attached entity, it is set to NULL. For example:

```
CONTENT_LENGTH = 9
```

CONTENT_TYPE

The value of this variable indicates the media type of the attached entity, if any. If there is no attached entity, it is also set to NULL. HTTP 1.0 uses MIME Content-Types, which provide an extensible and open mechanism for data typing and for data type negotiation.

With HTTP, you can represent different media like text, images, audio, and video. Within such media, there often exist various encoding methods. For instance, images can be encoded as jpeg, gif, ief, or tiff. The value of the CONTENT_TYPE variable for an attached gif image file could therefore be:

```
CONTENT_TYPE = image/gif
```

For HTTP requests, a client may provide a list of acceptable media types as part of its request header. This allows the client more autonomy in its use of unregistered media types. Although data providers are strongly encouraged to register their unique media types and subtypes with the Internet Assigned Numbers Authority (IANA), this does provide additional flexibility. But since both client and server must be able to handle unregistered items, media types registered with the IANA are preferred over unregistered extensions.

See Table 6-2 for the seven standard predefined MIME Content-Types. (The primary subtype is presented in italics.)

Table 6-2

MIME Registered Content-Types Used by HTTP

Type	Subtypes	Description
application	*octet-stream*	transmit application data
text	*plain*	textual information
multipart	*mixed*, alternative, digest, parallel	multiple parts of independent data types
message	*rfc822*, partial, external-body	an encapsulated message
image	gif, jpeg	image data
audio	*basic*	sound data
video	*mpeg*	video data

application

This MIME Content-Type describes transmitted application data. This is typically uninterpreted binary data. The primary subtype is 'octet-stream' intended to be used in the case of uninterpreted binary data. An additional subtype, 'PostScript', is defined for transporting PostScript documents within MIME bodies.

Subtype Specifications

Whenever an environment variable supports subtyping, note that some subtype specification is *mandatory* for that variable. That is, there are no default subtypes.

All type, subtype, and parameter names are case insensitive. For example, 'IMAGE', 'Image', and 'image' are all equivalent. The only constraint on subtype names is that their uses must not conflict. It would be undesirable to have two different uses of 'Content-Type: application/grunge'. The name provides a simple mechanism for publicizing its uses, not constraining them.

The simplest and most common action when a client requests 'application' MIME Content-Type data is to offer to write the information to a file. For example, the environment variable:

```
CONTENT_TYPE = application/octet-stream
```

would result in the client asking the user if he or she would like to save the binary data to a local file on his or her hard drive.

Other expected uses for 'application' could include things like spreadsheet data, data for mail-based scheduling systems, compressed binary data such as *gzip*, and languages for "active" e-mail.

text

This MIME Content-Type describes textual data. The primary subtype is 'plain'. This unformatted text requires no special software to render the text, although the indicated character set must be supported by the client. Text subtypes are forms of enriched text where software may enhance the presentation of the text. The most common non-registered text subtype used on the Web is 'html (text/html). This software must not be required in order to grasp the general idea of the text's content. One such possible subtype is 'richtext' which was introduced by RFC 1341.

An example of this environment variable is:

```
CONTENT_TYPE = text/plain; charset=us-ascii
```

For more information about 'richtext' and RFC 1341 see this URL:

```
http://www.cis.ohio-state.edu/htbin/rfc/rfc1341.html
```

Please note that since its publication, RFC 1341 has been superseded by RFC 1521, which incorporates some new material not mentioned in 1341. For current implementation details, please consult the most current version of any RFC. The full collection, which includes pointers from obsolete to current versions, can be accessed through the following URL:

```
http://www.cis.ohio-state.edu/hypertext/information/rfc.html
```

multipart

This MIME Content-Type describes data consisting of multiple parts of independent data types. There are four common subtypes.

1. 'mixed' is the primary subtype.
2. 'alternative' represents the same data type in multiple formats.
3. 'parallel' for parts intended to be viewed at the same time.
4. 'digest' for parts of type 'message'.

message

This MIME Content-Type subtype is an encapsulated message. A MIME body of Content-Type 'message' is itself all or part of a fully formatted message. This message must comply with the Internet Mail Header protocol described in RFC 822. This RFC 822–compliant message may contain its own completely different MIME Content-Type header field.

There are three subtypes:

1. 'rfc822' is the primary subtype.
2. 'partial' is defined for partial messages that allow fragmented transmission of MIME bodies deemed too large for normal mail transport facilities.
3. 'external-body' is for specifying large MIME bodies by reference to an external data source such as an image repository.

Here's an example of a standard e-mail text message:

```
CONTENT_TYPE = message/rfc822
```

image

This MIME Content-Type describes image data. The MIME Content-Type image requires a display device such as a graphical display, a FAX machine, or a printer to view the image data. There are two subtypes that are defined for two widely used image formats, jpeg and gif.

For example, data of a gif encoded image would be:

```
CONTENT_TYPE = image/gif
```

audio

This MIME Content-Type describes audio or sound data. The primary subtype is 'basic'. Audio requires an audio output device such as a speaker to display the contents.

An example of a MIDI–attached MIME body would be:

```
CONTENT_TYPE = audio/x-midi
```

NOTE: the "x" prefix declares this MIME Content-Type subtype to be an extended data type.

video

This MIME Content-Type describes video data. Video requires the capability to display moving images. This is typically accomplished with specialized hardware and software. The primary subtype is 'mpeg'.

An example of a video data entity would be:

```
CONTENT_TYPE = video/mpeg
```

For more information about the IANA, see this URL:

```
http://ds.internic.net/rfc/rfc1590.txt
```

GATEWAY_INTERFACE

This environment variable represents the version of the CGI specification to which the server that supplies this value complies. This variable is not request-specific and is set for all HTTP requests. An example value would be:

```
GATEWAY_INTERFACE = CGI/1.1
```

http_(string)

CGI environment variables beginning with the string 'HTTP_' contain HTTP header information supplied by the client. These are the MIME Content-Types that the client will accept, as supplied in HTTP request headers. Each data type in this list should be separated by a comma as required in the HTTP 1.0 specification.

The HTTP header name is converted to all uppercase characters. All "-" (hyphen) characters are replaced with "_" (underscore). Finally, the 'HTTP_' string is prepended, resulting in the set of HTTP_string environment variables.

The HTTP request header data sent by the client may be preserved, or it may be transformed, but it will not change its meaning. An example of this behavior occurs when a server may strip comment data from an HTTP request header. If necessary, the receiving server must transform the HTTP request header data to be consistent with the legal syntax for a CGI environment variable.

In the course of its operation, the WWW server handles many HTTP request headers. It is not required to create CGI environment variables for all received header data. In particular, the server should remove any headers containing authentication data such as 'Authorization'. This is valuable information that should not be available to other CGI applications. The following example identifies the MIME Content-Types that a server supports and services:

```
HTTP_ACCEPT = application/zip, audio/basic, audio/x-midi, application/x-rtf,
video/msvideo, video/quicktime, video/mpeg, image/targa, image/x-win-bmp,
image/jpeg, image/gif, application/postscript, audio/wav, text/plain,
text/html, audio/x-aiff, audio/basic, application/x-airmosaic-patch, applica-
tion/binary, application/http, www/mime
```

PATH_INFO

This variable represents extra path information, provided by a requesting client. It describes a resource to be returned by a CGI application once it completes successfully. Clients can access CGI applications using virtual pathnames, followed by extra information appended to this path. Because URLs use a special encoding method for character data, this path information will be decoded by the server if it comes from a URL before it is passed to a CGI application.

The value of the PATH_INFO variable can be one of the following:

1. It may be contained in some trailing part of the requesting client's URI.

2. It may be some string provided by the client to the server.

3. It may be the entire client's URI.

A CGI application cannot decipher how PATH_INFO was chosen or constructed based solely on its value. As a CGI programmer, you must determine the context in which this variable is to be used in your CGI application. An example of a valid PATH_INFO variable is:

```
PATH_INFO = /raising/arizona/
```

PATH_TRANSLATED

This variable represents the operating system path to a file on the system that a server would attempt to access for a client requesting an absolute URI containing the PATH_INFO data. The server provides a translated version of PATH_INFO, which takes the path data and does any virtual-to-physical file system mapping.

For security reasons, some servers do not support this variable and will set it to NULL. This variable need not be supported by a server. The algorithm a server uses to decode PATH_TRANSLATED is invariably operating-system dependent. Therefore, CGI applications utilizing PATH_TRANSLATED may have limited portability. Here's an example of an NCSA server's 'DocumentRoot' equal to '/u/Web' that builds on the preceding example:

```
PATH_TRANSLATED = /u/Web/raising/arizona/
```

QUERY_STRING

This variable represents a URL-encoded search string. The value of this variable follows the "?" character in the URL that referenced a CGI search application. The value of this variable is not decoded by the server, but is passed onto the CGI application untouched.

The information after the "?" in a URL can be added by one of the following:

- an HTML <ISINDEX> document
- an HTML <FORM> CGI application (using the GET method)

- manually appended by the HTML document's author in which the reference occurs, in an <A> (anchor statement)

The value of QUERY_STRING is encoded in the standard URL format of replacing a space with a "+" and encoding nonprintable characters with the hexadecimal encoding scheme of '%dd' where "d" is a digit. You will need to decode this hexadecimal information before you use it. (You will learn how to do this in Chapter 8.)

This variable is always set when there is query information requested by a client, regardless of any command-line decoding by the CGI application. An example of a client's query URL for a CGI search application ('places.pl') to locate a place named "Sunset Crater" could look like this:

```
http://www.flagstaff.az.us/cgi-bin/places.pl?Sunset_Crater
```

The resulting QUERY_STRING value for this URL would be:

```
QUERY_STRING = Sunset_Crater
```

REMOTE_ADDR

This CGI environment variable represents the Internet Protocol (IP) address for a requesting agent. This is not necessarily the address of the client, but could be the address of the host for that client, depending on the type of connection and operating system the client is using. Here's an example:

```
REMOTE_ADDR = 199.1.78.25
```

REMOTE_HOST

This variable represents the fully qualified domain name for a requesting agent. If the server cannot decipher this information, REMOTE_ADDR is set to NULL. Domain names are case insensitive. Here's an example:

```
REMOTE_HOST = ppp1.aus.sig.net
```

This is the address of the machine of one of the author's Internet service providers, where the client actually resides on his machine at home. It communicates to the Internet through the host via the Point to Point Protocol (PPP) — in this case, using connection 1 (which is why the first term in the domain name is "pppP1"). Thus, the agent is not necessarily the client.

REMOTE_IDENT

This variable represents the remote user's name retrieved from the server. This RFC 931 (Authentication Server) identification must be supported by the HTTP server. It is highly recommended that use of this CGI environment variable be limited to logging actions. The current RFC 931 documentation implies that the HTTP server must attempt to retrieve the identification data from the requesting agent if it supports this feature. Finally, the value of this variable is not appropriate for user authentication purposes. An example would be:

```
REMOTE_IDENT = inmate.state.prison.az.us
```

REMOTE_USER

The value of this environment variable is the authenticated user's name. Two conditions must apply for this variable's value to be set:

1. The server must support user authentication.
2. The CGI application must be protected from unauthorized access.

If the AUTH_TYPE variable's value is 'Basic', then the value for REMOTE_USER will be the user's identification sent by the requesting client:

```
REMOTE_USER = gail_snokes
```

REQUEST_METHOD

The value of this CGI environment variable represents the method with which the client request was made. For HTTP 1.0, this is GET, HEAD, POST, PUT, DELETE, LINK, and UNLINK. The method name is case sensitive. An example for a client posting HTML form data to a server is:

```
REQUEST_METHOD = POST
```

SCRIPT_NAME

This variable's value is the URI path that identifies a CGI application. It is the virtual path to a CGI application being executed by a server. In this example, the client's query URL of a CGI application that calculates an engine's maximum horsepower is:

```
http://www.muscle.cars.org/cgi-bin/calc_max_hp.pl
```

and the corresponding SCRIPT_NAME variable's value is:

```
SCRIPT_NAME = /cgi-bin/calc_max_hp.pl
```

SERVER_NAME

This variable represents the server's hostname, DNS alias, or IP address as it would appear in URLs. This variable is not request-specific and is set for all requests. An example is:

```
SERVER_NAME = www.hal.com
```

SERVER_PORT

This variable is the port on which a client request is received. This is deciphered from the appropriate part of a URL. Most HTTP server implementations use port 80 as the default port number. URLs that do not explicitly specify a port can be accessed via port 80. For example, the following URL specifies that port 8119 is the designated HTTP server port:

```
http://www.chevelle.org:8119/index.html
```

SERVER_PROTOCOL

This variable's value represents the name and revision of the information protocol that the requesting client utilizes. The protocol is similar to the URL scheme used by a requesting client, and it is case insensitive. An example is:

```
SERVER_PROTOCOL = HTTP/1.0
```

SERVER_SOFTWARE

This variable represents the name and version of the information server software. This variable is not request-specific and is set for all requests:

```
SERVER_SOFTWARE = NCSA/1.4
```

THE CGI COMMAND LINE

Some operating systems support methods for providing data to CGI applications via the command line. This technique is used only in the case of an HTML <ISINDEX> query.

A server identifies this type of request by the GET method, accompanied by a URI search string that does not contain any *unencode*d "=" characters. This method trusts the clients to encode the "=" character in an <ISINDEX> query. This practice was considered safe at the time of the design of the CGI specification and requires that you, as a CGI programmer, be careful to observe this restriction.

A server parses this string into words using the rules in the CGI specification, as follows:

1. The server decodes the query information by first splitting the string on the "+" characters in the URL (which map to spaces, following URL encoding techniques).

2. The server then performs any additional decoding before placing each split string into an array named 'argv'.

   - Typically, this consists of separating out individual variable strings by splitting the input stream at each ampersand ("&").
   - Then, the resulting substrings must be split again (at the equal sign "=" character) to establish name and value pairs, where the left-hand-side value provides the name of the variable, and the right-hand-side value supplies its corresponding value.

This approach follows the UNIX method for passing command-line information to applications. 'argv' is an array of pointers to strings, where the length of the 'argv' array is stored in the environment variable 'argc'. (Love that UNIX!)

If the server finds that it cannot send the 'argv' array to the CGI application, it will include *no* command-line information. Instead, it will provide the non-decoded query information within the environment variable QUERY_STRING. This failure may be attributed to internal limitations of the server like those imposed by *exec( )* or */bin/sh* command-line restrictions. Another example of such a failure occurs when the number of arguments sent by the server to the CGI application may exceed the operating system's or server's limitations. It may also occur when a string in the 'argv' array is not a valid argument for the CGI application that it enters.

For demonstrated examples of command-line usage see this URL:

```
http://hoohoo.ncsa.uiuc.edu/cgi/examples.html
```

Make sure when you run these examples that you pay close attention to the values for the command-line variables 'argc' and 'argv'. We'd argue strongly that the first integrity check on accepting CGI input in a program is to make sure that 'argv' is non-zero, and that the number matches the expected number of arguments to your program!

It's also noteworthy that this command-line data-passing is seldom used for handling HTML forms, which can contain arbitrarily large amounts of data. HTML forms normally utilize environment variables to pass data using the POST method, because this method bypasses command-line length restrictions and the occasional data-passing problem that context-switching can sometimes cause in the UNIX runtime environment.

CGI DATA INPUT

For requests with data attached following the HTTP request header, like HTTP POST or PUT, the data is delivered to the CGI application using a standard input file descriptor. All CGI applications follow this method of reading data. For UNIX operating systems, this uses the so-called standard input device, commonly referred to as *stdin*.

The server will send a number of bytes of information, at least as long as the value specified by the variable CONTENT_LENGTH, using the *stdin* file descriptor to pass the data to the CGI application. The CGI application is not required to read all of this data, but neither must it attempt to read more than CONTENT_LENGTH bytes.

The server also provides the CONTENT_TYPE for data passed to the CGI application. This permits the application to use this information to decide how to interpret the data it receives. At the end of the data stream, the server is not required to transmit an end-of-file marker; both server and application assume that reading will cease immediately after the CGI application reads the number of bytes specified by the value of CONTENT_LENGTH.

For example, let's assume you are working with an HTML form that provides its data using the <FORM> METHOD="POST". Let's say this form's results are 15 bytes encoded, and look like "one=bob&two=cat" (in decoded form).

In this example, the server will set CONTENT_LENGTH to '15' and CONTENT_TYPE to 'application/x-www-form-urlencoded'. The first byte on the script's standard input file descriptor will be the character "O", followed by the rest of the encoded string.

CGI DATA OUTPUT

A CGI application always returns *something* to the client that invokes it, or to the server. The CGI application sends its output to a standard output file descriptor. UNIX calls this *stdout*. The CGI application output might be a document generated by the application (typically HTML, destined for delivery to the client) or it might be data retrieval instructions to the server (e.g., to transfer a file to the client).

Output is usually returned in one of two ways. The first form is non-parsed header output. Using this form, a CGI application must return a complete HTTP response message.

The second form of returned data is parsed header output. A server is only required to support this form. In this case, the CGI application returns a CGI response message. This response consists of headers and a body, separated by a blank line. These headers are either CGI headers that will be interpreted by a server or they are HTTP headers to be included within the response message. Here, the body is optional; but if it is supplied, the body must be prefaced by a MIME Content-Type header.

If the body is excluded, the CGI application must transmit either a Location or Status header. The Location header is used to indicate to the server that the CGI application is returning a reference to a document rather than the document's bits and pieces. The Status header is utilized to provide information to the server about the status code the server should use in its response message to the client. For information about the syntax of these CGI headers, please consult the CGI specification (or at least Chapter 8, which covers CGI input and output in considerable detail).

Summary

In this chapter we presented the middleware needed to bridge the abyss between Web and non-Web information repositories. In the next chapter, we introduce you to some old and proven programming languages and also to some new and exciting programming languages that you can use to implement CGI applications.

7 CGI Programming Languages

*P*rogramming languages come in many different flavors: procedural (e.g., C, Basic, and FORTRAN), object-oriented (e.g., C++, Smalltalk, and Java), logic languages like Prolog, and functional languages like Lisp. There are more programming languages out there than most of us could ever learn, even in several lifetimes!

Every programming language has its own solution domain and its own philosophy; that is, each one best solves specific types of problems, and an application's design is influenced by the language's philosophy. For example, Lisp isn't practical for number crunching, nor is FORTRAN the best choice for heavy-duty string manipulation.

Languages taken from the same paradigm, like C and Pascal, have different syntaxes but you can translate between them with relative ease. Both are procedural languages with similar constructs and design principles.

Across the board, though, computer language philosophies can differ substantially, as can the expressive style in the resulting programs. The four computer language paradigms that we're concerned with in this book are:

- Procedural — describes the steps of an algorithm
- Object-oriented — describes interactions among objects
- Logical — deduces solution from predicates
- Functional — describes transformation functions

Remember, language philosophy influences program design. What does all this hooey have to do with CGI applications? Lots!

In this chapter we will take a close look at some considerations involved in choosing a CGI programming language. We will then peek under the hood of two compiled programming languages, C and C++. Then we'll delve into interpreted languages such as Perl, the C and Bourne shells, Python, and Tcl. Finally, we'll look at Java, which is a compiled and interpreted programming language. While there are numerous other choices possible for writing CGI programs, we decided that confining ourselves to accepted practice still left plenty of options open!

Choosing a CGI Programming Language

Choosing the right programming language should be the result of a thorough and painstaking problem analysis. In some cases, a language might be selected simply because the programmer understands the language and can use its constructs and syntax to their best advantage.

In other cases, languages are chosen because they have proved to be more understandable, more reliable, more efficient, or more extensible than others (where all these other things are true, there will usually also be a huge amount of public domain source code available, too).

When it comes to writing code, there is seldom much sense in reinventing the wheel. Working from public domain, freeware, or shareware source code is usually a great way to learn a new language because of the variety of algorithms implemented and examples available. In any case, once a language is chosen, there's no going back without considerable work, pain, and suffering.

The Five Primary Considerations

There are five primary considerations when choosing a language for CGI programming:

1. the amount of public source code in easily accessible repositories

2. the availability of support and infrastructure tools like debuggers, compilers, interpreters, tutorials, books, classes, and "language-aware" editors

3. your own level of knowledge of a particular language or class of languages

4. the desired throughput for data, compared to support for special operations

5. the "ilities" in the language: extensibility, modularity, usability, and reusability

All of these characteristics play an important role in your selection, but typically the first two or three outweigh the rest.

PUBLIC SOURCE CODE REPOSITORIES

This consideration for choosing a particular CGI programming language is probably the most popular. Many CGI programmers want to hit the road running: they want to code up a forms-handling CGI application as fast as they can type, aided only by fermented beverages and pizza. Right from the get-go, you can visit many different Internet sites with public CGI source code libraries (see Chapter 15 for more details).

These sites contain wonderful nuggets of code that any CGI applications programmer could slap together with very little effort. Voila! A near-instant CGI application. "Instant code" has great appeal, and many CGI programmers rely heavily on mining the Internet to fill their coffers with prefabricated code.

There is, however, some slight danger in reusing such code: A malicious programmer might donate a tainted piece of CGI software to a public source code repository. This code could have a bomb wedged deep inside, ready to go off and wipe out your entire hard drive.

Do yourself a favor: When reusing public CGI source code, check it for lines such as cd /; /bin/rm -rf *. These two nasty little commands seem harmless enough, but in combination can ruin your weekend, if not your life.

Also, be careful when downloading binary executables. You have no idea what has been rolled into these "black boxes" built from somebody else's code. A good example is a recently advertised DOS program that claimed to turn your read-only CD-ROM into a writeable CD-ROM. Instead of delivering the promised functionality, this program fired off a low-level disk format and went on to wipe out the whole hard disk.

When it comes to using other people's code: caveat emptor. Try it on a test system before letting it loose on your production system.

Language Support

Your site's own brilliant system administrator can be helpful in determining the level of support for any potential CGI programming language. This will require asking some detailed questions and, possibly, helping your administrator to figure out the answers.

First, determine the availability of programming languages at your site. On most UNIX systems you can look in either "/usr/local/bin" or "/usr/share/bin" for languages like Perl, C, C++, or Tcl. For example, if you want to determine if your UNIX site has Perl installed, look for the executable file "/usr/local/bin/perl". This is the Perl interpreter that executes a Perl program. You can also use the UNIX commands *which* and *whereis* to find these compilers and interpreters; for example:

```
% which perl
/usr/local/bin/perl
% whereis perl
perl: /usr/local/bin/perl /usr/local/perl5.000
```

Ask your system administrator if you have source-level debuggers like *xdbx* for C. If your site currently does not have source-level debuggers, ask your system administrator what it takes to get one installed (bribing them with lunch usually works). The C and Bourne shells and Perl include built-in shell debuggers, so this may not be much of an issue.

Finally, you'll need to determine the availability and the quality of programming language reference material. Your company's library may contain O'Reilly *Nutshell Handbooks* on Perl, the C and Bourne shells, or an extensive tutorial on Tcl stashed away on its dusty metal shelves in the technical library. This stuff can be invaluable.

You can also find out if your site has any online documentation *man* pages or *help*. For example, typing **man perl** at the command prompt on a UNIX machine will quickly let you know if you have access to a readable set of reference pages. If you get a "not found" message, don't give up quite yet: Maybe this *man* page is not in your path. See your system administrator if you don't know how to alter your *man* path.

YOUR LEVEL OF KNOWLEDGE AND UNDERSTANDING

This consideration is by no means purely quantitative. You are the only one who knows your level of understanding of a particular language or class of languages. You are also the one who best knows your strengths and weaknesses.

When considering a CGI language, take a good, hard look at your past experiences with programming languages. You should have a good feel for how long it would take you to master a how-to book on a new language that is a member of a familiar class of languages. If you're a hot-shot Bourne shell programmer, then learning another shell scripting language — like Perl — typically involves learning the new syntax and how to apply it. The intellectual overhead needed to switch to a new language within the same class should be small for the experienced programmer.

DESIRABLE DATA THROUGHPUT

Since the WWW was developed on UNIX, many of the repositories of public CGI source code contain UNIX-based languages like Perl, C shell, Tcl, Bourne shell, and C/C++. Each of these languages is native to UNIX machines and can be found on nearly every UNIX box.

There are two distinctions to be made among these six languages. Perl, the C and Bourne shells, and Tcl are all interpreted languages. This means that their source objects are not compiled into a binary format, loaded, and then executed. Each of these has an interpreter that reads every line of the source code each time it is run and slows down the interpreted application. It also slows down the throughput of the data.

By comparison, C and C++ are compiled into a binary executable, loaded into RAM, and executed at faster speeds, resulting in faster throughput. If you have a mission-critical or a real-time embedded application, an interpreted language won't cut it. In those cases, an executable binary object is just what the doctor ordered.

Finally, there is a language like Java, which is a combination of compiled and interpreted. Java requires a runtime system — including a Java interpreter — native to a platform and an "architecture-neutral" compiled binary object. The execution speed of a Java "application" is not notably different from the same type of program written in C or C++.

DESIRABLE "ILITIES"

Considering a few of the more important "ilities" is another popular way to decide on a CGI application programming language. These "ilities" include:

- **extensibility:** a measure of how easy it is to write applications that build upon core mechanisms while adding functionality; new methods or subclasses (depending on the paradigm).
- **modularity:** a measure of how easy and efficient it is to package each object into a self-contained unit.
- **reusability:** a measure of how easily and efficiently you can leverage prior work and art in your programs.
- **understandability:** a measure of the complexity of the language's concepts and constructs.

All of these elements are important, but how important they are depends on your circumstances. For instance, if you want to leverage existing code and public domain materials in your work, reusability will be most important. If you need to work with an unfamiliar language, understandability may be all-important.

Compiled CGI Programming Languages

Compiled languages create binary objects that are loaded and executed in the computer's main memory. These objects are the result of a compiler assembling ASCII source code into binary information (0s and 1s).

A compiler is typically native to a particular computer architecture and you can assume that binary objects from one architecture will not execute on another architecture. For example, don't expect Pascal code compiled into a binary object and run on a PC to execute successfully on a UNIX machine. Instead, the original Pascal source code must be compiled with a native UNIX Pascal compiler into a UNIX-compatible binary object.

In the sections that follow, we'll discuss some of the more popular compiled languages you can use to develop CGI applications.

C

The C language was first implemented in 1972 on an old dead and forgotten machine (a DEC PDP-8) that lay dormant in a hallway at Bell Labs. Brian Kernighan and Dennis Ritchie created C as a language for their own use and amusement. Over 20 years later, it's still one of the most popular languages in use.

C is a procedural program that describes the steps of an algorithm, like a procedure on how to install a water pump on a Chevy. You complete each successive step until you have a new and functional water pump installed, or your sorting algorithm assembles a list in ascending alphabetical order.

There are two primary advantages in choosing C as a CGI programming language. First, it can be compiled into a very tight binary object that takes up minimal space compared to interpreted languages. Some C compilers include command-line options that instruct it to create an optimized binary object. This results in an even smaller binary object. Second, binary objects typically execute faster than interpreted languages. If speed of execution is a major concern, you should definitely pick a compiled programming language. The primary disadvantage to using C for CGI programming is it that it is difficult to manipulate strings with C language constructs. Nearly 90% of all CGI applications involve heavy string manipulation. This means that character and string data must be massaged, transformed, converted, or translated from one form to another.

By contrast, integer and floating-point math CGI applications are few and far between. Most CGI applications take string and character data such as <FORM> data or query data and return other string and character data based on some embedded heuristics. For example, a typical CGI application gathers <FORM> data from a "Comments and Suggestions Form" interface. The CGI application then assembles the <FORM> data into a MIME mail message and mails it to the designated address. It can also record <FORM> data to a log file. "Heavy string manipulation" describes a day in the life of a typical CGI applications engineer.

C++

C++, a superset of C, is a member of the object-oriented (OO) paradigm of programming languages.

The Incremental Paradigm

One historical note: the "++" signifies that C++ is an increment of one paradigm from the procedural paradigm of its parent, the C language. In the C language, the unary operation "++" increments the value of a variable by one unit. Bjarne Stroustrup, who created C++ at AT&T, claims that C++ is much better than plain vanilla C.

Objected-oriented languages like C++ offer many advantages. They provide superior reusability of classes, which reduces the cost of development for similar applications. They also allow extensibility of core classes by allowing programmers to add functionality.

For example, a core class such as "Automobile" could have functions like "transport" or "stop". A programmer could add an "accelerate" function to the class without disrupting other already-deployed instances of the "Automobile" class. They also support modularity, which is the methodology of breaking a problem down into its smallest understandable units, where each module acts as a separate functional unit.

Finally, OO languages stress the reusability of classes across many different problem domains. Reusability of source code is a popular research topic because it reduces the cost of development. It can also increase the quality of source code but this depends heavily on the quality of the software engineering of the component classes in use. As yet, reusability is talked about far more than it's practiced, so its benefits remain more theoretical than actual.

The main disadvantage of using C++ is that it is belongs to the OO paradigm. OO development of source code is a completely different beast, requiring substantial training and street smarts. Designing classes for reusability, understanding the polymorphism of functions within a class, and providing effective management of classes within and across applications are new concepts for many applications engineers.

Shifting to a new programming paradigm is usually preceded by an act of nature — like an earthquake. Or more likely, you're a laid off COBOL programmer, and the classifieds are full of "OO Developers Desperately Needed" ads. Need we say more?

Another disadvantage to using C++ is that there is only limited public domain CGI source code available. This is probably because CGI is a relatively new area, and few OO CGI applications have been released for public consumption. But this should begin to change once software engineers begin to develop OO Web solutions (which we're expecting to see on the market any day now).

Interpreted CGI Programming Languages

In this section we look at some of the common interpreted languages you can use to create CGI applications — namely Perl, the C and Bourne shells, Python, and Tcl.

PERL

Perl, the Practical Extraction and Report Language, is an interpreted language optimized for easy manipulation of files, text, and processes. Perl is typically used when scanning text files, extracting text strings, and printing reports based on the information that's extracted. Perl was created by Larry Wall in the early 1980s.

Perl provides a lucid and succinct way to solve many programming problems typical in the CGI realm. Before Perl, these tasks were accomplished only with difficulty by C or shell applications which, unlike Perl, were not designed for heavy string, text, and file manipulation.

Perl is not yet a standard part of UNIX, but it is widespread and is likely to be available at your site. Consult your system administrator for more details. If Perl isn't on your system, it is available via anonymous ftp from various Internet sites. For more information about Perl, see this URL:

```
http://www.cis.ufl.edu/perl/
```

The Perl language is intended to be easy to use, but also to be complete and efficient, rather than tiny, elegant, and minimal. Perl combines some of the best features of C, *sed*, *awk,* and *sh*. Programmers familiar with these languages should have little difficulty learning and applying Perl.

Perl's syntax and structure is very similar to C. Many of the constructs in Perl like if, for, and while correspond to their counterparts in C. With Perl, you can manipulate and match regular expressions much easier than with *sed*, *awk*, or *lex*.

Unlike most UNIX utilities such as *sed* and *awk*, Perl does not arbitrarily limit the size of your data. Perl can incorporate your entire text file into a single string. Recursion has no depth restrictions. The only real restriction on these operations and data structures is your machine's memory size. Finally, hash tables used by associative arrays are gracefully built and handled to prevent wicked performance reductions.

Perl is the gem of the interpreted languages because of its ability to do heavy string manipulation (and we're not talking heavy in weight, but heavy in large amounts). It uses sophisticated pattern-matching techniques to scan vast amounts of text quickly and efficiently. Although optimized for scanning text, Perl can also manipulate binary data with the same ease as text.

Perl can also prevent security breaches through *setuid* applications. Such applications can be exploited in malicious ways in order to wreak havoc in a computer system, but Perl applications are safer than *setuid* C programs. A data flow tracing mechanism is implemented in Perl to avoid many foolish security holes.

Perl can make up for the limits of UNIX utilities you would otherwise use, like *sed*, *awk*, or *sh*. Some of these utilities have line-length limitations that do not exist for Perl. The translators that are usually part of the Perl distribution will turn existing *sed* and *awk* scripts into Perl scripts. Also, Perl will typically run a little faster than these utilities because of its design. Finally, if the prospect of writing a text file manipulation application in C drives you to distraction, pick up a Perl book and use it instead.

Today, most CGI applications use Perl because of its many positive characteristics. You will notice that in many of the public CGI source code repositories, more than half the code is written in Perl. You will find out later in this book where to find these sites and what to retrieve, so you can hit the road running when building your first CGI applications.

UNIX SHELL SCRIPTING LANGUAGES

There are two flavors of UNIX: Berkeley (BSD 4.3) and AT&T System V. There is a push to combine the best of both of these but that is yet another book (its topic, in case you're interested, would be "POSIX"). Within these two UNIX environments you will find three common shells: Bourne, Korn, and C. All of them support processes, pipes, directories, filters, and other standard UNIX functions.

The shell is the most important user interface on a UNIX computer. The shell is just another program; it has no special status. It can be updated and modified with little effort, resulting in different flavors of shells. These alternative shells can also live on a UNIX box that has a native shell. Each shell operates as a separate program, and each user can choose which interface or shell to use when working on a UNIX machine.

Here we'll look at two shells: the C shell and the Bourne shell. (The Korn shell has the same functionality as the Bourne shell and combines many of the features of the C shell.) The C and Bourne shells are not syntactically compatible. Each shell's interactive commands and script languages differ somewhat and each has unique behaviors and characteristics, atop a core of common functionality. Finally, each shell has its own scripting language that can be the foundation for writing CGI programs. Since that's why you're here, let's look at each one in turn.

The Bourne shell

UNIX machines typically have one native command interpreter or shell. On many machines this is the Bourne shell, named after S.R. Bourne in 1975. The Bourne shell is part of the standard configuration for every flavor of UNIX. Because it is smaller than the C and Korn shells, it is the most efficient for shell processing.

The Bourne shell is compact, executes quickly, and requires minimal resources. Developed at AT&T, it has become the most widely used shell. Major advantages of the Bourne shell include:

- It allows exception handling via the *trap* command that is unique to the Bourne shell.
- It supports both local and global variables.
- It takes advantage of System V's *named pipes*.

The scripting language is somewhat C-like, but works more like a conventional command language. While it is excellent for small, throwaway activities, the Bourne shell does not have the kind of flexibility and extensibility you'd look for in a "real" programming language.

The C shell

The shell that executes under most UNIX operating systems is the C shell, developed by Bill Joy while at the University of California at Berkeley. It is a command interpreter and provides an important user interface to the UNIX operating system.

The advantages of the C shell include its:

- *history* function, which keeps track of the commands as you input them and permits you to go back and execute them without retyping the command in the shell
- direct evaluation of built-in (native UNIX) commands
- aliasing mechanisms, which allow you to create mnemonic names for commands, files, paths, or other system objects
- control of foreground and background tasks
- syntax similar to the C programming language

Even though the C shell's scripting language is C-like, it works more like a conventional command language than a complete programming language. While it is useful for small, throwaway activities and applications, the C shell doesn't have the power and extensibility you'd look for in a "real" programming language.

Tcl

The Tool Command Language (Tcl, pronounced "tickle") is a simple scripting language for extending and controlling applications. Tcl can be embedded into C applications because its interpreter is implemented as a C library of procedures. Each application can extend the basic Tcl functions by creating new Tcl commands that are specific to a particular programming task.

Accompanying Tcl is a very popular Tcl extension called Tk (pronounced "tee-kay"). It is a toolkit for the X Window System found on many UNIX machines. Tk extends the basic Tcl functionality with commands to rapidly build Motif or X Window user interfaces. Tk is also implemented as a C library of procedures, allowing it to be used in many disparate applications. Like Tcl, Tk can be extended, typically by constructing new interface widgets and geometry managers in C.

The combination of Tcl and Tk (Tcl/Tk) is a programming system developed by John Ousterhout at the University of California at Berkeley. The Tcl/Tk system is easy to use and possesses powerful graphical interface capabilities. Tcl provides the scripting language, while Tk is a toolkit for creating and maintaining user interface widgets (widgets are graphical objects used in a user interface). These are similar to widgets found in other graphical user interface (GUI) toolkits, like OpenLook, Motif, and XView.

With Tcl/Tk, manipulation of GUI widgets does not require writing a C or C++ application. This differs from many of the other GUI toolkits. One of the true beauties of Tcl/Tk is that you can rapidly build a user interface, as compared to the pain and agony of writing a Motif application. Many C and C++ programmers want to use the Tk widgets in their own applications, so they should be pleased to learn that Tcl/Tk can work cooperatively with C and C++.

Since Tcl is interpreted, Tcl applications typically will not execute as fast as their C counterparts. For a small class of applications this may become a disadvantage but with the blinding speed of today's computer systems, Tcl/Tk represents an adequate applications system. If the speed of execution is critical in your application, don't fret. Tcl can be compiled or heavy-duty processing can be written in a compiled language such as C and C++, and the user interface programmed in Tcl/Tk. If this is unacceptable, create a throwaway prototype of the user interface using Tcl/Tk and get feedback from your target users to build a faster final implementation.

There are Tcl versions for different platforms and operating systems, which makes Tcl fairly portable. The one feature of Tcl that affects portability is its support for native operating system calls. If these facilities are used, portability will be sacrificed for convenience.

Tcl/Tk provides five benefits to applications developers:

- It allows any application to have a powerful scripting language (Tcl) by linking in the Tcl interpreter.

- It supports rapid development of applications; you can create GUI applications faster than using C and C++ applications.

- It can execute interpreted scripts on-the-fly without recompiling or restarting applications.

- It provides an embeddable "glue" language that allows developers to combine features from different programs into a single application.

- It is amazingly easy to learn.

Because of its extensibility and depth, Tcl/Tk is adequate for all but the most processor-intensive applications. It is particularly well suited for those that require complex graphical displays or sophisticated user interfaces.

More information about Tcl/Tk can be found at:

```
http://www.sco.com/Technology/tcl/Tcl.html
```

PYTHON

Python is an interpreted, interactive, object-oriented programming language. It combines an understandable and readable syntax with noteworthy power compared to other interpreted languages. It has modules, classes, exceptions, and dynamic data types and typing. Python also provides interfaces to many system calls and libraries, and to various windowing systems like X11, Motif, Tk, and Mac. Python can even be used as an "extension language" for applications that require a programmable interface. Finally, new built-in Python modules can be implemented in either C or C++.

Python executes on many platforms, including UNIX, Mac, OS/2, MS-DOS, Windows 3.1, and NT. Python is copyrighted but freely usable and distributable to individuals as well as commercial institutions.

Python has been used to implement a few WWW modules. Currently these modules include a CGI module, a library of URL modules, and a few modules dealing with Electronic Commerce. For information about these WWW applications of Python, see the URL:

```
http://www.eeel.nist.gov/python/
```

General information about Python is available at:

```
http://www.cwi.nl/~guido/Python.html
```

Compiled/Interpreted CGI Programming Languages

JAVA

Java is a new object-oriented programming language and environment from Sun Microsystems. Along with C and C++, Java is compiled into an architecture-neutral binary object and then interpreted like Perl or Tcl for a specific architecture. So, it's a dessert topping and a floor wax!

With Java, you can create either standalone "applications" or "applets" to be used within CGI applications. Sun characterizes Java using a standard, but formidable, set of industry buzzwords:

Java: A simple, object-oriented, distributed, interpreted, robust, secure, architecture-neutral, portable, high-performance, multithreaded, dynamic language.

Whew! Our take is that Java is a strictly-typed object-oriented language, similar to C++ sans many of that language's shortcomings. For instance, Java will not let you cast an integer type to a pointer.

Java applications can execute anywhere on a network, making it highly suitable for CGI applications. Another really interesting aspect of the language is that the Java compiler creates an "architecture-neutral" binary object. This object is executable on any platform that has a Java runtime system installed. You can write *one* Java program that can execute on all other supported platforms including Mac, UNIX, NT, and Windows.

Netscape Communications Corporation has licensed the Java language to implement within their Netscape Navigator browser. Their main motivation is to increase the extensibility of Navigator and to enable the creation of a new class of client/server networked applications.

Java and HotJava — the WWW browser from Sun written in Java — are freely available in binary form to individuals. Java can also be licensed to commercial institutions. Currently, the supported platforms for Java include Solaris, SunOS, Windows NT, and Windows 95. The Macintosh version has not been completed as of this writing but will probably be ready before you read this paragraph.

For more information about Java, see this URL:

```
http://java.sun.com/
```

Summary

Choosing a programming language for your CGI applications should not be done lightly. You'll want to carefully consider the amount of available public source code, the support available for the language, your level of knowledge of its programming paradigm, its data-handling abilities, and its extensibility, modularity, usability, and the reusability of its software components. Once you've considered these factors, selecting a language should be simple. Then you can worry about dealing with CGI inputs and outputs, which you'll learn about in the next chapter.

8

CGI Input and Output

*T*o programmers, it sometimes appears that if only they could get the right handle on their data, it would solve all their problems and answer all their prayers. We think this might be a bit overstated, but we're more than willing to concede that graceful handling of CGI input and output can be tedious and difficult. But hey, that's why they pay CGI programmers the big bucks, right?

Even so, it's become obvious to everybody that where CGI programming is concerned, the world is just one wide web of opportunity. CGI-savvy programmers are in high demand and it looks like it's going to stay that way for some time. That's why it's time to sharpen your CGI skills, clean up your keyboard, and mash the pedal to your CGI metal. That's why we'll start off with where the real CGI action begins (and ends): with accepting input from clients, and returning nicely formatted results for them to "ooh" and "aah" over.

In this chapter, you'll learn the ins and outs of CGI input and output. We'll cover the two HTTP methods, POST and GET. For GET, we'll look at <ISINDEX> and <FORM> examples. For POST, we'll look at a more complex (and interesting) <FORM> example.

A Different Sort of Input Method

The CGI specification supports two HTTP methods for handling CGI input: GET and POST. The METHOD field in HTTP indicates the method applied on an object identified by a URL. GET is always supported by

CGI (it's the default method, in fact), and POST by nine out of ten implementations.

A list of other methods accepted by your HTTP server will be returned in response to either an HTTP 'SimpleRequest' or 'FullRequest 'statement. Method names are case sensitive — so write 'em as you see 'em. For more information about these requests, please consult the HTTP 1.0 specification:

```
http://www.w3.org/hypertext/WWW/Protocols/HTTP/Request.html
```

GET IT WHILE YOU CAN

The GET method instructs a server to retrieve the data referenced by a URL, where the URL specifies a CGI application. For instance, a simple CGI application that echoes the CGI environment variables back to the client is coded in HTML as:

```
<A HREF="http://www.hal.com/hal-bin/test-cgi">
```

The value of the attribute, HREF, is a URL that refers to a CGI application residing on the referenced server — in the example just shown, the server is *www.hal.com* and the CGI script is */hal-bin/test-cgi.pl*. The following is the *test-cgi* Bourne shell script that will be used throughout this chapter:

```
#!/bin/sh
echo Content-Type: text/plain
echo
echo CGI/1.0 test-cgi script results:
echo
echo argc = $#  argv = "$*"
echo
echo SERVER_SOFTWARE   = $SERVER_SOFTWARE
echo SERVER_NAME       = $SERVER_NAME
echo GATEWAY_INTERFACE = $GATEWAY_INTERFACE
echo SERVER_PROTOCOL   = $SERVER_PROTOCOL
echo SERVER_PORT       = $SERVER_PORT
echo REQUEST_METHOD    = $REQUEST_METHOD
echo HTTP_ACCEPT       = "$HTTP_ACCEPT"
echo PATH_INFO         = $PATH_INFO
echo PATH_TRANSLATED   = $PATH_TRANSLATED
echo SCRIPT_NAME       = $SCRIPT_NAME
echo QUERY_STRING      = $QUERY_STRING
echo REMOTE_HOST       = $REMOTE_HOST
```

```
echo REMOTE_ADDR      = $REMOTE_ADDR
echo REMOTE_USER      = $REMOTE_USER
echo CONTENT_TYPE     = $CONTENT_TYPE
echo CONTENT_LENGTH   = $CONTENT_LENGTH
```

As well as being educational, this script is a handy testing tool to examine the values assigned to the most common environmental variables used in CGI programs. We find it quite useful for testing and debugging our environment and we think you will, too!

USING THE GET METHOD

<ISINDEX> Query

The main use for the GET method is to perform searches or to address queries to a database. In HTML 3.0, all you need to do is to add the <ISINDEX> tag to your document's head using an HREF attribute to the CGI program that will perform the search or query on your behalf. The necessary HTML looks like this:

```
<HEAD>
<ISINDEX HREF="http://www.hal.com/hal-bin/query">
</HEAD>
```

This supplies a URL for the CGI application that will service any <ISINDEX> queries elsewhere in your HTML document. The browser is responsible for assembling the query string; the CGI program referenced in the <ISINDEX> tag needs to be able to take it from there when it's delivered by the server.

The URL used with GET includes the URL defined in the <ISINDEX> statement, and adds a set of arguments for use in the CGI program. These arguments are preceded by a "?" (question mark). For instance, the browser would build a URL from the text entered by the user into the search text widget. For a search on the two keywords "blues" and "brothers," the resulting string passed to the server (and on to the CGI program) will be:

```
http://www.hal.com/hal-bin/query?blues+brothers
```

In such URLs, a special form of encoding, called URL-encoding, is used. That is, keywords are separated with a "+". Spaces (" "), plus signs

("+"), and other special characters are encoded as hexadecimal ASCII escape sequences. Remember, these numeric entities take the form: %## where "#" is a hexadecimal number — for example, space = %20, plus = %2B. Browsers that accept text input should map keywords separated by spaces to keywords separated by plus signs.

A finer level of content control that is invisible to users is sometimes supplied by more advanced browsers. These clients may allow multiple keywords as input, and require the use of the numeric entity "%20" to get a space (" ").

The <ISINDEX> query is built by appending a "?" to a URL followed by keywords separated by a "+" sign. For instance,

```
<A HREF="http://www.hal.com/hal-bin/test-cgi?one+two+three+four">
```

would send four keywords — namely, "one" "two" "three" "four" — to the CGI application *test-cgi* via the standard input device (*stdin*). For this kind of HTTP request, the default method is GET. Here's the result of this query:

```
CGI/1.0 test results:

argc = 4 argv is one two three four

PATH = /bin:/usr/bin:/usr/etc:/usr/ucb
SERVER_SOFTWARE = NCSA/1.3
SERVER_NAME = www.hal.com
GATEWAY_INTERFACE = CGI/1.1
SERVER_PROTOCOL = HTTP/1.0
SERVER_PORT = 80
REQUEST_METHOD = GET
HTTP_ACCEPT = */*
PATH_INFO =
PATH_TRANSLATED =
SCRIPT_NAME = /bin/test-cgi
QUERY_STRING = one+two+three+four
REMOTE_HOST = ppp2.aus.sig.net
REMOTE_ADDR = 199.1.78.26
...remaining elements empty and omitted for that reason...
```

Notice the value of the environment variable REQUEST_METHOD = GET. This is expected because GET is the default HTTP method. Also notice the value of the array 'argv'. It is the string of keywords separated by blanks "one two three four". This information is another form in the value of the QUERY_STRING variable, which is 'one+two+three+four'.

How would you parse the QUERY_STRING variable to get at the data and do something with it? You basically split the QUERY_STRING environment variable up into pieces by using the "+" as the separator between keywords. This bit of Perl code deciphers this variable for the method GET:

```
# determine the request method, make sure data is coming
# across STDIN, and determine if query string is defined
if ($#ARGV != -1  &&  $ENV{REQUEST_METHOD} eq 'GET' &&
                    $ENV{QUERY_STRING} ne ''){
    # split the query string into an array of keywords
    @keywords = split("+", $ENV{QUERY_STRING}); }
```

The array of keywords, '@keywords', has the value of:

```
@keywords = ( "one", "two", "three", "four")
```

You can now query an external database of indexes for the occurrence of each of these keywords and return the hit list in the form of an HTML document to the client via the server.

<FORM>

Form data may be sent to CGI applications for processing by using the GET method as well as the POST method. For example, this chunk of HTML code:

```
<FORM METHOD="GET" ACTION="http://www.hal.com/hal-bin/test-cgi">
<INPUT TYPE="submit" VALUE="Submit Query">
</FORM>
```

results in the following output from our *test-cgi* program:

```
CGI/1.0 test results:

argc = 0 argv is

PATH = /bin:/usr/bin:/usr/etc:/usr/ucb
SERVER_SOFTWARE = NCSA/1.3
SERVER_NAME = www.hal.com
GATEWAY_INTERFACE = CGI/1.1
SERVER_PROTOCOL = HTTP/1.0
SERVER_PORT = 80
REQUEST_METHOD = GET
HTTP_ACCEPT = */*
PATH_INFO =
```

```
PATH_TRANSLATED =
SCRIPT_NAME = /bin/test-cgi
QUERY_STRING =
REMOTE_HOST = ppp2.aus.sig.net
REMOTE_ADDR = 199.1.78.26
...remaining elements empty and omitted for that reason...
```

Notice that here again the value of REQUEST_METHOD is 'GET'. This matches the METHOD attribute of <FORM>. QUERY_STRING is empty because we didn't send it any arguments. This simple form will now give QUERY_STRING a value:

```
<FORM METHOD="GET" ACTION="http://www.hal.com/hal-bin/test-cgi">
Enter text: <INPUT NAME="widget1">
Enter text: <INPUT NAME="widget2">
<INPUT TYPE="submit" VALUE="Submit Query">
</FORM>
```

and produces these results:

```
CGI/1.0 test results:

argc = 0 argv is

PATH = /bin:/usr/bin:/usr/etc:/usr/ucb
SERVER_SOFTWARE = NCSA/1.3
SERVER_NAME = www.hal.com
GATEWAY_INTERFACE = CGI/1.1
SERVER_PROTOCOL = HTTP/1.0
SERVER_PORT = 80
REQUEST_METHOD = GET
HTTP_ACCEPT = */*
PATH_INFO =
PATH_TRANSLATED =
SCRIPT_NAME = /bin/test-cgi
QUERY_STRING = widget2=I%27d%20rather%20be%20sailing.&widget1=Gone%20fishin%27
REMOTE_HOST = ppp2.aus.sig.net
REMOTE_ADDR = 199.1.78.26
...remaining elements empty and omitted for that reason...
```

Look at the value of QUERY_STRING. Look funny? Its value is a series of text input widget name and value pairs. In this case, two widgets. Each variable/value pair in QUERY_STRING is separated by an ampersand ("&").

The funny-looking characters are ASCII hexadecimal representations for two different characters. In this example, apostrophe = %27, and space = %20. Notice the "." after "sailing" is *not* encoded. Why? The HTTP specification determines which characters to represent as hexadecimal and which to leave as written.

How should you decipher this version of QUERY_STRING? Extending our previous Perl code example, we now have to build an array of widgets, each having a name and an associated value, to match the name=value pairs returned by the form. Here's the extended Perl code:

```
# determine the request method, make sure data is coming
# across STDIN, and determine if query string is defined
if ($#ARGV != -1  &&  $ENV{REQUEST_METHOD} eq 'GET' &&
                    $ENV{QUERY_STRING} ne '') {
    # split the query string into an array of keywords
    foreach $widget (split("&", $ENV{QUERY_STRING})) {
        # get the keyword and value pair from the widget string
        if ($widget =~ /(.*)=(.*)/) {
            ($key, $value) = ($1, $2);
            $value =~ s/\+/ /g ; # replace "+" with " "
            # unescape ASCII hexadecimal characters
            $value =~ s/%(..)/pack('c',hex($1))/eg;
            $inputs{$key} = $value; # add keyword/value pair to a list
        }
    }
}
```

The associative array, '%inputs', has the value of:

```
%inputs = {
  widget1 = Gone fishin' ,
  widget2 = I'd rather be sailing.
}
```

Having acquired the associative array that lets you inquire about the value of forms elements by their names, you can proceed from here to write more code to handle these name=value pairs in any way you like. But please, remember to unescape those nasty ASCII hexadecimal characters before you use them (that is, to convert them from their hexadecimal representations to their ASCII equivalents).

That's all the coverage we plan to give the GET method. In fact, it's not recommended for most serious CGI programming, because it's limited in the number of characters it can safely accommodate for transfer between the browser and the host to an effective maximum of 255 characters (including the plus and equal signs used for URL encoding). That may sound like a lot, but for a complex form, it's nowhere near enough!

In the sections that follow, we'll take a gander at the POST HTTP method, preferred by most CGI programmers for serious data-passing, because it is not subject to the limitations that restrict GET's abilities to transfer data from the browser to the server (and on to your CGI programs).

THEY'RE AT THE POST!

The POST method is used to make a request to a server. This request is to accept the entity enclosed within the HTTP request as a new object for the server, which is subordinate to the object specified in the URL field in the Request line of the HTTP request that carries it. The contents of this new object (the data that we're trying to transfer to the server and on to a CGI program) is enclosed in the MIME body of the request.

For instance, this full HTTP request:

```
POST /hal-bin/test-cgi HTTP/1.0
```

asks the server to create a new object subordinate to the "/hal-bin/test-cgi" object. A URL will be allocated for the new object by the server and returned to the client. The new object is the data part of the request. For more detailed information about HTTP requests (and other methods and terminology), please consult the HTTP 1.0 specification at:

```
http://www.w3.org/hypertext/WWW/Protocols/HTTP/Request.html
```

POST allows a ubiquitous method for providing the following functions to a WWW client:

- posting a message to a bulletin board, mailing list, or newsgroup
- obtaining information about existing server resources
- providing form data to a CGI application

What does a POST query to a CGI application look like? You can make a connection to a WWW server with *telnet* if you know the server's name and its port number. The following example is a simple POST query of the *www.hal.com* server that is accepting WWW access requests on port 80:

```
austin 11: telnet www.hal.com 80
Trying...
Connected to hal-alt.hal.COM.
Escape character is '^]'.
POST /hal-bin/test-cgi HTTP/1.0
**** blank line here ****
```

Once telnet has connected, it sits and waits for your input. You can then enter an HTTP request. In the preceding example, we made a POST request and entered:

```
POST /hal-bin/test-cgi HTTP/1.0
```

After the POST request, the HTTP 1.0 Request specification requires a carriage return/line feed (CrLf). You must enter a blank line after the POST query. This is critical. So after typing in the POST query, hit the carriage return twice! Here's what is returned by the server in response to this request:

```
HTTP/1.0 200 OK
Date: Friday, 02-Jun-95 21:11:13 GMT
Server: NCSA/1.3
MIME-version: 1.0
Content-type: text/plain
```

This header information precedes the new object created by the server and returned to the requesting client. Here's what *test-cgi* has to tell us about the object that's returned:

```
CGI/1.0 test results:

argc = 0 argv is

PATH = /bin:/usr/bin:/usr/etc:/usr/ucb
SERVER_SOFTWARE = NCSA/1.3
SERVER_NAME = www.hal.com
GATEWAY_INTERFACE = CGI/1.1
SERVER_PROTOCOL = HTTP/1.0
SERVER_PORT = 80
REQUEST_METHOD = POST
HTTP_ACCEPT =
PATH_INFO =
PATH_TRANSLATED =
SCRIPT_NAME = /bin/test-cgi
QUERY_STRING =
REMOTE_HOST = austin.aus.sig.net
REMOTE_ADDR = 199.1.78.2
REMOTE_USER =
AUTH_TYPE =
CONTENT_TYPE =
CONTENT_LENGTH = -1
Connection closed by foreign host.
```

You can try some simple example POST queries of your own. *telnet* to *www.hal.com* and use port 80 (**telnet www.hal.com 80**). Try it and check the results:

```
POST /hal-bin/test-cgi?query HTTP/1.0
POST /hal-bin/test-cgi?simple+query HTTP/1.0
POST /hal-bin/test-cgi?widget1=Big+Block&widget2=Bow+Tie HTTP/1.0
```

These POST examples indicate how a WWW client sends information to a server. It creates an HTTP request and fires it off to the specified server. The server recognizes that a CGI application is referenced, and it passes the data downstream to that application.

The CGI application then creates a new object on the server. Once the CGI application terminates, it sends the server its output, which in turn sends that output back to the client. Later in this chapter, we'll look at CGI output. First, let's look at a <FORM> example that uses the POST method.

The Ins and Outs of <FORM> Data

HTML allows users to build extensive forms using <FORM> and its associated tags. Forms look good on most graphical WWW clients and are popular because they are incredibly useful and have commercial potential. (See Figure 8-1.)

With a form, your WWW site's visitor can do some of the following:

- provide you with feedback about your WWW site or your product line
- ask technical questions
- query a database of information
- leave his or her name in a guest book
- order a product or information about a product
- enter a travel request with your company's secretary

A set of form tags in HTML lets clients render a small set of input widgets. The form's user can enter text or choose options in the form; when it's complete, he or she submits the data to a targeted server where the data is processed. (These tags are discussed in more detail later in this chapter.)

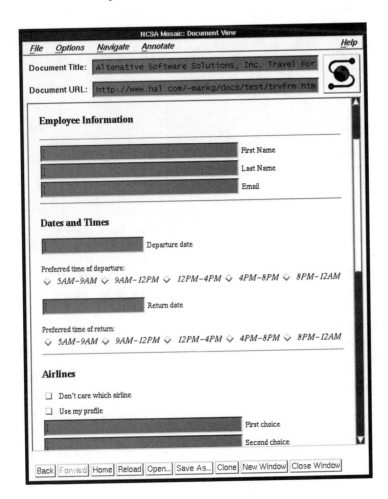

Figure 8-1
The HTML <FORM> tag permits easy construction of a simple travel request form.

The targeted server passes the form data as named variables with associated values to a CGI application specified in the initial <FORM> tag that sets up the form. This CGI application parses the data, performs whatever processing is required, and prepares a response — typically another HTML document that it constructs on the spot. Then, the application returns the output to the server, which in turn hands it back to the client. Figure 8-2 shows this interaction between the client, the server, and the CGI application, with the associated data flows.

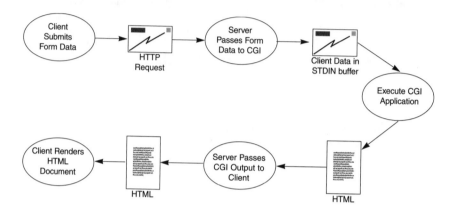

Figure 8-2

Data flows from the client to the server and on to the application for an HTML <FORM>, before reversing the journey to deliver its results.

In Figure 8-2, the client requests a form from a remote WWW server. It then renders that form on the user's display. Such a form can contain input widgets like:

- one-line text fields
- multiple-line text widgets
- checkboxes
- radio buttons
- scrollable menus of options

Users see forms and respond by entering data into their various input widgets. Once a user has completed all the input fields, or selected all the necessary input boxes and buttons, he or she typically chooses a "Submit" button on the form with an input device — a mouse or pointer, for example — to tell the browser to pack up the form's contents and deliver it to the server.

Once the form data has been received, the server determines that the client has requested services from a CGI application. Next, the server hands the form data to the customized CGI application named in the HTTP request.

The receiving CGI application deciphers the input data, does the right thing, and then returns its customized output back to the server. The server accepts the CGI output and finally pumps it back across the Internet to the requesting client where the output is rendered. Typically the output is an HTML document that was created on the fly. It can also be a reference to a document, like another URL, which will then be delivered to the client. Either way, the client gets an answer of some kind (which is all that clients typically care about).

<FORM> TAGS AND ATTRIBUTES

The IETF HTML working group considered many ways to implement forms handling, but they decided to extend the 1.0 HTML DTD and develop a forms language. These extensions are included in the IETF level 2 HTML DTD. This forms language makes it possible for a browser to retrieve a form, render it on the user's display, accept user input, and finally, send the form data to a specified server for further handling.

The <FORM> HTML tag allows an HTML author to create a small set of nice input widgets without writing any GUI application code. Therefore, you can rapidly build a useful graphical interface; for example, for your travel request form. Table 8-1 presents the HTML <FORM> tags and their attributes for the IETF level 2 HTML DTD.

Table 8-1

HTML 2.0 <FORM> Tags and Attributes

Tag	Description	Attributes
<FORM> </FORM>	input form	*ACTION*, METHOD*, ENCTYPE**
<INPUT>	input field	ALIGN, NAME, TYPE***, VALUE, CHECKED, SIZE, MAXLENGTH, SRC
<SELECT> </SELECT>	selection list	*NAME*, MULTIPLE, SIZE
<OPTION>	selection of a selection list; item of <SELECT>	SELECTED, VALUE
<TEXTAREA> </TEXTAREA>	multiple line text input	*NAME, ROWS, COLS*

Required ATTRIBUTES are in *italics*
* - default value = GET
** - default value = 'application/x-www-form-urlencoded'
*** - values: TEXT (default), PASSWORD, CHECKBOX, RADIO, SUBMIT, RESET, IMAGE, HIDDEN

Let's look at an in-depth example to examine the ins and outs of CGI data. Our example is based on the simple "Travel Request Form" shown in Figure 8-1.

An Example Form

To utilize the power of forms on the WWW, Alternative Software Solutions, Inc. builds a request form that their employees must fill out two weeks prior to traveling. On this form, all information is required — that is, all input widgets must be completed by the employee — after which it gets submitted to the company secretary via e-mail.

The secretary receives travel requests via e-mail, which are then booked with the company's travel agency, based on the information provided by the traveler. Here's the typical kinds of information required from traveling employees:

- first and last name
- department/billing code
- e-mail address
- acceptable departure and return dates
- preferred departure and return times
- preferred hotel accommodations
- purpose of trip

Here's the HTML for this form:

```
<!DOCTYPE HTML PUBLIC "-//IETF//DTD HTML 2.0//EN">
<HTML>
<HEAD>
<TITLE>Altenative Software Solutions, Inc. Travel Form</TITLE>
</HEAD>
<BODY>
<H1>Alternative Software Solutions, Inc. Travel Form</H1>
<P> Please try to give Biff (biff@ass.com) this information at least two
weeks in advance.
<HR>
<FORM METHOD="POST" ACTION="http://www.ass.com/cgi-bin/travel_request.pl">
<INPUT TYPE="reset" VALUE="Clear Form">
<HR>
```

```
<H2>Employee Information</H2>
<HR>
<INPUT SIZE=40 NAME="fname"> First Name<BR>
<INPUT SIZE=40 NAME="lname"> Last Name<BR>
<INPUT SIZE=40 NAME="email"> Email<BR>
<INPUT SIZE=25 NAME="billto"> Department Billing Code<BR>
<HR>
<H2>Dates and Times</H2>
<INPUT NAME="ddate"> Departure date
<P>Preferred time of departure:<BR>
<INPUT TYPE="radio" NAME="dtime" VALUE="5AM-9AM"> <i>5AM-9AM</I>
<INPUT TYPE="radio" NAME="dtime" VALUE="9AM-12PM"> <i>9AM-12PM</I>
<INPUT TYPE="radio" NAME="dtime" VALUE="12PM-4PM"> <i>12PM-4PM</I>
<INPUT TYPE="radio" NAME="dtime" VALUE="4PM-8PM"> <i>4PM-8PM</I>
<INPUT TYPE="radio" NAME="dtime" VALUE="8PM-12AM"> <i>8PM-12AM</I>
<P><INPUT NAME="rdate"> Return date
<P>Preferred time of return:<BR>
<INPUT TYPE="radio" NAME="rtime" VALUE="5AM-9AM"> <i>5AM-9AM</I>
<INPUT TYPE="radio" NAME="rtime" VALUE="9AM-12PM"> <i>9AM-12PM</I>
<INPUT TYPE="radio" NAME="rtime" VALUE="12PM-4PM"> <i>12PM-4PM</I>
<INPUT TYPE="radio" NAME="rtime" VALUE="4PM-8PM"> <i>4PM-8PM</I>
<INPUT TYPE="radio" NAME="rtime" VALUE="8PM-12AM"> <i>8PM-12AM</I>
<HR>
<H2>Airlines</H2>
<INPUT TYPE="checkbox" VALUE="indifferent" NAME="airline-ind"> Don't care
which airline<BR>
<INPUT TYPE="checkbox" VALUE="profile" NAME="airline-prof"> Use my profile<BR>
<INPUT SIZE=40 NAME="airline1"> First choice <BR>
<INPUT SIZE=40 NAME="airline2"> Second choice <P>
<H3>Airline Seating Preference</H3>
<DL>
<DD><INPUT TYPE="radio" VALUE="indifferent" NAME="seating"> Don't care about
seating
<DD><INPUT TYPE="radio" VALUE="profile" NAME="seating"> Use my profile
<DD><INPUT TYPE="radio" VALUE="window" NAME="seating"> Window
<DD><INPUT TYPE="radio" VALUE="aisle" NAME="seating"> Aisle
<DD><INPUT TYPE="radio" VALUE="emergency" NAME="seating"> Emergency row
</DL>
<HR>
<H2>Destination</H2>
<INPUT SIZE=45 NAME="city"> City<BR>
   <SELECT NAME="state" SIZE="3">
     <OPTION> Alabama
     <OPTION> Alaska
     <OPTION> Arizona
     <OPTION> Arkansas
     <OPTION> California
     <OPTION> Wyoming
</SELECT>State<BR>
<HR>
<P> Smoking preference:<BR>
<INPUT TYPE="radio" NAME="smoking" VALUE="no"> <i>Non-smoking</I> <INPUT
TYPE="radio" NAME="smoking" VALUE="yes"> <i>Smoking</I>
```

```
<HR>
<H2>Reasons for trip</H2>
<TEXTAREA NAME="reasons" ROWS="5" COLS="55"></TEXTAREA><BR>
<HR>
<P>
<INPUT TYPE="submit" VALUE="Submit Travel Plans to Biff">
</FORM>
<HR>
<ADDRESS> Last updated Mon 11 Jul 94 by elvis@ass.com</ADDRESS>
</BODY>
</HTML>
```

Reading the specification for the <FORM> tag, it's easy to see that
the HTTP method specified is POST — the value of the METHOD
attribute. This tells the browser what kind of request to make to the
server at the URL in the ACTION attribute — in our example, this is:

```
http://www.ass.com/cgi-bin/travel_request.pl
```

This URL is actually a request for a CGI application on the
www.ass.com server. The CGI application must read and parse the input
differently from the GET method. Let's take a closer look.

This bit of Perl handles CGI input using the POST method:

```perl
# flush stdout buffer
$| = 1;
# Print this MIME data no matter what
print "Content-type: text/html\n\n";
# check for the POST method
if ($ENV{'REQUEST_METHOD'} eq 'POST')
{
    # How many bytes are we supposed to receive?
    read(STDIN, $buffer, $ENV{'CONTENT_LENGTH'});
    # make a list of keyword/value pairs
    @pairs = split(/&/, $buffer);
    # cycle through each pair and decipher the values
    foreach $pair (@pairs)
    {
        # get the name/value pair strings
        ($name, $value) = split(/=/, $pair);
        # translate "+" to a space
        $value =~ tr/+/ /;
        # decipher ASCI hexidecimal escaped characters, if any
        $value =~ s/%([a-fA-F0-9][a-fA-F0-9])/pack("C", hex($1))/eg;
        # add the pair to a list keyed on the name of the variable
        $contents{$name} = $value;
    }
}
```

So, how do we get the data from the client? Remember, for the POST method, the standard input device (*stdin*) is the mechanism used. This bit of Perl code reads the *stdin* buffer:

```
# How many bytes are we supposed to receive?
read(STDIN, $buffer, $ENV{'CONTENT_LENGTH'});
```

The environment variable CONTENT_LENGTH determines the number of bytes of information to read from the *stdin* buffer. This buffer contains the data stream sent by the client to the server.

The server then passes this information via *stdin* to the CGI application. That is where we extract the input data. Once the buffer has been split into keyword/value pairs, we decipher each pair and store it in an associative array. This array allows us to access a variable's value instantly.

For instance, this bit of Perl code references the '%contents' associative array and its contents:

```
print <<"HTML";
<HTML>
<HEAD>
<TITLE>Travel Request for $contents{'name'}</TITLE>
</HEAD>
<BODY>
<H1>Travel Request from $contents{'name'}</H1>
</BODY>
</HTML>
HTML
```

As you can see from this example, the CGI application used the name of the user — $contents{'name'} to create an HTML document. Voilà! You have just dynamically created a custom HTML document. This document will be sent back to the traveler and rendered on his or her display.

The Inside Scoop on CGI Output

CGI output — the data returned to the requesting client — is also sent in the body of a MIME message. The standard output device, *stdout*, is the pipe that CGI uses to push data back to the requesting client. But before purging loads of data, the first thing a CGI application must write to *stdout* is a MIME Content-type header.

In the previous Perl examples, you might have noticed this declaration:

```
print "Content-type: text/html\n\n";
```

Look familiar? The CGI application is indicating that the type of MIME body it is returning to the requesting client is 'text/html'. Remember, 'text' is the type and 'html' is a subtype. This instructs the client to render the attached MIME body as an HTML document.

Later in this chapter, we'll look at a more complicated Content-type declaration. For now, lets look at a more complicated Perl script to handle the complete sample Travel Request form. In this example, notice how the input is parsed and put into an associated array. In this example we also begin to look at CGI output:

```perl
#!/usr/tools/bin/perl — -*-perl-*-
# Print this out no matter what
print "Content-type: text/html\n\n";
# flush stdout buffer
$| = 1;
if ($ENV{'REQUEST_METHOD'} eq 'POST')
{
    # How many bytes are we supposed to receive?
    read(STDIN, $buffer, $ENV{'CONTENT_LENGTH'});
    @pairs = split(/&/, $buffer);
    foreach $pair (@pairs)
    {
            ($name, $value) = split(/=/, $pair);
            $value =~ tr/+/ /;
            $value =~ s/%([a-fA-F0-9][a-fA-F0-9])/pack("C", hex($1))/eg;
            $contents{$name} = $value;
    }
}
chop($date = `date`);
################################################
# CGI Output: As HTML and as an email message
################################################
# Create an HTML document on the fly. Yee-haw!
print <<"HTML";
<HTML>
<HEAD><TITLE>A.S.S. Travel Form Entries</TITLE></HEAD>
<BODY>
<H1>Travel Request from $contents{'name'}</H1>
<P><HR><P>
<I>$date</I>
<UL>
```

```
<LI> Name = $contents{'name'}
<LI> Email = $contents{'email'}
<LI> Departure date = $contents{'ddate'}
<LI> Departure time range = $contents{'dtime'}
<LI> Return date = $contents{'rdate'}
<LI> Return time range = $contents{'rtime'}
HTML

# check the airline section of the form data
if($contents{'airline-ind'} eq 'indiffernt') { ; }
else {
    print "<LI> Airline (first choice) = $contents{'airline1'}\n";
    if($contents{'airline2'} ne '') {
  print "<LI> Airline (second choice) = $contents{'airline2'}\n";
    }
}
print <<"HTML";
<LI> Destination City = $contents{'city'}
<LI> Destination State = $contents{'state'}
<LI> Smoking preference = $contents{'smoking'}
<LI> Reason for trip = $contents{'reasons'}
HTML

if($contents{'reasons'} ne '') {
    print "<LI> Reasons = $contents{'reasons'}\n";
}
print <<"HTML";
</UL>
</BODY></HTML>
HTML

# Now create an email message and mail it.
$subject = "Travel Plans for " . $contents{'name'};
$sendto = "biff@ass.com";
# open a named UNIX pipe to send the mail
open (MAIL, "| /usr/lib/sendmail $sendto") || die "Can't send mail: $!\n";
# This selects the open pipe handle.
select(MAIL);
print <<"EMAIL";
Date: $date
From: $contents{'email'}
To: $sendto
Subject: $subject

Name = $contents{'name'}
Email = $contents{'email'}
Bill-to = $contents{'billto'}
Departure date = $contents{'ddate'}
Departure time range = $contents{'dtime'}
Return date = $contents{'rdate'}
Return time range = $contents{'rtime'}
EMAIL
```

```
if($contents{'airline-ind'} eq 'indiffernt') { ; }
else {
    print "Airline (first choice) = $contents{'airline1'}\n";
    if($contents{'airline2'} ne '') {
      print "Airline (second choice) = $contents{'airline2'}\n";
    }
}
print <<"EMAIL";
Destination City = $contents{'city'}
Destination State = $contents{'state'}
Smoking preference = $contents{'smoking'}
Reason for trip = $contents{'reasons'}
EMAIL

if($contents{'reasons'} ne '') {
    print "Reasons = $contents{'special'}\n";
}
close(MAIL);
exit;
```

This CGI Perl script echoes the data back to the user as an HTML document and the same information is mailed to Biff, the secretary who will make the travel arrangements. This information could have also been saved to a log file for future reference.

So far so good. As these things go, this is a fairly simple CGI application. Now, let's look a piece of a CGI application that has a complex MIME Content-type. What do you expect the requesting client to do with this MIME Content-type?

```
Content-type: application/octet-stream;type=tar;conversions=gzip
```

The primary subtype of 'application' is 'octet-stream'. This indicates that the MIME body contains binary data. The two parameters in this example are:

- 'type' — the general type of binary data
- 'conversions' — the set of operations that are performed on the data before writing it to *stdout*

The MIME specification recommends that the proper action for an implementation that receives 'application/octet-stream' information is to offer to put the binary data in a local file.

The 'application/octet-stream' parameters used here are two members of a larger set. In Chapter 18, you will become MIME masters. If you can't wait until then, you can find more information about MIME (RFC 1521) in section 7.4.1 at:

```
http://www.cis.ohio-state.edu/htbin/rfc/rfc1521.html
```

Summary

There are two primary methods for presenting data to a CGI application. GET is used for <ISINDEX> queries and is discouraged for form data. POST is the method of choice for forms because it is not limited by a system's command-line length limit. Output from a CGI application is in two parts, an HTTP header with an attached MIME body of Content-type. Once you've grabbed that data, though, the rest is up to you.

In the next chapter, we'll step up to the big picture and share our ideas about designing entire CGI applications!

9 Designing CGI Applications

The Requirements Analyzed

*C*GI development can be seen as an outgrowth of traditional structured programming, mixed with a scripting language framework, all rolled together into a single package. On the one hand, applications programs are constructed with *all* elements of the full-blown software engineering/development paradigm in mind, with formal techniques for eliciting information to drive the design of data structures, user interfaces, and APIs. On the other hand, CGI programs are normally viewed less as whole systems and more as the means to a particular end, to solve much less ambitious and more circumscribed information processing requirements.

Typically, you'll use a CGI in a gateway capacity or as middleware between two other processes (like, between a server and an application program or an engine, which defines the essence of the "gateway" part of CGI). Hence, CGIs are usually less concerned with providing interface delivery, other than what's hard-coded directly into the model, and more concerned with getting some particular job done (like recording and analyzing the input from an HTML <FORM>).

A Language for All Seasons

Because CGI programs are used differently from print-formatting applications (like Microsoft Word or Adobe Photoshop), their creation requires an approach different from typical application development. Typically, CGIs are minuscule in comparison with a full-featured spreadsheet program. More significantly, CGIs are far more likely to be updated on-the-fly, as dictated by their operating environments.

As times change, so must CGI code. Perhaps that's why CGI engineers favor using quick-and-dirty scripting languages, because they lend the greatest amount of control, flexibility, portability, and extensibility to their coding. This also explains why you'll seldom find an assembly language implementation of any of the popular CGIs out on the Net today (if ever).

This isn't to say that there's no place for C compilers in the land of CGI. We know of many C applications used to interface Web applications with a variety of systems. You would want to use a C program for a processor-intensive CGI, for things like complex calculations or large-scale data translation.

Interpreted scripts, on the other hand, are ideal for smaller, less intensive data crunching. They also excel at string manipulation and text parsing. This is the exact reason why we tend to "just whip out a little Perl" for our CGI solutions, rather than wheeling out the C preprocessor, compiler, and linker just to print a nice <BOLD>Hello World!</BOLD>. C programs have their places, just as do Perl scripts, and Korn or Bourne shell scripts.

For a good real-world example, we'll spend three chapters plotting the course of a CGI that we designed, created, and tested for another IDG Web-related book (whose Web site we are also happy to house and govern).

Throughout these chapters, we'll track the requirements, design, implementation, and ignition of a particular CGI resident on that home page; specifically, the interactive form that accepts and collates data entered by people who wish to register this book across the Web.

This chapter concerns itself with the design and requirements phase of the development process, as well as those goals that the resulting application will need to address. As we take you through this phase, we will also handle other important upfront design issues, ponder some variable scoping alternatives, and debate the need for ancillary programs to assist in handling the forms data over time.

Design of the Registration Form

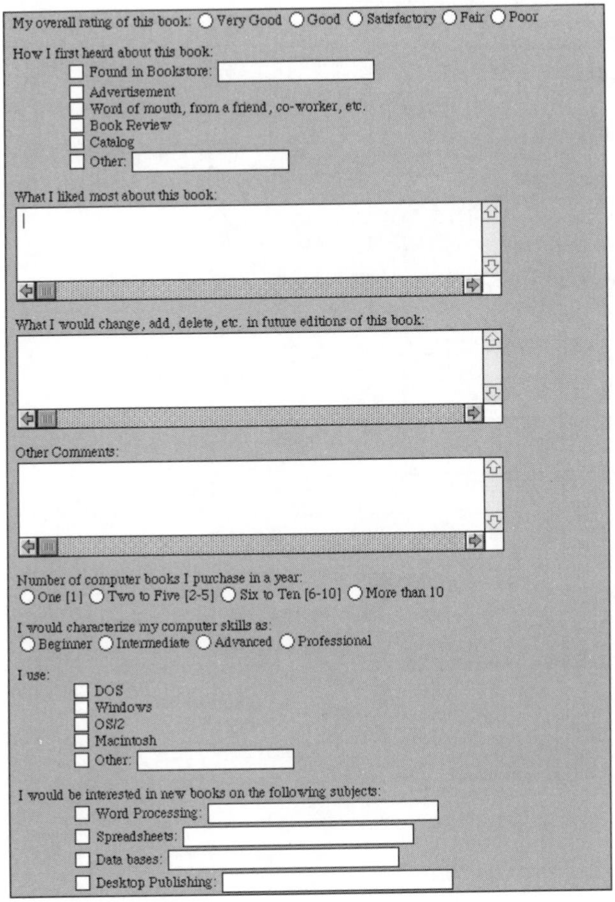

Figure 9-1

First part of the registration form.

Figures 9-1 and 9-2 illustrate that the basic building blocks for our registration script emerge quite clearly from the form it's supposed to handle. Based on the HTML code for the form (which we've included shortly to let you follow along), we set out to provide a CGI mechanism that accepts user input. The CGI application then writes the data to a common aggregate file, checking for errors where appropriate, and parses the data file into a summary report.

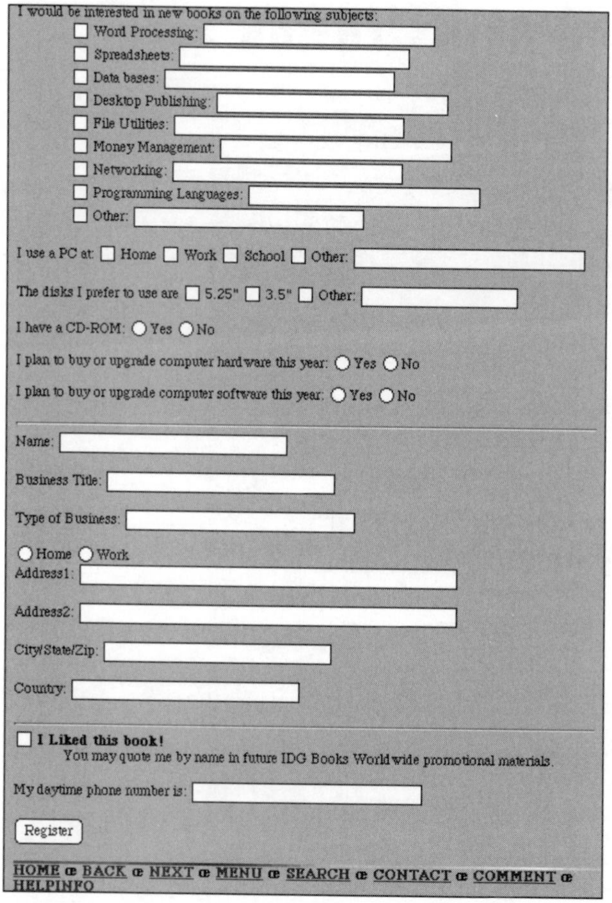

I would be interested in new books on the following subjects:
☐ Word Processing: ▢
☐ Spreadsheets: ▢
☐ Data bases: ▢
☐ Desktop Publishing: ▢
☐ File Utilities: ▢
☐ Money Management: ▢
☐ Networking: ▢
☐ Programming Languages: ▢
☐ Other: ▢

I use a PC at: ☐ Home ☐ Work ☐ School ☐ Other: ▢

The disks I prefer to use are ☐ 5.25" ☐ 3.5" ☐ Other: ▢

I have a CD-ROM: ○ Yes ○ No

I plan to buy or upgrade computer hardware this year: ○ Yes ○ No

I plan to buy or upgrade computer software this year: ○ Yes ○ No

Name: ▢

Business Title: ▢

Type of Business: ▢

○ Home ○ Work
Address1: ▢

Address2: ▢

City/State/Zip: ▢

Country: ▢

☐ **I Liked this book!**
　You may quote me by name in future IDG Books Worldwide promotional materials.

My daytime phone number is: ▢

[Register]

HOME ∝ BACK ∝ NEXT ∝ MENU ∝ SEARCH ∝ CONTACT ∝ COMMENT ∝
HELPINFO

Figure 9-2

Second part of the registration form.

```
<HTML>
<HEAD>
<TITLE>HTML for DUMMIES - IDG Books - IDG Registration
</TITLE>
<BODY>
<A NAME="top"></A><IMG SRC="graphics/line.gif"><BR>
<B><A HREF="html4dum.html">HOME</A> &#32;&#166;
<A HREF="comment.html">BACK</A> &#32;&#166;
<A HREF="ftpstuff.html#top">NEXT</A> &#32;&#166;
<A HREF="search4d.html#menu">MENU</A> &#32;&#166;
<A HREF="search4d.html#search4d">SEARCH</A> &#32;&#166;
<A HREF="contact.html">CONTACT</A> &#32;&#166;
```

```
<A HREF="comment.html">COMMENT</A> &#32;&#166;
<A HREF="helpinfo.html">HELPINFO</A></B><BR>
<IMG SRC="graphics/line.gif"><P>
<H1><IMG ALIGN=TOP SRC="graphics/dummyguy.gif">
IDG Online Registration</H1><P>
<IMG SRC="graphics/line.gif"><BR>
```

This page is the on-line version of the registration sheet in the book. If
you have purchased the book, you may use this page to register your purchase
and send comments to IDG. `<I>`Please use this form only if you have purchased
the book.`</I><P><form method="post" action="http://www.outer.net/cgi-bin/html4dum.register.pl">`

```
<H2>Title of this Book: <I>HTML for Dummies</I></H2><P>
My overall rating of this book:
<input type=radio name="overrate" value="VG">Very Good
<input type=radio name="overrate" value="G">Good
<input type=radio name="overrate" value="S">Satisfactory
<input type=radio name="overrate" value="F">Fair
<input type=radio name="overrate" value="P">Poor<P>
```

```
How I first heard about this book:<BR>
<IMG SRC="graphics/ind2.gif">
<input type="checkbox" name ="Bookstore">Found in Bookstore:
<input type="text" name="BSname" Value="" size=20><BR>
<IMG SRC="graphics/ind2.gif">
<input type="checkbox" name ="Ad">Advertisement<BR>
<IMG SRC="graphics/ind2.gif">
<input type="checkbox" name ="Word">Word of mouth, from a friend, co-worker, et
c.<BR>
<IMG SRC="graphics/ind2.gif">
<input type="checkbox" name ="Review">Book Review<BR>
<IMG SRC="graphics/ind2.gif">
<input type="checkbox" name ="Catalog">Catalog<BR>
<IMG SRC="graphics/ind2.gif">
<input type="checkbox" name ="Other">Other: <input type="text" name="othernm" V
alue="" size=20><P>
```

```
What I liked most about this book:<BR>
<TEXTAREA NAME="liked" ROWS=4 COLs=60></TEXTAREA><P>
```

```
What I would change, add, delete, etc. in future editions of this book:<BR>
<TEXTAREA NAME="change" ROWS=4 COLs=60></TEXTAREA><P>
```

```
Other Comments:<BR>
<TEXTAREA NAME="comments" ROWS=4 COLs=60></TEXTAREA><P>
```

```
Number of computer books I purchase in a year: <BR>
<input type=radio name="compnumb" value="1">One [1]
<input type=radio name="compnumb" value="2to5">Two to Five [2-5]
<input type=radio name="compnumb" value="6to10">Six to Ten [6-10]
<input type=radio name="compnumb" value="plus10">More than 10<P>
```

```
I would characterize my computer skills as: <BR>
<input type=radio name="compskil" value="Beginner">Beginner
<input type=radio name="compskil" value="Intermediate">Intermediate
<input type=radio name="compskil" value="Advanced">Advanced
<input type=radio name="compskil" value="Professional">Professional<P>

I use: <BR>
<IMG SRC="graphics/ind2.gif">
<input type="checkbox" name ="DOS">DOS<BR>
<IMG SRC="graphics/ind2.gif">
<input type="checkbox" name ="Windows">Windows<BR>
<IMG SRC="graphics/ind2.gif">
<input type="checkbox" name ="OS/2">OS/2<BR>
<IMG SRC="graphics/ind2.gif">
<input type="checkbox" name ="Macintosh">Macintosh<BR>
<IMG SRC="graphics/ind2.gif">
<input type="checkbox" name ="Other">Other: <input type="text" name="otherpc" V
alue="" size=20><P>

I would be interested in new books on the following subjects:<BR>
<IMG SRC="graphics/ind2.gif">
<input type="checkbox" name ="WordProc">Word Processing:
<input type="text" name="WordProcNm" Value="" size=30><BR>
<IMG SRC="graphics/ind2.gif">
<input type="checkbox" name ="Spreadsheets">Spreadsheets:
<input type="text" name="SpreadsheetsNm" Value="" size=30><BR>
<IMG SRC="graphics/ind2.gif">
<input type="checkbox" name ="Databases">Data bases:
<input type="text" name="DatabasesNm" Value="" size=30><BR>
<IMG SRC="graphics/ind2.gif">
<input type="checkbox" name ="Desktop">Desktop Publishing:
<input type="text" name="DesktopNm" Value="" size=30><BR>
<IMG SRC="graphics/ind2.gif">
<input type="checkbox" name ="FileUtil">File Utilities:
<input type="text" name="FileUtilNm" Value="" size=30><BR>
<IMG SRC="graphics/ind2.gif">
<input type="checkbox" name ="MoneyMng">Money Management:
<input type="text" name="MoneyMngNm" Value="" size=30><BR>
<IMG SRC="graphics/ind2.gif">
<input type="checkbox" name ="Networking">Networking:
<input type="text" name="NetworkingNm" Value="" size=30><BR>
<IMG SRC="graphics/ind2.gif">
<input type="checkbox" name ="ProgLang">Programming Languages:
<input type="text" name="ProgLangNm" Value="" size=30><BR>
<IMG SRC="graphics/ind2.gif">
<input type="checkbox" name ="Other">Other:
<input type="text" name="other" Value="" size=30><P>

I use a PC at:
<input type="checkbox" name ="PCHome">Home
<input type="checkbox" name ="PCWork">Work
<input type="checkbox" name ="PCSchool">School
<input type="checkbox" name ="PCOther">Other:
<input type="text" name="PCOtherNm" Value="" size=30><P>
```

```
The disks I prefer to use are
<input type="checkbox" name ="525">5.25&quot;
<input type="checkbox" name ="35">3.5&quot;
<input type="checkbox" name ="DiskOther">Other:
<input type="text" name="DiskOtherSize" Value="" size=20><P>


I have a CD-ROM:
<input type=radio name="CDROM" value="Yes">Yes
<input type=radio name="CDROM" value="No">No<P>


I plan to buy or upgrade computer hardware this year:
<input type=radio name="Hardware" value="Yes">Yes
<input type=radio name="Hardware" value="No">No<P>


I plan to buy or upgrade computer software this year:
<input type=radio name="Software" value="Yes">Yes
<input type=radio name="Software" value="No">No<P>


<HR>
Name: <input type="text" name="Name" Value="" size=30><P>
Business Title: <input type="text" name="Bustitle" Value="" size=30><P>
Type of Business: <input type="text" name="TypeBus" Value="" size=30><P>
<input type=radio name="AddrLoc" value="Home">Home
<input type=radio name="AddrLoc" value="Work">Work<BR>
Address1: <input type="text" name="Addr1" Value="" size=50><P>
Address2: <input type="text" name="Addr2" Value="" size=50><P>
City/State/Zip: <input type="text" name="CSZ" Value="" size=30><P>
Country: <input type="text" name="Country" Value="" size=30><P>
<HR>


<input type="checkbox" name ="QuoteMe"><B>I Liked this book!</B><BR>
<IMG SRC="graphics/ind2.gif">You may  quote me by name in future IDG
 Books Worldwide promotional materials.<P>
My daytime phone number is: <input type="text" name="DayPhone" Value="" size=30>
<P>
<INPUT TYPE="submit" NAME="Register" VALUE="Register"><P>


<IMG SRC="graphics/line.gif"><BR>
<B><A HREF="html4dum.html">HOME</A> &#32;&#166;
<A HREF="comment.html">BACK</A> &#32;&#166;
<A HREF="ftpstuff.html#top">NEXT</A> &#32;&#166;
<A HREF="search4d.html#menu">MENU</A> &#32;&#166;
<A HREF="search4d.html#search4d">SEARCH</A> &#32;&#166;
<A HREF="contact.html">CONTACT</A> &#32;&#166;
<A HREF="comment.html">COMMENT</A> &#32;&#166;
<A HREF="helpinfo.html">HELPINFO</A></B>
<IMG SRC="graphics/line.gif"><P>


<ADDRESS>
<A NAME="bottom"></A>
E-Mail: <A HREF="mailto:html4dum@outer.net">
HTML for Dummies at html4dum@outer.net</A><BR>
</ADDRESS>
```

```
URL: <A HREF="http://www.outer.net/html4dum/registrn.html">
http://www.outer.net/html4dum/registrn.html</A>
<BR>
Text - Copyright  &copy; 1995,  Ed Tittel &amp; Steve James.<BR>
Dummies Design and Art - Copyright  &copy; 1995,  IDG Books Worldwide, Inc.<BR>
Web Layout - Copyright  &copy; 1995, LANWrights &amp;
<A HREF="http://www.io.com/~mcintyre/homepage.html">IMPACT Online.</A><BR>
Revised — June 5th, 1995 [JMS - IMPACT Online]<BR>
</BODY>
</HTML>
```

First off, you'll notice that the form has many visual clues that help the user complete it without over-cluttering it with a ton of directions.

An essential step in the design process is the evaluation of the materials given as the base for you to work with. In this case, several versions of the data captured from the form were passed from the programmer to the administrative personnel and back again, to nail down the end product more exactly.

It's essential to understand that all parties involved in development — and this definitely includes its final users — must arrive at a common understanding of what will be delivered before any substantial development work should be undertaken. This understanding emerged from playing off what is desired against what can be delivered; inevitably, all participants will make some compromises along the way.

It's also important to note that many managers have a poor understanding of the resource requirements and delivery timeframes for development projects. Even though final decisions may be dictated by management, it's important to inject reality into the negotiation process surrounding these decisions. Otherwise, plans that hinge upon completion of projects could become unhinged, with potentially disastrous consequences for all parties involved.

After management and development participants arrive at a mutual understanding, the next logical step in CGI evolution is an assessment of the variables needed and their planned uses.

Mapping Fields to Variables

Throughout most of the HTML code and within our CGIs, we tend to pick meaningful names for variables. A short example would be that all of a user's comment would be stored in a TEXTAREA that is coincidentally enough called 'comments'.

```
Other Comments:<BR>
<TEXTAREA NAME="comments" ROWS=4 COLs=60></TEXTAREA><P>
```

Although it seems obvious to point this out, we've seen many occasions where programs are delivered as minefields, full of hastily engineered code replete with variables named '$x' and '$stuff' that do nothing but destroy the code's maintainability. It is always helpful to collect all of the variable names that you intend to use, before writing a single line of code. Such a variable dictionary can greatly simplify the act of writing the code thereafter.

A compelling reason for a smart naming scheme derives from the choice of Perl as the development language. By using a common library to parse your input environment variables, you can interact with your names directly. When it comes to deciphering array references like $in{a_really_big_string_2} or $in{the_Other_stuff} you'll quickly understand why using more descriptive names is a good idea.

For our HTML example, we chose simple, lowercase words (sans embedded punctuation to make them easier to type) wherever possible for variable names. This approach will make coding less of a stress-test. In the next chapter, where we explore writing the actual Perl script, you should be pleasantly surprised to discover that the code is quite readable and easy to produce.

Variable Error Checking

A common oversight for beginning CGI scriptwriters is the omission of even minimal error-handling routines. As any veteran programmer can attest, a good portion of any well-developed structure is framed by solid fall-through and failure mechanisms. In short, our advice is to "expect the unexpected."

Even if your description of what users should input into a field is *perfectly* clear, that won't prevent a three-year-old from hopping up onto the keyboard (while Daddy visits the loo) and spamming out a gaggle of

James Joyce at your CGI. At that point, you'd quickly realize how nice it would have been to check for redundant or ridiculous responses. That also confers an opportunity to either toss them or ask for clarification, rather than to process them blindly (and uncaringly, as your end users might conclude).

For our registration example, we decided that we wanted to respond to the omission of the registrant's name, address, or phone number from the form. Since these fields are paramount to the owner of the site, we planned to program the gateway to reject a form missing these essential details and to politely request that these required fields be completed before continuing further.

Although our example is simple and our demands pretty soft, it does illustrate the need to address error handling and control from the onset of the design process. Imagine instead, a set of forms designed to be front-ends to a database engine; one, in fact, that is very choosy about the input it is willing to accept. Under these circumstances, a ton of pre-parsing and error-handling is necessary just to ensure that input is valid before it ever hits the database engine.

Alternate Methods of Data Capture

One characteristic prevalent in the early days of the Web, but almost uniformly overlooked today, is that not everyone has a forms-capable browser. Some of us are still forced to use what we have at our disposal, such as Lynx, a text-based browser. When sketching out preliminary forms designs and the CGI programs that will ultimately handle them, be sure to include a data delivery path for users who cannot interact with your forms directly.

One good way to include the whole client base is to provide multiple equivalent data request mechanisms that let users choose how they wish to send and receive such information. You could, for instance, automatically e-mail a standard questionnaire to the recipient, who could then fill it out and reply via e-mail. Another equivalent mechanism is to include your questionnaire as a text page, so that users could print out the Web page, fill in the answers, and fax the results to a data collection point. With the same approach, they could capture the text page elec tronically and fill it out more legibly. As you ponder the alternatives, you'll quickly realize that there are many options that will allow your users to communicate with you.

Designing the Output File Format

In our example, the intention is to funnel all customer responses received from the form into a single file. This makes the design of the file format important to the longevity and usefulness of the CGI. Since the format of the data in the file will determine how difficult it will be to program any post-capture processing, we will pay special attention to our planned uses for this file. Finding a happy medium between "easy to capture" and "easy to post-process" is therefore an important design goal for the file format.

After serious deliberation, we agreed that the format for the data file should be similar in structure and function to the HTML page that drives it. Each category is therefore prefaced by its name, followed by a colon, followed by the data extracted from the user's entry for that category.

Multiple-entry questions will use some infrequently occurring character as a separator. Finally, we decided that multiple-line entries (from TEXTAREA fields) would always occupy the same number of lines in the data file, whether they were completely occupied or not.

Because the data file will be used by several other applications, including some CGIs, consistency in the file format, layout, and data representations is critical. If we miss or add a single line, or have an accident in our programming (hit a bug, if you will), this could cause everything to go haywire. Because these concerns are so important to the successful operation of the program, they also point out the need for rigorous testing following implementation.

Our final decision involves choosing a record separator; because we write the input from multiple users to the same file, we have to be able to distinguish the contents of one user's information from another. We chose a line of equal signs to denote the end of one record and the beginning of the next one.

When you sit down to address such issues in your own project design meetings, be aware that the data file to be created is dependent and driven by the applications that will later use it. Therefore, you should get a require-ments specification for each of the intended uses for your data files. Then, you can concoct a format that will handle all of their needs simultaneously.

A format that drives other programs (rather than a program that drives other formats) will eventually become mixed up and unsuitable, or possibly even unusable over several generations of changes. A strong inital focus that understands and ties together all of a CGI's uses should be fully planned out and produced. Even if you don't take our word for it, experience will teach you that this is the only way to go!

Designing a Report Writer

Now that the structure and layout requirements for the data file are con-firmed, it's time to consider adding another application to post-process the data file on a regular (or occasional) basis. In other words, you'll need to build a reporting engine to take the data file as input, analyze its contents, and use this information to generate a summary report.

Because many of the questions that drive the contents of the data file are multiple-choice, or "pick-the-responses(s)-that-apply," a good way to report on such information is to break down responses for each item into percentages by category. For instance, the total number of respondents who favor DOS/Windows as their platform of choice can easily be tabulated and returned as a percentage of the total answers.

Other information collected in the form — like raw comment text — could be sampled at random and inserted into another report or ignored altogether. Since only a few administrators will want to read every such reply once or twice a year, this collation across records isn't necessary for the initial implementation. The simple series of percentages and totals is all that's required for the first pass, since the users are currently interested only in a monthly summary report.

In writing your own report generators, you may feel the need to gateway your information to a database back-end for processing, which is perfect in today's multi-solution market. If so, you might need to spend more time in the design of the data file to make it best fit the requirements of the DBMS's import utility.

Building in Counters and Status

The last little bit of code that needs to be written is in conjunction with the main registration database but isn't essential for its operation. We thought it would be nice to offer a ticket number (so to speak) to each visitor who fills out the form, giving each of them an idea of how many respondents had visited before them.

This is absurdly easy to accomplish using a simple counter that updates another file. Many large, busy sites like to show off their traffic stats by indicating that "you were visitor number 21,346." Our registration database will probably not include this feature, but we can play the statistics game, too, if we have to!

Here's one final touch that's all too often overlooked — namely, the return page sent to the user after all of the CGI processing is complete. Usually consisting entirely of a string of Perl print statements filled with the appropriate HTML, these statements tell the user what needs to be done next, and whether the CGI succeeded. With the registration CGI, we opted to send our users a standard banner for the site, along with either a simple "thank you" message if the database updated properly, or a "sorry: please retry" message otherwise.

When designing your programs or scripts, it pays to consider all the aspects of HTML forms and CGI development. If you spend the time up-front to worry about the details, it will definitely pay a handsome return in easier coding, simpler debugging, and appropriate default behavior when the software is built. It's either "Pay (a little) now" or "Pay (a lot) later!"

Overall Design Thoughts

REUSABILITY

Code developed for your WWW site should be resuable, if at all possible, for other projects or other reasons. If you make your code generic and simple enough for multiple uses, you'll enable rapid prototyping for your other CGI projects. This also helps to justify the time and effort it'll take you to learn some of the standard CGI utilities and libraries (which we'll cover in Chapter 15 and elsewhere throughout this book).

If you think carefully about the scope of your CGI project during the design phase, you'll consider other possible applications that it might suit as well. This will help you create broader functionality that may have more uses later on, as well as solving your current data-handling needs.

For our registration database example, we intend to write its code so that if another book project needs a quick registration form, only three or four lines of code would need to change. We could also run our registration database against a selection of general question-and-answer forms, with only slight modifications, thereby making it applicable to other projects. And of course we've included it here in this book, for you to reuse as well!

PORTABILITY

The selection of a scripting language or environment for portability is another important facet of CGI development. By using Perl, as most WebMasters do, we can transfer our scripts from one UNIX box to another, with no recompiling or re-engineering necessary.

By using an interpreted language like Perl, scripts will usually run without modification, regardless of the system architecture involved. In this day and age, when some pundits believe that Windows NT will soon rule the world, portability is a favorable feature that may pay unexpected dividends or ensure longer-term viability of code.

EXPANDABILITY

As your Web site grows, you will need to grow with it. The ability to maintain and control the continued and ongoing development of your CGIs over time should also be a major focus for design groups. By *expandability* we refer to the eventual and inevitable need to update or alter your CGI scripts to fit a new or expanded set of requirements. By designing a growth path into your software, future changes will be easier to handle.

How do you do this? By heavily documenting your code, so that you (and others who follow in your steps) will be able to understand what your code does and how it works; by using intelligent variable names and assignments to improve readability; and by using data files to configure your programs from separate input or a finite-state machine-modeling tool to create formal descriptions of complex parsing and data-handling tasks. All of these approaches make your code easier to understand and maintain, and they also make it easier to change and enhance.

LIBRARYIZING

You might also consider collecting your work into a programming library, so that others who make use of CGIs on your site may access them. Or you could even publish them on the Web. By collecting, sanitizing, and bundling your CGIs into a library, other users may not have to repeat the development processes you've already perfected. And because libraries are easy to invoke and efficient to use, they won't impose too much overhead on you or your development efforts.

Summary

In this chapter, we've taken you through a quick design process for a group of our CGIs as they were actually produced. Further, we've demonstrated the need to write clear, independent code, wherever possible. We've also left clues about how to build low-maintenance, powerful CGIs by using the planning stage to nail everything down. Finally, we discussed some overall design strategies that should be worth following in all your projects to help guarantee their success.

II The Bridge to CGI Implementation

*T*he eight chapters in Part II supply the examples, reference materials, and basic techniques you'll need to begin creating your own CGI applications. Chapters 10 and 11 continue the elaboration of the forms-handling example introduced in Chapter 9. Chapter 10 steps you through the implementation process of a registration form-handling CGI, with an attendant report generator to abstract the acquired data. Chapter 11 tackles the testing and debugging process, using this same program as the focus for its remarks and advice.

Chapters 12 through 17 cover a number of issues that CGI developers must address before they begin serious implementation. Chapter 12 discusses the authors' choices of Web server platform and operating system, programming languages, tools, and other implementation specifics, along with possible alternatives.

Chapter 13 explains some techniques for surfing the Web for additional CGI information (the traditional and still informative master source for Web programming tips, tools, tricks, and techniques). Chapter 14 explains how to build simple, standard scaffolding for creating the "return page" HTML documents so common in CGI programs.

Chapter 15 examines some of the best of the many CGI code resources on the Net, with a particular emphasis on useful CGI programming libraries. Chapter 16 discusses the need for forms alternatives and introduces several techniques to solicit input from users whose Web browsers may not be forms-enabled.

In Chapter 17, we conclude this part of the book with a discussion of some common CGI programming gotchas and pitfalls, in the hope that you can learn from our mistakes and avoid well-known hazards on the road to CGI mastery.

10 Building and Installing CGI Applications

*I*n the previous chapter we discussed the steps taken to identify the need for a CGI, to define the specific functions necessary, and to design the algorithms that would fulfill the original need. Once we are satisfied with our design and specification, we can begin coding our CGI.

We typically develop CGIs in Perl, since as an interpreted language it lends itself well to debugging and tweaking. It's very easy to write small chunks of code in Perl and then run the script to make sure it's going to do what you intended.

It may be necessary to modify your code somewhat in order to test it fully. Basic syntax and typos can be checked just by feeding the script or fragment to the Perl interpreter, and more subtle context and interpretation issues can be discovered using Perl's *-w* switch.

But to test higher-level attributes of a script, like adherence to a design specification, you may have to either fake some input data or modify the script to work with existing data while debugging. These testing tricks are universal and can apply to the development of any sort of tool or program.

When writing CGIs, however, you are likely to run into snags peculiar to this kind of development. Since a CGI script is expecting to receive its input from a Web browser and to send its output back to the same browser, it can be tricky to test. A crashing bug of any sort will return an error code 500 to the browser, complete with a message about the server not being able to complete your request. Unfortunately this is not very informative, particularly when you're trying to debug your code.

You could try to test your CGI scripts from the UNIX shell command line, but two things make this difficult:

1. All output will be returned in HTML format and may therefore be difficult to interpret correctly.

2. Many scripts must be called from a form using the POST or GET methods. As such, they depend on obtaining input data from the URL-encoded values supplied by HTTP environment variables. If the data isn't where it's supposed to be or isn't in the proper form, the CGI's behavior can be erratic, to say the least.

In fact, the Perl library we customarily use in our scripts, "formlib.pl", checks for form data and if it isn't present, returns an error page with the following message:

```
Error in 'GetFormArgs'

this script needs to be called from a FORM, either by POST or GET.

if you need help, call whoever wrote the script you're using.
```

This isn't very informative, either. The same message would be produced by running the script from the shell. In these cases, you may want to use a *debugging routine*, a chunk of code that will return all the data sent to it from the browser. We'll discuss this in more depth once we have some script code to work on.

html4dum.register.pl
Anatomy of a Perl Script

SETUP AND INITIALIZATION

The first part of any shell script consists of the magic line used to invoke the script's interpreter, in this case, Perl 4.036. From there we try to include a descriptive name for the script, identify its author(s), the date it was started, and finally, current version information. When writing a CGI, it is also worthwhile to include the URL for the form that calls the script (since they're so strongly related, if for no other reason). Here's the beginning of our CGI script:

```
#!/usr/local/bin/perl
# HTML4dummies Registration CGI
# 6/5/95 - singe@outer.net
# called by http://www.outer.net/html4dum/registrn.html
#
# 1.0 - collects data from the user's submitted registration form,
# parses it and translates where necessary into an intelligible
# format then writes the whole thing to the data file for future
# use.
#
# 1.1 - error handling added
#
```

Next, we'll perform the setup and initialization steps, load Brigette Jellinek's forms library, and use its procedures to parse the form data:

```
require "/www/cgi-bin/formlib.pl";
$| = 1;                      # output NOT buffered
chop ($date = `/bin/date`);
# for the 'this page created' line at the bottom
&GetFormArgs();
# parse arguments passed from FORM (now in %in)
$ENV{PATH_INFO} ne '' && &GetPathArgs($ENV{PATH_INFO});
print "Content-Type: text/html\n\n";
######################################################################
```

The lines that bear special attention are the output unbuffering the usage error checking. By setting Perl's built-in variable called '$|' to '1', we ensure that no data can languish in a memory buffer when the connection is broken from the browser to the CGI through the Web server.

The lines that invoke Brigette's library procedures 'GetFormArgs' and 'GetPathArgs' extract the data from both POST and GET method invocations, and return the error message described above if both subroutines fail to find any data.

The final line of this fragment outputs the mandatory 'Content-Type' header, and the following blank line signals the end of headers and the beginning of data. From here on in, any output to STDOUT will make its way straight back to the browser that invoked it.

Now it's time to set up the beginning of our HTML document:

```
print "<HTML><HEAD><TITLE>HTML for Dummies",
"Registration</TITLE></HEAD>";

unless ( $in{Name} && ($in{Addr1} || $in{DayPhone})) {
    # the user did not send us the minimum amount of information,
    # spit out an error
```

```
print "<H1><IMG ALIGN=TOP SRC=",
"\"http://www.outer.net/html4dum/graphics/dummyguy.gif\">",
"ERROR!</H1>\n";
print "There was a problem with the data you entered. You ",
    "need to supply at least: <B>name, address and ",
    "phone number.</B><P>",
    "If you wish to correct your data, ",
    "<A HREF=\"http://www.outer.net/html4dum/registrn.html\">",
    "return to the registration form.</A><HR>",
    "<ADDRESS>Registration form CGI by",
    "singe@outer.net<P>$date</ADDRESS></HTML>";

exit (1); # end the CGI right here.
```

Here, we've signaled the browser that we're creating HTML output with the <HTML> tag and then we want to print our static <HEAD> portion of the document, which consists only of our <TITLE>.

Next, we perform error checking specific to our data and reject the user's input if a name, an address, or a phone number is missing. Note the link back to the registration form at the bottom of the error message. It's exceptionally bad form (pun alert!) to chastise users for bad data and not give them an easy way to correct the mistake. Note also the use of **exit()** as a way to instantly terminate the CGI.

In the next section, we'll build our standard navigation bar for the set of Web pages the form belongs to:

```
} else {
   # we now continue with our regularly scheduled CGI

      print "<BODY> <A NAME=\"top\"></A> ",
      "<IMG SRC=\"http://www.outer.net/html4dum/graphics/line.gif\"><BR>",
      "<B><A HREF = \"http://www.outer.net/html4dum/html4dum.html\">
HOME</A> &#32;&#166;",
      "<A HREF = \"http://www.outer.net/html4dum/contact.html#top\">
BACK</A> &#32;&#166;",
      "<A HREF = \"http://www.outer.net/html4dum/ftpstuff.html#top\">
NEXT</A> &#32;&#166;",
      "<A HREF = \"http://www.outer.net/html4dum/search4d.html#menu\">
MENU</A> &#32;&#166;",
      "<A HREF = \"http://www.outer.net/html4dum/search4d.html#search4d\">
SEARCH</A> &#32;&#166;",
      "<A HREF = \"http://www.outer.net/html4dum/contact.html\"> CONTACT</A>
&#32;&#166;",
      "<A HREF = \"http://www.outer.net/html4dum/comment.html\"> COMMENT</A>
&#32;&#166;",
      "<A HREF = \"http://www.outer.net/html4dum/helpinfo.html\">
HELPINFO</A></B><BR>",
      "<IMG SRC=\"http://www.outer.net/html4dum/graphics/line.gif\"><P>",
      "<IMG ALIGN=TOP
SRC=\"http://www.outer.net/html4dum/graphics/dummyguy.gif\"> ";
```

This enormous print statement sets up the clickable navigation bar at the top of our return page. This could have come after we did our business with the user's data, but it's a good idea to get some data out to the browser before embarking on behind-the-scenes data manipulation.

Here's why: our processing may run into a system or network bottleneck that slows it down to the point that the browser times out. If we send some initial data straight out to the user before any potentially time-consuming tasks, the browser will give us quite a bit more time before timing out and delivering an error message instead of a registration form!

PROCESSING USER INPUT

From here on out, we'll get right into the meat of the script. First, we open the file handle to append to our raw data file and write the user's data out to that file:

```
while (-e "/www/httpdocs/html4dum/data/registrations.LCK") {
system ("sleep 3");
}
open (LOCK, ">> /www/httpdocs/html4dum/data/registrations.LCK");
open (REGISTER, ">>/www/httpdocs/html4dum/data/registrations");

print REGISTER "Overall Rating: $in{overrate}\nHeard from: ";
```

Note our rudimentary file locking — if a lock file exists, we make the script sleep for three seconds and then check again. This could result in an endless loop if a lock file was left behind by some previous execution of the script, but the user's browser will time out in this case so we're probably safe.

The first input area is the user's rating of the book, which is a <SELECT> input area with a single selection, and therefore doesn't need any special handling. The general format for the data file is **Fieldname: value** with one field per line:

```
if ($in{Bookstore}) {
    print REGISTER "Bookstore";

    if ($in{BSname}) {
       print REGISTER " ($in{BSname})";
       $join = "|";
    }
}
```

```
        print REGISTER "\t";

if ($in{Ad}) {
    print REGISTER "${join}Advertisement";
    $join = "|";
}

if ($in{Word}) {
    print REGISTER "${join}Word of mouth";
    $join = "|";
}

if ($in{Review}) {
    print REGISTER "${join}Review";
    $join = "|";
}

if ($in{Catalog}) {
    print REGISTER "${join}Catalog";
    $join = "|";
}

if ($in{Other}) {
    print REGISTER "${join}Other";
    $join = "|";
}

if ($in{othernm}) {
    print REGISTER " ($in{othernm})"
}

$join = "";
```

We've now completed the **Heard from** entry. On the registration form, the user is presented with a series of checkboxed options and allowed to choose as many as were applicable. In addition, if the user chooses **Bookstore** or **Other**, they must also fill in a text input box with the specific source, that is, the bookstore name or the **Other** source.

To handle this indeterminate amount of data, we use a series of if statements to test all the applicable input names for checked boxes. If one is defined, we print a label that describes this source to our file along with the variable '$join'. This variable is set to the value '|' if any of the checkboxes are defined, so that if there is more than one answer, the resulting labels will be separated by |.

To put this another way, if the variable '$in{Advertisement}' is defined, the user has indicated that they heard about the book from an advertisement. We print '$join' and 'Advertisement' to the data file, so that if a previous box was checked, '$join' will be defined as '|' and the two values will be separated by this character. The vertical line character was chosen for human- and machine readability when the data is parsed for a summary report.

After writing the label to the data file we define '$join' to '|' so that, if 'Advertisement' is the first checkbox the user selected, the dividing line is now in place so any further checkbox values will print properly.

The final piece of this input-handling code widget must handle any write-in specifics on the user's form; that is, when the user checks 'Other' and then types the specific source into the text entry field. We check for the existence of a value in the variables associated with those text fields and, if a value exists, add it to the data file, surrounded by parentheses:

```
print REGISTER "\nLiked: $in{liked}\nWould Change: $in{change}\nComments:
$in{comments}";
```

```
print REGISTER "\nComputer Books Purchased Per Year: $in{compnumb}\nSkill
level: $in{compskil}\n";
```

Here, three free-form text areas are printed as-is to the data file, and two radio button inputs are dumped directly to the file. Radio-button answers are handled differently from checkbox answers, since they are single choice only. They don't require any of the fancy state-testing or text concatenation of the "check all that apply" questions:

```
print REGISTER "Type of Computer used: ";
if ($in{DOS}) {
    print REGISTER "${join}DOS";
    $join = "|";
}

if ($in{Windows}) {
    print REGISTER "${join}Windows";
    $join = "|";
}

if ($in{OS/2}) {
    print REGISTER "${join}OS/2";
    $join = "|";
}

if ($in{Macintosh}) {
    print REGISTER "${join}Macintosh";
    $join = "|";
}
```

```
if ($in{Other}) {
   print REGISTER "${join}Other";
   $join = "|";
}

if ($in{other}) {
   print REGISTER " ($in{otherpc})";
}

$join = "";
```

Another multiple-answer question is handled, complete with type-in answers. It is worth noting that the '$join' variable is cleared between questions that will be using it. This is to avoid a situation where the first answer to a given question is preceded by an unnecessary | because it was used by a previous question.

Our next fragment takes care of the remaining multiple-answer questions:

```
print REGISTER "\n";

print REGISTER "Interested in: ";

if ($in{WordProc}) {
   print REGISTER "Word Processing";
   $join = "|";
}

if ($in{WordProcNm}) {
   print REGISTER " ($in{WordProcNm})"
}

if ($in{Spreadsheets}) {
   print REGISTER "${join}Spreadsheets";
   $join = "|";
}

if ($in{SpreadsheetsNm}) {
   print REGISTER " ($in{SpreadsheetsNm})"
}

if ($in{Databases}) {
   print REGISTER "${join}Data bases";
   $join = "|";
}

if ($in{DatabasesNm}) {
   print REGISTER " ($in{DatabasesNm})"
}
```

```
if ($in{Desktop}) {
   print REGISTER "${join}Desktop Publishing";
   $join = "|";
}

if ($in{DesktopNm}) {
   print REGISTER " ($in{DesktopNm})"
}

if ($in{FileUtil}) {
   print REGISTER "${join}File Utilities";
   $join = "|";
}

if ($in{FileUtilNm}) {
   print REGISTER " ($in{FileUtilNm})"
}

if ($in{MoneyMng}) {
   print REGISTER "${join}Money Management";
   $join = "|";
}

if ($in{MoneyMngNm}) {
   print REGISTER " ($in{MoneyMngNm})"
}

if ($in{Networking}) {
   print REGISTER "${join}Networking";
   $join = "|";
}

if ($in{NetworkingNm}) {
   print REGISTER " ($in{NetworkingNm})"
}

if ($in{ProgLang}) {
   print REGISTER "${join}Programming Languages";
   $join = "|";
}

if ($in{ProgLangNm}) {
   print REGISTER " ($in{ProgLangNm})"
}

if ($in{Other}) {
   print REGISTER "${join}Other";
   $join = "|";
}

if ($in{other}) {
   print REGISTER " ($in{other})"
}

$join = "";
```

This tortuous fragment is for one question with many options, each with a text area in which a user could specify his or her interest by name. Generally this kind of mixed-mode, multiple-answer form is not recommended when you need to do back-end parsing of this type.

But in this case, the form was meant to duplicate the format for the printed registration card included in the actual book, and it arrived as a *fait accompli*. If you're designing a form and the back-end at the same time, we recommend that you consider ways to control the user's input more closely.

In the next section, we handle the user's computer-usage profile:

```
print REGISTER "\nUses a PC at:\t";

    if ($in{PCHome}) {
       print REGISTER "Home";
       $join = "|";
    }

    if ($in{PCWork}) {
       print REGISTER "${join}Work";
       $join = "|";
    }

    if ($in{PCSchool}) {
       print REGISTER "${join}School";
       $join = "|";
    }

    if ($in{PCOther}) {
       print REGISTER "${join}Other";
       $join = "|";
    }

    if ($in{PCOtherNm}) {
       print REGISTER " ($in{PCOtherNm})"
    }

    ${join} = "";

    print REGISTER "\nPreferred Disks:\t";

     if ($in{525}) {
       print REGISTER "5.25";
       $join = "|";
    }

    if ($in{35}) {
       print REGISTER "${join}3.5";
       $join = "|";
    }
```

```
if ($in{DiskOther}) {
    print REGISTER "${join}Other";
    $join = "|";
}

if ($in{DiskOtherSize}) {
    print REGISTER " ($in{DiskOtherSize})"
}
```

We're on the home stretch. The last three single-answer questions can be printed directly to the data file as-is. The contact information will also be printed directly, with the exception of the three address fields, which must be printed on a single line, separated by colons:

```
print REGISTER "\nHas a CD-ROM:\t$in{CDROM}\n";

print REGISTER "Plans to buy or upgrade computer hardware this
year:\t$in{Hardware}\n";

print REGISTER "Plans to buy or upgrade computer software this
year:\t$in{Software}\n";

print REGISTER  "Name: $in{Name}\n";

print REGISTER  "Business Title: $in{Bustitle}\n";
print REGISTER  "Type of Business: $in{TypeBus}\n";
print REGISTER  "$in{AddrLoc} Address:
$in{Addr1}:$in{Addr2}:$in{CSZ}:$in{Country}\n";
    if ($in{QuoteMe} eq "on") {
        $quote = "Yes";
    }
    else {
        $quote = "No";
    }
    print REGISTER  "Agrees to be quoted: $quote\n";
    print REGISTER  "Daytime phone number: $in{DayPhone}\n";
    print REGISTER
"===========================================================\n\n";
    close (REGISTER);
```

CLOSING ARGUMENTS

Finally, we're done with the form! If the quote button is on, we note explicitly that the user agrees to be quoted, and if it's off, we note that instead. The entry in the data file is capped off with a line of equal signs as a record delimiter, which aids parsing the file later on when we're summarizing the data.

It's also worth mentioning that the unbuffering of our data performed at the beginning of the script only applies to the default file handle. This is *stdout()*, unless explicitly changed in the script. In other words, any print statements that do not specify a file handle go to the default, *stdout()*, and are not buffered. Those that do specify a file handle, like our print statements directed at REGISTER, will still be buffered. We don't have to worry about losing data, however, since we are explicitly closing the file handle after writing data to it. This flushes any buffers that exist before terminating the connection to the file.

All that remains is to acknowledge the user's registration and close our <HTML> tag. The browser should now notify the user in some way that the document is finished loading — usually some kind of "Document done" message — and the user is free to move on to another page:

```
print "<H2>Thanks for your registration information!</H2>";
print "<ADDRESS>Registration form CGI by
singe@outer.net<P>$date</ADDRESS></HTML>";
}
```

DEBUGGING IS A STATE OF MIND

When developing this CGI, we took a few steps to aid in debugging. The most basic of these was to run the script from the command line, invoking Perl with the *-w* flag, to make sure it could compile and execute the script and return the proper "must be called from a form" error message.

If we needed to test beyond this stage, we would have to modify our script slightly. A CGI script called "handleforms.pl" is available as a companion piece to "formlib.pl". It can be called in a FORM ACTION tag and will return the values for all the input fields in your form. Similar test CGIs exist for nearly every library used to extract data from forms. This helps to avoid the environment variable assignment problem we discussed at the beginning of the chapter and makes a developer's life much easier.

What is more useful is to convert such a CGI into a Perl library subroutine that we can call from within our script. By stripping out the portion of the code that parses the form data, making the data summary code a procedure by wrapping it in sub <name> {}, and making the last line read simply 1; this is fairly easy to accomplish. Save the resulting script under a different name, "debugforms.pl" perhaps, and you're ready to use it in your script.

In our registration CGI, if we wanted to use the debug code and we had named the subroutine debug, we'd include the following lines near the top of the script:

```
require "debugforms.pl";
&debug;
```

This approach lets us keep an eye on our data, comparing our expectations to what we actually get. Another method that produces similar results is to use *tail* to watch what's being written to the "registrations" file as it's being written, like this:

```
tail -f registrations
```

We can even background this task and continue to edit or configure from the shell. Whenever the script is run and data written to the file, we'll see it on-screen.

Finally, you might want to consider redirecting *stderr( )*, where any runtime errors will show up. Usually *stderr( )* is equivalent to *stdout( )*, but in the case of CGIs, *stderr( )* ends up assigned to a null device (i.e., you can't read its contents), unless you explicitly direct it somewhere useful. Here's an example:

```
open (STDERR, ">>/tmp/CGI.errors");
```

This file can also be *tail*ed to keep an eye on it.

The Raw Data File

The file produced by the collective output of the registration form is, in and of itself, a database of our registered readers. We could browse this file to look at the data directly. If we did, this is what we'd see:

```
Overall Rating: VG
Heard from:    Other (Wrote it!)
Liked: The endearing sense of humor regarding the importance of DTDs and
validation.
Would Change: Update for final 2.0 DTD, then for 3.0 DTD.
Comments:
Computer Books Purchased Per Year: plus10
Skill level: Professional
Type of Computer used: DOS, Windows, Other
Interested in: Networking (CGI, TCP/IP, NetBIOS), Programming Languages
(Perl, Tcl/Tk, Java), Other
Uses a PC at:   Home, Work
Preferred Disks:   3.5
Has a CD-ROM:   Yes
Plans to buy or upgrade computer hardware this year:   Yes
Plans to buy or upgrade computer software this year:   Yes
Name: Ed Tittel
Business Title: Principal
Type of Business: Network consulting & writing
Work Address: 5810 Lookout Mountain Drive:Austin, TX 78731-3618:USA
Agrees to be quoted: Yes
Daytime phone number: 512-452-3768
================================================================
```

This might be useful to get a general sense of our readership, but it isn't useful at all if we want to get a precise picture of our respondents' answers to our questions. This is where statistics come in.

Registration Statistics Summarizer

To get any useful information out of the registration data file as a whole, we'll need to develop a tool that can understand its data, compile results, and present us with a summary report. Happily, text parsing and twiddling was Perl's original purpose, so we can stay in the same development environment that we used for the CGI.

The basic model for the report generator is to collate the entries made in a given month and to count the number of occurrences of each answer for each question. Once the entire data file is processed, we'll know the total number of respondents and can calculate the distribution percentages for each answer.

So, without further ado, here's the initial chunk of report writer code:

```
#!/usr/local/bin/perl
#
# reggie-reporter.pl
# singe@outer.net
# 1.0 6/23/95
#
# registration report generator for HTML for Dummies Web site.
# run once a month from cron, generates summary report.
#
```

The preceding should look familiar by now, including the magic shell invocation for Perl and the script's name, author, date, and description.

The next line uses Perl's ability to dip into the UNIX shell with back quotes to run a utility program and grab its output. In this case the utility is *date*, which we're using to get today's date in the form "06.23.95" and assign it to the variable '$date':

```
chop ($date = `/bin/date '+%m.%d.%y'`); # get today's date for date stamp

# first we'll move the current registration data aside, to freeze it for our
reporting.

rename ("/www/httpdocs/html4dum/data/registrations",
"/www/httpdocs/html4dum/data/registrations.$date");

# open raw registration data file
open (RAW, "/www/httpdocs/html4dum/data/registrations.$date") || die "Can't
open registration data!";

# open files to write comments and contact information to
open (COMMENTS, ">> /www/httpdocs/html4dum/data/comments");
open (CONTACT, ">> /www/httpdocs/html4dum/data/contacts");


print COMMENTS "$date\n"; # print date stamp to contact and comment
print CONTACT "$date\n";  # files

while (<RAW>) {


    if (/^=+$/) { # new registration begins on a line of equals

        $reg_count++;  # count another registrant

        print CONTACT "\n";
        # end contact info for previous registrant
```

We're reading through the raw data file now, counting each registrant by the number of lines of equal signs encountered. The meat of the script comes next, with a long series of **elseif** statements testing the current line of the data file for the presence of our field names:

```
} elsif (/^Overall Rating:\s*([a-zA-Z]*)/) {
    $rating{$1}++;
```

The preceding code fragment handles a typical field with a single value. The field name is recognized by the beginning of the regular expression, or *regex*, and the field's value is captured by the wildcard expression in the parentheses. The wildcard portion of the regular expression very precisely matches zero or more lower- or uppercase letters that follow the space or spaces after the colon.

Once matched, the matching text is automatically placed into the variable '$1'. Perl does this because the matching text is enclosed in parentheses. Finally, we increment an associative array using the field value as a key. We'll create a new associative array for each question as we find it, to keep track of the answers recorded in the log:

```
} elsif (/^Heard from:\s*(.*)/) {
    @answers = split ('\|', $1);

    foreach $item (@answers) { #count each check box
        $item =~ s/\s*\((.*)\)\s*//;

        if ($item =~ /([a-zA-Z]+)/) {
        # if it contains data, count it.
            $heard{$item}++;
        }
    }
```

This widget differs from the previous ones because it is looking for a field that may have multiple values. We capture that field's value or values in the same way as with the single value field. Once the variable '$1' is populated with our captured value, its contents are placed in the array '@answers'. It is placed in the array using the function **split**, which divides the scalar value of a variable into a list suitable to assign it to an array. We're using the character | as our divider, since, as you remember, we used it to divide multiple answers in the registration CGI.

Equipped with our array, filled with as many answers as the user provided for this question field, we now step through this array using the **foreach** command, placing each element in the variable '$item' as we go along. Next we strip off any specifics — the values typed in by the

user and enclosed in parentheses in our data. This is accomplished using
another regular expression operator, this one the substitution modifier,
invoked in the line:

```
$item =~ s/\s*\(.*\)//;
```

Here the =~ operator signals Perl that we will be searching the variable '$item' using a regular expression. The **s** modifier before the begin-
ning of the regular expression indicates that we will be changing the
data matched in the first part of the following regex. The regex then
begins, matching any data surrounded by parentheses and substituting it
with the data in the part of the regex between the middle and last /, in
this case, nothing. In this one operation, we have efficiently sliced off
any extra spaces and parenthetical data.

Why have we discarded this extra data? The free-form nature of data
typed in directly by any number of registrants is beyond the scope of
this script's parsing and reporting abilities. For the time being, we focus
only on quantifiable data whose values fall within defined ranges.

Now trimmed down, the variable '$item' is next examined in an if
statement to see if it contains any data. If it passes the test, we increment a pair in the associative array for this question, here named with
'$item' as the key:

```
} elsif (/^Liked:/) {
   print COMMENTS $_
} elsif (/^Would Change:/) {
   print COMMENTS $_
} elsif (/^Comments:/) {
   print COMMENTS $_
```

These three free-form text fields are separated out to the comments
file as raw data. The rationale for duplicating this is to build a summary
of these answers or for any future data processing that may be required.
In other words, since we acquired the data so laboriously, we don't
want to lose it!

The script continues in this manner for the remainder of the input
fields, alternating between parsing single-answer and multiple-answer
fields:

```
} elsif (/Computer Books Purchased Per Year: ([a-zA-Z0-9]*)/) {
   $booksbought{$1}++
```

```
} elsif (/^Skill level: ([a-zA-Z0-9]*)/) {
    $skill{$1}++
} elsif (/^Type of Computer used: (.*)/) {
    @answers = split ('\|', $1);
    foreach $item  (@answers) { #count each check box
        $item =~ s/\s*\(.*\)//;

        if ($item =~ /[a-zA-Z]+/) {
            $computerused{$item}++;
        }
    }
}
```

We'll spare you the gory details, but the original script is on the CD. The next portion of the script that we'll look at includes some special attention for the contact information:

```
} elsif (/^Name:\s*(.*)/) {
    print CONTACT $1, ":";

    } elsif (/^Business Title:\s*(.*)/) {
        print CONTACT $1, ":";

    } elsif (/^Type of Business:\s*(.*)/) {
        print CONTACT $1, ":";

    } elsif (/^Home Address:\s*(.*)/) {
        print CONTACT "Home:$1:"

    } elsif (/^Business Address:\s*(.*)/) {
        print CONTACT "Business:$1:"

    } elsif (/^Agrees to be quoted:\s*(.*)/) {
        if ($1 =~ /Yes/) {
            $quote = 1;
            print CONTACT "Likes the book:";
        }

    } elsif (/^Daytime phone number: ([0-9\(\)\- ]+)/ && $quote) {
        print CONTACT $1, ":"
    }

} # end while
```

All the registrant's contact data is printed to a single line in a separate file. The resulting file is more suitable for a contact database with colon-delimited values and one person per line:

```
close CONTACT;
close COMMENTS;
```

```
# now we summarize stats collected above

open (REPORT, "> /www/httpdocs/html4dum/data/report.$date");
select REPORT;
# make it stdout, so we don't have to keep typing in the file handle
```

We open the file handle to the report in preparation for the actual statistics code. We then use the **select** function to make this file handle our default output. This makes naming the file handle after every print statement unnecessary. It also makes it easier to debug the script during development, since you can comment out two lines (the **open** and **select** statements), and the report will print to STDOUT.

Now we get ready to print the actual stats:

```
print " Registration Summary Report for HTML for Dummies\n",
      "===================================================\n\n",
      "Total number of respondents for month ending $date: $reg_count\n";
```

Remember, '$reg_count' is from the number of lines of equal signs we encountered and represents the number of registrants who have submitted data. Next we'll revisit each of the associative arrays that contain the answers encountered and the frequency for each of those answers, like this:

```
print "Overall Rating:\n———-\n";
%question = %rating;
&collate_and_staple;

print "\nHeard From:\n———\n";
%question = %heard;
&collate_and_staple;
```

What's happening here is that we're printing a heading for each question, assigning the question's associative array to a common array name, and then calling a subroutine. The reason we use this kludge to pass the associative array to the subroutine is that Perl stores parameters passed to a subroutine in a regular array, which destroys the associative array.

We'll skip the rest of the questions, since they all follow the pattern for the two shown above and go right to the statistical powerhouse at the heart of this script:

```
sub collate_and_staple {
# take data in an associative array (passed as parameter) and
# calculate frequency and percentage of each answer.
```

```
foreach $category (sort keys(%question)) {
  $percent =  sprintf ("%.2f",$question{$category}/$reg_count*100);
  printf ("%-30s%10d%10s%%)\n",$category.":",$question{$category},
    "(".$percent);
      }
}
```

This subroutine is what each subroutine passes through. It uses the **foreach** control structure like that used to step through the arrays earlier. This time, however, we use it to step through an associative array, so we need to specify that we want the 'keys' for the array, rather than the values. We also add the operator **sort** so that we retrieve the keys in alphabetical order. Each key is stored in the variable '$category'.

The next line uses the **sprintf** function, or formatted string print. Perl borrowed this construct from C, and it behaves the way it would in that language. Its formatting rules form the bedrock for the philosophy that underlies every aspect of C, and as such are beyond the scope of our present discussion. Suffice it to say that here the function is used to take the calculated percentage of the total number of respondents who gave this answer and chop it down to two decimal points.

Finally, we use **printf**, a close relative of **sprintf**, to output the name of the answer, the number of times it occurred in the data file, and the percentage of respondents who answered this way.

The final bit of the script simply cleans up and mails the finished report out to all interested parties:

```
close REPORT;
unlink ("/www/httpdocs/html4dum/data/registrations.LCK");

open (MAIL, "| /usr/bin/mailx -s 'HTML Summary Report' html4dum");
open (REPORT, "/www/httpdocs/html4dum/data/report.$date");
while (<REPORT>) { print MAIL }
close MAIL;
close REPORT;
```

File handles are marvelously flexible: in this script alone, we've used them to read data from a file, to write out to a brand new file, to append data to an existing file, and here, to pipe data to a UNIX *mail* program. (Just thought we'd point that out.)

THE FINAL OUTPUT

When complete, the form looks like this:

```
Registration Summary Report for HTML for Dummies
======================================================

Total number of respondents for month ending 06.24.95: 10
Overall Rating:
--------

G:                                   2      (20.00%)
VG:                                  8      (80.00%)


Heard From:
------

Other:                               7      (70.00%)
Review:                              1      (10.00%)
Word of mouth:                       1      (10.00%)


Computer Books Purchased Per Year:
--------------------

2to5:                                3      (30.00%)
6to10:                               3      (30.00%)
plus10:                              4      (40.00%)


Skill level:
-------

Advanced:                            4      (40.00%)
Intermediate:                        1      (10.00%)
Professional:                        5      (50.00%)


Type of Computer used:
---------

DOS:                                 6      (60.00%)
Macintosh:                           3      (30.00%)
Other:                               7      (70.00%)
Windows:                             9      (90.00%)
```

It continues on in this way for a while, but we won't bore you with
the whole thing. Note that the percentages can add up to more or less
than 100%, since they reflect the percentage of respondents, not
responses, to a given question. A given question can get 30 answers
from 15 users or 10 from 20.

Final Touches

Once both the scripts have been tested, they can be turned loose on the world. The CGI should reside in the "cgi-bin" directory, and the path as called from the registration Web form verified. The report script could live anywhere, since it uses absolute paths to get to its data. We chose to place it in the same directory as the data itself, so that no one will stumble across it, wonder what it's meant to do, and remove it.

The permissions would have to be set properly, with the CGI as world-executable, and the report writer as whatever you see fit. Once again, we chose to make it owned by *root* and only executable by the owner, to keep meddling fingers away.

The final step in installing the scripts is to add a *crontab* entry for *root* so that the report generator, here named "reggie-reporter.pl", automatically gets run at the end of each month.

What's Next?

Whenever you complete a forms-based system like this, you will inevitably think of five new enhancements or features that the system needs. One that should be a given whenever dealing with Web forms is an alternative for those without forms-capable browsers. Thus, our next priority is to develop a way for the user to retrieve a text-only template of our registration form (this is covered in Chapter 16). Graphically challenged users could then fill out the text-based form equivalent using a text editor, and e-mail it in. A cousin of the CGI and the report writer could intercept these responses based on the mail's address or subject, parse the data, and add it to the registrations file.

Second, after a couple months of operation we'd probably want to see statistics not only on the previous month's registrants, but also on all the data we've collected to that point. Once again, an adaptation of "reggie-reporter.pl" could be developed and pressed into action, with perhaps the core code for the original transformed into a procedure that is called first for the past month, and then on a file that represents the total history for all registrations.

Summary

When it comes to implementing specifications, there's no substitute for experience. That's why we recommend that you build a few throwaway programs if you're a CGI beginner or if you're changing from one language to another. The more practice you get in handling CGI input; performing operations on the data; and building output for users, programs, and data-gathering, the better you'll be able to handle the rigors of production code when that becomes necessary!

CHAPTER 11

Testing and Installing CGI Applications

*T*he design of your CGI application describes how the software will satisfy its specifications, usually at several levels of detail. The highest level of detail normally identifies and describes the software's major components. Through a process sometimes called *stepwise refinement*, finer levels evolve to describe each component within the system in glorious detail. For example, a design might describe each component's interface and its required inputs and outputs. As a result of this process, a detailed design document — an artifact of the software life cycle — will be produced.

When a design is more or less complete, implementation follows. During this phase of the software life cycle, the specification for the software gets turned into code. At this point also, the development effort may be divided among individuals or teams who will take responsibility for the implementation of individual software components, usually called *subsystems* by their developers.

Although each subsystem is normally tested at this stage of development, overall product testing to ensure that all implemented components function correctly within the system is not performed until those components are assembled into a complete system. Thus, testing of a complete system is initiated only after the entire system has been implemented. The point at which all the individual subsystems are combined into a total system is often called the *integration phase*.

The integration phase joins all subsystems into a single system that must be determined to work properly. Normally this proceeds in incremental steps, where a particular subsystem is treated as the core component and tested thoroughly by itself. Then, as each subsequent subsystem gets integrated with the growing collection of subsystems, the resulting collection is tested and debugged. Eventually, after all the subsystems and components have been fused together, the system is tested as a whole.

It's a Dirty Job, but...

The least glamorous phase in the software life cycle is testing. Testing is tedious and can appear uninteresting, yet it is essential to the delivery of a properly functioning system. Only after a successful conclusion of the testing process can you begin the last and final step of the development process: the installation of your CGI application onto your production server, where it can be accessed by your user community.

Once you've caught and killed all the bugs in your CGI application, you might decide it's time to install it. But wait, there's more to testing than making the code work — and certainly more than just getting it to compile and run!

Once the code appears to be working, you'll still need to test its input and output behavior. You not only want to make sure that it provides the right output when handed the right input, but that it can deal with "wrong" input as well.

In this chapter, you'll learn how to thoroughly test your CGI applications in a non-production test environment and why this is a good idea. You'll also learn what defines good and bad data, and how to write a simple test plan. Once these testing requirements are fully met, only then can you finally install your CGI applications onto your production Web.

Setting Up a Test Environment

It's always a good idea to test your CGI applications in a "test Web." This allows you to tweak your CGI code unobtrusively, without the public breathing down your neck.

Modifying CGI applications that affect your production Web can be dangerous and painful. Here's why: if you introduce errors into your CGI application in a production Web, you could render your CGI-dependent form inoperative. This could easily confuse your users; worse, it could make them exceedingly unhappy and might even drive them away.

We've learned from experience that 99% of all unhappy users will fill out your Web's comment form with objections, whining, and complaints, compared to the 1% of happy users who send compliments. If you develop your CGI applications out of your users' sight, you can avoid many of the causes of unhappiness. This is where the concept of a test Web comes in really handy.

THE TEST WEB IS THE BEST WEB!

A test Web can be a small Web that exhibits the same behavior and structure as your production Web, but is not publicly accessible. Regardless of your server's operating system, the best way to test CGI applications is to create and modify them in your test Web. Only when they pass your test plan should they be installed onto your production Web server, where they'll be available to the browsing public.

The rest of this section assumes that you are able to install your own test Web. If you can't install a test server yourself, ask your local Web-Master if your system already has a test Web. If not, you might set up a personal CGI directory where only you can execute the programs it contains. Either approach results in creating a good place to test CGI applications before they're used by the outside world.

The example we'll use for the remainder of this chapter contains some UNIX-specific details. This is as much due to the maturity of UNIX servers (which in our opinion still far surpass the others) as it is to the fact that all of the authors use UNIX-based Web servers. But this is not meant to belittle the considerable capabilities of Mac, Windows, and OS/2 servers. The example program we're testing here is taken from an online book registration form used for another book written by several of this book's authors. If you care to follow along, its URL is:

```
http://www.outer.net/html4dum/registrn.html
```

INSTALLING A TEST SERVER

Setting up your test Web is much easier than you think. Jay Weber at EIT has created a forms-based "Webmaster Starter Kit" that builds a UNIX-based WWW server for you. It's as easy as filling in the form. For more information about this service, see this URL:

```
http://wsk.eit.com/wsk/doc/
```

This service does not require you to have root access or privileges on your target system. This makes it easy for you to install your very own test Web. The only constraint you should honor is to establish the communications port for your test Web's HTTP listener on a port greater than 1024. In the UNIX world, applications — like your test HTTP server — that use port addresses greater than 1025 are not required to run as *root*. A typical port number for a test server is 8001.

Using our registration form on the *www.outer.net* machine as an example, let's compare a production URL:

```
http://www.outer.net/html4dum/registrn.html
```

to a URL on our test server:

```
http://www.outer.net:8001/html4dum/registrn.html
```

Notice the resemblance between these two URLs. The clue that the second URL connects to a test Web is the explicit port address of 8001. Remember, the default port number for UNIX HTTP servers is port 80; if your server listens on this port, its number can be omitted from the URL. If you don't advertise that port 8001 is active to your users, you can generally develop CGI applications out of the public eye, and therefore, out of the line of fire.

Please notice another thing — that both the production server and the test server run on the same machine. One of UNIX's strengths is its ability to execute and manage multiple processes on a single machine.

Another approach to building a test server might be to install it on a different machine. But this can create some logistical difficulties. If the two machines aren't able to mount each other's file systems, moving files between them will require *ftp,* or worse, "sneaker net." In the same vein, mirroring a production Web is not nearly as manageable as using symbolic links on the same machine. Therefore, to simplify our example, both the production and test servers will be on the same machine.

Once you have successfully installed your new test Web server, the next thing to do is to mirror the desired portions of your production Web structure that you will be manipulating. In a UNIX environment, this is best done using symbolic links from your test Web to your production Web. We recommend that you mirror those parts of the production Web space that are common to all HTML documents in your Web. This includes things like directories of icons, which may include graphical dividers, bullets, and warnings, but should also include frequently used elements like boilerplate information and copyright or license agreements.

Symbolic Links

Here's a quick lesson on symbolic links: a link's source is listed first followed by the target in the *ln -s* UNIX command. For instance, this UNIX command (the *%* is the command-line prompt for UNIX):

```
% ln -s /www/docs/images/*.gif .
```

creates a symbolic link from all the GIF images in the directory "/www/docs/images" to the current UNIX working directory. It could have also been specified as:

```
% ln -s /www/docs/images/*.gif /www/test/images/
```

To link to an entire directory, you would enter:

```
% ln -s /www/docs/images/ /www/test/images/
```

which creates a symbolic link from the "/www/docs/images/" directory to the "/www/test/images/" directory. Using this approach will let you grab all of the elements you need (but don't plan to change) from your production Web without having to create extra copies.

THE ROOT OF ALL TESTING

To continue the installation of our example registration form in our test Web, we need to specify the 'DocumentRoot' for the test server. This needs to be different from the production Web's document root. If it's not, you will create filename collisions and you will not remain insulated from the general public.

For example, on an NCSA HTTP server, you must specify a path in your file system that represents the root for all HTML documents and associated objects whose value the server will return upon request. Any HTML document requested outside the scope of this document root will be refused by the server. This protects system directories and files outside the document tree from prying eyes.

If we look at the document root specification for the production Web, we'd see something like:

```
DocumentRoot   /www/docs/
```

This specifies that if you open a URL like:

```
http://www.outer.net/
```

for this site without specifying a specific HTML document, you can rely on the server to append a default HTML filename to that URL, and the server will map this logical request to a physical path in the file system:

```
/www/docs/index.html
```

Likewise, opening this URL:

```
http://www.outer.net/hypertext/images/GTO.gif
```

will be mapped to a physical path of:

```
/www/docs/hypertext/images/GTO.gif
```

by the server. The underlying HTTP GET request for this file actually looks like this:

```
GET /hypertext/images/GTO.gif HTTP/1.0
*** blank line here ***
```

This GET request retrieves the following data:

```
GET / HTTP/1.0
*** blank line here ***
```

That's correct, the root symbol / is equivalent to the physical file "/www/docs/index.html". The / indicates to the server that it should retrieve the default HTML filename at the document root.

We've set the document root on our test server to:

```
DocumentRoot  /www/test/
```

so a comparison of the two document roots would look like this:

```
DocumentRoot  /www/docs/   # Production server
DocumentRoot  /www/test/   # Test server
```

Because physical file mappings are controlled by the document root for each server, this avoids filename contention and filename collisions that would inevitably result in damage to production HTML documents.

AN ALIAS BY ANY OTHER NAME

Next, we need to specify the script alias for the test server. This is an alias that a WWW client uses to reference CGI applications in a particular physical location on the server. This alias allows the server administrator to hide where actual applications reside in the file system. It's not only a good security measure for CGIs, but it can protect the rest of the file system from compromise as well.

For instance, following the NCSA server conventions, the production server's script alias could be specified as:

```
ScriptAlias  /cgi-bin/  /www/cgi-bin/
```

This specifies that if a client submits a URL like:

```
http://www.outer.net/cgi-bin/register.pl
```

the server will actually call the "/www/cgi-bin/register.pl" CGI application. The alias is mapped to the physical location in the server's file system indicated by the final argument in the *ScriptAlias* command.

Our test server actually specifies its script alias as follows:

```
ScriptAlias  /cgi-bin/  /www/test-cgi-bin/
```

Using this specification, a URL like:

```
http://www.outer.net:8001/cgi-bin/register.pl
```

would call a CGI application named "register.pl" in the test CGI area on the test server ("/www/test-cgi-bin/register.pl").

Comparing the two script alias specifications for the test and production servers, you'd see the following:

```
ScriptAlias  /cgi-bin/  /www/cgi-bin/       # Production server
ScriptAlias  /cgi-bin/  /www/test-cgi-bin/  # Test server
```

Even though the test CGI directory uses the same URL as the production CGI directory, the test server maps that alias to a different directory. Here again we avoid filename collisions, yet keep our environments distinct. This is the real benefit of symbolic links: they allow you to reference distinct environments by changing pointers to the file system (aliases) rather than changing HTML code or CGI programs. Ultimately this makes life simpler and reduces the chances of introducing errors in the changeover from testing to production modes.

Sometimes you may have to create symbolic links from the test area to the production area. For example, you may need to link the "/www/test-cgi-bin/register.pl" file to the production CGI application "/www/cgi-bin/register.pl". This is acceptable when the "register.pl" application is required by another CGI application you are testing and modifying, but you should always proceed with caution when exposing elements of your test environment to the production environment.

As a rule of thumb, it's only safe to make symbolic links from the test to the production environment for documents and programs that are required but will not be modified. If you ever need to modify one of these items, you can simply remove the symbolic link and make a physical copy of the file to the test area. You could then proceed to alter the test copy without affecting the production version (which is now separate and distinct).

THE ACT OF CREATION IS BEST DONE IN PRIVATE

When you first create a CGI application or an HTML document, always do it in its respective test area. These areas should therefore be used for incremental development, as well as for maintenance.

To perform maintenance on our "register.pl" CGI application, for example, we would begin by copying the source code from the production CGI area to the test area. If a source code management system is part of your development environment, you should check out the latest version of the application and then copy it to the test area. For our examples, we'll assume a CVS source code system is deployed.

We'll also assume that some maintenance is required on the "register.pl" CGI application. The next step in the process is to check out the latest version of the application from the CVS repository. Once this is accomplished, we'd then copy the source code to the test area.

From examination of the source code, we realize that a Perl library will be required. To make this available during testing, we create a symbolic link to the required library which is named "formlib.pl". Thus, if we use the UNIX command *ls -la* to obtain a long listing of the test CGI directory "/www/test-cgi-bin/", we'd see one file and one symbolic link, as follows:

```
lrwxrwxrwx 1 www formlib.pl -> /www/cgi-bin/formlib.pl
-rwxr-xr-x 1 www register.pl
```

Now we can begin modifications to "register.pl". But first, a few words about source code management...

Once our application has been completely and successfully tested, it can then be checked into our source code control system. We strongly suggest that you use a source code control system to manage versions of your CGI applications, especially if you have more than a handful of them to manage. This confers many benefits, the most notable of which is *version control*. While a discussion of version control is outside the scope of this book, suffice it to say that such control makes sure that the most current, tested version of a program or document is what users see, rather than some mistakenly grabbed older version or some untested version still in the development process.

Source Code Repository Automatic Installation into Your Web

A useful application of a source code management system is to instruct it to automatically install all WWW objects, such as CGI applications or HTML documents, into the production Web once any such object has been checked into the repository. This guarantees that all objects are under some control.

This technique is particularly interesting if the source code management system can execute other applications as well.

For instance, a CVS could also validate an HTML file with an SGML parser once that file is committed to its repository. Not until the document is valid (that is, it parses successfully), will the HTML document be placed into the production Web. This guarantees that the production Web only contains valid HTML documents, without requiring a human being to remember to manually perform a validation step for each file checked into the CVS system.

The Good, the Bad, and the Boundary

What constitutes good CGI data? Bad CGI data? It is dependent on the type of data, its intended use, and how it is specified by the user. If you provide the user with a hypertext link like:

```
http://www.search.org/cgi-bin/search?moe+larry+curly
```

your CGI application should not require any extensive testing since the HTML author carefully crafted this URL. On the other hand, for forms data, this is a different story.

Forms allow users to input data into widgets where some have restricted input like a CHECKBOX input widget while others will cheerfully accept any printable characters, as in TEXT input widgets or TEXTAREAs. This type of input needs to be checked for omission or invalid characters.

For instance, if you'd like users to input their phone numbers, you'd expect the widget's value string to include digits and possibly a couple of - (hyphen) characters or even a pair of parentheses. You would not expect characters such as [A -Z]. It's a good idea to check the input to make sure your expectations are met! Users don't always follow the rules, and they might even sometimes take advantage of your poor form's gullible nature...

In our registration CGI, "register.pl", we have numerous input widgets that need checking. Let's look at the very last TEXT input labeled **My daytime phone number is:**. The HTML markup for this widget is:

```
My daytime phone number is: <INPUT TYPE="text" NAME="DayPhone" SIZE="30">
```

On the client side, there is no way to check the value of the 'DayPhone' variable; this must occur on the server side. The only restriction the client can enforce is the SIZE or number of characters shown in the input widget — namely, the width of the rendered widget may be only 30 characters wide. If the user enters more characters, the text area scrolls right as characters are input.

Don't confuse this with the MAXLENGTH attribute of <INPUT> that restricts the number of characters allowable in an input widget. In this case, the user can only enter up 30 characters. The SIZE and MAXLENGTH attributes do not need to be equal in value but if SIZE is less than MAXLENGTH, all data entered scrolls right until the number of characters equals the MAXLENGTH. If SIZE is greater than MAXLENGTH, the widget accepts only up to MAXLENGTH number of characters and the rest of the widget is left unused.

Data boundaries can be set for each type of form widget. For checkboxes and radio buttons, this point is moot because they are either checked or not. But for INPUT elements, users can enter any printable characters into the widget through their keyboard. One way to establish data boundaries is to evaluate the type of data input into the widget.

Here's an example taken from the registration form:

- text — any printable character
- phone number — [0-9], "-", ".", "(", ")", " "(blank). Here are some examples of expected data:
    ```
    (555) 123-1234
    555.123.1234
    555-123-1234
    555 123 1234
    ```

If there had been text input widgets that expected a pure integer, then you could set a boundary for integer input. For example, if the registration form had asked the user to enter "The number of copies you purchased", you would expect this integer to be greater than 1. This is our first boundary (the lower bound).

The second boundary (the upper bound) is a little more difficult. Your widget could handle anything up to the maximum value your specific operating system can handle, or you could put an artificial limit on it, say 5000. But the odds of someone buying 5000 copies is small, so you might want to set it even lower.

At this point, you've established a lower and upper bound on the integer input into this widget. Now your CGI application that handles the form can check the value of the 'number-of-copies' variable for boundary errors.

A Simple Test Strategy

There are many formal testing techniques and tools used by organizations that design, implement, and sell software products. These tools may or may not be suitable for your system or your site. Often, less formal testing techniques are appropriate, but there's always a tradeoff between the convenience that a tool can supply against its costs and complexity.

A simple and easy method for testing your CGI applications is to develop a test plan, where a simple test plan can be derived directly from your detailed design document. This document will typically contain a description of an application's interface, where the input and output are specified in detail. This information is often sufficient to determine boundary checks, as well as tests for accuracy and correctness (where applicable).

If you don't have a detailed design document, you can still proceed with development of a testing strategy without a written test plan. It is always a good idea to sketch out the steps you plan to run your CGI application through, the boundaries for each input widget, and some sample data.

What follows next is a simple test plan for our "register.pl" CGI application. It is organized for each input widget for the registration form.

TEST PLAN FOR REGISTER.PL CGI APPLICATION

```
Widget name: overrate
Widget type: radio
Test Data:
    Pass:   VG,G,S,F,P


Widget name: Bookstore
Widget type: checkbox
Data boundary:
Test Data:
    Pass: on, NULL

Widget name: BSname
Widget type: text
Data boundary: any printable character
Test Data:
    Pass:
        "test name"
        " test name"
        " test name"
        "\ntest name"
        "\ttest name"
        "\ttest name\n"
        "\ntest name\t"


    Fail:
        "" (NULL)


    Notes:
eliminate preceding and trailing whitespace
issue warning on input of expletive words or phrases
remove any carriage returns
escape any shell metacharacters such as "!", "&", and "|"


Widget name: liked
Widget type: textarea
Data boundary: any printable character
Test Data:
    Pass:
        "This is a test.
         This is a test."
    Fail:
        "" (NULL)
    Notes:
issue warning on input of expletive words or phrases
escape any shell metacharacters such as "!", "&", and "|"


Widget name: DayPhone
Widget type: text
Data boundary: [0-9], ".", "-", "(", ")", " "(space)
Test Data:
```

```
Pass:
  "(555) 123-1234"
  "(555)-123-1234"
  "555-123-1234"
  "555.123.1234"

Fail:
  "(abc) 123-1234"
  "(555)!123_1234"
  "abc-abcd"
  ""  (NULL)
```

With this test plan in hand, a professional tester can run all the necessary data needed for testing through the CGI application. For instance, a test person could enter the specified test data for the **BSname** input widget specified in the plan, including the data that passes and the data that fails.

The tester should record the results for each test. When problems are found, these can be communicated to the CGI applications engineer. A test report should include a detailed description of each failure, the input data that caused or accompanied the failure, and the resulting behavior of the CGI application. This is very important and ensures that the CGI application will be nearly bulletproof by the time testing is concluded.

Installing Your CGI Application

Finally, after coding, debugging, and testing your CGI application, you can go ahead and install your CGI application into your production Web. In most software development companies this is embedded in the "check-in" activity in a CVS system. Here, the check-in task enters a new revision for the source code into a common source code version control system.

Source code management is usually mandated by your institution. It requires a common repository for source code and binary objects that are to be controlled and managed by software. Some typical UNIX source code management systems are the Revision Control System (RCS) and the Concurrent Version System (CVS). Both of these systems track and manage source code and executable objects.

Once the source code for your CGI application has successfully been checked into the source code repository, you can install it. This may be as easy as copying the application to the proper CGI applications directory on your local server, or as difficult as transferring the application from your machine at home to your remote Web server hosted by an Internet Service Provider (ISP).

In either case, make sure that the permissions on the application are suitable. For UNIX applications, this means to make sure the permissions are at least 755 (executable by you, group, and the world). You need only satisfy the server. Most NCSA servers run as *nobody*, a special UNIX user name with limited functionality and access. Check with your local Web server administrator for the correct permissions.

After that, perform one final test to make sure that the installation has been successful. Then — assuming things are working properly — you can stand back and let the world in through your front door!

Summary

Testing applications can be performed by inspection, but we recommend a more formal testing phase accompanied by a test plan. We also recommend that you test your CGI application out of your user's sight, either in an unknown corner of your Web or, better still, in a completely separate test environment. When you're ready to share your work with the world, you can do so with confidence that it will be well behaved and that your code will work as expected!

CHAPTER 12

Our Foundations Development Environment

*T*his chapter briefly documents the development environment that we used to build and test the code for this book. Its purpose is to explain to you what platforms, operating systems, languages, libraries, and tools we used. We'll also discuss some potential stumbling blocks you may encounter as you try to take our work — and the code we include on the CD-ROM — and apply it to your own particular circumstances.

Basic Assumptions

Because we couldn't develop parallel versions of everyone's code that's discussed here (some of which appears on the CD-ROM), we had to make some assumptions about what environment, tools, and programming languages to target for the development efforts and advice you'll find in this book. In the sections that follow, we'll lay out exactly what we assumed, try to explain why we made such outrageous assumptions, and explain how you might take the ideas and capabilities we cover and use them under other circumstances.

For Better or Worse, Our Platform Is UNIX

We'll start this section with our profound and humble apologies to the developers who use a Web server running under OS/2, on some version of Microsoft Windows, or on the Macintosh. In our survey of the current state of the art, we decided that because the overwhelming majority of Web servers in use today run on some form of UNIX, that UNIX would be our target development platform.

If you're running UNIX, you'll be pleased to hear that we tested our code on the following versions or implementations:

- 4.3 BSDI
- Linux (Slackware 1.2.10)
- A/UX 3.1.1 (System 5–compatible)
- Sun/OS 4.13 (no Solaris, sorry)

Even if you're not running one of these particular flavors but are using some kind of UNIX on your system, you should be able to take nearly all of the code included with this book — ours and other people's — and use it on your systems without too much effort.

If you've never ported code from one version of UNIX to another, you might want to talk to someone who has. You should also search the USENET newsgroup list for groups that discuss one of the flavors mentioned above, and probably also the flavor you're using. If you don't have a text-only listing of all the newsgroups available from your ISP, you can usually get one just by asking for it. You can then use a text editor with a *search* command to look for UNIX version names (that is, look for *bsd* or *linux* rather than *unix*). Finally, you'll probably want to obtain a manual of system calls for both versions of UNIX involved (the one you're porting from and the one you're porting to) so you can figure out how to translate or kludge the capabilities of the source system on your target of choice.

If you're working on a non-UNIX system, take heart in our inclusion of source code and in the willingness of most authors whose work appears on the Internet to offer the same. Even though most of the authors whose work we included here — including our own — make occasional to heavy use of system functions in their CGI programs, this is merely a hump to get over in most cases, rather than a death knell to the usability of the work that's included here.

Because system calls vary, alas, from operating system to operating system, we can't really give you much useful advice on exactly what to do to port our CGIs to your system. In some cases — most notably, the

Macintosh running Mac/OS — it will be necessary to recode everything in AppleScript anyway. In other cases, you should be able to find a Perl variant for your platform that will gladly accommodate the non-system-dependent aspects of the programs for you. The problem remains one of mapping UNIX system calls to those calls supported by your system (or faking your way around them), but this is doable.

In the final analysis, we hope this explains why we've taken so much time in the book to talk about approaches and methods and have used code primarily for illustration. Hopefully, you'll be able to take our ideas and those of the many fine authors whose code we discuss in the book and use them as you see fit in your own programming environment, whatever that may be.

Take comfort from this: although *httpd* implementations vary, nearly all of them follow the same approach to accepting input from clients and passing it on to CGI programs. Likewise, nearly all of them handle CGI program output the same way. Working within a standard environment like the Web means there's only so much ugliness and eccentricity that the development community will tolerate, no matter what platform is hosting a server!

OUR LANGUAGE OF CHOICE IS PERL4

Even though Larry Wall and his colleagues have been laboring mightily on Perl5, the object-oriented and entirely worthy successor to Perl4, we've made Perl4 the language of choice for this book.

Here's why. Our Perl4 is actually version 4.036. It's been heavily tested, widely used, and the bulk of the shareware, freeware, and public domain CGIs we located on the Net work for that version. Perl5 is interesting and offers nice new capabilities, but it's an object-oriented language that diverges considerably from its Perl4 ancestor.

Because there's just not that much code or experience coming out of Perl5 right now, we stuck to the more familiar version. Besides, most of the system administrators we talked to indicated that they would be running both versions in parallel on their systems. Since most of the tools in use today were written for Perl4, we expect parallel use to continue for some time to come.

You'll find that there are lots of other languages used for CGIs on the Net — most notably C, or some UNIX shell variant — but we chose Perl because of its outstanding string-handling capabilities. And since implementations are currently available for UNIX, Windows NT, DOS, OS/2, and the Mac/OS, your platforms won't be too constrained by our choice of language. We just happen to think it's the most efficient and expedient language for CGI programming available today. You're certainly entitled to think otherwise, and we won't argue with you — we'll simply point out that you shouldn't have too much difficulty translating our Perl code into that language, since it's also pretty easy to learn and understand.

Finally, we chose Perl because of its outstanding debugger, which permits step-by-step execution, halts at predefined breakpoints, and variable inspection and interactive value assignment. All of these things make it easier to deal with HTTP's use of *stdin* and *stdout* for handling input and output during program execution.

We've also come to know and love many of the tools and libraries mentioned in this book (most of which are in Perl for some strange reason or another), which have become comfortable and familiar through repeated use. Here again, you can think and use what you want, but we've found the selection of Perl tools and utilities to be consistently superior to others that we've looked at (however cursorily).

Here again, we reemphasize the book's focus on concepts, ideas, and programming approaches, rather than a single-minded concentration on programming details. We think that if you understand the solutions that CGIs are supposed to provide and the common techniques that have been used to implement them, you'll be able to take it from there!

WE'LL WORK WITH EITHER CERN OR NCSA HTTPD

Even though there are some significant configuration and structural differences between the two major UNIX implementations of the HTTP daemon, *httpd*, we're equally at home working with both. Both of these systems are well documented and broadly used. You'll find differences between them when it comes to image-handling, mapfiles, configuration details, and directory structures, but these are all elements that can be flushed out and dealt with.

Even if you choose a non-UNIX *httpd*, you'll find that it resembles one or the other of these two major variants. Here again, this derives as much from the standard nature of the TCP/IP networking world, where a certain amount of individual variation is tolerated but outright nonconformity is usually ignored. As long as vendors or implementers build other versions, you can rest assured they want them to be used; this, we would argue, guarantees a basic level of conformity that should be comforting.

When systems do diverge from one or the other of these norms, you'll observe also that such divergence is heavily documented. Where things are different, the implementers are usually keenly aware of the differences. And since they're keen on having you use their implementation, they're usually also keen on letting you know how and why, and what needs to be done about it. This is equally true for the OS/2, Windows NT, Macintosh, and commercial UNIX implementations we've investigated.

WE TAKE GOOD TOOLS WHEREVER WE CAN GET THEM!

Most of the programmers involved in this project learned, to their surprise (and sense of synchronicity) that they had begun using "formlib.pl" (a library of Perl code for handling HTML <FORM> input) more or less independently, starting about two years ago. Its author, Brigitte Jellinek of the University of Salzburg in Austria, has done a superb job of making forms input easy to accommodate and handle within Perl programs. It remains the common programming denominator across the entire group of authors and writers.

Many other tools or toolsets have come and gone. The best way to decide how usable a library or toolset might be is to force yourself to read its documentation. If that looks interesting, there's no substitute for hands-on experience. That's why using these tools, however briefly, is the only way to honestly evaluate them. Sure, this takes time (sometimes lots of it) and effort, but it's the only way to distinguish a tool that "looks nice" from one that helps your programming go more smoothly.

We've tried to recommend only those tools that we've used for a while with good results, or those that have been highly rated by other programmers whose opinions we trust. In the final analysis, a live test in your environment is the only way you can decide what to use. If you're willing to spend some time and dig in deeply, you may find your programming skills improving at the same time that your program's capabilities begin to blossom.

As programmers, we can think of no better way to learn than by reading the work of others, both seriously and deeply. Even though you may end up rejecting most of what you examine, you'll have ample opportunities to learn new programming approaches, constructs, algorithms, and techniques!

Summary

When it comes to building real-live Web services and applications, at some point you have to disengage from the realm of possibility and settle into the real world. This means making platform, operating system, programming language, and other choices that constitute your development environment. In this chapter, we've tried to explain the environment we used to write this book and why we chose it. We've also explained some of the trials and tribulations you might have to go through in order to take a different tack.

At the end of the day, however, the need to provide your users with effective, intelligent Web services is what we hope gives value to this book, no matter how our choices for assembling a development environment differ from yours. Therefore, our primary goal in this book is to help you understand concepts, techniques, and approaches to programming CGI, rather than leading you by the hand through a mass of what could all too easily be irrelevant details.

If we can share a common understanding of the programming process and the kinds of solutions you can provide to your users, you should be able to puzzle out the details for yourself. If not, we'll try to point you to numerous other sources of information and points of view, so that you can illuminate your understanding from many angles and ultimately find the information that will let you proceed to build the solutions you want!

CHAPTER

13

Locating CGI Resources

G iven the ever-changing nature of the WWW, it should come as no surprise that the Web is also the right place to look for CGI information, programs, and other related resources. In fact, the Internet contains a plethora of information on CGI and other topics that can add capabilities to your own Web pages. All you need to do is establish the habit of monitoring what's new and interesting in order to keep up with the latest and greatest CGI ideas, tools, and techniques.

Here are a few suggestions for information-trolling on the Internet:

- Follow ongoing debates and information exchanges about CGI programming to keep abreast of the hot topics and burning issues. You'll develop a sense of who the real players are, what they're keen on, and the cutting-edge capabilities they discuss, as well as the more mundane — and practical — topics that others may be researching.

- Watch the regular online Question & Answer (Q&A) exchanges for essential clues to the kinds of problems or stumbling blocks that you may eventually encounter in your own CGI programming. Often you'll also gain access to the solutions or workarounds necessary to fix or avoid these potential gotchas without learning about them the hard way!

- Peruse the collections of code, tools, and information available online. You may find ready-to-use versions of programs or routines that you would otherwise have to build from scratch. Why reinvent the wheel when wheels of all kinds and sizes are there for the (re)using?

■ Observe the traffic devoted to particular CGI widgets, algorithms, and data-handling problems. You'll be exposed to new programming ideas and approaches to enrich your abilities and the code you write. It'll force you to think about aspects of data structures, parameter passing, and variable manipulations that you might never have considered on your own. In short, exposure to new, innovative methods and ideas will help you to grow as a programmer.

We could go on and on about the joys and beauties of online information mining, but we hope you've gotten the idea by now. Suffice it to say that there's tons of interesting CGI stuff out there, a surprising amount of which can be educational, enlightening, and labor-saving, to boot!

Then, too, there are other sources of CGI information besides those that are online. We'll try to make sure you hear about the best of these and that you know where to find current information about the more conventional forms of these sources.

Going Straight to the Internet Sources

The Internet is truly an infinite information resource, so locating the "right stuff" requires a certain amount of savvy. It also requires a tight focus (to avoid the Web's many distractions), a sense of direction (to avoid looking for CGI in all the wrong places), and enough knowledge of how the Internet works to know what kinds of resources are worth investigating further.

In this chapter, we'll try to help you stay in focus, to give the best directions we can, and to point out the relevant workings of the Internet to let you become savvy enough to use it effectively. This requires knowing what kinds of resources are available and how to use them appropriately.

In the following sections, we'll lay out a set of Internet resource types. Then we'll discuss each type in detail to get you comfortable enough to do your own investigating after that. Along the way, we'll try to equip you with information on related tools, locations, and techniques for using each type of resource to the max!

> ## "Learning How to Learn" about the Internet
>
> If it helps you, please treat this chapter as an extension of the old proverb:
>
> *Give a man a fish, and you feed him for a day. Teach a man to fish, and you feed him for a lifetime.*
>
> In your case, it means that we want you to learn to recognize these kinds of resources and to master the techniques for identifying and locating them. That's not because we want to feed you for a lifetime, it's because anything specific we tell you about any Internet resource available today is likely to be passé in a matter of months. If you know how to look for what's current, you'll be able to quickly locate the information you need.

INTERNET RESOURCE TYPES

While there is more "stuff" out there than you can shake a stick at, there really aren't that many different kinds of materials to reckon with. That's why we'll begin with a brief overview of the types and locations of Internet resources.

In a search for CGI information, specifications, and examples, here's what you're most likely to find:

FOCUSED NEWSGROUPS

Focused newsgroups are groups of interested individuals who congregate around a specific topic on USENET, BITNET, or one of the other regular message exchange areas on the Internet.

Where CGI is concerned, this involves a handful of primarily USENET newsgroups with varying levels of interest in (and coverage of) CGI-specific or related topics, like CGI itself, programming languages used for CGI, Web authoring and programming, and other related areas.

When we cover these newsgroups, we'll also briefly explain the USENET hierarchy and how to go looking for CGI topics.

FOCUSED MAILING LISTS

Focused mailing lists originate from targeted mail servers that collect message traffic from active correspondents, and then broadcast the accumulated traffic to anyone who signs up for the mailing list.

Entering and leaving a mailing list takes a little more effort than subscribing to or leaving a USENET newsgroup, but otherwise these two categories provide the same kind of information: daily message traffic — sometimes quite voluminous — focused on CGI or related topics.

Locating mailing lists can sometimes be tricky. We'll try to give you some pointers to help locate them when we discuss what's available for CGI-related topics. We'll also talk about advertising methods and the ins and outs of subscribing to and exiting from mailing lists.

INFORMATION COLLECTIONS FROM "INTERESTED PARTIES"

Sometimes individuals with special interests in a particular area — like CGI — will collect information about their area of concern and publish it in a variety of forms ranging from Web pages to file archives on private or public servers.

While such collections can often be eclectic and idiosyncratic, the best of them can offer outstanding "jumping-off points" for investigating any particular topic. This is as true for CGI as it is for other topics.

Like mailing lists, finding these gems can be a matter of hit or miss. We'll try to give you some tips to help improve your batting average!

INFORMATION FROM SPECIAL INTEREST GROUPS

Special interest groups cover a multitude of approaches to their topics: they can be trade or industry organizations, research or standards groups, or even companies involved in particular activities.

Often the groups with vested interests in a technology will provide information on that technology, along with pointers to other sources. This is as true for CGI as it is for other topics, but because these groups are nonpareils of Web and Internet presence, they are often among the best places to start looking.

As we explore these groups and organizations in more detail, we'll introduce you to interested parties from all these sectors, and then some!

It's often been said that "It's not *what* you know, it's *who* you know, that counts." When it comes to locating Internet resources, this may sometimes seem more like "*where* you know," but the principle remains pretty much the same. By the time you finish this chapter, our goal is to make sure you've gotten some familiarity with all five W's regarding Internet resources, including *who, what,* and *where,* but also *when* and *why*!

OTHER SOURCES WORTH INVESTIGATING

Even though they may not be as dynamic and interactive as online resources, don't overlook the information you can glean from conventional print-based publications. (We know you've got to be somewhat open-minded in this regard, because you're reading this book!) We'll do our best to acquaint you with some books, magazines, and publishers to check out in your quest for the latest and greatest CGI information.

In the final analysis of information resources, whether online or otherwise, it all comes back to people. To conclude our review of important CGI resources, we'll also identify some key individuals and groups as sources of further enlightenment when all other avenues dry up.

Please, please, *please,* be humble and courteous when you deal with CGI gurus: Since these people are ultimately the source of all CGI wisdom, it's a good idea to approach them respectfully and circumspectly, and not to demand too much from them. As with successful and knowledgeable people in any niche, they're all very busy, and might not be able to drop whatever they're doing just to talk to you. E-mail is a great interactive technique when approaching the great ones, since it lets them choose if and when to consider your requests, and how to reply.

FOR EVERY RESOURCE TYPE, THERE'S A SEARCH METHOD

As we investigate the various sources for CGI information on the Internet (and elsewhere), we'll also try to tell you how to best explore and exploit each resource. For some types this can mean simple searching techniques or access to *pro forma* documents; for other types, you may actually use specialized tools or ask some questions in the right places to help you find where to look for CGI enlightenment.

We hope you'll agree that simply knowing that these types of resources exist is a good thing. We also hope that you'll be able to appreciate the value of the questions and answers, the code fragments and programs, and the other goodies you'll find as you begin to explore them. In the sections that follow we'll treat each type of resource in more detail and provide examples for each one. Once you've finished our coverage, though, we can only suggest that you take the I-way to the destinations of your choice, since only you know what you *really* need to know!

CGI-Related Newsgroups

When it comes to dealing with USENET and related collections of news-groups (like BITNET, IMSI, MAIL, etc.), there's plenty of raw material to be found that sometimes relates to CGI. The secret to locating the right resources is knowing how to cast your net.

To begin with, you'll want to obtain a list of the newsgroups that your Internet Service Provider (ISP) carries. You probably already have access to this list through whatever newsreader you're using, but you can usually get a plain-text version of this list just by asking for it.

The names for USENET and other newsgroups consist of strings of lowercase names separated by periods. For example,

```
comp.infosystems.www.authoring.cgi
```

is a part of the computing infosystems hierarchy on USENET, in the area devoted to World Wide Web (www) topics that are related to authoring. As its name suggests, this newsgroup focuses entirely on CGI-related matters and technologies, and is a prime source for CGI-related information.

As it also happens, *comp.infosystems.www.authoring.cgi* is the only newsgroup we found with "cgi" anywhere in its name. But it's not the only newsgroup that covers relevant information, so we'd like to suggest some additional terms to search on when perusing the list of available newsgroups from your ISP:

- "www" will help you locate all the Web-related newsgroups that are available. Our search turned up 24 of them. Not all of these are necessarily focused on, or even related to CGI, but most of them are worth checking out. This is the list we came up with from our own ISP:

```
bit.listserv.www-vm
cern.www.announce
cern.www.talk
comp.infosystems.www
comp.infosystems.www.advocacy
comp.infosystems.www.announce
comp.infosystems.www.authoring.cgi
comp.infosystems.www.authoring.html
comp.infosystems.www.authoring.images
comp.infosystems.www.authoring.misc
comp.infosystems.www.browsers.mac
comp.infosystems.www.browsers.misc
comp.infosystems.www.browsers.ms-windows
comp.infosystems.www.misc
comp.infosystems.www.providers
comp.infosystems.www.providers
comp.infosystems.www.servers.mac
comp.infosystems.www.servers.misc
comp.infosystems.www.servers.unix
comp.infosystems.www.users
comp.os.os2.networking.www
imsi.mail.www-talk
list.www-de
mail.www
```

From experience, we know that the groups most worth following belong to the *comp.infosystems.www.authoring* hierarchy, since that's the collection of newsgroups devoted to constructing Web pages, programs, and more. For those of you with interests in particular platforms — like Macintosh, Windows, or UNIX — the newsgroups that cover the intersection of the Web and these platforms will be helpful, if only as a source of pointers to where the real stuff is. As for the rest, the only way to find out if they're worthwhile is to drop in and see!

- Another USENET hierarchy worth watching falls within the *comp.lang* newsgroups, which are devoted to particular computer languages. We've found useful CGI scripts in the following newsgroups:

```
comp.lang.c
comp.lang.c++
comp.lang.perl
comp.lang.perl.misc
comp.lang.python
```

but you should consider following whatever languages you use to build your CGI programs, as a source of inspiration, information, and code fragments galore!

One last recommendation for the USENET newsgroup hierarchy is to keep tabs on *news.announce.newusers*; that's the group where new newsgroups are announced and it's worth polling at least once a month to see if any new CGI groups have popped up.

CGI-Related Mailing Lists

The thing about Internet mailing lists is that you'll hear about them only in the most off-handed ways. Even our favorite search engines (see the section entitled "Searching for Satisfaction" at the end of this chapter) turned up very little information on CGI-related mailing lists.

Yet when we started reading the USENET and other newsgroups and following particular conversations, we quickly learned about a handful of such lists. Despite the accidental nature of our learning — which, by the way, makes it very hard to teach — keeping an ear to the groundswell of information about CGI appears to offer your best hope for locating a CGI-related list that's right for your needs.

Here's what we came up with:

- *cgi-pm@webstorm.com*
  type: Majordomo

  This list covers lots of interesting CGI issues and regularly features interesting code samples and example programs. Old threads are archived at the following URL:

  `http://www.webstorm.com/local/cgi-perl/`

  To subscribe to this mailing list, send e-mail to the address on the first line, with the word "subscribe" as the message body. If your mailing insists on attaching a ".sig" (signature) file at the end of your messages, follow the word "subscribe" with the word "end" on the next line. Thus, the body of your message would look like this:

  ```
  subscribe
  end
  ```

- *webedge-talk@webedge.com*
  type: Majordomo

  This list springs from the WebEdge Technology Conference, hosted twice a year, that brings Apple-focused Web developers together. This particular list covers many CGI-related topics, but primarily those focused on AppleScript, Apple's scripting language for use on the MacHTTPd software. The URL for Webedge is:

```
http://www.webedge.com/
```

  To subscribe to this mailing list, send e-mail to the address on the first line, with the words "subscribe webedge-talk" as the message body. If your mailing insists on attaching a ".sig" (signature) file at the end of your messages, follow the word "subscribe" with the word "end" on the next line. Thus, the body of your message would look like this:

```
subscribe webedge-talk
end
```

  If you're not a budding or current Mac WebMaster, this list may not be for you; but if you are, you'll find it fascinating.

  When reading mailing lists, as with USENET newsgroups, you have to be willing to overcome what's called the "signal to noise" ratio: that is, the ratio of helpful, interesting, or informative messages to irrelevant and useless ones. Only you can decide if it's worth the effort, but be aware that for some of these lists or groups, the noise can sometimes be deafening!

Parties Interested in CGI

As you read through the newsgroups and mailing lists, you'll begin to notice that certain people are very active in these areas. You'll also come to appreciate that some of them are witty and knowledgeable, and that a few will offer gems of wisdom or programming expertise that leave you thoroughly bedazzled.

When you find somebody who proves him- or herself to be worth listening to about CGI, try to see if they've got a personal Web page or hotlist that you might be able to use. You can look for URLs in their ".sig" files (often a dead giveaway), or use the UNIX *finger* command to see if they've published any URLs in their personal profiles. These individual resources can often be very useful, especially if the person's interests or expertise overlaps substantially with your own.

If you see that someone is conversant on a particular topic that catches your fancy, or might help you solve a problem but they don't publish a URL, send them e-mail asking for more information. Be sure to ask them if they know of any good Web resources, mailing lists, or file archives with information on the subject. This kind of direct inquiry can also turn up resources that you might never have known existed.

Just remember that while it never hurts to ask for help or information, it's always a good idea to ask politely. E-mail is a very good way to get (and give) information, but don't expect instant or incredibly detailed responses. It's an unwritten but powerful rule on the Internet that you shouldn't demand any more from others than you are willing to give in return (a digital version of the Golden Rule, as it were). Be nice, be terse, and be patient, and you'll probably get all the help you can stand!

CGI-Focused Groups and Organizations

When it comes to dealing with CGI, there are certain groups that naturally spring to mind. All of these organizations have a more than casual interest in the technology; some have an interest in CGI that could accurately be called proprietary. Who do we mean?

This list includes organizations responsible for the CGI specification, who actually implement CGI for their HTTP servers, or who use CGI as routine elements of their professional activities. Table 13-1 lists some of these organizations and their URLs.

Each of these URLs is a treasure trove of CGI information that can lead you to other sources as well. The only way to find out what they have to offer is to spend some time surfing — not such a bad assignment!

This is by no means an exhaustive list of possible organizations, either; we'd also recommend that you check out the home pages for the browser vendors (like Netscape Communications Corporation).

Table 13-1
CGI-Focused Organizations

Organization	Who are these guys?	URL
World Wide Web Organization (W30)	joint venture between CERN, MIT, and others to manage the World Wide Web	http://www.w3.org/hypertext/ WWW/Daemon/User_3.0/ CGI/Overview.html
National Center for Supercomputing Applications (NCSA)	developer of MOSAIC Web browser and another key httpd implementation	http://hoohoo.ncsa.uiuc.edu/ cgi/Overview.html
WWW Virtual Library (a W30 project); be SURE to use their built-in search engine on "CGI"	comprehensive catalog of online info; URL is for the Web Developer's Library	http://WWW.Stars.com/
Enterprise Integration Technologies (EIT); be sure to check out their "WebMaster's Starter Kit"	a Stanford spin-off; tools for installing and maintaining Web services	http://wsk.eit.com/wsk/doc/

CGI-Related Publications and Off-Line Resources

At present, we're not aware of any books that specifically target CGI programming (but since we're writing one, we figure others are working in the same area). However, there are lots of good resources worth checking out.

For one thing, most Web- and HTML-focused books cover CGI at some level of detail. For another, most of them point to a variety of useful resources. We've found the following books to be particularly useful:

- *Mary E. Morris, **HTML for Fun and Profit**, Prentice-Hall, Upper Saddle River, NJ, 1995. (List Price $35.95; ISBN 0-13-359290-1.) Some of the best coverage on CGI tools and techniques we've seen anywhere.*

- *Ed Tittel and Steve James,* **HTML For Dummies**, *IDG Books Worldwide, Indianapolis, IN, 1995. (List Price: $29.99; ISBN 1-56884-330-5.) Includes basic coverage of CGI with some useful sample programs.*

- *Laura LeMay,* **Teach Yourself Web Publishing with HTML in a Week**, *SAMS Publishing, Indianapolis, IN, 1995. (List Price: $25.00; ISBN 0-672-30667-0.) Includes basic coverage of CGI and related terminology.*

- *Ian S. Graham,* **The HTML Sourcebook**, *John Wiley & Sons, New York, 1995. (List Price: $29.95; ISBN 0-471-11849-4.) Features a chapter devoted to coverage of CGI design, specification, programming, and usage.*

Don't forget also that there are plenty of magazines that cover the Internet (some, more or less exclusively). We've found the following ones to be particularly informative:

- **Internet World**, a monthly publication aimed specifically at Internet topics and technology, so new Web-related announcements proliferate here. Send inquiries via e-mail to info@mecklermedia.com or call +1-203-226-6967. Address: 20 Ketchum Street, Westport, CT, 06880.

- **IWAY**, a bimonthly, hands-on publication aimed at the Internet, with coverage for beginning to intermediate users trying to master related tools and technologies. Send your queries via e-mail to editors@iway.mv.com or call +1-603-924-9334. Address: 80 Elm Street, Peterborough, NH, 03458.

- **NetGuide**, an online services magazine that covers all of the major online information services by category and includes occasional coverage of programming topics. Submit queries via e-mail to netmail@netguide.cmp.com or call +1-526-562-5000. Address: 600 Community Drive, Manhasset, NY, 11030.

- **Wired**, this is the trendiest and most fashionable of the online coverage magazines. Chances are that CGI-related information will only appear if it's something catchy or outrageous. Submit queries via e-mail to editor@wired.com or fax to +1-415-222-6249. Address: 520 Third Street, San Francisco, CA, 94107.

We can't say that you'll walk away from any of these sources completely enlightened about CGI (or anything else, for that matter), but we've found all of them to contain occasional nuggets of useful information. When it comes to the magazines, maybe you could borrow someone else's copies or buy single issues from a newsstand, before plunking down your hard-earned cash for any subscriptions!

Searching for Satisfaction

Using the right tools makes researching the Web much simpler. There is a class of software tools called *search engines* that can examine huge amounts of information to help you locate Web sites of potential interest. Here's how most of them work:

- Somewhere in the background, laboring in patient anonymity, you'll find automated Web-traversing programs, often called *robots* or *spiders*, that do nothing but follow link after link around the Web, ad infinitum. Each time they get to a new Web document, they peruse and catalog its contents, storing the information for transmission to a database elsewhere on the Web. (For more information, see Chapter 23.)

- At regular intervals these automated information gatherers transmit their recent acquisitions to a parent database, where the information is sifted, categorized, and stored.

- When you run a search engine, you're actually searching the database that's been compiled and managed through the initial efforts of the robots and spiders, but which is handled by a fully functional database management system that communicates with the CGI program for your search form.

- Using the keywords or search terms you provide to the form, the database locates "hits" (exact matches) and also "near-hits" (matches with less than the full set of terms supplied, or based on educated guesses about what you're *really* trying to locate).

- The hits are returned to the CGI program by the database, where they are transformed into a Web document to return the results of the search for your perusal.

If you're lucky, all this activity will produce references to some materials that you can actually use!

We'd like to share some pointers to our favorite search engines with you, which you'll find in Table 13-2. This is not an exhaustive catalog of such tools, but all of them will produce interesting results if you use "CGI" or "CGI scripts" as search input.

Table 13-2
Web Search Engines

Search engine name anf info	URL
ElNet Galaxy MCI spinoff ElNet's engine	http://www.einet.net
Lycos Carnegie-Mellon engine	http://lycos.cs.cmu.edu
W3 Org Virtual Library W3 Org outsourced project	http://www.stars.com
Wandex MIT spinoff's engine	http://www.netgen.com/cgi/wandex
WebCrawler University of Washington engine	http://webcrawler.com
World Wide Web Worm (WWWW) University of Colorado engine	http://www.cs.colorado.edu:80/ home/mcbryan/WWWW.html
Yahoo	http://www.yahoo.com

When you're using these search tools, the most important thing to remember is that the more specific you can make your search request, the more relevant the results. Thus, if you're looking for CGI program listings, you might try using "CGI program listings" or "CGI scripts" as your search terms instead of simply "CGI." While you may get plenty of nothing when using search terms that are too specific, that's better than looking through a plenitude of irrelevant materials when nothing is all that's in there!

Summary

When it comes to finding information about Web-related stuff, the Web's a good place to look! But there are other valuable sources of information available, both on and off the Internet. In this chapter, you've learned where to look for Web and CGI programming information and how to make an effective information search. Hopefully this will stand you in good stead when you go out looking for the "ultimate widget." In the next chapter, we'll help you get a leg up on building HTML documents within your CGI programs, as you take a look at some snazzy CGI return-page templates.

CHAPTER

14

CGI Return Page Templates

*M*ost of the output that CGI programs create consists of HTML docu-ments generated in response to the input submitted by users. While it's true that some CGI programs may simply return a URL for an existing Web document or an application-specific file to download, most of them take user input, massage that data, and then use the resulting information to build a *return page* for feedback, results, or further interaction.

In this chapter, we'll examine some tips for improving your program-ming productivity when building such pages in your CGI programs. We'll also share some tricks that depend on using preformatted building blocks to make your job easier. We'll even try to warn you about some of the common pitfalls that you're likely to encounter when building Web documents programmatically and try to steer you around them whenever possible.

Before we launch into our discussion, we'd like you to ruminate on the concept behind this chapter — namely, that of a *template*. In its original application, a template was a kind of "master form" that pre–Industrial Revolution craftsmen would use to create copies in order to make items or components (like gunstocks, chair spindles, or anything else that required a reasonably standard part) when building a weapon, a chair, or whatever. This approach helped to make certain aspects of construction more routine and predictable (and more suitable for apprentices who had not completely mastered their crafts).

If this expresses the idea of constructing reusable parts in a cus-tomized environment, then we've succeeded in getting our inspiration for this chapter across. If not, think of the elements covered herein as a set of approaches for building low-level elements of reusable code that you can incorporate when building HTML documents inside your CGI programs.

What's in a Page?

To begin with, let's take a look at the major building blocks of a Web page so that we can examine the process of construction. At the highest level, a Web page consists of two contiguous blocks of text:

1. The HTTP header, required to tell the browser how to handle an incoming Web document or the server how to accommodate its content.

2. The document body, which may come in many formats. For the purposes of this chapter, we assume that the only format involved is CONTENT_TYPE=text/html. From an HTML perspective, this means all text that occurs between <HTML> ... </HTML> tags, including those tags themselves.

But since our focus is exclusively on HTML documents, we'd like to treat Item number 2 as if it consisted of three parts, in keeping with HTML's own document structure:

1. The HTML document header, which consists of all text between <HEAD> ... </HEAD> tags.

2. The HTML document content, which consists of most of the text between <BODY> ... </BODY> tags.

3. The HTML document footer, which consists of some standard text right at the bottom of the document, just before the </BODY> tag. At a minimum, this includes copy inside <ADDRESS> ... </ADDRESS> tags, but we'll recommend some other items you might want to consider including in your footer as well.

Static Versus Dynamic Content

When you get ready to write the part of your CGI program that creates an HTML document, some of the information will be constant or will not change very often, while much of the information will be determined by the input that's been passed to you in a query, form, or some other kind of user interaction. The part that stays more or less constant is what we'll call *static* content, while the part that is based entirely on user input we'll call *dynamic* content.

GIVE ME SOME STATIC!

Here are some examples of static content that you'll probably recognize:

- The basic HTTP header information:

```
Content-type: text/html
```

- Required HTML markup: by this we mean the basic tags that you're required to place into each HTML document in order to be DTD-compliant. These include structure tags like <HTML> ... </HTML>, <HEAD> ... </HEAD>, <BODY> ... </BODY>, etc.
- The HTML DTD identification comment (or some other appropriate SGML-derived prolog, as covered in Chapter 4):

```
<!DOCTYPE PUBLIC HTML "-//IETF//DTD HTML 2.0//EN" >
```

- Your <ADDRESS> information, which normally includes author attribution, contact information, and the like at the foot of a page. For example, here's the <ADDRESS> information from Ed Tittel's LAN-Wrights Web pages:

```
<ADDRESS>
<A NAME = "bottom"></A>
E-Mail: <A HREF="mailto:etittel@zilker.net">LANWrights via
etittel@zilker.net</A><BR>
Snail-mail: 5810 Lookout Mountain Drive<BR>
Austin, TX 78731-3618 USA
</ADDRESS>
```

Notice that this HTML code includes a standard anchor to help the browser find the bottom of the page (i.e., <A NAME="bottom"></A>). Notice also that it includes Ed's e-mail address, using a "mailto: " URL. Finally, it includes his snail-mail address.

The best way to isolate static elements in your HTML documents is to go through half a dozen picked at random. Look for recurring elements that stay the same from page to page and build yourself a list, as you locate them.

Static elements, once identified, can easily be included into your CGI programs using any of several techniques that we'll cover later in the chapter. Once you figure out what these static elements are, handling them is easy, but the technique you'll use will probably depend on the amount of text involved.

THE HAPPY MEDIUM: DYNAMIC BUT CONSTANT

Before we briefly address the completely dynamic aspects of your return pages (since they are so dynamic, they don't fit our template model terribly well), we'd also like to point out that there are some elements in HTML documents that recur regularly but that also include dynamic elements.

Some good examples of recurrent but ever-changing elements include:

- The entire <HEAD> section of an HTML document. Normally, the only things that change in this section are the text for document titles. Sometimes, however, additional pointers for things like the <BASE> URL, the <LINK> link type information, or a <NEXTID> URL, to point to a logical successor to a document, may also appear.

  Each of these includes recurring markup along with dynamic values. Together, they follow a fairly customary order. By building a template that allows the insertion of string-valued variables, you can actually build an entirely static <HEAD> section for your document that can be completed simply by forcing your CGI script to insert the values for these variables in the right places.

- Preformatted text (enclosed between <PRE> ... </PRE>) normally comes from other sources, anyway. By using a *file include* in your program, bracketed by the necessary HTML tags, you can handle such text quickly and easily.

- It's not totally commonplace, but it is good practice to include the URL for a page somewhere on the page itself. We generally do this as a part of our footers. That way, if a document gets mirrored somewhere, or a user downloads the HTML source code but forgets to grab its URL, he or she can always return to the original. The text surrounding this information can be static and the URL inserted by the CGI program using a string variable.

If you wanted to carry this concept to its logical extreme, you could even build programmatic wrappers for lots of different kinds of HTML tags, so that you'd only need to call a short routine with the necessary dynamic values to reference links, headings, or other HTML elements. We think this may be carrying things a bit too far, but you can reevaluate this thinking on your own. If you write lots of CGI code, it might be worth the effort to build such a set of widgets. If not, it would probably be overkill.

THE TRULY DYNAMIC

Most of the really interesting stuff that you'll put onto your CGI-constructed HTML documents will vary each time a user runs your program. It could be the results of a particular database query, a computation of their biorhythms, or even just an echo of some forms feedback to let your users know their information came through correctly.

Even so, when this information has to be packaged in HTML format, the HTML itself will stay fairly consistent. Although the content changes each time, you'll want to shoot for a consistent appearance for your pages. If you or your organization has a style defined for its Web pages, you'll want to make your programmatically created pages look just like your handcrafted ones.

Either way, this means that consistent elements of style and appearance will repeat from page to page, and from document to document. If you can isolate the recurring parts here, too, you may be able to save yourself some programming effort by figuring out how to insert them using static code and string-valued variables, rather than hacking out the same information time and time again.

This technique works particularly well for recurring page elements like graphical icons or mandated images (like your logo or various types of visual signposts), navigation bars, or forms widgets. With a little abstraction and some inspired programming, you can build pages quickly and easily. When you've debugged and validated the resulting HTML during the testing process, you can assume that the output from your CGIs will be valid as well.

Building the HTTP Header

This is almost too simple for words, so let's show you some code instead. Here's a Perl example for constructing an HTTP header:

```
print "Content-type> text/html\n\n";
print "<HTML>";
print '<!DOCTYPE PUBLIC HTML "-//IETF//DTD HTML 2.0//EN" >',"\n";
```

Notice double "/n"s

That's all there is to it, but please notice that there are some subtleties.

First of all, the **Content-type** output statement ends with two \n characters. This is because the HTTP server requires that a blank line follow the content-type statement. A newline may be represented by any of several characters — a carriage return (CR), a linefeed (LF), or most commonly, by a CrLf pair — in most operating systems.

In Perl, the ASCII newline character \n handles this job (the interpreter will figure out what actual character to use, depending on the system it's running on). Thus, the first \n ends the line that contains the content-type declaration, while the second \n writes a blank line to *stdout*. The Web server interprets this blank line as a delimiter that precedes the rest of the document body, so it must precede any other contents in the file. Even if you don't use Perl to write your document-building code, you *must* remember to write a blank line after the content-type declaration.

The second line of Perl also includes some interesting subtleties. Notice the use of single quotes (') around the SGML DTD identifier; we took this approach because this tells Perl to treat all the text within the quoted string as literal characters. Otherwise, Perl would have tried to end the string at the first double quote that we wanted to quote for the name of the DTD (i.e., "-//IETF//DTD HTML 2.0//EN").

What this really means to you as a CGI programmer is that you must become aware of the quotation techniques for whatever language you use to build your CGIs. In particular, you will have to observe which of the special HTML characters are also special characters for your language and learn how to produce them as literals for output to the HTML document file, rather than as instructions to the programming language. Where Perl is concerned, this means learning how to deal with the following characters properly:

- double quote (")
- dollar sign ($)
- hash mark or pound sign (#)
- at sign (@)
- percent sign (%)

In one form or fashion, Perl wants to treat these characters as flags for particular kinds of values. In many cases, it will be smart enough to know that when they occur in a quoted string, they shouldn't be treated as flags and interpreted. But in some cases — particularly for the double quote and the dollar sign — Perl will behave very strangely unless you learn how to quote them properly.

Be Careful When Naming <FORM> Fields

If you're using Perl, you also need to be careful when naming form fields in HTML forms. The safest approach to take is to use uppercase characters only for field names or to make sure that no field names match any Perl reserved words (like language terms, function names, etc.).

Otherwise, you could end up trying to index an associate array using a variable name that is being treated as a reserved word, and end up wondering why your program doesn't work correctly. We learned this the hard way, by naming a form variable **sub**; since this happens to be the reserved word that calls a subroutine in Perl, it wouldn't function properly as an array index!

This wouldn't have been a problem at all, if the language had called us to task with an appropriate error message. But since it simply skipped any statements that tried to use this index and behaved correctly otherwise, we were left scratching our heads for a pretty good while. So, please, learn from our mistake!

Building the HTML Header

Since most of the information in an HTML header is pro forma, you could take an approach like this to construct a nearly static header:

```
$Q = '"';
print "<HTML>\n";
print "<HEAD>\n";
print "<TITLE> $Title </TITLE>\n";
if ($BASE gt "") {print "<BASE HREF=",$Q,$BASE,$Q, ">"};
if ($NEXTID gt "") {print "<NEXTID N=",$Q,$NEXTID,$Q, ">"};
print "</HEAD>\n";
print "<BODY>\n";
```

We'll use $Q to quote the quote character ' " '

This approach lets you build a single set of code for all HTML headers, but requires that you supply this fragment — which could easily be repackaged as a subroutine — with values for the variables needed. In other words, as long as you've defined a value for the title of the HTML document, $TITLE, this code will create a syntactically valid HTML header for your document.

If you supply values for either a BASE URL and/or a NEXTID, the code will output one or both of them for you inside the header. Since these values are optional, they will be included in the HTML document only when a value exists. And since your CGI program is responsible for supplying these values, we assume that you'll use one or both of these options only when you need to!

The HTML Document Body

This is where the real action is. We won't, therefore, dwell on this much, except to point out some possible areas where a little programming can save you some work.

THE BEGINNING OF THE BODY

The body of an HTML document should begin with a <BODY> tag, and end with its </BODY> closing counterpart. To be sure to create valid HTML every time, we recommend that you add the opening <BODY>

tag to the end of the <HEAD> ... </HEAD> piece of code (that's why we did it in the preceding example).

DEALING WITH RECURRENT ELEMENTS

While there are many potential candidates for this kind of treatment, we'll pick a navigation bar taken from Ed Tittel's LANWrights pages as an example. If you'd like to check this page for reference, its URL is:

```
http://www.io.com/~mcintyre/lanwrght/
```

Here again, we make use of string-valued variables to convey dynamic information into what is otherwise a static structure. For the navigation bar shown in Figure 14-1, the corresponding HTML looks like this:

```
<B><A HREF = "#b2"> NEXT BOOK</A> &#32;&#166;
<A HREF = "#top"> TOP OF PAGE</A> &#32;&#166;
<A HREF = "lanwrght.html"> HOME</A> &#32;&#166;
<A HREF = "lanwcmmt.html"> COMMENT</A></B>
```

Each of the books in the list is separated by a navigation bar that reads the same as the one depicted in Figure 14-1; for each book, only the value for **NEXT BOOK** needs to change.

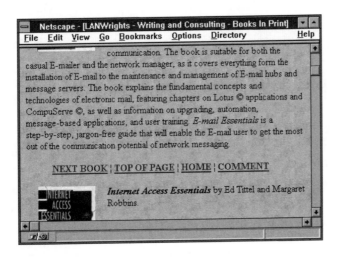

Figure 14-1
The LANWrights navigation bar lets you jump from book to book or to other standard menus and locations.

Therefore, the corresponding Perl code would look like this:

```
$Q = '"';
print "<B><A HREF = ",$Q,$NEXT_BOOK, '</A> &#32;&#166;',"\n";
print '<A HREF = "#top"> TOP OF PAGE</A> &#32;&#166;',"\n";
print '<A HREF = "lanwrght.html"> HOME</A> &#32;&#166;',"\n";
print '<A HREF = "lanwcmmt.html"> COMMENT</A></B>',"\n";
```

The only variable that's required to make this work for each invocation of the navigation bar is the name of the anchor, **$NEXT_BOOK**, for the next book in the list. Here again, repackaging as a subroutine would make it easy to insert the navigation bar wherever it's needed. And by using a naming convention that can be incremented as we did here (**B1** for book one, **B2** for book two, etc.), you could even generate the anchor tags programmatically.

INCORPORATING PREFORMATTED TEXT

Since most preformatted text is probably being created by some other program or utility, it should be easy to deliver it to your CGI program as a text file. If you can arrange for that to happen, all you need to do is instruct your CGI program to write the text to *stdout* between <PRE> ... </PRE> tags. In Perl, here's all the programming effort required:

```
print"<PRE>\n";
open (HTML_PRE, "/path/to/the/right/file.txt");
while (<HTML_PRE>) {
    print
}
close HTML_PRE;
print "</PRE>\n";
```

Copies every line in "file.txt" to stdout( )

Granted, we think that <PRE>-formatted text looks pretty ugly, but this certainly makes it easy to incorporate output from other programs into your CGI program's output. This technique will also work for incorporating HTML-formatted information as well, so if you ever got real ambitious, you could write a parser-cum-HTML-formatter for the same output and produce some good-looking output instead!

Handling <PRE>-Formatted Text

Because <PRE>-formatted text is usually rendered in an ugly, monospaced font (like Courier), your program will have to deliver the text with layout determined for such a display. This means that you want to use spaces to align text elements (tabs don't work the same way across all browsers). It also means that you'll want to limit your lines to 72 characters, maximum. That way, you can be sure your content will fit on most people's displays without unsightly (or unplanned) line wraps.

ENCODING HTML MARKUP

Earlier, we mentioned the possibility that you might want to write special code to handle more complex elements of HTML markup programmatically. We also added that you probably wouldn't find the effort justified unless you had to write lots of CGI programs. Even so, there are certain categories of markup that may work better than others when applied programmatically.

This applies especially for indexing long HTML documents, particularly for Webified versions of long or complex documents, like an HTML DTD. We're not going to give this approach much coverage here, but we would like to refer you to an outstanding example of this genre that's available on the Web. If you consult the following URL:

```
http://hopf.math.nwu.edu/docs/utility.html#indexmaker
```

you'll find a complete set of documents that describe this index-building tool, as well as some other interesting Perl CGI programs.

In order to download the *indexmaker* program (and the rest of the WN utilities), please download the file named "wn.tar.gz", uncompress it, and untar it to make the "/WN" source directory hierarchy. This file is available via anonymous ftp from *ftp.acns.nwu.edu* in the directory "/pub/wn".

If you read through the source code for this program, you'll probably get some excellent ideas about how to encapsulate markup in code and also have a chance to play with an excellent tool!

Handling HTML Document Footers

Once you've processed the content for the body of an HTML document within your CGI program, the only part that remains to be handled is the footer. Taking the <ADDRESS> information presented earlier in this chapter and adding some additional variables to the code, here's the Perl code to close out your HTML document:

```
$Q = '"';
print "<HR>";
print "<ADDRESS>\n";
print '<A NAME = "bottom"></A>',"\n";
print 'E-Mail: <A HREF="mailto:etittel@zilker.net">LANWrights via
etittel@zilker.net</A><BR>',"\n";
print 'Snail-mail: 5810 Lookout Mountain Drive<BR>',"\n";
print 'Austin, TX 78731-3618 USA',"\n";
print '</ADDRESS>',"\n";
print "URL: <A HREF =",$Q,$URL,$Q, ">\n",$URL, "</A>\n";
print "Revised — June 5th, 1995 [JMS - IMPACT Online]<BR>\n";
print "</BODY>\n";
print "</HTML>\n";
```

Here, we've slid in another string variable — this time, to let the URL for the current page be included in the HTML document. If the page you're building with your CGI program is evanescent and won't be around any longer than it takes to service your user's request for information, we suggest you insert your home page URL here. If so, you could use a static string instead of a variable (but you might want to use a variable anyway, in case you ever need to relocate your Web pages to another server).

Other Template Tricks

In general, the key to building good, reusable templates is to keep an eye on your CGI programming activities. When you find yourself coding the same lines repeatedly, you've located some good potential fodder for the template approach.

This might relate to some particular requirements for your own pages, like a set of icons for a navigation bar, or a text-only navigation bar. Or, it might be an offshoot of some particular stylistic requirements for your organization's Web pages, like a common set of graphics and horizontal rules at the beginning and end of each document.

To a certain extent, this kind of repetition is a good thing, because it gives your Web documents a consistent look and feel. Common controls and icons also make it easy for users to find their way around your Web site, by making things consistent and familiar. In this case, good design leads to labor-saving programming, since these repeated elements are excellent candidates for implementation as templates.

Summary

In this chapter, we've covered the analysis and implementation of common HTTP and HTML elements from the return pages that you'll need to build in your CGI programs. Along the way, we discussed the kinds of elements that are good candidates for simplified coding and have mentioned some techniques for using string variables to make semi-dynamic HTML easy to handle.

Don't forget the power of the occasional *file include* within your return pages, especially for <PRE>-formatted text. If you can detect repeated elements and code them for easy reuse, you can make assembling your pages as easy as stacking building blocks together!

15

The Major CGI Libraries

*A*ctually, the title of this chapter is something of a misnomer. Since there's no formal rating for CGI libraries, whether major, minor, or otherwise, we're making a brash claim about the collections of code that we're going to cover here. So we'll start by confessing that the title's just a ploy to pique your interest in some of the better CGI materials we've encountered in our wanderings around the Net.

In this chapter, we'll take you on a tour of a number of interesting online CGI collections — we hope you'll eventually agree that they're useful as well. We'll begin the chapter with some information about how we located these resources in the first place and then proceed to tackle these treasure troves in more or less alphabetical order (by URL, that is). We'll end the chapter with a few well-chosen caveats on reusing other people's work and on deciding whether your own work is worth sharing with others.

Before we explain how we found this stuff, we'd like you to pause a moment and thank your lucky stars — or perhaps the Big Spider herself — that so many individuals and organizations have seen fit to share their hard work and valuable programs with the Internet community. We strongly believe that one of the key factors behind the success of the Internet in general, and the Web in particular, has been the selfless efforts of all the people who've contributed their work to the greater good.

If it wasn't for the generosity of others, we wouldn't be able to tell you about the many keen collections of CGI programs and code you can find on the Web. Not only would that be too bad for us (we'd have nothing to write about), it would also be too bad for you (you'd have to build all the CGI widgets and tools you'd need yourself, instead of being able to stand on the shoulders of the giants who've gone before you)!

Looking for CGI Nirvana

When it comes to locating the real storehouses of knowledge on the Web, there's no substitute for knowing where — and how — to start looking. Fortunately, we have been mired in Web programming long enough to know where and how to look for CGI information. For the benefit of those who may not be similarly mired, we'd like to share some of our favorite techniques with you. If the resources we mention don't include the widget you need, you can prospect for it on your own.

ROUND UP THE USUAL SUSPECTS

We're pretty sure that this section heading (cheerfully stolen from the movie, *Casablanca*) appears somewhat out of its original context. In this case, we mean that you should check out the usual jumping-off points for HTML- and CGI-related information searches.

What does this mean? Here's a list of possible answers:

- **Check the "official" information resources.** This means looking in the Web pages for the W3C and at NCSA. All of the relevant locations have useful CGI information, including code libraries, specifications, and pointers to other sites. Some of the most relevant URLs are:

  ```
  http://hoohoo.ncsa.uiuc.edu/cgi/
  http://hoohoo.ncsa.uiuc.edu/cgi/interface.html
  http://www.w3.org/hypertext/WWW/Daemon/User/CGI/Overview.html
  ```

- **Use a search engine.** We had the best luck with the search strings *CGI script, CGI program,* and *CGI library.* You, too, can run a search on one or more of these strings at any of the following URLs (if we've omitted your favorite search engine, please forgive us in advance):

  ```
  http://www.yahoo.com/search.html
  http://query1.lycos.cs.cmu.edu/lycos-form.html
  http://nmt.edu/~mfisk/websearch.cgi
  http://www.cs.colorado.edu/home/mcbryan/WWWW.html
  ```

- **Consult Chapter 13, "Looking for CGI Resources."** If we didn't cover it here, we definitely covered it there (take a look, if you haven't already)!

Since knowing where to start looking for information is a key ingre-dient for a successful Web information search, we're glad to help you start off on the right foot. But before you run off to look for yourself, read the rest of this chapter. You may want to hit some of the other resources in here first, instead of finding them on your own!

ASK AN EXPERT!

By all means, if you know somebody who's been hacking CGIs since the WWW was a just a small skein in an out-of-the-way research lab in Switzerland, ask them for input on good CGI resources. They may even share some of their own stuff with you. Other places to ask for pointers should include the relevant newsgroups and mailing lists (see Chapter 13) and Doctor Web, available at:

```
http:/www.stars.com/Dr.Web/
```

DO SOME READING

There are lots of good resources out there (so we can't tell you how *thrilled* we are that you're reading our book). In addition to the informa-tion that these pages contain, you should take a trip to your favorite bookstore and consult titles in any or all of the following areas:

- HTML information, programming, and design.
- Computer languages, especially Perl, Java, Python, and C.
- CGI or Web programming (while our book is the only one in this category right now, we don't expect it to stay that way for long!).

You'll also find useful information in weekly or monthly computer magazines like *PC Week*, *PC Magazine*, *Internet World*, *IWAY*, *NetGuide*, and others. Please consult Chapter 13 for contact/subscription informa-tion on these resources. They all cover the Web regularly and often include useful information on new and interesting CGI libraries, tools, or techniques.

By the time you've waded through all this material, you'll have amassed enough URLs to check to keep you busy for a week. If they're not on the list covered in the sites mentioned in this chapter, you may have undiscovered riches yet to explore!

Some Select CGI Sites

In this section, we'll take you on a tour of half a dozen CGI sites on the Web that we've found to contain useful pointers, usable code, and/or useful programming information. We'll present these sites by their URLs in alphabetical order, followed by a brief description of their contents, coverage, and value to both budding and horribly experienced CGI programmers.

HTTP://HOOHOO.NCSA.UIUC.EDU/CGI/INTERFACE.HTML

Description

This is the "front page" for CGI information at the National Center for Supercomputing Applications, NCSA, one of the primary sources for Web server software and technology on the Web today. This site offers a rich collection of information about CGI, including numerous specifications, programming guides, and other documentation. It also includes a large collection of CGI programs, source code, and pointers to other related references.

CGI Collections

NCSA maintains a large collection of CGI programs in an FTP archive on its server. The URL for this collection is:

```
ftp://ftp.ncsa.uiuc.edu/Web/httpd/Unix/ncsa_httpd/cgi/
```

Figure 15-1 shows a screenshot from the file listing in this archive, which just scratches the surface of what's available here. You'll find everything from CGIs for forms-handling to online comics retrieval routines — hey, would we kid you about something as important as the comics?

Netscape - [Directory of /Web/httpd/Unix/ncsa_httpd/cgi]

File   Edit   View   Go   Bookmarks   Options   Directory   Help

Back   Forward   Home   Reload   Images   Open   Print   Find   Stop

Location: ftp://ftp.ncsa.uiuc.edu/Web/httpd/Unix/ncsa_httpd/cgi/   N

```
Up to higher level directory
   .message              416 bytes Sun Jun 04 21:39:00 1995
   AA-1.2.tar.Z            9 Kb    Thu Jul 07 00:00:00 1994 compressed fi
   README                413 bytes Thu Jul 07 00:00:00 1994
   bbc_man2html           21 Kb    Thu Jul 07 00:00:00 1994
   cgi-lib.pl.Z            2 Kb    Tue May 02 11:33:00 1995 compressed fi
   cgi-src/                        Wed May 03 05:45:00 1995 Directory
   cgi_handlers.pl.Z       2 Kb    Thu Jul 07 00:00:00 1994 compressed fi
   form-mail-1.3.tar.Z    16 Kb    Thu Jul 07 00:00:00 1994 compressed fi
   htcache.pl.Z            6 Kb    Thu Jul 07 00:00:00 1994 compressed fi
   htmlfinger              3 Kb    Thu Jul 07 00:00:00 1994
   mailin.c.Z              1 Kb    Thu Jul 07 00:00:00 1994 compressed fi
   ncsa-default.tar.Z     33 Kb    Thu Jul 07 00:00:00 1994 compressed fi
   read-comics.Z           5 Kb    Thu Jul 07 00:00:00 1994 compressed fi
   saytime.tar.Z           2 Kb    Thu Jul 07 00:00:00 1994 compressed fi
   sh-post.tar.Z           2 Kb    Thu Jul 07 00:00:00 1994 compressed fi
```

Figure 15-1
The FTP listing for the NCSA CGI archive shows most of the items it contains.

Because of the wealth of information as well as the software that this site contains, we can't recommend it highly enough. Please do check it out.

http://www-genome.wi.mit.edu/ftp/pub /software/WWW/cgi_docs.html

Description

This is an outstanding library of forms-handling CGI routines, written in Perl by L. Stein of the MIT Human Genome project. This library, known as "CGI.pm", uses objects to create Web fill-out forms on-the-fly and to parse their contents.

"CGI.pm" supplies a simple interface for parsing and handling query strings passed to CGI programs. It also offers a set of functions for creating fill-out forms in HTML. Instead of using HTML syntax for forms elements, the document is created by Perl function calls.

In "CGI.pm" all actions occur through a *CGI* object. When you create an object, it examines the environment for a query string, parses it, and stores the results. You can then ask that object to return or modify query values. CGI objects can handle either POST or GET methods, and can correctly distinguish between scripts called from <ISINDEX> documents and form-based documents. "CGI.pm" even allows you to debug your scripts from the command line without worrying about setting up environment variables.

CGI Collections

"CGI.pm" is stored on the server in a UNIX compressed (*.Z*) format. It can be downloaded via an HTTP file transfer right on the page. Because the compressed version of the library is less than 46 Kbytes, it's quick and easy to grab. Figure 15-2 shows the link to the file.

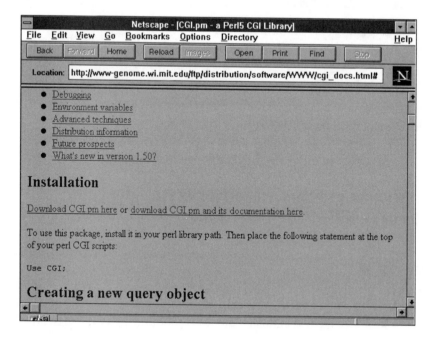

Figure 15-2
The CGI.pm library can be downloaded right from a link on this page.

HTTP://WWW.COSY.SBG.AC.AT/WWW-DOKU/TOOLS/ BJSCRIPTS.HTML

Description

This is a collection of CGI scripts assembled by Brigitte Jellinek, of the University of Salzburg, in Austria. It includes a spiffy guestbook application, some system administration utilities, and some log file handling CGIs, in addition to the forms-handling library that won our hearts. Figure 15-3 shows a listing of what Ms. Jellinek has to offer.

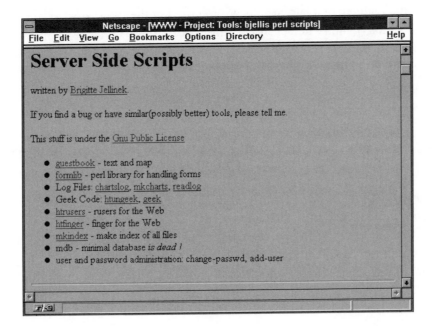

Figure 15-3
A forms-handling library is just one of the gems in Ms. Jellinek's collection.

CGI Collections

"Formlib.pl" contains three Perl subroutines that can help you handle input from HTML forms. For forms that use the POST method, you'll need to use the 'GetPostArgs' routine, and for those that use the GET method, the 'GetFormArgs'.

All three of these subroutines read and parse the input appropriately, and deliver their arguments in an associative array named '%in'. Thus if you had an input field named 'color' in your form, and the user entered 'red' in that field, you'd find that:

```
$in('color') == 'red'.
```

Ms. Jellinek also includes a subroutine 'GetPathArgs' to parse arguments passed via the PATH, where she assumes the format will be:

```
/var1=value1/var2=value2...
```

for the path. Here again, results are returned in the associative array, '%in'.

As Ms. Jellinek herself notes, this can be quite convenient should you want to access the same program from several forms: some of them general and some of them specialized (perhaps with fixed or hidden values).

HTTP://WWW.OAC.UCI.EDU/INDIV/EHOOD/PERLWWW/

Description

This is a collection of pointers to Perl CGI programs and other tools maintained by Earl Hood, of Convex Computer Corporation in the Dallas area in Texas, another name that pops up frequently in CGI programming circles. This page contains a broad selection of applications, HTML browsers, file conversion programs, widgets, utilities, and other goodies.

CGI Collections

Earl's page includes a category called "Development" that features pointers to CGI libraries and archives, including both "cgi-lib.pl" and "CGI.pm" (mentioned elsewhere in this section). It also provides pointers to four other major libraries. Other sections include pointers to a bunch of useful Perl-based tools and widgets; aspiring authors can also contact Mr. Hood to see about getting their own Perl libraries or programs listed.

HTTP://WWW.STARS.COM/VLIB/PROVIDERS/CGI.HTML

Description

This collection of CGI resources is part of the Web Developer's Virtual Library project, implemented by Alan Richmond at *stars.com* (also the home of Doctor Web). Here's what *Netsurfer Digest* (April 21, 1995) has to say about this site:

> *The WWW Virtual Library section on Web Development has over 1,000 links to sites with information of interest. Whatever you want to know about the World Wide Web can probably be found in one of the sites pointed to by their extensive topical list. This site makes it quick and easy to find sites containing more information.*

Their CGI section is no exception to this; it contains pointers to innumerable sources of code, specifications, and other information about CGI. Figure 15-4 only hints at the wealth of information you'll find at this URL.

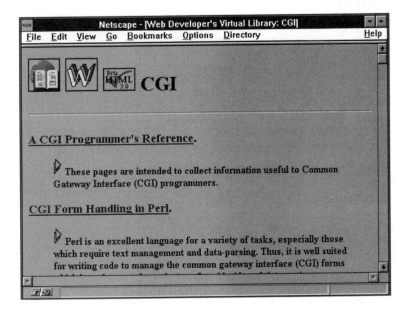

Figure 15-4
The W3 Developer's Virtual Library has an extensive listing of CGI-related topics.

CGI Collections

The Virtual Library listing for CGI includes 27 entries, of which 12 or 13 contain useful CGI code samples, libraries, or programs. It includes almost all of the other resources we cover in this chapter, in addition to the primary sources of documentation and server-specific information.

HTTP://WWW.W3.ORG/HYPERTEXT/WWW/ DAEMON/USER/CGI/OVERVIEW.HTML

Description

This URL points to the CERN *httpd* site, and includes an in-depth discussion of the CGI interface for that particular server. In addition to providing good background information and implementation details on CGI, these documents include multiple code samples inline, as well as pointers to numerous example programs.

CGI Collections

You'll find pointers to a date conversion program (*calendar*) and a Web gateway to the UNIX *finger* command, as well as the nearly ubiquitous *cgi-parse* program (used to parse input variables using the POST method). These pages also include useful installation and server-handling information (specific to the CERN implementation) regarding CGI scripts.

HTTP://WWW.WEBEDGE.COM/WEB.DEV.HTML

Description

This document comprises Carl de Cordova's "Web Development Pointers," which is surely one of the most comprehensive sets of Macintosh-related Web development pointers available anywhere. Figure 15-5 doesn't begin to do justice to the breadth of coverage that this page contains, but it provides pointers to some very interesting AppleScript resources.

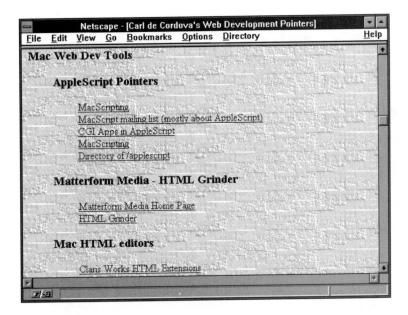

Figure 15-5
The WebEdge Developer's page includes pointers to nearly everything development-related for the Macintosh.

CGI Collections

In addition to the many AppleScript resources depicted in Figure 15-5, the WebEdge server is host to a large collection of CGIs authored by WebEdge attendees. At this site, you'll find the best collection of Macintosh CGIs available anywhere!

HTTP://WWW.YAHOO.COM/COMPUTERS/WORLD_WIDE _WEB/CGI_COMMON_GATEWAY_INTERFACE/

Description

Yahoo stands for "Yet Another Hierarchical Officious Oracle"; it's a database written and maintained by David Filo and Jerry Yang, who style themselves "self-proclaimed Yahoos." This is an inauspicious introduction to one of the real treasures of the World Wide Web. This particular URL takes you to the compendium of CGI-related resources that Yahoo can lead you to. Figure 15-6 can only hint at the wealth of information and material included in the 23 entries listed here.

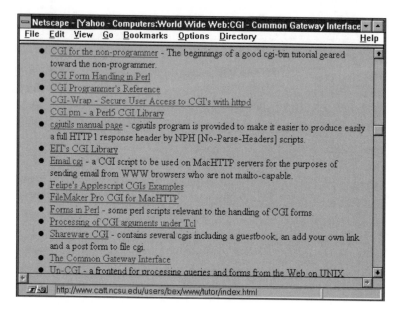

Figure 15-6
The Yahoo listings for "CGI" include a bunch of great code collections.

CGI Collections

You'll find that 17 of the 23 entries (at least, at the time of this writing) point to collections of CGI code from platforms ranging from the Amiga to UNIX. And the resources linked herein include only minimal overlap with our own picks, as well as those lists provided by other hotlists and link pages. This collection is worth visiting and revisiting, as you mine the libraries and programs for goodies worth grabbing and reusing!

Using CGI Programs Effectively

We've got to confess that one of the libraries we mentioned in this chapter — namely, Brigitte Jellinek's "form.pl" — didn't exactly pop out of any searches. Though we did find her by name on the Web, this library didn't show up on any of our search engines. Instead, her reputation preceded her entry into this book: as we looked through our own CGIs and those of others, her code kept showing up all over the place.

This points to one of the key benefits of joining the Internet community in general, and the fraternity of CGI programmers in particular: good tools spread like wildfire and become part of what "everybody knows." We don't know who first heard about Brigitte's work, or how we first obtained a copy, but among the authors of this book, "everybody knows" that "forms.pl" is an invaluable tool. What this should tell you is that this Perl program is quite worth checking out. It also suggests that reading lots of CGIs and looking for other common elements may help you to locate other treasures that might not register on the CGI radar any other way.

By exclusion, this also points out another potential gotcha when using CGIs taken off the Net. Not every tool or program is as usable as "form.pl". Sometimes, the work of others takes more time and effort to master and incorporate into your own code, than building the equivalent functionality yourself. While you're perusing these libraries, keep reminding yourself of this tradeoff and stay away from things that appear hard to understand. If it looks too hard to use, it probably is!

In other words, the best proof of reusability is repeated use in other CGIs. If you stick to the tools that you find used most often by others, you may not live on the bleeding edge of programming technology. But until you become a CGI guru yourself, living on the edge may be a little ambitious anyway.

Besides, there'll come a time, sooner or later, when you have to build or use some brand-spanking new tool, algorithm, or technology because you have no other choice. You can have your fun teetering on the bleeding edge when that happens — in the meantime, stick to those tools and programs that have withstood the use and abuse of your colleagues, and you'll be less likely to wind up bleeding all over your late and broken CGI code!

Publish and/or Perish!

When you've covered all the bases for a particular widget or program and haven't come up with a solution, you may be forced to write a widget or program of your own someday. If that happens to you, it may cause you to think about sharing your work with others and publishing your CGI on the Web.

We think this is a great idea, but you have to be certain that what you have to offer is both general and useful enough to be worth publishing. This means that if your widget lets a system administrator assign a new user account name and password, that you take the time to test it on multiple versions of UNIX before you release it to the world. It also means that you'll want to release it privately to a small circle of would-be users and incorporate their feedback before you loose your tool on an unsuspecting world.

Then, when you do publish your CGI program or widget, you can do so with confidence that it works as advertised and that it provides functionality that others can actually use. Anything less, as they say, is simply unacceptable! And when you've published your work, be open to the feedback from users that will come your way and be prepared to refine and improve your work over time. This will keep your widget or program useful, rather than making it obsolete.

Summary

In this chapter, we've covered a number of key Web sites where you'll find CGI programs ready for the taking (if not for the using). We've also tried to point out some useful resources and approaches for finding other sites and code we may not have mentioned in the select set of resources that we do cover.

Hopefully, this combination of goodies includes the very CGI widget or program you're looking for. If not, you may have to write the code yourself. If you do, you can think about publishing your own work on the Web when it's written, tested, and ready for prime time.

Don't forget that using "other people's code" is nearly as easy and as much fun as spending "other people's money." Just remember: you don't know where that code has been, so be careful what you use and how you use it. As always, practice "safe computing"!

16 <FORM> Alternatives

*T*he HTML <FORM> tag, and its several relatives — <INPUT>, <TEXTAREA>, <SELECT>, and <OPTION> — have probably been the cause of more CGI programming than any other single capability on the Web. Given the ease of building an on-screen form and the many tools and techniques available to write CGIs to process their input, it may come as a shock to hear that many users aren't capable of handling forms at all.

Estimates vary among the pundits, but the experts we asked opined that anywhere between 1 out of 2 and 1 out of 4 people cruising the Web today can't use interactive forms. That's because they may be using browsers that can't display forms (character-mode browsers like Lynx) or that can't handle forms input in any way, shape, or form (most HTML 1.0-era software, or older).

You may be tempted to blow off this segment of the audience, especially since it's shrinking daily. On the other hand, if you're really interested in getting feedback from everybody who visits your pages, you may be interested to hear that these "graphically challenged" users can be accommodated on your Web pages with a small amount of additional thought and programming effort.

In this chapter, we'll examine a number of methods for presenting text-based alternatives to on-screen forms input. We'll also discuss how to design the text information you'll send to these users to make it easy to parse and incorporate into your forms-based data logs or databases. Along the way, we'll take a look at an online book registration form and describe how to build a text alternative.

From <FORM> to Text?

When you design an on-screen form in HTML, you'll most often start from a document of some kind, or even a preprinted form. Whatever your source of inspiration and design, be sure to save it, because that source will come in handy for the creation of a text-based equivalent.

Creating a pure-text version of a nicely-formatted on-screen form or a professionally printed paper form may seem like a step in the wrong direction, especially in terms of "look and feel." So why are we encouraging you to take this giant leap backward in appearance? It's simple: you can be sure of delivering plain text to just about any kind of computer on the Internet without getting tripped up by formatting problems, character set incompatibilities, or what-have-you.

The same cannot be said for most other ways of presenting data to users on a computer; at best, if you can assume they have access to a common display engine (like Adobe Acrobat or WordPerfect Envoy), you can send them something they can print out and write in by hand. But that means somebody will have to key in this data later on, before it can become a part of your online data empire.

The pure-text approach, while sometimes ugly and always full of nit-picky little details, adds to universal deliverability the advantage of being editable on all platforms. If you simply include an e-mail address with your text file and request that users e-mail you that text form, the minute details of platform-specific file formatting (that is, "end of line" handling and character codes) can be neatly sidestepped by the delivery mechanisms inherent in SMTP mail and MIME encoding (text/ASCII).

From HTML Back to Text

To begin with, the listing that follows defines the HTML for an online registration form for an IDG book. It's production-level HTML that's been cleaned up a bit to protect the innocent (or at least, to keep the guilty parties safely anonymous):

```
<HTML>
<HEAD>
<TITLE>Foundation Programming - IDG Books - IDG Registration
```

```
</TITLE>
<BODY>
<A NAME="top"></A><IMG SRC="graphics/line.gif"><BR>
<B><A HREF="twf.html">HOME</A> &#32;&#166;
<A HREF="comment.html">BACK</A> &#32;&#166;
<A HREF="ftpstuff.html#top">NEXT</A> &#32;&#166;
<A HREF="searchtwf.html#menu">MENU</A> &#32;&#166;
<A HREF="searchtwf.html#search4d">SEARCH</A> &#32;&#166;
<A HREF="contact.html">CONTACT</A> &#32;&#166;
<A HREF="comment.html">COMMENT</A> &#32;&#166;
<A HREF="helpinfo.html">HELPINFO</A></B><BR>
<IMG SRC="graphics/line.gif"><P>
<H1><IMG ALIGN=TOP SRC="graphics/found1.gif">
IDG Online Registration</H1><P>
<IMG SRC="graphics/line.gif"><BR>

This page is the on-line version of the registration sheet in the book. If
you have purchased the book, you may use this page to register your purchase
and send comments to IDG. <I>Please use this form only if you have purchased
the book.</I><P>
<FORM METHOD="POST"
 ACTION="http://www.outer.net/cgi-bin/twf.register.pl">

<H2>Title of this Book: <I>Foundation Programming</I></H2><P>
My overall rating of this book:
<INPUT TYPE="RADIO" NAME="overrate" VALUE="VG">Very Good
<INPUT TYPE="RADIO" NAME="overrate" VALUE="G">Good
<INPUT TYPE="RADIO" NAME="overrate" VALUE="S">Satisfactory
<INPUT TYPE="RADIO" NAME="overrate" VALUE="F">Fair
<INPUT TYPE="RADIO" NAME="overrate" VALUE="P">Poor<P>

How I first heard about this book:<BR>
<IMG SRC="graphics/ind2.gif">
<INPUT TYPE="CHECKBOX" NAME ="Bookstore">Found in Bookstore:
<INPUT TYPE="TEXT" NAME="BSname" VALUE="" SIZE="20"><BR>
<IMG SRC="graphics/ind2.gif">
<INPUT TYPE="CHECKBOX" NAME ="Ad">Advertisement<BR>
<IMG SRC="graphics/ind2.gif">
<INPUT TYPE="CHECKBOX" NAME ="Word">Word of mouth, from a friend, co-worker,
etc.<BR>
<IMG SRC="graphics/ind2.gif">
<INPUT TYPE="checkbox" NAME ="Review">Book Review<BR>
<IMG SRC="graphics/ind2.gif">
<INPUT TYPE="checkbox" NAME ="Catalog">Catalog<BR>
<IMG SRC="graphics/ind2.gif">
<INPUT TYPE="CHECKBOX" NAME ="Other">Other: <INPUT TYPE="TEXT" NAME="othernm"
Value="" SIZE="20"><P>

What I liked most about this book:<BR>
<TEXTAREA NAME="liked" ROWS="4" COLs="60"></TEXTAREA><P>

What I would change, add, delete, etc. in future editions of this book:<BR>
<TEXTAREA NAME="change" ROWS="4" COLs="60"></TEXTAREA><P>
```

```
Other Comments:<BR>
<TEXTAREA NAME="comments" ROWS="4" COLs="60"></TEXTAREA><P>

Number of computer books I purchase in a year: <BR>
<INPUT TYPE="RADIO" NAME="compnumb" VALUE="1">One [1]
<INPUT TYPE="RADIO" NAME="compnumb" VALUE="2to5">Two to Five [2-5]
<INPUT TYPE="RADIO" NAME="compnumb" VALUE="6to10">Six to Ten [6-10]
<INPUT TYPE="RADIO" NAME="compnumb" VALUE="plus10">More than 10<P>

I would characterize my computer skills as: <BR>
<INPUT TYPE="RADIO" NAME="compskil" VALUE="Beginner">Beginner
<INPUT TYPE="RADIO" NAME="compskil" VALUE="Intermediate">Intermediate
<INPUT TYPE="RADIO" NAME="compskil" VALUE="Advanced">Advanced
<INPUT TYPE="RADIO" NAME="compskil" VALUE="Professional">Professional<P>

I use: <BR>
<IMG SRC="graphics/ind2.gif">
<INPUT TYPE="CHECKBOX" NAME ="DOS">DOS<BR>
<IMG SRC="graphics/ind2.gif">
<INPUT TYPE="CHECKBOX" NAME ="Windows">Windows<BR>
<IMG SRC="graphics/ind2.gif">
<INPUT TYPE="CHECKBOX" NAME ="OS/2">OS/2<BR>
<IMG SRC="graphics/ind2.gif">
<INPUT TYPE="CHECKBOX" NAME ="Macintosh">Macintosh<BR>
<IMG SRC="graphics/ind2.gif">
<INPUT TYPE="CHECKBOX" NAME ="Other">Other: <INPUT TYPE="TEXT" NAME="otherpc"
VALUE="" SIZE="20"><P>

I would be interested in new books on the following subjects:<BR>
<IMG SRC="graphics/ind2.gif">
<INPUT TYPE="CHECKBOX" NAME ="WordProc">Word Processing:
<INPUT TYPE="TEXT" NAME="WordProcNm" VALUE="" SIZE="30"><BR>
<IMG SRC="graphics/ind2.gif">
<INPUT TYPE="CHECKBOX" NAME ="Spreadsheets">Spreadsheets:
<INPUT TYPE="TEXT" NAME="SpreadsheetsNm" VALUE="" SIZE="30"><BR>
<IMG SRC="graphics/ind2.gif">
<INPUT TYPE="CHECKBOX" NAME ="Databases">Data bases:
<INPUT TYPE="TEXT" NAME="DatabasesNm" VALUE="" SIZE="30"><BR>
<IMG SRC="graphics/ind2.gif">
<INPUT TYPE="CHECKBOX" NAME ="Desktop">Desktop Publishing:
<INPUT TYPE="TEXT" NAME="DesktopNm" VALUE="" SIZE="30"><BR>
<IMG SRC="graphics/ind2.gif">
<INPUT TYPE="CHECKBOX" NAME ="FileUtil">File Utilities:
<INPUT TYPE="TEXT" NAME="FileUtilNm" VALUE="" SIZE="30"><BR>
<IMG SRC="graphics/ind2.gif">
<INPUT TYPE="CHECKBOX" NAME ="MoneyMng">Money Management:
<INPUT TYPE="TEXT" NAME="MoneyMngNm" VALUE="" SIZE="30"><BR>
<IMG SRC="graphics/ind2.gif">
<INPUT TYPE="CHECKBOX" NAME ="Networking">Networking:
<INPUT TYPE="TEXT" NAME="NetworkingNm" VALUE="" size="30"><BR>
<IMG SRC="graphics/ind2.gif">
<INPUT TYPE="CHECKBOX" NAME ="ProgLang">Programming Languages:
<INPUT TYPE="TEXT" NAME="ProgLangNm" VALUE="" SIZE="30"><BR>
```

```
<IMG SRC="graphics/ind2.gif">
<INPUT TYPE="CHECKBOX" NAME ="Other">Other:
<INPUT TYPE="TEXT" NAME="other" VALUE="" SIZE=30><P>


I use a PC at:
<INPUT TYPE="CHECKBOX" NAME ="PCHome">Home
<INPUT TYPE="CHECKBOX" NAME ="PCWork">Work
<INPUT TYPE="CHECKBOX" NAME ="PCSchool">School
<INPUT TYPE="CHECKBOX" NAME ="PCOther">Other:
<INPUT TYPE="TEXT" NAME="PCOtherNm" VALUE="" SIZE="30"><P>


The disks I prefer to use are
<INPUT TYPE="CHECKBOX" NAME ="525">5.25&quot;
<INPUT TYPE="CHECKBOX" NAME ="35">3.5&quot;
<INPUT TYPE="CHECKBOX" NAME ="DiskOther">Other:
<INPUT TYPE="TEXT" NAME="DiskOtherSize" VALUE="" size="20"><P>


I have a CD-ROM:
<INPUT TYPE=RADIO NAME="CDROM" VALUE="Yes">Yes
<INPUT TYPE=RADIO NAME="CDROM" VALUE="No">No<P>


I plan to buy or upgrade computer hardware this year:
<INPUT TYPE=RADIO NAME="Hardware" VALUE="Yes">Yes
<INPUT TYPE=RADIO NAME="Hardware" VALUE="No">No<P>


I plan to buy or upgrade computer software this year:
<INPUT TYPE=RADIO NAME="Software" VALUE="Yes">Yes
<INPUT TYPE=RADIO NAME="Software" VALUE="No">No<P>


<HR>
Name: <INPUT TYPE="TEXT" NAME="Name" VALUE="" SIZE="30"><P>
Business Title: <INPUT TYPE="TEXT" NAME="Bustitle" VALUE="" SIZE="30"><P>
Type of Business: <INPUT TYPE="TEXT" NAME="TypeBus" VALUE="" SIZE="30"><P>
<INPUT TYPE=RADIO NAME="AddrLoc" VALUE="Home">Home
<INPUT TYPE=RADIO NAME="AddrLoc" VALUE="Work">Work<BR>
Address1: <INPUT TYPE="TEXT" NAME="Addr1" VALUE="" SIZE="50"><P>
Address2: <INPUT TYPE="TEXT" NAME="Addr2" VALUE="" SIZE="50"><P>
City/State/Zip: <INPUT TYPE="TEXT" NAME="CSZ" VALUE="" SIZE="30"><P>
Country: <INPUT TYPE="TEXT" NAME="Country" VALUE="" SIZE="30"><P>
<HR>

<INPUT TYPE="CHECKBOX" NAME ="QuoteMe"><B>I Liked this book!</B><BR>
<IMG SRC="graphics/ind2.gif">You may quote me by name in future IDG
  Books Worldwide promotional materials.<P>
My daytime phone number is: <INPUT TYPE="TEXT" NAME="DayPhone" VALUE=""
SIZE="30"><P>


<INPUT TYPE="submit" NAME="Register" VALUE="Register"><P>


<IMG SRC="graphics/line.gif"><BR>
<B><A HREF="twf.html">HOME</A> &#32;&#166;
<A HREF="comment.html">BACK</A> &#32;&#166;
<A HREF="ftpstuff.html#top">NEXT</A> &#32;&#166;
```

```
<A HREF="searchtwf.html#menu">MENU</A> &#32;&#166;
<A HREF="searchtwf.html#search4d">SEARCH</A> &#32;&#166;
<A HREF="contact.html">CONTACT</A> &#32;&#166;
<A HREF="comment.html">COMMENT</A> &#32;&#166;
<A HREF="helpinfo.html">HELPINFO</A></B>
<IMG SRC="graphics/line.gif"><P>

<ADDRESS>
<A NAME="bottom"></A>
E-Mail: <A HREF="mailto:twf@outer.net">
Foundations Programming at twf@outer.net</A><BR>
</ADDRESS>
URL: <A HREF="http://www.outer.net/twf/registrn.html">
http://www.outer.net/twf/registrn.html</A>
<BR>
Text - Copyright &copy; 1995, Ed Tittel, Mark Gaither, Mike Erwin &amp;
Sebastian Hassinger.<BR>
Foundations Design and Art - Copyright &copy; 1995, IDG Books Worldwide,
Inc.<BR>
Web Layout - Copyright &copy; 1995, LANWrights &amp;
<A HREF="http://www.io.com/~mcintyre/homepage.html">IMPACT Online.</A><BR>
Revised — June 23rd, 1995 [JMS - IMPACT Online]<BR>
</BODY>
</HTML>
```

This is a lot of HTML to digest, but as we discuss Figures 16-1 through 16-5 in the sections that follow, we'll show you what this looks like a screenful at a time, as we explain how to turn this HTML back into text.

The Art of Textification

When converting a form into a text-based equivalent, the most important thing to remember is that any line that contains user input will have to be parsed and the user input extracted. Making this easy should be a prime design consideration (you'll save yourself extra programming effort that way). We strongly recommend structuring the text file so that input occurs at the end of any given line, after a separator (like a colon, as in our example) or on a line by itself. You'll see this principle at work in the subsections that follow.

Be sure to begin your file with some user instructions, to let them know a computer will be reading the form. Be sure to end the file with the e-mail address where the data should be sent, so it can begin to take its rightful place in your collection of end-user data.

REGISTRATION FORM, PART 1

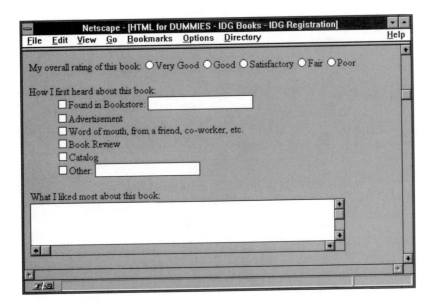

Figure 16-1
The first screenful from the registration form includes rating and product discovery information.

Figure 16-1 picks up where the user input begins, after the form's actual introduction. We'll start you off with the text-based version's opening instructions, to lay the groundwork for user completion, and then follow with the text equivalent of the information included in the figure:

```
            The Foundations Programming Registration Form

Dear Reader:
   Welcome to the Foundations Programming Registration Form! We'd like you
to fill this out to the best of your ability and e-mail it to us at the
following address:
   twf-form@outer.net
If you have any comments or questions about the form, or the book, please
e-mail:
   twf-support@outer.net
We'll be happy to answer any of your questions and help you find your way
through our materials!
```

```
Instructions:
1. Please edit this file with an ASCII editor, or save the output
   from your editor as "text-only."
2. Please do not remove or edit item tags at the head of each
   question line; item tags are surrounded by square brackets
   ("[ ]") and contain sequence numbers.
3. Please do not remove the colon (":") that ends each input line
   on the form; it's what we use to tell the computer where to start
   reading your information.
4. Any changes to the form that make it unreadable to our mail-
   handling program will result in a return mail message to you
   containing a blank form. It this happens to you, and you can't
   figure out why, please e-mail us at the support address.
Thanks! (You may delete any part of this form, up to the line of
        equal signs that follows below, before mailing.)
=======================================================================
[1]  My overall rating of this book (place an "X" to the right of
     your selection)
     [1.1]  Very Good:
     [1.2]  Good:
     [1.3]  Satisfactory:
     [1.4]  Fair:
     [1.5]  Poor:

[2]  How I first heard about this book (place an "X" to the right of
     your selection, or add appropriate text where requested)
     [2.1]  Found in bookstore:
     [2.2]  Name of bookstore:
     [2.3]  Advertisement:
     [2.4]  Word of mouth (from a friend, co-worker, etc.):
     [2.5]  Book Review:
     [2.6]  Catalog:
     [2.7]  Other:
     [2.8]  Please explain:

[3]  What I liked most about this book (you may write up to four
     lines of text for your answer)
```

Please note that we've given a unique bracketed label for each item and that we've kept items one to a line whenever possible. Note also that the textarea question (item [3]) is followed by the maximum number of lines of input allowed for an answer.

REGISTRATION FORM, PART 2

Figure 16-2 concludes the overall commentary on the form with open-ended questions about what might need changing in the book, along with a request for other comments. It then commences the user profile section of the form, requesting information about book-buying habits and a self-assessment of the reader's computer skills:

```
[4]   What I would change, add, delete, etc. in future editions of
      this book (you may enter up to 4 lines of text for your answer)




[5]   Other Comments (you may enter up to 4 lines of text for your
      comments)




[6]   Number of computer books I purchase in a year (place an "X" to
      the right of your selection).
      [6.1]   One (1):
      [6.2]   Two to Five (2-5):
      [6.3]   Six to Ten (6-10):
      [6.4]   More than 10:

[7]   I would characterize my computer skills as (place an "X" to the
      right of your selection).
      [7.1]   Beginner:
      [7.2]   Intermediate:
      [7.3]   Advanced:
      [7.4]   Professional:
```

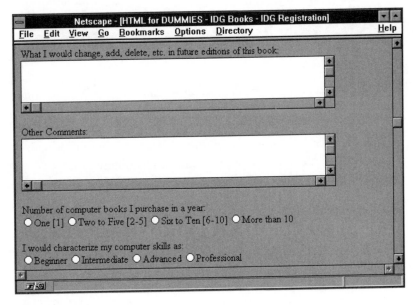

Figure 16-2
This part of the registration form asks for suggestions for change, other comments, and starts a user computer profile.

Here again, we've provided the maximum number of input lines allowed as blank lines in an essay-question format.

REGISTRATION FORM, PART 3

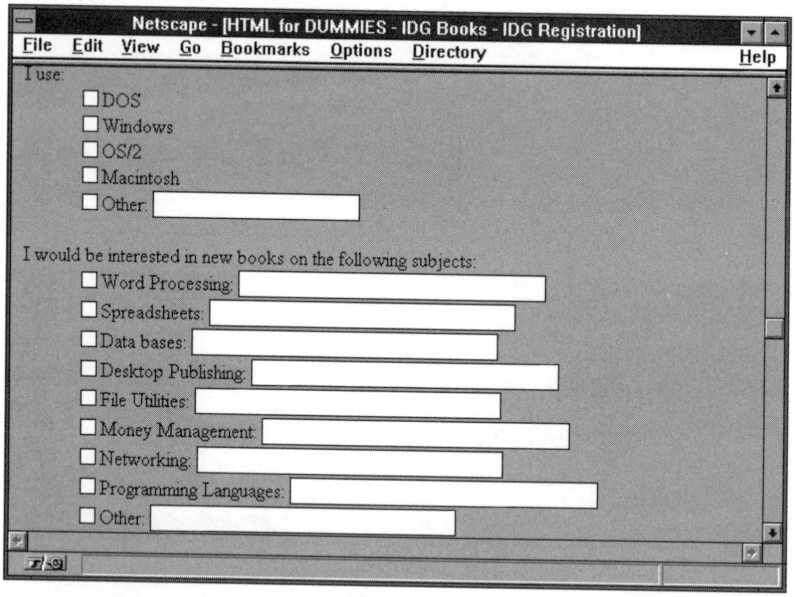

Figure 16-3
This part of the form continues the reader's computer profile, capturing information about platforms and software used.

In this part of the form (see Figure 16-3), we solicit information about the reader's computer platform and their potential interest in other software or hardware topics. This part includes selection of interest areas and free-form input on the HTML; we'll simplify it with text instructions instead:

```
[8]   I use (place an "X" to the right of the software you use, or
      write in what you use if you select "Other.")
      [8.1]   DOS:
      [8.2]   Windows:
      [8.3]   OS/2:
      [8.4]   Macintosh:
      [8.5]   Other:
```

```
[9]   I would be interested in new books on the following subjects
      (write in topics or suggestions to the right of the subject):
      [9.1]  Word Processing:
      [9.2]  Spreadsheets:
      [9.3]  Databases:
      [9.4]  Desktop Publishing:
      [9.5]  File Utilities:
      [9.6]  Memory Management:
      [9.7]  Networking:
      [9.8]  Programming Languages:
      [9.9]  Other:
```

REGISTRATION FORM, PART 4

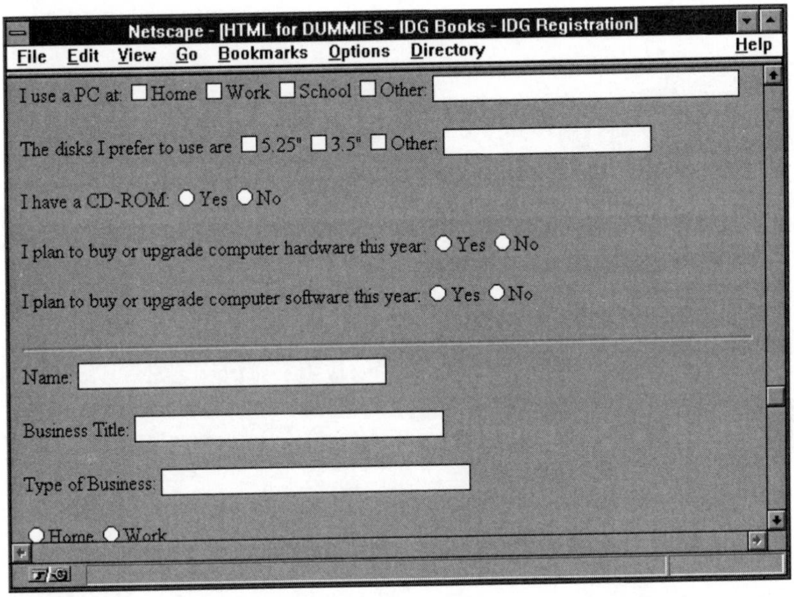

Figure 16-4
This part of the form completes the reader's computer profile and begins to capture his or her identification information.

We conclude the survey of the reader's computer involvement and expertise here, with questions about PC use, diskette size, and equipment ownership and buying plans (see Figure 16-4). After the horizontal rule, we begin the section that captures the reader's name, address, and employment information:

```
[10] I use a PC at (place an "X" to the right of your selection; if
     you select "Other" tell us where you use it):
     [10.1] Home:
     [10.2] Work:
     [10.4] Other:

[11] The disks I prefer to use are (place an "X" to the right of
     your selection; if you select "Other" tell us what kind):
     [11.1] 5.25":
     [11.2] 3.5":
     [11.3] Other:

[12] I have a CD-ROM (place an "X" to the right of your selection):
     [12.1] Yes:
     [12.2] No:

[13] I plan to buy or upgrade computer hardware this year (place an
     "X" to the right of your selection):
     [13.1] Yes:
     [13.2] No:

[14] I plan to buy or upgrade computer software this year (place an
     "X" to the right of your selection):
     [14.1] Yes:
     [14.2] No:

On the next three lines, enter your information to the right of the field.
[15] Name:
[16] Business Title:
[17] Type of Business:

[18] Please mark to the right to identify the address that follows:
     [18.1] Home:
     [18.2] Office:
```

REGISTRATION FORM, PART 5

As shown in Figure 16-5, by keeping formats regular and consistent, using the colon as a field delimiter, and informing users about the rules for filling out a text-only form successfully, you can make it easy for them to understand what's expected of them:

```
[19] Please provide your street address, including mail stop or
     other internal routing information. You can use up to two lines
     of text.

[20] Please provide your City, State or Province, ZIP or Postal
     code, and Country information on the lines that follow:
```

```
    [20.1] City:
    [20.2] State/Province:
    [20.3] ZIP/Postal Code:
    [20.4] Country:

[21] Please place an "X" to the right of the "Yes!" below if we can
     quote from your response to this questionnaire.
     [21.1] Yes!:

[22] Please provide your daytime telephone number (optional):
     [22.1] Phone:

Thanks for filling out our questionnaire. Remember to save it as a text-only
file (ASCII format), and e-mail it to twf-form@outer.net.
```

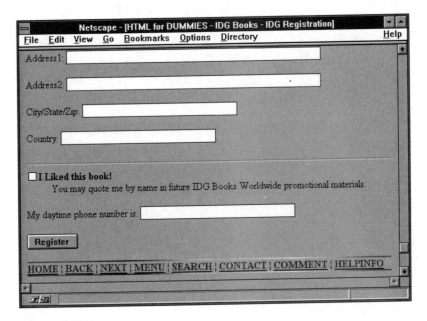

Figure 16-5
This portion of the form concludes the user contact information and repeats the necessary e-mail address.

Better still, it will make your programming job easier, when it comes to decoding the reader input that the form can provide. By reading the tags and searching for values beyond the colon, it'll be easy to tell what fields have been filled in and to associate those values with the proper field names.

We'd recommend writing a program that reads this input and creates an input stream that matches the input that HTTP delivers to the CGI for the original form; that way, you can use the same software to handle e-mail input processing as well as Web-based input. Remember, you won't need to create an HTML document for feedback or to acknowledge receipt of the data, but you may want to send a one-line e-mail back to the submitter indicating receipt of their data.

Shipping the Text-Only Form File

When it comes to delivering the data to readers who lack forms capability in their browsers, you have several options for delivering that information to them. The easiest and most intuitive is just to include a link on your page that downloads the file to them when they select it. By creating a link with an HREF that points to a file with a MIME content-type other than text/html, most browsers will allow users to download the file for handling by a helper application. Because of its ease and simplicity, this approach is the one we recommend.

Of course, since e-mail will be the vehicle for returning input from the user, why not use it to deliver the blank form in the first place. If all browsers could reliably capture a user's e-mail address, this would be just a matter of reading the right environment variable(s). But since parsing the 'REMOTE_HOST' variable, or concatenating 'REMOTE_HOST' with 'REMOTE_USER' doesn't always produce a correct e-mail address, what's a CGI programmer to do?

We think a good approach is to set up an e-mail autoresponder, and let e-mail handle the whole thing. If the browser they're using supports e-mail, you could use a MAILTO: URL right on the same page. But alas, the same browsers that don't support forms, also don't support the MAILTO: URL.

An autoresponder is an e-mail program that sends a reply to anyone who sends an e-mail to its address. For example, if the handling software were properly configured, sending a message to the account *xxy@info.net* might produce a reply that contains a set of randomly generated lottery picks. In your case, we recommend that you set up an autoresponder that replies to all incoming messages with a message that contains the text for a blank form. If you do, make sure that the instructions about where to send the completed form are clear: if they use their e-mail package's *reply* command, they'll simply get a new blank form back in return!

Summary

In this chapter, we've covered some techniques for designing a text-only form replacement for those users whose browsers won't allow them to complete forms interactively. We also covered the best techniques for delivering these text-only forms.

Providing text-only forms helps you to broaden your ability to communicate with users and empowers users to communicate who might otherwise escape your notice. When the folks using older or less feature-rich browsers get added to your feedback community, you might even learn some things about your Web pages or their content that will help you improve their value to everyone. At worst, you'll simply establish communications with a broader segment of your reader community!

CHAPTER

17

Gotchas, Warnings, and No-Nos

*I*n this chapter, we'll share with you the many things we learned to avoid, stop doing, and not even think about, when it comes to working with Web development. Starting with a discussion of HTML-related topics, we'll present a list of things that you should always do, or never do, to help you get your documents right. Then we'll apply the same emphasis to CGI programming, to steer you away from the rocks of despair, toward the harbor of peace and contentment!

HTML's Barest Necessities

- Don't overlap tags anywhere. For example, this is invalid HTML:

  ```
  <B>This is <EM>emphatic!</B></EM>
  ```

- SGML comments begin with the string <!-- and end with -->. Some browsers do not recognize SGML comments correctly. Here's an example of a proper SGML comment:

  ```
  <!-- This is a proper SGML comment -->
  ```

- An SGML prolog should be the very first line in an HTML document; if you're creating an HTML document in a CGI program, it should be the third line (the first one will be the Content-type assignment, and the second one must be blank). As of this writing, you can choose from the following list depending on which DTD you plan to follow:

```
— Ways to refer to Level 3: most general to most specific —
<!DOCTYPE HTML PUBLIC  "-//IETF//DTD HTML//EN//3.0">
<!DOCTYPE HTML PUBLIC  "-//W3O//DTD W3 HTML 3.0//EN//">
<!DOCTYPE HTML PUBLIC  "-//IETF//DTD HTML 3.0//EN">
<!DOCTYPE HTML PUBLIC  "-//IETF//DTD HTML 3.0//EN//">
<!DOCTYPE HTML PUBLIC  "-//IETF//DTD HTML Level 3//EN">
<!DOCTYPE HTML PUBLIC  "-//IETF//DTD HTML Level 3//EN//3.0">

— Ways to refer to strict Level 3: most general to most specific —
<!DOCTYPE HTML PUBLIC  "-//IETF//DTD HTML Strict//EN//3.0">
<!DOCTYPE HTML PUBLIC  "-//W3O//DTD W3 HTML Strict 3.0//EN//">
<!DOCTYPE HTML PUBLIC  "-//IETF//DTD HTML Strict Level 3//EN">
<!DOCTYPE HTML PUBLIC  "-//IETF//DTD HTML Strict Level 3//EN//3.0">

— Ways to refer to Level 2: most general to most specific —
<!DOCTYPE HTML PUBLIC  "HTML"
<!DOCTYPE HTML PUBLIC  "-//IETF//DTD HTML//EN">
<!DOCTYPE HTML PUBLIC  "-//IETF//DTD HTML//EN//2.0">
<!DOCTYPE HTML PUBLIC  "-//IETF//DTD HTML 2.0//EN">
<!DOCTYPE HTML PUBLIC  "-//IETF//DTD HTML Level 2//EN">
<!DOCTYPE HTML PUBLIC  "-//IETF//DTD HTML Level 2//EN//2.0">

— Ways to refer to Strict Level 2 —
<!DOCTYPE HTML PUBLIC  "-//IETF//DTD HTML Strict//EN">
<!DOCTYPE HTML PUBLIC  "-//IETF//DTD HTML Strict//EN//2.0">
<!DOCTYPE HTML PUBLIC  "-//IETF//DTD HTML Strict Level 2//EN">
<!DOCTYPE HTML PUBLIC  "-//IETF//DTD HTML Strict Level 2//EN//2.0">

— Ways to refer to Netscape extensions HTML —
<!DOCTYPE HTML PUBLIC "-//Netscape Comm. Corp.//DTD HTML//EN">
```

- Make sure you enclose all attribute values in double quotes. This is not a requirement for valid HTML per se, but it can avoid headaches and loss of sleep. For example, in this HTML fragment:

```
<INPUT TYPE="checkbox" NAME=Smoking Preference CHECKED>
```

it's difficult for human readers to determine if the name of the widget is **Smoking Preference CHECKED** or **Smoking Preference**. To avoid this situation, always enclose an attribute's value in double quotes, for example:

```
<INPUT TYPE="checkbox" NAME="Smoking Preference" CHECKED>
```

CGI Programming Gotchas

- Remember, two sets of carriage return/line feed (CrLf) characters must occur in a file written to the server on *stdout* after an HTTP request. The safest way to do this is to write an extra blank line after writing the link that contains the HTTP request. In this example, the octal representations for Cr (\015) and Lf (\012) are used:

```
GET /hal-bin/test-cgi\015\102
\015\012
```

- Print your 'Content-type:' declaration at the very head of your document, preceding all other statements.

  If your 'Content-type:' declaration appears deep in a CGI application, some servers will time out and return a blank document to the requesting client. For instance, on some servers this Perl script returns a blank document because the server times out:

```
#!/usr/tools/bin/perl
sleep(200);
print "Content-type: text/html\n\n";
print "<HTML><BODY><P>Print this</BODY></HTML>";
exit;
```

  while this script produces an HTML document:

```
#!/usr/tools/bin/perl
print "Content-type: text/html\n\n";
sleep(200);
print "<HTML><BODY><P>Print this</BODY></HTML>";
exit;
```

  The crucial difference here, apparently, is that forcing the CGI to immediately send data to the server helps to ensure that it will not time out as quickly as it otherwise might.

- Avoid using reserved words for form variable names.

  For example, if you have a Perl CGI application handling a form, don't name a text input widget 'sub', 'main', or 'fork'. These names are case sensitive, so you can capitalize the first letter in each variable name (or the whole thing) and be safe.

- Don't allow users to run commands on your machine through a forms interface.

  Don't allow users to enter any system commands from within any text input widgets; for example, an input widget like 'Enter a UNIX *man* command'. The motivation for this widget might be that you want to let your users view man pages on your server interactively. But beware, someone could enter the following text:

  ```
  man fake; cd /; /bin/rm -rf *;.
  ```

  This would fail for the *man* command, but the *rm* command will delete some or all of the files managed by your Web server. You could offer this service through a Web page, but you'd want to disallow commands like *cd*, *rm*, or *boot*, to protect your system from ignorant or malicious users.

- If you make calls to any derivatives of *system()*, *fork()*, or *exec()*, escape all metacharacters that might occur within forms variables.

  For instance, we could enter a very long bogus string of characters with a ! character somewhere in the string into a text input widget. This character is called a *bang* and on most UNIX machines will invoke a command-line interpreter. If you perform a *system()* call with this string of characters, it just might recognize the **bang** character and start a shell for the current user.

  To handle this possibility, do something like the following in Perl to avoid this:

  ```
  s/\!/\\!/g;    # substitute an escaped bang character
  s/\|/\\|/g;    # substitute an escaped pipe character
  s/\&/\\&/g;    # substitute an escaped ampersand
  ```

  Always escape dangerous characters!

  Also, if you unescape SGML character entities in your CGI application, be sure you escape the !, &, and | characters. For example, we could enter this string into a text input widget:

  ```
  "&#47;bin&#47;rm&#32;&#173;rf&#32;&#42;"
  ```

  Your CGI application would unescape these character entities as */bin/rm -rf* *. If you do a *system()* call with this new string, you are looking for trouble.

- When debugging CGI Perl applications, make sure you comment out any *select* statements other than *select(STDOUT)* or *select(STDERR)*. If you forget to do this, you will not get any of your variable/value print statements.

- When creating files in your file system from a CGI application, make sure that you give an absolute path to the file. It's a big mistake to give a relative path to this file. For instance, an NCSA server assumes this is relative to the 'DocumentRoot' for the server and will not find the file.

  Conversely, when creating files within your Web space — in the NCSA example, under the 'DocumentRoot' specified directory — you can specify these files relative to the 'DocumentRoot' directory for the NCSA server.

- If you are writing to a log file from a CGI application for the first time, make sure the file's permissions allow the server to write to this file.

  In a UNIX environment, most servers run as anonymous entities such as *nobody* or *www*. These vague entities need permission to write to your log from within your CGI application. In most cases, the permissions value of 664 is sufficient (but dangerous).

- Reusing an input widget NAME attribute won't erase any previous value. The server appends new value after a # character.

  This can lead to subtle errors. For instance, this HTML fragment:

```
<INPUT SIZE=40 NAME="fname"> First Name<BR>
<INPUT SIZE=40 NAME="lname"> Last Name<BR>
<INPUT SIZE=40 NAME="email"> Email<BR>
<INPUT SIZE=40 NAME="fname"> Bank Name<BR>
```

  results in fname=Mark#Austin Bank if for the first widget labeled First Name you entered Mark and for the fourth widget labeled Bank Name you entered Austin Bank.

- Be careful when using user input to create other CGI applications (meta-applications).

  Messing with HTML within HTML is tricky, since <FORM>, <HTML>, <TEXTAREA>, and others can get you in trouble. This is applicable anywhere a user is allowed to input stuff that is going to be imbedded in HTML later, such as in a guest book or threaded discussions.

- Be careful when specifying directories in a server's configuration files.

  Any mistake in specifying a system directory can possibly open you up for security back doors and eventually, death by hackers. There is a very slim possibility of this happening, but it's best to be careful.

Miscellaneous

- Upgrading your *http* daemon can trash your current "mime.types" file.

  When upgrading HTTP servers, for instance installing NCSA *httpd* 1.4 over 1.3, copy your current "mime.types" file to a new file such as "mime.types.1.3". Install your new server and then examine the differences between the new "mime.types" file included with the server and your "mime.types.1.3". The new "mime.types" file should reflect your old file plus any new MIME Content-Types.

- Protect yourself from electronic graffiti.

  If you provide comment or suggestion forms for your users to give you feedback through a form, occasionally you might get some explicit and offensive comments. If you feel that this is inappropriate, you can either filter the offensive words or phrases or return a message such as, "I'm sorry, Dave, those kinds of words are not appropriate here. Thank you, drive through!"

  Here's a little Perl script to intercept the use of the "seven words you can't say on TV" made famous by George Carlin (we have substituted non-words for some of the seven words):

```
# check text entered for nasties and unlawful acts
    if($In{'comments'} =~ /[ ]*(smeg|prat|nimnal)[ \t\n]/i) {
        print "<HTML><BODY><P>";
        print "I'm sorry, those kinds of words aren't
                appropriate here. Thank you, drive through!";
        print "</BODY></HTML>";
        exit;
    }
```

- If you have a spot where you collect valuable information within your Web as by-products of CGI applications such as a log directory, it's a good idea to create a dummy default HTML file in this directory.

For instance, if you have a directory where you keep logs for all your CGI applications and this directory is under the document root for your server, browsing can get to these files. For example, let's say you have a directory named "/www/docs/apps/logs/" and your document root is "/www/docs", then your log files could be viewed by a WWW browser. All you need to do is open the URL:

```
http://www.flake.com/apps/logs/
```

If there isn't a default HTML file in this directory, you will get an *ftp* listing of the files in this directory. Oooops! The fix is to put a file named identically to the default HTML filename for your server in this directory. For example, you might create a dummy "index.html" file in this directory. This circumvents the file display behavior, which also could be avoided by using user authentication within this directory.

- Servers append default HTML document filename to incomplete URLs.

  An incomplete URL is one that does not explicitly specify a particular HTML document. For example, if your server's default HTML file name is "index.html", then these URLs would reference the "index.html" file:

```
http://www.snap.org/
http://www.snap.org
```

  In the first example, the server completes the URL by appending "index.html". In the second example, the server will append "/index.html". Both of these result in referencing the default HTML document named "index.html" if it exists. If it doesn't, guess what, you will get an *ftp* directory listing of the document root. This might create unwanted exposure, and helps to explain why it's a good idea to *always* create a default HTML file in the root directory.

- When your server's configuration changes, make sure your user authentication access files are not misconfigured.

  Sometimes our WebMasters work in the back room, late at night, and make server configuration changes without notifying their Web users. For instance, the server might have been updated to handle user authentication. You might find old and broken user authentication access files (".htaccess" — NCSA *httpd* specific) laying around in some of your directories. The files in this directory were accessible yesterday, but today you keep getting a "500 Server Configuration Error" when making a reference. Look for and move the ".htaccess" files to another name and try accessing the URLs again.

This problem can also happen when you move your Web from one server to another.

■ When configuring your HTTP server, be wary of 'FollowSymLinks' (for NCSA servers, this is in the "access.conf" file).

Specifying this keyword allows symbolic links in either the document root directory or the server root directory to be followed by Web clients. Some unknowing Web authors could add a symbolic link from their Web directory under the document root to a private directory outside of the document root. For example: links to "/etc" or "/bin" should be avoided.

■ User authentication should not be used for access that requires a protected or encrypted data stream.

Financial transactions, orders for products, or any personal information (including credit card numbers) should not be included in pages verified by the .htaccess type of user authentication.

Summary

This chapter is meant to distill our own misadventures in the Web trade, as we've made countless mistakes in the course of learning what to do, and what to avoid like the plague. Hopefully, you'll be enlightened enough to learn from other people's mistakes, instead of having to repeat them for yourself!

III Basic CGI Programming Elements and Techniques

*T*he nine chapters in Part III investigate some basic topics and applications that the majority of CGI programmers will want to investigate, to aid in the construction of quality CGI applications and significant enhancements to their Web's capabilities.

Chapter 18 begins this process with an in-depth discussion of the Multipurpose Internet Mail Extensions (MIME), a set of file formats originally created to enhance the Internet's Simple Mail Transfer Protocol (SMTP) e-mail capabilities, now also used to describe the format of the files supplied by Web servers.

Chapters 19 and 20 discuss providing access to large bodies of data through Web pages, as Chapter 19 investigates tools to link Web pages to a Wide Area Information Services (WAIS) server, and Chapter 20 explains how to use indexing tools. Chapter 21 explores the tools available to create searchable indexes for large data collections. Chapter 22 discusses a perennial favorite of CGI programmers — monitoring Web page access and usage, and massaging the resulting statistics to create compelling charts and graphs.

Chapter 23 shifts focus to examine the software automatons called spiders, robots, or wanderers that are commonly used to prowl the Web for the raw materials available from global search engines like Yahoo, EINet, Lycos, and others of that ilk.

Chapter 24 discusses "webifying" various document types, and includes a description of the tools currently available to automate this process.

In Chapter 25, the topic turns to graphics, specifically the graphics tools and techniques used for Web navigation through clickable image maps. Chapter 26 investigates on-the-fly creation of HTML documents — to add the elements of customization and interactivity to your Web pages. Finally, in Chapter 27, we cover the major options available for choosing the Web server that will host your CGI applications, a decision that will have a profound impact on implementation choices and programming details.

CHAPTER

18 Mastering MIME

Extending Internet and Electronic Mail

*I*n 1982, RFC (Request For Comments) 822 formally defined the format for standard electronic mail (e-mail) messages on the Internet. Since its formal definition over ten years ago, e-mail has been getting a little gray on top. While RFC 822 specifies a format for text-based e-mail messages, there is no mention of non-text messages, like audio or images.

A major limitation of mail systems based on RFC 822 is that the contents of e-mail messages is restricted to short lines of 7-bit ASCII text. That's why users must typically convert any non-textual data into 7-bit bytes before launching their mail programs. This also explains why encoding schemes like hexadecimal and *uuencode* (UNIX-to-UNIX encode) have become indispensable add-ons to modern e-mail software.

In addition to its intolerance for non-text data, RFC 822 is also incapable of handling other types of text messages. Furthermore, there is no support for languages requiring character sets other than US ASCII. Since RFC 822 does not provide support or mechanisms for mail containing Pacific Rim language text, multimedia, or even most European language text, additional functionality is needed.

In June 1992, a new standard, RFC 1341, was released. RFC 1341 is a description and specification for the Multipurpose Internet Mail Extensions (MIME). MIME supplies vital technology for extending the capabilities and functionality of standard Internet e-mail.

You can find RFC 822, 1341, and other RFC documents at:

```
ftp://ds.internic.net/rfc
```

MIME provides four main mechanisms that solve the text limitations and non-text message shortcomings of the antiquated RFC 822. These mechanisms are specified in header fields that provide the following information:

- **MIME version** — identifies the version of MIME to which the message conforms.
- **Content-Type** — specifies the general type and subtype of data in the body of a message.
- **Content-Transfer-Encoding** — specifies an ancillary encoding applied to the data.
- **Content-ID** — a unique message id (optional).
- **Content-Description** — text description of body content (optional).

MIME provides numerous mechanisms for describing and specifying the format of an Internet message body. It also provides extensions to e-mail, including the ability to handle images, audio, and video objects within an ordinary Internet e-mail message body.

MIME message bodies can now include the following kinds of information:

- Multimedia messages (images, audio, and video)
- Binary or application-specific data
- Character sets other than 7-bit ASCII
- Multiple objects within a single message body
- Messages with multiple fonts
- Text with unlimited line lengths

We think you'll agree that this is a significant improvement over RFC 822, because it lets e-mail software worry about how to transfer the data, rather than forcing end users to pre-encode non-textual messages. We always like it better when the computer does all the work!

The Marriage of MIME and HTTP

In HTTP, messages are passed in a format similar to that used by
Internet Mail (RFC 822) and MIME (RFC 1341, RFC 1521). The HTTP
messaging protocol uses a request/response paradigm. A client — the
requesting application — makes a connection over TCP/IP to a server —
a receiving application. Once the connection is made, the client sends a
request to the server in the form of a MIME message with a special
header. This request consists of:

- a request method,
- a URI, and
- the protocol version,
- followed by a MIME message including client data, request attributes,
  and optional MIME body content.

In Chapter 8 we presented an example similar to such a request:

```
POST /hal-bin/test-cgi HTTP/1.0
```

In this example, the request method is 'POST', the URI is "/hal-bin/
test-cgi", the protocol version is 'HTTP/1.0', and the body content was
omitted (we'll look further at MIME messages and body contents a little
later in this chapter).

The server responds to the request with a status line that includes
the server's HTTP protocol version and a status code. The status line is
followed by a MIME message containing server information and an
optional body with content. Here's an example of the response for the
request in the previous example:

```
HTTP/1.0 200 OK
Date: Friday, 02-Jun-95 21:11:13 GMT
Server: NCSA/1.3
MIME-version: 1.0
Content-type: text/plain
```

The status line is 'HTTP/1.0 200 OK', and the 'Date', 'Server', and
'MIME-version' lines represent the specific server information returned
to the client. The 'Content-Type' line identifies the attached MIME body

as type 'text/plain'. This is the basic header information of an HTTP response.

Here's the rest of the response to the client:

```
CGI/1.0 test results:

argc = 0 argv is

PATH = /bin:/usr/bin:/usr/etc:/usr/ucb
SERVER_SOFTWARE = NCSA/1.3
SERVER_NAME = www.hal.com
GATEWAY_INTERFACE = CGI/1.1
SERVER_PROTOCOL = HTTP/1.0
SERVER_PORT = 80
REQUEST_METHOD = POST
HTTP_ACCEPT =
PATH_INFO =
PATH_TRANSLATED =
SCRIPT_NAME = /bin/test-cgi
QUERY_STRING =
REMOTE_HOST = austin.aus.sig.net
REMOTE_ADDR = 199.1.78.2
REMOTE_USER =
AUTH_TYPE =
CONTENT_TYPE =
CONTENT_LENGTH = -1
```

Notice that there is no HTML markup in the included MIME body. The clue comes from the value of the 'Content-Type', in this case 'text/plain'. If the return MIME body included HTML markup, the value of the 'Content-Type' would have been 'text/html'. Also, if the body had been a binary object, the 'Content-Type' would take the value 'application/octet-stream' (also covered in Chapter 8 in our discussion of HTTP headers).

The 1.0 version of HTTP incorporates many of the concepts and constructs of Internet mail and MIME to transport data across TCP/IP connections. This allows transmitted objects to exist in many representations. These networked entities can also be transported by extensible mechanisms of HTTP.

HTTP does not conform completely to MIME, however. The performance of HTTP versus e-mail differs radically. Since HTTP is not limited by the constraints of existing e-mail gateways and protocols, it complies strictly with RFC 822 and MIME to ensure proper delivery of messages within the WWW.

DIVERGENCE OF HTTP FROM MIME

There are distinct areas where HTTP varies from MIME, and these variations and differences must be communicated to TCP/IP transport gateways for MIME-compliant protocols. In turn, these gateways must provide the correct protocol conversions.

MIME requires converting an entity to its canonical form before it can be transferred, but in the WWW world HTTP does not require this conversion. It manages this through a kind of technological sleight of hand: HTTP actually changes the definition of "canonical form" for text types.

That is, HTTP alters the canonical form requirements for text and application types. It redefines the canonical form of text types to permit multiple octet sequences for identifying line breaks in text. The preferred MIME form for a line break is a carriage return (CR) and line feed (LF) pair (CrLf). But here is another place HTTP strays from strict MIME. Because of the nature of text documents that include naturally occurring line breaks, HTTP applications have to accept a bare CR or LF alone in the data stream.

Furthermore, HTTP may use text media represented by a character set that does not use octets 13 and 10 for CR and LF, respectively (as is the case for some multibyte character sets). HTTP overcomes these specific character value requirements by allowing the use of various character set definitions. These allow it to represent the equivalents of the CrLf pair, as well as a bare CR, and a bare LF using codes that may be specific to your system.

HTTP Provides Special Handling

Some multibyte character sets define CR and LF differently than the typical %13 and %10, respectively. HTTP makes only one assumption — namely, that a client must be capable of using such a character set and must know the appropriate hexadecimal representation for line breaks within the referenced character set. This permits a much better-looking (and acting) display of text on-screen, and helps to keep Web documents readable.

For HTTP, the interpretation of line breaks is applied only to the contents of a MIME body. All other HTTP constructs use CrLf exclusively to indicate line breaks. For example, when constructing a 'POST' request via telnet, the CrLf is required after the 'POST' line. If you just enter the 'POST' line during a telnet session and hit return, nothing happens because HTTP is waiting for a CrLf pair before it processes the POST request. Here's an example:

```
POST /hal-bin/test-cgi HTTP/1.0\015\012
\015\012
```

The \015\012 sequence is the CrLf pair in octal. This could also have been specified in hexadecimal sequences, \x13\x10. This is an explicit CrLf sequence. On most systems, hitting the return key of your keyboard accomplishes the same thing.

If you were creating your own simple WWW client, you would need to put these characters explicitly into the data stream. Here's a bit of Perl code to provide an example of a simple WWW client using the octal representation for Cr (\015) and Lf (\012):

```
print <<"COMMAND";
GET /pubs/documents/localbld.html HTTP/1.0\015\012
\015\102
COMMAND
```

After your client makes a socket connection to the server, the client assembles the HTTP request shown above. This request is for an HTML document named "localbld.html" located in the Web space of the server. The document's location is specified relative to the server's 'Document-Root' designation and the */pubs/documents* path.

The client makes this request for the document and then sleeps, waiting for the HTTP header and attached MIME body that it receives in response from the server. Please notice the CrLf pair at the end of the GET method line, and after that line. This is necessary because the first CRLF pair ends the GET method line, and the second terminates the HTTP request. The HTTP server must see this blank line before it can begin to process the HTTP request from the server. Without this second CrLf pair, the server will time out and the transmission will be unsuccessful.

HTTP also redefines the default character set for text-based MIME entities. A client may make a request for a resource of type 'text/plain'. It can then further request that the character set for the plain text be set to US ASCII. For example, a client could set the HTTP environment variable 'Content-Type', which governs the type of MIME-attached entity that will be sent as the message body, with an attribute to control the character set, as follows:

```
CONTENT_TYPE = text/plain; charset=us-ascii
```

The attribute 'charset' is set to 'us-ascii', which specifies that the requesting client requires its plain text to conform to the character set named "US ASCII."

If a text-type MIME entity is requested, HTTP changes the default character set to "ISO-8859-1" (also known as ISO Latin-1). The ISO-8859-1 character set is a superset of US ASCII. This means that all of the US ASCII characters are included (octets 0-127) in the ISO-8859-1 character set, plus some additional characters. The server can override the client's request for a specific character set by adding a character set parameter value in the 'Content-Type' response header field.

MIME and CGI Applications

CGI applications take input in the form of an HTTP request header, manipulate the input data, and then return some kind of response — typically, an HTML document. In this section, we'll look at a simple WWW client written in Perl. This client accepts an absolute URL as input, connects to the server through a socket, makes an HTTP request, and finally echoes the HTML document to the screen. Here's the source code:

```
#! /usr/tools/bin/perl
#%%%%%%%%%%%%%%%%%%%%%%%%%%%%%%%%%%%%%%%%%%%%%%%%%%%%%%%%%%%%%%%%%%%%
#% PROGRAM : rtrurl.pl
#% CREATOR : Mark Gaither
#% CREATION DATE : Mon Nov 7 14:14:39 CST 1994
#% DESCRIPTION : Retrieve URL from a WWW server
#%%%%%%%%%%%%%%%%%%%%%%%%%%%%%%%%%%%%%%%%%%%%%%%%%%%%%%%%%%%%%%%%%%%%
```

```
$usage = 'Usage: rtrurl.pl -u url
 -u = required URL
';

require "getopts.pl"; # include a Perl library call
&Getopts('hu:'); # get the command line options and values

if(defined($opt_h)) { print $usage; exit; } # usage message
if(!defined($opt_u)) { print $usage; exit; }
else { $url = $opt_u; } # get URL value

$object = ''; # initialize the object to retrieve

# decipher the absolute URL
if($url =~ /^([a-z]+)\:\/\/([^:\/]+)(:\d+)?([^ ]*)$/) {
 $protocol = $1; # determine protocol (typically http)
 $server = $2; # get server DNS name
 $port = $3; # determine which port number
 $object = $4; # get the object to retrieve
 if(!defined($port)) { $port = 80; } # default port
 else { $port =~ s/://; } # remove ":" from server name
}

if($protocol ne 'http') { exit; } # restricted to HTTP only

###########################################################################
# Build the GET HTTP command
###########################################################################

# if the leading slash is omitted in the object, try adding one
if($object eq '') { $object = "/"; }

# HTTP GET command - notice two line break octal character pairs
$command = "GET $object HTTP/1.0\015\012\015\012";

# write the string to the open socket
&write_command($server,$port,$command);

exit;

###########################################################################
# Write the HTTP command to the open socket
###########################################################################
sub write_command {
 local($server,$port,$stream) = @_; # get parameters
 local($name,$aliases,$proto); # define local variables

 $name = $aliases = $proto = ''; # initialize local variables
 $AF_INET = 2; # required TCP/IP junk
 $SOCK_STREAM = 1; # ditto
 $sockaddr = 'S n a4 x8'; # more TCP/IP specific stuff
```

The right-hand bit of code handles URL-encoded text.

```perl
chop($hostname = 'hostname'); # remove the CR from the hostname

# Next few lines are required for a TCP/IP connection
($name,$aliases,$proto) = getprotobyname('tcp');
($name,$aliases,$port) = getservbyname($port,'tcp') unless $port =~
/^\d+$/;;
($name,$aliases,$type,$len,$thisaddr) = gethostbyname($hostname);
($name,$aliases,$type,$len,$thataddr) = gethostbyname($server);

if($name eq '') { die $!; } # handle gethostbyname failure
# determine network addresses
$this = pack($sockaddr,$AF_INET,0,$thisaddr);
$that = pack($sockaddr,$AF_INET,$port,$thataddr);

# make the socket filehandle
if (!socket(S,$AF_INET,$SOCK_STREAM,$proto)) { die $!; };

# give the socket an address
if (!bind(S,$this)) { die $!; }

#call up the server
if (!connect(S,$that)) { die $!; }

# set socket to be command buffered
select(S);
$| = 1; # flush stdout buffer
select(STDOUT);

# write the GET command we built previously to the open socket
print S $stream;
$_ = <S>; # read first line of the response from the server

# look for the status line in the response from the server
if(/^HTTP/) {

# continue reading the response from the open socket
while(<S>) {

# look for first blank line — first CRLF!
  if(/^\w/) { next; }
  else {

    # finally, the MIME entity is returned - typically of
    # type "text/html" or "text/plain". It is printed to the
    # 'stdout' file handle.
    while(<S>) { print STDOUT $_; }
  }
  }
 }
}
```

Denotes read all input from open socket (<S>)

This simple WWW client illustrates how to assemble an HTTP request programmatically. A CGI application, like the HaLSoft HTML Validation Service, could then utilize this client to retrieve a specified URL, where the URL was entered into a text input widget by the user. The CGI application deciphers the URL from the *stdin* buffer and then launches the above client.

Content-Type

Let's look at an example of a more complex HTTP response. The HaL-Soft HTML Check Toolkit builds a customized HTML validation toolkit for a user. Here's how it works:

- The user fills in a series of forms, entering information like user name, organization, and e-mail address.

- Following this, the user indicates the operating system type, the paths to install the custom-built binaries and the man pages, and finally the type of compression the user prefers. (Right now, this toolkit is for UNIX boxes only.)

- Finally, the user submits the request to build a custom HTML Check Toolkit utilizing HaLSoft's WWW server.

- The server builds the compressed tar file and then automagically prompts the user for a local filename to save the binary data.

The real question here is: how does the server direct the client to pop up a dialog box? Why, through the HTTP response header, of course! More specifically, through the MIME Content-type the server sends back to the requesting client. Here's what's involved:

```
# Print this out no matter what
print <<"OUT";
Content-type: application/octet-stream;type=tar;conversions=gzip
OUT
```

This MIME 'Content-Type' declaration states that the enclosed MIME body type is 'application'. The subtype is 'octet-stream' which is the primary subtype of 'application'. The 'type' and 'conversions' are two of a set of 'octet-stream' parameters. 'octet-stream' indicates that a MIME body entity contains binary data. The possible 'octet-stream' parameters include:

- **name** — a suggested filename for the binary data.

- **type** — the category of binary data. No automatic processing by the client uses this information. It is for the human reader only.

- **conversions** — the operations performed on the data prior to transmission. You can specify multiple conversions which must be separated by commas in the order they are to be applied. As you would expect, the order in which a client undoes these conversions is the reverse of the specification — that is, from right to left. The MIME specification (RFC 1521) does not specify any particular conversion operations; in practice, this means any methods commonly available to both server and client may be used.

- **padding** — append a number of bits to the data stream. These bits supply the contents necessary to produce a completely enclosed byte-oriented data stream. This parameter is used when the MIME body content contains a bitstream that is not a perfect multiple of the byte size.

An example of a common UNIX-specific HTTP response might be:

```
Content-Type: application/octet-stream;
name=html-check; type=tar;
conversions="x-encrypt,x-compress"
```

This example HTTP response header fragment would cause the client to pop up a dialog box so the user could save the incoming binary data to a named file (the default is 'html-check'). Remember, this is an appropriate action for the client when receiving 'application/octet-stream' MIME data.

The client would then apply the conversions to the binary data in the order 'x-compress' followed by 'x-encrypt'. How does the client know which local applications to call to perform these operations? The answer lies in the ".mailcap" file (we'll look at this later in this chapter).

Be careful! The use of such conversions is not always portable, because each site can have a different ".mailcap" file entry for 'application/octet-stream;type=x-encrypt'. The use of *uuencode* (UNIX-to-UNIX-encode) is particularly discouraged. You really should use the 'Content-Transfer-Encoding' mechanism of the HTTP response header instead; it's more standardized and portable across Internet mail gateways.

Many Content-Types specify binary or 8-bit character data. For many Internet transport protocols, these data types must be encoded or converted; as you can probably guess, Internet e-mail is one of these protocols (because of RFC 822 limitations). SMTP requires messages to be converted to 7-bit US ASCII data, with a size limit of 1,000 characters per message line. But with MIME handling specified for each 'Content-Type', such conversions can be handled in the background by software.

Finally, RFC 1341 strongly discourages developers from implementing executable or process-oriented mechanisms that might be named in the 'Content-Type' parameter like this:

```
Content-Type: application/x-interpreter
```

In this example, the 'x-interpreter' subtype is a script that takes the MIME message body as input and executes any system directives that it might contain. This could be extremely dangerous, because a malicious person could send anything in the message body. If, for instance, it included the following sequence of commands:

```
"cd /; /bin/rm -rf *;"
```

it would erase your entire hard disk and make your weekend (or your continued well-being) highly stressful!

Content-Transfer-Encoding

The 'Content-Transfer-Encoding' header field in an HTTP response header represents an attempt to define a standard mechanism for re-encoding data into the 7-bit US ASCII short-line format. This field is used to identify the type of re-encoding applied to the data prior to transport. This field also specifies a mapping between the native format of data and a format that maps to 7-bit mail transport protocols, like the Simple Mail Transfer Protocol (SMTP). The value of the field that specifies the type of encoding is not case sensitive and all of the allowed values are formally defined in RFC 1341 as:

```
Content-Transfer-Encoding :=
"8bit" / "7bit" /
"base64" / "quoted-printable" /
"binary" / x-token
```

In other words, message data can be physically formatted as:

- **7bit** — short-line US ASCII
- **8bit** — short-line non-ASCII characters
- **binary** — long-line non-ASCII characters
- **base64** — arbitrary sequences of octets that are not human readable
- **quoted-printable** — consists of octets mapping to printable ASCII characters

These values for 'Content-Transfer-Encoding' imply nothing about the 'Content-Type' of a message, other than the encoding algorithm used to generate that data. It also implies nothing about the transport system requirements if the data remains unencoded.

If the 'Content-Transfer-Encoding' header field is omitted, the default value is '7bit'. This requires that the message body already be in a 7-bit mail-ready representation. The 'x-token' value represents external encoding schemes, where the 'x' prefix indicates any such token in the MIME specification is externally defined, and nonstandard in status. This allows the extension of HTTP and MIME mechanisms. For example, developers could define new encoding types like:

```
Content-Transfer-Encoding = "x-your-new-encoding-scheme"
```

One word of caution from RFC 1341: the creation of new 'Content-Transfer-Encoding' mechanisms is both explicitly and strongly discouraged because it hinders the interoperability between HTTP and WWW applications. Any extensions would have to be supported by both the client and the server side, eliminating uninformed or casual clients from correctly interpreting any such encoded information.

Let's look at an example using the 'Content-Transfer-Encoding' mechanism. For instance, a fragment of an HTTP response header from a server might look like this:

```
Content-Type: text/plain; charset=ISO-8859-1
Content-transfer-encoding: base64
```

In this example, the contents of the MIME message body encoded as 'base64' ASCII originated from an ISO-8859-1 format. Upon receipt by the client and after decoding, the message content would be restored to its ISO-8859-1 form. One reason for encoding the data as 'base64' ASCII is to impose a limited type of security typical of mail user agents based on the Privacy Enhanced Mail protocol (RFC 1113).

The MIME .mailcap File

A ".mailcap" file lists the mappings between MIME types and external applications — typically known as viewers. The ".mailcap" format is formally defined by RFC 1524.

For example, you can configure your WWW client to map the 'image/gif' MIME 'Content-Type' to your particular local gif image viewer, *xv*, which can be found typically in */usr/local/bin* of most UNIX machines. This instructs the WWW client to call upon a helper application or external viewer named *xv* to view the image externally, if it receives a MIME message body of the type 'image' and subtype 'gif'. In a typical client environment, the *xv* helper application must be in the user's path of executable applications.

Here is a sample ".mailcap" file:

```
# This is a simple mailcap file.
# Lines starting with '#' are comments.
# Note that '%s' means substitute the
# datafilename when the viewer is executed.

# Map all types of audio to the viewer 'showaudio'.
audio/*; showaudio %s

# Map all types of images to the viewer 'xv'.
image/*; xv %s

# Map MPEG video to the viewer 'mpeg_play'.
video/mpeg; mpeg_play %s

# Map all types of video *other than MPEG* to the viewer
# 'genericmovie'.
video/*; genericmovie %s

# Map all PostScript data to view 'ghostview'.
application/postscript; ghostview %s

# Map all device independent (dvi) data to viewer 'xdvi'.
application/x-dvi; xdvi %s
```

Typically, WWW clients like *Mosaic* use ".mailcap" files. Other MIME-capable multimedia mail handler applications use them also, like *metamail* or *Ishmail* from HaLSoft.

GLOBAL AND PERSONAL .MAILCAP FILES

Most WWW clients rely on the ".mailcap" file to determine the helper applications available to handle the array of MIME 'Content-Type' messages. Most notable among these is *Mosaic*.

There are two kinds of ".mailcap" files, global and personal. The global ".mailcap" file is the default ".mailcap" file for a site or system. Users of MIME-capable applications, like *Mosaic*, need not create their own specialized ".mailcap" file. They can rely on their system administrators to create and maintain this file which contains system and site configurations for MIME types and their associated external viewers.

Second, you can have your own personal ".mailcap" file to control the external viewers that your MIME-capable application utilizes. You might want to use a different application to view ".gif" images other than the site-configured viewer. Normally, the personal ".mailcap" file overrides any and all previously defined global external viewers.

For UNIX *Mosaic* sites, the global ".mailcap" file has the following pathname:

```
"/usr/local/lib/mosaic/mailcap"
```

This controls and configures *Mosaic*'s external viewers. The X resource variable for *Mosaic* for the global ".mailcap" file is 'global-TypeMap'. Its value is the absolute path to the ".mailcap" file in the system. The variable and its value is placed in a global ".Xdefaults" file, which lists all global X resources for a site or system.

For a personal ".mailcap" file, you would need to change your local ".Xdefaults" file to include the *Mosaic* X resource variable named 'personal-TypeMap'. Again, the value of this X resource variable is a path to your local ".mailcap" file — for example:

```
Mosaic: personalTypeMap="/u/markg/.mailcap"
```

This would direct my *Mosaic* WWW client to use my own personal ".mailcap" file when mapping MIME Content-Types to helper applications. Entries in your personal ".mailcap" file override entries in the global ".mailcap" file which override the built-in defaults of most MIME-capable applications like *Mosaic*.

Summary

If a MIME would talk, what would she say? She would probably tell you about the divergence of HTTP from the explicit MIME specification, because of its diverse message data types like video and images. She would also tell you how to utilize the 'Content-Type' header field of the HTTP response header to direct clients to do some specific action. She would also explain to you about Content-Transfer-Encoding mechanisms and how they work. Finally, she would describe to you how to map MIME 'Content-Type' to actual helper applications. But MIMEs don't talk, do they? Maybe that's a good thing...

CHAPTER

19 Using WAIS with CGIs

Welcome to the Wide World of WAIS

*T*he World Wide Web is a vast resource of interconnected computers, each sporting its own individual data pool. To help manage and deliver this data to interested parties, many popular search and retrieval engines have been deployed in the past few years.

Many of the best general-purpose search engines are not particularly suited for Web- or Internet-related activities. Most are large-scale database management systems used to aggregate and sift a large company's total information flow. These include industry giants like Oracle, Sybase, GSQL, and RBase, to name just a few. The WAIS system, however, is uniquely suited for Web applications as well as offering an enterprise-capable search and retrieval system. Developed primarily on the UNIX operating system, WAIS systems have been employed to deliver data to virtually all popular desktop machines in use today.

WAIS (Wide Area Information Servers, pronounced "ways") is a network of publishing systems designed to distribute all types of data to a variety of clients. The core WAIS engine is simple to install, easy to use, and, when pointed at relevant data, will compile indices for easy assimilation.

WAIS was originally implemented as a large distributed database of interconnected content servers located on both regional and international networks. This original framework is still supported by present versions of the search engine. However, each content server is independently capable of answering queries by searching through its local datastore. Even though a user can cause a few thousand back-end search engines to respond to a single query, this is generally not necessary because many servers are configured only to access their own local databases.

In this chapter, our discussion will focus primarily on *freeWAIS*, a version of the WAIS software package that's publicly available through the Internet. We'll also explore what's worth indexing, how to index it, and how to retrieve information by using a Web-based WAIS interface. Furthermore, we'll illustrate examples of the various WWW gateway methods used by programmers and administrators. This should serve nicely to showcase WAIS's real power as a back-end application to your CGI programs.

We will also explain in detail how to set up and configure the various gateways discussed in this chapter, as well as the WAIS server itself. Finally, we'll warn you about some of the peculiarities of the WAIS system and provide a selection of Net pointers to help you on your journey to WAIS wisdom. We'll begin at the foundations of WAIS with some background material.

WAIS Architecture Unmasked

WAIS was originally developed as a joint project among Thinking Machines, Apple Computer, Dow Jones, and the KPMG Peat Marwick group. The "free" version of WAIS that is bouncing around the Internet today is very much like the one that its founders created. This version gives you full access to the server's source code, the engine that indexes the data, and some utility programs for managing the resulting information pool.

Considering the simplicity of use and power afforded by the WAIS engine, it's no surprise that a couple of forks in the development path have arisen. Thinking Machines, for one, no longer supports the publicly distributed WAIS (as of WAIS-8-b5.1). Support and development of the free WAIS system is now being handled by CNIDR (Clearinghouse for Networked Information Discovery and Retrieval).

Current CNIDR releases, called *freeWAIS*, are available from most of the popular Internet software archive sites. For more information on CNIDR, consult this URL:

```
http://cnidr.org/welcome.html
```

 Or visit this one to download a copy of *freeWAIS*:

```
http://cnidr.org/cnidr_projects/freewais.html
```

The commercial aspects of WAIS development and support are now handled by WAIS, Inc., founded by most of WAIS's original developers. Although WAIS, Inc., does sell commercial servers with extra features and full support, they continue to provide other freely redistributable tools. Information about WAIS, Inc. can be found at

```
http://www.wais.com/
```

WAIS was designed to create a distributed network publishing system that could help people find information simply by asking questions. These questions may be expressed in natural language (for example, English) or through the use of more formal query statements like literal phrases (search strings), Boolean syntax, or specific field values. WAIS software allows users to search for and retrieve documents from local or remote information sources all over the world; for our purposes, we'll only be using it for local data.

One of WAIS's many strengths is that it allows indexing and retrieval of a large number of different data types, including nontextual information. Client applications can search on, and retrieve information from, these nontextual documents, according to predefined translation standards. Many of the popular WAIS clients on the market today support most of the elements detailed in Table 19-1.

To illustrate the benefits of using these different document types, consider your business or organization and the myriad of choices that an individual must make when creating a document. By supporting the most frequently used document types, the indexing and retrieval of your financial data — stored as Microsoft Excel spreadsheets, for instance — is certainly possible. The same is true for other commonly used applications.

Table 19-1

Standard Display Formats Supported by WAIS

Format	Description
HTML	HyperText Markup Language
MIME	Multipurpose Internet Mail Extensions
GIF	Graphics Interchange Format
TIFF	Tagged Image File Format
PICT	Apple PICT Image
PS	PostScript
DVI	Device-Independent Printer Output
TEXT	ASCII Text
TEXT-FTP	FTP File Format
QUICKTIME	Apple QuickTime Movie
PERSUASION	Aldus Persuasion
MS-WORD	Microsoft Word Document
MS-POWERPOINT	Microsoft PowerPoint Slides
MS-EXCEL	Microsoft Excel Spreadsheet
WQST	WAIS Source/Question Format

WAIS PROTOCOLS

Even though the *Wide Area* part of WAIS would imply the use of a large network such as the Internet to interconnect servers and clients, WAIS can be used on a LAN (Local Area Network) quite effectively and has been configured for use on a single machine. You'll find that the WAIS engine is a powerful system that can be modified or adjusted to suit almost any of your needs.

WAIS information servers use TCP/IP protocols to exchange information with their various client applications. In the future, we may see LAN versions of WAIS that support other protocol stacks (like AppleTalk and IPX) with gateways to the TCP/IP version running on the Internet. In this manner, a WAIS system could be used to house an organization's internal data, with its public documents advertised to the global Internet.

WAIS uses the Z39.50 query protocol for its standard communications. This protocol is used by the thousands of WAIS servers across the Internet, from which there are some 500 or more databases normally available, with topics ranging from recent movie reviews to technical documentation, as well as a host of archival information. Although this broad scope is sometimes useful, it is generally not necessary because most WAIS administrators only index and serve their local data.

The use of WAIS as a back-end server engine with a World Wide Web browser as its front end makes for a powerful, yet simple means for cataloging and presenting information to the rest of the world in a friendly and sophisticated way.

WAIS AS A CLIENT AND A SERVER

The most important aspect of the WAIS system, from a design standpoint, is that it is a traditional client/server application. What this means is that the WAIS system is inherently efficient, scalable, and capable of supporting different kinds of clients. A Microsoft Windows WAIS client, native to the DOS/Windows operating system, retains its ability to converse with the server using a rigidly defined protocol. It is this common exchange that makes WAIS both portable and scalable.

Compare this to a library catalog system that forces its users to employ or emulate a particular type of hardware (probably a VT100 terminal), as well as forcing them to interact with the host system using a proprietary interface. The WAIS server, on the other hand, exchanges question–and–answer information with a whole variety of clients using a standard protocol, independent of the OS the client uses, and regardless of the client's intentions toward the resulting data it delivers.

WAIS DATABASES REVEALED

Indexing 101
The key ingredient for cooking up a WAIS database is a collection of information that does not necessarily have to be of the same type, along with a WAIS index for that data. Because WAIS can index and handle

different kinds of information, this collection may include a variety of file formats and application-specific information.

Since a single document is the smallest retrievable piece of information from a WAIS engine, it stands to reason that you need to construct your data pool from a collection of documents in your file system's directory hierarchy. The WAIS indexing system uses a text-parsing process to extract words from documents, as well as a headline, both of which are used to present hitlists back to querying clients.

At indexing time, which generally occurs nightly, the WAIS system creates a set of indexes from your original materials. In building this index, a series of headlines and word counts is constructed from your data tree. Depending upon your publishing habits and the timeliness of your materials, you may need to index more often, perhaps twice a day.

Because it is capable of tearing through multiple document styles to create the index, the parsing engine is the real workhorse of the WAIS system. It can handle PostScript files, newsgroups, dvi, or even graphics documents, all of which may be parsed, indexed, and searched on demand. This lets organizations focus on content rather than format, and is therefore a real boon for information managers. A complete list of supported formats can be found in Table 19-2.

During the indexing process, the WAIS parser/indexer also supports a list of customizable stop words (words that are ignored, usually because they appear so frequently), an option for incremental indexing, and techniques to derive word variations (called *stemming*).

Incremental indexing is especially powerful because it allows the server to add, modify, or delete data from the original store without having to suspend server activity. Incremental indexing is also much faster than re-indexing an entire database.

HOW IS THE INDEX USED?

Client processes contact the server by reading the source description file. This lets multiple servers, each with different sets of data, participate in a single retrieval process. Upon receipt of a query, the server checks its access list to see if the client has permission, and if so, the server processes the query. For most local WAIS servers, this step is unimportant because queries are usually generated from a known pool of clients, which will only search those servers that you have personally configured.

Table 19-2

Standard Parse Formats Supported by WAIS

Format	Description
dash	In the dash format, each document is separated by a row containing a minimum of 20 dash characters, "-". The line following the dashed line is expected to contain a headline, followed by the text of the document.
dvi	For Device-Independent Printer Output files.
filename	Treats each file as a single document and uses the filename as the headline. The contents of the file, however, are generally not parsed. This method is used for most binary files not listed elsewhere.
first-line	Specifies that each file contains a single document, and that the first non-blank line of the file is the headline, and that the remainder of the file is parsed as words.
first-words	The first-words parse format is similar to first-line, except that the headline is the first 100 non-whitespace characters in the file.
gif	CompuServe's Graphics Interchange Format.
html	HyperText Markup Language.
mail-digest	For standard Internet mail digest files. Each message is parsed as a separate document with the subject line the headline.
mail-or-rmail	For UNIX mail files. Parsed like mail-digest.
netnews	For Internet Network News files.
one-line	Treats each line of a file as a separate document with the line as the headline.
paragraph	Each paragraph is separated by one or more blank lines. The first line of each paragraph is the headline, which is followed by the text of the document.
pict	Apple PICT image files.
ps	PostScript files.
source	The source file format is a file format generated by the WAIS indexer for the Directory of Servers. The file typically contains information about the database and is parsed exactly like the text file format.
text	Each file is treated as a single document; the filename is used as the headline, and the contents of the file are parsed as words.
tiff	Tagged Image File Format.

During initial query decomposition and processing, the WAIS server proceeds to match query words against its index of document words. The match-ups it finds are used to produce a list of headlines, which are returned to the browser for display to the end user.

Do I Need a Gateway? What for?

Now that we've covered WAIS operations, let's illustrate its interaction with common Web clients. To facilitate this analysis, we assume that the client's software environment uses a WAIS gateway. Gateways are applications or scripts that run as CGIs on a Web server in tandem with the HTTP server. Gateways provide a common channel for the Web–to–WAIS, and WAIS–to–Web data flow that its client/server architecture demands.

Most of the popular Web clients don't support WAIS access directly; this explains the need for CGI programs to act as WAIS gateways. In the following sections, we'll explore seven of the many available WAIS gateway options that we found while surfing the Net for usable WAIS–to–Web CGI implementations.

We expect that in the not-so-distant future you'll see the need for such gateways dwindle substantially, to include only those sites that perform extended WAIS searches themselves, or who provide their data in nonstandard formats (perhaps as output from proprietary applications). Those organizations that require proprietary data formats will probably continue to use gateways, but we expect that otherwise most browsers will draw on built-in WAIS support.

Finding WAIS Gateways

It shouldn't be a surprise that using a WAIS-based search engine to locate WAIS-based tools and CGI scripts works pretty well. You can try to find other samples of this genre with your own electronic quest, but here's what we uncovered (and decided to keep, based on user scuttlebutt on the newsgroups and some hands-on experience in working with these tools).

WAIS.PL

The first, simplest, and most common CGI script is the "wais.pl" script included with the NCSA server application. Because it is a simple configuration, it's a good place for you to start your WAIS education. We'll take you on a quick tour of its configuration and operation as a warm-up exercise.

You'll need to modify only four lines at the top of this script to make it fully operational. This presupposes that you have already installed the WAIS server and have it running under its own power. It is common for such gateway scripts to use the *waisq* (an abbreviation for "WAIS query") application for communication with the WAIS server.

The location of this executable should be established in the first lines of the configuration. The '$waisd' variable should set the location of your source directory, the place where you store all of your indexes. The '$src' variable should be the library you wish to search, and finally, the '$title' field is merely for decoration:

```
$waisq = "/usr/local/bin/wais/waisq";
$waisd = "/wais/";
$src = "TIL";
$title = "Local Web Server Documentation";
```

In using this configuration, we were able to search against a database running on Apple's Web server, from which the output of "wais.pl" is captured in Figure 19-1. As you can see, the results appear somewhat mysterious.

SON-OF-WAIS.PL

For a slightly more advanced version of "wais.pl", you might try tracking this program down, since the generic "wais.pl" leaves a lot to be desired. Luckily, the configuration for both "son-of-wais.pl" — and the next example, "kidofwais.pl" — are almost identical to that of "wais.pl". The source code and some quick reference materials about son-of-wais can be found at

http://dewey.lib.ncsu.edu/staff/morgan/son-of-wais.html

KIDOFWAIS.PL

This is probably the best of the three simple one-script Perl treatments of the standard WAIS CGI gateway. This script supports debugging, table titles, formatting options, and a whole ton of other whiz-bang features.

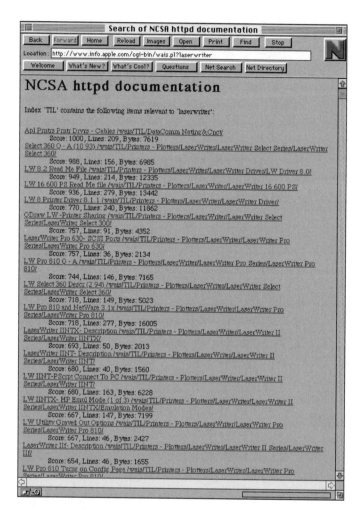

Figure 19-1

wais.pl return screen.

To get a good feel for how this gateway operates, you need only run through the same configuration as the "wais.pl" script mentioned earlier. Notice in Figure 19-2 how attractive the resulting screen output looks. Of course, it's not a fully customized HTML document, but it's quite nice for a quick-and-dirty 10-minute configuration.

The documentation and source for "kidofwais.pl" lives at

```
http://ewshp2.cso.uiuc.edu/Source_table
```

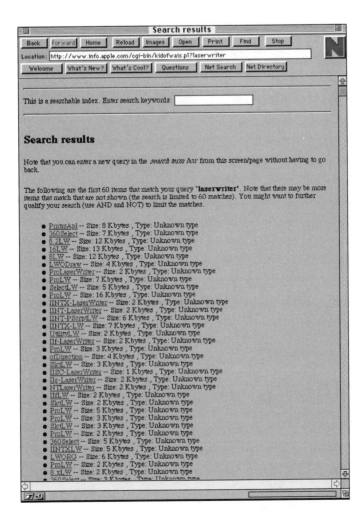

Figure 19-2
kidofwais.pl return screen.

SFGATE

One of the more powerful gateway script systems was programmed by
Miao-Jane Lin and Ulrich Pfeifer, copyrighted by the University of Dort-
mund. This is a series of scripts that interact as a conduit for information
between your WAIS server and your Web server. Thankfully, the creators

of these scripts were nice enough to enclose a configuration and installation routine along with the standard distribution, so that setup is a breeze.

Notice in Figure 19-3 that SFgate gives you more control over what areas of the WAIS server you may use for your query strings. Authors and titles, as well as the body of the text, can be searched en masse or independently. This flexibility helps to produce more usable search results.

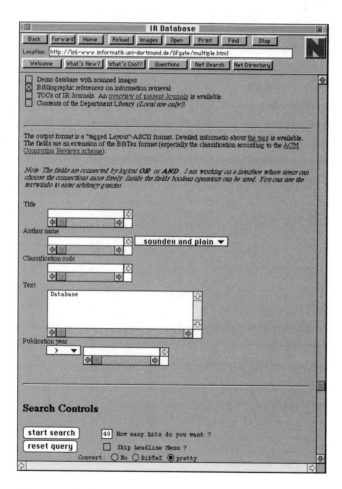

Figure 19-3
SFgate search screen.

To get the latest word on what is happening with SFgate or for more information on its designers, point your browser at

http://ls6-www.informatik.uni-dortmund.de/SFgate/SFgate.html

FWAIS.PL

The "fwais.pl" script is entirely functional. It allows the user to execute the script and to pull a list of the sources that the WAIS server can search. A fully selectable list of "libraries" is presented to the user, of which several sources may be used to generate the query.

    http://waisqvarsa.er.usgs.gov/public/fwais.pl

WWWWAIS.C, VERSION 2.5

Probably the most powerful of the search and retrieval CGI gateways to WAIS is this small C program created by Kevin Hughes from EIT. We were able to compile and configure "wwwwais.c" for several different flavors of UNIX without any hassles. It is a very robust system that is well worth getting to know. To create the diagram in Figure 19-4, we used the EIT gateway itself to illustrate what the interface looks and feels like.

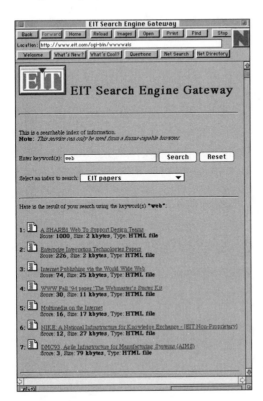

Figure 19-4

wwwwais.c in action.

The whole application is controlled by a few design files along with one big configuration file named "wwwwais.conf". One of the nice features this program provides is its ability to allow and disallow use of the gateway, based on the IP address of the requesting machine. A short clip from the configuration file explains this capability best:

```
AddrMask all
# Only addresses specified here will be allowed to use the gateway.
# For the above mask option, these rules apply:
# 1) You can use asterisks in specifying the string, at either
#    ends of the string:
#    "192.100.*", "*100*", "*2.100.2"
# 2) You can make lists of masks:
#    "*192.58.2,*.2", "*.100,*171.128*", ".58.2,*100"
# 3) A mask without asterisks will match EXACTLY:
#    "192.100.58.2"
# 4) Define as "all" to allow all sites.
```

For more information on the *wwwwais.c* application or to read about how to make full use of its features, check out the following URL:

```
http://www.eit.com/software/wwwwais/wwwwais.html
```

WAISGATE (WEB-TO-WAIS GATEWAY)

WAISGate is a commercial product of WAIS, Inc., the company formed when Thinking Machines no longer supported or upgraded the WAIS code. WAISGate is a rich set of CGI tools that will allow a WEB or WAIS administrator to get off to a flying start. This is a toolset well worth investigating and you'll find it at

```
http://server.wais.com/waisgate-announce.html
```

Exploring WAIS as a User

You're probably already familiar with using search engines that are available on the Web, such as the ever-popular Yahoo site. To illustrate, we will visit Apple Computer's Web site and point out some of the common features used in creating a Web–to–WAIS interface. Other search engines you will find on the Internet are similar in attitude and form to Apple's.

Figure 19-5 reveals that Apple chose to include two pop-up menus with relevant keywords to help searchers find documents. For those interested in a possible purchase of a new Power Macintosh, you could select the "Specification Sheet" keyword from the left pop-up, then select "Power Macintosh" from the right pop-up, and type "8100-110" for the model number in the fill-in space provided.

Figure 19-5

Apple's Web site, found at: http://www.info.apple.com/til.html.

After hitting the "Start Search" button, the Web server executes a CGI gateway program — in this case, a Perl script on a UNIX machine — that interfaces itself to the WAIS engine by presenting the search string, and retrieving a hitlist when it's ready (see Figure 19-6).

Figure 19-6

Hitlist results from the search shown in Figure 19-5.

As you might expect, the first item on the hitlist of documents returned is the article that we were interested in, "Pwr Mac 8100 10-110 Tech Specs."

Ranked Relevance Revealed

The criteria used for ranking relevancy include: words found that match the search string, the proximity of the words to each other in the document, and the overall relevance of the document compared with the other documents found. WAIS presents more pertinent documents first so that searchers sift through less irrelevant material.

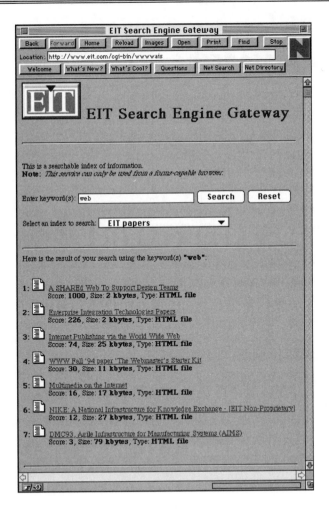

Figure 19-7

Pwr Mac 8100 10-110 Tech Specs document.

Finally, Figure 19-7 shows the actual data retrieved from the Web server and translated by the gateway. In designing your own hitlists, you should be sure to return a list of items as URLs that link off to the actual documents presented or the appropriate scripts for handling them. This way, users won't be hampered by difficult or obscure WAIS results and will be able to access their data quickly and easily.

What's the Difference Between *waisq* and *waissearch*?

The normal operation of obtaining return information from an active WAIS server is usually handled by one of two widely available programs, either the *waisq* or the *waissearch* program. Both are included with the *freeWAIS* distribution and will search through available WAIS information databases on your behalf. *waisq*'s purpose is to look in databases resident on your local server, while *waissearch* is for querying remote WAIS servers.

waissearch works its magic by connecting to a remote machine on a well-known port address reserved for incoming WAIS queries. The port ID used for WAIS is generally 210, and most WAIS UNIX configurations choose this value by default. Nothing should stop you from using another port address (we'd recommend allocating one that isn't commonly reserved for some other IP server) if you want to keep your server private or if you intend to control access closely.

You might run your WAIS server with a command that looks something like the following, should you wish to change the default port of your own server:

```
/wais/waisserver -p 2010 -d /wais/sources -e /tmp/wais.log &
```

This will start a WAIS server running on port 2010 and will log appropriate stuff to a file named "wais.log". Also, the "/wais/sources" directory will be consulted for all databases that the server needs in order to load an index.

Other Topics

You've nearly reached the end of our WAIS tour, so we want to leave you with a few well-chosen bits of miscellany that you might find interesting. Read on for more potential sources of WAIS information.

SWISH

For a very simple indexing system to handle indexing the HTML pages that you are serving, you might try out SWISH. SWISH (Simple Web Indexing System for Humans) is a very trim program that is more a proof of concept than a full-fledged application, but there is a beauty to its simplicity.

You can find the SWISH documentation at

```
http://www.eit.com/software/swish/swish.html
```

And the source code is here:

```
ftp://ftp.eit.com/Web.software/swish/
```

SWISH is similar to WAIS in the way that it indexes datastores but is almost entirely devoted to handling smaller, lower-volume data resources. For that reason, though, it may be of considerable interest to those of you who have private or company-specific collections of data to compile, index, and search.

INDEXING HIERARCHIES OF HTML DOCUMENTS

More and more, people who are already using WAIS to publish a database of information via the WWW have come to the realization that WAIS would be a powerful ally in indexing the actual contents of the WEB server itself. By using WAIS to catalog a directory of HTML pages, users are given the option to query for a particular page by keyword or by browsing for related information across many Web pages.

Sometimes is can be helpful to see an overview of the contents of a Web server that deals specifically with one topic that you are researching. Several of the larger Internet Service Providers already offer a variety of search and retrieval systems to construct such overviews for their Web pages. You, too, can set this up with a WAIS system as your back-end. For a more detailed discussion of this approach, please consult Chapter 12.

WAIS and HTTP Integration

Probably the hottest topic in the WAIS–to–Web gateway arena is the enhancement of Web browsers to handle WAIS back-end engines directly. This eliminates the need for a gateway and represents what we believe will be the next logical step of Web–to–WAIS, WAIS–to–Web evolution. The best resource found on this subject is:

```
http://wintermute.ncsa.uiuc.edu:8080/wais-tutorial/wais-and-http.html
```

Usenet News Archives

If you have any questions about WAIS in general, or problems with the creation and maintenance of your WAIS databases, the USENET newsgroup hierarchy offers a wealth of good information and informal technical support resources. Try posting to *comp.infosystems.wais* if you would like to join an ongoing conference on WAIS issues and directions. It's a real goldmine of information!

Mailing Lists

The mailing lists in Table 19-3 include topics related primarily to WAIS (wais-interest, wais-discussion, wais-talk, and SIG-WAIS). The other two lists cover issues related to the Z39.50 protocol used for WAIS communications (Z3950IW and ZIP). If you send e-mail to any of the server addresses listed in column two, include the word "info" as your message body to get the details on how to subscribe to each list.

Table 19-3
The Best of the WAIS Mailing Lists

LIST NAME	Contact Address
SIG-WAIS	Contact: sig-wais-info@cnidr.org
WAISCUST	Contact: listserv@rice.edu
wais-discussion	Contact: wais-discussion-request@think.com
wais-interest	Contact: wais-interestrequest@think.com
wais-talk	Contact: wais-talk-request@think.com
Z3950IW	Contact: LISTSERV@nervm.nerdc.ufl.edu
ZIP	Contact: zip-request@kudzu.concert.net

FUTURES AND COOL ENGINES

For a glimpse at the future of Web-based database search and retrieval well beyond what conventional WAIS engines can support today, we'd recommend that you examine both the Glimpse and Harvest tools we encountered on our own search for "search and retrieval" enlightenment. You'll locate each of these outstanding tools at its eponymous site:

```
http://glimpse.cs.arizona.edu:1994/
http://harvest.cs.colorado.edu/
```

Summary

With the rise of more public datastores across the Internet, the advent of more robust technology based on Web–to–WAIS gateways should soon be available. This promises to strengthen the Web–to–WAIS connection and ensure its ongoing longevity.

To start you on the road to information publishing, this chapter dealt with the best of the WAIS CGIs available, with a brief mention of some of the more advanced work underway. Should you have a large pool of information resources that you want to advertise — and deliver — to the world, setting up a WAIS gateway could be the start of something big!

20 Indexing Your Web Site

Lost in the Funhouse

*T*hink of your Web system as a castle. It has huge hallways filled with Impressionist art, balconies that deliver vivid views of the landscape, a fine library stocked to overflowing with every conceivable text, and of course there's a dungeon. It's murky and damp, but it supplies the foundation for everything else.

To your friends and colleagues, finding their way around your castle is a simple matter because they visit it regularly. To a stranger, it's bound to be far more mysterious and the long passageways deep into the dungeon's recesses can be especially forbidding, easier to avoid than explore.

We view the data that a Web server houses as an intricately structured collection of interlinked documents. It's almost like a castle that's grown since the Middle Ages; its floor plan long since overwhelmed by additions, escarpments, turrets, and what not.

You grew up here; there's no chance you'd ever get lost. But what if there's no road map to lead the way for visitors, nor guideposts to help them find their way when they get lost? When viewed from the perspective of someone who enters your Web for the first time, its structure can sometimes be confusing, to say the least.

But this confusion is as much a matter of perspective as anything else. If only these visitors could view the whole collection from above, its structure would reveal itself. A 10,000-foot view would let them go right to the information that interests them most.

By indexing the actual HTML documents that comprise your Web site, you can build a practical and powerful solution for your visitors — one that allows them to find almost anything they may need. In the previous chapter, we talked in detail about the WAIS search and retrieval engine and how it is used to provide access to almost any sort of information: text, PostScript, graphics, etc. The WAIS system proves to be quite an ally when it comes to designing and implementing a database management system with ties to the WWW.

In this chapter, you'll learn how to use the WAIS system to its fullest extent. We'll show you how to configure the main engine and how to use it to index some data (mainly Web pages). We'll also show you how to use CGI scripts to present that data to your visitors.

Even though the bulk of our discussion revolves around the WAIS system and its uses, we'll also address other indexing and locational tools for Web documents. We'll also examine some of the possibilities in the not-so-distant future of Web crawling, to give you an idea of where these tools may lead us.

What to Include

The larger and more varied a Web site becomes, the more necessary it is to provide a simple search mechanism. It may simply be for your own good and nobody else's, just to preserve your sanity as the Web's administrator. Whether for your own benefit or for everyone's, the first real step in indexing your site is to decide which HTML documents you want to be able to search.

We manage some very large Web sites, some with thousands of HTML documents on a single server. This can make it tough to cull out those documents that shouldn't be included. "Why would we need to ignore some files?" you ask. "Aren't they *all* important?" The answer, unfortunately is, "yes and no." As our own experience has shown after about a year of chugging along, dishing out full service to the Internet, the structure of the data in just about any Web site starts to aggregate into its own unique form.

Every site's data mix is original and unique. It's also independent of all the other sites worldwide, and it's that very individuality that supplies the framework that underlies your data. As the number of HTML documents increases, the size of the associated index grows apace, possibly even as a multiple of the growth of the documents involved. As your collection of documents continues to grow, you'll also want to start indexing it more frequently — we recommend that you do it nightly for large collections (1,000 documents or more) and weekly for smaller ones.

For its ability to search an entire HTML document tree in just a few seconds, indexing programs rely heavily on an index file that contains all of the relevant associations between various words and documents. These index files should be rebuilt regularly; we recommend you schedule this kind of activity deep into the wee hours of the morning, so as not to impede the process of clients connecting with your server during prime-time hours.

It's normal for an index file to exceed the size of the original data used to produce the index. Most text-parsing systems, including our example WAIS engine, allow users to select the size and scope of their customized index files. This means indexes can grow arbitrarily large and complex, based on user queries (and patience, because a large amount of material takes more time to search, abstract, and deliver to the user than a smaller amount). Nevertheless, this requires building a master index or a collection of related indexes, with nearly every conceivable term for your pages that users can draw from.

What follows is an exact listing from the *man* page for *waisindex*, a UNIX application that parses Web pages and builds index files. The important thing to note is the line in boldface that states that WAIS has a current limitation of 16MB per index. Please be careful what you include in your main data set to be parsed. For performance reasons, it is always better to have more, smaller indexes than to create only one or two gargantuan, all-encompassing ones.

```
BUGS
      It temporarily takes twice the space it needs for an index.

      Due to some compile time constants the document table is
      limited to 16 Megabytes. This limits the indexer to data-
      bases with headlines that add up to less than 16 megabytes
      (since that's the principal component of the table). This is
      typically a problem for database types where a record is
      essentially a headline (one_line, archie).

Thinking Machines      Last change: Sun May 10 1992            3
```

Watch Those Index Sizes!

The larger your site, the more there is to index. The larger the index, the longer it takes to create files, and the slower searches proceed. The best approach is to keep things relatively trim: include as much as you can but be smart about what you include.

In your quest to decide what to include and what to toss, you must consider what data is essential to your site's operation and what data is mere fluff. You might postulate that most of the graphic images that make a site look dynamic and professional are useless in an index (we'd be inclined to agree with you). Of course, this doesn't preclude the possibility that on your site, you might have an entire catalog of antiques, complete with images, that is your Web server's mainstay. In this case, you would clearly want to index the graphics alongside the HTML code.

Our point is that data organization differs from site to site, sometimes wildly. It's ultimately up to a site's administrator — and its users — to decide what should be indexed and what should be ignored. Since site administrators are usually the ones responsible for making this decision, they can get user input in one of two ways:

1. By observation: use statistics tools to measure which pages and files get visited (covered in Chapter 22).

2. The direct approach: include survey forms and solicit user feedback directly.

Another good idea is to spend some time using the site yourself, every day; your own instincts will help guide the decision about what to index and what to ignore.

As a rule of thumb, if you have the available disk space and the computing resources required to rebuild indexes every night, then re-index the whole thing nightly. Your users won't be disappointed with the results, and neither will you! If you don't have the necessary space and CPU cycles, rebuild a portion of the index nightly and try to cover the entire site at least every three or four days.

Installing and Configuring freeWAIS

For the purposes of this discussion, we assume that you've downloaded the latest version of *freeWAIS* (or at least loaded the version from the CD-ROM that came with this book) and successfully compiled it on your UNIX system. If you're not using a UNIX system or don't have access to one, you might want to skip to the end of this chapter where we cover options for other platforms like the Macintosh and the PC.

Once installed, WAIS remains more or less dormant on your system until you decide which directories on your site you wish to include in an index. An effective approach that we use on systems we administrate consists of using symbolic links to create a repository for each Web directory tree.

Here's how you might proceed to do the same thing:

- Make a new directory in your main WAIS sources directory entitled "WEB".
- Link off other directories that contain HTML files.

By indexing all or part of that "WEB" directory, you can easily arrange and rearrange all of your "WEB" indexing without ever having to touch the layout of your Web site.

The application that you'll use for this purpose is called *waisindex*. It should be in the same directory with all of your other WAIS tools. In the following example, we index three major HTML directories on our site, using the UNIX *cron* facility:

```
# Crontable
# WAIS Indexing for the public Web Server
#
# Index our Customer's Pages for easy retrieval
#
30 4 1-31 * 0-6 /wais/waisindex -l 1 -e /dev/null -d /wais/WEB/customers
-r -mem 6 /wais/customers > /dev/null;
#
# Index our own pages
#
30 5 1-31 * 0-6 /wais/waisindex -l 1 -e /dev/null -d "/wais/WEB/baseWeb
-r -mem 6 /wais/baseWeb > /dev/null;
```

"30 4" means 4:30 "1-31" means everyday

```
#
#  Index our pointers to other sites
#
30 6 1-31 * 0-6 /wais/waisindex -l 1 -e /dev/null -d "/wais/WEB/pointers -r
-mem 6 /wais/pointers > /dev/null;
```

The *cron* daemon allows you to specify when a particular job should be executed. In this case, we use *waisindex* to fully re-index each of our three major catalogs at 4:30, 5:30, and 6:30 a.m. Please notice that we use the -e parameter to redirect error messages to "/dev/null". (But when you set up your system, you should dump them to a disk file so that you can see what these error messages look like and what they're trying to tell you.)

The *-r* parameter instructs the process to recursively parse enclosed subdirectories; this is how the process is able to traverse entire directory trees. The *-m* parameter tweaks the amount of memory the indexer uses and thus controls how fast it can index and demand system resources. The *-l* field determines the verbosity of the logging level: the larger the number, the more detailed the log, and the more output produced. Please also note that the redirects to "/dev/null" at the end of the commands aren't absolutely required, but they do prevent our finicky *cron* daemon from sending us e-mail when the job has completed.

Once these indexes are created, the next important step is to test the search capability of the system with the *waisq* command. In the next example, we search our "/WEB/customers" index for Jean Smith's home page:

```
/wais/waisq -m 100 -c /wais/ -f - -S customers.src -g Jean Smith
```

The server should respond with output like the following:

```
Searching customers.src...Initializing connection...Found 13 items.
  (:question
    :version  2
    :seed-words "Jean Smith"
```

The system should produce several lines of text containing the search strings used and the results for the query. It is this output that you'll concern yourself with when building results to send back to search engine users. In other words, you'll have to write the CGI programs necessary to parse this information, grab the data they need, and create the HTML necessary to present that data to the end user who issued the query.

As covered in Chapter 19, there are a variety of scripts suitable for reading this output and transforming it into a human-readable form, complete with HTML tags. Please remember that when using a search engine, the resulting hits produce a list of files containing the search string. This list of files can be opened and parsed by your script or simply returned as a larger list of Address Tags.

Using CGIs to Format the Output

There are a few resources currently available that allow you to input your WAIS (or SWISH) indexing sources, to run a script, and get back a nicely formatted list of URLs in return. We briefly covered the best of these tools, called *wwwwais,* in Chapter 19. *wwwwais* is an elegant C program that acts as a traffic cop between WAIS or SWISH systems and the WWW, through a CGI program like yours.

To use *wwwwais,* you must first configure the program to support those WAIS databases that you indexed earlier to retrieve Web searches. Here's the URL that can get you the information you'll need to use this program, and the software that comes along with it:

```
http://www.eit.com/software/wwwwais/wwwwais.html
```

To get underway, please edit the "wwwwais.25.c" file. Here, the only line that you need to be concerned with is:

```
#define CONFFILE "/www/conf/wwwwais.conf"
```

This defines the location of the file that *wwwwais* uses for all of its on-the-fly configuration. Once the application program is built, you will never need to edit the source code, so all changes to your WWW environment can be handled gracefully by editing the "wwwwais.conf" file that you specified in the program.

Following we have included a listing from one of Apple's servers that shows a simple configuration for one WAIS source and one SWISH source. The index files were created by both programs using the same directory as a base, for the purposes of this example:

```
# wwwwais.conf
#
# WWWWAIS configuration file
# 6/5/95
# Kevin Hughes, kevinh@eit.com
# Documentation at http://www.eit.com/software/wwwwais/wwwwais.html
#
# Apple configuration: Contact: Mike Erwin (mikee@austin.apple.com)
#
PageTitle "Web search of www.info.apple.com"

# If this is a string, it will be a title only.
# If it specifies an HTML file, this file will be prepended to
# wwwwais results.


SelfURL "http://www.info.apple.com/cgi-bin/wwwwais"
# The self-referencing URL for wwwwais.

MaxHits 40
# The maximum number of results to return.

SortType score
# How results are sorted. This can be "score", "lines", "bytes",
# "title", or "type".

AddrMask all
# Only addresses specified here will be allowed to use the gateway.
# For the above mask option, these rules apply:
# 1) You can use asterisks in specifying the string, at either
#    ends of the string:
#    "192.100.*", "*100*", "*2.100.2"
# 2) You can make lists of masks:
#    "*192.58.2,*.2", "*.100,*171.128*", ".58.2,*100"
# 3) A mask without asterisks will match EXACTLY:
#    "192.100.58.2"
# 4) Define as "all" to allow all sites.

WaisqBin /wais/waisq
# The full path to your waisq program.
WaissearchBin /wais/waissearch
# The full path to your waissearch program.
SwishBin /www/cgi-bin/swish/swish
# The full path to your swish program.

WaisSource info.apple.com 210 WEB "Search Apple's WEB (WAIS)"
SourceRules replace "/wais/WEB" "http://www.info.apple.com/"
SwishSource /www/cgi-bin/swish/index.swish "Search Apple's WEB (Swish)"
# WAIS source file descriptions.
# For waisq sources:
#    WaisSource full_path_to_source/source.src "description"
# For waissearch sources:
#    WaisSource host.name port source "description"
```

```
UseIcons yes
# Define as "yes" or "no" if you do or don't want to use icons.

IconUrl http://www.info.apple.com/icons
# Where all your icons are kept.

TypeDef .html "HTML file" $ICONURL/text.xbm text/html
TypeDef .htm "HTML file" $ICONURL/text.xbm text/html
TypeDef .txt "text file" $ICONURL/text.xbm text/plain
TypeDef .ps "PostScript file" $ICONURL/image.xbm application/postscript
TypeDef .eps "PostScript file" $ICONURL/image.xbm application/postscript
TypeDef .man "man page" $ICONURL/text.xbm application/x-troff-man
TypeDef .gif "GIF image" $ICONURL/image.xbm image/gif
TypeDef .jpg "JPEG image" $ICONURL/image.xbm image/jpeg
TypeDef .pict "PICT image" $ICONURL/image.xbm image/x-pict
TypeDef .xbm "X bitmap image" $ICONURL/image.xbm image/x-xbitmap
TypeDef .au "Sun audio file" $ICONURL/sound.xbm audio/basic
TypeDef .snd "Mac audio file" $ICONURL/sound.xbm audio/basic
TypeDef .mpg "MPEG movie" $ICONURL/movie.xbm video/mpeg
TypeDef .mov "QuickTime movie" $ICONURL/movie.xbm video/quicktime
TypeDef .Z "compressed file" $ICONURL/compressed.xbm application/compress
TypeDef .gz "compressed file" $ICONURL/compressed.xbm application/gnuzip
TypeDef .zip "zipped file" $ICONURL/compressed.xbm application/zip
TypeDef .uu "uuencoded file" $ICONURL/uu.xbm application/uudecode
TypeDef .hqx "Binhex file" $ICONURL/binhex.xbm application/mac-binhex40
TypeDef .tar "tar'red file" $ICONURL/tar.xbm application/x-tar
TypeDef .c "C source" $ICONURL/text.xbm text/plain
TypeDef .pl "Perl source" $ICONURL/text.xbm text/plain
TypeDef .py "Python source" $ICONURL/text.xbm text/plain
TypeDef .tcl "TCL source" $ICONURL/text.xbm text/plain
TypeDef .src "WAIS index" $ICONURL/index.xbm text/plain
TypeDef .?? "unknown" $ICONURL/unknown.xbm text/plain
# Information for figuring out file types based on suffix.
# Suffix matching is case insensitive.
#    TypeDef .suffix "description" file://url.to.icon.for.this.type/
#    MIME-type
# You can use $ICONURL in the icon URL to substitute the root icon
# directory.
```

Much of the *wwwwais* configuration file is self-explanatory, but we'll mention a few problems that might occur when using it. Pay close attention to the permissions and locations of the applications that *wwwwais* needs to execute to get its query results back. The *WaisqBin*, *WaissearchBin*, and *SwishBin* directives control what and where these important files are. Figure 20-1 shows the results of a WAIS search.

Also important are the 'SourceRules' and sources as they are defined. These templates are used as options to your searching application and to parse the results returned when they exit. As a bonus, *wwwwais* puts a nice icon at the beginning of each file that it finds and the system uses a lookup table to assign these graphics. The end of the configuration file is primarily concerned with the MIME types and locations for the helper icons.

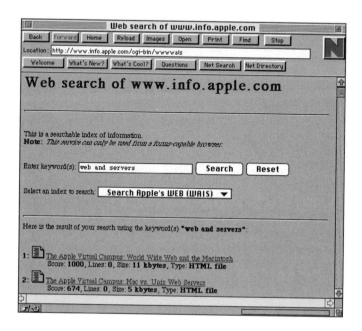

Figure 20-1

wwwwais' search/retrieve screen shows the results of a WAIS search.

The pop-up menu entitled "Select an index to search:" is populated with the title fields that are entered as sources for the query. In the preceding example, both the "Search Apple's WEB (WAIS)" and the "Search Apple's WEB (Swish)" items are what the user sees when the interface is employed.

We believe that *wwwwais* is a powerful tool that can bring some genuine sophistication to Web sites that use it. It is simple to install and easy to use, but it could be more robust as far as its configurability is concerned.

The WebMaster is unable to change the *wwwwais* user interface without modifying the C source code and recompiling, which can be tedious at times. We're sure that a more serviceable version should be available in the future; we'd recommend that you be on the lookout for it (we'll be looking for it, too).

Using SWISH to INDEX Your Site

SWISH is another indexing tool that we covered briefly in Chapter 19. SWISH (Simple Web Indexing System for Humans) is a good first choice database engine for use in Web applications because it is easier to configure and use than WAIS. Although many of its principles are the same, the SWISH system is more geared to providing answers that a WEB system can handle without modification.

But which engine you use depends on your search needs. If your intention is only to present a search engine for your Web-related data, SWISH is a good starting point. If you're just getting your feet wet and are hoping to move to a more capable search system, you might try configuring WAIS right out of the bag.

Since SWISH is simple to compile and set up, it should be a good exercise to download it and work through the examples that follow. SWISH is available from the Enterprise Integration Technologies Corporation (EIT) at the following URL:

```
http://www.eit.com/software/swish/swish.html
```

The first thing to do, as always, is to consult the "/swish.11/src/config.h" file for changes specific to your system. Machine-dependent elements as well as some default indexer behavior are controlled from this file. Some important variables to set are the 'PLIMIT' and 'FLIMIT' settings that ultimately control the speed and size of the resulting index. You should test various configurations before settling on what is right for your site.

The second thing to do is to edit the SWISH configuration file, usually found in the same directory as the application itself. The sample file included with the online distribution materials requires only a few changes to be made to get things running. Here's the listing for Apple's SWISH configuration:

```
# Sample SWISH configuration file
# Kevin Hughes, kevinh@eit.com, 3/11/95

IndexDir /wais/WEB

# This is a space-separated list of files and
# directories you want indexed. You can specify
# more than one of these directives.
```

```
IndexFile index.swish
# This is what the generated index file will be.

IndexName "Index of Apple's Web"
IndexDescription "This is a full index of Apple's Web site."
IndexPointer "http://www.info.apple.com/cgi-bin/wwwwais/"
IndexAdmin "Mike W. Erwin (mikee@austin.apple.com)"
# Extra information you can include in the index file.

IndexOnly .html .htm .txt .gif .xbm .au .mov .mpg
# Only files with these suffixes will be indexed.

IndexReport 3
# This is how detailed you want reporting. You can specify numbers
# 0 to 3 - 0 is totally silent, 3 is the most verbose.

FollowSymLinks yes
# Put "yes" to follow symbolic links in indexing, else "no".

NoContents .gif .xbm .au .mov .mpg
# Files with these suffixes will not have their contents indexed -
# only their file names will be indexed.

ReplaceRules replace "/wais/WEB" "http://www.info.apple.com"
# ReplaceRules allow you to make changes to file pathnames
# before they're indexed.

FileRules pathname contains admin testing demo trash construction confiden-
tial
FileRules filename is index.html
FileRules filename contains # % ~ .bak .orig .old old.
FileRules title contains construction example pointers
FileRules directory contains .htaccess
# Files matching the above criteria will *not* be indexed.

IgnoreLimit 50 100
# This automatically omits words that appear too often in the files
# (these words are called stopwords). Specify a whole percentage
# and a number, such as "80 256". This omits words that occur in
# over 80% of the files and appear in over 256 files. Comment out
# to turn of auto-stopwording.

IgnoreWords SwishDefault
# The IgnoreWords option allows you to specify words to ignore.
# Comment out for no stopwords; the word "SwishDefault" will
# include a list of default stopwords. Words should be separated by
# spaces and may span multiple directives.
```

As you can see, there is little in the SWISH configuration file for you
to change. You can control SWISH entirely from the command line anyway, or you may process a prefabricated indexing model. This is where
the "swish.conf" file comes in handy.

Comparing INDEX Sizes

```
Original Data Size:           20.1 M
SWISH Index Size:             0.9 M
WAIS Index Size (dct+inv):    9.9 M
```

The files indexed include a random collection of text, graphics, code, and archive files (one the author's home directories). As these file sizes indicate, WAIS indexes are large (they can sometimes even exceed the size of the indexed data). Because of this size disparity, a noticeable difference can be detected in the time to completion for a search performed on each of these various databases. Everything comes with a price; in this case, there's a definite tradeoff between complexity (or completeness) and search time.

We find that it is desirable to configure a few of these configuration files for various directories with various different attributes, and then to use the *swish* program to index them from a *cron* process. By using the *-c* command-line switch, a configuration file from anywhere on the drive may be used to specify all of the other indexing parameters. In this way, you can maintain a collection of "swish.conf" files for different purposes.

Here's a short example of the program's output:

```
Checking dir "/home/mikee/trans"...
  applesearch.html (4 words)
  bugs-pl (105 words)
  date (21 words)
  feedtest.pl (105 words)
  fortune (22 words)
  get.top.30.pl (125 words)
  lister-pl (86 words)
  listproc-pl (202 words)
  newsoftware-pl (25 words)
  parse (30 words)
  phf (78 words)
  post-query (57 words)
  query (102 words)
  srch.cgi (242 words)
  sw.handler-pl (148 words)
  test-cgi (100 words)
  test-cgi.tcl (160 words)
  til.script.pl (355 words)
  til.script.pl.old (257 words)
  top.30.wais (232 words)
  top.30.wais.fn (no words)
```

```
Checking file "/home/mikee/zones"...
  zones (34 words)

Removing very common words... no words removed.
Writing main index... 41519 unique words indexed.
Writing file index... 296 files indexed.
Running time: 12 minutes, 16 seconds.
Indexing done!
```

Although not billed as a complete solution, SWISH definitely has both advantages and drawbacks. The documentation is unclear on whether the application can handle really large data collections, but since we've never subjected it to anything larger than around 50MB, we can't confirm or deny its suitability for such situations. On the other hand, it is quick, convenient, and easy to use!

CUSTOMIZING SEARCH RESULTS

Once a search is complete, the final programming task is to handle the resulting output. If you don't have the time or patience to write a Perl script to customize the output for either a *waisq* or a *swish* search, *wwwwais* offers a perfect solution.

If you'll refer again to Figure 20-1, you can see that once the application is compiled and installed, you're set. *wwwwais* includes a built-in forms generator capable of recursively calling itself on successive calls. This means you can use its output-formatting capabilities instead of writing your own. This approach has the virtues of simplicity and minimal effort, but it produces generic-looking output.

You may, however, need a customized results screen. This might be because you must follow formats specified by a corporate or organizational style sheet for Web pages. It might also be because you've entertained the thought of piping the search output to another script for intermediate processing. Either way, you'll need to study the output of your retrieval engine and take the appropriate measures to deliver properly formatted data.

We've had extensive experience in writing customized output routines, and it is our opinion that tweaking the search data into the form you need is fairly easy. It even becomes routine if done regularly. Some fancy results can often be achieved with only a few hours' investment. At this point, we'll wish you "Good luck, and happy indexing!"

Other OS Options

Of course, there are Web servers out there running on systems other than UNIX. We've concentrated on UNIX for this book because it represents the largest installed base of Web servers in use today, and because it supports the biggest collection of tools, techniques, and wisdom about serving up Web pages. That doesn't mean the other platforms aren't any good; in fact, some would argue that other platforms — most notably, the Macintosh and Windows NT — are actually better than UNIX as Web servers. We're not entirely convinced of this, but here are some tools that you'll want to investigate if you are using a non-UNIX platform for your Web server.

APPLE MACINTOSH

Global HTTP Contents 1.0, programmed as an AppleScript applet, will generate an HTML-formatted text document that contains a hierarchical list of the contents of a folder and all of its subfolders. Although not quite in the same class as the UNIX parsing engines discussed earlier, it is helpful for the Macintosh Web administrator.

The product can be found at:

DOS/WINDOWS/WINDOWS NT

If you're a Windows NT user, you may be interested in a recently developed Web server that runs on NT. WebSite (TM) from O'Reilly & Associates is a 32-bit Web server with an intuitive graphical interface. It provides a tree-like display of all the documents and links on your server, with a simple solution for finding and fixing broken links. WebSite combines the power and flexibility of a UNIX server with ease of use of a Windows application. Read all about it at the following URL:

```
http://gnn.com/gnn/bus/ora/item/website.html
```

Summary

Hopefully, we've made search engines, and the prospect of indexing your entire site, attractive enough that you'll be willing to do the work necessary to let the world sort and sift through your HTML documents. By using catalog systems with advanced retrieval engines linked to the WWW via intelligent scripts, site navigation can aspire to heights beyond a fancy navigation bar slapped at the bottom of every page.

If you become familiar with the search programs that do the work on the back end, you'll ensure yourself a place in the future of the Web. When it is necessary to make large pools of information available to everyone in a simple fashion, you'll be well equipped to handle the job!

CHAPTER 21

Getting Hyper: Principles of Hypertext Design

*A*lthough hypertext is new and exciting technology, the legacy of thousands of years of linear text is hard to overcome. In other words, even though document designers can do incredibly nifty and creative things with linking and hypermedia, they have to fight the nearly overwhelming tendency to make their documents read like books.

Even though hypertext can make lots of interesting displays and links available, a hypertext document won't live up to its potential unless you exploit these capabilities in the most appealing and useful ways. This means modeling document structure to follow the flow of information.

As suggested in the discussion on *chunking* in Chapter 24, the process of converting linear text from other electronic or hard-copy sources depends in large part on mapping logical segments or sections of such documents into individual HTML files. At best, this helps to fit linear text into the hypertext model and helps maintain the readability of linear materials.

But what about documents designed from scratch for hypertext implementation? How can you avoid the burden of history and build useful, intuitively connected documents without following a linear approach? As you see later on, linear flow is good for some things, but not for others. Providing a good match between the structure of the content and the structure of the HTML document that contains the content is the best solution.

In the sections that follow, you'll have a chance to examine some common organizational techniques for building documents for the World Wide Web. Then we'll take a look at some different kinds of data and discuss how they can best be modeled in HTML documents. We'll conclude with a discussion of a set of principles for building hypertext documents that should stand you in good stead as you begin construction of a new world of information and representation.

Stringing Pages Together, the Old-Fashioned Way

Despite the nonlinear and interconnected structures that HTML can facilitate, some pages demand to be read in sequence. Narrative is a good example of materials that must be read in sequence — each narrative element builds on those elements that precede it. Other materials, like recipes or how-to's, also demand the same treatment because they depend on following a particular sequence to deliver the correct information.

In cases like these, it's a good idea to string pages together, as outlined in Figure 21-1. A document of five pages or more — if you believe Tim Berners-Lee in his *Hypertext Online Style Guide* — should be chained together in this manner anyway.

Figure 21-1
Chain pages together to read them in sequence.

The URL for TBL's document is:

```
http://www.w3.org/hypertext/WWW/Provider/Style/Overview.html
```

The nice thing about hypertext is that you can chain pages together forward and backward, making it easy to "turn" pages in either direction. Don't be afraid to include other appropriate links in this basic structure (e.g., to other HTML documents, a glossary, or other points inside your document).

Hierarchies Are Easy to Model in HTML

If you're used to constructing a document from an outline, a hierarchical approach to document links should be immediately intelligible. Most outlines start with major ideas and divisions, which get refined and elaborated, ultimately winding up with all the details you want to include in your final document.

Figure 21-2 shows a four-level hierarchical document structure that organizes an entire large, complex work (it could make a pretty good model for a hypertext version of this book, for instance).

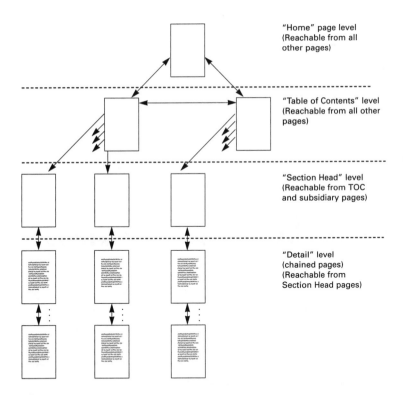

"Home" page level
(Reachable from all
other pages)

"Table of Contents" level
(Reachable from all other
pages)

"Section Head" level
(Reachable from TOC
and subsidiary pages)

"Detail" level
(chained pages)
(Reachable from
Section Head pages)

Figure 21-2
Four levels of document hierarchy is usually plenty of structure, even for the most complex collection of pages.

HTML imposes no limits on the kinds of hierarchies that you can build. The only limits should be your own imagination and your audience's ability to handle complexity. For both your sakes, we'd suggest keeping the hierarchy from getting too big or too deep. Some experts recommend no more than two or three levels of hierarchy, but we're still fixated on the famous study on human memory published in the 1970s, entitled "The Magic Number 7, Plus or Minus 2."

In actual practice, when it comes to building document hierarchies, you'll learn that you basically have two choices:

1. A document hierarchy may be *broad*; that is, it covers a lot of technical, lexical, or factual territory. This would work for something like a dictionary, which includes definitions for lots of words but doesn't provide much detail about any of them.

2. Alternatively, a document hierarchy may be *deep*, which means that it includes lots of details about a narrow range of topics or materials.

Most people can readily deal with either type of hierarchy but will have trouble dealing with one that is both deep *and* broad. Even though there's nothing inherent in HTML that prevents such a structure from being built, it's probably not a good idea to try!

Multiple Tracks for Multiple Audiences

It isn't unusual to build a single document collection that includes different levels or kinds of information to meet the needs of different audiences. HTML makes it easy to interlink basic introductory documents (like a tutorial or a technical overview) with more pointed, in-depth reference materials. That way, you could design a home page that points beginners at a tutorial, then leads them through an overview, before assaulting them with the down-and-dirty details of your "real" content.

This kind of organization, depicted in Figure 21-3, lets you notify experienced readers how to access your in-depth content directly, bypassing introductory and explanatory materials. Such an approach lets you design for multiple audiences, without creating multiple document collections for each audience. Instead, HTML lets you create certain *pathways* into your materials, so that your audience can pick the approach that suits it best.

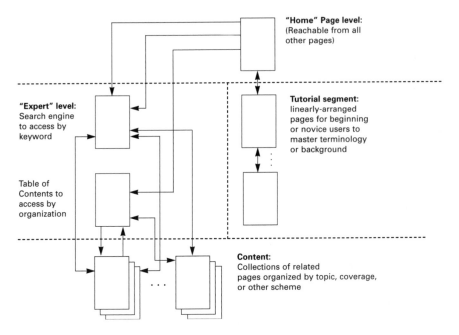

Figure 21-3

Multiple tracks through a document can serve several audiences.

The organization in Figure 21-3 differs somewhat from those depicted in Figures 21-1 and 21-2. This collection of documents includes three separate areas, interlinked with a home page, that emphasizes the links between related documents more than the flow of pages within individual collections.

In fact, the kind of document pictured in Figure 21-3 would probably combine elements from both a linear and a hierarchical structure in its actual page flows. A tutorial is typically meant to be read from front to back, or at least a chapter at a time, while reference materials will usually be consulted by topic and only rarely read all the way through. That's why the tutorial on the right is presented as a linear sequence of pages, and the content collection on the bottom is primarily accessible through a table of contents and/or a search engine.

Just as the access methods for information vary by use, so also does the organization of the documents that present that information. That's why designing hypertext documents depends strongly on analyzing the content that a document collection is supposed to present.

In the section that follows, we'll examine a highly successful document collection that should help to illustrate all of these organizational ideas at work.

The RFC Library

Where TCP/IP is concerned, the architectural standards and the United States Internet are governed by the Internet Architecture Board (IAB), previously known as the Internet Activities Board. This group has ultimate custody of all the RFCs as well.

The IAB delegates its responsibilities for development, operations, and management of the Internet and related protocols and services to various subcommittees, working groups, and suborganizations that it controls. It also contracts with other commercial companies specializing in communications, computing, and various types of consulting to help provide and manage key aspects of the Internet's infrastructure.

The subgroup that is chartered with protocol development and implementation is the Internet Engineering Task Force (IETF). It is comprised of a steering committee that reports to the IAB and a collection of working groups, each of which is responsible for various protocols and services under development or in maintenance mode. The bulk of Internet protocol development and standardization activity is handled by the working groups within the IETF.

The documents that specify and describe TCP/IP protocols and services are called *Request For Comments*, otherwise known as *RFCs*. RFCs are assigned in numeric order by the IETF and are referred to by number. The document that describes the Internet Official Protocol Standards is RFC 1610, which is close to the top end of the range of assigned numbers (the current ceiling is 1814, assigned 6/22/95).

Even though "Request For Comments" sounds more like a question to solicit feedback on an idea (which is how the bulk of RFCs actually function), standard RFCs have the weight of law (or at least, decree) in the Internet and TCP/IP communities. These documents represent only a fraction of the total collection of RFCs, but they literally dictate how protocols behave and what functions they must perform.

Failure to conform to these definitions — especially for required or recommended protocols — can cost a vendor the opportunity of doing business with the DoD and all the other bodies and agencies that adhere to its guidelines (of which there are many, both inside and outside the U.S.). In matters of dispute or in questions regarding the protocols, the RFCs are the final authority and the IETF the final source of resolution.

RFCs may be obtained from the Internet host named *ds.internic.net* via *ftp*, *WAIS*, or e-mail. Using *ftp*, RFCs are stored as "rfc/rfcnnnn.txt" or "rfc/rfcnnnn.ps" where 'nnnn' is the RFC number, '.txt' is the ASCII version, and '.ps' the PostScript version of the file. Using *WAIS*, *telnet* to *ds.internet.net* and search the database 'rfcs'.

But the best way to access the RFC collection, as you might guess from the focus of this book, is via the Web. If you point your browser at the following URL:

```
http://www.cis.ohio-state.edu/hypertext/information/rfc.html
```

you'll gain access to the home page for the entire collection. You can access RFCs directly by number using the following notation:

```
http://www.cis.ohio-state.edu/htbin/rfc/rfcnnn(n).html
```

where 'nnn(n)' is the three- or four-digit representation for the RFC number (older RFCs numbered less than 1000 are entered as such; e.g., 'rfc1610' or 'rfc822').

The RFC library at Ohio State is complex and many-sided. This library displays a number of valuable characteristics:

- It supports access to any document directly by its RFC (document) number.

- It includes a search engine that provides keyword search for the text of all documents in the library.

- It provides a comprehensive index with links to every RFC and all necessary supporting documentation.

- It includes pointers to relevant FAQs and orientation materials, to help naive or first-time users better understand the library. These include overviews, a glossary, a complete list of protocols, a bibliography, and a subject index for the RFCs.

- As RFCs age, they become obsoleted by other higher-numbered documents; each RFC includes a pointer to the chain of documents that preceded it and the chain that follows it. This makes it easy to get from any known RFC to its most current implementation and to read through the entire history of a subject, protocol, or operations document.

- RFCs function as a true collection — that is, they draw on the contents and information stored in other RFCs. The Web version also includes pointers to a list of "related RFCs," which makes it easy to understand the context and content of any individual RFC.

The last two elements of this list, the RFC "history chain" and the pointers to "related RFCs," are probably the most useful aspects of this collection. But the real utility of this library is a function of its organization as a document collection. It's also a function of the underlying database from which these documents are drawn and the search and formatting tools that make Web access possible.

If you examine Figure 21-4, you'll see a high-level approximation of how this document collection is created, maintained, and organized. This diagram shows the following key elements:

- the home page, which contains pointers to all of the collection's facilities

- the comprehensive index, which provides pointers to all individual documents

- the search engine, which permits all documents to be searched by keyword

- the internal history and relationship pointers inside the individual RFCs, which describe the historical progression of and relationships among RFCs

- the Webification tool, which takes RFCs in their mandated PostScript format and transforms them into HTML documents

- the indexing tool, which adds history, relationship, and keyword indexing information to the HTML documents that result from translation

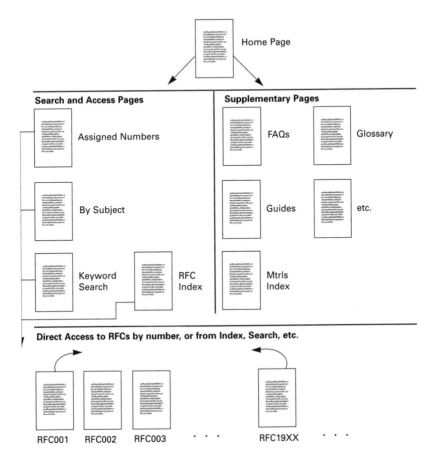

Figure 21-4

The RFC Library combines hierarchical, historical organization with explanatory materials and indexing tools to create a multidimensional information repository.

Because the collection of RFCs is ever-changing and growing, organization and access are particularly important. As draft documents become standards, they'll stop changing and that's also when new draft versions will typically be added. This structure shows that the model outlined for hierarchical (deep) and broad (lots of documents) information collections can be successfully combined. The RFC library is an excellent working model for how to serve up a large, complex collection of data that meets its consumers' needs very well.

The Principles of Hypertext

In the sections that follow, we're going to abstract the basic concepts for organizing effective hypertext documents from the materials we've covered so far in this chapter and from relevant materials elsewhere in the book (where appropriate, we'll provide cross-references). The idea here is to boil the design process down to a series of short rules of thumb that should be easy to understand, remember, and apply.

ANNOTATE ALL EXTERNAL REFERENCES

Any time you include a link to an external document, provide a description of what's on the other side of the link. The more your readers know about what's connected to the link, the better able they'll be to decide when (and if) to follow it.

Because external links remove readers from your document set, consider using *indirection* for accessing such links. That is, link from inside one of your documents to an annotated jump page and then to the external document, rather than from a link inside document content straight to other material. This provides the information necessary to decide when to make the jump and helps readers to explore your pages more fully before leaving them.

INDICATE THE SCOPE AND SIZE OF YOUR MATERIALS

If your document set is large and complex, it's a good idea to let your readers know what kinds of materials they contain, how large the collection is, and the best methods for navigating through those materials. If readers are prepared to step through a complex or large set of materials, they'll be much less likely to get frustrated (and thus, less likely to jump out of your document set) than if they find themselves in an "information thicket" from which there is no apparent means of escape nor mode of orientation or navigation.

LIMIT THE COMPLEXITY OF YOUR INDEX

The RFC library actually provides three ways to access information, spread over four or five levels. But it uses the index, the table of contents, the search engine, and document–to–document pointers to make it easy to approach the document collection from any of a number of dimensions. These range from:

- direct access to a known RFC
- the ability to browse descriptive information or a comprehensive index of all information
- the ability to search for specific keywords using a search engine
- the ability to follow historical or contextual relationships among documents

Because users will want to slice the collection at some moments and dice it at others, the collection offers multiple methods of access. But each method is simple and coherent and has certain obvious applications for particular circumstances. This approach limits perceived complexity and is nothing short of ingenious.

MATCH YOUR STRUCTURE TO YOUR CONTENT

The RFC collection can be organized in many ways:

- as an incremental succession of numbered documents
- as an historical progression of versions of the same document
- as a collection of textual information that can be searched by keyword or topic
- as a set of multiple collections of documents, each of which is interrelated by common technologies, subject areas, protocols, or implementers

The beauty of the HTML implementation of the library is that it implements all of these organizations simultaneously. The utility of this implementation is that it provides simple rules (structuring of individual RFC document names) and tools (index, TOC, and search engine) to exploit each aspect of the structure as needed.

PRESENT DISTINCT TOPICS AS DISTINCT DOCUMENTS

The individual RFC supplies a natural granule for the composition of the library's document collection. This body is composed of over 1,800 individual documents, intertwined and interlinked by historical and factual relationships. Yet each individual one has a separate existence and can easily be accessed as such.

Likewise, the supporting materials (including the many external references included on the home page) share a topical focus. Each element provides a specific view of the library itself, individual aspects of its subject matter, or supplementary information (e.g., glossary, bibliography, protocol list, and subject index) to help locate and understand particular topics and documents.

PROVIDE APPROPRIATE ACCESS METHODS

Nearly any collection of information will benefit from a table of contents and a set of orientation materials, especially for collections with different pathways designed for different types of users (as with the collection depicted in Figure 21-3).

Where documents have a regular, predictable structure (as with the naming convention used for RFCs), document names and organization should reflect that structure.

Where large collections of information exist, supplying programmatic access through a search engine or on-the-fly indexing tool is quite appropriate (the online DTDs mentioned in Chapters 3 and 5 are good examples here, in addition to the search engine available in the RFC library).

In real life, they say that "form follows function," but when it comes to document collections, it's probably more appropriate to say that the data access functions supplied should follow (and enhance) the structure of the data as much as possible.

SUPPLY EASY, CONSISTENT NAVIGATION TOOLS

The broader or deeper a collection of documents, the easier it is to get lost in the swamp. If you provide users a map of the overall layout when they enter your collection (or better yet, make it available at any point) and place regular signposts along the way, your users will be able to find their way around your content, no matter how large or complex the collection may actually be.

At a bare minimum, every page layout you deliver to your users — especially pages generated on-the-fly from CGI programs — should include a navigation bar (or some graphical equivalent) that points to the following elements:

- the home page (probable label: "Home")
- the previous page (probable label: "Back")
- the table of contents (suggested label: "TOC")
- the index (if applicable; suggested label: "Index")
- the search engine (if applicable; suggested label: "Search")
- the next document (if a logical successor exists; probable label: "Next")
- an explanation of the document collection or a map of its structure (suggested labels: "Help" or "Map")

If this approach to navigation is presented clearly and consistently throughout your document collection, users will be able to zip in and out with ease. They'll also be better equipped to find what they're looking for.

One final word of advice: if you structure your pages so that users never have to scroll more than one screen up or down to find a navigation bar, they'll love you forever!

USE LINKS AS REFERENCES

Finally, it's important to understand that hypertext links provide the glue that ties related elements in a document collection together. Any time you wish to refer to materials contained elsewhere in your document set, it's legitimate to place a clearly labeled link that lets readers pursue more information on the topic, if they so choose.

Likewise, when presenting off-line graphics, video, sound, etc., use icons to indicate the type of data involved. Also tell users how big the information on the other side of the link is, so they can decide whether it's worth the wait to retrieve it. Here again, providing choice (and control) to users is "the right thing" to do.

Finally, you should avoid the temptation to use links as a kind of footnote. Where items are relevant and tie to other major or minor topics in your content, a link is completely appropriate.

Where you wish to digress or dive into low-level details, you should use the indirection technique we recommended earlier for external document links (that is, take your readers to an annotated link to this information and let them decide whether they wish to pursue the content further). The idea is to provide a rich and informative structure through linking, not an amorphous, disorganized one. HTML 3.0, which currently includes support for footnotes, may render these exhortations moot.

Summary

When it comes to organizing hypertext documents, it's wise to let go of the two-dimensional legacy of traditional linear text. By allowing the structure of the underlying data or content to dictate document organization, you can create a collection of documents that provides easy access to the content. Then, by including the right mix of access methods and tools, you can provide appropriate ways to search for and retrieve information. Finally, by supplying the right kinds of internal links and relationships, you can let these documents express the underlying structures to which they belong.

CHAPTER

22 Monitoring Web Server Activity

Who's That Knocking at My Door?

Since the advent of the World Wide Web, it seems that everyone — users, administrators, managers, and executives — has been trying to understand just what the Web really is. Is it a marketing tool, a research and educational resource, a new venue for commerce, or is it all or none of these? No one truly knows the answers yet, but the search for enlightenment continues and the need for information is almost insatiable.

Statistics are the tools we turn to when dealing with an indeterminate social phenomenon. If quantitative, objective scales can be derived from and applied to a phenomenon, we can begin to construct a better picture of what variables are involved and how they change over time. From this a larger picture may be derived — namely, the complex, organic process spawned from chaotic societal currents and eddies that some might even call a "trend."

The first measure to apply to the question "What is the Web?" is scale. There are two distinct realms at work within the Web that are most worth looking at. The Web can be looked at on two different levels, macro and micro. The macro level is the World Wide Web as a whole, but collecting statistics on this scale is a job best left to the denizens of the Ivory Tower. No one does big-time statistical modeling better than the academic research community; all the proof you'll ever need for this assertion can be found at the Virtual Library, whose URL is:

```
http://www.charm.net/~web/Vlib/Misc/Statistics.html
```

On the micro level, Web activity occurs right in your face. After all, if you've gone through the effort of publishing materials on the Web, you probably want to know how they're being perceived by your audience and how much traffic your pages are getting. Then, too, if you could collect data on the people who actually use it, or what those users are doing on your site, what better place to look than on your own server?

A large number of tools exist to help you collect and understand Web server statistics. Ranging from the simplest of usage summaries to the most complex, configurable, graphical analysis engines, these tools have one common goal: to provide a close-up of your particular corner of the Web. We'll take a look at some of the best tools available, as we cover the whole range of Web monitors, from simple to complex.

Talking with the Log Lady: HTTP Log Analysis, Parsing, and Summaries

Some of the most valuable sources of information about the Web come from the Web servers themselves. Like most Internet services, Web servers can typically be configured to log some or all of their activities to one or more text files. The formatting and specific information in these files will vary from one WWW server to another, but at least one aspect of the log will remain consistent: it contains all of the raw material you'll ever need to analyze your server's activity.

A sample line from an NCSA *httpd*'s "access_log" file should serve to demonstrate:

```
way.outer.net 204.96.111.64 singe [02/Jun/1995:00:48:54 -0500] "GET
/singe/MilkCheese.gif HTTP/1.0" 200 16860
```

First, this NCSA *http* server saves its log using the "Common Log Format," an agreed-upon standard for WWW servers. NCSA and CERN were among the earliest *httpd* developers to adopt this standard, with a host of others quickly following suit. Unless otherwise stated, all of the packages we cover in this chapter support the "Common Log Format" on UNIX.

Now let's examine the items in the log entry. The first entries include the name and IP number of the host making the http request of your server (way.outer.net 204.96.111.64). The next entry shows the requesting user's name if the document or server being accessed requires authentication (*singe*).

This is followed by a date and time stamp ([02/Jun/1995 :00:48:54 - 0500]); then the actual HTTP request as received from the browser, in this case a GET command, the path to the requested file, and the version of HTTP being used (GET /singe/MilkCheese.gif HTTP/1.0).

Finally the server's result code and the number of bytes transferred back to the browser are recorded (*200 16860*). In order to become completely fluent in Log-ese, you'll need to understand the HTTP commands and result codes. They're covered online at:

```
http://www.w3.org/hypertext/WWW/Protocols/HTTP/HTRESP.html
```

Even a cursory glance at the log entry above should tell you that with a little work and the right tools you could extract the number of times a specific machine accessed your site, how many unique machines accessed it, which were your most popular documents, and much, much more. Server statistics packages take this raw data as presented by the server, parse it, filter out and collect the pertinent data, and then output a report summarizing the results. What could be simpler, right?

WHAT'S A *WAMP*?

A personalized version of this sort of summary is precisely what *WAMP* offers. A nifty little Perl script, *WAMP*'s default behavior is to run through the current NCSA *httpd* access log file looking for references to the username of the person who is running it. For example, if the user *singe* runs *WAMP* with no command-line options, *WAMP* will produce a list of machines that have accessed pages with *singe* in their names or paths. Most often, pages that contain references to the user's name in the filename or path will be part of the user's home page, so in that way *WAMP* provides the information for which it is an acronym: Who's Accessing My Pages? (Sorry, it has nothing to do with wabbits, wascally or otherwise.)

You can find WAMP at:

```
http://www.wwu.edu/~n9146070/wamp.html
```

By using command-line options in *WAMP*, we can get the counts to indicate how often a particular document has been accessed, and a breakdown of accessing machines by domain. Still logged in as *singe*, we typed **wamp -url -a** at the shell prompt, and as you can see from our sample output, no one in particular is interested in our home pages:

```
Welcome to WAMP, singe
Reading logfile.....
Reading complete....
Sites parsed...
prisoner.austin.apple.com        6
tarragon.lcs.mit.edu             3
way.outer.net                    9
/singe/                          4
/forms/dns.html                  1
/forms/todo.outer.html           1
/forms/customer_entry.html       3
/singe/felix08.GIF               1
/singe/navbar.GIF                2
/singe/home.html                 3
/forms/line_item_real.html       1
/singe/MilkCheese.gif            1
/forms/todo.html                 1
com                              6
edu                              3
net                              9
WAMP complete.
```

WAMP also allows you to specify a different username via its *-u* command line switch. As attractive as *WAMP* is for its simplicity, the above output betrays a flaw in the program's design: Because it looks for the username with a free-form pattern-recognition scheme, *WAMP* counts every time the username appeared *anywhere* in the log entries. Therefore, the document "/~jane/singers.html" would be counted as *singe*'s document even though it belongs to *jane*.

In any event, a web developer's bag of tricks needs representation at every level of complexity and *WAMP* does what it does quite elegantly. You should try it out yourself!

SWISS ARMY STATISTICS FROM GETSTATS

If *WAMP* does one thing well, *getstats* attempts to do *everything* well. A C program written by Kevin Hughes at EIT, *getstats'* source and documentation are available at:

```
ftp://ftp.eit.com/pub/web.software/getstats
http://www.eit.com/software/getstats/getstats.html
```

Where *WAMP* was personal, looking at one user's pages at a time, *getstats* uses a wide-angle lens to show you your server as a whole.

The program installs easily, just make sure you set the user defines in the source before compiling. Of particular note are: 'SERVERSITE', the URL of your *http* server; the top-level directory for your Web server, called 'ROOTDIR'; 'HOMEPAGE', the page to serve when a URL has no document specified; the path to the server's 'LOGFILE'; the 'SERVER-TYPE', defined as 'NCSA', 'CERN', 'PLEXUS', 'GN', 'MAC', or 'GOPHER'; and a boolean called 'COMMON' that defines whether your server is using the "Common Log Format" mentioned earlier.

We must place the utmost stress on the importance of the 'COMMON' define, because if it is not set properly, *getstats* will behave badly. If the program seems to work but never exits or returns any statistics, most likely you have not defined "COMMON". Take our word for it — this is practical experience speaking!

Compiling *getstats* should be a simple matter of:

```
cc getstats.c -o getstats
```

on most flavors of UNIX. The program's author recommends *gcc*, and it worked beautifully on SunOS, Linux, and A/UX, where we performed our testing (*gcc* is the Gnu C Compiler, one of the terrific products from Richard Stallman's Free Software Foundation).

It also bears mentioning that all of *getstats.c* defines can be over-ridden by its command-line options, and that once you get to know the program you may want to go back and recompile it with your favorite defaults.

Once all the *cc* rigamarole is out of your hair (but hey, that's what we love about UNIX, isn't it?), you can actually run the program and start generating statistics. *getstats* plain-vanilla default behavior is to generate a concise summary report in this form:

```
HTTP Server General Statistics
Server: http://www.outer.net/ (NCSA Common)
Local date: Sun Jun 04 22:36:00 PM CDT 1995
Covers: 05/29/95 to 06/04/95 (7 days).
All dates are in local time.
Requests last 7 days: 4489
New unique hosts last 7 days: 550
Total unique hosts: 550
Number of HTML requests: 698
Number of script requests: 201
Number of non-HTML requests: 3590
Number of malformed requests (all dates): 817
Total number of all requests/errors: 5306
Average requests/hour: 32.6, requests/day: 783.4
Running time: 10 seconds.
```

You get this summary along with all of *getstats'* copious report options.

One command-line switch we recommend always choosing when running *getstats* from the shell is the progress meter option, *-p*. It's just the thing to calm our Attention-Deficient Disordered nerves while *getstats* churns through 30,000 or so lines of HTTP log files. Another helpful aid is the *-t* switch, which specifies how many lines of each report we want to see, making it delightfully simple to generate those top 10, 20, or 30 lists that management is always after.

Some of *getstats'* other, more utilitarian highlights include reporting either hosts or domains accessing the site, or files requested. Reports can be sorted by number of accesses, time of last access, host name, or bytes transferred. The log can be filtered either to include or exclude entries with host names, or requests containing a specific regular expression. The latter feature can be used to generate reports for specific offerings on your Web site, much like *WAMP*. For example, invoking *getstats* with the command line:

```
getstats -p -fa -t 10 -sr "/singe*"
```

generates the following report:

```
HTTP Server General Statistics
Server: http://www.outer.net/ (NCSA Common)
Local date: Mon Jun 05 00:14:57 AM CDT 1995
Covers: 05/30/95 to 06/04/95 (6 days).
All dates are in local time.
Requests last 7 days: 13
New unique hosts last 7 days: 2
Total unique hosts: 2
Number of HTML requests: 3
```

```
Number of script requests: 0
Number of non-HTML requests: 10
Number of malformed requests (all dates): 819
Total number of all requests/errors: 832
Average requests/hour: 7.5, requests/day: 180.4
Running time: 6 seconds.

HTTP Server Full Statistics
Covers: 05/30/95 to 06/04/95 (6 days).
All dates are in local time.
Sorted by number of requests.

# of Requests : Last Access (M/D/Y) : Hostname
_____


10 : 06/04/95 : way.outer.net
 3 : 05/30/95 : tarragon.lcs.mit.edu
```

In other words, *getstats* shows the same pitiful lack of interest in Sebastian's home page that *WAMP* illustrated, but in much more detail. We feel compelled to clarify that Sebastian just put his home page on this server a few days ago, so the world at large is not really showing a total lack of interest. It doesn't know about his pages; therefore it hasn't yet had a chance to ignore him.

Returning to the report, you should notice that the concise report has also been constrained to requests containing the regular expression **/singe*** giving a tidy overview of general activity on a specific Web offering.

Finally, *getstats* can also generate traffic reports with bar graphs drawn with ASCII characters showing the numbers of requests and bytes served by the hour, day, week, and month. The same constraints for strings can be applied to traffic reports.

One final note: with the *-ht* option, *getstats'* output is formatted for an HTML browser; this has cool implications that we'll consider shortly.

BEAN COUNTER'S WET DREAM: WWWstat

"Exhaustive" is the word that *WWWstat* conjures up. A Perl script written by Roy Fielding at the University of California at Irvine, this tool leaves no stone unturned, or at least no statistic goes unreported. Slightly less configurable than *getstats*, *WWWstat* nonetheless has some distinct advantages.

First, its output simply must be seen to be appreciated. As a sample output, you can look at the statistics of the university's own server:

```
http://www.ics.uci.edu/Admin/wwwstats.html
```

With its extremely lucid presentation of the numbers and its reports structured in a completely logical way, you get an incredibly complete picture of the server. *WWWstat* reports the server-wide information first, followed by accesses by host, domain, and reverse lookup, concluding with the activity for the documents available on the server.

Various reporting features can be turned on or off with command-line options, but this tool's maximum impact is achieved by letting it do what it's programmed to do. *WWWstat* does have some of *getstats'* power in terms of excluding or including hosts and/or documents via regular expression filters, but where it really falls down is its failure to allow the user to change its sort criteria and to limit the number of entries printed.

WWWstat's output is always HTML-ized, so this is a tool that creates Web reports that are themselves served on the Web. The documentation is quite clear about how you should implement it on your site — namely, as a *cron* job that runs nightly, replacing the previous day's report when it's done.

Like so many aspects of the Web, log analyzers were almost predestined to become self-referential, reporting on the medium that serves as transport for the reports it generates.

MAC SEE, MAC DO: WEBSTAT

Log analysis is not limited to UNIX platform *http* servers. WebSTAR, an *http* server formerly known as MacHTTP, provides a level of logging activity adequate to support its own statistics-reporting applications.

One such application is *WebStat*, written by Phil Harvey at Queen's University in Canada. To install *WebStat*, the program and its configuration and format file must be placed in the same folder as WebSTAR. The "WebStat.config" and "WebStat.format" files must be customized to suit your site's needs, and then the application is ready to run. It creates a file

called "WebStat.html", which may be linked to an appropriate
reference on one of your Web pages for viewing.

WebStat's report will appear familiar. That is because the data structure and format is largely based on WWWstat's. Also like WWWstat,
WebStat's report is HTML-formatted to take advantage of the layout and
linking power of the Web.

Figure Painting: Making the Leap from ASCII to GIF

How long it took the unknown Web developer to make the leap from
HTML-formatted columns of access and byte counts to CGI-generated
graphs the world will never know, but we'd like to think it was only
milliseconds. Everyone knows that pretty pictures and flashy colors catch
and hold our attention better than stacks of digits, and the power of the
Web makes possible the nearly instant translation of raw numbers to
finalized graphical data.

There are two uniquely Web-like aspects to most of the packages
that change server stats into pie charts or bar graphs:

1. They build from the efforts to massage the raw data of the access
   log into an intelligible report, as detailed earlier, instead of starting
   over from scratch. That is, these packages use one of the programs
   described earlier to do all the grunt work and confine themselves to
   fussing with the resulting data.

2. They also use pre-existing tools to draw their graphs. The Internet
   lends itself to this kind of collaboration incredibly well, with one
   person leveraging off the hard work of another to create something
   that transcends both.

With an introduction like this, you're probably expecting some pretty
snazzy displays. If you check out these tools, we're sure you won't be
disappointed!

GETGRAPH.PL

Remember the ASCII character bars in *getstats*? If any one part of a Web statistics package cries out for color and shape, it is those bars of asterisks and plus signs. Martien Verbruggen must have thought the same way, because he created *getgraph.pl*, which does just that (See Figure 22-1). Using *gnuplot*, *GIFtrans,* and *ppmtogif,* Martien's Perl script parses *getstats* output and translates it into attractive, transparent GIFs suitable for Web viewing.

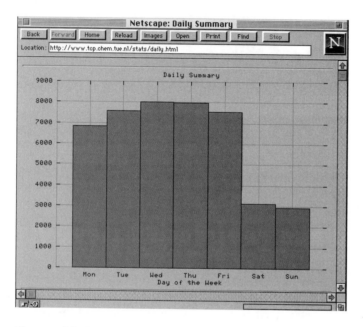

Figure 22-1

A daily summary chart generated by getgraph.pl.

It's more work to install *getgraph.pl* than *getstats*, because of all the other packages it depends on. Your version of UNIX — how standard or nonstandard it is — may make installation difficult, but with these pictures, isn't it worth a try?

All of the necessary sources can be found at the following URLs:

```
http://www.cs.dartmouth.edu/gnuplot_info.html
ftp://ftp.chem.tue.nl/pub/sysutils/GIFtrans.c
ftp://ftp.x.org/R5contrib/
```

Here's how all the pieces fit together: the Perl script *getgraph.pl* parses the numerical data from the output of *getstats*. *getgraph.pl* then feeds the data to *gnuplot,* which creates a "ppm" file, a portable plot file format supported by Jef Poskanzer's kitchen sink UNIX graphics utilities suite, *pbmplus.* One of the *pbmplus* tools, *ppmtogif,* then translates the "ppm" file to the GIF standard, and finally the file is passed off to *GIFtrans,* a simple utility that converts the GIF to GIF87a and sets its background to transparent. The file is now ready to be delivered to any graphical Web browser. You'll find more *getgraph.pl* examples at:

    http://www.tcp.chem.tue.nl/stats/

GWSTAT

Another add-on, *gwstat* leverages off the work done by *WWWstat.* It takes *WWWstat's* copious output and condenses it into a series of highly effective graphs. Written by Qiegang Long at the University of Massachusetts, *gwstat* also uses pre-existing Graphics Tools to create raw graphics files and then converts them to Web browser readable GIFs. These packages, called *Xmgr,* are available at:

    ftp://ftp.teleport.com/pub/users/pturner/acegr/

The process from raw numbers to bar graphs in *gwstat* is quite similar to *getgraph.pl,* in that the Perl script shuffles the raw data through an X-Windows package that converts it to a portable image file, then through the *ImageMagick* graphics utility to end up with a GIF. The end results are also fairly similar.

You'll find *ImageMagick* at:

    ftp://ftp.digex.com/pub/X11/contrib/applications/ImageMagick

Figure 22-2 illustrates a *gwstat* graph. Look for more examples at:

    http://dis.cs.umass.edu/stats/gwstat.html

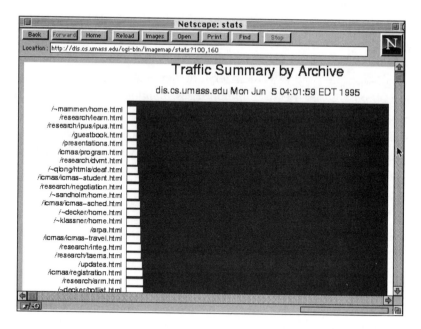

Figure 22-2

gwstat's "usage by document" graph.

WUSAGE

Written in C by Thomas Boutell of the Quest Protein Database Center (and keeper of the WWW-related FAQs for the WWW newsgroups), *wusage* is unique in that it has all the necessary pieces for collecting the data and presenting it as built-in GIFs. As he explains in his online documentation, Boutell based his GIF support code on the code found in *pbmplus*, the package mentioned above, which was in turn based on the code in *GIFENCOD*.

The Electronic Palimpsest

Isn't the Internet a marvelous thing? It's a living history of code, maintained, improved, and archived by the high priests of the information age, the programmers and developers. Each generation of cool tool stands on the shoulders of the previous one. And sometimes — like now — it adds up to something great!

Since it's a C program, you'll have to go through the process of compiling *wusage*, but the author claims this shouldn't be too difficult. As always, this depends entirely on your flavor of UNIX. Once compiled, *wusage* can be configured and then executed as a nightly *cron* job, to update the statistics for your server.

wusage has the advantage of being small, relatively portable, and self-contained, rather than a complex, interconnected system of programs, scripts, and utilities. Where it is somewhat lacking is in options, since the traffic overview chart shown in Figure 22-3 is the only report it will generate.

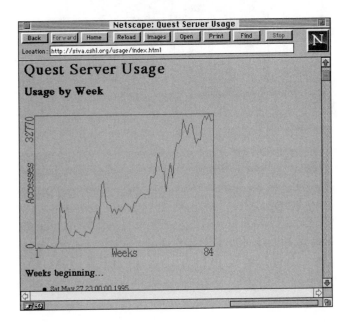

Figure 22-3
Statistics generated by wusage 3.2 for the Quest WWW server,
http://siva.cshl.org/.

VB-STAT

So that we cannot be accused of platform-chauvinism, we will now mention a Visual Basic program designed to run on a Windows NT, 95, or 3.1 *http* server. It is a run-time package, so Visual Basic is not required to install *VB-stats* on the server. As you can see in Figure 22-4, its output is pleasantly three-dimensional and the author, Web developer Robert Denny, writes that the installer/configuration wizard included with the package handles most of the setup chores.

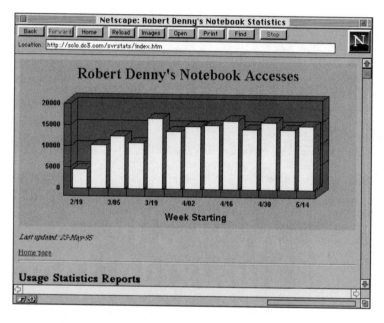

Figure 22-4
Robert Denny's VB-stat output, http://solo.dc3.com/.

Unfortunately, like *wusage*, *VB-stat* is confined to only one report format.

For Those of You Who Can't Get Enough Data

PROFESSIONAL HELP

What if you need more information than is typically captured in your http server's log? Have no fear. No matter how deep-rooted your love for numerical data, there is someone who loves it more. Take, for example, David-Michael Lincke, at the Institut für Wirtschaftsinformatik at the University of St. Gallen, Switzerland, who has hacked the NCSA *httpd* server to log referrer documents and user agents, as well.

What this means is that when someone accesses one of your documents, the server logs the document you came from — that is, the location of the link to your document. User agent logging keeps track of what kind of browsers are hitting your site. David has written Perl scripts to demonstrate his logging extensions, and the results are fascinating:

```
%Reqs Requests  WWW Browser
---------------|-----------------------------
73.94  678639  | Netscape
16.56  151944  | NCSA Mosaic and enhanced Versions
 2.66   24436  | Lynx
 2.44   22416  | IBM WebExplorer
 1.34   12319  | Netcom NetCruiser
 3.06   28048  | Others
```

You can find out more about these *httpd* extensions at:

```
http://www-iwi.unisg.ch/~dlincke/httpd-ext.html
```

CASE STUDIES

It's important that we don't forget to mention another logging tool — CGIs can be built to log their own activity. The advantage here is that you can tailor the information you need to know about the use of that specific CGI and build the logging into the functionality of program or script.

In fact, many CGIs' primary function is to log their own activity, often in the form of e-mailed feedback to the script's owner or answers collected from a form. Don't be afraid to create your own log file with your CGI and make it write to the collected HTTP log directory so you can keep track. Watch your results carefully to make sure you designed it correctly and that you're getting the information you need.

FUTURE LOGGING MODELS

All the preceding tools for collecting and analyzing logs have a couple of characteristics in common. They all distill large amounts of information into smaller, summarized pieces of data. They all do so in a strictly linear way — that is, they order the data according to time or size or number of requests on a specific document or host. And they all produce misleading reports.

Why? Because one of the most basic questions we are trying to answer with all of this is "how big is the audience for my site?" This question has a lot of other attendant issues as well, like "how long does the average user spend at a time on your site," "which are the most-traveled sets of links," and so on.

All information is almost entirely absent from the tools we've discussed here. To enable this type of analysis, our tool would have to track a user's session from start to finish. This is not an easy task in a medium that is asynchronous and non-linear, and at the moment we are aware of no such tools.

But, as with most good ideas on the Web, that void will probably not last long. Someone will decide it's too good an idea and too tempting not to implement. In fact, perhaps *you* could create such a beast, and the collective Web will beat a path to your home page. And you can watch your traffic statistics go off the CGI-created graph!

23 Robots, Spiders, and WebCrawlers

*T*he useful information returned by search engines on the Web doesn't just come out of nowhere. Rather, it is laboriously gathered by software automatons that cruise the Web, with either broadly or narrowly defined objectives and read through all the HTML documents they encounter, harvesting or calculating all information that meets their programming criteria.

These programs are called *Web robots,* or simply *robots.* Sometimes, you'll hear them referred to as *spiders* or *WebCrawlers.* No matter what they're called, these programs all perform similar tasks: they pick up selected pieces of information from the Web documents they find — at least the URL and the title, if not more — and report their findings back to a logging program on the originator's server. This log is massaged, inspected, and digested to create the database from which search engines pluck their responses to your queries.

In reality, a robot is nothing more than a browser-like program that uses ordinary HTTP protocols to request access to Web resources and documents. Robots typically understand links, URLs, and other selected HTML tags and information. They know how to catalog these tags or how to abstract statistics based on what they encounter. Since they don't actually display anything, you could think of them as a kind of "headless browser," that chew their way around the Net with an inexhaustible appetite for any new links that might come their way.

In this chapter, we'll examine some of the more common robots in use on the Web today. We'll also present a rationale for designing robots and then discuss the pros and cons of actually implementing one. You'll also learn about an informal standard for restricting the resources that robots will access on your Web site and what to do if your server is overrun by a robot on a rampage.

A Robot Taxonomy

Let's trot out a more formal definition of a robot. According to David Eichmann, Assistant Professor of Computer Science at the University of Houston-Clear Lake and the author of an excellent Web document entitled "Ethical Web Agents," a robot is ...

> ... *a program that autonomously explores the structure of the Web and takes some action on the artifacts thereby encountered. This action might be as simple as counting the number of artifacts found, or as complex as a full text indexing of the contents of an artifact.*

Taken from:

http://www.ncsa.uiuc.edu/SDG/IT94/Proceedings/Agents/eichmann.ethical/eichmann.html

Robots have been designed for numerous tasks, including:

- cataloging any and all pages
- cataloging pages that meet specific search criteria
- gathering Web statistics
- synchronizing files across mirrored servers

Basically, robots exist to permit the ongoing acquisition of information about the Web, whether content-, site-, or activity-related.

Robots also differ in the scope of their activities. Up to now, we've described robots as free- and far-ranging programs able to go anywhere on the Web. Yet some of the most useful robots are kept localized to a single server or a single collection of servers to provide local cataloging information and statistics.

Is the World Ready For Yet Another Robot?

Given that robots are good at gathering information, why might you hesitate before adding another one to the collection available on the Internet? For one thing, there are already 30-odd robots running somewhere on the Net as you're reading this. For a look at the most up-to-date collection of robots we've seen anywhere, please consult Martijn Koster's outstanding catalog of active and inactive robots at:

```
http://web.nexor.co.uk/mak/doc/robots/active.html
```

As we were writing this chapter, his catalog included 37 robots; 33 active and only 4 inactive.

Unfortunately robots can put a considerable strain on network resources and tax the very servers whose contents they may be cataloging or measuring. Whereas a human might try to read and comprehend some of each document that he or she examines, robots can zip from one link to the next at dizzying rates.

Given the sizable number of robots already in existence, you might want to consider whether one of them could perform the kinds of tasks you're after, rather than creating a new one. Likewise, you might want to investigate one or more of the publicly available search engines like CUSI, ALIWeb, or CityScape's Global On-Line Directory, if all you're looking for is a search engine. Look for these resources at:

```
http://pubweb.nexor.co.uk/public/cusi/cusi.html
http://web.nexor.co.uk/public/aliweb/aliweb.html
http://www.gold.net/gold/
```

If you can find another tool that does the job, why clutter the Web with another robot? You could save yourself time and energy and help keep the overhead of tracking the Web from overtaking the bandwidth consumed by human seekers for truth and enlightenment (or at least, entertainment).

A Rationale for Robot Creation

If you decide to proceed with a robot of your own despite our exhortations to do otherwise, we'd like to suggest a rationale for approaching the task. We'd also like to suggest a few do's and don'ts that will probably stand you in good stead with the rest of the Internet community, or at least keep the heat turned down on any flames headed your way! Finally, we'd like to point you to the source for much of this good advice, Martijn Koster's outstanding "Guidelines for Robot Writers":

```
http://web.nexor.co.uk/mak/doc/robots/guidelines.html
```

IDENTIFY YOURSELF AND YOUR ROBOT

If you build a robot, make sure that you include contact information in your program so that if it starts making trouble at some sites, administrators or users can contact you and alert you to the need for corrective action. In particular, this means that you should do the following:

- **Use the HTTP codes.** HTTP supports an environment variable called **USER-AGENT** to identify all Web browsers. Since a robot is a kind of browser, use this field to supply a name for your robot (e.g., "Cyber-Picker/1.1"). It's customary to include both the robot's name and its current version, as our example is meant to indicate. This identification allows server maintainers to recognize your robot as such, and to handle it appropriately as compared to normal human users running interactive browsers.

- **Tell them where you're from.** HTTP also supports a **FROM** field to identify the user who's running a browser. Use this field to supply your e-mail address (e.g., *etittel@zilker.net* or *mikee@outer.net*). This provides a method of contact in case your robot ever causes any problems, so that sites experiencing difficulties can get you involved quickly and easily.

- **Use an autoresponder.** Alternatively, you might set up an auto-responder e-mail account for your robot that includes instructions on how to kill it and how an administrator might make his or her site unvisitable by your robot. In this case, you'd supply the e-mail name for the autoresponder in the FROM field, so that anyone seeking instructions could do so 24 hours a day.

By identifying your robot and yourself as its creator, you can easily dispel any paranoid fantasies that some sites might entertain regarding your robot's intentions or capabilities. Since you're a programming artist, why not autograph your work?

SPREAD THE WORD

Before you unleash your robot on the Net, post a message to *comp.infosystems.www.providers* to let the world know that you're about to begin using it. If site administrators know about your robot in advance, they can watch for its appearance and be ready to report any problems that might occur. You'll also want to e-mail Martijn Koster at *m.koster@nexor.co.uk* because he maintains the list of active robots mentioned earlier in this chapter.

STAY IN TOUCH

When you set your robot loose on the Net, don't take off immediately thereafter for a two-week vacation to the jungles of Borneo. It's a good idea to stay logged into the machine that's running your robot, so people with problems or questions can use *finger* and *talk* to contact you. If you do have to leave your machine, turn your robot off; that way, there's no chance that problems could crop up on somebody else's server when you're unavailable.

NOTIFY THE AUTHORITIES

Because robots can consume lots of system resources and network bandwidth, you'll want to warn your ISP or your system administrator and let him or her know that you're going to be launching a robot. It's usually a good idea to offer to coordinate with them to keep the robot from consuming scarce resources during peak processing periods. You could even consider such notification a form of common courtesy because if your robot screws up anywhere, your provider will probably hear about it, too!

Don't Be a Resource Hog

Robots can suck up CPU cycles and network bandwidth like nobody's business (it's that speed differential between man and machine). Do what you can to minimize your robot's impact on your own system, and on the servers it visits. Here's how:

- **Accept only what you can handle.** HTTP includes an ACCEPT field that lets browsers specify what kinds of documents they can handle in advance. If your robot can only handle certain kinds of content types (e.g., text/html and text/ascii), make sure you tell the server you're accessing about these limitations. That way, properly configured servers won't try to send your robot data that it can't handle anyway.

  Likewise, if your program can't handle compressed files, you can parse URLs to look for file extensions like ".zip", ".Z", ".gz", or ".tar" and avoid requesting them altogether. The same is true for graphics files or other data files that feature common file extensions or file-naming conventions.

  Finally, if your robot can't work with non-HTTP protocols, scan URLs for alternative services like "ftp://", "wais://", "mailto:", etc. You'll be able to avoid asking for input that the robot can't digest, thereby saving the server and the network unnecessary traffic and activity.

- **Always check results.** Keep track of recent responses from all servers; if a server continues to refuse your robot's document requests, it may be trying to tell you something (like, for instance: "your robot's not welcome here!").

  Likewise, keep a list of sites and URLs that your robot has already visited; that way, you can avoid unnecessary repetition or looping. In the same vein, check physical IP addresses for servers as well as DNS names, because it's likely that some Internet hosts may advertise multiple DNS names for the same machine.

- **Don't overdo it.** Properly begun, robots don't need to run that frequently; Martijn Koster recommends quarterly (every three months) and not more than every other month. Actual frequency will depend on the volatility of the data you're investigating, but if you start with "What's new" information or with previously unvisited sites, you'll be much more likely to avoid revisiting documents that haven't changed since your last access.

- **Don't use query facilities.** Some documents support search facilities (e.g., <ISINDEX>) or contain search forms. Don't let your robot interact with such facilities; they can produce bogus searches with equally bogus results.

- **Run during off-peak hours.** One of the benefits of notifying local authorities is that they can tell you when the machine is most likely to be lightly loaded, so that your robot can run without adversely affecting others. If you plan to access a regular list of sites, e-mail their administrators to find out the most opportune times to visit.

- **Run silent, run deep.** Build your code so that your robot doesn't try to access too many documents in any given time interval. Generally it's a good idea to keep document accesses to one or two per minute, since that's not too different from normal human usage patterns. This will require some extra effort when coding your robot (use a counter and add a "sleep cycle"). As an alternative, consider rotating your retrievals among a pool of servers, rather than trying to consume documents a server at a time.

- **Use your head.** If your applications can take advantage of the HTTP HEAD facility to read only document headers, rather than GET which retrieves entire documents, please do so. This will lower the amount of data that needs to be transferred over the Net, sometimes substantially.

By following these simple tips, you can keep your robot from making too much of a nuisance of itself at other sites. Even so, you'll want to keep an eye on things while your robot is running and constantly monitor its activities.

STAY IN CHARGE

It's especially important that you maintain control over your robot when you first unleash it, but it's no less important to remain aware of its activities and behavior at other Web sites. By observing its behavior and its consumption of system and network resources, you can keep your robot from becoming a drain on the network.

In particular, you'll want to build data collection, monitoring, and explicit controls into the robot, so that you can manage it quickly and correctly. Here are more details about what kinds of functionality you'll want to include in your robot:

- **Be ready to act!** In the course of normal operations, your robot might visit hundreds to thousands of sites. It may upset or excite some administrators or users along the way, so be ready to react when requests for information or assistance come your way. Remember that your robot is running on somebody else's site, and act accordingly. That's why our next item is entitled "Include explicit controls."

- **Include explicit controls.** Although robots can run unattended, there's no reason they can only work that way. You'll quickly learn that interactive controls, such as to suspend or kill the robot, can be quite helpful.

    Likewise, you'll want to be able to steer your robot toward (or away from) particular sites. Configuration files that can include and exclude servers by name, subnet mask, or IP address are quite useful.

- **Log activities and maintain statistics.** Log all sites and pages visited, links traversed, and anomalies encountered (the latter can be essential during testing or in diagnosing problems). Keep track of vital statistics as well, like counts of successful and failed retrievals, average file sizes, and number of hosts visited.

    Make sure the program uses these logs to avoid repeated or duplicate visits. Watch your disk space consumption for logs, too — it may be necessary to scale back your searches, to allocate more space for logs, or both.

- **Observe the rules of the road.** An informal standard for excluding robots from servers has been defined (it's covered later in this chapter). Learn about it and adhere to its rules. This will really help to keep your robot out of trouble (or at least away from where it's not wanted).

Likewise, if a system administrator or user from a particular site indicates that they don't want your robot on their server, keep it away from that site. You could, of course, figure a way around any barriers to entry they might erect for your robot, but that's not acceptable behavior.

If you know what your robot is doing and how it is behaving on its visits to other Web sites, you'll be able to respond directly and effectively if trouble should ever arise. Also, by monitoring your robot's consumption of resources, you'll be able to tune it to keep it from overusing other people's resources.

SHARE YOUR ROBOT'S WEALTH

Once you've gotten a robot up and running, you'll want to return some value to the Internet community whose resources you've been consuming. The best way to do that is to make it easy for others to observe and examine the information that your robot's been collecting and to remain receptive to other people's feedback about what and how to report that information.

In particular, you'll find the following elements to be crucial in maintaining the goodwill of your fellow Internauts:

- **Keep good records.** The whole point of using a robot is to acquire and maintain information. Make sure that what you acquire is well organized and easy to access and understand. Keep as much historical data as you can, to help interested parties look for trends, usage patterns, or other statistically derivable results. (Large collections of data tend to acquire certain followings in the research and academic communities, just because they're grist for statistical methods.)

- **Maintain raw data.** The huge amounts of information your robot collects will be massaged to produce results, observe patterns, draw conclusions, etc. But the raw data that led to the final results may also have value; therefore, consider making this available to others for research or investigation as well. If you can afford the disk space, make it available through an FTP archive; if not, offer to provide archival copies on demand for a modest fee.

- **Publish your results.** The reason for running a robot is to fulfill some information-gathering or reporting task. Once that task is complete, make the results available to the Net. This is another way of paying back the community, and it can also provide valuable information to other researchers, programmers, and Netizens of all stripes.

  Make sure your results are intelligible and easy to follow. Try providing graphical as well as textual or numeric presentations of your information. The more forms your results can take, the more likely they are to be useful to someone else.

- **Report errors and problems.** Robots will inevitably encounter stale or erroneous links on their perambulations around the Web. If you log this information, you can create and publish error reports (after checking to make sure the errors are legitimate, not a function of some fault with your robot). This information will be useful to those sites where such errors or problems are detected; you should inform the appropriate authorities by e-mail.

By making your data, your results, and your observations of the Net available to others, your robot's efforts are guaranteed to provide value to a larger community. That's why we've recommended making your information available to others in as many forms as possible.

A Standard for Robot Exclusion

We really can't conclude a discussion of Web robots without covering the results of an informal agreement among the participants of the robot-focused mailing list *robots-request@nexor.co.uk* on June 30, 1994. In short, this agreement defines a facility jointly created by a large number of robot developers to protect Web servers against unwanted accesses by their robots. At any time, the most current version of Martijn Koster's document "A Standard for Robot Exclusion" may be found at:

```
http://web.nexor.co.uk/mak/doc/robots/norobots.html
```

This document outlines an approach that depends on the presence of a URL pointing to a file named "/robots.txt" at any given Web site. Based on perusal of this file, any robot can determine if its presence is at all welcome and if there are certain areas on the server that it should avoid.

The choice of the filename "/robots.txt" was deliberate, motivated by the following concerns:

- A desire to fit the filenaming requirements for all common operating systems (hence the DOS-like 8x3 name used).

- No special file extensions that might require server configuration tuning (hence the extension ".txt").

- The filename should be self-descriptive and easy to remember.

- To minimize possible collisions with other Web-related files.

Remarkably, "/robots.txt" manages to meet all of these criteria.

As its name implies, "robots.txt" is a pure-text file that resides in the root directory for the entire Web server. This file consists of one or more records, separated by blank lines that may be denoted by any of the common methods (i.e., CR, LF, or CrLf). Each record contains lines that take the form:

```
<field>:<optionalspace><value><optionalspace>
```

where:

- Comments begin with a pound sign (#); the remainder of any line of text after the pound sign will be ignored.

- <field> names are case insensitive and may be either **User-agent** or **Disallow.**

- <value> data is alphanumeric and will supply the name of the robot for which an access policy is described if the <field> name is **User-agent,** or the access policy description, if the <field> name is **Disallow.** Access policy values may include full pathnames or partial paths; any URL that starts with a partial value will be disallowed; an empty value indicates that all URLs may be accessed. At least one **Disallow** field is required per record.

- If a list of **User-agent** fields precedes a **Disallow** field, all of the robots named in those records will be subject to the access policy defined in the **Disallow** field.

- If an asterisk is used in a **User-agent** field, it acts as a wildcard character to identify any robot not named in other **Disallow** records.

Some examples of this file should help to cement your understanding of its workings. Here are a couple of heavily commented "robot.txt" files for your edification:

```
#robots.txt for http://www.outer.net/
User-agent:*
Disallow:/cypherdocs/map/     #this is a private URL space
Disallow:/tmp/                #temporary files, please ignore
# Interpretation:
# This file applies to all User-agents ('*')—that is, all robots
# All URLs within the /cypherdocs/map/ hierarchy are disallowed
# All URLs within the /tmp/hierarchy are disallowed

#robots.txt for http://www.io.com/
User-agent: *
Disallow: /docs/              #system administrator URL space

User-agent: localbot
Disallow:
# Interpretation
# This file applies to all external User-agents ('*')
# Notice the blank line that separates the first & second records
# The second, empty "Disallow" grants the User-agent "localbot"
# access to all URLs
```

Even though the notation for "robot.txt" is fairly primitive, it is expressive enough to provide access controls by robot name over the full range of URLs available on any given server. Even though this "standard" isn't really a standard, we suggest strongly that any robots you build take cognizance of it and that you let its directives guide your robot's behavior.

More Robot Hangouts

Throughout the course of this chapter, we've exposed you to most of the robot-related resources available at *www.nexor.co.uk,* including a number of URLs and a mailing list. Even though this site is extremely well plugged into the Web robot world, here are a couple of other URLs that we recommend visiting:

```
http://www.yahoo.com/Reference/Searching_the_Web/Robots__Spiders__etc_/
http://www.stir.ac.uk/jsbin/jsii
```

The first URL is for the Yahoo server's page on Robots, Spiders, Wanderers, Worms, and more. It's a great hotlist for robot information and source code access. The second URL is for the JumpStation II front page; it's a way of searching documents, servers, URLs, and for adding information on a variety of topics to the local database. Both of these resources add to the information provided at *www.nexor.co.uk* but *www.nexor.co.uk* remains the best source of robot-related information on the Net, bar none!

Summary

In this chapter, we've investigated the whys and wherefores of that busiest of Web beasts: the robot, spider, or wanderer that perambulates the Web's highways and byways in search of information. While we can argue that creating another robot may not be the best use of your programming efforts, we can also agree that investigation of source code for a robot can be a real education in CGI programming.

That's why we think it's worth your time to investigate at least some of the many resources we've pointed out during our discussion of Web robotics. And, should you feel compelled to build one yourself, we've also provided a set of guidelines that should help you remain a good Netizen while adding yet another robot to the World Wide Web!

24 Webifying Documents

*I*n the electronic jungle, documentation has proliferated in many formats — WordStar, MS Word, FrameMaker, PageMaker, and QuarkXpress, to name just a few and flowered wildly on many platforms. New proprietary document formats continue to quietly enter the desktop publishing underbrush at a fast pace.

Sharing electronic documents under these circumstances is difficult; sometimes it's nearly impossible. Our manuscript, created with QuarkXpress, doesn't make sense to your MS Word editor unless it's converted to a common format. Your MS Word 6.0a documents may not even be translated into a colleague's MS Word 2.0 without some loss of formatting information.

What all this means to us is that we have to continually update our tools and processes for transforming, translating, filtering, and converting these formats into HTML. Another solution might be to junk your desktop publishing system for one of the new SGML-based authoring environments like ArborText's SGML Publisher or SoftQuad's Author/Editor. (As Chapter 4 suggests, you'll probably need to modify your document management process as well.)

In this chapter, you'll learn about a philosophy of Webification and how it can play an important role in making your valuable information suitable for online publication. You'll also learn about tools and environments that can help you prepare your documents. Finally, you'll encounter the basic principles of document analysis and learn how to *chunk* your HTML documents.

The Zen of Webification

Webification requires you to apply tools or processes to an electronic document that result in the creation of an HTML document with equivalent content. Figure 24-1 depicts a typical process specification whose focus is the transformation of a document into HTML.

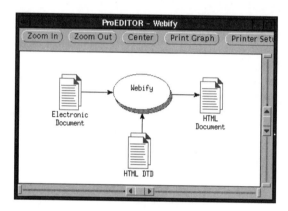

Figure 24-1

A process definition for Webifying a document.

Notice the composite task labeled *Webify* in the center of the figure. Here Webify means to convert, transform, translate, or filter an existing document into HTML. It is a high-level term that describes these processes without revealing their details.

Electronic document formats are diverse; they can range from pure ASCII to text with embedded control characters, tags, and process instructions. Without further processing, different formats create problems when sharing electronic documents among different desktop publishing applications.

The tasks involved in Webification may be further defined as follows:

- **Conversion** — The process of changing from one form to another. For example, conversion may occur between a hard-copy document and its soft-copy equivalent.

- **Transformation** — The process of changing one structure to another. For example, transformation of a document from one governing DTD to another DTD can involve significant changes in structure.

- **Translation** — The process of rendering a document in terms of one language to an equivalent rendering in another. For example, a document could be translated from LaTeX markup to an HTML equivalent. Translation is always difficult because no two languages share exactly the same terms, syntax, or concepts.

- **Filtering** — The process of removing certain objects from a document. For example, removing processing instructions important to a specific scheme that are not used in a general markup scheme would eliminate unintelligible code from a document.

One, some, or all of these operations may be required to Webify a particular document. Notice also that these operations may be required only once or every time a document is Webified. Let's take a closer look at each of these and see how they fit into the philosophy of Webification.

CONVERSION

This operation converts existing hard-copy documents such as User's Manuals or company catalogs into soft-copy or electronic documents stored on a computer. The cost of conversion is determined by the amount of existing hard-copy and the resulting soft-copy quality desired.

There are many methods of conversion. You could use an optical scanner to convert hard-copy pages to bitmapped pages. These bitmaps could then be analyzed by software programs like Optical Character Recognition (OCR) or Intelligent Character Recognition (ICR) to produce ASCII text from the bitmaps.

Typically, OCR and ICR programs are measured by the percentage of correct conversion of bitmapped characters to ASCII characters. Some of these programs tout results as high as 99% conversion, but that's dependent on a variety of characteristics. These include the font used to print the hard copy; its quality; the number of tables, figures, and graphics it contains; and the orientation of the copy as it passes through the scanner. Any skew to a page can cripple OCR and ICR software, resulting in low conversion rates.

Based on the DoD CALS initiative, many feasibility studies have analyzed OCR of hard copy. Their conclusions haven't been promising:

one study reveals that it's cheaper to manually reproduce a medium to large volume of hard-copy documentation rather than to scan and OCR that copy.

TRANSFORMATION

Transformation is the process of changing an electronic document's structure to another structure. This process involves creating a map of one element to another (one–to–one), many document elements onto one (many–to–one), and one element or structure to many others (one-to-many).

Some elements may not fit into another document structure at all. They may have to be omitted altogether, resulting in a non-isomorphic transformation — a transformation that involves a loss of data. This is also called *down transforming*. An example is down transforming an HTML 3.0 document to HTML 2.0. Even though tables could be reproduced using the <PRE> tag, retransforming the resulting HTML 2.0 document back into HTML 3.0 would not restore the table to its original state.

A mapping strategy is derived as the result of a document analysis process discussed later in this chapter. In order to create such a mapping, you need a formal description of each of the document's structures. When it comes to HTML, this is best served by a DTD.

Even then, DTD–to–DTD transformations are still difficult unless the document types that the DTDs specify are similar in structure. For instance, mapping a JOURNAL document type to a MAGAZINE document type would probably be rather straightforward. But mapping the same JOURNAL to a BOOK might be difficult and time consuming. This is because many of the JOURNAL document elements may not naturally occur in BOOK, or vice versa. And if that sounds challenging, try mapping a JOURNAL to a BROCHURE!

TRANSLATION

Translation is the process of interpreting one language into another. For instance, you might translate a document from Rich Text Format (RTF) or LaTeX to HTML. Fortunately, there have been technical advances in tools to automate this process; many are already publicly available (some of these will be discussed later in this chapter).

Translating documents is quite similar to spoken language translation. A translator, whether human or program, must understand both languages, including their respective sentence structures, words and phrases, and verb conjugations. Likewise for each language's syntax and structure. For programs, semantics are largely irrelevant, but the same can't be said for human translation.

A translation process involves analyzing the syntax of each language and identifying both common and unique elements. This is similar to transformation, but translation does not operate on document structure; it turns one document element or group of elements from one language into a comparable form in another language. For instance, the RTF representation of **this is bold** looks like:

```
{\b this is bold}
```

Translating this to HTML results in:

```
<B>this is bold</B>
```

From this simple example we can see that to translate a bold phrase, you would want to map the { character to the equivalent HTML character <.

Next, consider the type of element involved. The RTF element type is specified by the character sequence of \b which represents **bold**. This maps to the HTML character sequence of **B** which is appended to the < character. In order to make this a valid SGML open tag string, we need to append a >. This results in the open tag string for an HTML bold element: <B>.

The end tag is not so straightforward, because we need some upstream information — the current element type. The } maps to the HTML tag character >. But what about the rest of the end tag? It requires the element type that we already deciphered when assembling the start tag — \b in this example. Finally, from all this information the proper HTML end tag is assembled — </B>.

The content of the phrase is intact. This is considered an isomorphic translation because no data is lost in the process. No content is lost either, and the presentation is retained.

If the content was retained, for instance, but some processing information was lost in the translation, this would be considered a non-isomorphic translation. This is not bad in most cases. For instance, if you have a centered italic heading in *troff*, a translation to HTML 2.0 would result in a left-justified highlighted heading. The content remains intact but the presentation is modified. In most cases, this is also acceptable.

Our translation example is typical of most automated translation processes. Most translation tools require you to identify elements in your source and target languages to help create the most useful mappings.

FILTERING

The filtering process removes certain elements from a document that are deemed frivolous, not required, or damaging to its structural integrity. A good example of filtering is the removal of processing instructions associated with an element of a procedural markup language that are unimportant or unused in a descriptive markup language. When going from MS Word to HTML, this might consist of eliminating a border around a block of text or changing an outline font to a plain font.

Tools and Environments

There are numerous tools and environments that can aid your preparation of electronic documents for the Web. In this section, you'll learn about commercial applications as well as public-domain tools. But we need to discuss the characteristics required from your electronic documents before you can proceed.

Preparing electronic documents for the Web requires the source data to have certain characteristics:

- Text, process instructions, control characters, and embedded tags must be represented in ASCII.
- The logical elements of a document must fit into a hierarchical structure.
- Markup in the document must represent logical elements or process instructions on logical elements.
- Markup must be descriptive, not procedural.

Examples of translatable data representations include FrameMaker documents, which can be exported as Maker Interchange Format (MIF). Likewise, starting from MS Word 6.0, you could export a document using Rich Text Format (RTF). Most other desktop publishing applications can export their documents into a form that can be Webified. Finally, there are some typesetting languages such as Scribe and LaTeX that already match these characteristics.

Data representations that don't meet these requirements include the following:

- PostScript, because it's interpreted, not static.

- WordPerfect and QuarkXpress, because they do not describe logical elements or represent hierarchical structures.

- Databases, because they do not represent data with an ASCII stream.

Granted, you could use Ghostscript to capture a PostScript file as a GIF file, and then render the entire document as a GIF within an HTML document, but would you want to download it from home with a 14.4 modem? Plus, you'd completely lose any ability to access or manipulate the document's content.

The four elements of Webification are commonly used in combination. Translation, transformation, and filtering are vital elements of the Webifying process that frequently occur together. Conversion is not included here because we assume that your document is already in an electronic form that matches the characteristics of static form, hierarchical structure, logical elements, and descriptive markup.

At this point, we'll examine some tools and environments for preparing your electronic documents for the Web. Because of their ready availability and low cost, we concentrate on public domain applications (we'll mention some commercial applications for the sake of completeness).

We're making the following distinction between tools and environments:

- **tools** — add-on filters to a word processor for exporting HTML

- **environments** — standalone applications that aid in the translation and transformation of documents

In the sections that follow, we examine a handful of tools and environments that you may find useful in your efforts to Webify documents created in other environments.

THE INTEGRATED CHAMELEON ARCHITECTURE

The Integrated Chameleon Architecture (ICA) is an environment for UNIX machines that uses X Windows. It is a suite of tools that helps you create translators for your documents. ICA's primary platform is Sun-4 with SunOS 4.1.x using X11R4 from MIT. ICA is publicly available at:

```
ftp://ftp.cis.ohio-state.edu/pub/chameleon/
```

ICA requires that you understand the specifics of the markup scheme of your documents in detail; that you be able to tokenize and parse your documents; and that you understand SGML and HTML. ICA decomposes the task of translation into subtasks, where each subtask must be performed in a certain order and fashion. In ICA, regular expressions describe the data and tags and grammars define the document structure.

One vital step before using the ICA toolset is to perform a content analysis of your document. The hardest part of utilizing HTML is analyzing your document set's content. One reason this is so hard is that your brain does all the work; there isn't yet any sophisticated software for performing document analysis.

Given that the objective is to facilitate translation into HTML, the document analyst must determine how the document content should be marked up — that is, the set of tags to be used, their corresponding attributes, and the overall structure of the document. Because the HTML 2.0 or 3.0 DTD dictates these, all that's left to do in this step is to identify the logical elements in your document set — such as chapters, sections, table of contents, indexes, and tables and figures — and to map them to equivalent HTML markup.

The benefits of ICA include the following:

- ICA is a code-generating system — it generates C, lex, yacc, and DTDs.
- ICA aids complicated, repeated translations.
- ICA generates complete and correct translators.

- ICA, while time consuming, is relatively easy to use.

- ICA translators are easy to modify.

- ICA translators are easy to share — they are executable C programs.

- ICA's retagging tools can be used independently of the architecture.

- Using ICA, you can generate SGML DTDs for your documents independent of the architecture.

ICA transforms documents in three distinct phases:

1. *General Description Phase* — In this phase, you develop a general markup scheme — that is, a grammar that describes the structure of an intermediate document. This grammar drives the rest of the tools in the ICA suite.

2. *Build Phase* — This phase involves two separate toolsets:

   - Retagging Toolset — It consists of a "Retagger," which specifies the mappings to replace specific source markup tags that eventually translate into explicit markup in the target document and an "Insert Tagger," which requires that you specify information to make implicit tags in the source document explicit. This toolset produces a retagger application that is applied to the source document.

   - Structural Mapping — This toolset contains the "Map Specific to General Structure" tool, for which you must specify certain structural features of a specific markup scheme. This tool produces a specific–to–general translator. The "Map General to Specific Structure" tool is where you specify the permutations of the strings from the general markup scheme into a single string in the specific markup scheme for each permutation. With these two tools, you can reorder the tags of a specific markup scheme to fit the same order as the intermediate general markup scheme.

3. *Use Phase* — This phase is where you apply the retagging application to the document that produces an explicitly marked-up document. This document is then input to a specific–to–general translator that results in a general marked-up document. This document is then input to a general–to–specific translator that produces the target document.

ICA can be used to build a gateway environment. In such an environment, authors can continue to create and modify documents using a desktop publishing application. They can "offer" their documents to a gateway that translates them into the general markup scheme. They can also "ask for" a document that translates the general markup scheme back into the native desktop publishing markup scheme.

Only when a document is ready for the Web, is a general–to–specific translator applied to the general markup document to produce HTML. For more information about ICA, we recommend the Prentice Hall book, *The Integrated Chameleon Architecture: Translating Electronic Documents with Style* by Sandra Mamrak, Conleth O'Connell, and Julie Barnes (Englewood Cliffs, NJ, 1994, ISBN: 0-13-056418-4).

RAINBOW

In 1993, Electronic Book Technologies (EBT) announced a new "public technology platform" to facilitate the translation from common proprietary word processing formats to SGML. The goal of Rainbow is to provide a stable document data format that can then be input to translation tools.

Rainbow specifies a single DTD that is an *enabler* between a word processor format and SGML. This DTD represents a wide variety of word processing formats. A *Rainbow Maker* is a tool that translates proprietary word processing formats into an intermediate document that conforms to the Rainbow DTD. Only then can *Rainbow Translators* and other tools extract SGML and HTML structure from the intermediate Rainbow document. This is similar to the ICA approach to translation based on an intermediate general markup scheme.

Rainbow Makers are currently available for Microsoft RTF, Frame, and Interleaf. You can get free copies of Rainbow Makers and the annotated Rainbow DTD through anonymous *ftp* at:

```
ftp://ftp.ebt.com/pub/nv/dtd/rainbow/
```

OTHER PUBLICLY AVAILABLE TOOLS

During the earliest days of the WWW, authors either created their documents using a plain ASCII editor (like *vi*) or they used a semi-native HTML editor (like *Emacs* in html-mode). Starting a couple of years ago, authors began to use structured SGML editors to create HTML (like ArborText's SGML Publisher). Last year, SoftQuad introduced a structured HTML editor called HoTMetaL that allowed authors to create HTML documents using a native HTML editor.

But authors who have document collections in other forms must resort to writing translators from their original document formats to HTML. Fortunately, there are numerous public domain applications that can translate documents into HTML. These include the following word processing or document formats:

BibTeX	DECwrite	FrameMaker MIF
Interleaf	LaTeX	Linuxdoc-SGML
MS RTF	PageMaker	PostScript
PowerPoint	QuarkXpress	Rainbow
Scribe	Texinfo	troff
VAX Document	Word Perfect	WS Word RTF

Another set of public domain applications is available for translating computer programming languages to HTML. These include the following:

Ada	C	C++
Fortran	Lisp	Literate Programming
Web		

In addition to these applications, other utilities exist to translate the following formats into HTML with publicly available code:

AmigaGuide hypertext documents	ASCII
e-mail archives	Emacs info files
FAQs	GML
help files (Mac, Windows, or other formats)	Lotus Notes databases
man pages	Mathematica notebooks
MS Excel tables	SGML

Many of these applications, as well as others we didn't mention here, are available at:

```
http://www.w3.org/hypertext/WWW/Tools/Filters.html
```

If you have specific translation needs or requirements, you'll find this URL well worth visiting.

Life After Translation

Once you have translated your documents into HTML, then what? The first thing you'll want to do is to evaluate the resulting HTML documents. There will definitely be items to be added; like navigational aids, visual elements, footers, and more. They might also need to be chunked into smaller pieces.

CHUNKING

Chunking a document means to break it up into salient nodes of information. Each of these nodes should contain a single concept or idea and be able to stand on its own content. These atomic chunks can be linked into a larger logical document or collection of documents. This is a way to share common information among hypertext documents. For instance, you need only write company boilerplate or copyright and trade restrictions once, but this information can be linked to many other HTML documents.

The process of chunking isn't easy. Chunks might be too large and cumbersome, yet very small chunks can be difficult to manage. As part of your document analysis, you should determine how big to make the average size of the chunks you'll create from your document set, or what kind of organizational units to turn into individual documents.

For instance, most documents can be chunked easily by sections. This means that for each section in your original document, you will create a corresponding HTML file. These files may be interlinked to match the structure of the original through a table of contents, indexes, inter-document references, or navigational aids. This helps to match the necessities of network retrieval where grabbing information in smaller pieces is more efficient, against the desire to replicate a large, complex document structure.

INTEGRATION

The organization of files to create your document on the Web is vital. When it comes to organization, there are two basic ways you can go:

1. Put all the document's HTML files in a single directory.
2. Store the HTML files under a subdirectory that represents your document's structure.

For instance, a chapter subdirectory could contain all the HTML files and images for that chapter. If you chunked at the section level this would make the most sense, since chapters typically contain multiple sections. Here again, the decision is yours; based on our experience, we prefer the second approach.

External images and figures should be organized the same way as the text. Images should accompany their respective sections in their directories. This narrows the locality of images and also maintains a consistent relationship between images and HTML files. Sometimes this may not be possible, especially if images include icons from your server's icon repository or if images are reused from other documents, but it's a good rule to try to follow whenever possible.

For large documents that consist of many chunks, it's a good idea to create a page that contains an abstract, author information, keywords, and the table of contents (TOC) for each document. In the Web world, a TOC is a list of hypertext links to the chunks for the document, either to a chunk itself or to a particular named anchor within a chunk.

Each chunk should include a navigational aid, be it a flashy navigation bar or a simpler text equivalent. For example, a classic text navigational command set typically includes:

- Up — traverse up a level in the document hierarchy.
- Previous — traverse back to the previous chunk in the TOC.
- Next — traverse to the next chunk in the TOC.
- TOC — go back to the TOC.
- Part of — this document is part of a larger name collection.

Most well-executed Web sites provide such navigational aids as a part of each HTML chunk in a large HTML document set. Individual pages that are not part of a large collection of interrelated chunks require different navigational tools. Notice that this navigation metaphor works especially well for highly structured linear documents represented as hypertext.

One final note: during the integration of your documents into your Web, you will likely want to change some documents' names to fit your server's document model. For instance, the NCSA HTTP server allows the person who configures the server to specify a filename for a default HTML file.

If someone opens this URL:

```
http://www.idgbooks.com/
```

what HTML file should the server return to the requesting client? For the NCSA server, the default filename is appended to this URL and then the HTML document is retrieved. For example, NCSA servers use "index.html" as the default HTML filename. Thus the generic URL just mentioned would end up looking like this:

```
http://www.idgbooks.com/index.html
```

This is a complete URL that is now intelligible to the server. This leads us to our last point: let's assume that you've successfully translated and chunked a large User's Guide at the section level. You've created a directory in your Web space called "UsersGuide". In this case, the incomplete URL for your guide might look like:

```
http://www.server.org/products/software/UsersGuide/
```

What part of the User's Guide structure should users obtain by default? We suggest that it be the very HTML file that includes the document's abstract, its author information, and its TOC.

Therefore, this URL should point to the User's Guide TOC. This means you will have to rename your TOC HTML file to "index.html" following our previous example. Or you could bypass this by specifying the URL for your User's Guide as follows:

```
http://www.server.org/products/software/UsersGuide/TOC.html
```

However, this is harder to remember and it does not inform the reader that the file also includes an abstract, keywords, and author information. Such a detailed URL would be a mess!

Although the details for the default page vary by server type (e.g., CERN or NCSA), it's still a good idea to specify Welcome or Home Pages this way. Thus, for each directory within your Web space, you would create an "index.html" as the Welcome Page for that directory. These index files could even be assembled into a master index for better access to your Web space. By working from your original formats to this kind of structure, your documents will truly be Webified!

Summary

Webifying your documents can be a one-time ordeal, or it can be a repetitive task. It can involve conversion from hard copy to soft copy, transformation from one DTD to another, translation from one language to another, or filtering spurious markup. Whichever activity suits your needs, you can transform your valuable documentation into a vital part of the WWW. By applying the right mix of tools and common sense, you should be able to create a process that can work for your documents without having to do everything by hand.

CHAPTER

25 Image Maps

The Art of GIF-Giving

*R*egular HTML is pretty plain, especially in this weaned-on-television, CD-ROM-playing world we now live in. Even in-line GIFs can be clunky when slick navigation is what you're after. This is where image maps come in. Image maps, also known as clickable maps, allow you to cook up the coolest user interface in the graphics package of your choice, then link the appropriate URL to coordinate points on the graphic. Good-bye, lifeless unnumbered lists of "click here to see..."; hello 3D, multicolored, 21st Century user interface!

First we'll examine some real-world examples of image maps already in use in both standard and more unusual applications. Next we'll look at several tools for creating an image map configuration file.

From tools, we'll move to the engines that serve maps on the Web and highlight some of the most popular and powerful image map CGIs available today. We'll look at the installation and configuration of these programs, scripts, and code libraries. Wrapping things up will be a collection of tips and tricks for using clickable images on the Web, culled from our own experience both as Web developers and users.

AIDS TO NAVIGATION

To get a better sense of what kinds of applications image maps lend themselves to, it may be a good idea to fire up your Web browser and take a look at some cool maps. Slick navigational tools are the most obvious use for image maps and Apple Computer Inc.'s home page (see Figure 25-1) is a perfect example.

Figure 25-1
Notice how graphics are used to navigate Apple's Web at http://www.info.apple.com/.

On the Apple home page, instead of a bulleted list of links or links embedded in dry marketing copy, your eye is immediately drawn toward the graphic elements, the 3D buttons, and the stylish logo art. These naturally lead your cursor to the linked areas of the image, where a click leads deeper into Apple's Web of pages.

GREAT FRAMES FOR INTERACTIVE INPUT

Navigation is just one of many possible uses for image maps. On the California Museum of Photography's Virtual Magnifying Glass Web page (see Figures 25-2 and 25-3), an image map takes input from the user and that determines the next image the user will see.

The entire image is mapped and the area the user clicks on determines which part of the picture gets magnified, drawing the user deeper into the photograph.

Figure 25-2
*A view from the gallery at http://cmp1.ucr.edu/exhibitions/
mapped_photos/magnifying_glass.html.*

Figure 25-3
The magnified detail from Figure 25-2.

OTHER EXOTIC APPLICATIONS

All kinds of user feedback can benefit from an image map interface.
Some Web pages use image maps to control video cameras on robot
arms, to modify parameters in geometric calculations, and many other
wonderful, practical applications. The only limitation lies with the image
map developer's imagination.

MAKING IMAGE MAPS WORK

The mechanism behind image maps is pretty simple: the image you wish to use is divided into *hot spots* — areas that you wish to link to URLs when the user clicks on them — and the coordinates that define these areas are determined and recorded.

For example, a rectangular area is defined by its upper left-hand corner and its bottom right-hand corner. These coordinates and the URLs for each hot spot are combined into a configuration file in a format appropriate to the image mapping CGI application in use. The resulting file — called a *map file* — is then uploaded or placed on your server, ready to interpret click locations and select appropriate links.

When your image is properly situated on the HTML page, you need only add the tag ISMAP to turn it into a clickable map, like this:

```
<IMG SRC="path/to/your/image/image.GIF" ISMAP>
```

Then, use the image tag as the focus of a hypertext link to your *imagemap* CGI program, as follows:

```
<A HREF="http://server.name.here/path/to/cgi/imagemap.cgi">
<IMG SRC="path/to/your/image/image.GIF" ISMAP></A>
```

In this way, you instruct the user's Web browser to pass the coordinates of any mouse click to the image map CGI through the *http* server.

You can observe mapping in operation by moving your mouse over an ISMAP image in a browser that dynamically displays the link over which your mouse is situated, like Netscape, MacWeb, or WinWeb. The link shows up as the URL for your imagemap program, followed by a question mark and the mouse's current x and y coordinates, separated by a comma.

You can observe mapping in operation by moving your mouse over an image map in a browser (such as MacWeb or WinWeb) that dynamically displays the image map URL. The hot spots' coordinates are checked against the configuration file for your image by the image map CGI, to determine which region has been selected (or to return a default value, if no defined region is chosen). This determination also selects the appropriate URL, which is then passed back to the user's browser.

Creating Hot Spot Definitions

Sometimes, defining the coordinates for a given hot spot can be tedious. Graphics packages that display your mouse's current location will help, but applications that display dimension information about selections you make on an image in pixels are even better. Even so, these features can be difficult to find in a graphics package and they may occasionally have serious limitations.

Because paint and image manipulation programs aren't written with image map CGIs in mind, the information they provide is not going to be tailored specifically for this use. There are, however, several tools available for designing image maps. We'll take a quick look at a few of them in the sections that follow.

WebMap for Macintosh

For the Macintosh family, one such application is WebMap (see Figure 25-4), by Rowland Smith of City Net Express. Version 1.0.1 is the current shareware version, but we recommend that you obtain version 2.0. It's currently at beta 8 as of this writing and will be available in a full commercial version by the time you read this.

WebMap opens GIF or PICT formats and allows you to create any number of geometric shapes, associating URLs and comments with the shapes as you go along. It doesn't currently support JPEG images but that is a minor shortcoming, since a large number of the Web browsers in use don't support JPEGs either.

WebMap also supplies a fully standard Macintosh interface for creating rectangles, circles, ovals, polygons, and points. This allows you to resize and move these shapes and ultimately to associate your URL with each one.

Once you've finished, WebMap can export NCSA or CERN image map configuration files (these are the two major UNIX *http* servers; we discuss their implementations of image maps later in this chapter).

If you want to save the map along with the image, instead of exporting a text version, WebMap will do this as well. It saves your shapes, comments, and URLs for future tweaking. The clever thing about this is that WebMap saves the map information so that the original image is not modified. Open the same picture with a graphics application, and there is no evidence of polygons, comments, or URLs.

Figure 25-4

WebMap for Macintosh builds map files for any clickable areas on your image that you select.

IMAGE MAP EDITORS ON THE WEB: MAPMAKER

MapMaker is a unique image map tool to build configuration files for your images right on the Web. Created by the folks at Telemedia, Networks, and Systems Group (a research group headed by Professor David Tennenhouse at the MIT Laboratory for Computer Science), MapMaker uses an image map to gather the coordinates for the vertices of the polygonal shapes you define by clicking on your screen.

To use MapMaker (see Figure 25-5), point your browser at its home page:

```
http://www.tns.lcs.mit.edu/cgi-bin/mapmaker
```

You'll get a form to specify the URL for the document containing the graphic you want to make a clickable image. MapMaker then applies an image map to your graphic allowing you to locate the vertices for as many polygonal hot spots as you want.

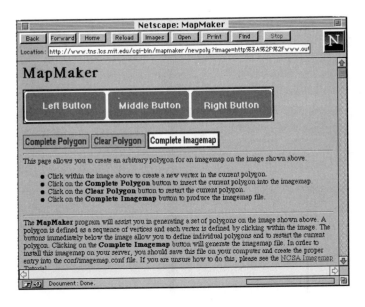

Figure 25-5

MapMaker's image map creation page.

Once you finish creating polygons, click on the "Complete Imagemap" button to create configuration files for both CERN and NCSA image map CGIs. All that's left is to install the appropriate file onto your server and configure your CGI for the new image map. We like this approach and think you will, too!

MAPEDIT: CREATING IMAGE MAPS IN WINDOWS

mapedit (see Figure 25-6) is almost to Windows what WebMap is to the Macintosh. mapedit also opens GIF files and allows you to define circular, rectangular, and polygonal clickable areas on the image, while associating a URL and a comment of arbitrary length with each selected area.

While *mapedit*, like WebMap, does allow you to select clickable areas once created, your control over a selected area is limited to deleting that area — you can't move or resize it as you could with WebMap.

Once your map is defined, you may export your work as a configuration file compatible with either the NCSA or CERN image map formats.

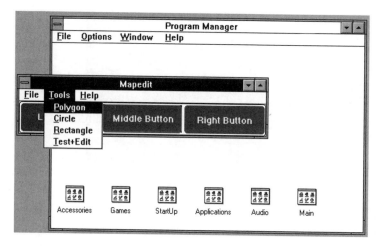

Figure 25-6
mapedit in action.

Imagemap CGIs

The final, and most important piece of the image mapping puzzle is, of course, the CGI program that handles coordinate translation. It receives the mouse click coordinates from the browser, matches those coordinates to the proper hot spot definition, and redirects the client's Web browser to the desired URL. No small feat of programming, but fortunately it's no big deal to find one of these programs.

In fact, there are image map CGIs available for all the major *http* servers, on all the popular Internet server platforms. Though the end results are virtually the same, the various servers' methods, configurations, and implementations are different enough to warrant a quick overview of what's out there. Here goes:

NCSA IMAGEMAP

Without a doubt, the most prevalent image map CGI is the eponymous C program distributed with the NCSA *httpd* server for the UNIX operating system, available at:

```
http://hoohoo.ncsa.uiuc.edu/docs/tutorials/imagemap.txt
```

imagemap is distributed as a source file and must be compiled with your system's C compiler, using a command that looks like this:

```
cc -o imagemap imagemap.c
```

Once compiled, *imagemap* should be copied to the *httpd* server's *root directory*. This is located in the top-level *httpd* directory and named */cgi-bin*.

Once compiled, *imagemap* should be copied to *httpd/cgi-bin*. The imagemap configuration file must be located in the *httpd* configuration directory, *conf*, also usually located in *httpd*'s top-level directory. This file must be named "imagemap.conf" and contain one entry for each image you wish to serve with *imagemap*. Each entry points the *imagemap* CGI to the hot spot definition file for that image. The format for each entry in "imagemap.conf" looks like this:

```
imagename: /path/to/imagemap/definition/mapfile.map
```

The choice for the 'imagename' is arbitrary but the convention is to use the name of your GIF image, without the '.gif' suffix.

Also, the map file is typically located in the same directory as the image itself, as in this example, but this isn't an ironclad requirement. If, for example, you were serving an image map using the file "navbar.gif", and that file was located in the directory */Webmall/main*, the entry in the "imagemap.conf" file would read:

```
menu: /Webmall/main/navbar.map
```

The actual map definition file contains one line for each defined hot spot, with lines beginning with # interpreted as comments. Every other non-blank line consists of the following:

```
method URL coordinate1 coordinate2 ... coordn
```

Coordinates take the form x,y. The number of coordinates depends on the *method*, or type of hot spot. A method may be one of the following:

- **default:** The default URL is returned to the Web browser whenever the mouse click falls outside any of the defined hot spots in the map file. For obvious reasons (we hope!) no coordinates are required.

- **circle:** A circle is defined by the coordinates of the center point and an edgepoint (for a radius).

- **poly:** Describes a polygon of at most 100 vertices, where each coordinate pair represents a vertex.

- **rect:** Describes a rectangle. The coordinates are its upper-left and lower-right corners.

- **point:** For the region closely surrounding a point, where the coordinate pair defines the point itself.

The URL supplied for a hot spot can be a fully-qualified URL to a resource with protocol, server, and path spelled completely out, or a relative pathname to a file elsewhere on your server.

The map file "navbar.map", for our "navbar.gif" image map example given earlier, might look like the following:

```
point http://www.outer.net/Webmall/retail/pets.html 251,13
rect /retail/gifts.html 2,2 133,46
poly http://www.outer.net/Webmall/services/therapist.html 268,3 395,3 397,44
269,45
circle http://www.outer.net/Webmall/food/pizza.html 161,17 193,49
default http://www.outer.net/Webmall/main/information.html
```

The matching routine reads through the entire file each time a pair of coordinates is passed from the user's browser. Therefore, if any defined areas overlap, the area that appears last in the map file is the one returned to the browser.

Finally, the correct way to call *imagemap* from your HTML page is to place the <IMG> tag inside a link to imagemap. In addition, *imagemap* takes a command-line argument that specifies the name of the image map file (this is why the URL in the anchor statement ends with */navbar*). Here's how we'd call our example from within an HTML document:

```
<A HREF="http://www.outer.net/cgi-bin/imagemap/navbar">
<IMG SRC="http://www.outer.net/Webmall/main/navbar.gif" ISMAP></A>
```

When the image is clicked, the entire process occurs, to allow *imagemap* to redirect the Web browser by means of a Location: header. This works like a charm, unless you've set up your map file or your link reference incorrectly, in which case it's time to troubleshoot your image map and HTML document.

CERN HTIMAGE

The image map CGI distributed with "the other *httpd*" — CERN's WWW server for the UNIX operating system — shares many attributes with NCSA's *imagemap*. It, too, is provided as a C source file and must be compiled into a binary executable on your UNIX server in much the same way as *imagemap*.

Also like NCSA's *imagemap*, *htimage* is installed in the same directory where all your CGI scripts and binaries reside. The only real difference in the respective installations is that *htimage* does not require the central configuration file to point it to the various image map files it serves. Instead, the map file is called directly from the HTML link that calls *htimage*. The earlier image map link example, if served off a CERN Web server running *htimage*, needs to be rewritten like this:

```
<A HREF="http://www.outer.net/htbin/htimage/Webmall/main/navbar.map">
<IMG SRC="http://www.outer.net/Webmall/main/navbar.gif" ISMAP></A>
```

The map file requires some significant alteration as well. *htimage* supports a default URL, as well as circles, rectangles, and polygons, but it doesn't do points.

One major difference between the two is that for *htimage*, each area definition line must take the form:

```
method (coordinate pair) ... URL
```

Coordinate pairs are written (x,y) and the number of coordinates and some slight differences are dictated by the specific method involved.

Methods (abbreviated **def**, **circ**, **rect**, and **poly**) are defined in *htimage* as follows:

- **default:** No coordinates necessary. Matched when browser's coordinates fall outside any defined area.

- **circle:** A single pair of coordinates followed by a single digit that equals the radius.

- **rectangle:** Two pairs of coordinates that define any two opposing corners.

- **polygon:** As many coordinates as the polygon has vertices. If the path given is not closed, i.e., the first and last coordinate pairs aren't the same, *htimage* will connect the first and last coordinate pairs.

Hot spot definitions are checked in the order of appearance in the map file, and the URL corresponding to the first match is returned. If none matches, the default URL is returned.

IMAGE MAPS ON MACINTOSH WEB SERVERS

Perhaps it is a testimony to the popularity of image maps that, despite the recent arrival of a Web server for the Macintosh operating system, there are already three separate image map CGIs for the platform. Chuck Shotten's MacHTTP, now marketed as WebSTAR, turns a Mac on the Internet into a full-featured Web server, including the ability to run CGIs and serve image maps much like its older brothers running on UNIX servers.

Imagemap 1.6

The first of the CGIs is a port of the *imagemap* program included with the NCSA Web server and discussed earlier. Rewritten in MacPerl, "imagemap.cgi" operates almost exactly the same way NCSA's *imagemap* does, serving the same methods and sharing the same configuration file format.

The first step in configuring "imagemap.cgi" is slightly hairy, requiring the use of ResEdit (a resource editing program from Apple Computer Inc., guaranteed to inspire fear and loathing in all but the most seasoned Mac developers). In actual fact, the operation is fairly simple. Launch ResEdit, then open the Perl script and locate the 'TEXT' resource and open it. There should be a single resource inside, with the ID#128, named !. Open this and find the lines:

```
#————————Configure This————————#


$server_home = "Macintosh HD:Communication ƒ:MacHTTP Software:";


#——————————————————————#
```

Replace the pathname in quotes with the appropriate pathname for your server's home directory. Save the file and quit ResEdit.

Place the edited CGI in the folder where WebSTAR is located, and create an NCSA-formatted *imagemap* configuration file for each map you want to serve.

Once everything is in place, the "imagemap.cgi" is called more after the fashion of the CERN *htimage*, since it does not have a central image map configuration file. Instead, the command-line arguments passed to the CGI include the path to the map file itself.

To revisit our previous example, on a Macintosh running "imagemap.cgi" our link would look like this:

```
<A HREF="http://wwwmac.outer.net/imagemap.cgi$Main/navbar.map>
<IMG SRC="http://www.outer.net/Webmall/main/navbar.gif" ISMAP></A>
```

MacImagemap

Another take on NCSA's *imagemap*, this CGI is a standalone program written in C. It complies fairly closely with the behavior and configuration of the original *imagemap*. It even uses a single central configuration file to define the image maps being served, along with the path to each one's map file. This configuration file, named "imagemap. config", must reside in the same folder as MacImagemap. MacImagemap's folder, in turn, must be placed inside WebSTAR's folder in order to work properly.

The map file itself is identical to the format and specification for the NCSA map file described earlier. Here's how to reference MacImagemap in your ISMAP link:

```
<A HREF="http://wwwmac.outer.net/imagemap.cgi$navbar>
<IMG SRC="http://www.outer.net/Webmall/main/navbar.gif" ISMAP></A>
```

MapServe

Finally, we come to MapServe, another standalone CGI for use with WebSTAR. Like MacImagemap, place the MapServe folder in the folder that contains WebSTAR to install the software.

MapServe does not have a central configuration file, using instead a map file for each image it serves. The map file is in NCSA format and must also reside in the MapServe folder.

An image map link that utilizes MapServe looks quite similar to the CERN *htimage* link:

```
<A HREF="http://wwwmac.outer.net/mapserve.cgi$navbar.map>
<IMG SRC="http://www.outer.net/Webmall/main/navbar.gif" ISMAP></A>
```

Oddities and Cool Stuff

Variations and extensions of the image map concept are now cropping up on the Web. These take the basic idea of a CGI that serves a click-able ISMAP GIF in an HTML document and push its boundaries, some-times creating something weird and wonderful in the process. Here are a few tasty examples:

GLORGOX

One variation is called Glorgox, written by Tom Rathbone of UUNET Canada for use with a UNIX-based WWW server. It, too, is based on the NCSA imagemap CGI, but instead of tying hot spot definitions to geo-metric shapes, Glorgox's image maps are resolved by a color-coded map that you create for the image you wish to serve. An auxiliary GIF file is maintained on the server for the ISMAP GIF, and this second image con-tains a color-coded map of the clickable areas on the image visible from the Web. The easiest way to understand this is to look at Tom's own example (see Figures 25-7 and 25-8) available at the following URL:

```
http://www.uunet.ca:80/~tomr/glorglox/demo/
```

Figure 25-7
Image-mapped document served to the Web.

Figure 25-8
The auxiliary image for the image in Figure 25-7.

Each differently colored portion of the auxiliary image is linked to a different URL. The image is paletted, so each map can contain 255 different hot spots, one for each of the allowable colors in the palette. The map file contains the path and name of the auxiliary file and an entry for each color present in that file, along with the URL to return if the mouse click falls on that color. The colors are referenced by their numerical codes, as in this line from the map file for Tom's demo:

```
2 http://www.uunet.ca/~tomr/glorglox/demo/imap.html
```

This would return a URL if the mouse was clicked on a red area of the auxiliary map, since red is color number two. Creating the auxiliary files for use with Glorgox may be more difficult than for orthodox image map CGIs, because it requires some work with a high-end graphics application, but the results are unlike anything else on the Web. Way cool!

CYBERVIEW3D DOCUMENT GENERATOR

Someone who has taken the image map paradigm and catapulted it far into the future is Paul Burchard of the University of Minnesota's Geometry Center. Developed using W3Kit, a code library for manipulating three-dimensional geometrical figures and building off of WebOOGL, an object-oriented graphics scripting language with support for HTML tags, Paul's CGI shows us a glimpse of the Web's future, when Virtual Reality and three-dimensional navigation will be the norm.

With Cyberview3D, the user can load and view GIFs of three-dimensional objects and with a click of the mouse rotate the object or view the data behind the image. It truly must be seen and played with to be believed. Cyberview3D's home page is at:

```
http://www.geom.umn.edu/apps/cyberview3d/about.html
```

Caveats and Tips to Click

If, at this moment, you're thinking that image maps are the coolest thing since hypertext, then we have succeeded in helping you appreciate the power of the clickable image. Image maps are indeed a good thing, bringing a third dimension to the traditionally two-dimensional ASCII universe common to most Internet user interfaces. In fact, we think of image maps as a colorful, freeform third dimension to the Web, limited only by the WWW developer's imagination. Before you run off to convert your entire Web site into one gigantic image map, consider the following caveats.

SMALL IS BEAUTIFUL

Small is beautiful. Use as few colors as possible, and if possible save your file as an indexed GIF (gif89). Adobe Photoshop, for example, is an application that gives you this option. An indexed GIF reduces the color palette information saved with your image, thereby reducing its file size. As a rule of thumb, fifty to a hundred kilobytes is about the limit for a workable map image. On the other hand, you might decide to dither your image, and end up reducing its display time and file size (two wins for the price of one!).

PRESENT ALTERNATIVES

Remember that some people don't have Ethernet connections to the Internet. Some people don't even have v.34 modems or even a graphical Web client. To accommodate your audience, be sure to follow each image map with a text-only version of your interface, or at least a link that leads off to the text version. It's called backwards-compatibility, and it makes (and keeps) friends.

KEEP IT SIMPLE

Interface design is a highly technical artform and should be treated with respect. Don't overdo the ornamentation or go nuts with graphics and clickable images all over the place.

KEEP IT PROFESSIONAL

This advice is doubly true if the map is part of a commercial Web site. Computers have brought tremendous graphics power to our desktops but that hasn't made us all into Michaelangelos. Hire a graphic designer, someone who does it for a living, and the money spent on graphics can get you the most bang for your Web-site-development bucks!

USE YOUR IMAGINATION!

Above all, keep your mind open and your imagination active. Image maps, like many Web features, are by themselves rather crude, but they do lend themselves to just about any application. If you can visualize it, there is probably a way to make it real. Go ahead, give it a shot!

ONE MORE VERY IMPORTANT POINT

There is a runtime penalty with image maps. Each click on an image map results in two files being opened (the image itself and the map file). Besides, hot spot matching requires some processing, so map files shouldn't be made too large. To reduce this advice to its minimal form: Don't overdo the image maps!

CHAPTER

26 HTML Document Creation On-the-Fly

A recurrent theme throughout this book is an underlying approach to interactive Web communication that we call *HTML-on-the-fly*. By this, we mean a wide range of actual techniques, tools, and concepts to automate the creation of, and updates, to a Web site.

We've learned, however, that this simple explanation does not do justice to the power that can be tapped when HTML-on-the-fly is fully appreciated and understood. The average developer's epiphany on this subject arrives with the understanding that HTML tags and formatting act as a filter through which information flows.

This elevates the concept of HTML-on-the-fly from mere batch translation of text to an understanding of what's involved in building dynamic, on-demand, individually created documents. Sites that employ this approach can take Web users to places they've never been before.

Using this approach, a UNIX-based *httpd* server and all its attendant tools, languages, and helpers act as a unified whole — that is, as a sort of *megaserver* capable of feeding customized multimedia content to all visitors. Every nook and cranny in that environment can be accessible to those propeller-heads with a propensity to tweak, customize, and generally hotrod their Web sites.

In this kind of Web environment, your Web server becomes a custom application with its own unique interface. It can present choices and tailor every aspect of its output to your users' needs and desires.

Though we have touched at least tangentially on this aspect of HTML and the Web in almost every chapter in this book, it is a subject important and subtle enough to warrant a focused discussion. In this chapter, we'll look at a few packages found on the Web that implement some aspects of HTML-on-the-fly. Along the way, we'll also highlight the issues and possibilities that each package offers. Once you grasp the core of this concept and the potential it promises, we believe you'll be anxious to start applying some of what you've learned to your own Web site!

Browsing Mail

As a medium, electronic mail is particularly *simpatico* with the Web — so much so, in fact, that we devoted Chapter 31 entirely to this subject. If a CGI needs to translate a document into HTML when a user requests it, you want to be sure that the document's native format is fairly consistent.

E-mail is a medium that offers large quantities of data in ASCII files on servers everywhere in the Internet universe. E-mail also uses a fairly static, dependable format for that data. It is, therefore, perfectly well suited as a base form for your data. That's why it's no surprise that such a conversion tool is already available.

MAIL2HTML

A Perl script written by Nate Sammons at Colorado State University, *mail2html* allows a user to browse e-mail mail boxes using the Web. Parsing messages in a mailbox and generating the necessary HTML on demand is simple, since *mail2html* depends on the SMTP header syntax to demarcate the beginning and end of each message.

Installing this CGI is simple. First, make sure the initial line of the script is properly formed, as you would with any executable script, making sure the path to *Perl* is correct for your system; also, check the ownership and permissions. Next, for each mailbox you want to make accessible from the Web, create a value pair in the associative array named '%index', the key to which is the mailbox name and the value the path to the file that contains it. The following example is taken from Nate's code:

```
$index{'varsity-announce'} =
    "/home/admin/majordomo/archive/varsity-announce/varsity-announce.full";
```

Finally, you may customize the footer information, contained in the variable '$footer'. Nate's code for the footer reads as follows:

```
$footer = "<P><hr>\n<em>Generated by mail2html, written by " .
  "<a href=\"http://www.vis.colostate.edu/info/staff/nate\">" .
  "Nate Sammons</a>, nate@vis.colostate.edu<P>\n";
```

This code sets what appears at the foot of each HTML document.

If you do modify this code we're compelled to point out that, like all publicly accessible code on the Internet, it's common courtesy to make sure the original author gets full credit for his or her work in a visible place in your program. (We think a "Credits" comment section in the beginning or at the end of your source code is a good way to do this!)

Once installed, *mail2html* can be called to either return a listing of the contents of a mailbox or provide a view of a specific message. A typical use for *mail2html* is to share a communal mailbox via the Web. In the example shown in Figure 26-1, these messages are sent to a mailing list called "nclug" accessed through *mail2html*.

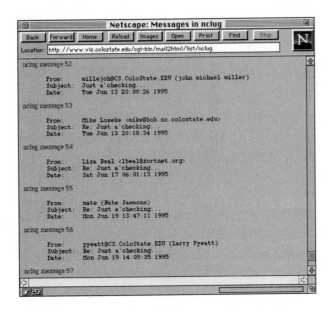

Figure 26-1

A listing of messages in the nclug's mailbox, courtesy of mail2html.

This listing is called by a link to *mail2html* in the following manner:

```
http://www.outer.net/cgi-bin/mail2html/list/"mailbox_name"
```

The "list" portion of the link informs *mail2html* that the user is requesting a listing of the mailbox named at the end of the link (e.g., "mailbox_name"; in reality, you'd use a real mailbox name, like "kwhite"). The actual list is built by scanning the mailbox and looking for "From:" headers. Each new "From:" is treated as a new message and is separated and stored for final output. Here's the code that performs this task:

```
open(MBOX, $index{$mbox});
while(<MBOX>) {
  if (substr($_, 0, 5) eq "From: ") {
    ++$i;
    @tmp = split(/\s+/, $_);
    shift @tmp;
    @from[$i] = shift @tmp;
    while ($q = shift @tmp) { @date[$i] .= "$q "; }
  }
  elsif (substr($_, 0, 9) eq "Subject: ") && (!@subject[$i])) {
    @subject[$i] = substr($_, 9);
    chop @subject[$i];
  }
  @listing[$i] .= $_;
}
close(MBOX);
```

Picks-out From: lines

Picks out Subject: lines

As you can see, when a "From:" is encountered, a pointer is incremented, the sender and date values extracted and stored, and the entire line stored in an array element for that message. If a subject line is found, it too is parsed and stored.

Once all the messages in the mailbox have been preprocessed, *mail2html* kicks into its HTML mode. The message array ('mbox') is traversed and each message is emitted with links and tags. The following code accomplishes this:

```
print "Content-type: text/html\n\n";

print "<title>Messages in $mbox</title>\n";
print "<h1>Messages in $mbox</h1>\n";

foreach $i (1..(@listing -1)) {
  print "<dl><dt><a href=\"/cgi-bin/mail2html/view/$mbox/$i\">$mbox message
$i</a><br>\n";
  print "<dd><xmp>From:      " . @from[$i] . "\n";
  print "Subject:   " . @subject[$i] . "\n";
  print "Date:      " . @date[$i] . "</xmp></dl><P>\n\n";
}

print $footer;
}
```

Prints out each message in turn

The **foreach** control structure steps through the array one message listing at a time. A link is created pointing back to *mail2html* with the "view" command; and the "From:", "Subject:", and "Date:" headers are printed with appropriate formatting tags.

When a single message's link is selected, *mail2html* is called again, this time with the "view" command between the CGI name and the mailbox name. The final argument in the URL supplies the message number. In this way the URL

```
http://www.outer.net/cgi-bin/mail2html/view/mailbox_name/3
```

returns something resembling the information depicted in Figure 26-2 (this is an example taken from the "nclug" mailing list).

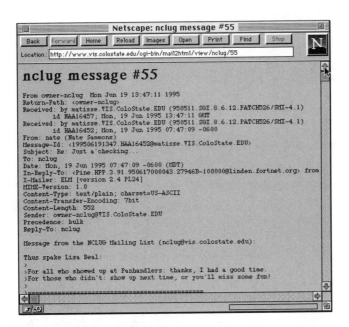

Figure 26-2
mail2html displays a single message selected from a listing.

The script retrieves the specified message and formats as indicated in the listing display. It opens the mailbox as a file handle, reads it through, counting each "From:" header as a message, until it reaches the desired message number. At this point the message is read into an array until the end of the message is encountered, then it is printed from the array to the requesting user's *httpd* session, with the requisite headers and formatting.

As you can see, Nate has chosen to leave the message view portion of *mail2html* fairly plain, with just the title of the mailbox and the number of the message highlighted, and the rest of the text and headers preformatted. There is no reason why he couldn't have added filters to place different formatting tags for the headers and the message. Also, some kind of navigation aid might be helpful, either back to a home page, or even better, to the next and previous messages in the mailbox.

What Nate's CGI demonstrates is a lesson you could learn from any HTML formatting-on-the-fly tool. That is, any type of consistently-formatted ASCII text is ideally suited to HTML formatting-on-the-fly, especially when using Perl. The text can be pulled apart easily and any kind of formatting applied.

Webified Man Pages

man pages are a useful source of reference information on any UNIX operating system.

For the novice, they represent an entrée into the rarefied command-line interface, and for the experienced user or administrator, they provide a crutch for overtaxed memories. Therefore it seems natural, if somewhat heretical, that several authors have written CGIs to translate *man* pages from their native format into HTML, to be browsed via the Web.

MAN2HTML

One such CGI is Brooks Cutter's interpretation of *man2html*. An outgrowth of other people's stabs at scripts also named *man2html*, Brooks' script, written in Perl, took the idea from a command-line *man* page translator that spat HTML-formatted text to STDOUT and adapted it to live translation via the Web.

```
http://www.vis.colostate.edu/info/staff/nate/geek_code.html
```

man pages lend themselves to this type of translation because they, too, conform quite strictly to a predefined format. A typical *man* page consists of a series of headings (NAME, SYNOPSIS, ARGUMENTS,

LIMITATIONS, SEE ALSO, etc.), all of which are followed by information of a relatively predictable type.

man2html uses this predictability to its advantage, formatting heading names and parsing the text that follows the headers accordingly. Figure 26-3 shows an example of Brooks' program at work on the *cp(1)* man page.

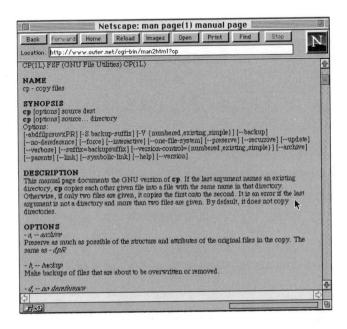

Figure 26-3

man2html's translation of the cp(1) man page.

The script also draws on the power of *rman*, or Rosetta Man, a very clever *man* page formatter. You can see from its output that *man2html* takes cues such as command-line options at the beginning of a line or a recurrence of the name of the subject of the man page. In these examples, the text that cues the script is then made italic and bold, respectively.

One of *man2html's* most powerful automatic formatting tricks comes at the end of a *man* page, where most such pages list other, related commands that may provide additional information to a knowledge-seeking user. These entries (which occur under "SEE ALSO") are formatted with links back to *man2html*.

In this way, *man2html* provides built-in navigation in its own output. Here again, like *mail2html*, more navigational aids would be helpful but this approach works reasonably well.

Another distinguishing feature of *man2html* is that it presents the user with a search page, as shown in Figure 26-4, when called with no arguments. This lets users enter the command via a form, rather than on a command line.

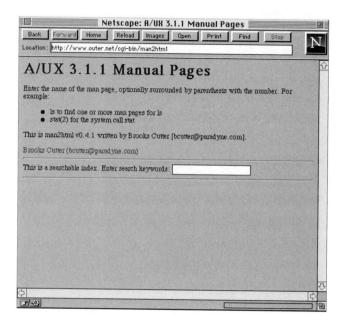

Figure 26-4

man2html's search page.

This page uses the native HTML <ISINDEX>, so browsers with no forms support don't present any problems. It's a nice feature and one that is strangely absent from many CGI scripts. Command-line utilities in UNIX typically will give a usage or copyright message when invoked with no arguments or with improper arguments, so it makes sense that a CGI should give some helpful response for this kind of input.

FTP Browsing

Though we look at FTP on the Web in another chapter, the subject bears mention here because it illustrates yet another area in which HTML-on-the-fly really shines.

FTPB

http://www.vis.colostate.edu/info/staff/nate/geek_code.html

Yet another Nate Sammons script, *ftpb* is a Perl-based FTP browser that uses a very simple method to build HTML documents on demand. Examining *ftpb*'s output, as shown in Figure 26-5, reveals the secret of its simplicity.

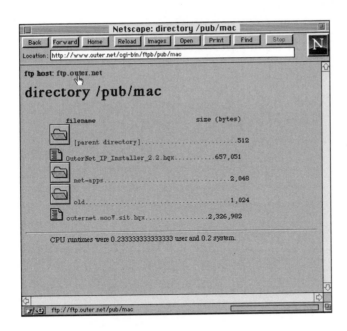

Figure 26-5
ftpb's HTML-formatted output.

If you think the listing bears a striking resemblance to a UNIX *ls* listing, you're not far off. That's because Nate's CGI uses the same UNIX system call, *stat*, to get a file's information. The script takes its command-line argument as a relative path to a directory on the server's ftp archive, opens the directory using Perl's opendir and readdir functions, and stats the files one at a time.

The output of that command is translated directly to HTML and directed back to the user's browser. This is achieved using the following piece of Perl code:

```
sub pref {
   my ($file, $href, $label) = @_;
   if ($fancy) {
       my @stat = stat("$root/$file");
       my $type;
       if (-d _)     { $type = 'dir';  }
       elsif (-T _) { $type = 'text'; }
       elsif (-B _) { $type = 'bin';  }
       print $icon{$type},
             "<a href=\"$href\">$label</a>",
             &buffer($label, 35, $spacer),
             &rprint(&nicenum($stat[7]), 12, $spacer),
             "\n";
   }
   else {
     print "<a href=\"$href\">$label</a><br>\n";
   }
}
```

You can see how Nate's code determines the type of data the file contains and constructs an HTML-formatted entry for each item. Other subroutines handle the text layout and add the appropriate icons to the document before returning it to the user.

Finally, *ftpb* has the ability to read and display text files from each directory, according to the name of a file. The default filenames to display are stored in the associative array named 'messages', that is initialized with this statement:

```
@messages      = ('.welcome.msg',     ## welcome messages, etc.
                  '.message' );       ## add more as needed
```

Therefore, any time *ftpb* encounters a directory with files whose names appear in '@messages', it will read the contents of that file and display the contents on the browser, as shown in Figure 26-6.

This particular feature gives the administrator a fair degree of flexibility, since the text file can vary according to the contents of the directory.

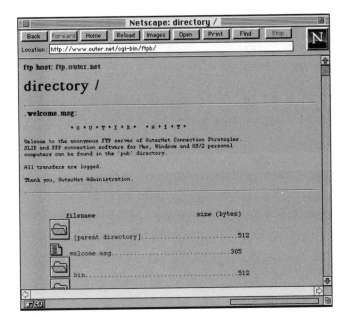

Figure 26-6

".welcome.msg" and ".message" displayed by ftpb.

The relevance of this particular CGI to our current topic of discussion comes from its reliance on a UNIX file system as the framework for its data. The way in which UNIX manages files, directories, and symbolic links is extremely efficient, flexible, and robust, and by no means an undesirable hook upon which to hang the inner workings of a WWW CGI. In fact, translating file and directory information and navigation into HTML is just the bare minimum of the potential held by this technique.

Any type of application that requires an hierarchical data structure, even a simple database, can use Perl's prodigious file-manipulation tools to create and use a directory tree populated with files. These directories and files can serve admirably to organize and maintain your data, and with a modicum of clever design, users need never know what underlies the HTML documents served to them.

Best of all, data can be extracted from a UNIX file system very quickly, a primary requirement for HTML-on-the-fly systems.

Oddments, Helpers, and Horizons

The preceding examples should start you thinking about other text formats that are consistently laid out and would therefore lend themselves to on-demand HTML formatting. PostScript, tab-delimited database files, *texinfo* format, and *setext* formats come to mind almost instantly.

All of these format types, and many more, could be periodically translated to HTML in batches. In fact, there are plenty of tools out there that would allow you to do so. However, when your data changes often or when duplicating it lock, stock, and barrel in a second format is not convenient, consider formatting it on demand.

This approach is also appropriate when the data must stay in its native format for any reason whatsoever. If you have a collection of articles authored and maintained in *setext* or *texinfo*, for example, HTML-on-the-fly techniques support continued manipulation of the data in its original format.

These same techniques can solve a problem often faced by the Web server administrator. In many cases, a team of content providers may want to publish information to the Web but might not have the skills required to format that information in HTML. If the team is receptive to the approach, you may want to consider creating an agreed-upon format to serve as an intermediary between their native format and HTML. This custom format could be as simple a set of rules as

- First line of the document always supplies the name of a graphic file to include in HTML.

- Any line of text followed by a line of equal signs is an <H1>.

- Any line of text followed by a line of hyphens is an <H2>.

- A bulleted list will be translated to a <UL> (unordered list).

This simple example illustrates how easy it would be for authors to follow these rules and for a translator to convert such text files into HTML-on-demand with a script.

GHOSTSCRIPT: GIFS-ON-THE-FLY

HTML is not the only commonly served format on the Web. All graphical WWW browsers are capable of displaying GIF images, and for the time being this has become the *lingua franca* for images on the Web. Nevertheless, images exist in a plethora of formats Internet-wide, and depending on your platform and the software you use, one or another of these formats may be more convenient to work in than GIFs.

If this describes you or if you have to work with a large store of graphics that are not GIFs but need to be served on the Web, don't despair, for there is a program that can come to your aid. It's called *Ghostscript*.

Developed originally as a software PostScript processor for producing printed matter, *Ghostscript* has evolved into a jack-of-all-graphics-formats. Distributed as a GNU package, it is available on any FTP server that carries GNU software, including the mothership site at

```
ftp://prep.ai.mit.edu:/pub/gnu.
```

Compiling *Ghostscript* can be difficult, since it is a large package with many system library dependencies, but this will depend on your platform. Many flavors of UNIX will actually compile the entire package easily, so long as you can answer the "Configure" script's questions about your system's idiosyncrasies.

When compiling, make sure that you include the "gif8" output device, since it allows *Ghostscript* to translate to a GIF file. It is included with the current version, 2.6.1. Once built, using *Ghostscript* to convert files to GIFs from within Perl scripts is quite easy, as in this sample code:

gs is the name of the Ghostscript program

```
if (! -e $gifpathname) {
        system ("cp $pathname /home/transfer/bill.ps");
        system ("/usr/bin/remsh goanna '/usr/bin/gs -q -dNOPAUSE -r80x67 -
dMAGSTEP=.5 -sDEVICE=gif8 -sOutputFile=/home/transfer/bill.gif --
/home/transfer/bill.ps'");
        system ("cp /home/transfer/bill.gif $gifpathname");
        system ("rm -f /home/transfer/bill.gif /home/transfer/bill.ps");
}
```

As a standalone package of utilities, *Ghostscript* can translate among the following graphics formats: BMP, GIF, PCX, PBM, PPM, TIFF, and PGM.

If you want to expand those capabilities, you can download another graphics utility package, Jef Poskanzer's *pbmplus*. It supports a host of exotic graphics formats, including Group III fax, MacPaint, UNIX plot, and ASCII. *pbmplus* is available from

```
<ftp://ee.utah.edu//pbmplus/pbmplus10dec91_tar.gz>
```

Not only can the resulting arsenal of graphics utilities translate from one graphics file to another, but, with the addition of *gnuplot,* discussed in Chapter 25, you can create graphics out of thin air. Data from statistics packages, existing databases, or user input can be processed and fed to *gnuplot* for conversion to a UNIX plot file. The resulting plot can be converted to a GIF by either *Ghostscript* or *pbmplus*, and finally returned to the browser. The potential uses for this type of on-the-fly automatic document creation fairly boggles the mind.

NETCLOAK

netcloak is a package that extends MacHTTP or WebSTAR in ways that make these Macintosh-based Web servers much more conducive to dynamic document creation. Run as a sort of CGI coprocessor, *netcloak* preprocesses your documents, interpreting certain extended tags according to a number of conditions.

These extensions are fairly simple to implement in your documents and add the ability to insert variables; hide and show parts of documents according to the user's domain, browser client, or referring document; or password-protect portions of documents. The variables available for insertion include the date and time, and the number of times the document has been accessed.

In this way, static documents containing *netcloak*'s custom tags achieve quite a high degree of customization once the preprocessing is completed.

Summary

In your adventures as a WWW developer, we are certain that you will encounter some situations that will demand one or more of the HTML-on-the-fly techniques we've covered in this chapter. Especially when you must deal with data that cannot be changed from native, non-HTML formats, the best solutions will often emerge from custom CGIs that apply HTML as a sort of filter through which that data must pass on its way to your users.

This sort of approach works for pre-existing collections of data or as a way to ease the authors' learning curves for the content being served at your Web site. For the latter case, if you create the data in plain text, using simple, prearranged formatting rules, your CGI can give the final shove that pushes the text the rest of the way to users on the Web.

When designing a CGI that returns dynamically created HTML to the user, you may want to create a static page as a boilerplate for your script. This document can then be inserted into your Perl script as a series of print statements with appropriate variable substitutions to capture the dynamic content. This adds the benefit of making you more aware of how your users experience the resulting output from your script.

There are some elements that are particularly useful to work into dynamic HTML documents, especially elements that enhance the user interface presented. First and foremost among these should be navigational aids. Too often a CGI's output consists only of a simple page of formatted output with no way back to the referring page, or to the next or previous pages of your data.

Error handling is also important for dynamically created CGIs. The URL that includes a CGI often features a long, tortuous UNIX file path and/or a collection of options and arguments. Any user trying to find help or an index to your data may try to call your CGI without including the information originally used to call the specific file or record. It's essential to make your CGI behave in some useful way when it is called without all the proper arguments, perhaps by presenting a table of contents, a help page, or a search form to the user.

Finally, when designing an HTML formatting-on-the-fly system, never underestimate the utility of the UNIX file system. From hierarchical data organization to information about individual files, a UNIX directory tree has a lot to offer in terms of infrastructure for your scripts.

We would hope that the way *ftpb* reads and displays the contents of certain files on the fly suggests the incredible potential for these techniques. Merging this behavior with the idea of formatting text for easier HTML translation, you can build systems in which complex layouts for text and graphics is generated on demand.

If your data is formatted, named, and placed in directories according to a simple set of rules, a CGI can take that data and insert it into a template that is as complex and sophisticated as you like. No more preformatted, monospaced text — your HTML-on-the-fly documents can include headings, lists, and images, and your users need never know that what they're viewing never existed until they requested it!

CHAPTER

27

Getting the Best Buy For Your Bucks

*T*he process of selecting a server platform can be a difficult one, especially for a new WebMaster. What type of server is best for your intended application? How much traffic can it handle? Is it better to get a cheap PC or a Mac, or should you invest in a big UNIX box with lots of memory? These questions are paramount to any Web designer. By analyzing your network and your Web system's possible uses, you can establish an accurate proposal for hardware and software before you start development work.

The most important phase in evaluating server needs is "planning and requirements analysis." Gather together all the groups within your organization that intend to publish information on your Web server and sit them down for a presentation. Define what is possible and what is unlikely or unreasonable, and then you can elicit information from each group about their particular wants and needs. You may get useful information from your initial meeting with everybody, but you'll also want to follow up with additional meetings with each group (and with individuals from each group, if necessary). Don't quit asking questions until you're absolutely sure you've heard everything there is to hear about what they want "their" Web server to do.

The next step is to lay out an implementation plan that encompasses each of these requirements. Be sure to pay careful attention to projections of activity and to the level of service your organization intends to offer.

A project that entails offering your full product list online, with a search engine and a database gateway, that allows potential Web customers to browse, query, and actually purchase your products online would be a giant undertaking. It also requires commitments from several departments to supply person- as well as machine-power to meet such goals.

In this chapter we discuss the many options available to you in setting up your first Web server on the Internet. Although it may seem simple, there are subtle issues that can sometimes prove to be large hurdles upon closer inspection. Specifically, you'll learn to determine which server platforms are best for particular tasks, what kinds of Internet connections you should choose, and some strategies for keeping everything on schedule.

We'll start by offering you a good comparison and contrast page between the major flavors of Web server software currently available. This "WWW Servers Comparison Chart" is generally up-to-date and is well-stocked with useful information, like ease of setup, maintenance requirements, and log formats. Point your favorite browser to this URL:

```
http://www.proper.com/www/servers-chart.html
```

For completeness' sake, we have enclosed a copy of this page for your quick perusal, dated June 1995.

```
The server software programs listed in this document are:

AP Apache HTTP from the Apache Project
GN GN from John Franks
GO GoServe from Mike Cowlishaw
HC httpd from CERN
HN httpd from NCSA
HS HTTPS from European Microsoft Windows NT Academic Centre (EMWAC)
MH MacHTTP from BIAP Systems
NM NetMagic Webserver from NetMagic
NP NetPublisher from Ameritech Library Services
NS Netscape Communications and Netscape Commerce from Netscape Communications
OP WebServer and Secure WebServer from Open Market
PV Purveyor from Process Software
PX Plexus from Tony Sanders at BSDI
R6 Region 6 Threaded HTTP Server
WN WN from John Franks
WS WebSTAR from StarNine Technologies
WT WebSite from O'Reilly and Associates
```

Features of the Servers

	AP	GN	GO	HC	HN	HS	MH	NM	NP	NS	OP	PV	PX	R6	WN	WS	WT
Runs under:																	
Unix	Y	Y	N	Y	Y	N	N	N	N	Y	Y	N	Y	N	Y	N	N
Windows NT	N	N	N	Y	Y	Y	N	Y	Y	Y	N	Y	Y	N	N	N	Y
VMS	N	N	N	Y	N	N	N	N	N	N	N	N	Y	N	N	N	N
Macintosh OS	N	N	N	N	N	N	Y	N	N	N	N	N	N	N	N	Y	N
OS/2	N	N	Y	N	N	N	N	N	N	N	N	N	N	N	N	N	N
Windows 3.1	N	N	N	N	Y	N	N	N	N	N	N	N	N	N	N	N	N
Launching:																	
Can run from inetd	NR	Y	X	NR	NR	X	X	X	N	Y	N	X	NR	N	Y	X	X
Logging with syslog	N	Y	X	N	N	X	X	X	N	Y	Y	X	Y	N	Y	X	X
CERN/NCSA common log format	YL	N	YS	Y	YL	N	N	N	N	YL	Y	Y	N	YD	YL	YL	Y
Protocol support:																	
Server-side includes	Y	N	YS	N	Y	N	N	N	TM	Y	SO	Y	Y	Y	Y	N	N
Reply with any status code without using CGI	Y	N	YS	N	Y	N	N	Y	Y	Y	Y	N	Y	Y	Y	N	Y
Emits 500-level status codes	Y	Y	YS	Y	Y	Y	Y	Y	Y	N	Y	Y	Y	Y	Y	Y	Y
Headers:																	
Automatic response to If-Modified-Since	Y	Y	Y	Y	Y	Y	Y	Y	Y	N	Y	Y	Y	Y	Y	Y	Y
Select files based on Accept header	Y	N	YS	Y	Y	N	N	N	N	Y	N	Y	Y	N	N	Y	N
Change actions based on User-Agent header	Y	N	YS	N	Y	N	N	N	N	Y	Y	N	N	N	N	Y	N
Security:																	
Can require password (Authorization: user)	Y	N	YS	Y	Y	N	Y	Y	N	Y	Y	Y	Y	YP	Y	Y	Y
Supports SSL	N	N	N	N	N	N	N	N	N	Y	N	N	N	N	N	Y	N
Supports S-HTTP	N	N	N	N	N	N	N	N	N	Y	N	N	N	N	N	N	N
File security model	AU	DU	FS	DU	AU	NS	AU	AG	DU	AU	AU	AG	AU	DU	DU	AU	AG
Prohibit by IP address	Y	Y	YS	Y	Y	N	Y	Y	Y	Y	Y	Y	Y	Y	Y	Y	Y
Prohibit by domain name	Y	Y	YS	N	Y	N	Y	Y	N	Y	Y	Y	Y	Y	Y	Y	Y
Additional security features	CG	GS	SS	CC	CG	N	MS	N	N	NE	AX	PS	AX	YP	GS	MS	N
Other:																	
GUI-based setup	N	N	Y	N	Y	Y	Y	Y	Y	Y	Y	N	N	N	N	Y	Y
GUI-based maintenance	N	N	N	N	N	Y	Y	Y	Y	Y	N	Y	N	N	N	Y	Y
Script or action based on output file type	Y	Y	YS	N	Y	N	N	Y	N	Y	N	Y	Y	Y	Y	N	Y
Also serves other protocols	N	GO	GO	N	N	N	N	N	GZ	N	N	N	N	N	N	N	N
Automatic directory tree	Y	N	YS	Y	Y	Y	N	Y	Y	Y	Y	Y	Y	Y	Y	Y	Y
User directories	Y	N	YS	Y	Y	Y	N	X	N	Y	Y	Y	Y	Y	Y	X	N
Search engine	IE	IE	N	N	IE	NW	AP	Y	Z3	N	PL	NW	WO	Y	IE	AP	Y
Cost	FR	FR	FR	FR	FR	FR	CO	CO	CO	CO	CO	CO	CO	FR	FR	FR	CO

```
Legend

Y Yes
N No
? Not sure
X Not applicable
AG Allow access to all files unless listed in an access file; can make groups
of users and allow access by group name
AP Interfaces to AppleSearch search engine
AU Allow access to all files unless listed in an access file
AX The security model is easily extensible (code examples included). Can also
make groups of users and allow access by group name and allows security locks
to be kept outside of the protected directory.
CC Can make groups of users and allow access by group name, and allows security
locks to be kept outside of the protected directory
CG Can make groups of users and allow access by group name
CO Commercial software (costs money to license)
DU Deny access to all files unless listed in an access file
FR Free software (may be public domain or GNUish public license)
FS File-level security through a script
GO Serves Gopher (not Gopher+)
GS Allows security locks to be kept outside of the protected directory (for
example, to allow partial access only to CD-ROMs)
GZ Serves Gopher & Z39.50
IE Internal search engine as well as freeWAIS support
IW Internal WAIS engine
MS Allows extensions to the security model through CGIs that interpret password
info. It also allows groups of users to be assigned to specific realms which
contain one or more files.
NE Netscape Commerce has public-key encryption and authentication
NR Yes but not recommended
NS No file-level security
NW Uses the WAIS Toolkit for Windows NT
PL Through Personal Library Software engine
PS Can allow/deny based on virtual paths outside the hierarchy; also allow/deny
based on access method
SO For Secure-HTTP only
SS All requests are filtered by a script to which any kind of security can be
added.
TM Includes are created with an HTML template wizard
WO FreeWAIS, grep, and others
YD Yes plus configurable diagnostic trace
YL Yes and additional logs can log other headers.
YP Comes with customizable authentication server that provides access checks via
password
YS Yes, through a script
Z3 Internal & external Z39.50
```

If you visit this site, you'll be happy to note that the links at the bottom consist of URLs that point to each of the referenced servers' home pages.

Consequently, if you are interested only in UNIX servers, the following link supplies a nice discussion of the UNIX options available today:

```
http://mistral.enst.fr/~pioch/httpd/
```

Where to Begin

There are several important matters to address before your Web server can be brought online. A few of these considerations are listed below and we'll discuss each of these throughout this chapter, but because each set of circumstances — yours, for instance — is unique, the actual list of considerations will change.

- **Connection:** How fast does your server's Internet connection have to be? T1 (1.544Mbp/s) is a typical connection for fairly large organizations, with 64kbp/s lines more common for smaller businesses and individuals.

- **Platform:** Are you going to reuse equipment that you already have, or do you need to select and purchase equipment for this project? Most servers run on UNIX platforms already in use for other tasks, but there is a growing tendency for smaller Web hosts to use microcomputers or workstations as their platforms.

- **Scalability:** Will you outgrow this box in one year? Will you need several other servers down the line to work in tandem with this one? Will you need to purchase ancillary equipment to offload some of the other tasks this Web server will handle (like CGI applications, for instance)? The amount of CPU speed, disk space, and multitasking required for your expected user load will influence your answer.

- **Statistics:** What kind of reporting will be required from this machine? Will you need to invest in programming a custom solution, or are the public ones good enough?

- **Interoperability:** Will your selected server platform work well with the systems that you already have in place? What will you need to do to ensure easy data transport or migration?

- **Personnel:** Will you need a full-time administrator, or will current staff handle the server's management responsibilities?
- **Publishing:** Will your chosen platform make it difficult or easy to post and change your HTML documents? What systems need to be in place to ensure a simple Web publishing chain?

Our discussion begins with your connection options. If you are part of a large corporation or are already well connected, this may not be a factor for you. But if you are a small business or an individual, you may have to scope out the Internet Service Providers (ISPs) in your area before you tackle any Web server issues. In the next section we will give you a clearer picture of the different options available for connecting a server to the Internet.

Getting Connected

THROUGHPUTS AND COSTS

Table 27-1 should give you some idea about what kind of connection you'll need for your server. Warning! These costs included are *general averages*; they will vary significantly from city to city, as well as from provider to provider. Also, as Telco resources become more advanced, their prices for new lines are guaranteed to be different. In determining your connection needs, be sure to consult the Web server FAQ available at:

```
http://sunsite.unc.edu/boutell/faq/bandwidth.html
```

This page provides valuable clues about what to make of throughput measurements, especially "connections per minute," and "total hits per day."

When it comes to picking line speeds, remember that bandwidth is a strange beast. Sometimes, it is difficult to quantify just what engineers mean by *latency*, and real *network utilization*. In our experience, only enormous sites (500 simultaneous users or more) really justify a full T1 connection, whereas most sites could get by with a fractional T1, or even a 64/128k ISDN line.

In closing, we suggest that you shop around for as many different options as you can find in your area. Because competition is stiff among ISPs these days, you may find some bargains along the way. And don't forget to play one off against the other, especially if you like one ISP's prices and another one's services.

LINE SPEEDS AND LATENCY

Table 27-1
Line Speeds and Costs

Connection Speed	Description	Approximate Cost Startup + (Monthly)*
28.8k	*Dedicated Modem Connection:* Modem required and a phone line.	$450 ($50–$250)
56/64k	*Leased Line:* Modem and a leased line required.	$650 ($125–$750)
56/64k	*ISDN (Integrated Services Digital Network):* A bridge/router and ISDN line are required.	$3,000+ ($400–$750)
128k	*Fractional T1:* An IP router and CSU/DSU required along with the local loop.	$5,000+ ($1,800–$2,500)
256k	*Fractional T1:* An IP router and CSU/DSU required along with the local loop.	$5,000+ ($2,200–$2,800)
512k	*Fractional T1:* An IP router and CSU/DSU required along with the local loop.	$5,000+ ($2,500–$3,500)
T1	*Full 1.54 Mbits/sec:* An IP router and CSU/DSU required along with the local loop.	$5,000+ ($2,900–$3,800)
Fractional T3	Not available everywhere; special equipment required.	$15,000+ ($12,000+)
Full T3	Not available everywhere; special equipment required.	$15,000+ ($25,000+)

*Startup costs include average equipment costs and the monthly charges include line charges from your Telco along with ISP charges.

Housing a Server at Your Site

Let's say you've decided to use a 64k ISDN connection, and that you will be running your server across that wire more or less exclusively. Let's assume further that your company sells comic books and collectible figurines, and that you wish to drum up some business across the Internet, as well as attract this new clientele to your online establishment.

This scenario also assumes that you will need a connection only for your Web server and a couple of other machines for administration. The minimal list of equipment requirements based on these assumptions follows:

- Server platform (486 PC running free BSD)
- Admin & Workstation platforms (one Macintosh and one PC)
- ISDN bridge/router (Ascend Pipeline HX-50)
- LAN cabling and cards (NICs — Network Interface Cards — for all three machines, with three segments of thinwire Ethernet cable)

Using this configuration, you can be up and running within a week, providing you have immediate access to the equipment, and that the telecommunications installations go smoothly and quickly. Since you have a network of only four nodes, the ISP you selected would have designated you a subsegment of a Class C network range (probably an 8- or a 16-machine subnet, using the CIDR (Classless Inter-Domain Routing) approach). This allows each of your machines to conduct peer-to-peer transactions with any other machine on the network, as well as with each other.

When hosting a Web server at your residence or business, your equipment obtains Internet access by placing a phone call to establish a network presence (whether via analog modem, an ISDN bridge, or a router). In these circumstances, be warned that electrical storms, phone company activity, or even unexplained incidents can knock you off-line.

Although adequate for handling such disconnects, this kind of equipment is generally less reliable than what you'd use for a dedicated circuit (e.g., CSU/DSU and a T1 line). For some of you, this won't matter because you can't afford the additional costs, but we wanted you to understand this tradeoff anyway. It means you do need to keep an eye on your server and network connection, though, to make sure both are running properly at all times.

Housing Your Server at the ISP

Some ISPs sell space in their office, granting you the ability to place equipment on their backbone connection to the Net. This is typically both faster and more reliable than dealing with modems and bridges. There are two drawbacks to this approach:

1. Security for your server is left to the service provider and its staff.

2. You lose control over the server's hardware, including access to the machine's floppy drive and/or peripheral equipment. (Physical access to a machine is rarely essential but can sometimes be convenient.)

If you don't have the staff to run a server at your site, the space to house it properly, or the inclination to take on a 7-day-a-week, 24-hour-a-day maintenance job, housing a server at an ISP is a good idea. The main reason why more individuals and organizations don't take this route is because they don't want to pay the associated costs.

If you do go the ISP route, most service providers offer some sort of Uninterruptible Power Supply (UPS) for your server, as well as a backup strategy for your data. This can help justify the extra costs of housing your Web server away from home.

WHAT DO I NEED TO WATCH FOR?

When your server is not physically attached to your network, you may want to consider paying for a phone line connected directly to that machine, for monitoring and management access. A cheaper solution consists of a couple of dial-in accounts from the service provider. Either way, you can always dial in to do system administration or to check network status.

If your site has no other network connections, you might also look into getting a dedicated SLIP or PPP link. SLIP stands for Serial Line Interface Protocol and PPP for Point-to-Point Protocol; both are methods for using ordinary phone lines to establish "real" network connections. Or an ISDN account might make more sense to facilitate remote administration of your server.

Why Not Lease Space on a Server?

Sure thing. If you have a particularly small site, or one that is better-suited to remote operation (for instance, if you travel a lot and wouldn't be around to take care of a server yourself), then there are plenty of providers that offer Web space for rent. A good place to start looking for such providers is at the following URL:

```
http://union.ncsa.uiuc.edu/HyperNews/get/www/leasing.html
```

What Do I Need to Watch For?

By offering your pages on somebody else's site, one annoyance is that most Web servers will not permit you to "spoof" domain names to Web directories. Here's what this means in English: If your domain was *curtains.com* and you contracted *big.Web.com* to serve your pages, you would more than likely share that machine with other patrons.

The access point for your Web pages would probably look something like: "http://www.curtains.com/curtains" or even "http://www.curtains.com/~curtains/curtains.html." Any outside user's attempt to open up "http://www.curtains.com" would produce *big.Web.com*'s home page rather than yours. Although it's merely an annoyance, we've heard many people voice their displeasure at the required "/curtains" part of their home pages. (There are several workarounds for this, but they go beyond the scope of this book.)

The most important thing to consider when purchasing rental space on another company's Web server is the system of CGIs in place. When you're running your own server, *you* have full control over what applications you'd like to run as gateways; if you need another one, you can always add it.

If you're renting, the CGI system may be out of your control. Since CGIs, if mismanaged, could be a potential point of compromise, Web-Masters tend to be very conservative regarding their management and operation. We suggest that you ponder this hard when shopping for a provider to house your site.

Comparing UNIX Servers

UNIX Web server applications are quite similar in their configuration and management. In a recent study by Robert E. McGrath (mcgrath@ncsa.uiuc.edu) of NCSA, the best-performing servers include the NCSA 1.4 (pre-forking) server and the NetSite Communications Server. Both servers were capable of delivering consistently superior performance when compared to the NCSA version 1.3 server or the CERN 3.0 server.

The results of his tests can be found at:

```
http://www.ncsa.uiuc.edu/InformationServers/Performance/V1.4/
report.html
```

Other Platforms

Though our own preferences are clearly spelled out in Chapter 12, we're not afraid to admit that there are more viable options for serving up a Web than our beloved UNIX. In the sections that follow, we'll discuss some of these, including the Macintosh and Microsoft-based options.

CHOOSING A MAC SERVER

For the Macintosh platform, there is only one choice for your Web server, and a great choice it is, too. Marketed under its new name, *WebSTAR*, the MacHTTP server developed by Chuck Shotton, is currently distributed by StarNine Products. The commercial version differs from the free version, which is available from BIAP Systems, Inc., in that it supports the System 7.5 thread manager which allows for speedier responses from the server when handling CGIs. Also, it's programmed in 601 native PowerMac code. Look for it at:

```
http://www.starnine.com/
http://www.biap.com/
```

Using the Macintosh as a server platform is a fantastic way to get started as a WebMaster; it is easily configured and administered. The Macintosh has fewer security headaches, and the new version rivals the performance of some UNIX machines. All in all, it's a good option and well worth the money, both for the necessary hardware and software.

CHOOSING A DOS/WINDOWS PC SERVER

For the original DOS/Windows platform, there are only limited choices. The NCSA server is really the best of what's available, although the KA9Q server offers more services in addition to HTTP (such as *gopher*, *ntp*, *finger*, and *mail*, to name just a few).

The Windows NCSA server can be found through NCSA's major UNIX distribution site (its URL also appears below as ...win-httpd), while the KA9q server can be found at the eponymous URL:

```
http://www.city.net/win-httpd/
http://inorganic5.chem.ufl.edu/ka9q/ka9q.html
```

CHOOSING A WINDOWS NT SERVER

By contrast to the limited options available for the Mac and the DOS/Windows, Windows NT offers a nice selection of Web server packages. Along with the standard NCSA server distribution (they support most everything), NetMagic, NetPublisher, and Netscape all offer advanced, reliable Web server implementations.

A secure version of the server software (which supports SHTTP) is available from the European Microsoft Windows NT Academic Centre (EMWAC). Also, the Purveyor server software by Process Software; Web-Site from O'Reilly and Associates; and Plexus, by Tony Sanders at BSDI, should not be omitted. Here is a list of the URLs related to these servers:

```
NetMagic:      http://www.aristosoft.com/netmagic/company.html
NetPublisher:  http://netpub.notis.com
Netscape:      http://www.netscape.com/comprod/netscape_commun.html
Purveyor:      http://www.process.com/prodinfo/purvdata.htm
Plexus:        http://www.bsdi.com/server/doc/plexus.html
WebSite:       http://Website.ora.com/
```

Web Server Miscellany

PROXIES

You may have heard about using a "proxy server" to deliver Web traffic to your site as a security precaution. Proxies are guaranteed routes through a firewall that isolate an internal network from an external one. If your company has placed restrictions on your network that prevent you from accessing a Web site on the Internet even though your company is connected to the Net, you might benefit from a proxy.

By running a version of Web server software that supports a proxy operation, a machine that is on the internal net can conduct transactions with an external machine by using the proxy as an intermediary. Traffic is funneled through this proxy machine, which can be vetted by your network security personnel to maintain a firewall. Generally, the CERN software is the best solution for configuring a proxy Web server (as another alternative, a package called SOCKS lets Web clients be modified to connect to servers outside their firewalls).

LOAD BALANCING STRATEGIES

What if your server becomes notorious and starts to bog down because of the load? That's when load balancing, which means spreading the processing load across multiple servers, can help. The simplest method for load balancing can be built right into your HTML pages as they are created, or even added afterwards, if necessary.

By distributing the pages evenly between two machines, or by placing all of the CGI traffic on a single machine and the HTML on the other, you can off-load the overloaded machine and balance the load across the two machines.

You may also consider running a "Round Robin" version of BIND, which provides a selection of IP addresses for a single name each time an Internet client asks. This option is nicely scalable, but becomes a headache when it comes to synchronizing the information on each of the mirror machines. The more machines you have in the cycle, the more time and effort you'll spend in keeping all of them up-to-date. Many really huge sites employ this method by using powerful machines and splitting the load three or four ways.

Summary

Given that there is a server platform for almost any need, on almost any platform, selection can be quite a pain. We hope that by detailing the decisions we've had to make in setting up servers, both large and small, that you've gained a clearer picture of what kinds of resources — equipment, personnel, and software — you'll need. You should be prepared to deal with various connectivity options, server types and platforms, and mechanics of handling server loads. Now, make up your mind and get that server running!

IV Advanced CGI Programming Tools and Techniques

*T*he seven chapters in Part IV expand our discussion of CGI and Web programming to deal with advanced tools and techniques, and also to look at nascent, but exciting, areas of Web development that should interest forward-looking CGI programmers.

We begin our discussion in Chapter 28 with an examination of file retrieval tools and aids, to support access to ftp- or Web-based file archives through your Web pages. In Chapter 29, we investigate the options available today for accessing full-blown Database Management Systems (like Oracle, Informix, and Sybase) through CGI programs, including a sample application to illustrate the programming elements required. In Chapter 30, we explore approaches and software available to support audio, video, and multimedia capture and communications via the Web.

Chapter 31 returns to the Internet's very roots, as we explore the sometimes wonderful synergy that a combination of electronic mail and the Web can create, with an investigation of mail server gateways and related tools. In Chapter 32, we discuss security concerns for Web servers and services, as we cover the most important bases involved in protecting UNIX-based Web servers from compromise. We also cover the issues and technology involved in "Secure HTTP," an emerging Web protocol that promises to make the Web safe for electronic commerce and other secure Web-based transactions.

In Chapter 33, the focus shifts to the issues involved in making the Web "truly interactive," and examines some of the tools and applications that are moving the Web inexorably in that direction.

In Chapter 34, we close our Web programming investigations with a brief discussion of the CD-ROM included in this book, a road map of its layout, and some recommendations for how you can use it most effectively.

CHAPTER

28

File Access Through the Web

The Software and How to Get It

On the Internet, if you want to download data to your machine, more often than not you will be using the File Transfer Protocol, or *FTP*. Like most Internet services of a certain age, FTP is immensely powerful and very intimidating to anyone short of a UNIX-weenie. FTP's command-line interface, with its seemingly infinite features and options, will remain an obstacle to users until it can be replaced with a more intuitive, approachable interface.

The World Wide Web is not the "killer app" of the Internet; it is the *front-end* to the killer app, which is the Internet itself and all its associated services, FTP included. As the user interface to the Internet, the Web does its job very well, so that one arcane, UNIX-spawned protocol or service after another has been made easier to use and less frightening to the unititiated.

Although such diverse services as mailing lists, database lookups, and a host of other tools and utilities both useful and whimsical have been retrofitted with Web front-ends, FTP remains a holdout. Examples do exist of various methods for easing the complexity of FTP's normal file location and retrieval syntax, but these are few and far between.

Our analysis of the current Web situation *vis-à-vis* file retrieval, shows that there are at least two features that are slowing the widespread development of full-featured Web solutions to the problem. Let's discuss...

All Browsers Are Not Created Equal

First, most popular Web clients directly support File Transfer Protocol. Thus Web front-ends can be used for displaying file listing and downloading even if the FTP sites are not running a Web server.

This lessens the immediate need for customized Web interfaces to particular sites, since even a machine with no running HTTP server can be accessed with Netscape, MacWeb, WinWeb, and the Mosaic family. However, this generic view is not the most desirable, for a number of reasons.

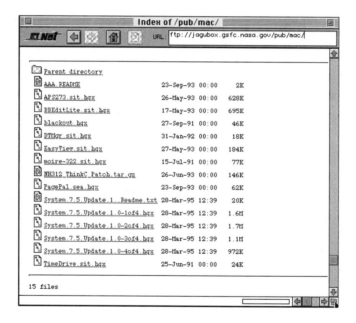

Figure 28-1
MacWeb's generic FTP file listing.

Every FTP site on the Internet looks exactly the same, no matter where that site is, who runs it, or what it contains. For example, the first, most obvious thing about MacWeb's built-in FTP browser is that it *looks* generic (see Figure 28-1). All the power of the Web to customize, personalize, and generally hotrod the data is missing and presumed lost.

Even Netscape, the self-proclaimed Cadillac of Web browsers, has a generic FTP site listing-view that leaves much to be desired. All these browsers attempt to interpret file suffixes to guess at file formats; many can identify a number of Mac, DOS, and UNIX formats. All can use the file type to display an icon specific to the file's format. All can parse a directory listing and display file sizes and modification dates. They can also allow the user to change to a parent directory, display a "README" file from the current working directory, or display a directory's name at the top of the page.

But there's no reason why file retrieval through the Web should begin and end with such generic views. These browsers get the information they need to present the directory listings to the user from parsing the output of the FTP server. That same information could be made available to your tools or CGIs in any number of ways, so that you could create your own customized FTP browsing view.

With customization, you could attach abstracts describing software files using a link to that software's listing. You could display custom icons associated with the software or with the FTP site's owner. You could also add further explanatory notes to directories, embed navigation aids to the rest of your services, or massage file listings into more pleasing layouts.

With a little more imagination and sweat, you could also allow the middleware — the CGIs and scripts that create and maintain the HTML code — to add features such as load balancing, mirror access, or file compressions to the old-fashioned FTP protocol they are "dressing up."

Through a Glass, Darkly

Strangely, there are very few FTP sites available via a custom Web front-end, and absolutely no readily available, generalized tools or CGIs designed to aid in creating such a site. There are, however, a few individually developed solutions that you can examine to get a clear picture of what is required to develop such a Web site yourself.

When designing a front-end for file retrieval, a few key distinctions must be drawn and decisions made. First, you must determine whether you need to design a general-purpose solution for your entire site, or whether you're simply trying to facilitate the retrieval of a few key files.

THE WHOLE FTP BOATLOAD

If you need a full-site Web front-end — that is, one that allows your users to browse and download files from your entire FTP site, or at least a large part of it — a further distinction must be made. This is the determination of how often these files, their parent directories, and the accompanying information that goes with both are updated.

Typically, there are two useful categories for this frequency: daily, which requires batch translation of the entire FTP site's directory listings into HTML; or instantaneous, which requires CGIs that translate file and directory information into HTML on demand.

CGIs: THE BENEDICTINE MONKS OF THE WEB

For nightly translations *en masse* from your FTP site's directory tree into HTML, you're looking at a design and implementation that requires tools to be run from *cron* (or an equivalent clock daemon on non-UNIX systems) to produce your desired HTML output. This kind of translation is loosely defined and could range anywhere from a simple mirroring of the FTP site to a more complex process involving extracting "README" files, formatting their contents, indexing for keyword or filename searches, and the like. The only essential elements are links to the various directories, whose contents must be represented either in separate HTML files or in separate sections of the same file, and links to the files themselves for downloading.

The Hyperarchive at MIT is a Web mirror site of the Info-Mac archive. Steven Ward, the site's administrator, uses a *Perl5* script called *mirror* to do just that — perform a nightly update of his mirror of the multi-gigabyte file archive. Once he has copied the directory structure and all the files and file abstracts locally, he runs a home-grown C program to generate the hierarchy of HTML documents that constitutes the browsable *hyperarchive*. This program also produces an index file suitable for use in searches. Another custom C CGI handles search requests, using *grep* to do the actual work and returning a clickable hit list to the user.

As you can see in Figure 28-2, Steve's "FTP tree-to-HTML documents" program is more than a little clever. Instead of a straight translation of one hierarchy of files to another, he takes advantage of HTML's strengths and adds a link to each package's abstract, which goes a long way to reducing traffic on downloads of software the user doesn't actually want. His abstracting tool creates a number of other methods for looking at files from the raw listings. These compose the page you see in Figure 28-2, summarizing recent additions to the Info-Mac archive in reverse chronological order, as well as an index listing by author name and by package name.

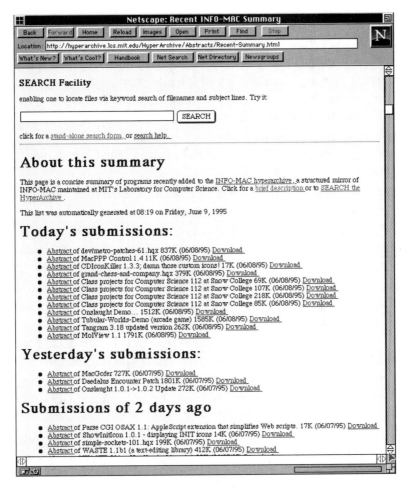

Figure 28-2

The Info-Mac Hyperarchive's page summarizing recent additions.

Steve Ward's "Hyperarchive" package is included on the accompanying CD-ROM, but we warn you that the package is provided in the state in which it was developed — that is, as a specific solution for his own mirror/Web site. It should be adaptable to any site, with a little work, but that work will definitely be required. For more information, check out the following URL:

```
http://hyperarchive.lcs.mit.edu/HyperArchive/Abstracts/Recent-Summary.html
```

MIRROR DECISIONS AND ISSUES

One benefit of Ward's method is that it lends itself very well to remote mirroring or distributed archiving. A Web site that is updated nightly doesn't need direct access to the central file system upon which the software resides. To perform an update, it might first retrieve a full listing of the site, normally saved at the root level of the archive and named "ls-lR" or "00INDEX" or some such. It could then scan the listing for changes and connect again to that site only to retrieve needed files. Alternatively, NFS or AFS could be used to access that file system remotely.

Another possibility might be that the Web version of the FTP site need not contain files at all, but could act merely as an interface to the actual FTP site. In this scenario, the index file retrieved from the FTP site would be used to build HTML pages with links that point back to the original FTP site. The user need not know that the Web front-end and the file archive back-end reside in two different locations.

It also bears mentioning that a collection of downloadable files provided through an HTML document need not reside on a single server. If mirroring is involved, your site can collect collections of files from several servers, the only constraint obviously being your available drive space. With a "virtual Web mirror" of the type just described, serving multiple FTP sites is even easier, since the only management issue is to ensure that the link for any given file points to its proper host and directory specification.

Even more intriguing is the possibility of a crude load-balancing system. If you're presented with a situation where you have a popular collection of files, this could give rise to concerns about your FTP server being overloaded by the demand for those files. In such a case, the archive could be physically duplicated across a number of FTP hosts.

Such a distributed archive could then be accessed through a single Web site interface that varies the host links for any given file according to whatever algorithm you might wish to use. You could cycle through a list of hosts as your program writes the links, or it could be determined by a more complex scheme if your servers have different handling capacities.

If the files you are serving reside on the same Web server that hosts the hyperarchive, you have a choice regarding the protocol you use to deliver these files. The most obvious solution would be to run an FTP server on the same host, in addition to the HTTP server that handles the Web services, and then to link all your files using FTP, where file URLs would take the following form:

```
ftp://your.host.name/path/to/file/filename.extension
```

FTP Versus HTTP as a File Retrieval Protocol

Alternatively, HTTP can be used as a file retrieval method. This could contribute to a performance gain, since your HTTP server would be able to retrieve files directly for users. This would probably be more efficient than if the user's browser were to be redirected to a separate FTP server.

The reason for this performance gain is twofold. First, there is no login and password negotiation required for HTTP as there is for FTP (even with anonymous FTP). Second, HTTP is a higher-performance data-transfer protocol than FTP.

To do this, it may be neccessary to edit your "mime.types" file to correctly represent the types of files your Web site serves. For example, all BinHex-encoded files would require you to add a line to your "/conf/mime.types" file to associate the file suffix ".hqx" with a corresponding MIME type. For our example this would look like:

```
application/BinHex 4.0  hqx
```

This will ensure that if the file itself does not have the proper HTML header lines declaring its type, the server will add this header before passing it off to the client. At that point, the client looks up its own list of MIME types to find the "helper application" associated with that file type. Then, after the download is complete, the browser will attempt to submit the resulting file to that helper application for decoding or display.

The only drawback to the "direct HTTP approach" is that it imposes an extra load on the machine running the HTTP server. If high performance is a requirement and your Web server has the necessary capacity, HTTP is the way to go!

Less Automation, More Sweat

For another example of batched conversion and updating of a Web/FTP site let's turn to the Office of Telecommunication Services' FTP server at the University of Texas. Here the administrator of this site, Chris Johnson, maintains a gorgeous Web version of the Macintosh archive at the University of Texas. Its home URL is:

```
http://wwwhost.ots.utexas.edu/mac/main.html
```

Chris has expanded on the concept of providing additional information to help users find and choose software prior to downloading. Not only does his site provide each file's author, date, and package name using indices much like the Hyperarchive, but each package is also presented on its own informational index-card-like listing. (See Figure 28-3.)

Each file on OTS/Mac has been abstracted, its icon extracted, and key data such as system requirements, mirror sites, and cost is presented in an associated abstract. Author contact information, including a functional **MAILTO** tag where available, is also present. As you can plainly see, this amount of cogent information can make users' file-browsing experiences much more productive and informative.

It should be noted that Chris's development and maintenance for this site requires significant grunt work. The abstracting and data extraction for each package takes time and energy on his part, and the automation tools only perform certain parts of the updates. At this time, those tools are also highly site-specific, but OTS/Mac nevertheless serves as a good example of the frontiers of excellence in offering FTP archives on the Web.

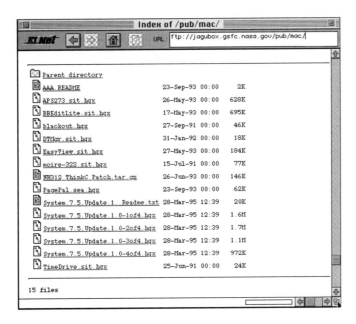

Figure 28-3
An OTS/Mac file listing, featuring Alberto Ricci's Sound Effect 0.92.

More Automation, No Sweat

The aim of any useful implementation of technology is to decrease the amount of work you do. Administering a Web FTP site by hand is a task you will abhor, so we suggest that you make plans to automate, starting with the very first steps you take toward developing an FTP site.

One way to dramatically decrease the amount of labor involved is to do away with HTML pages altogether. What we mean by this is to accept the idea that text documents residing on a server, *no matter how often they are updated*, will always be obsolete.

Once that realization sets in, there is something you can do about it. When a user wishes to see the contents of a directory, have your server create the necessary HTML-formatted text on the fly. When a user wants to look at a particular package, create that HTML on demand as well. No pages ever sit idle, therefore no pages ever need updating. What could be more simple?

Lister, You Lazy Sod!

The means to realizing a completely on-the-fly file delivery service already exists in the form of CGI scripts or programs. Friends to the obsessively lazy, CGIs can accomplish with a single piece of code what would otherwise require hours of slaving over tags, and the endless process of updating content. Even the batch processing described earlier lacks something by comparison with dynamically-created HTML.

lister-pl is a perl CGI that Sebastian Hassinger, one of the authors of this book, developed as a proof-of-concept for the idea of dynamically-created FTP offerings in HTML. Instead of creating all the necessary pages in huge periodic sweeps, *lister-pl* gets a listing of the directory the user wishes to see and converts it into formatted HTML with valid links.

This instant conversion is accomplished by parsing the */bin/ls -l* output for each item's name and type. If a given item is a directory, its link is created in such a way that it points back at *lister-pl*. Since *lister* takes a command-line argument that is the path to the directory it will list, this may be accomplished as follows:

```
http://www.outer.net/cgi-bin/lister?path/to/your/directory
```

If an item is a file, the file suffix is matched to the appropriate icon GIF, and the entire thing is embedded in a link that can retrieve the file via FTP. (See Figure 28-4.)

To snazz things up a bit, after directory listings have been dealt with and the resulting links stored in an associative array (of Perl), a graphic and a title are delivered first to the user's browser. These are followed by a dump of the associative arrays, which results in icons, names, and links for all the files and directories present in the target directory appearing in the browser window. Finally, the footer information is sent to the browser, the CGI script exits, and the link from the server to the browser is severed.

Either type of FTP-to-HTML conversion (using FTP as a service, or MIME type to have HTML handle file transfer) is as subject to disaster as any other programmed behavior on a computer. With the batch processing method, things can get more dire — if something goes awry, it can affect your entire hierarchy of Web pages.

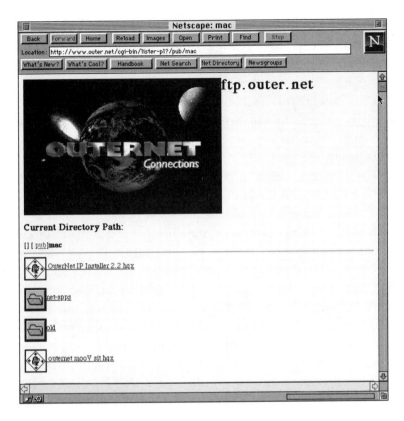

Figure 28-4
Lister-pl's output from the URL http://www.outer.net/cgi-bin/lister-pl.

If a CGI chokes and dies, at worst it's ruined a page of output being served to a single user. If it's a programming bug that's causing the malfunction, a single correction to the CGI makes every page it serves from then on perfect again. A buggy batch translating tool would necessitate rerunning the entire batch, in most cases.

It could be argued that reading a file off a drive taxes the CPU less than running an entire compiled program or, even worse, interpreting a script every time a user's browser issues a **GET** or a **POST**. On the other hand, clever programming and careful use of system calls and resources can result in a CGI that puts a minimum strain on your server for a major gain in features and functionality.

lister mutates

As a proof-of-concept, *lister-pl* suggests the possibility of more features than it actually implements. Since it uses the long version of the */bin/ls* UNIX system utility, it could conceivably use any of the information provided in that listing. This could include file sizes, the date last modified, and perhaps a flag as to whether the "anonymous" user has permission to touch each particular file and directory.

Additionally, the load balancing concept mentioned earlier could also be implemented. If a variety of hosts were available with the same file archive, a *lister*-like CGI could distribute the file links it created across all the hosts with as complex an algorithm as you wished to create.

Even more exciting, perhaps, is the idea that a CGI could produce file listings as sophisticated as those presented on OTS/Mac, but created on the fly rather than by hand. Here's how this could happen: if a package was placed in a directory of the same name as the package along with an HTML text file with all the pertinent information and any necessary graphics, the CGI could find and load all these elements *en masse*.

The same CGI program could then output them according to a preset layout, so that the graphic, abstract, and "Download" button would appear consistently across the entire site. Your abstract need not even be HTML to begin with, if your CGI is capable of interpreting and HTML-izing plain text on the fly.

File Index Searching

In addition to file listings and retrieval, of course, the Web has the capability to aid in the search of any number of FTP indices.

ARCHIE

The grandaddy of all Internet FTP databases, Archie resides on servers the world over, and has until recently been accessible only via Telnet, e-mail, or custom clients. Now, like every other aspect of the entire universe, Archie has a Web front-end, shown in Figure 28-5.

Archie's form interface is a good thing, as it is in almost any case where a graphic interface is applied to a command-line application. In graphical form, options are clear and readily available to the user. Other Archie servers and forms are linked to the page, as is further information about the Archie database and searching tips.

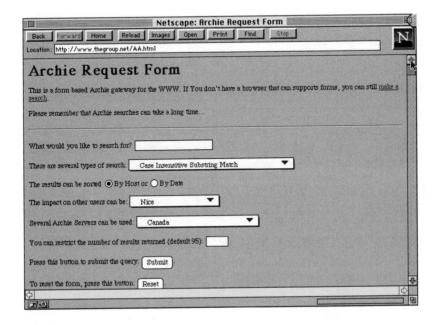

Figure 28-5
The Archie Web form can be found at http://www.thegroup.net/AA.html.

c|net: The Computer Network

The current contender for Archie's success is the Virtual Software Library (VSL), and its underlying search engine. This library indexes thousands of public domain and shareware programs available at over 20 so-called "front desks" for the library, scattered throughout the world.

VSL's main advantage over Archie is the flexibility of its searches, whic you allow you to search by platform type (DOS, Windows, Macintosh, UNIX, etc.) as well as by file names, descriptions, dates, and sizes. It is thus dependent on the file abstracts found at managed file archives such as SimTel, Info-Mac, CICA, and the like.

As you can see from Figure 28-6, the VSL search form provides numerous options for selecting files by keywords, file names, and other indexical features. It's quite a bit more focused and powerful than Archie, at the expense of its uncluttered elegance.

The VSL home page is at:

```
http://vsl.cnet.com
```

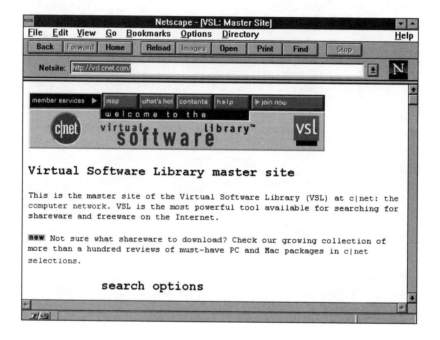

Figure 28-6
The Virtual Shareware Library search form.

LOCAL INDICES

The Info-Mac Hyperarchive includes a simple search of its own listings, and this is, in general, a good practice for Web-based file archives. A local search can be implemented in any number of ways, including participating in one of the large indexing efforts such as Archie, SHASE, or Harvest. Alternatively, you can run one of the site-indexing tools described in Chapter 20, or roll your own indexing and searching engines, if you have a small site or like a challenge.

Individual File Retrieval and Whatnots

In some instances, the number of files you may wish to serve will be much smaller and much more specialized than an entire FTP archive. If what you are developing is simply a tiny FTP site with a manageable number of files, then hand-formatted, custom browsing pages may be the right solution. However, if the files are in a different format than HTML on your server — PostScript or RTF, for example — you may want to investigate the possibility of converting on the fly.

Another instance where a CGI may be appropriate even for a small number of files occurs when you need a script to be executable, browseable, and retrievable. A script that displays the source of the script, instead of executing it, is at:

```
http://wsk.eit.com
```

This lets users examine scripts, as well as run them, and can be a powerful instructional tool. It can also save you lots of time answering the question: "How did you DO that?"

Attack of the Killer httpd Server

In its rampage through the herd of existing Internet services, HTTP proves itself time and time again one of the most powerful and certainly the most flexible of the protocols currently available. Gopher fell first, its traffic falling to nearly unmeasurable levels at a rate proportionate to the increase in popularity of Mosaic.

It seems to us that FTP might very well be next. To begin with, an older protocol hamstrings FTP, because it was written for long-bygone, low bandwidth days. But its arcane, complex command interface is what probably spells its doom: Today we expect graphical input, fast connections, customizable pages, and HTML. HTTP can deliver all of these, hence our cause for wondering how long FTP can hang on to dear life.

CHAPTER

29 Database Management Tools

*A*n organization's Database Management System (DBMS) can be dauntingly unapproachable as well as dizzyingly complex. A DBMS can erect a formidable obstacle for system administrators to include in their overall Web designs.

In most organizations, a typical DBMS houses inventory tracking, order entry, financial and accounting records, and perhaps sensitive personnel information. Such monstrous databases act like centers of gravity that pull in all sorts of extraneous data, with varying degrees of significance and usefulness.

The applications for DBMS-derived information will affect the entire organization and almost every constituency will have an opinion on what should or should not be included. Many individual groups will build and use their own custom set of programs to sift and sort their own particular segment of the overall data pool.

Large database engines usually come wrapped inside a standard access package, each with its own peculiar development environment and application programming interfaces (APIs). Oracle systems are probably the most common, with other standard flavors including DBMSs like Ingres, Unify, Sybase, RBase, and FileMaker Pro.

In previous chapters we've talked about using smaller, more agile engines to index Web-specific data. In this chapter, we will touch briefly upon what should be considered when the time comes to tie your mainframe (or at least, an organizational-level DBMS) to the Web.

WHAT MAKES ONE DATABASE UNLIKE ANOTHER?

Most Web applications use search and retrieval engines, rather than traditional DBMSs. The most prolific ones — like WAIS — are intended primarily for indexing large collections of documents or other data. A directory tree of documents is parsed into the word elements that comprise them; then a search engine finds the right document, providing it is given a query string that matches those word elements. Using a DBMS, all you really have is an advanced card catalog system without the associative logic or indexing capabilities that make WAIS so special.

Database Management Systems are based on a *sort and sift* model. Data elements are broken down into their component parts (fields) and given meaning in conjunction with other elements. The field customer_name means nothing to a WAIS index process, but as a lookup field in an Oracle database, it can yield a specific record by matching a query string to a field value (or set of such values). Further, by using a standard search language (such as SQL, Structured Query Language), all kinds of data manipulation become possible.

As the ease of interfacing with these DBMSs becomes easier and their prices drop, a corresponding increase in the demand for such services has occurred. This also makes DBMS interfaces more important and necessary. Web systems will ultimately provide simple, portable, and robust DBMS interfaces to excite significant development efforts. Today, alas, that technology is not ready.

In this chapter we will cover a design strategy for fitting relational databases into your organizational mold and into your Web environment. We will give you practical advice on where to begin with your infrastructure goals, how to steer them, and what tripwires you might encounter along the way. We understand the complexities inherent in this kind of configuration and hope to provide you with some attainable stepping stones for your journey.

Relational Databases Overview

Network programmers or system administrators (probably the bulk of the people reading this book) usually work for a Telecom group in most larger organizations. Being of the same mind, we authors know that the DBMS end of the IT world can be strikingly different from your own. You could even use the words *puzzling* or *frightening* without going too far over the edge. In this section, we'll take a few minutes to overview how relational databases work and the purposes they fulfill.

Databases store information mainly as a series of *tables* that are collected together into a logical, interrelated collection called a *database*. The best way to visualize a database is to imagine a spreadsheet program that knows what column titles mean and how they relate to one another.

In the example that follows, we use a simple table containing rows of Web server data to illustrate our point. We'll call it the SITE TABLE:

SITE_NO	WEB_MGR	DATE_UPD	SITE_NAME	IP_ADDR
20937	BRUNZWYK	11-11-94	zone.alpha.com	207.223.4.4
23463	GOMEZ	9-8-94	www.perly.com	199.98.15.74
92375	RICE	2-12-95	xray.zebra.com	202.19.123.2

In this example, the indexed field (a column that can be searched on quickly because that's how the records are ordered) is the SITE_NO column.

Each record in a relational database is considered a *row* and usually contains one data element for each field (*column*). There are several common types that you might use to specify what kind of data may be placed in each field (like number, string, or date).

Now suppose that you have another table called the WEB_MANAGER TABLE that looks like this:

WEB_MGR	MANAGER	HIRE_DATE	E_MAIL
BRUNZWYK	BRADY	3-13-93	brun@alpha.com
STEVENS	CLEAVER	4-4-94	stevens@basket.net
GOMEZ	PARTRIDGE	8-9-88	gomez@indigo.mail.net
RICE	CLEAVER	3-19-91	basmati@colored.zebra.com

The real functionality of a relational DBMS comes from the ability to look up information by joining the two tables where appropriate. By cross-referencing the Web Manager table with the site table, you can get from the IP address to the e-mail address.

Here is some SQL that would produce the desired results:

```
select mgr.E_MAIL from WEB_MANAGER mgr, SITE s where
((s.IP_ADDR='202.19.123.2') and (s.WEB_MGR=mgr.WEB_MGR));
```

Of course, real databases have much more extensive tables with a whole range of fields available for use. Thus, performing SQL queries would probably merit several lines of source code or even a whole SQL program that might take several hours to complete.

Why Connect a DBMS to the Web?

Because DBMSs house so much of what most organizations term *essential* data, it will become increasingly useful to intermix Web and database interaction in the future. For internal uses, a company could set up an HTTP server (it wouldn't even have to be connected to the Internet) that could allow them to serve their personnel database to the whole company. Order-entry people could check on product availability; production groups could use the Web server for large-scale, company-wide document management. The list of applications that the Web–database combination could serve is almost limitless.

Externally, an organization might publish product announcements to the Web. The corporate database might provide a link to the internal inventory and pricing system, allowing customers to check on their orders. Here again, almost anything you can dream of doing with the Web–database combination can be done (with enough time and money).

Another bonus that comes from using CGI programs to tie the Web to your database is that configuration and maintenance is generally very easy. By using a couple of well-engineered Perl scripts, you could handle the bulk of your CGI requirements for maintenance and upkeep quite easily.

Finally, consider the possibility of merging your internal and external networks — with the appropriate firewalls — so that you could hire a data-entry company from the other side of the globe. They could access your main database (no Net replication, long-distance fees, or mailing of *tar* tapes needed). And best of all, the interface is something they already know (the Web)!

Composing an Interface

The construction of a good interface that allows your users to get the best use out of your database is paramount to a good reception in the user community. With your DBMS already primed and configured for pumping out data using whatever system you've already constructed, you'll gain the benefit of making a superior Web interface.

Figure 29-1 is an edit screen from our customer account database, which is unfortunately not a popular SQL database, but rather a custom program designed and built in-house. Nevertheless, it illustrates the benefits of giving your users enough access to get their jobs done, but not so much that they are inundated by fields and buttons.

You'll notice that the account screen is a bit clumsy. As with so many systems, it was developed rapidly with only scant care for the overall framework. By thinking out what our data requirements would have been a month, a year, and two years down the road, we could have saved ourselves the extra programming effort that was spent in expanding and building the Web interface.

Create Your Own CGI

Now that you know what you can accomplish and the kinds of design cues you'll need, let's jump to the quest for appropriate CGIs that can interface your designs with an actual DBMS.

For this chapter, we searched high and low for any such CGIs and found only slim pickings. This reflects the Internet-centric nature of so many CGIs — which derives from the Web's origins and its most pressing initial programming tasks. Unfortunately, the Web has not yet inherited its rightful place as an interface for full-scale production systems. As the Internet and the production world come closer and closer to merging, the availability of CGIs for DBMSs should increase. At present, we found a good selection of Oracle CGIs, several Sybase CGIs, and a few stragglers that could be applied to any of the generic SQL systems.

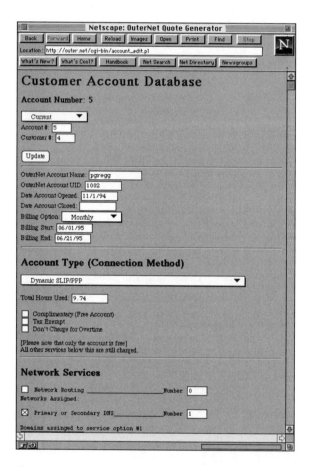

Figure 29-1
OuterNet's account edit screen.

To provide a simple example of what these CGIs could accomplish, we wrote a small Perl script that will run in tandem with an Oracle database on a UNIX operating system. Using the table information from the examples earlier in this chapter, we connected to a generic Oracle database (using the username/password of 'scott/tiger') and created two new tables (SITE and WEB_MANAGER). We then inserted the same data produced in the SITE and WEB_MANAGER tables into the database so that our form would retrieve results. Here's the Perl script:

```
#!/usr/local/bin/perl
#
#  /www/cgi-bin/ora_search.pl
#
#   A CGI test for accessing an Oracle DB
#   Author: Mike Erwin
#   e-mail: mikee@outer.net
#   Version: 1.0  -  6/23/95
#   Revision History:-- Very Simple-- Proof of Concept only.
#
#############################################################################
require "/www/cgi-bin/formlib.pl";

#   Various Startup Variables and whatnots
#############################################################################

$|                  = 1;
$datestr            = `date '+%m/%d/%y %H:%M:%S'`;    #
$timedate           = `date '+%H%M%S'`;
chop ($datestr);
chop ($timedate);

&GetFormArgs();          # parse arguments passed from FORM (now in %in)
$ENV{PATH_INFO} ne '' && &GetPathArgs($ENV{PATH_INFO});

$sSITE_NO                      =$in{sSITE_NO};
$sWEB_MGR                      =$in{sWEB_MGR};
$sDATE_UPD                     =$in{sDATE_UPD};
$sSITE_NAME                    =$in{sSITE_NAME};
$sIP_ADDR                      =$in{sIP_ADDR};

if ($sSITE_NO || $sWEB_MGR || $sDATE_UPD || $sSITE_NAME || $sIP_ADDR) {
      $use_site = 1;
}
$mWEB_MGR                      =$in{mWEB_MGR};
$mMANAGER                      =$in{mMANAGER};
$mHIRE_DATE                    =$in{mHIRE_DATE};
$mE_MAIL                       =$in{mE_MAIL};

if ($mWEB_MGR || $mMANAGER || $mHIRE_DATE || $mE_MAIL) {
      $use_mgr = 1;
}
$TMP_FILE                      ="/tmp/query.sql";
$SQL_APP                       ="/usr/oracle/bin/sqldba";

print STDOUT "Content-Type: text/html\n\n\n";

open(QUERY,"> $TMP_FILE");
print QUERY "connect scott/tiger;\n";
if ($use_site) {
    print QUERY "select * from SITE where ";
    if ($sSITE_NO) {
        print QUERY "SITE_NO='$sSITE_NO'";
```

For a "real" imple-mentation you'd pause the program for keyboard entry of the password here.

```
        }
        if ($sWEB_MGR) {
            print QUERY "WEB_MGR='$sWEB_MGR'";
            }
        if ($sDATE_UPD) {
            print QUERY "DATE_UPD=$sDATE_UPD";
        }
        if ($sSITE_NAME) {
            print QUERY "SITE_NAME=$sSITE_NAME";
        }
        if ($sIP_ADDR) {
            print QUERY "IP_ADDR=$sIP_ADDR";
        }
}
if ($use_mgr) {
print QUERY "select * from WEB_MANAGER where ";
        if ($mWEB_MGR) {
            print QUERY "WEB_MGR='$mWEB_MGR'";
        }
        if ($mMANAGER) {
            print QUERY "MANAGER='$mMANAGER'";
        }
        if ($mHIRE_DATE) {
            print QUERY "HIRE_DATE=$sDATE_UPD";
        }
        if ($mE_MAIL) {
            print QUERY "E_MAIL=$mE_MAIL";
        }
}

print QUERY ";\n";
close (QUERY);

print STDOUT "<h2>Query Result</h2><pre>";

$ENV{'PATH'} .= ":/usr/oracle/bin";
$ENV{'ORACLE_SID'} = "SAMP";
$ENV{'ORACLE_HOME'} = "/usr/oracle";

open (ORACLE,"$SQL_APP < $TMP_FILE |");
while(<ORACLE>) {
        print STDOUT "$_";
}
close (ORACLE);
print STDOUT "</pre>";
```

This little script is intended merely as a "proof of concept" and not much else. For a real implementation, it would need to handle multiple databases, updates, index fields, and a whole selection of other features.

This script only does one thing: it gets values for any of the fields that exist in the SITE or WEB_MANAGER tables and it performs an SQL 'select' on them by passing control off to the *sqldba* application. Results are not processed in any way and are returned to the query client almost unmodified. As you might imagine, the results could be parsed into other queries or formatted into a table or another Web form before being returned to the user.

The interface that lets Web browsers access the database is delivered from the following HTML code. The user's view of this code appears in Figure 29-2, right after the HTML listing. The results of hitting the "submit" button appear in Figure 29-3.

```
<HTML>
<HEAD>
<TITLE>Oracle Test DB Engine</TITLE>
</HEAD><BODY>
<h1>Test Web Database</h1><HR>
<FORM METHOD="POST" ACTION="http://sneech.austin.apple.com/
cgi-bin/ora_search.pl">
<H3>SITE Table</H3>
Site Number:            <INPUT TYPE="text" NAME="sSITE_NO" SIZE=10><BR>
Site Manager:           <INPUT TYPE="text" NAME="sWEB_MGR" SIZE=20><BR>
Date of Last Update:    <INPUT TYPE="text" NAME="sDATE_UPD" SIZE=20><BR>
Site Name:              <INPUT TYPE="text" NAME="sSITE_NAME" SIZE=40><BR>
Site Address:           <INPUT TYPE="text" NAME="sIP_ADDR" SIZE=16><P>
<H3>WEB_MANAGER Table</H3>
Site Manager:           <INPUT TYPE="text" NAME="mWEB_MGR" SIZE=20><BR>
Personnel Manager:      <INPUT TYPE="text" NAME="mMANAGER" SIZE=20><BR>
Hire Date:               <INPUT TYPE="text" NAME="mHIRE_DATE" SIZE=20><BR>
E-Mail Address:         <INPUT TYPE="text" NAME="mE_MAIL" SIZE=40><P>
<INPUT TYPE="submit" NAME="Search" VALUE="Search">
</BODY>
</HTML>
```

Let's explore how it operates. First, let's assume that the user is interested in finding all the site managers in the WEB_MANAGER table whose direct manager is **CLEAVER**. This result can be produced by typing the search string **CLEAVER** into the field that we wish to search. Figure 29-2 shows what we did.

As mentioned earlier, the results are returned to the user basically unmodified by the CGI, complete with the correct information as shown in Figure 29-3.

As you can see, improving upon this system would be an absolute necessity but its simplicity demonstrates *how* to ask a running Oracle database for some information. In your configuration of a Web–to–DBMS gateway, keep in mind that you will need to exercise a great deal of care in defining the different aspects of your system. It's also a certainty that a more robust script will be required.

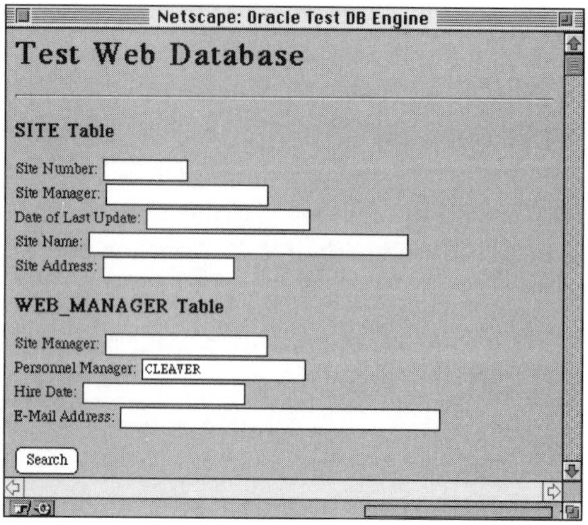

Figure 29-2
Web interface for the "ora_search.pl" CGI.

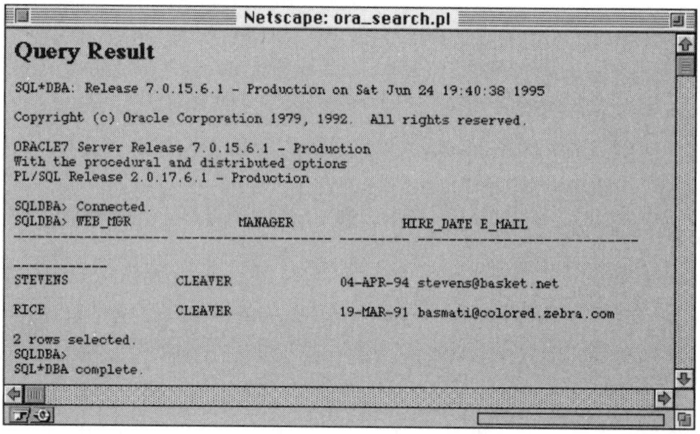

Figure 29-3
The results from running "ora_search.pl".

Consult the Oracle

Because the biggest selection of CGIs on the Net today communicate
with Oracle databases, we will explore some of the goodies we found

while surfing. First and foremost, the most up-to-date list of Oracle goodies can be found at Yahoo; here's the URL:

```
http://www.yahoo.com/Computers/World_Wide_Web/Databases_and_Searching/Oracle/
```

ORACLE WORLD WIDE WEB INTERFACE KIT

The most complete treatment of Oracle-related Web tools lives at the Oracle site. Oracle has done a great job of collecting and packaging all of the CGIs that interoperate with their databases. Oracle distributes these tools as a single package known as the "Oracle World Wide Web Interface Kit," located at

```
http://dozer.us.oracle.com:8080/
```

The packages that are included with the kit include the items listed in Table 29-1. Although Oracle has done a nice job of collecting and distributing these CGIs, please note that Oracle does not support them "officially."

Table 29-1

Packages Included with the Kit

Package	Description
WOW	"Web-Oracle-Web" — A tool for developing gateways using PL/SQL-stored programs. The WOW gateway acts as an RPC server so that the database may be accessed from any allowed node on the network.
Decoux	A set of three different gateways that are run as "OraPerl" scripts or Pro*C executables. Makes use of pseudo-HTML tags (<SQL>), which get replaced when the database returns data.
ORAYWWW	Another OraPerl example that is used to browse tables and return HTML output.
WORA	Another Pro*C CGI that is used only to extract table information without the capability of updating it. The interface model allows you to use checkboxes and selection lists as well as the standard text-input box.
TSS	A Meta Text Search System with the capability of browsing any type of data along with information that is stored in an Oracle database. It was designed as two daemon processes with the Oracle interface written in PL/SQL.

Most of the helper applications and gateways in the Interface Kit make use of the Oracle Pro*C Development Language that ships with Oracle 7. Pro*C is an ANSI standard embedded SQL parser that allows you to mix C code and SQL to produce binary code that knows how to interface with your Oracle database. If your copy of Oracle lacks Pro*C (as ours unfortunately does), you can make only limited use of these packages.

WHAT IS ORAPERL?

OraPerl is a Pro*C/Perl integration application that constructs a version of Perl capable of processing embedded SQL commands. Many of the CGIs that come with the Oracle Interface Kit listed in Table 29-1 require its use.

To build the *OraPerl* environment, you will need a source code tree for Perl that supports *Usersubs*, a C compiler (such as *gcc*), and the *OraPerl* distribution, which we had a hard time finding, but which *is* included on the CD that comes with this book. Currently the *OraPerl* package only operates with Oracle Databases, but there are other embedded SQL languages out there for engines like Informix or Sybase.

Sybase

As Oracle has done with its Interface Kit, Sybase has done with those CGI scripts that can interact with its database. You'll notice that many of the same tools that we've discussed have been reimplemented to accommodate a Sybase host. For a concise listing of the currently available Sybase CGIs, point your browser directly at Sybase:

```
http://www.sybase.com/WWW/
```

SYBPERL

sybperl is much like *OraPerl* in that it is a collection of extensions to Perl5 that supports database interaction using embedded SQL. Likewise, *sybperl* needs the same componentry as *OraPerl*: an ANSI C compiler,

Perl5 source code with Perl5 libraries, and the *sybperl* distribution. As you might expect, *sybperl* has been used by quite a few CGI designers and is required for most of the examples that they give. To get the software and the full skinny on *sybperl,* link to this site:

```
http://www.sybase.com:80/WWW/Sybperl/index.html
```

WEB/GENERA

Web/Genera is a software toolset that helps with the integration of Sybase Databases to WWW applications. It uses a high-level schema notation that controls both the interface to the Sybase data engine, as well as the HTML output that creates the desired interface. This CGI tool behaves much like GSQL (discussed next), in that there is an application program that manages both ends of the equation (WEB and DBMS), much like a traffic cop. For more information, please look at this page:

```
http://gdbdoc.gdb.org/letovsky/genera/genera.html
```

GSQL

Probably the most promising Web–to–DBMS technology to come along is the GSQL package, which makes no assumptions as to the kind of SQL DBMS you will use as a data pump. By requiring users of the GSQL system to write their own database interface, it separates out the Webification part of the process, leaving the actual SQL interface to another (more appropriate) application.

GSQL's real power comes from its capability to create HTML forms based on rules and commands found in "proc" files. Proc files contain a list of commands and interface designs that are then passed to the *gsql* application, which then return either an HTML page so that users may interact with the database, or (if there are arguments) passes them to the DBMS for processing. The same CGI application is used for both purposes and differentiates its action by the inclusion or lack of arguments.

The best place to learn about GSQL, including where to obtain the software or to sample some databases using GSQL, is at this URL:

```
http://www.ncsa.uiuc.edu/SDG/People/jason/pub/gsql/starthere.html
```

Summary

In our short tour of the DBMS world, we hope that we've supplied you with some good starting points to begin your journey toward integrating your information management systems and the World Wide Web. Although the tools we covered were *primordial* at best, we're hopeful that they represent the first steps toward what could be the Web's most effective use yet!

Audio-Video Capture and Real-Time Pages

Video

*I*n striving to build a world where everything is at your fingertips and all information is instantly accessible and easy to locate, we constantly push the limits of how much of our reality we can distribute across a computer network. By digitizing the world around us and then using devices to encode and deliver those bits of our "here and now" to another person's "there and now," we can work and play better together.

It has been a long-standing ambition for many Net explorers to be able to converse in real time with other people around the globe, to sample a concert that is playing in Sussex, England, or to offer someone the chance to interact with a piece of your local world. The Internet is a natural playground for such activities and has witnessed significant advancements in these areas in the past few years. Audio and video compression techniques have improved dramatically, and worldwide standardization of multimedia types makes it simpler to communicate across a variety of architectures and networks.

In this chapter, we'll explore some video and audio connection strategies used on the WWW and how some of their designers helped to develop a whole new world of networked multimedia.

In our video section, we start by showcasing some sites that offer a "point-and-shoot" camera connected to the Internet. We follow up with some more interactive sites that allow you to influence what you see, and close with a discussion of the move towards real-time full-motion video on the Net.

In the audio section, we address the use of sound in normal Web layouts, demonstrate some of the interactive sound pages like the "Blue Dog Can Count" page, and finish with a discussion of possible future uses for this emerging audio technology.

Finally, we wrap things up by investigating the potential benefits that networked audio-video transport can deliver. We will trace the path to see where these efforts might lead and touch briefly upon the dynamics of what multimedia services can provide to users.

REFRESHED IMAGES AT A CLICK AND A GLANCE

Our first foray into the video arena is to check out sites that offer up-to-the-minute pictures when you return a form. These sites typically have a camera connected to a computer with a CGI running that can capture a graphics file, convert it to a Net-suitable format, and then make it available to the requester.

Sometimes this process is set up as an automated job that occurs every 10 minutes or so to give users an *almost current* feel for what is going on at the server's location. More commonly, such cameras are configured to snap a picture when the user submits a form. In the sections that follow, you'll learn about some of the many sites that use video to illustrate their surroundings or capabilities.

Rear window — a view for the Net

By pointing a camera out the window, you can give the world a nice view of what your corner has to offer. Figure 30-1 shows a view of Cambridge, England, that gives you the choice of seven different buildings or areas on which to focus for a more detailed transmission. Interestingly enough, most of the links depicted bring you to that site's Web page or login prompt if accessed. Here's the URL for this location:

```
http://www.cam-orl.co.uk/cgi-bin/pangen
```

As you can see from comparing the system clock at the top of Figure 30-1 (11:06 PM) to the page that we retrieved at 4:52 PM on England's local time, the image is real-time, even if it's off by a few minutes. The large difference between our clocks is due to distance between GMT and CDT, our respective time zones.

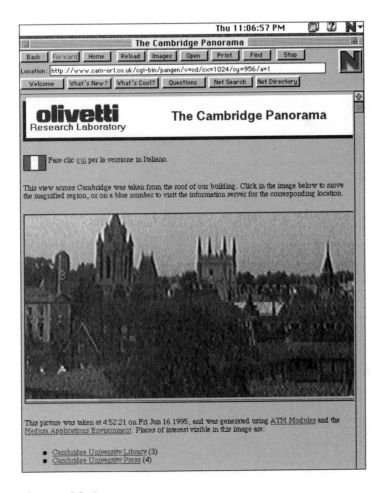

Figure 30-1
Out the window, a shot of the River Cam.

The Cambridge site uses an interface card (ATMos) in conjunction with a camera module, all made by Olivetti Research Laboratories and wired on an ATM network to deliver the graphics as compressed JPEGs to its Web server.

In Figure 30-2 we visit Stockholm, Sweden, for a moment. Please notice that this site in Stockholm has added a time, temperature, and a sun, and moon stamp to liven things up a bit. Here's the URL for this site:

```
http://www.ausys.se/weather/weather.exe?medium+eng
```

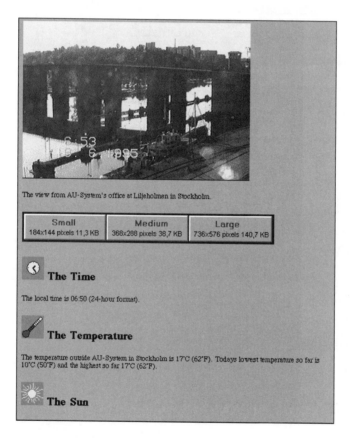

Figure 30-2

The Stockholm site adds more local information.

And Figure 30-3 is an image of what we got for two weeks running as we attempted to connect with one of the Net's most infamous sites, the "live iguana" page, at

```
http://iguana.images.com
```

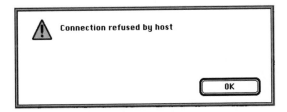

Figure 30-3
Busy sites are almost impossible to hit!

A site that lets visitors poke their metaphorical heads out into the local world has considerable curiosity value. This gives users a sense of the uniqueness (and distance) that the Internet usually masks so well. Although they're simple, these graphics point the way for future servers that will handle full-motion video communications in much the same way that we send e-mail messages today.

Some interactive sites offer more

In Japan, there's a Web site with a camera that allows you to not only view a real-time GIF picture, but also to download an MPEG movie of recent action (see Figure 30-4). As a picture is worth a thousand words, so is a movie worth a thousand pictures; sometimes, literally! Of course, there's a penalty to pay while waiting for the download to complete. The URL for this site is

```
http://match.sfc.keio.ac.jp/peephole.html
```

The movie we downloaded from Japan took about two minutes using a 14.4Kbps modem. The software used to run the video to online graphics conversion was written by Eto Kouichirou. It is basically a collection of Perl and shell scripts with some off-the-Internet utilities. (We weren't able to determine exactly what type of camera he was using, however.)

Web control, Robby-the-Robot style!

The controllable robot arm at the University of Western Australia, located in Perth, is probably the site that is the most complex and, consequently, the most fun. By giving you full control over a robotic arm for three minutes (sometimes longer), the Department of Mechanical Engineering lets you maneuver around a grid covered with rectangular blocks.

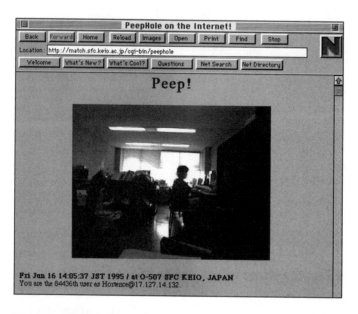

Figure 30-4
You'll find stills and movies at this site in Japan.

Using a Web form that asks for different movement vectors for the arm, your mission is to reposition the blocks on the table — remotely. You are given the two images from two different angles for orientation, along with six line-art drawings that plot the location of the blocks in relation to each other and to the robotic hand. This is shown in Figure 30-5.

Figure 30-6 depicts the legal form inputs, which in turn are passed to the robot to be executed. You have control over the position of the hand in three-dimensional space above the table, as well as the different orientations of the hand itself, described using the flying-terms pitch (front-to-back inclination) and yaw (side-to-side inclination).

To play with the Robot Arm, try linking to this site:

```
http://telerobot.mech.uwa.edu.au
```

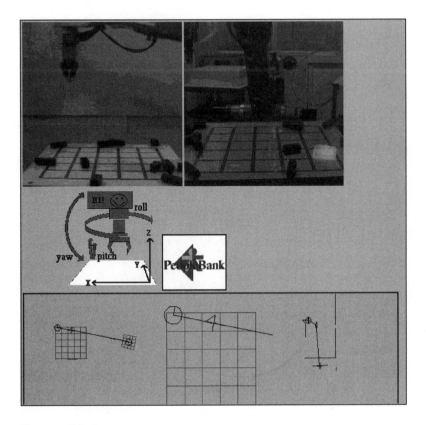

Figure 30-5

A view of the Robot Arm's landscape and blocks.

○ Change Image__ ○ Reset Robot__ ○ Open Gripper__ ○ Close Gripper__ □ Don't update 1st Camera.__ □ Don't update 2nd Camera.__ □ Don't show wire frame.

The origin is at bottom right of grid in 1st camera view and the grid squares are 100 millimetres. Angular position is in degrees. Enter values and submit or click on the wire frame.

◉ Move Relatively__ ○ Move Absolutely : X Increases Left: `0` Y Increases Away: `0` Z Increases Up: `0`

Roll: `0` Pitch: `0` Yaw: `0` [**Submit**] [**Clear**] The images above are 6982 and 10058 bytes respectively. Didn't move? Look in the log.

You have exclusive control while you use the robot within 3 minutes. You have been on since Fri Jun 16 14:19:51 1995 , it is now Fri Jun 16 14:26:55 1995 . Leave your comments or read the other comments.

Figure 30-6

The HTML form that controls the Robot Arm includes all the necessary positioning details.

REAL-TIME TRAFFIC WATCH

The benefits of using real-time graphics and video are best illustrated with a real-world example. Several up-to-the-minute traffic report pages can be found on the *yahoo* server, including the one from San Diego depicted in Figure 30-7.

Figure 30-7
The San Diego traffic scene.

This particular site covers much of the San Diego area and is a good illustration of the kinds of information that real-time systems can provide. Sure, it isn't world shattering, but it quickly conveys useful information (especially if you're a San Diego commuter).

As long as there's data readily available to drive such displays, this kind of service is ideally suited for Web implementations. To visit this site, or some of the other sites that the Department of Transportation for the State of California currently monitors and displays, point your favorite Web browser to

```
http://www.scubed.com:8001/caltrans/caltrans.html
```

CONSTANTLY REFRESHED PICTURES

As we move closer and closer to a system that allows real-time full-motion video transmission and reception, our next stop on this

is the *server push* and *client pull* directives of the new Netscape browser.

In the continuously refreshed BirdCam video sequence shown in Figure 30-8, you can see that this client/server relationship resembles that of an ongoing communications session. When connecting to most Web sites, your browser requests a page, gets all of its associated data and links, and then closes up shop. This creates only a single transitory connection.

As you sit at your workstation and stare at the Web information that's displayed on your screen, there's no client–to–server discussion going on in the background. As far as the software is concerned, you are done communicating until you select another hypertext link that might even take you to another site altogether.

The server push/client pull mechanism redefines this ordinary connection to handle a continuous stream of graphical data to be updated in as close to real time as the client's browser can manage. In this case, you'd see a series of images arriving on your screen until you selected another link, or until your machine freaked out and crashed (don't laugh — this happened to us a couple of times). In other words, the Netscape server directives offer a quick and dirty way to get real-time video running from your site.

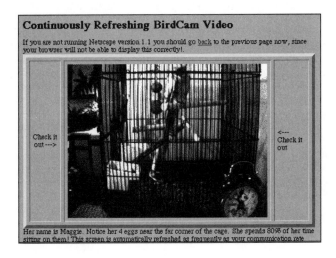

Figure 30-8
BirdCam from http://bizserve.com/ascott/cam.html.

The client pull directive, conversely, is not an open connection like the server push directive. In a client pull, the client is instructed when it should open a new connection and what to get when the connection is established. A more technical discussion of these topics can be found at the following URL:

```
http://bizserve.com/ascott/pushpull.html
```

Even though this is only an approximation of real video communications, it's still worth investigating, especially if your content requires regularly updated graphical displays.

REAL-TIME VIDEO

The real challenge for many Web developers is to offer MPEG movies on demand. Just as the tangible, up-to-the-minute feel of a real-time graphic is exciting to the viewer, more so is the ability to witness a short sequence of scenes. This is like going to the movies, except that the participants and action are true to life.

With the surge in development related to video on demand, we expect to see a world where movies can be purchased or viewed across the Internet from home; where live feeds from almost anywhere can be aggregated into a global participatory conference; and where the current craze for role-playing games will offer its devotees a more realistic experience. In the sections that follow, we'll profile some sites that are moving in this direction.

FallsCam at Niagara Falls

One of the better sites that allows Web users to download a movie is the Niagara Falls video-capture site. Found at the following URL, we downloaded a nice, 2-minute picture of the waterfall in action from a perch high above the action, with good image quality:

```
http://fallscam.niagara.com
```

SOME IMPLEMENTATION EXAMPLES

To set up an automated video server quickly and easily, several solutions for the Macintosh are readily available. One of the best ones is the publicly available *save-25-cents* CGI written by Eric Lease Morgan. Its requirements include a Macintosh computer, a video input device like a Connectix QuickCam or a video camera connected to the Mac via an A/V card, AppleScript, PhotoCapture version 1.1, the Clip2gif software, the save-25-cents CGI, and the MacHTTP server software (or WebStar).

The only real configuration involved is telling the CGI where to look for saved files, where to log things, and where to put the files that it converts. Other than that, turning this script on is a real breeze. We're convinced you'll be satisfied with the results. Here's a URL for the site that explains this software in greater detail and that can deliver the necessary CGI:

```
http://www.lib.ncsu.edu/staff/morgan/save-25-cents-cgi.html
```

Another good Macintosh AppleScript CGI for automatic picture generation is the *FrameServer* CGI. It was programmed by Roel Vertegaal at the University of the Netherlands. This software is just as simple to install as the save-25-cents version above; you'll find it at the following site:

```
http://mirror.apple.com/mirrors/Info-Mac.Archive/comm/tcp/frame-server.hqx
```

Finally, there's also a good home page you can visit that contains a third CGI, as well as a nice description of the author's trials and tribulations in setting up his server to snap a picture of whatever TV show he's watching:

```
http://www.csua.berkeley.edu/~milesm/how.html
```

THE FUTURE OF NET VIDEO

In the section that follows we'll examine some programming tools that should help to extend the video capabilities of the World Wide Web.

Anyone need a cup of joe?

Where is all this leading, you might ask. We think it's leading to a world of interactive video, combined with elements of virtual reality, sprinkled with a controlling language somewhat akin to HTML but more suited for the manipulation of video and audio objects.

Imagine sitting down at a friend's computer, putting on some Net goggles and a glove, and navigating back to your office for some data, all with real-world-like objects that you can control by virtual manipulation. To check on your infant daughter back at home, you could open a video feed from her room and sneak a peek at her napping. There are countless opportunities for implementation using these kinds of components, the beginnings of which are already in development.

To help extend HTTP to better handle such requirements, Sun Microsystems has developed a new object-oriented programming language called Java. Java is an interpreted language, much like PostScript or Perl, that allows the developer to quickly create, debug, test, release, and maintain the source code, and it can also be compiled.

Java's other strengths include its portability, which strongly resembles HTML's, and its speedy execution. Multithreaded, highly secure, and object-oriented architectures give Java the structure and representational abilities to service real-time audio and video needs. For a proof of concept, a tour of the HotJava facility, and a quick history lesson in its origins, follow the primary link to

```
http://java.sun.com
```

Virtual worlds await

For our final stop in the wide world of Web video, we'll visit the home page for the *Virtual Reality Modeling Language*, more commonly known as VRML, where we find its developers hard at work creating a language capable of sending full Virtual Reality from machine to machine in the form of marked-up text with inserted graphics (like HTML).

With practical applications in cartography, architecture, and interior design (to name just a few), as well as a whole array of interactive games, Virtual Reality is no longer a dream of the few but a mission for the many. Legions of engineers and would-be users have been constantly advancing the science (or art) of VR to a point where VR is looming as a real Internet possibility in the near term. We look forward to seeing what it has to offer in the next few years; it is bound to be both exciting and illuminating.

The best place to start learning about current VR work and about what's being planned is at the following Web site:

```
http://www.yahoo.com/Entertainment/Virtual_Reality/Virtual_Reality_Modeling_
Language__VRML_/
```

Audio

Just as video can enhance users' experiences in navigating the Web, so can sounds. Used in different capacities and for different reasons, both video and audio are similar in that they both record a "stitch in time" for later reuse. Consequently, real-time delivery is a concern that both of these information media share.

INTERACTIVE SOUND SITES

The Computer Science Club at the University of Waterloo has developed an interesting Net microphone using a PC running Linux with a Gravis UltraSound card. Several Perl scripts written in conjunction with the VoxWare sound utilities allow WWW users to record sounds. Here's the URL:

```
http://csclub.uwaterloo.ca/gadgets.html
```

On the more interactive side of things, the "Blue Dog Can Count" form page allows users to enter two numbers and select a mathematical operation: addition, multiplication, or division. When that form is submitted, the CGI encodes a sound file containing the right number of "barks" for Blue Dog's answer. We know it's kind of silly, but this page (shown in Figure 30-9) does a good job of demonstrating that almost anything is possible with a little hard work. Here's where to go to hear from Blue Dog:

```
http://kao.ini.cmu.edu:5550/bdf.html
```

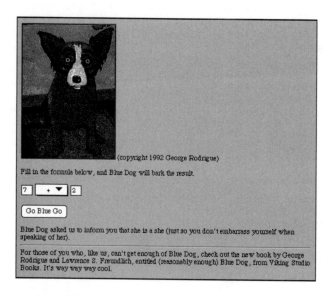

(copyright 1992 George Rodrigue)

Fill in the formula below, and Blue Dog will bark the result.

7 + ▼ 2

Go Blue Go

Blue Dog asked us to inform you that she is a she (just so you don't embarrass yourself when speaking of her).

For those of you who, like us, can't get enough of Blue Dog, check out the new book by George Rodrigue and Lawrence S. Freundlich, entitled (reasonably enough) Blue Dog, from Viking Studio Books. It's way way way cool.

Figure 30-9
The Blue Dog Can Count page in action.

EXTERNAL APPS

Until there is a common standard for the transmission of sound across the WWW (right now there are about five commonly used formats), sound applications will remain the provenance of external helper applications. Within the next few years, we expect to see a movement to integrate a single sound format directly into browser software that all platforms will support. Until this happens, users will be forced to use external applications.

We'll look at two such programs: RealAudio by Progressive Networks and NetPhone by the Electric Magic Company.

RealAudio

The RealAudio system involves both server and client pieces to help manage and distribute large audio files across the Internet. Currently, RealAudio's server software runs on a Windows NT server as well as on standard UNIX platforms. This software complies with the HTTP logs format and is capable of handling proxy server situations, where security is an overriding concern.

The RealAudio player is designed to work with popular stock Web browsers and offers complete control over the audio stream, including functions like rewind, fast forward, and pause. The information we downloaded suggests that using the client-end software resembles using a tape recorder, making the interface both simple and familiar. The client software can even be configured to handle WWW bookmarks, to give users direct access to RealAudio server sites.

To get more information, connect to the RealAudio site at

```
http://www.realaudio.com
```

NetPhone

Although it only supports the Apple Macintosh at this time, Electric Magic, the maker of NetPhone, promises it will soon interoperate with the ubiquitous CU-SeeMe interactive video software (covered in the next section) for connections to those with PCs or UNIX machines as well.

NetPhone is possibly the only application that delivers full duplex transport to users. This means all parties talking can listen and speak at the same time, much like using a real telephone. NetPhone supports multiple connections, includes WWW interface support, and supplies an address book for contacting other call recipients.

NetPhone's most interesting feature is its notion of a "NetPub" a public chat area where users can mingle or use the area as a jump point or a meeting place for multiparty interaction. NetPubs may turn out to be public discussion arenas, much like USENET, or what Internet Relay Chat (IRC) provides today. We are sure that this field will blossom quickly and provide users with many potential benefits.

To get the latest information from Electric Magic, connect to its Web site:

```
http://www.emagic.com/netphone/mainblurb.html
```

AV: Together at Last

AV is shorthand for audio-video, and it describes the kind of multimedia support that most users want — namely, synchronized pictures and sound — to provide the most realistic two-dimensional approximation of real life possible on the Internet. In the subsection that follows, we'll cover the most popular interactive video format on the Net today — CU-SeeMe (pronounced "See You, See Me").

CU-SeeMe

White Pine Software and Cornell University are the joint authors of CU-SeeMe, the outstanding audio-video conferencing utility. Although CU-SeeMe does not directly interconnect with either a Web server or a Web client, this capability shouldn't be too hard to implement. Therefore, we're confident that Web access to this software will soon be possible.

CU-SeeMe consists of a client-side application that runs on either a Windows machine or a Macintosh. It utilizes TCP/IP for transport to connect to a server-like application called a *reflector*. Reflectors provide a common meeting ground for potential conferencers and allow participants to communicate simultaneously.

CU-SeeMe's method for broadcasting multimedia has been developed with low-bandwidth connections in mind (like 28.8 modems) and performs decently across them. CU-SeeMe supports most common computers and low-cost video equipment and is also easy to configure and operate.

Desktop video-conferencing is sure to become a booming industry in the next few years as network speeds increase and home access points to the Internet proliferate. Likewise, planned bandwidth enhancements — like ISDN — should improve overall behavior and support more realistic frame rates. White Pine distributes an excellent demo version of its software that shows the product in action.

To read more about CU-SeeMe, point your browser to the White Pine site:

```
http://www.wpine.com/cuseeme.html
```

Summary

In this chapter, we have only scratched the surface of the booming multimedia capabilities in the offing for CGI programmers. We've explored some sites that support video or audio, and some that make use of both. By implementing a server that delivers access to multimedia applications, you can create a unique and helpful system that users will appreciate.

To close, here's a list of some other good repositories of audio-video Web sites that we think you'll find worth visiting:

```
http://www-cgi.cs.cmu.edu/afs/cs.cmu.edu/user/bsy/www/iam.html
http://www.evo.net/video/
http://www.yahoo.com/Computers/Internet/Interesting_Devices_Connected_to_the_Net/
```

CHAPTER

31 Electronic Mail Gateways

The Proto-Web

*I*n the days before the World Wide Web was born and before Gopher came along, the only services available on the Internet were Telnet, FTP, USENET news, and e-mail. Of these, e-mail was the only platform that hinted at the Internet's true potential. Telnet, FTP, and USENET were really like the "big brothers" of capabilities that were also available on local Bulletin Board Services.

It's true that on the Internet you could telnet to a site in Norway as easily (and cheaply) as you could to one in your home town, but in neither case would your activities exhibit any of the characteristics that define the WWW. And e-mail has always been pretty much a pure text environment, so it has never had the same cachet as the Web. But only e-mail was (and is) as asynchronous, user-driven, customizable, and decentralized as the Web would later become.

Those services that used e-mail for information delivery, like Archie, ftp-by-mail, list servers, and others, displayed these characteristics in the following ways:

- They were asynchronous — your "session" could stop and start repeatedly and could stretch over days or weeks.
- They were user-driven — they waited for users to make requests or issue commands before acting.
- They were customizable — the interface within an e-mail container was entirely up to the designer, which indeed led to unique and recognizable interfaces for these services.

- They were decentralized — a service's command interpreter could reside on one machine, its data files on another, administration on yet another, and all this was invisible to the users.

Now that the Web has arrived and taken these features to a new level, it seems fitting that e-mail should maintain a strong presence on Web pages. Many CGIs exist solely to tie the flash of HTML to the steadfast utility and dependability of e-mail.

E-mail appears on the Web in several different forms. Its simplest application is usually a basic form-based mail interface that provides a conduit for feedback from users to a site's owner or WebMaster. At the other end of the scale, you'll find Web-based interfaces that can simplify the use of the most popular mailing list servers. In between, you'll find scripts to view mailboxes via HTML or to manage, search, or display mailing list archives on the Web, or even to "spoof" Internet e-mail! In this chapter, we'll take a look at all of them.

Have Your CGI Mail My CGI

Every major platform that supports HTTP offers at least one CGI to take forms input and mail it to a designated recipient. E-mail is not only a launching point for CGI development, it's also a useful function to include on your pages.

Besides, e-mail can make it simple to perform any of the following information-gathering tasks:

- Collect feedback on your Web offerings.
- Field requests for more information or technical help.
- Register users and collect profile or contact information.

In fact, this list could go on and on; these are just a few of the potential uses of mail from the Web.

The simplest Web-based e-mail implementation could be a form with fields for a user's name and return e-mail address, along with a text area to type in a message. When submitted, the CGI script specified in the

ACTION tag would extract this information and place it into a mail message. This is such a simple task that it could easily serve as a CGI anatomy lesson.

We'll write such a CGI from scratch, assuming a UNIX platform running *sendmail* and *perl,* and the availability of Brigitte Jellinek's "formlib.pl":

```
#!/usr/local/bin/perl
# the above is the standard 'magic' to inform the shell to feed this
# file to the program named after the bang.
#
# simple CGI to intercept a form and mail the contents to the page's
# owner
#
# HTML4dummies Comment remailer
# 6/5/95 - singe@outer.net
# called by /html4dum/comment.html
#
require "/www/cgi-bin/formlib.pl";
                        # this executes the perl library script,
                        # making the subroutines contained therein
                        # available to our script.

$| = 1;                 # output NOT buffered - this prevents perl
                        # from buffering the script's output to STDOUT
                        # from being buffered -- since STDOUT is our
                        # conduit back to the user's browser, we want
                        # to ensure that our data gets out as we
                        # create it. If the connection goes away while
                        # we still have data in memory, the user will
                        # never see it.

&GetFormArgs();         # parse FORM arguments (now in %in)

$ENV{PATH_INFO} ne '' && &GetPathArgs($ENV{PATH_INFO});
                        # the existence of the PATH_INFO environment
                        # variable and the successful parsing of the
                        # information contained within are the tests
                        # that prove the CGI was called properly from
                        # a form

# both the preceding lines of code use sub-routines supplied in
# Brigette Jellinek's excellent formlib.pl - a library of tools for
# parsing form data into usable variables (see Chapter 15 for more
# info).

chop ($date = `/bin/date`);
                        # set the variable $date to the output of the
                        # UNIX program 'date', chopping the trailing
                        # carriage return from the result
```

```
print "Content-Type: text/html\n\n";
                        # set the return document's MIME type

# [output page's title, header info, etc.]

open (COMMENT,"| /usr/bin/mailx -s \"HTML4DUM Comments: $in{subject}\"
html4dum" );
# open filehandle which is a pipe to the UNIX mailx program, setting # the
mail's subject and recipient

print COMMENT "$date:";
print COMMENT "Comments from: $in{name}\t($in{from})\n";
print COMMENT "\n$in{body}";
print COMMENT "\n================================================================
========\n\n";
close (COMMENT);

# print date and explanatory infomation, and user's input to the
# mail filehandle, closing it when done to ensure delivery.

print STDOUT "<H1>Thank you for your comments!</H1><P>",
             "You have submitted the following comments:<P>",
             "<HR><PRE>$in{body}</PRE><P>";

print STDOUT "<B>If you have purchased the book <I>HTML for
 Dummies</I> you can",
"<A HREF = \"registrn.html\"> register on-line!</A></B><P>",
"<ADDRESS>Sample form CGI by singe@outer.net<P>$date</ADDRESS>";

# finish off with the footer info
```

The preceding program is somewhat inflexible, however. While it could be called by any number of forms, assuming they contained fields with the same names, it would mail the data to the same person every time. Any extra data submitted by the form would be lost, and the subject of the mail message would be identical every time.

PROPRIETARY TAGGING

A solution to this is presented in the MAILTO tag that is part of the Netscape extensions to HTML 2.0. Such a tag is written in the form

```
<A HREF="MAILTO:biff@outer.net">I'm lonely!</A>
```

Clicking on it opens Netscape's built-in mailer, which offers subject header and message boxes that may be completed by the user and then sent. Netscape handles its own SMTP negotiation, so the message gets passed directly from the Web browser to a mail daemon without requiring a CGI's intervention.

This approach is easy, clean, and economical, but it does have some significant drawbacks. Netscape's built-in mailer is not customizable in the least, whereas a form page can contain whatever you want, formatted however you want it. The built-in mailer cannot specify a subject line to ease filtering for the mail's recipient.

You cannot add additional forms input, like *radio buttons* or *selects* to the mailer. Most important, as with any of the other Netscape extensions, other browsers will not be able to interpret a MAILTO tag, and consequently will not be able to create mail.

BUILDING A BETTER MAIL HANDLER

Taking the straightforward Perl script that we just presented and making it universally customizable was Doug Stevenson's aim when he first set out to write his WWW Mail Gateway script. This resulted in a tool that provides many of the same advantages of the Netscape MAILTO tag, with none of the drawbacks.

Stevenson's script can be implemented on any Web browser that supports the GET method of form action, which is to say, on *any* graphical Web browser. It can be called from any number of forms, with a different recipient's address and subject line specified for each instantiation. It can handle any amount of additional data from the submitting form. It is impressively easy to install and implement, and therefore we recommend it highly.

Also written in Perl, Doug's script, named "mailto.pl", allows you to specify the following variables from the form that calls "mailto.pl":

- **to:** the recipient of the mail.
- **cc:** specifies carbon copy addresses for the outgoing mail message.
- **from:** who the mail should appear as being from. If not specified, it is created using the CGI variables REMOTE_IDENT and REMOTE_HOST to guess at a mail address. If the browser submitting the form is Netscape, the REMOTE_USER variable is used instead. A manually specified address supersedes these methods.

- **sub:** default subject for the message.
- **body:** supplies a default body text for the message.
- **nexturl:** once the mail has been sent, the script will redirect the user to the URL specified by this variable. If undefined, they will get a generic "mail sent" message.

Installing and Using mailto.pl

In order to use *mailto.pl* at your own site, simply place the Perl script in your "cgi-bin" directory and open it with a text editor like *vi* or *pico*. Only two variables need to be set for *mailto.pl* to work, with a few additional options to consider.

You must set the variable named '$sendmail' to the full pathname for your sendmail executable, which is usually either "/usr/lib/sendmail" or "/etc/sendmail". Next, you must set the variable named '$script_http' to the URL for the *mailto.pl* script itself.

Of *mailto.pl's* many optional features, the most useful is enabling logging for *mailto.pl* activities. This is specified by setting the value of the '$logging' variable to '1', and by specifying a file that "mailto.pl" can write to as the value for the variable named '$logfile'.

The final step is to save the edited copy of "mailto.pl" and change its permissions to allow universal execution. Once this is completed, the CGI script can be called from a simple link. The GET method passes variables to the script — in other words, it dumps variable names and values onto the command line for the script to interpret. Here's an example where the recipient's address is *biffo@outer.net* and the subject (See Figure 31-1) line is "Test of Mailto.pl CGI":

```
<A HREF="http://www.outer.net/cgi-bin/
mailto.pl?to=biffo@outer.net&sub=Test+of+Mailto.pl+CGI">Mail me!</A>
```

Note that variable/value pairs are separated by ampersands and that spaces are replaced by plus signs — in other words, standard URL encoding is used. If you wish to specify a static message body, you would simply add a "body=message" variable/value pair to the link. The message would be constrained by the standard GET limitations, mainly the maximum length command line that the shell will accept. (This is covered in detail in Chapter 8.)

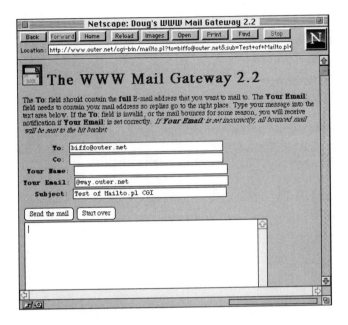

Figure 31-1

mailto.pl's *mail input form.*

The page returned from this link consists of a fill-in form with the "To:" and "Subject:" headers filled in as specified. Users may then enter the body of the message themselves and, when submitted, *mailto.pl* will rigorously error-check their input.

The final noteworthy aspect of *mailto.pl* is its ability to present a limited set of addresses to which the user may send mail. This set is defined as an associative array within the script or externally from a text file, and choices are placed in a *select* widget on the input form. Also, actual e-mail addresses may be hidden and users given a choice of a range of "real names" rather than addresses.

mailto.pl is capable of meeting the needs of almost any situation where e-mail must be sent, including support for mailing list subscriptions.

TOO COMPLEX? E-MAIL GETS SIMPLER

If the feature set of *mailto.pl* is more than you had in mind for your CGIs, you might consider *email,* a CGI written in C by Thomas Boutell.

Instead of the customizable form interface provided by a link to *mailto.pl*, *email* passes your data to "/bin/mail", which simply mails it to the designated user.

Compiling *email* is simple. The only configuration you'll need to do is to change the line in "email.c" that reads

```
#define EMAIL_CONF_PATH "/home/www/email.conf"
```

to reflect the path where you want *email*'s configuration file to reside. This configuration file simply contains the addresses of the people who should receive mail from *email*, followed by the URL of the page you wish the user to be presented with after sending the mail.

Thus, if *email* is called to send mail to *biffo@outer.net* and that address does not exist in the configuration file, the mail will be rejected. If it is present in the file, the data will be passed to "/bin/mail" and from there mailed to *biffo@outer.net*. After the mail is accepted, the user is informed that the message has been sent, and is presented with a link to the URL that follows the address in the configuration file.

In order to use *email* on the Web, simply create a form like the following:

```
<FORM METHOD="POST" ACTION="http://www.outer.net/cgi-bin/email.cgi">
Your Name: <INPUT NAME="name"><P>
Your Email Address: <INPUT NAME="email"><P>
<INPUT NAME="subject">Subject<P>
<INPUT NAME="recipient" VALUE="singe" TYPE="hidden">
<P>Text:<P>
<TEXTAREA NAME="content" ROWS=10 COLS=60></TEXTAREA> <P>
Click <INPUT TYPE="submit" VALUE="submit"> to submit your
message. Click <INPUT TYPE="reset" VALUE="reset"> to clear
your message and start over.
</FORM>
```

The 'name' and 'email' fields are error-checked, and the mail will be rejected if they are left blank. The 'recipient' field is of type "hidden" and is therefore not visible to the user. It is this field that determines who will receive the mail. Finally, the 'content' field contains the body of the message.

If your needs are simple, or if you want a small form integrated into a larger, preexisting form, *email* should suit your needs perfectly.

NEXT VERSE, SAME AS THE FIRST (ON MACOS)

For those of you running a Macintosh-based HTTP server, there is a CGI available that does much the same thing as *email*, called *email.cgi*. Since it's Mac-based, it is written in AppleScript and must reside in the MacHTTP or WebSTAR folder.

Written by Eric Lease Morgan at NCSU, *email.cgi* is meant as an alternative to the MAILTO tag, like the other packages discussed here. Its implementation is quite simple: in addition to MacHTTP or WebSTAR, you will also need to install AppleScript and the following OSAX (scripting extensions): "Tokenize", "Decode URL", and "TCP Scripting Additions version 1.1.2".

In your HTML document, simply create a form that matches this example:

```
<FORM METHOD="POST" ACTION="http://machttp.outer.net/email.cgi">

<INPUT TYPE="hidden" NAME="recipient" VALUE="biffo@outer.net">
<INPUT TYPE="hidden" NAME="mailer" VALUE="mail.outer.net">

Your Name:<INPUT TYPE="text" NAME="user" SIZE="40" MAXLENGTH="40"><P>

Your E-Mail adddress:<INPUT TYPE="text" NAME="address" SIZE="40"
MAXLENGTH="40"><P>

Subject:<INPUT TYPE="text" NAME="subject" SIZE="40" MAXLENGTH="40"><P>

<TEXTAREA NAME="message" ROWS=6 COLS=40></TEXTAREA><P>
<INPUT TYPE="Submit" VALUE="Send the message"> <INPUT TYPE="reset" VALUE="Reset">
</FORM>
```

Once again, the text input fields match up to variables used internally in *email.cgi*. Specifically, 'user' is the sender's name, 'address' is the e-mail address, and 'message' is the body of the mail. The two hidden fields, 'recipient' and 'mailer', are used to address the mail and to set the relay host — a machine running an SMTP mailer that can forward the message to the recipient.

Mailing List Interface

E-mail makes for a messy user experience. Address formats vary from one system to another, signatures clutter the message with noise, and even if all else is equal, any two people will have different ways of typing a message. This environment makes any attempts to send commands back and forth through mail unreliable.

Inconsistency is a problem for all mailing list software. Almost everyone who has used mailing lists has experienced their misinterpreted commands and their endless help files. The Web can offer a controlled interface for reliably collecting data.

A package that implements a full suite of commands from a large variety of mailing list servers is *mailserv*, which is yet another sterling Perl CGI script. It's quite elegantly written and fully documented online, and currently supports *listprocessor, listserv, majordomo,* and manually administered lists. Other unsupported mailing list servers can be added using *mailserv's* extensible ".cf" file format.

For each mailing list, *mailserv* presents a simple text input and radio button interface (shown in Figure 31-2). The user's e-mail address is specified and then the user chooses as many of the available commands he or she desires and submits the form when done. These commands are submitted to the server, which executes them and sends the results back to the user.

Installing *mailserv* is simple: unpack the archive in the "/cgi-bin" directory or a subdirectory under "/cgi-bin". For each mailing list server you wish to support with *mailserv*, create a soft link from the script to the name of the server; i.e., for *listproc* type:

```
ln -s mailserv listproc
```

From there on, it's simply a matter of setting the owner's address and the location of *mailserv* and its support files, and the script is ready to run.

The actual features offered by *mailserv* will vary, depending on the mailing list package you serve with it. At the very least, all the supported systems have *subscribe* and *unsubscribe* commands. Depending on the sophistication of the software, other commands will list other mailing lists hosted on the same server, tell who is on a particular list, and retrieve archive listings and individual items from the archives. In all cases, the mailing list server responds to your request as though you had submitted it via e-mail — that is, with a piece of e-mail of its own, sent to your mailbox.

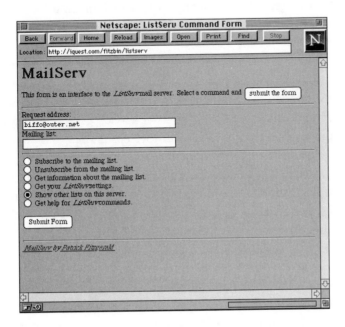

Figure 31-2

mailserv's interface for the listproc mailing list server.

This last point also describes the major drawback presented by *mailserv*. On the one hand, it's wonderful to be presented with a menu of commands for the server and to know that your choices will be accepted by the server with virtually no margin for error. On the other hand, if the response you receive requires you to follow up with a further dialog with the mailing list server, *mailserv* is no longer there to help. Any further commands to the mailing list server must travel via e-mail, with all the inherent difficulties this can entail.

This weakness is particularly evident when dealing with searching and retrieving files from the mailing list's archives. In that case, it is not surprising that there are other packages available to ease and automate these types of procedures.

Search and Retrieval

It is not unusual for the participants of a mailing list to believe that their communications deserve some measure of immortality, and *list archives* exist for that reason. As a living history of a mailing list, the archive can prove to be an invaluable aid to anyone interested in the list's topic or focus.

Even so, searching an archive and retrieving the relevant portions can be a challenge. There are a few CGI-based packages designed to ease this process. As with everything else we've discussed thus far, slapping a Web front-end onto an existing Internet service goes a long way to making it more usable, even for relative novices.

One such package is Eric Lease Morgan's *ListwebberII* (see Figure 31-3). Written in Perl, *ListwebberII* can ease the pain of searching for and retrieving files from mailing lists. It supports both UNIX and VMS-based *listproc* and *listserv* lists, which make up a large portion of the public mailing lists on the Internet. In fact, *listserv* was the original mailing list program, the first popular large-scale server to serve lists off VAXen on the BITNET network.

Popular though it may be, the original syntax for searching and retrieving that was carried out by the UNIX adaptation of *listserv (listproc)* is not pretty. It requires that you not only specify a search string but also that you name the archive you wish to search. *Listwebber II* simplifies this with a selection of the lists that it serves, and a single input field for the desired search string.

ListwebberII also collects your real name and e-mail address so that once your query has been submitted, the servers' responses may be sent directly to your mailbox (see Figure 31-4). A particularly nice feature of *ListwebberII* is the response page to a user's query. It recaps the servers queried and the query string, and explains the time frame in which to expect responses.

This is helpful, since a dedicated Web surfer needs to be reminded that a gateway to an e-mail-based system does not offer the instant gratification available from an entirely Web-based service.

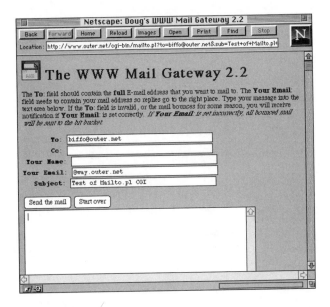

Figure 31-3

Listwebber II's query form interface.

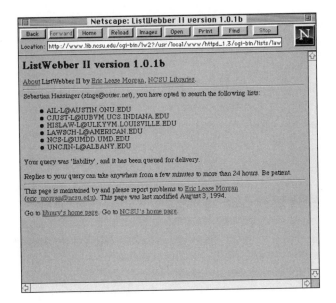

Figure 31-4:

A typical Listwebber II reply page.

When the response *does* come, *ListwebberII* can help the user yet again. A typical e-mail response looks like this:

```
Date:        Sat, 10 Jun 1995 12:55:52 -0400
From: "L-Soft list server at ALBNYVM1 (1.8b)"
<LISTSERV@UACSC2.ALBANY.EDU>
Subject:       File: "DATABASE OUTPUT"
To: singe@outer.net

> S liability in UNCJIN-L
--> Database UNCJIN-L, 17 hits.

> I
Item #   Date    Time   Recs   Subject
------   ----    ----   ----   -------
000058 94/01/06 11:49    40    Hal on racism and white-collar crime
000353 94/01/29 12:51   200    Hal on media, crime, and search and seizure--3+
ss+
000467 94/02/17 21:05    73    SRCL CONFERENCE, Corporation and Criminal Law,
Dec+
000480 94/02/20 14:24    24    pardon my 3rd (short!) post of the day on Phil
Jen+
000505 94/02/22 12:14   217    Hal P.: getting specific about evidence of
satanic+
000510 94/02/22 19:31    46    Re: Hal P.: getting specific about evidence of
sat+
000670 94/03/24 10:51   221    law and politics book review
```

Armed with this data, you could go back to the *ListwebberII* form and click on the 'retrieve' radio button. Next you would select the same server that sent the response, in this case "UNCJIN-L". The query in this case would be the 'Item #' for the message you wish to retrieve. Submit that command and the server responds with the file via e-mail.

List Administration Tools

Strangely, this area of Web–to–e-mail interfaces has not been exploited. Most mailing list administration falls victim to the same pitfalls described earlier. The commands are often nonintuitive, and slight variations in the way commands are written to the server can cause untold difficulties.

This seems ripe territory for development. Though a centralized server is normally administered by someone with sufficient expertise to deal with the system's complexities, owners of individual lists are not always as knowledgeable. Typically, a list owner is little more than a regular user with an enthusiasm for a particular topic. Easing the difficulties encountered by these list owners is often the largest part of an administrator's responsibilities.

With this in mind, it's easy to see that a Web interface for adding and deleting subscribers, administrating message and file archives, and approving messages to a moderated list would be useful, indeed. As we have seen from the scope and power of the interfaces to the various aspects of e-mail described earlier, this is entirely feasible — it's just that nobody's done it yet.

Summary

With tools like the ones we've described, both existing and suggested, the circle is complete, linking the first implemented time-, space-, and host-independent service — e-mail — to the newest emerging technology — the Web. By beautifying, simplifying, and standardizing interfaces, the Web is slowly enveloping e-mail-based services. It can be said, in fact, that the Web is doing the same, slowly but surely, to everything on the Internet — consuming the very idea of a distributed, wide-area network, and regurgitating it as an HTML form.

32 WWW Server and CGI Security

*S*ince there is tremendous interest in enhancing Web security, many well-renowned Internet agencies have been furiously developing the next generation of communications protocols. This boiling pot of security buzzwords is being tossed around the popular media today and captures, in essence, what a hot topic it is for everyone.

The varying needs for secure systems range from the small requirements of "Joe's Generic Web Service," to a complex configuration requiring multiple secure keys that employs a military grade cryptosystem used by a giant interconnected corporation. Our discussion will only address the needs and issues of ordinary Web users and the middleware applications available to service their needs.

An Open Door Is Not Always Good...

CGIs that reside on a host server can be viewed as an open door to possible compromise. The misconfiguration or unintentional misuse of certain CGIs could lead to system-wide havoc, perhaps even a completely hacked-apart Web server.

Most HTTP servers run as a separate process on a machine using some variant of the UNIX operating system, despite the growing tendency in many companies to use other, more secure systems for their basic Web management. In essence, CGI programs operate as the core of any Web system. They provide system administrators with the ability to completely configure and program their Web servers, allowing them to interact with other aspects of the system. When you allow other applications to control the system using a CGI, it stands to reason that the security of the CGI and how it is used should be carefully guarded.

Since CGI programs are not part of the *httpd* server, it has no control over them, other than to completely allow or disallow their use. Because CGI programs are so important and valuable, they are usually allowed to run *en masse*, which potentially opens up a possible point of entry for system snoops and other electronic lowlifes.

In this chapter we address the possible security holes present on a UNIX operating system running *httpd* server software. Since a large part of what we suggest is common practice for good system administrators, our intent is to provide practical exposure to those of you with less system administration experience.

We also explore some of the recent efforts undertaken by various organizations to provide secure transmission of information across the Web. We touch lightly upon the different types of encryption used in the computer industry today, to guide our discussion of those kinds considered suitable for secure operations on the Internet. Finally, we wrap up by providing starting points that you can use to collect information on products and services that employ some of these new secure approaches to the Web.

The following URL is a good place to go for a quick peek at what's going on with security and WWW:

```
http://www.w3.org/hypertext/WWW/Security/Overview.html
```

Security Is Like Mowing the Lawn...

Strange though it may seem, security needs to become an ongoing activity, not just as a "set-up-and-ignore" task. Although it may seem simple to begin with, the ever-changing aspects of a company's network make security management a demanding and challenging role for anyone.

If your company is like the ones that we've been around, things change on an almost-daily basis. New people move in, other people migrate to far corners of the globe, and some take on new roles. This creates nearly daily challenges for the system administrator, who may already be wearing several hats or who might have recently changed jobs him- or herself.

We recommend that you re-evaluate your security configuration at least quarterly and that you check up on its operation monthly. We aren't advocating a policy of "eternal vigilance," but we believe there is justifiable cause to merit ongoing activity, even if it's only moderate and sporadic.

A Typical UNIX httpd Configuration

If you are afraid of UNIX, join the club. We know a handful of accomplished engineers actively engaged in the computer industry for over 20 years, all of whom still get woozy when asked to administer a "typical" UNIX system.

First of all, UNIX is never as *typical* as writers of technical books — or for that matter, the designers of the UNIX operating system — would like you to believe. That's because UNIX's greatest strength — and weakness — is that it gives anyone the ability to program a totally customized operating system environment using easily accessible, built-in tools. Ultimate control and configurability is really neat, but it's also what makes your UNIX box just a little different from your neighbor's.

For the security-conscious administrator, the first and foremost system control to quarantine is the *user* and *group* designations for your *httpd* server. This configuration is controlled by the "httpd.conf" file, and usually lives in the */www/conf* directory, where www is the *httpd* directory root.

Here's a copy of our "httpd.conf" file in its entirety. Please note that we've bolded the sections most pertinent to this discussion.

```
#                    HTTPD.CONF
# This is the main server configuration file. It is best to
# leave the directives in this file in the order they are in, or
# things may not go the way you'd like.
#
# Do NOT simply read the instructions in here without understanding
# what they do; if you are unsure, consult the online docs. You have
# been warned!!!
#
```

```
# Rob McCool (comments, questions to httpd@ncsa.uiuc.edu)

# ServerType is either inetd, or standalone.

ServerType standalone

# If you are running from inetd, go to "ServerAdmin".
# Port: The port the standalone listens to. For ports < 1023, you
# will need httpd to be run as root initially.

Port 80

# If you wish httpd to run as a different user or group, you must
# run httpd as root initially and it will switch.

# User/Group: The name (or #number) of the user/group to
# run httpd as.

User www
Group httpd

# ServerAdmin: Your address, where problems with the server should
# be e-mailed.

ServerAdmin www@www.outer.net


# ServerRoot: The directory the server's config, error, and log
# files are kept in

ServerRoot /usr/local/www/httpd-1.3

# ErrorLog: The location of the error log file. If this does not
# start with /, ServerRoot is prepended to it.

ErrorLog logs/error_log

# TransferLog: The location of the transfer log file. If this does
# not start with /, ServerRoot is prepended to it.

TransferLog logs/access_log

# PidFile: The file the server should log its pid to

PidFile logs/httpd.pid

# ServerName allows you to set a host name which is sent back to
# clients.

ServerName www.outer.net

TimeOut 60
IdentityCheck off
```

Using the reserved keywords *User* and *Group*, the administrator can change the daemon's user designation when it executes. When the *httpd* daemon is first started — usually from the "/etc/rc.local" file at system boot-up — a full process list reveals that the server process is owned by *root*, rather than the user designation that you've selected.

What's happened here? Because root starts the process, the map retains that fact. In the listing below, you'll notice that children forked by the *httpd* daemon to service incoming clients do report the proper user id:

```
root 190     1 0  May 30   ?   3:18 /usr/local/www/httpd-1.3/httpd
www  14648  190 0 01:34:49   ?   0:00 /usr/local/www/httpd-1.3/httpd
www  14650  190 1 01:34:50   ?   0:00 /usr/local/www/httpd-1.3/httpd
```

Also highlighted in the "httpd.conf" file, please notice the *Port 80* command. Although you might not think of the server's activity as a security concern, consider that many institutions and network managers use router-based firewalls to manage unwanted and unsecure traffic.

Normally, the WWW server (on almost any platform) defaults to listening to port 80 for incoming client connections. Port 80 is regarded as the "well known socket" or "well known port" address for handling Web traffic. By specifying another port in the configuration file, server administrators (who have taken the appropriate measures at their border gateway routers) can elect to keep their Web server local by operating on a firewalled port.

Many network administrators firewall ports greater than 1023, because these ports are not specifically reserved for any particular type of connection. By disallowing connection attempts at the router for port addresses higher than 1023, a Web server can be guaranteed privacy simply by operating in that range.

*ServerType Run from inetd

The server can also be started from *inetd* (the Internet Daemon), used on some systems to control other, more specific daemons (like *news* and *mail*, or *httpd*). The configuration file offers another reserved word — namely, "ServerType" — for such use. This, too, can keep the unauthorized from taking advantage of the unwary!

In all cases where a directory name is specified in one of the various configuration files for *httpd*, any mistake or miscalculation in its specification can produce unexpected results or lead to possible security hazards.

Although it's difficult to compromise the security of a marginally misconfigured server, it remains a potentially dangerous problem because it might expose some hole (no matter how small) for a hacker to crack at.

System hacking/cracking is typically 98% brute force, fueled by persistence and time. The longer a hole exists, the longer a chisel can be applied. By the way, the other 2% is Lady Luck. She's almost impossible to keep out of your system (but why would you want to?).

SRM.CONF

The Server Resource Map, or "srm.file" that we have included below contains some server control directives that you'll want to consider when configuring your *httpd* program. First, and probably most important, is the location where the server obtains HTML documents. By using the 'DocumentRoot' directive as we have done below, any client's **GET** requests on your web server will be limited to the scope of the */usr/local/www/httpd-1.3/httpdocs* directory.

By disallowing requests for documents outside of a known location, the administrator can establish greater control over what users see. Consider the option where the whole "/" drive is accessible to a requestor. Web clients would then be able to download system specific files like the "/etc/passwd" file or the "/etc/hosts" file in attempts to gain more information about the system hosting the Web service. Clearly, this is a poor idea. In the same fashion, the 'UserDir' directive can be misconfigured to give clients access to areas that are equally off limits.

```
# With this document, you define the name space that users see on
# your http server.
#
# See the tutorials at http://hoohoo.ncsa.uiuc.edu/docs/tutorials/
# for more information.
#

# DocumentRoot: The directory from which you will serve your
# documents. By default, all requests are taken from this directory,
# but symbolic links and aliases may be used to point to other
# locations.

DocumentRoot /usr/local/www/httpd-1.3/httpdocs
```

```
# UserDir: The name of the directory which is appended onto a user's
# home directory if a user request is received.

UserDir public_html

# DirectoryIndex: Name of the file to use as a pre-written HTML
# directory index

DirectoryIndex index.html

# FancyIndexing is whether you want fancy directory indexing or
# standard

FancyIndexing on

# AddIcon tells the server which icon to show for different files or
# filename extensions

AddIconByType (TXT,/icons/text.xbm) text/*
AddIconByType (IMG,/icons/image.xbm) image/*
AddIconByType (SND,/icons/sound.xbm) audio/*
AddIcon /icons/movie.xbm .mpg .qt
AddIcon /icons/binary.xbm .bin .Z .gz .tar
AddIcon /icons/back.xbm ..
AddIcon /icons/menu.xbm ^^DIRECTORY^^
AddIcon /icons/blank.xbm ^^BLANKICON^^

# DefaultIcon is which icon to show for files which do not have an
# icon explicitly set.

DefaultIcon /icons/unknown.xbm

# AddDescription allows you to place a short description after a
# file in server-generated indexes.
# Format: AddDescription "description" filename

# ReadmeName is the name of the README file the server will look for
# by default. Format: ReadmeName name
#
# The server will first look for name.html, include it if found, and
# it will then look for name and include it as plaintext if found.
#
# HeaderName is the name of a file which should be prepended to
# directory indexes.

ReadmeName AAA.README
HeaderName HEADER

# IndexIgnore is a set of filenames which directory indexing should # ignore
Format: IndexIgnore name1 name2...

IndexIgnore */.??* *~ *# */HEADER* */README*
```

```
# AccessFileName: The name of the file to look for in each
# directory for access control information.

AccessFileName .htaccess

# DefaultType is the default MIME type for documents which the
# server cannot find the type of from filename extensions.

DefaultType text/html

# AddType allows you to tweak mime.types without actually editing
# it, or to make certain files to be certain types.
# Format: AddType type/subtype ext1

# AddEncoding allows you to use certain browsers (Mosaic/X 2.1+)
# uncompress information on the fly. Note: Not all browsers support
# this.

#AddEncoding x-compress Z
#AddEncoding x-gzip gz

# Redirect allows you to tell clients about documents which used to
# exist in your server's namespace, but not anymore. This allows
# you to tell clients where to look for relocated documents.
# Format: Redirect fakename url


# Aliases: Add here as many aliases as you need, up to 20. The
# format is Alias fakename realname

Alias /icons/ /usr/local/www/httpd-1.3/icons/

# ScriptAlias: This controls which directories contain
# server scripts. Format: ScriptAlias fakename realname

ScriptAlias /cgi-bin/ /usr/local/www/httpd-1.3/cgi-bin/

# If you want to use server side includes, or CGI outside
# ScriptAliased directories, uncomment the following lines.

#AddType text/x-server-parsed-html .shtml
#AddType application/x-httpd-cgi .cgi
```

The 'ScriptAlias' directive in "srm.conf" should be considered the most lethal possible security hole if it's configured incorrectly. As we mentioned earlier, by granting too much access to a server's private system files, unwanted attempts to either get or execute files are likely to occur.

Just as the 'DocumentRoot' command limits GET calls to a known location, the 'ScriptAlias' command limits requests to run CGI programs. Hence, by allowing a Web client to *execute* anything anywhere on a system, a security compromise can almost be predicted. We recommend instead that you limit your CGI applications to a single directory, and that you absolutely do not put any soft-links to other directories into this tree.

UNIX Permissions and Ownerships

An old friend of ours — a serious UNIX guru and a terrific tutor — once told us that most all problems in UNIX stem from permission-related traumas. Since permissions are easily changed and so easy to forget, we will point out some of the more sobering traumas that deal with *httpd*.

First of all, here's a listing of the permissions we suggest you use on your UNIX system:

```
drwxrwxr-x  10 www    httpd       512 Apr 19 00:02 ./
drwxr-xr-x   3 root   managemt    512 Sep  6 1994  ../
drwxrwx---   2 root   httpd       512 May 31 01:00 auth/
drwxrwxr-x   7 www    httpd      3584 May 31 16:58 cgi-bin/
drwxrwx---   2 root   httpd       512 Dec  6 16:24 cgi-src/
drwxrwxr-x   2 www    httpd       512 Feb 27 10:54 conf/
-rwxr-xr-x   1 www    httpd    138480 Mar 13 15:28 httpd*
lrwxrwxrwx   1 root   httpd        14 Apr 18 23:27 httpdocs/
drwxrwxr-x   2 www    httpd       512 Sep  6 1994  icons/
drwxrwxr-x   2 www    httpd       512 May 29 04:00 logs/
drwxrwx---   2 root   managemt    512 Sep  6 1994  src/
drwxrwxr-x   3 www    httpd       512 Sep  6 1994  support/
```

Limiting Access to Internal Servers

Earlier, we mentioned a method for securing a server to an internal network by using a routing firewall, and then altering the port where the server listens for connection requests. This is usually beyond what a normal Web administrator has in mind when limiting access to a server.

A simpler method is to utilize the *Allow From* keywords to specify hosts (either IP addresses, or Fully Qualified Host Names [FQHNs]) in the "access.conf" configuration file. Partial domain names may also be used to specify a subsection of a domain rather than a network. Here is an example of a configuration that would deny all Web traffic except for hosts in *outer.net*:

```
<Limit GET>
order deny,allow
allow from *.ibm.com
allow from ibm.com
deny from all
</Limit>
```

The following configuration denies all Web traffic except for hosts that conform to the following IP addresses, or IP address ranges. The single machine "18.72.0.3" and the single machine "130.164.13.248" are allowed to connect to the Web server and so are any of the machines that begin with a 17 as the first dotted quad in their IP address (as a class "A" IP address, this is a huge range of machines).

```
<Limit GET>
order deny,allow
allow from 18.72.0.3
allow from 130.164.13.248
allow from 17
deny from all
</Limit>
```

As you can see, this configuration file is quite simple. But when applied with the potent imagination of a system administrator, you could easily create a complex and varied security system.

ACCESS.CONF

The access control file, "access.conf" is listed on the next page. This file contains some server-wide configurations to grant permissions to various areas of the Web server system.

Watch Out for FollowSymLinks

Be careful of the "**FollowSymLinks**" keyword. Because it allows symbolic links in either the document root directory or the server root directory to be followed by Web clients, unintentional links to private directories could lead to publishing personal information. For example, links to /etc or /bin would be inadvisable.

```
# access.conf: Global access configuration
# Online docs at http://hoohoo.ncsa.uiuc.edu/
# I suggest you consult them; this is important and confusing stuff.

# /usr/local/etc/httpd/ should be changed to whatever you # set ServerRoot to.

<Directory /usr/local/www/httpd-1.3/cgi-bin>
Options Indexes FollowSymLinks
</Directory>

# This should be changed to whatever you set DocumentRoot
# to.

<Directory /usr/local/www/httpd-1.3/httpdocs>

# This may also be "None", "All", or any combination of "Indexes",
# "Includes", or "FollowSymLinks"

Options Indexes FollowSymLinks

# This controls which options the .htaccess files in
# directories can override. Can also be "None", or any
# combination of "Options", "FileInfo", "AuthConfig", and
# "Limit"

AllowOverride All

# Controls who can get stuff from this server.

<Limit GET>
order deny,allow
allow from all
</Limit>

</Directory>

# You may place any other directories you wish to have access
# information for after this one.
```

.htaccess Gives You Power

In the "access.conf" file shown earlier in this chapter, please notice that the 'AllowOverride All' option instructs the Web server to override all options in a directory if the ".htaccess" file exists. The access control file may be different on your system, but since the default is for *httpd* to ship with it is named ".htaccess" we will continue to refer to it by that name. Change the name of the access file on the 'AccessFileName' line in "srm.conf".

WHAT DOES .HTACCESS CONTAIN?

Let's assume that you want to publish some pages on your Web server that only you and several other people may access. The built-in (*.htaccess*) security system provides a perfect mechanism for doing this. Although there are drawbacks to using it — for instance, the actual data that is transmitted as Web pages is sent as clear text — it is a good start toward demonstrating what you can do with UNIX authorization systems.

Assume that you want yourself (felix) and your colleagues (boris and chico) to have access to a whole tree of HTML documents in a project you're working on together (Mercury). The following example shows the ".htaccess" file, which you should place at the root of the directory that you wish to control:

```
AuthUserFile /www/auth/.htpasswd
AuthGroupFile /dev/null
AuthName Project_Mercury_Access
AuthType Basic

<Limit GET>
require user felix
require user boris
require user chico
</Limit>
```

Please notice that the 'AuthGroupFile' directive is used to create a group of people that need access to the restricted files, and that the 'AuthName' is merely a tag and can be assigned to anything that you like. Generally 'AuthName' is used to help identify a directory before the user must provide an authorization. But by using the '<Limit GET>' command, this restricts all clients attempting to execute the 'GET' server command anywhere within this directory tree. Specific users can be authenticated by specifying them with the 'require user' directive within this file.

HOW WOULD YOU EMPLOY THE .HTACCESS FILE?

The user file ("AuthUserFile") tells the Web server to perform verifications by reading usernames and encrypted passwords from the file located at */www/auth/.htpasswd*.

A simple method for creating users and their associated encrypted passwords can be simplified by an application that is normally included with the *httpd* distribution. Try running the *htpasswd* program with the intended username to get a DES-encrypted entry for your ".htpasswd" file. Here's how we added a password for felix:

```
htpasswd -c /www/auth/.htpasswd felix
```

Here's an example of the ""htpasswd" file:

```
felix:F9CXrjJfkvnc.
boris:M5RZrwWk2pz0k
chico:quIM.8lfVk4QE
```

You'll notice that the password field looks like the standard UNIX 13-character DES encrypted password from the "/etc/passwd" file. This is because *httpd* and Web clients support DES for this mode of authorization. Pay careful attention to the format of this file, as well as its contents. Simple errors in case or transposition can be hard to track down.

The *.htaccess* system should NOT be used for access that requires a protected or encrypted data stream. Financial transactions, orders for products, or any personal information (including credit card numbers) should not be included in pages verified by the *.htaccess* system.

Even though the DES encryption scheme is used to create the password, little else actually happens when a client connects to the server. When a Web client requests a page from a controlled access area on the server, the user must supply a password in order to gain access to those protected pages. A nice little authentication box pops up and the user supplies the appropriate username and password.

The security hole here is that the password is sent across the network to the server as a simple uuencoded entry, *not* in a protected stream. Anyone clever enough with a packet capture utility could easily trap the password, *uudecode* it, and then gain access to other areas on the system.

Our recommendation is that you use the basic authentication system very sparingly until a more secure method is approved and in production.

To UNIX or Not to UNIX?

The most compelling reason for using a UNIX host as a primary Web server is because the UNIX operating system has been around for more than 25 years and has been heavily debugged. UNIX machines, designed to provide multiuser, multitasking operations from a single CPU, are also enhanced to provide support for multiple, simultaneous network connections.

It's hard to find a UNIX version that doesn't ship preconfigured with a generic TCP/IP stack and a networking-enabled kernel. This also explains why UNIX machines increase the risk of compromise when they run on the Internet. Supporting a whole host of different networking options, from the Network Time Protocol to a whole slew of Remote Procedure Calls, UNIX machines typically include a number of possible security threats right out of the box.

We are not trying to discourage you from using a UNIX Web server; we just want to make it plain that these security issues need to be considered for any complex system. On the plus side, UNIX machines are great at providing network services to a large number of clients. They are capable of servicing a huge number of HTTP requests and are usually stable systems in general.

With this in mind, we would like to suggest that using an alternate operating platform eliminates some of the inherent risks associated with UNIX. For example, the Macintosh HTTP Daemon is almost impervious to TCP/IP attacks. Given that there is no "command-line interface" to the Mac operating system, and that the only software running that allows TCP/IP traffic is the Web Server Software, it poses a significant challenge to any would-be security hack. The same argument is true for a DOS/Windows platform.

Because Windows NT and OS/2 are designed to act more like UNIX and less like personal workstations, they have a more complex set of security points to address. While they are thus more vulnerable to security attacks than DOS/Windows or the Macintosh, their weaknesses are also nowhere near as well-known or -documented as UNIX's.

The Benefits of Secure Transit

Why be concerned about secure transit? What data could be important enough to require an almost unbreakable encryption scheme on both ends, just to ensure its inviolability? On today's bullet train toward progress, our lives are quickly turning into an online affair at every turn. Banks are going online, and many large stores are investigating the Internet in hopes of hanging out a shingle on the Iway.

As interested parties get closer and closer to offering real products and services via the Net, the need for secure communications becomes increasingly necessary. Financial transactions, which have been in the limelight lately, only represent a small percentage of sensitive information destined for Internet transactions.

Secure-HTTP

Secure-HTTP (S-HTTP), a superset of the WWW's existing HTTP protocol, provides security for both clients and servers. S-HTTP was designed to enhance the current protocol, not to fix its deficiencies. This structure allows for separate (but not totally independent) development paths for the two protocols. It is the simple correlation of S-HTTP to HTTP that will prove to be its greatest advantage.

There is a huge development community actively engaged in the creation and testing of S-HTTP applications. And at the writing of this book, there are probably tens of thousands of servers and possibly more than a million core users on the Web, with the numbers increasing daily. With this level of activity, it is evident that demand for a common security mechanism will be fulfilled by the year's end. S-HTTP represents one of the leading efforts in this direction.

If you are interested in the current plans for S-HTTP, follow this URL:

```
http://www.eit.com/projects/s-http/index.html
```

OTHER WWW SECURITY MECHANISMS

The *Shen* proposal for World Wide Web security, developed by Phillip M. Hallam-Baker of CERN, is probably one of the largest parallel proposals to S-HTTP. *Shen* is basically concerned with the specifics of local security policies, trust models, message formats, and implementation issues. S-HTTP, by contrast, restricts itself only to a definition of protocols (message formats), and does not attempt to handle implementation or policy details.

We think because it focuses exclusively on the delivery layer, S-HTTP will prove to support a wider variety of usage models. This will ultimately make S-HTTP one of the most successful and flexible designs for Web security. Several other developments in the secure HTTP arena include:

- IP Address Authentication — This is the most commonly used architecture today, but it is not robust enough for electronic commerce.

- Basic Authentication — Also very popular, and also not robust enough for electronic commerce.

- PEM/PGP Encapsulation — This option is largely unused.

- Kerberos — A latecomer, one of two key security services used in distributed IP environments (it serves as the security model for DCE, the Distributed Computing Environment), but it has yet to be widely adopted for Web usage.

THE S-HTTP SPECIFICATION AND DESIGN GOALS

S-HTTP was designed not only with commercial transactions in mind, but also with a myriad of other uses possible for such a dynamic system. The varying types of server-based security implementations, as well as the whole collection of Web clients that already exist (and will be created in the future) were incorporated into the S-HTTP design and specification. In general, its goals were to provide reasonable security for a broad base of clients, suitable for protecting sensitive financial and authentication information in the wide-open-free-for-all affectionately known as the Internet.

For a formal treatment of S-HTTP's technical details, point your browser here:

    http://www.eit.com/projects/s-http/shttp.txt

WHAT CAN WE DO WITH S-HTTP?

In a recent presentation given by Allan Schiffman (one of the principle architects of S-HTTP) at Interop 94, some real-world examples bubbled up from the froth. S-HTTP is capable of providing full credit card transactions in a secure manner, IRS income tax filing as well as payment, full online banking, Internet checks drafted off one of the cyberbanks, and provisions for the spec'ing and purchasing of soft-products (software or data).

In the future, S-HTTP will provide facilities for encryption and authentication, as well as RSA-based digital signature. By mixing and matching delivery agents, a whole scheme of security can be erected by almost any Net entity, whose wide-ranging scope could include just about anybody with a computer. It will be interesting to see how this technology matures and what kinds of development it leads to. If you're thinking about any commerce-related Web applications, S-HTTP is certainly worth following.

Some Places to Go...

The following URL includes a great collection of Security, Encryption, and Privacy issues:

    http://www.cs.purdue.edu/homes/spaf/hotlists/csec.html

Summary

Security is as much a state of mind as it is a set of operational procedures and controls. If you adopt the attitude that your server is an asset worth protecting, you'll be more than halfway to keeping your valuable information out of danger. By remaining aware of the potential holes in your server and alert to potential attempts to compromise its security, you can head off the worst of all possible outcomes: compromise without cognizance! The rest is pure routine...

User Interaction Through HTML

Everybody's Doing It

*E*very aspect of the Internet is moving toward increased interactivity, and the Web is no exception. The impetus for this book, in fact, is the quest for interactivity on the Web. For WWW publishing purposes, HTML does just fine all by itself unless you want your pages to include even the slightest bit of interaction with the audience. To do that, you need to program some of the goodies we cover in these pages.

So, if interaction is one of the ideas woven into the fabric of every discussion that goes on in this book, why does it need its own chapter, too? The answer is, that like many wide-ranging and powerful ideas, approaches to interaction can become a category all its own.

The quest for interaction through HTML takes many forms. The earliest examples followed the first flurries of development after the advent of the CGI standard. These usually took the form of scripts that allowed users to add data onto the end of an HTML document, such as *guestbook* and *addlink* scripts.

As the Web's potential has become better realized, forays into interaction are increasingly sophisticated. First came CGIs that facilitated threaded discussion groups in the USENET style, such as *hypernews*. Next came "live" chat or talker-type CGIs, with pages that updated as quickly as possible to reflect all the comments typed in by any number of users.

The most recent developments include serious efforts to create standards and models for annotation on Web documents, and the arrival of the kind of large, throbbing buzzwords that so often fund research grants, such as *collaboration* and *groupware*.

That said, it's time to take a look at some representatives of each of these categories and examine the issues involved in making your Web site both interactive and sophisticated.

Basic Interaction Through HTML

We've already looked at CGIs that incorporate those principles elaborated by the developers of the first user-interactive CGIs. Simply put, they provide the ability to append data to existing documents. This becomes interactive when modified documents are served back to the user who has added the text, and to the Web at large, ready for further input, and so on.

ADDLINK

The idea of allowing users to add links to your home page must have been appealing from the very start, especially for those of us who tend toward laziness. Imagine a hotlist that grows all by itself!

From a programming standpoint, this is simple to do. Thus, there are many implementations of this type of CGI available on the Net. All of them follow the same basic model:

- They present the user with a form input in which to type an http link, along with an optional description.

- Once submitted, the link is imbedded in an <A HREF=...> tag, with a description (if it exists) or the link itself as the anchoring text.

- The resulting link is written to the end of a file that in most cases is statically linked from the user's home page.

  Voilà, instant an self-perpetuating hotlist.
  Some *addlink* packages you may want to take a closer look at are

- Adam Radulovic's "add a link" program:

  http://www.i-link.net/cgi-bin/adamlistlinks

- the *Widow's Web* library of CGI programs:

  `http://128.172.69.106:8080/cgis/addlink.html`

- Matt's *Free For All Link Page*:

  `http://alpha.prl.k12.co.us/~mattw/links/links.html`

All of these URLs include pointers to the code you can use to let users add links to your Web pages.

GUESTBOOK

Guestbook CGIs arose out of a desire to allow page owners to see who had accessed the page and also to allow subsequent users to browse the listings of previous visitors. Either purpose may easily be served with basic access log parsing or a form that appends user information to a plain text file for the owner's perusal. Yet either solution would lack style and readability, because the results would be presented in preformatted text or worse yet, machine-generated preformmated text (in the case of the log file parsing).

It's safe to say that the guestbook concept has been taken to its utmost by Brigitte Jellinek, whose *guestbook* program can be found at

`http://www.cosy.sbg.ac.at/ftp/pub/people/bjelli/webscripts/guest/guestbook.html`

Not only can users add text to Brigitte's guestbook file through the CGI, guestbook also cleverly includes a way for users to pinpoint their locations on a world map (see Figure 33-1).

Guestbook is actually a collection of CGIs used to collect user input, locate positions and markup maps, and organize and present the resulting pages. It also depends upon "formlib.pl"; the *pnm* library from *pbmplus*; *dblookup* from *netfind*; and, of course, *perl* 4.018 or higher; and *httpd* 1.2 (or higher) with *imagemap* installed.

If you wish to install *guestbook* on your Web site, the source can be downloaded from Brigitte's pages. When you *untar* the archive, it creates a hierarchy under the directory named "guestbook". There are two files in "guestbook/src" that will need editing, namely "config.pl" and "config.sh". Both simply need paths to dependencies, the hostname, the necessary URLs. When satisfied with your changes, you can type **make all** and the packages will be generated automatically.

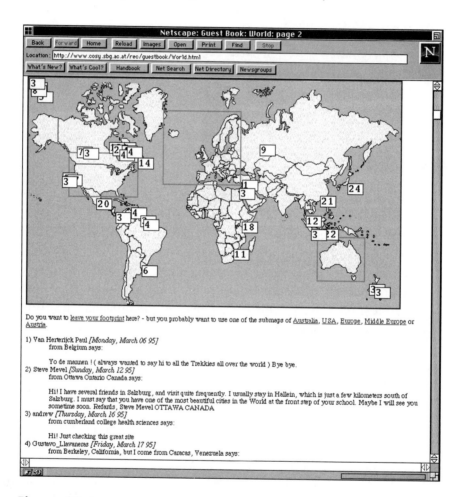

Figure 33-1

Brigitte Jellinek's guestbook with world map.

From there, you can modify "header.htinc" and "footer.htinc" in the "guestbook" directory. These files define which HTML documents or text you want to have printed at the top and bottom of each of *guestbook*'s pages.

Finally, each of the "*.map" files will need to be modified. These are the imagemap configuration files for serving the world map images associated with the *guestbook* sign-in form. The only modifications you will need to make in these files will be to change the path to reflect the situation at your site.

In picking a home directory for *guestbook,* you'll want to make sure that your Web server can run CGIs from files in the desired path. You may copy the entire hierarchy there, or even *untar* it in place. After verifying that the file permissions will allow the world to execute the scripts and read the data files, you should be ready to go.

As users add their entries to the guestbook, the data file will grow. Each person who views the guestbook will cause the viewing CGI to read in the data file, wrap it in the header and footer information, add the relevant map image, and output the result to the user's browser. Of course, this means that any HTML typed in by the user, including links to other documents or inline images, will be displayed with the proper formatting by the browser.

It is this ability to step outside the plain-text world of *IRC* or *talk* that serves as one of the forces driving the development of interactive HTML applications.

The Current State Of the Interactive Web

From an application of Web technology such as *guestbook*, it takes only a small leap to see that users' entries can interrelate with one another, and the amount of interaction going on will increase geometrically. This interrelation can be both contextual, in the sense that one user can comment on the comments of another, and logical. CGIs that keep track of comment threads, common keywords, topics, etc., can establish such logical relationships by providing tools to the user for browsing on, and responding to, comments.

Replace the term *comments* with *articles* in the preceding paragraph, and you have a basic description of a threaded discussion group of the sort that underlies USENET. Next we focus on a program called *hypernews* that implements this very capability.

HYPERNEWS

This is precisely the idea that Daniel Laliberte took and applied to create his *hypernews* program. Modeled closely after USENET but a distinctively Web-based service, *hypernews* allows users to participate in threaded discussion groups created by *hypernews* administrators.

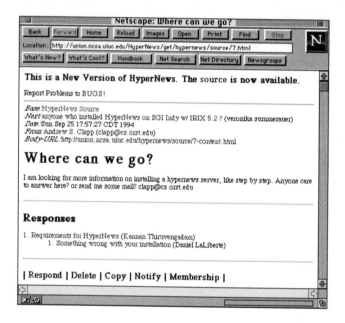

Figure 33-2

A typical hypernews article with navigation and response tools.

As you can see in Figure 33-2, the format of a *hypernews* article is static header information, followed by the headers for the current article. These headers take the form of links to the thread's root article, to the next article in the thread, to the current article's author, and to the URL for the article's body.

These headers are followed by the body text, which can have embedded HTML formatting, followed by links to actions the user can take on the current article. These actions include responding to, deleting, or copying the article (the latter two actions are only available to *hypernews* administrators with proper authentication). The two remaining options deserve close attention, since Daniel has done a large amount of work to squeeze a lot of utility into his CGIs.

At the end of each article there's a link entitled "Membership", that, if clicked, brings the user to a form for personal information, including name, e-mail address, URL, and password for the site. Once you are a member, *hypernews* allows access to additional features of the server and also keeps track of articles that you post or subscribe to. Membership information may be changed at any time, but new passwords take some time to be updated in *hypernews'* access control file.

The final user tool at the bottom of each article is a link named "Notify". When followed, this link brings the user to a form that allows him or her to "subscribe" to any or all of the articles in the current thread. When a user has subscribed to a thread, he or she is automatically notified by e-mail whenever any subscribed articles are modified.

What is especially impressive about *hypernews* is the effortlessness with which it generates hierarchies of articles and responses on-the-fly. Each article has both a link to the article to which it responds, and a link to the next article in its headers. Most informatively, a tree representation of the thread structures appears beneath the body of each article.

These navigation tools make it easy for users to navigate within a large, complex body of data. This is yet another of HTML's strengths that help make it so useful for interactive applications.

If you wish to get *hypernews* up and running on your UNIX Web site, you may do so by *untarring* the archive in your "cgi-bin" directory. The only file you will need to edit is "hnrc". It contains the configuration options for *hypernews,* most of which consist of paths to its homes in both the "cgi-bin" and document root directories. Make sure to specify your e-mail address as an administrator, and leave all the security options the way they are, for the time being.

The only possible gotcha we encountered while installing *hypernews* resulted from its need for up-to-date and accessible ".ph" files. These are the "Perl-ized" C system library files, where *hypernews* depends in particular on "socket.ph".

A tool for converting your system's ".h" files is included with Perl and is called *h2ph*. It's an under-documented tool, so we'll confess that we were only able to make it work by changing our working directory to "/usr/include" and typing the command

```
h2ph * sys/*
```

You may have to check the file permissions for the resulting ".ph" files, which should end up in your Perl library directory. If *hypernews* cannot find "socket.ph", you will experience **500 Server Errors** whenever you try to run these scripts from a browser.

Once you're satisfied that your installation is working, start using *hypernews* by setting up your user profile. Do this by using the "edit-personal.pl" script so that pointing toward a URL on your server runs the script that should load the correct form. Enter your e-mail address and password, and any other information you wish to specify, and submit the form. Now you can begin your first thread.

It's easiest to start a thread with an existing document, so you may want to create some sort of introductory article and save it to the *hypernews*' directory in the server's document tree. Then run the CGI named "edit-article.pl". This is in the "SECURED" directory under the *hypernews* binary home directory, so remember to add that to your URL's path. You'll also need to enter your e-mail address and password as specified on your membership form.

The form used to create a thread includes a space for you to point toward the document you created, and for its *virtual path* — that is, the way you want the users to access the thread. For example, the virtual path "/intro" results in a thread whose home article is accessible through this URL:

```
/cgi-bin/HyperNews/get/intro.html
```

While *hypernews* can be interesting to experiment with and could even prove a useful tool in facilitating interaction between your users, it still does not challenge the biggest obstacle facing interactive HTML. This obstacle is *time. hypernews* is asynchronous, so the lag between an article and its responses is completely arbitrary. For true interactivity, you'd want your users to be able to see communications in as close to real time as the Web can get. This is where *WebChat* and its ilk come in.

WebChat

Originally developed by Michael Fremont, *WebChat* is now described as "an open collaborative project" based on the GNU Software License. Essentially, this means that *WebChat* joins in the grand Internet tradition of collaborative development and sharing brain cycles amongst the community at large. This is fitting, since what *WebChat* attempts to do is to make possible live chat via the Web.

With an interface that looks essentially like a *guestbook* type application (see Figure 33-3), *WebChat* allows you to type text and links into a text area and, when submitted, your comment becomes visible to everyone who is following the chat.

The source code available for downloading and installing on your server is version 0.2. It is quite simple to install, consisting of one form, two GIFs, and two Perl scripts. Some paths need to be changed in the "nph-client" and "init_transcript_file" scripts, but the documentation is very simple and clear on this point.

The newest version, running at

```
http://www.irsociety.com/webchat/webchat.html
```

is quite a bit more feature-rich. It offers multiple chat rooms and the ability to create a temporary conference room of your own. Most notably, it uses Netscape's client pull to offer automatic updates.

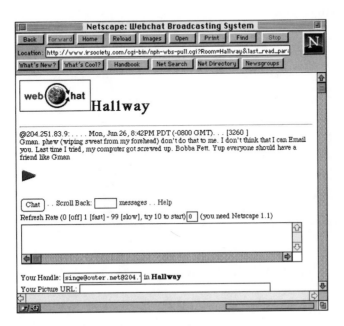

Figure 33-3
WebChat's chat form and listing.

By typing a value into the "Refresh Rate" field, the user will get an update of the chat page every few seconds, without reloading the page manually. As such, it brings talk on the Web several steps closer to true interactivity.

IRC W3 GATEWAY AND TALKER

Of course, *WebChat* is not the only talk-type CGI application out on the WWW. Two other examples are the *IRC W3 Gateway* (see Figure 33-4) and *Talker*. Both follow similar models, presenting the user with a text area to type into, and requiring reloads to see the most recent comments added to the page. The *IRC* gateway CGI is notable because it leverages the considerable power already wielded by the *IRC* protocol and its many servers.

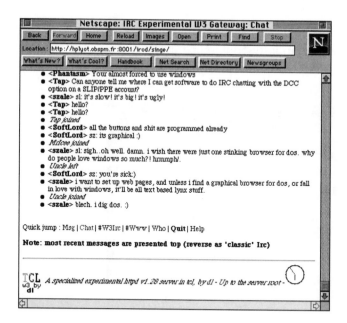

Figure 33-4
IRC W3 Gateway's familiar look and feel.

It remains simply a proof of concept at the moment, but it already has the beginnings of the familiar *IRC* interface. As the product develops, we hope to see all the power of the *IRC* client show up in the WWW gateway client, including the abilities to create channels, message people directly, find people online, and kick people off channels.

STORYBASE ANNOTATION

The next stage of development beyond chat and discussion is to open up interaction to include document text itself. Instead of users simply adding text to the end of a linear document, an annotation engine allows them to add text to any portion of a document. Some baby steps have been made toward this type of system, both in theoretical and practical work.

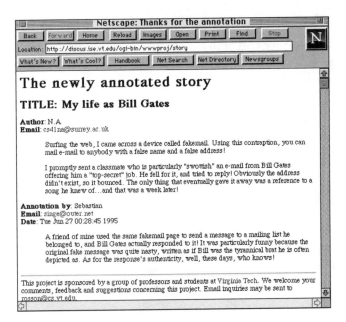

Figure 33-5
The Storybase Annotation server.

As you can see in Figure 33-5, the *Storybase Annotation* system resembles *hypernews*, with fewer navigational and action tools. Its annotations simply follow the original text and as such don't really break from the linear nature of all the interactive systems we've seen thus far.

In fact, it could be argued that since you can respond to articles located at any point in a thread, *hypernews* has already broken those bonds.

However, truly nonlinear annotation would allow precise linking of annotations directly to the text that the annotation addresses. Doug Englebart, Wayne Gramlich, and others have done excellent theoretical work in this area, and the W3 Consortium maintains a page with links to the best of this information:

```
http://www.w3.org/hypertext/WWW/Collaboration/Overview.html
```

The Future: Shared Space

By now it should be obvious that although many enthusiastic participants have done substantial groundwork, truly interactive HTML applications aren't ready for prime time. When compared to commercial products that integrate shared workspaces, collaborative document creation, or real-time voice and video conferencing, the Web's present shortcomings are all too apparent.

COMMERCIAL PRODUCTS CROSSOVER

There is, however, a movement afoot from many of the commercial developers of collaborative products toward the Web that confirms what we already suspected — that the future of many of these technologies is linked to the Web. The idea of distributed, multimedia, client/server systems that are also open-ended development platforms is far too powerful to resist.

Like so many other segments of the computer industry, the Web is becoming a sort of holy grail for groupware, shared space servers, collaborative applications, and other niche products that have been looking desperately for their place in the market. One example is Ubique's client (see Figure 33-6) and server products that offer the Web with integrated shared spaces.

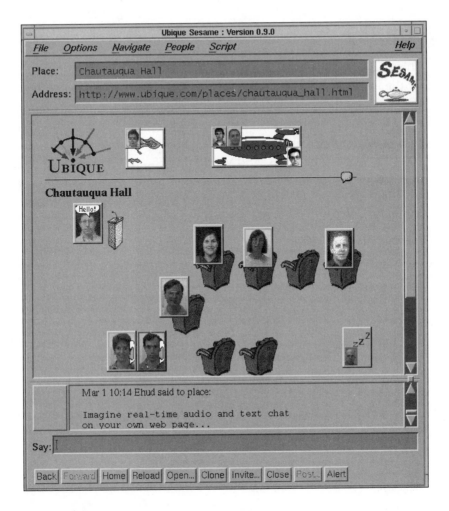

Figure 33-6
Ubique's XWindows Virtual Places client.

This product consists of a server and client that offer interaction in a virtual space and WYSIWIS (What You See Is What I See), shared whiteboard-like features over the Web. More information about these products can be found at

http://www.ubique.com/

Summary

This migration of commercial products and the seeds of possibility planted by the freely available packages we've looked at signify that the day is not far off when the Web will become truly interactive.

Interactive: even to say that it's the buzzword of the day is a cliché. Everything is interactive — television, computers, even appliances — now the World Wide Web. And yet all this effort to increase the total interactivity of our world isn't surprising. After all, it's what we've done since the dawn of time. It's just that we used to call it *communication*.

CHAPTER 34

Foundations of WWW Programming with HTML and CGI

Go Home...

*A*s a companion piece to this book, we've included, a CD-ROM filled with the goodies we've been telling you about. The disk is mastered following the ISO-9660 standard, so it should be mountable and readable from DOS/Windows, Macintosh, and UNIX machines alike (as well as any other platforms that adhere to this standard).

As much as possible, the software discussed in this book is included on the companion CD. It is organized into browsable directories, one for each chapter. But in order to utilize the resources of the disk to your best advantage, you will want a Web browser for your computer and a live connection to the Internet.

In addition to the software collection, the CD contains a number of HTML documents. These may be opened from the CD by any of the popular Web browsers, including Netscape, WinWeb, MacWeb, any Mosaic offshoot, and many others. The first document you should open is named "HOME.HTM" and is located at the root of the CD-ROM.

Once opened, the CD's home page should look like Figure 34-1.

From this page, you'll be able to follow links to a brief help file (basically an expanded version of the document you're reading now, with links to code examples, HTML documents, and more). We've also provided a jump page that inlcudes all of the URLs mentioned in the book and a browsable index of the CD.

The browsable index consists of a hierarchical, hypertext listing of the entire contents of the disk. One listing is sorted by chapter, the other alphabetically. Clicking on the name of one of the packages provides a listing of its contents, and a brief "read me" file or the package's actual documentation where available.

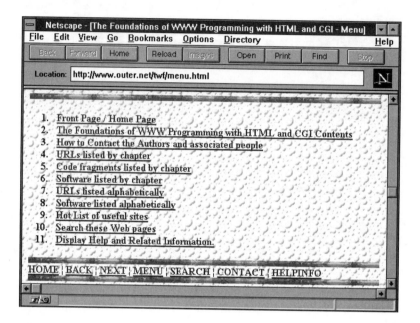

Figure 34-1

Foundations of World Wide Programming with HTML and CGI Programming CD home page.

In order to provide all our readers with a searchable index, we have duplicated the contents of the disk on a Web server, available through this URL:

```
http://www.outer.net/twf/
```

For this online version of our materials, we've created a WAIS index. Therefore, if you follow the link to the search form, you'll be able to type in search strings and submit queries. The resulting hitlists will provide paths to the appropriate files on your CD-ROM player or, when clicked, will download another (possibly more up-to-date) copy of the package from our site.

This search form follows the same basic format as that for a typical WAIS gateway, as we discussed in Chapter 19. You can type in a word or phrase that you think may be associated with your area of interest, and the search engine returns pointers to files that register hits on your search string.

If you don't have access to the Internet or prefer doing searches locally, you can duplicate our WAIS database on your own server. On a UNIX machine, you would accomplish this in much the same way we did when creating the index for our site.

After installing and configuring *freeWAIS* as described in Chapter 19, create an index of the contents of the CD. If you have sufficient disk space you will probably want to copy the CD onto your hard disk, owing to performance considerations. If you do not have the requisite amount of free disk space, you'll have to mount the CD at a mount point in WAIS' home directory.

Once the index is created, you may either query it with any WAIS client or set up a gateway to your Web server. Again, Chapter 19 contains information about a large number of freely available packages that will allow you to perform such searches.

If you do not have access to a UNIX server, you may be able to find an alternative method for indexing and searching your CD locally. On the Macintosh platform, AppleSearch is a very WAIS-like package that allows you to index an information source and then query the index server via a Mac or Windows AppleSearch client application.

Unfortunately, we weren't able to locate any equivalent capabilities for DOS or Windows, but please drop in on our Web server occasionally — by the time you read this, we may have located just the right tool for your needs!

Summary

This chapter concludes our adventures in programming for the World Wide Web. We've come a long way since the beginning of this book, and we hope your journey with us has been enjoyable. Mostly, we hope you've learned enough to be productive in your Web-related design and programming activities, and that you've been exposed to enough information resources and investigative techniques to go out and learn whatever else you need to know.

Please drop by our Web pages and share your feedback with us. Also, if you develop exciting new Web software or tools, drop us an e-mail and let us know about it. We might want to include your work in the next edition of this book. Thanks again for traveling the Web with us!

Glossary

#PCDATA. An SGML term that stands for "parsed character data," it refers to zero or more characters that occur in a context in which text is parsed and markup is recognized.

.gz. An abbreviation for GNU zip, a (primarily UNIX-based) file compression technique; this is a common file extension for files compressed using this technique.

.hqx. A format designator associated with the (primarily Macintosh) Bin-Hex program. To compress a file with this utility, you'd go from binary to hexadecimal; to decompress, from hexadecimal to binary.

.tar. An abbreviation for tape archival, *tar* is the eponymous UNIX compression command that creates ".tar"-formatted files. *untar* is the term used to name the operation of decompressing a *tar*red file, even though you'd use the command *tar -xvf junk.tar* to decompress the file named "junk.tar".

.Z. A format designator associated with the UNIX *compress* program. Use the UNIX *uncompress* program to decompress .Z-formatted files.

.zip. A format designator associated with PKWare's PKZIP utilities. In a DOS environment, you'd use *PKZIP* to compress a file, and *PKUNZIP* to decompress it; in Windows, we recommend Niko Mak's outstanding WinZIP utility.

abstract. A brief restatement of the contents of a file or document.

AFS (Andrew File System). Named after Andrew Carnegie by its inventors at Carnegie-Mellon University, AFS is a distributed file system available for many flavors of UNIX and a handful of other operating systems.

algorithm. A step-by-step, programmatic "recipe" for producing a certain set of results in a computer program.

alias. A computer system name that points to another name, instead of to an underlying object. Most Web URLs are either wholly or partly aliases (to protect the underlying file system on the Web server they point at).

America Online. An online information provider, usually known by its initials (AOL), which got its start as a dial-up service off the Internet and which now moving onto the Internet in a big way.

anchor. An HTML term for the destination end of a link; it may sometimes be used as a synonym for hypertext links of all kinds.

ANSI (American National Standards Institute). One of the primary standards-setting bodies for computer technology in the United States.

API (Application Programming Interface). Usually, a set of interface subroutines or library calls that define the methods for programs to access external services (i.e., to somebody else's system or program).

AppleScript. Apple Computer's scripting language for the Macintosh OS, AppleScript is commonly used to program CGIs for Macintosh-based Web servers (among other uses).

AppleSearch. A WAIS-like search engine developed for use under the Macintosh operating system.

application-independent. A format or facility is said to be application-independent when it works in multiple environments and doesn't depend on a specific application to understand or use its contents.

archie. A program that catalogs files on over a thousand *anonymous ftp* servers worldwide and lets users search against this database using interactive queries, e-mail, or through other programs like *gopher* or a Web browser.

architecture neutral. A buzzword applied to Sun's Java programming language that is meant to imply its ability to execute under a number of computer architectures without requiring recompilation or code changes.

argc. In UNIX, a counter of the number of arguments in the *argv* input argument array variable.

argv. In UNIX, *argv* is an array of variables used to pass input between programs or processes on a given machine.

associative array. A programming construct where individual elements are associated with specific names, rather than array positions or locations. Perl offers an especially good implementation of such arrays.

asynchronous. Literally, *not at the same time*, the term refers to computer communications where sender and receiver do not communicate directly with one another, but rather through accessing a common pick-up/drop-off point for information.

attribute. In SGML, HTML, and most object-oriented programming languages, an attribute is a named component of an object or term, with specific value typing, element definitions, and requirements and default status.

authentication. A method for identifying a user prior to granting permission to access, change, or delete a system or network resource. It usually depends on a password or some other method of proving that "User A" really is "User A."

autoresponder. An e-mail program that sends a predefined response back to anyone who sends a message to a particular e-mail address.

awk. An input-processing and pattern-matching language, *awk* scans each of its input filenames for lines that match any of a set of patterns specified in a program. All input filenames are read in order; the standard input is read if there are no filenames.

back end. Computer science jargon for a service that runs on a machine elsewhere on the network, usually driven by an interface or query facility from another machine elsewhere on the network (the front end).

backbone. A high-speed connection designed to interconnect multiple networks. A typical backbone connects only routers; normal network nodes occur only seldom if ever on backbones.

BASIC (Beginners All-purpose Symbolic Instruction Code). Basic is a computer language invented by John Kemeny at Dartmouth College in the late 1960s. It's popular because it's easy to learn and use.

BBS (Bulletin Board System). A synonym for *electronic bulletin board*, a BBS usually consists of a PC, modem(s), and communications software attached to the end of one or more phone lines. Callers dial up the BBS, where they can send and receive messages and download software.

binary. Literally, this means that a file is formatted as a collection of ones and zeros; actually, this means that a file is formatted to be intelligible only to a certain application, or that it is itself an executable file.

binary executables. Files created by compiling (and/or linking) source code modules to create executable files.

BIND (Berkeley Internet Name Domain). BIND is the most popular implementation of the Internet Domain Name Service in use today. Written by Kevin Dunlap for 4.3BSD UNIX, BIND supplies a distributed database capability that lets multiple

DNS servers cooperate to resolve Internet names into correct IP addresses.

BITNET (Because It's Time NETwork). A network that communicates via the Remote Job Entry (RJE) protocols that work over serial lines as well as TCP/IP. BITNET mail is sent through a gateway to the Internet.

black box. A computer-speak euphemism for a program or service whose internal workings are unknown, but that produces a predictable set of outputs for a particular set of inputs.

boilerplate. One of the few computer terms to originate in the legal profession, *boilerplate* refers to elements of text or documents that appear consistently in many or all documents (e.g., a copyright notice).

boot. Used as a verb, *boot* means to start up a computer from its turn-off state. As an adjective (e.g., *boot-time*), it refers to the computer while it's in the startup phase.

bottleneck. A point in a computer or a network where things become congested and slow down.

boundary errors. In programming, errors can occur within the range of the expected data, outside that range, or right on the edges of the expected range. When errors occur at the edges, they're called *boundary errors* (e.g., if a number between 1 and 100 is acceptable, what happens with 1 or 100?).

Bourne shell. UNIX machines typically have one native command interpreter or shell. On many machines, this is the Bourne shell, named after S.R. Bourne in 1975. The Bourne shell is part of the standard configuration for every flavor of UNIX.

breakpoints. A marked location in a program, usually set with a debugger or an equivalent tool, where the program will halt execution so that the programmer can examine the values of its variables, parameters, settings, etc.

bridge. A piece of internetworking equipment that operates at Layer 2 of the ISO model, and forwards packets from one network segment to another without checking address information (see also *router*).

browser. An Internet application that lets users access WWW servers and surf the Net.

BSDI (Berkeley Software Distribution, Inc.). BDSI remains one of the major flavors of UNIX available today, except that now it's distributed by a spinoff business and not the University of California at Berkeley (see *Vendor List* for contact info).

bug. Programmer-speak for an error, glitch, gotcha, problem, or "unsolved mystery" in a computer program.

C. A programming language developed by some of the founders of UNIX, Brian Kernighan and Dennis Ritchie, still very much in vogue among UNIX-heads.

C++. A programming language developed by Bjarne Stroustrup, C++ is a successor to the C language mentioned above. It is an object-oriented (OO) implementation of C.

CALS (Computer Aided Logistics System). A documentation system devised by industry and the U.S. military, primarily used for building and maintaining MilSpec documents.

case sensitive. Means that upper- and lowercase letters are not equivalent (e.g., UNIX filenames are case sensitive; "TEXT.TXT" is not the same as "text.txt").

cc (C compiler). The name of the standard C compiler program on a UNIX system.

cd (change directory). The name of the change directory UNIX command (also used in DOS).

CD-ROM (Compact Disk Read-Only Memory). A read-only computer medium that looks just like a music compact disk, but contains computer data instead of music.

CERN (Centre European Researche Nucleare). The European Center for Particle Physics, where the WWW began.

CGI (Common Gateway Interface). The parameter-passing and invocation technique used to let Web clients pass input to Web servers (and on to specific programs written to the CGI specification).

cgi-parse. A CGI for parsing standard input variables in CGI programs, available from the NCSA CGI library (see Chapter 15 or the CD-ROM for the URL).

"Cha Ching!" The noise a cash register makes when opened; used in this book to indicate the possibility of incoming cash.

character entities. Named SGML or HTML, variables that stand for otherwise unusable characters; in HTML entities are preceded by a, **&** and end with a ; (e.g., **<** stands for **<**).

charset (character set). A defined set of characters used to define legal character values and appearance in HTML or SGML documents.

checkbox. An HTML term for a graphical form widget that may either be checked (to indicate the presence of an associated value) or unchecked (to indicate its absence).

CIDR (Classless Inter-Domain Routing). A way of subdividing large collections of IP addresses into smaller groups (defined by subnet masks) and routing to them individually (allowing more people to share the same address blocks).

class. An object-oriented programming term, *class* refers to a method for defining a set of related objects that can inherit or share certain characteristics.

clickable image. A graphic in an HTML document that has been associated to a pixel-mapping CGI on the server; users can click on locations of the graphic and thereby retrieve an associated URL.

client pull. A Netscape method where a Web client can instruct a server to send it a particular set of data (e.g., client-initiated data transfer).

client/server. A computing paradigm wherein processing is divided between a graphical front-end application running on a user's desktop machine, and a back-end server that performs data- or storage-intensive processing tasks in response to client service requests.

client. Used as (a) a synonym for Web browser (i.e., *Web client*), or (b) as a requesting, front-end member for a client/server applications (like WWW).

close. A formal communications term that refers to session teardown and termination, usually at the end of a networked information transaction.

CNIDR (Clearinghouse for Networked Information Discovery and Retrieval). The industry group responsible for maintenance and distribution of the *freeWAIS* program.

COBOL (Common Business Oriented Language). An old-fashioned programming language invented by Rear Admiral Grace Hopper, still in use for many legacy business applications today.

collaterals. Marketing-speak for product promotional materials, like brochures, spec sheets, whitepapers, etc.

common log format. A data format agreed upon between NCSA and CERN for creating HTTP logs, used by most *httpd* implementers and vendors today.

compiler. A software program that reads the source code for a programming language and creates a binary executable version of that code.

compliant. Conforms to a defined standard of some kind.

CompuServe. An information service provider based in Columbus, Ohio, that hosts a large online user community (regarded as a prime source for technical support information, CompuServe is second only to the Internet in number of users).

connection. A link opened between two computers for the purposes of some specific communication.

content. The hard, usable information contained in a document. Users surf the Web looking for content.

Content-type. The MIME designation for file types to be transported by electronic mail and HTTP.

conversion. The process of changing from one form to another. For example, conversion may occur between a hard-copy document and its soft-copy equivalent.

crawlers. A class of programs designed to ceaselessly search the Web, looking for specific content or simply following links to see where they go.

CrLf (Carriage return/Line feed). One common combination of ASCII characters used to end one line of text and start a new one.

cron. A UNIX system utility that allows tasks to be executed at regularly scheduled intervals (e.g., indexing a large data collection for use by a search engine).

CSU/DSU (Channel Service Unit/Data Service Unit). A device to terminate a digital telephone channel on a customer's premises (commonly used to terminate T1 or higher bandwidth connections).

CVS (Concurrent Version System). A document management or version control system widely used for larger-scale software development projects to track progress and status of code modules. Such systems are widespread in most UNIX-based document and program production operations.

daemon. A UNIX term for a program that runs constantly, listening for requests for a particular connection or service (which it will answer and then spawn off a child process to fulfill).

DARPA (Defense Advanced Research Projects Agency, originally known as *ARPA*). The branch of the DoD that funds advanced research, including the initial work that led to the development and deployment of the Internet.

data content model. SGML-speak for the occurrence notation that describes what other markup is legal within the context of a specific markup element.

datagram. The smallest independent data unit within the IP layer of the TCP/IP protocol stack.

DBMS (Database Management System). A complex system of programs and utilities used to define, maintain, and manage access to large collections of online data.

de facto. A set of common practices that attains the value of standards through widespread and repeated usage.

debugger. A programming tool used to control the execution of programs under development so that they can be halted and queried at any point during execution.

delimiter. A special text character that indicates a record or field boundary within a text stream, rather than being interpreted as an actual part of the text itself (e.g., the characters < and > act as delimiters for HTML tags).

deprecated. Within the context of the HTML DTDs, a deprecated term is one whose use is no longer recommended, but which is still supported for backward compatibility.

descriptive markup. A descriptive markup system uses embedded codes to describe or annotate document elements, like paragraphs or quotations. These codes or tags simply supply names for a document's structural elements.

development environment. The collection of tools, compilers, debuggers, and source code management resources used as part of the software development process.

directory structure. The hierarchical organization of files in a directory tree.

DNS (Domain Name Service). An Internet service that maps symbolic names to IP addresses by distributing queries among the available pool of DNS servers.

document annotation. The process of attaching comments, instructions, or additional information to a document (usually with annotation software for electronic copy).

document root. The base of a Web server's document tree, the root defines the scope of all the documents that Web users may access (i.e., access is allowed to the root and all its children, but not to any of the root's peers or parents).

document tree. A description of the collection of all directories underneath the document root, with all the documents that each such directory contains.

DoD (Department of Defense). The people who brought you the Internet, among other things (see *DARPA*).

DTD (Document Type Definition). An SGML specification that defines the markup elements, their content-models, and other aspects of a markup language.

Dr. Web. A group of dedicated individuals who answer Web-related questions about the Web through a Web screen form available at *http://www.stars.com/Dr.Web/*.

DVI (DeVice Independent file). An intermediate output format created by TeX and related programs when printing from those markup environments.

e-mail (electronic mail). The service that lets users exchange messages across a network; the major e-mail technology in use on the Internet is based on SMTP (Simple Mail Transfer Protocol).

editor. A program used to edit a file; editors for specific programming languages, markup languages, and text formats are all available.

element. A basic unit of text or markup within a descriptive markup language.

element type. The kind of value that an element can take (text, number, tag, etc.).

emacs. A powerful, programmable text editor common on many UNIX systems, *emacs* can be configured as an HTML or SGML editor.

en. In typography, an en is a unit of width equal to one-half the point size of the type.

encoding. A technique for expressing values according to a particular notation (e.g., binary, ASCII, EBCDIC, etc.).

end tag. In HTML, an end tag closes the section of text to which a particular markup operation will be applied when that text is rendered.

entity. In HTML and SGML, an entity is a named or numbered reference to a particular character value, which

may not be otherwise expressible (because it will be interpreted if it's simply dropped into the text stream).

environment variables. Like other UNIX programs, CGIs obtain and store their input rather than reading it in every time it's needed. This stored information — in the form of environment variables — is passed to the program by the HTTP server (from the submitting client). An environment variable, therefore, is a value passed into a program or script by the runtime environment on the system where it's running.

error checking. The process of examining input data to make sure it is both appropriate (within specified value or scalar ranges) and accurate (correctly reflects the input).

Ethernet. A network access method developed by Digital Equipment Corporation, Intel, and Xerox in the early 1970s, Ethernet is the most widely used local-area network technology available today.

exception handling. If a program behaves abnormally, encounters an unexpected input, or detects an anomaly in its operation, it must react to such an event. This is called *exception handling*.

extensibility. A measure of how easy it is to write applications that build upon core mechanisms while adding functionality, new methods or subclasses (depending on the paradigm).

extension language. A programming language, like Python, that can be used to extend the functionality of programmable languages or interfaces.

external entities. Data elements or entities defined outside the context of a formal definition environment (like SGML).

FAQs (Frequently Asked Questions). A list of common questions with their answers, maintained by most special interest groups on the Internet as a way of lowering the frequency of basic technical questions.

field. In a database, a named component of a record and its associated values; in an HTML form, a named input widget or text area and its associated value.

file mapping. A method of supplying a filename to the outside world that does not reveal the complete internal file structures involved (see also *alias*).

filtering. The process of removing certain objects from a document. For example, removing processing instructions important to a specific scheme not used in a general markup scheme eliminates unintelligible materials.

finger. A UNIX command that provides identification information about Internet servers and user names.

fork. A UNIX command that's become synonymous with an execution style where one process splits off another to perform a particular subtask.

FORTRAN (FORmula TRANslation language). An old-fashioned computer language originally developed for calculation-intensive applications, still widely used in the engineering community today.

front end. The user interface side of a client/server application, the *front end* is what users see and interact with.

FTP (File Transfer Protocol). An Internet protocol and service that provides network file transfer between any two network nodes for which a user has file access rights (especially a remote host and your local host or desktop machine).

functional. A type of programming language for which all operations are defined through the evaluation of functions (e.g., LISP).

gateway. A program or service that knows how to convert input from one type of system to another type of system. The word Gateway is central to CGI because it handles input from Web clients as an extension of the Web server and supplies output to those same clients.

gcc (GNU C Compiler). A version of the C compiler implemented as part of the GNU Tools that is highly regarded in the UNIX development community.

general–to–specific. A component of a formal translation scheme that converts data from a generic, canonical format to the specific requirements of a particular system. Such a component is therefore the final element in a text or document conversion system like ICA or Rainbow.

GET. An HTTP method for moving input from the client to the server, GET delivers all of the input parameters inside the command line parameter's value.

gif (Graphics Interchange Format, also GIF). A compressed graphics file format patented by Unisys, and widely used in HTML documents for inline graphical elements.

graphical dividers. Visual elements in an HTML document used to divide text regions. For example, <HR> is a built-in graphical divider, but very often, HTML authors use special graphical elements for the same purpose for more visual impact.

GUI (Graphical User Interface). A generic name for any computer interface that uses graphics, windows, and a pointing device (like a mouse or trackball) instead of a purely character-mode interface. Windows, MacOS, and X11 are all examples of GUI interfaces.

gzip (GNU zip). The name of the program that produces ".gz" compressed file formats, primarily used in the UNIX world.

hash table. A computer data structure that performs a mathematical calculation on a field identifier (called a *hash*) to determine where a data element in a large table or index is located.

headless browser. An intentional synonym for a spider, robot, or wanderer meant to emphasize that it behaves like a browser, without actually displaying any of the data it finds.

helper applications. Applications invoked outside a Web browser to render, display, or play back data that the browser itself cannot handle (e.g., video or multimedia files).

hexadecimal. A form of computer data format where all values are expressed as a sequence of Base 16 digits (0–9, A–F).

hierarchical. A form of document or file structure, also known as a *tree structure*, where all elements except the root have parents, and all elements may or may not have children.

HTML+. An early successor to HTML 2.0 developed by Dave Raggett and since abandoned by the IETF, HTML+ prefigured many of the elements now under consideration for HTML 3.0.

HTML-on-the-fly. The method of creating HTML documents on demand, whenever the output from a CGI program or a request for information from a client requires delivery of such a document.

HTTP (HyperText Transfer Protocol). The TCP/IP-based communications protocol developed for use by WWW, HTTP defines how clients and servers communicate over the Web.

httpd (HTTP daemon). The daemon (or listener) program that runs on a Web server, listening for and ready to respond to requests for Web documents or CGI-based services.

hypermedia. Any of the methods of computer-based information delivery, including text, graphics, video, animation, sound, etc., that can be interlinked and treated as a single collection of information.

hypertext. A method of organizing text, graphics, and other kinds of data for computer use, which lets individual data elements point to one another; a nonlinear method of organizing information, especially text.

I-way. A synonym for *information superhighway*, it usually refers to the Internet as the only example of the highway that's working today.

IAB (Internet Architecture Board, formerly Internet Activities Board). The governing body for the Internet, which manages standards, contracts

certain aspects of the network's operation, and handles what little administration there is over the Internet.

IANA (Internet Assigned Numbers Authority). The arm of the IAB that assigns new IP address ranges to those who request them (and meet other necessary criteria).

ICA (Integrated Chameleon Architecture). An environment for UNIX machines that uses X Windows. It is a suite of tools that helps you create translators for your documents.

ICR (Intelligent Character Recognition). A type of software used to convert scanned documents (bitmaps) into electronic text.

IETF (Internet Engineering Task Force). The technical arm of the IAB responsible for meeting current engineering needs on the Internet, the IETF also has custody of RFC content and related standards status.

imagemap. An HTML construct identified by the <ISMAP> tag, an imagemap is a graphical image that has an associated map file that lets users select links by clicking on certain portions of the image.

instance. A particular incarnation of an object, class, or record, an instance includes the data for one single specific item in a data collection.

inter-document. Used as a modifier for a document link, this refers to a link that points from one document to a different document.

interface. The particular sub-routines, parameter-passing mechanisms, and data that define the way in which two systems (which may be on the same or different machines) communicate with one another.

international standard. In generic terms, an *international standard* is one that is honored by more than one country; in practice, this usually refers to a standard controlled or honored by the International Standards Organization (ISO).

Internet. The name for a worldwide, TCP/IP-based networked computing community with millions of users worldwide that links government, business, research, industry, and education together.

interpreter. A software program that reads source code from a programming language every time it is run, to interpret the instruction it contains. The alternative is to use a compiler, which translates source code into a binary form only once and which is executed thereafter instead.

intra-document. A hypertext link that points from one location inside a document to another location inside the same document. This capability lets hypertext provide good navigation within documents, as well as between them.

IP (Internet Protocol). The primary network layer protocol for the TCP/IP protocol suite, IP is probably the most widely used network protocol in the world.

ISDN (Integrated Services Digital Network). A high-bandwidth communications service, ISDN combines voice and digital services over a single medium, enabling telephone lines to handle both on a single wire. ISDN is a subset of the CCITT broadband ISDN (B-ISDN) standard.

ISO-Latin-1. An ISO-standard character set used as the default character set within HTML.

ISO-8879. The ISO standard that governs SGML.

ISP (Internet Service Provider). Any organization that will provide Internet access to a consumer, usually for a fee.

Java. A new object-oriented programming language and environment from Sun Microsystems. Along with C and C++, Java is compiled into an architecture-neutral binary object and then interpreted like Perl or Tcl for a specific computer architecture.

jpeg (Joint Photographic Experts Group, also JPEG). A highly compressible graphics format designed to handle computer images of high-resolution photographs as efficiently as possible.

kerberos. In Greek mythology, Kerberos was the three-headed dog who guarded the gates of hell against escapees. On the Internet, kerberos is one of a number of security servers that guard access to network resources. It's also the name for an authentication mechanism for use on networks, developed at MIT.

keyword. An essential or definitive term that can be used for indexing data, for later search and retrieval.

kludge. A programming term for a workaround or an inelegant solution to a problem.

LALR (Look Ahead Left-Recursive parser). A common parser architecture, LALR parsers are used for most programming languages.

LAN (Local Area Network). A network linked together by physical cables or short-haul connections, with a span that is generally less than one mile.

latency. The time interval between when a network node seeks access to a transmission channel and when access is granted or received.

lex. A lexical analyzer program commonly used in the UNIX environment, *lex* usually helps programmers build the front ends of parsers (which recognize individual terms or lexical units).

library. A collection of programs or code modules that programmers can link to their own code to provide standard, predefined functionality.

linear structure. A way of organizing text or information flow, so that one element follows after another, in linear fashion.

link. A basic element of hypertext, a link provides a method for jumping from one point in a document to another point in the same document, or another document altogether.

Lisp (LISt Processing language). A functional, self-modifying programming language commonly used for artificial intelligence applications and other complex programming tasks.

load balancing. The process of involving multiple computers in serving a common processing task to divide the work and, therefore, to balance the load between or among them.

logic. A type of computer language that implements some type of logical notation (e.g., predicate calculus) as its processing paradigm.

lower bound. The lowest value in the range of acceptable data for a particular attribute or variable.

Lynx. A character-mode (nongraphical) Web browser.

Mac/OS. An abbreviation for the Macintosh Operating System, currently version 7.5.

macro. A series of special instructions for a program or a metalanguage (like SGML) that allows a name to be substituted for a repeated sequence of operations or text within a document or a program.

mail server. Any member of a class of Internet programs (e.g., *majordomo, listserv, mailserv,* etc.) that allows users to participate in ongoing data exchanges or file retrieval via electronic mail.

mailing list. The list of participants who exchange electronic mail messages regularly, usually focused on a particular topic or concern.

man. The UNIX command used to produce manual pages (aka *help files*) for system commands, utilities, etc.

map files. The boundary definitions for a clickable image, stored in a file format for a particular HTTP server implementation (usually NCSA or CERN), used to assign URLs to regions on an image for user navigation.

markup. A special form of text embedded in a document that describes elements of document structure, layout, presentation, or delivery.

message traffic. The amount of information that circulates on a mailing list or newsgroup on a regular basis. A

mailing list with one or two messages a day has light traffic; a list with 100 or more a day has heavy traffic.

metalanguage. A formal language like SGML that is used to describe other languages.

METHOD. The HTML approach to passing input data from a browser to the server (and possibly on to a CGI program).

MIF (Maker Interchange Format). The export format produced by FrameMaker for sharing data with other word processors or text-handling systems (like HTML).

MIME (Multipurpose Internet Mail Extensions). Extensions to the RFC822 mail message format to permit more complex data and file types than plain text. Today, MIME types include sound, video, graphics, PostScript, and HTML, among others.

minimization. When a markup element is defined without a closing tag, it is said to be minimized. While this makes parsing the resulting markup language more difficult, it makes coding markup tags a lot easier for authors.

mirrored servers. Heavily used file archives, Web servers, or other network servers may be copied in toto and located around a network, to lower the demand on any one such server and to reduce long-distance network traffic. Whenever one server acts as a full copy of another, the second server is said to be a *mirror* of the first.

mnemonic. Programmer-speak for a name that's easy to remember.

modularity. The concept that a program should be broken into components, each of which supplies a particular function or capability.

monospaced. A type of screen or type font where all characters have the same width (like a typewriter font).

Motif. A UNIX-based GUI.

Mozilla (A cross between Mosaic and Godzilla). The name of the DTD and the language description for the Netscape extensions to HTML 2.0.

multithreaded. A computer run-time environment that uses a light-weight process control mechanism, called *threading*, to switch contexts among multiple tasks. Whereas a full-context switch may require 150 or more instructions in some operating systems, a thread switch can occur in as little as 30 instructions on some operating systems.

navigation. The act of finding one's way around the WWW.

navigation bar. A graphical or lexical set of controls on a Web page, intended to assist the process of Web navigation.

NCSA (National Center for Super-computing Applications). An arm of the University of Illinois, where Mosaic (one of the best of the Web browsers) was originally developed.

net-pointers. URLs, *ftp* addresses, or other locations on the Internet where you can go to get the "good stuff."

Netizens. Citizens or denizens of the Internet.

network services. Access to shared files, printers, data, or other applications (e.g., e-mail, scheduling, etc.) across a network.

network utilization. The amount of network usage, usually expressed as the percentage of bandwidth consumed on the medium, for a specific period of time (peak utilization of 80% is no big deal; sustained utilization of 80 percent usually means it's time to divide and grow your network).

newsgroups. On USENET, individual topic areas are called *newsgroups*. Such groups exchange regular message traffic and are a great source of information for technical topics of all kinds.

NFS (Network File System). A distributed file system originated by Sun Microsystems that's in wide use in TCP/IP networking environments today. NFS lets users access remote file systems as if they were an extension of their local hard drives.

NIC (Network Interface Card). The hardware that lets your computer talk to a network and vice versa.

NULL. In programming and UNIX terms, the representation for a missing or empty value.

numeric entities. In SGML or HTML, a way of referring to characters using a numeric notation (e.g., in HTML the string © is the numeric entity for the copyright symbol ©).

Nutshell Handbook. A series of books from O'Reilly and Associates, the *Nutshell Handbooks* provide excellent learning tools about UNIX programs and facilities.

object-oriented. A programming paradigm that concentrates on defining data objects and the methods that may be applied to them.

obsoleted. In the context of the HTML DTD, a markup element, tag, etc., is said to be *obsoleted* when it is no longer supported by the current official DTD.

occurrence indicators. In SGML, occurrence indicators are used to create regular expressions for content data models, to establish the rule for occurrence of tags within other tags.

OCR (Optical Character Recognition). OCR is a kind of software that can recognize characters as they occur in bitmapped data (faxes or scanned documents) and convert them into ASCII or other character codes.

octet stream. An HTML Content-type, octet-stream is the basic type for binary data, since it's nothing but a stream of 8-character bytes.

OO. Abbreviation for *object-oriented*; see object-oriented.

padding. Additional null values added to the end of a data or byte stream, usually to make sure it consists of an even number (or some other specified minimum) number of bytes.

parameter. A value passed into or out of a program, subroutine, or across an interface, whenever code components communicate with one another.

parameter entity. In SGML, parameter entities refer to the entities within a DTD or other document that will be occupied by whatever value for that entity is passed in as input when rendering or analyzing the document.

parse tree. A graphical representation of the designation of, and relationships between, tokens or lexical elements in an input stream after that stream has been parsed.

pattern matching. A computerized search operation whereby input values are treated as patterns and matches are sought in a search database. Whenever exact matches occur, this is called a *hit*; the results of a search produce a list of hits for further investigation.

PCL (Hewlett-Packard's Printer Control Language). The print description language developed for HP's laser printers, now used by many other laser printer manufacturers as well.

PEM/PGP Encapsulation (Privacy Enhanced Mail and Pretty Good Privacy). These two techniques use private/public key encryption to protect e-mail and networked communications, respectively. *Encapsulation* means that these techniques are applied to full-formed messages on the sending end and removed on the receiving end, acting as an extra "security envelope" around information.

Perl. An interpreted programming language developed by Larry Wall, Perl offers superb string-handling and pattern-matching capabilities and is a favorite among CGI programmers.

pixel (PICTure ELement). A single addressable location on a computer display, a pixel is the most primitive individual element for controlling graphics (it's also how image maps are measured and specified).

placeholder. A parameter is an ideal example of a placeholder, because it is a symbolic representation that will be manipulated by a program, but only when it's running and an initial input value is defined.

While the code is being written, all parameters are merely placeholders.

platform independent. Indicates that a program or device will work on any computer, irrespective of make, model, or type.

port address. In TCP/IP-speak, a port address refers to the socket identifier that a program or a service seeks to address for a specific type of communications. Most TCP/IP protocols have "well-known port addresses" associated to them (e.g., HTTP's is 80), but system configurations allow other port addresses to be used (which can sometimes be a good idea for security reasons).

port (short for transport, usually used as a verb). In computer jargon, *porting code* refers to the effort involved in taking a program written for one system and altering it to run on another system.

POST. An HTTP method whereby an array of associated names and values is passed to the server (and on to a CGI program) for further analysis and handling. POST permits arbitrarily long and complex collections of parameters unlike GET; which is limited to a maximum of 255 characters for most versions of UNIX.

PostScript. A page description language defined by Adobe Systems, PostScript files usually carry the extension ".ps" in the UNIX world and are a common format for exchanging nicely formatted print files.

PPP (Point-to-Point Protocol). A newer, more efficient asynchronous TCP/IP protocol, designed specifically for users who wish to make the most of a dial-in connection to the Internet.

principle of locality. In computer science terms, this idea conveys the notion that it's a good idea to stay in your own data neighborhood whenever possible. It's a way of designing data retrieval programs to access the hard disk or other, slower forms of storage as seldom as possible, by grabbing larger chunks of information and dealing with them as completely as possible before asking the operating system to deliver more.

problem domain. A topic or area of interest or concern that a particular application covers (e.g., the problem domain for a statistics program might be "the analysis and interpretation of correlations in specific populations").

procedural markup. A way of describing document contents and layout that emphasizes the *how* of display, rather than the structural elements embodied in the document. Procedural markup is common in proprietary document formats, since they are concerned with telling a single program how to display (or print) a file.

processor-intensive. An application that consumes lots of CPU cycles (i.e., runs for a long time) is said to be processor-intensive. Good examples include heavy graphics

rendering like ray-tracing, animation, CAD, and other programs that combine lots of number-crunching with intensive display requirements.

production Web. A Web server, or collection of Web documents that's used for everyday work or access.

propeller-heads. A synonym for *nerd*, a propeller-head is someone who delights in figuring out the optimal algorithm for the traveling salesman problem. If you don't know what we mean, you ain't one!

proprietary. Technology that's owned or controlled by a company or organization, and that may or may not be widely used.

protocol suite. A collection of networking protocols that together define a complete set of tools and communications facilities for network access and use (e.g., TCI/IP, OSI, or IPX/SPX).

ps (abbreviation for *PostScript*). A common file extension for PostScript files, used as a method to supply print images all over the Internet.

public-key encryption. A method of encrypting information for delivery across a public medium that relies on the combination of a widely available decryption key (the *public key* that must be combined with a unique *private key*) in order for decryption to occur. This is regarded as a highly reliable security technique.

Python. Python is an interpreted, interactive, object-oriented programming language that combines an understandable and readable syntax with noteworthy power.

query decomposition. The process of analyzing a database query for delivery to multiple underlying database servers or data collections for data access and retrieval.

query string. The parameters passed to a Web-based search engine, usually using the GET method (because search strings are nearly always short, this is quite safe).

QuickTime. Apple Computer, Inc.'s format for multimedia data files.

radio button. An HTML input widget used in forms where only a single choice may be made among a predefined set of choices (i.e., only a single button may be pushed at any one time in a set).

RCS (Revision Control System). A source code control system used in some UNIX environments to manage the software development process.

regex (abbreviation for *regular expression*). A formal notation for pattern specification for input to a search engine or language, regular expressions make use of wildcard characters and placeholders to let patterns match a variety of strings, as well as specific strings.

remote location. A site or machine elsewhere on the network, *remote location* can also refer to a machine that is only intermittently connected to a network (usually via a dial-up connection).

render. To interpret the contents of a document, image, or other file so that it can be displayed or played back on a computer.

replication. The process of duplicating information on multiple servers, usually according to some strict synchronization protocol or scheme, so that a copy can be said to be an exact replica of the original.

repository. A place where data is kept, like a file archive, database server, document management system, etc.

request. A network message from a client to a server that states the need for a particular item of information or service.

request header. The preamble to a request, the header must identify the requester and provide authentication and formatting information where applicable. This lets the server know where to send a response, whether or not that request should be honored, and what formats it may be allowed to take.

response. A network message from a server to a client that contains a reply to a request for service.

response header. The preamble to a response, the header identifies the sender and the application to which the response should be supplied.

response time. The amount of time that elapses between the transmission of a request for service and the arrival of the corresponding response.

retagger. An application used in document conversion, a retagger replaces implicit markup from a (usually procedural) markup language with explicit markup for a (usually descriptive) markup language.

reusability. The degree to which programs, modules, or subroutines have been designed and implemented for multi function use. The easier it is to take the same code and employ it in a number of applications, the higher that code's degree of reusability.

rm (remove). The UNIX file delete command.

robot. An autonomous Web-traversing program that seeks out and records information about Web documents that it encounters and examines during its travels. *spider* and *wanderer* are synonyms for *robot*; these programs collect data that is used in Web search engines.

router. An internetwork device or program that reads the addresses of incoming packets and forwards them to their destination or to other routers that can bring them closer to that destination.

RSA (Rivest Shamir Adelman, an encryption algorithm named for its inventors at MIT). RSA encryption uses a public/private key approach and is regarded as one of the secure methods for protecting data on the Internet. Many companies have adopted RSA (e.g., IBM, Novell, Microsoft, etc.) for their encryption needs, and it is widely used around the Internet.

RTF (Rich Text Format). An export file format supported by many word processors and desktop publishing programs.

runtime variables. Program input or output values that cannot be assigned until the program is running.

scalable. Able to accommodate arbitrarily large or small processing loads.

script. A synonym for *program*; programmers usually refer to their work as a script when it is written in an interpreted language (because, like a script, it is read all the way through each time it's run).

search string. The input passed for keyword search and pattern matching in an index to a search engine or database management system.

S-HTTP (Secure HTTP). A new form of the HTTP protocol that includes built-in encryption to provide more secure communications on the Web.

sed. A UNIX program, *sed* is a powerful stream editor that includes a variety of pattern-matching and substitution capabilities.

server push. A Netscape-designed technique to let a server initiate data transfer, especially useful for time-sensitive data like voice or video, where rapid delivery is crucial for continuity and intelligibility.

server. A network machine.

setext. A text markup notation used in an application called EasyView that recognizes various elements of descriptive markup for on-screen display (primarily in UNIX systems).

setuid. Unix command that allows a UNIX application to run at a different privilege or file permissions level from its owner for the duration of execution (this permits certain kinds of operations that would otherwise be impossible for some programs). It's a dangerous thing to do and should be used with great care in Web programs.

SGML (Standard Generalized Markup Language). A metalanguage suitable for describing all kinds of markup languages, including HTML.

sgmls. An application developed by James Clark that provides powerful SGML parsing and validation capabilities. Now superseded by his *sp* program.

shell. A UNIX user interface language, a shell provides the basic command environment for the UNIX operating system.

signal to noise. The ratio of good information to irrelevant junk in a newsgroup or mailing list.

singleton. A minimized markup tag (no end tag) consists of a single markup element. Because it stands alone, we call it a singleton.

sleep. A technique for momentarily pausing an application by suspending execution (usually for a specified period of time).

Smalltalk. An object-oriented programming language widely used for system prototyping and rapid applications development.

snail mail. The antithesis of e-mail, snail mail requires envelopes and stamps, and takes a whole lot longer to get there (at least, when the network's up).

source code. The original text files containing instructions in a particular programming language that programmers write when creating software. If you can see the source code, you have a good shot at understanding what a program is and how it works.

sp. James Clark's replacement for *sgmls*, a powerful SGML parsing and validation program.

specific–to–general. A software program used in the document conversion process that converts documents from a specific — and usually proprietary — form to a standard, generic intermediate form.

specification. A document that describes the requirements, inputs and outputs, and capabilities of a protocol, service, language, or software program (a kind of "blueprint" for a computer system or service of some kind).

spider (synonyms: *robot, wanderer, crawler*). A class of programs designed to ceaselessly search the Web, looking for specific content or simply following links to see where they go.

spoof. To instruct a router or bridge to act as if certain kinds of network traffic were being received; in general, a technique for instructing software to act as if certain conditions that may not prevail are true.

SQL (Structured Query Language). A database query language developed at IBM in broad use in DBMS's worldwide (an ANSI-standard version has been defined).

standard. A program, system, protocol, or other computer component that has been declared to be standard may be the subject of an official published standard from some standards-setting body, or it may simply have acquired that status through widespread or long-term use. When talking about standards, it's always important to find out if the designation is official or otherwise.

standards aware. Describes software that understands standards and can work within their constraints.

standards compliant. Describes software that rigorously implements all of a standard's requirements and capabilities; it's a lot more work than *standards aware*.

start tag. A markup up element that marks the beginning of a block of text to which a specific markup operation is to be applied.

stateless. A stateless protocol needs no information about what's happened in the past (or is expected to happen in the future) about communications between sender and receiver. It's the easiest and most efficient kind of network communication to implement.

static content. Document elements that remain consistent and don't have to change, even for on-the-fly information.

stdin. The UNIX standard input device, *stdin* is the default input source for programs and facilities, including Web servers and clients.

stdout. The UNIX standard output device, *stdout* is the default output source for programs and facilities, including Web servers and clients.

step–by–step execution. When debugging a program, locating the exact line of code where an error occurs can be essential to detecting and fixing the problem. Debuggers let developers *step through* their code for this very reason.

stepwise refinement. A phrase coined by Edsger Dijkstra to indicate the repeated respecification and analysis of program elements needed to create elegant designs and implementations.

string. In programmer-speak, a string consists of character data like "Mark" or "Sebastian".

style guide. A set of guidelines for document layouts, structures, and presentations.

style sheet. A set of named formats, suitable for inclusion in documents that make it easy to distinguish among an individual document's elements (and easy to use such definitions when authoring such documents).

sub-elements. Component parts of a document element (e.g., a single item in a list of attribute values, individual attributes, etc.).

symbolic link. A mechanism whereby one name points to another name in a system, rather than directly to an object. Symbolic names are common for Web servers, document roots, and other system objects.

synchronous. A method of communications wherein all communicating parties interact with one another at the same time.

syntax. The rules for placing and ordering terms, punctuation, and values, when writing statements in a particular language (including programming languages, where the rules tend to be pretty exact).

system administrator. The individual responsible for maintaining a computer system, managing the network, setting up accounts, installing applications, etc.

system clock. A built-in time counter available in most computer systems that keeps track of what time it is, in addition to other responsibilities.

T1. A digital transmission link with a capacity of 1.544Mbps. T1 (also written T-1) is a standard for digital transmission in the U.S., Canada, Hong Kong, and Japan.

tar (Tape ARchival program). A UNIX utility used to compress and uncompress files (files compressed with this program normally have the extension ".tar").

Tcl (Tool Command Language, pronounced *tickle*). Tcl is a simple scripting language for extending and controlling applications. Tcl can be embedded into C applications because its interpreter is implemented as a C library of procedures. Each application can extend the basic Tcl functions by creating new Tcl commands that are specific to a particular programming task.

TCP/IP (Transmission Control Protocol/Internet Protocol). The basic suite of protocols upon which the Internet runs.

telnet. A TCP/IP protocol and service that lets a user on one computer emulate a terminal attached to another computer.

template. An example or pattern for a program or document that acts as a predefined skeleton that only needs to be filled in to be complete.

test plan. A formal document that describes the steps required to test a software application, the data values to be tested, and the actions to be taken when bugs are discovered.

test Web. A separate implementation of a Web document collection, where new HTML documents and CGI programs can be tested and debugged before exposure to the public at large.

TeX. A text-based markup language developed by Donald Knuth of Stanford University when he discovered that existing typesetting environments couldn't handle his need for mathematical notation and text controls. Widely used in research, academia, and book publishing.

text widget. In HTML-speak a text widget is any <FORM> input element that permits text entry (e.g., <TEXTAREA> and <INPUT TYPE="TEXT"...>).

text/html. The MIME Content-type for HTML documents (most commonly used by HTTP and CGI programs for output and Web browsers for input).

text/plain. The MIME Content-type for plain text (will be displayed as-is as preformatted text by most Web browsers).

tiff (Tagged Image File Format). A popular graphics file format, most often seen as a file extension (on PCs, tif).

title. In HTML, the <TITLE> is inside the <HEAD> ... </HEAD> elements that identify an HTML document. It's important not only for displaying the document, but as a data element for spiders or robots seeking to identify information on the Web. Therefore, titles should be as descriptive as possible but not too long.

toolset. A collection of software tools useful for performing certain tasks (e.g., CGI input handling or imagemap creation).

traffic reports. Information on the number of visits to a Web site or to specific documents.

transformation. The process of changing one structure to another. For example, transformation of a document from one governing DTD to another DTD can involve significant changes in structure.

tree. A hierarchical structure for organizing data or documents, common examples of which include file system directories and family trees.

troff. A UNIX text-formatting program that uses procedural markup.

unbuffering. The process of unpacking data from a storage area in a program, usually as it's being parsed or otherwise digested.

unescape. To restore character codes from hexadecimal format into whatever format is normal for the processing environment. Special care must be taken to avoid introducing spurious instructions or unintended behavior during this process.

UNIX. The powerful operating system developed by Brian Kernighan and Dennis Ritchie as a form of recreation at Bell Labs in the late 60s, still running strong today.

upper bound. The highest value in the range of acceptable data for a particular attribute or variable.

URI (Uniform Resource Identifier). Any of a class of objects that identify resources available to the Web;

both URLs and URNs are instances of a URI.

URL (Uniform Resource Locator). The primary naming scheme used to identify Web resources, URLs define the protocols to be used, the domain name of the Web server where a resource resides, the port address to be used for communication, and the directory path to access a named Web document or resource.

URL encoding. A method for passing information requests and URL specifications to Web servers from browsers, URL encoding replaces spaces with plus signs, and substitutes hex codes for a range of otherwise irreproducible characters. This method is used to pass document queries (via the GET method) from browser to servers (and on to CGIs).

URN (Uniform Resource Name). A permanent, unchanging name for a Web resource (seldom used in today's Web environment).

USENET. An Internet protocol and service that provides access to a vast array of named *newsgroups*, where users congregate to exchange information and materials related to specific topics or concerns.

USENET hierarchy. The way in which newsgroups are organized is hierarchical. The most interesting collection of newsgroups, from the standpoint of this book, is the *comp.infosystems.www* hierarchy.

USPS (United States Postal Service). See *snail mail*.

valid HTML. An HTML document that's survived the rigors of validation; i.e., has successfully passed through HTMLchek or an equivalent program.

version control. An important aspect of a source code or document management system, *version control* refers to the ability to associate particular versions of documents or programs together (which may be necessary to maintain a production version and a development version for a program).

vi. A powerful and popular UNIX text editor.

virtual Web mirror. A collection of Web documents and related CGIs that completely reflects the contents of some other Web server.

W3 (World Wide Web).

W3C (World Wide Web Consortium). The consortium that includes CERN, MIT, and other organizations that currently have custody over HTTP, HTML, and other Web-related software and standards.

WAIS (Wide Area Information Service). A collection of programs that implement a specific protocol for information retrieval, able to index large-scale collections of data around the Internet. WAIS provides content-oriented query services to WAIS clients and is one of the most powerful Internet search tools available.

wanderer (synonyms: *robot*, *spider*, *crawler*). A class of programs designed to ceaselessly search the Web, looking for specific content or simply following links to see where they go.

Web sites. Individual Web document collections named by home pages or other unique URLs.

WebCrawler (synonyms: *robot*, *spider*, *crawler*). A class of programs designed to ceaselessly search the Web, looking for specific content or simply following links to see where they go.

Webification. The act of turning complex electronic documents in some other format into HTML, usually programmatically rather than by hand.

Webify. The verb form of *Webification*; see preceding definition.

WebMaster. The individual responsible for managing a specific Web site.

whitespace. The all-important, unoccupied space on a page or electronic document that provides the "breathing room" for text and graphical elements.

widget. In HTML-speak, any of the <FORM INPUT> types, which may be TEXT, CHECKBOX, RADIO BUTTON, etc.

X11. A GUI standard controlled by the X/Open Corporation (also the owner of the UNIX trademark and design).

Xanadu. Ted Nelson's original hypertext design, still regarded by many as an implementation worth striving toward.

Yahoo (Yet Another Hierarchical Officious Oracle). A database written and maintained by David Filo and Jerry Yang, who style themselves "self-proclaimed Yahoos." This is an inauspicious introduction to one of the best search engines for the World Wide Web. When we go surfing, we often start from Yahoo!

Z39.50. The name of the data transfer protocol used for WAIS requests and responses.

Contact List

Dave Raggett, Håkon W Lie, Henrik Frystyk, Phill Hallam-Baker
see W3C for info
arena@w3.org
http://www.w3.org/hypertext/WWW/Arena/
Arena

Alan Richmond
web@sowebo.charm.net
http://www.charm.net/~web/
Virtual Library

Allan Schiffman
info@terisa.com
http://www.eit.com/presentations/shttp-ams/index.html
Secure HTTP: Safe Transactions for the World Wide Web

Ameritech Library Services
library@www.ameritech.com
http://netpub.notis.com/
NetPublisher

ArborText, Inc.
1000 Victors Way Suite #400
Ann Arbor, MI 48108 USA
(313) 996-3566
FAX: (313) 996-3573
info@arbortext.com
http://www.arbortext.com/

Arthur Yasinski
webmaster@nofc.forestry.ca
http://www.nofc.forestry.ca/features/script.html
OraPerl

Ascend
1275 Harbor Bay Parkway
Alameda, CA 94502 USA
(510) 769-6001
FAX: (510) 814-2300
info@ascend.com
http://www.ascend.com/
Ascend Pipeline HX-50

BIAP Systems, Inc.
16323 Hazy Pines Ct.
Houston, TX 77059 USA
info@biap.com
http://www.biap.com/biap_contact.html

Chris Johnson
chrisj@mail.utexas.edu
http://wwwhost.ots.utexas.edu/mac/main.html
University of Texas Macintosh freeware and shareware archive

Chuck Shotton
BIAP Systems, Inc.
16323 Hazy Pines Ct.
Houston, TX 77059 USA
cshotton@biap.com
http://www.biap.com/
MacHTTP aka WebSTAR

Convex Computer Corporation
3000 Waterview Parkway
P.O. Box 833851
Richardson, TX 75083-3851 USA
(214) 497-4000
FAX: (214) 497-4848
webmaster@convex.com
http://www.convex.com/

CSC Internet-To-Real-World Gadgets
http://csclub.uwaterloo.ca/gadgets.html

Data Transfer Group
guy@jw.estec.esa.nl
http://www.thegroup.net/AA.html
Archie Request Form

Davenport Group
http://www.ora.com/davenport

David Eichmann
eichmann@rbse.jsc.nasa.gov
http://rbse.jsc.nasa.gov:80/eichmann/

David-Michael Lincke
dlincke@SGCL1.UNISG.CH
http://www-iwi.unisg.ch/about/team/dal.html

Doug Stevenson
http://www.declab.usu.edu:8080/Mailto/
mailto.pl

Earl Hood
ehood@convex.com
http://www.oac.uci.edu/indiv/ehood/man2html.doc.html
man2html

EINet
3636 Executive Center Drive
Austin, TX 78731 USA
(800) 844-4638
info@einet.net
http://www.einet.net/EINet/EINet.html
MacWeb, WinWeb

Electric Magic Company
http://www.emagic.com/netphone/mainblurb.html
NetPhone

Electronic Book Technologies
One Richmond Square
Providence, RI 02906 USA
(401) 421-9550
FAX: (401) 421-9551
info@ebt.com
http://www.ebt.com/
Rainbow

Enterprise Integration Technologies (EIT)
800 El Camino Real, Fourth Floor
Menlo Park, CA * 94025 USA
(415) 617-8000
FAX: (415) 617-8019
info@eit.com
http://www.eit.com/

Eric Lease Morgan
eric_morgan@ncsu.edu
http://www.lib.ncsu.edu/staff/morgan/
Save-25-Cents or 'Is Eric in?': The Script, email.cgi, Listwebber II,
son-of-wais.pl

Eto Kouichirou
t91069ke@sfc.keio.ac.jp
http://match.sfc.keio.ac.jp/peephole.html
Peep Hole

European Microsoft Windows NT Academic Centre (EMWAC)
emwac@ed.ac.uk
httpd for Windows NT
http://emwac.ed.ac.uk/

Frame Technologies Corporation
333 W. San Carlos St.
San Jose, CA 95110-2711 USA
(800) 843-7263
FAX: (408) 975-6799
webmaster@frame.com
http://www.frame.com/index.html
FrameMaker

Free Software Foundation
675 Mass Avenue
Cambridge, MA 02139 USA
GNU tools and software

George Rodrigue
honus+@cmu.edu
http://kao.ini.cmu.edu:5550/bdf.html
Blue Dog

H. Churchyard
churchh@uts.cc.utexas.edu
http://uts.cc.utexas.edu/~churchh/htmlchek.html
htmlchek

HaL Software Systems
3006A Longhorn Boulevard
Austin, Texas 78758 USA
(512) 834-9962
FAX: (512) 834-9963
lang@halsoft.com
http://www.halsoft.com/

Harvest
harvest-dvl@cs.colorado.edu
http://harvest.cs.colorado.edu/

Ingres Communications
info@ingress.com
http://www.ingress.com/

International Standards Organization
1, rue de Varembé
Case postale 56
CH-1211 Genève 20 Switzerland
+ 41 22 749 01 11
FAX: + 41 22 733 34 30
central@isocs.iso.ch
http://www.iso.ch/

INTERNET CONNECT NIAGARA INC
http://fallscam.niagara.com
Niagra Falls

James Clark
jjc@jclark.com
http://www.jclark.com/
SGMLS, SP

Jason Ng
likkai@ncsa.uiuc.edu
http://www.ncsa.uiuc.edu/SDG/People/jason/pub/gsql/starthere.html
GSQL

Jef Poskanzer
jef@river.org
http://home.river.org/~jef/
pbmplus

Jim Fullton
CNIDR, MCNC Information Technologies Division
3021 Cornwallis Road
Research Triangle Park, NC 27709 USA
Jim.Fullton@cnidr.org
http://cnidr.org/cnidr_projects/freewais.html
freeWAIS

Jon Lewis
jlewis@inorganic5.chem.ufl.edu
http://inorganic5.chem.ufl.edu/ka9q/ka9q.html
KA9Q

Jonny Goldman
http://waisqvarsa.er.usgs.gov/public/fwais.pl
fwais.pl

Kevin Hughes
kevinh@eit.com
http://www.eit.com/software/
wwwais.c, SWISH, getstats

LCS HyperArchive
hyperarchive@lcs.mit.edu
http://hyperarchive.lcs.mit.edu/HyperArchive.html
Hyperarchive

Lutz Weimann
weimann@zib-berlin.de
http://weyl.zib-berlin.de/imagemap/Mac-ImageMap.html
Mac Imagemap

Martien Verbruggen
tgtcmv@chem.tue.nl
http://www.tcp.chem.tue.nl/stats/script/
getgraph.pl

Maxum Development
john@maxum.com
http://www.maxum.com/maxum/
netcloak

Maxwell Labs
http://www.scubed.com:8001/caltrans/sd/big_map.shtml
Traffic Watch

Microrim, Inc.
15395 Southeast 30th Place, Ste. 200
Bellevue, WA 98007-9918 USA
(800) 248-2001
FAX: (206) 649-2785
RBase

Microsoft
One Microsoft Way
Redmond, WA 98052-6399 USA
(800) 426-9400
FAX: (206) 93-MSFAX
www@microsoft.com
http://www.microsoft.com/

Mike Grady
m-grady@uiuc.edu
http://www.cso.uiuc.edu/grady.html
kidofwais.pl

Nate Sammons
nate@vis.colostate.edu
ftp://ftp.vis.colostate.edu/pub/nate/misc/
mail2html, ftpd, ftpuue

NCSA
605 E. Springfield Ave.
Champaign, IL 61820-5518 USA
(217) 244-3473
pubs@ncsa.uiuc.edu
http://www.ncsa.uiuc.edu/
Mosaic

NetMagic
7041 Koll Center Parkway, Suite 160
Pleasanton CA 94566 USA
http://www.aristosoft.com/netmagic/company.html

Netscape Communications Corp.
501 E. Middlefield Rd.
Mountain View, CA 94043 USA
(415) 528-2555
FAX: (415) 528-4124
info@netscape.com
http://home.netscape.com/

Nico Mak Computing, Inc.
P.O. Box 919
Bristol, CT 06010 USA
support@winzip.com
http://www.winzip.com/winzip/
WinZip

O'Reilly & Associates
103A Morris Street
Sebastopol, CA 95472 USA
(800) 998-9938
FAX: (707) 829-0104
website@ora.com
http://website.ora.com/
WebSite

Oracle
500 Oracle Parkway
Redwood Shores, CA 94065 USA
(415) 506-7000
FAX: (415) 506-7200
webmaster@us.oracle.com
http://www.oracle.com/

Patrick Fitzgerald
fitz@iquest.com
http://iquest.com/~fitz/www/mailserv/
Mailserv

Paul Burchard
software@geom.umn.edu
http://www.geom.umn.edu/apps/cyberview3d/about.html
Cyberview3D

Paul Klark
paul@cs.arizona.edu
http://glimpse.cs.arizona.edu:1994/
Glimpse

Paul Sijben
sijben@pegasus.esprit.ec.org
http://www.pegasus.esprit.ec.org/people/sijben/statistics/dvertisment.html
WebStat

Phillip M. Hallam-Baker
hallam@alws.cern.ch
http://www.w3.org/hypertext/WWW/Shen/ref/shen.html
shen

PKWARE, Inc.
9025 N. Deerwood Drive
Brown Deer, WI 53223-2437 ,USA
(414)354-8699
FAX: (414)354-8559
http://www.pkware.com/
PKZip

Process Software Corporation
959 Concord Street
Framingham, MA 01701 USA
(800) 722-7770
FAX: (508) 879-0042
info@process.com
http://www.process.com/prodinfo/purvdata.htm
Purveyor

Professor James Trevelyan
jamest@shiralee.mech.uwa.edu.au
http://telerobot.mech.uwa.edu.au
Telerobot

Qiegang Long
qlong@cs.umass.edu
http://dis.cs.umass.edu/stats/gwstat.html
gwstat

Progressive Networks
616 First Avenue, Suite 701
Seattle, WA 98104
(206) 447-0567
http://www.realaudio.com
system

Robert Denny
rdenny@netcom.com
ftp://ftp.alisa.com/pub/win-httpd/util-support/vbstat31.zip
vbstats

Roel Vertegaal
R.Vertegaal@wmw.utwente.nl
http://mirror.apple.com/mirrors/Info-Mac.Archive/comm/tcp/frameserver.hqx
FrameServer CGI

Rowland Smith
(503) 232-9193
rowland@city.net
http://www.city.net/cnx/software/webmap.html
WebMap

Roy Fielding
fielding@ics.uci.edu
http://www.ics.uci.edu/WebSoft/wwwstat/
WWWstat

Russell Lang
rjl@eng.monash.edu.au
http://www.cs.wisc.edu/~ghost/
Ghostscript

Russell Owen
owen@astro.washington.edu
http://rowen.astro.washington.edu/
FileMaker Pro CGI

Scott Atwood
atwood@cs.stanford.edu
http://weyl.zib-berlin.de/imagemap/Mac-ImageMap.html
imagemap

SoftQuad Inc.
56 Aberfoyle Crescent
Toronto, Ontario, Canada, M8X 2W4
(416) 239-4801
FAX: (416) 239-7105
mail@sq.com
http://www.sq.com/
Author/Editor, HoTMetaL Pro

Stanley Letovsky
letovsky@gdb.org
http://gdbdoc.gdb.org/letovsky/genera/genera.html
Web/Genera

StarNine Technologies
2550 Ninth Street, Suite 112
Berkeley, CA 94710 USA
(510) 649-4949
FAX: (510) 548-0393
info@starnine.com
http://www.starnine.com/

Summer Institute of Linguistics
7500 W. Camp Wisdom Road
Dallas, TX 75236 USA
www@sil.org
http://www.sil.org/

Sybase
6475 Christie Ave
Emeryville, CA 94608 USA
(800) 792-2731
FAX: (510) 922-9441
webmaster@sybase.com
http://www.sybase.com/

Telemedia, Networks, and Systems Group
Room 508, MIT Laboratory for Computer Science
545 Technology Square
Cambridge, MA 02139 USA
(617) 253-6005
FAX: (617) 253-2673
webmaster@www.tns.lcs.mit.edu
http://www.tns.lcs.mit.edu/cgi-bin/mapmaker
MapMaker

Thomas Boutell
boutell@netcom.com
http://sunsite.unc.edu/~boutell/
pbmplus, email.c

Tom Rathbone
tomr@uunet.ca
http://www.uunet.ca/~tomr/glorglox/
Glorglox

Tony Sanders
sanders@bsdi.com
http://www.bsdi.com/server/doc/plexus.html
Plexus, wais.pl

Ulrich Pfeifer
pfeifer@ls6.informatik.uni-dortmund.de
http://ls6-www.informatik.uni-dortmund.de/SFgate/SFgate.html
SFgate

Unify
3901 Lennane Dr.
Sacramento, CA 95834-1922 USA
(800) UNIFY-IT
FAX: (916) 928-6406

Virtual Reality Modeling Language
http://vrml.wired.com/vrml.tech/vrml10-3.html

W3 Consortium
Massachusetts Institute of Technology
77 Massachusetts Avenue
Cambridge, MA 02139, USA
(617) 253-3856
FAX: (617) 253-4734
timbl@w3.org
http://www.w3.org/hypertext/WWW/Consortium/

WAIS, Inc.
690 Fifth Street
San Francisco, CA 94107 USA
(415) 356-5400
FAX: (415) 356-5444
Webmaster@wais.com
http://www.wais.com/

White Pine Software
40 Simon St., Ste. 201
Nashua, NH 03060-3043 USA
(800) 241-PINE
FAX: (603) 886-9051
http://magneto.csc.ncsu.edu/Multimedia/Classes/Spring94/
projects/proj6/cu-seeme.html
CU-SeeMe

WordPerfect
1555 N. Technology Way
Orem, Utah 84057-2399 USA
(800) 451-5151
FAX: (801) 222-5077
http://www.wordperfect.com/

Ziga Turk
ziga.turk@fagg.uni-lj.si
http://www.fagg.uni-lj.si/SHASE/
Virtual Shareware Library

IDG Books Worldwide License Agreement

law. If the Software is an update or has been updated, any transfer must include the most recent update and all prior versions. Each shareware program has its own use permissions and limitations. These limitations are contained in the individual license agreements that are on the software discs. The restrictions include a requirement that after using the program for a period of time specified in its text, the user must pay a registration fee or discontinue use. By opening the package which contains the software disc, you will be agreeing to abide by the licenses and restrictions for these programs. Do not open the software package unless you agree to be bound by the license agreements.

4. **Limited Warranty.** IDG Warrants that the Software and disc are free from defects in materials and workmanship for a period of sixty (60) days from the date of purchase of this Book. If IDG receives notification within the warranty period of defects in material or workmanship, IDG will replace the defective disc. IDG's entire liability and your exclusive remedy shall be limited to replacement of the Software, which is returned to IDG with a copy of your receipt. This Limited Warranty is void if failure of the Software has resulted from accident, abuse, or misapplication. Any replacement Software will be warranted for the remainder of the original warranty period or thirty (30) days, whichever is longer.

5. **No Other Warranties.** To the maximum extent permitted by applicable law, IDG and the author disclaim all other warranties, express or implied, including but not limited to implied warranties of merchantability and fitness for a particular purpose, with respect to the Software, the programs, the source code contained therein and/or the techniques described in this Book. This limited warranty gives you specific legal rights. You may have others which vary from state/jurisdiction to state/jurisdiction.

6. **No Liability For Consequential Damages.** To the extent permitted by applicable law, in no event shall IDG or the author be liable for any damages whatsoever (including without limitation, damages for loss of business profits, business interruption, loss of business information, or any other pecuniary loss) arising out of the use of or inability to use the Book or the Software, even if IDG has been advised of the possibility of such damages. Because some states/jurisdictions do not allow the exclusion or limitation of liability for consequential or incidental damages, the above limitation may not apply to you.

7. **U.S.Government Restricted Rights.** Use, duplication, or disclosure of the Software by the U.S. Government is subject to restrictions stated in paragraph (c) (1) (ii) of the Rights in Technical Data and Computer Software clause of DFARS 252.227-7013, and in subparagraphs (a) through (d) of the Commercial Computer—Restricted Rights clause at FAR 52.227-19, and in similar clauses in the NASA FAR supplement, when applicable.

Index

HTML Tag Quick Reference

(continued)

CD Errata

MACINTOSH USERS PLEASE NOTE

There is an issue with some of the copies of the TWF CD-ROM currently in circulation. If present, it will affect your ability to view the CD-ROM using a Web browser. The CD volume name has an option-hyphen character embedded in it, which will prevent all relative path URLs from working if, as instructed in the CD's read-me, you create the BASE HREF with a regular hyphen. Instead, you must replace the hyphen with the hexadecimal code for the option-hyphen. The portion of the URL that reads:

```
CD-ROM
```

should instead read:

```
CD%D0ROM
```

With this modification to the twf.html document, the rest of the CD should be browsable.

5/8/95

Order Center: **(800) 762-2974** *(8 a.m.–6 p.m., EST, weekdays)*

Quantity	ISBN	Title	Price	Total

Shipping & Handling Charges

	Description	First book	Each additional book	Total
Domestic	Normal	$4.50	$1.50	$
	Two Day Air	$8.50	$2.50	$
	Overnight	$18.00	$3.00	$
International	Surface	$8.00	$8.00	$
	Airmail	$16.00	$16.00	$
	DHL Air	$17.00	$17.00	$

*For large quantities call for shipping & handling charges.
**Prices are subject to change without notice.

Subtotal _____

CA residents add
applicable sales tax _____

IN, MA, and MD
residents add
5% sales tax _____

IL residents add
6.25% sales tax _____

RI residents add
7% sales tax _____

TX residents add
8.25% sales tax _____

Shipping _____

Total _____

Ship to:

Name _____

Company _____

Address _____

City/State/Zip _____

Daytime Phone _____

Payment: ☐ Check to IDG Books (US Funds Only)

☐ VISA   ☐ MasterCard   ☐ American Express

Card # _____ Expires _____

Signature _____

Please send this order form to:

IDG Books Worldwide
7260 Shadeland Station, Suite 100
Indianapolis, IN 46256

Allow up to 3 weeks for delivery.
Thank you!

IDG BOOKS WORLDWIDE REGISTRATION CARD

Title of this book: Foundation of World Wide Web Programming with HTML and CGI

My overall rating of this book: ❑ Very good [1] ❑ Good [2] ❑ Satisfactory [3] ❑ Fair [4] ❑ Poor [5]

How I first heard about this book:

❑ Found in bookstore; name: [6] _____

❑ Advertisement: [8]

❑ Word of mouth; heard about book from friend, co-worker, etc.: [10]

❑ Book review: [7]

❑ Catalog: [9]

❑ Other: [11]

What I liked most about this book:

_____

_____

_____

What I would change, add, delete, etc., in future editions of this book:

_____

_____

Other comments:

_____

Number of computer books I purchase in a year: ❑ 1 [12] ❑ 2-5 [13] ❑ 6-10 [14] ❑ More than 10 [15]

I would characterize my computer skills as: ❑ Beginner [16] ❑ Intermediate [17] ❑ Advanced [18] ❑ Professional [19]

I use ❑ DOS [20] ❑ Windows [21] ❑ OS/2 [22] ❑ Unix [23] ❑ Macintosh [24] ❑ Other: [25] _____
(please specify)

I would be interested in new books on the following subjects:
(please check all that apply, and use the spaces provided to identify specific software)

❑ Word processing: [26]

❑ Data bases: [28]

❑ File Utilities: [30]

❑ Networking: [32]

❑ Other: [34]

❑ Spreadsheets: [27]

❑ Desktop publishing: [29]

❑ Money management: [31]

❑ Programming languages: [33]

I use a PC at (please check all that apply): ❑ home [35] ❑ work [36] ❑ school [37] ❑ other: [38] _____

The disks I prefer to use are ❑ 5.25 [39] ❑ 3.5 [40] ❑ other: [41] _____

I have a CD ROM: ❑ yes [42] ❑ no [43]

I plan to buy or upgrade computer hardware this year: ❑ yes [44] ❑ no [45]

I plan to buy or upgrade computer software this year: ❑ yes [46] ❑ no [47]

Name: _____ Business title: [48] _____ Type of Business: [49] _____

Address (❑ home [50] ❑ work [51]/Company name: _____)

Street/Suite# _____

City [52]/State [53]/Zipcode [54]: _____ Country [55] _____

❑ **I liked this book!** You may quote me by name in future
IDG Books Worldwide promotional materials.

My daytime phone number is _____

IDG BOOKS

THE WORLD OF
COMPUTER
KNOWLEDGE

❑ YES!
Please keep me informed about IDG's World of Computer Knowledge.
Send me the latest IDG Books catalog.